THE MERITS OF FLEXIBLE
EXCHANGE RATES

THE MERITS OF FLEXIBLE EXCHANGE RATES

AN ANTHOLOGY

Edited by
Leo Melamed

George Mason University Press
Fairfax, Virginia

Library of Congress Cataloging-in-Publication Data

The Merits of flexible exchange rates : an anthology / edited by Leo Melamed.
p. cm.
1. Foreign exchange problem. I. Melamed, Leo.
HG3852.M47   1988
332.4'562—dc 19   88–12214 CIP
ISBN 0–913969–14–1 (alk. paper)
ISBN 0–913969–15–X (pbk. : alk. paper)

CONTENTS

FOREWORD   **Leo Melamed**   ix

INTRODUCTION   **Milton Friedman**   xix

PART I   **HISTORICAL OVERVIEW AND BACKGROUND**

1.   The Case for Flexible Exchange Rates   3
Milton Friedman

2.   The Case for Flexible Exchange Rates, 1969   43
Harry G. Johnson

3.   Reflections on the Exchange Rate System   71
J. Carter Murphy

4.   Functioning of the Current International Financial System: Strengths, Weaknesses and Criteria for Evaluation   81
Thomas D. Willett

PART II   **FLEXIBLE EXCHANGE RATES AND INTERNATIONAL TRADE**

5.   The International Monetary System and Proposals for International Policy Coordination   125
Gottfried Haberler

6.   The International Monetary System— Once Again   159
Gottfried Haberler

7. Growth Rates, Trade Balances and
    Exchange Rates   167
    Fritz Machlup

8. A Guide to Target Zones   183
    Jacob A. Frenkel and Morris Goldstein

9. Unexpected Real Consequences of
    Floating Exchange Rates   223
    Rachel McCulloch

PART III   BALANCE OF PAYMENTS, BUDGET DEFICITS
           AND FLEXIBLE EXCHANGE RATES

10. Domestic Saving and International Capital
     Movements in the Long Run and the
     Short Run   247
     Martin Feldstein

11. International Aspects of U.S. Monetary
     and Fiscal Policy   273
     Paul R. Krugman

12. Excerpts from the Council of Economic
     Advisers *Report to the President,* 1975, 1976,
     1977   297
     Alan Greenspan

PART IV   INTERNATIONAL FINANCIAL INSTITUTIONS
          AND THE POLICY OF INTERVENTION UNDER
          FLEXIBLE EXCHANGE RATES

13. The Role of Official Intervention   331
     Michael L. Mussa

14. Economic Structure and Policy for
     External Balance   361
     William H. Branson

15. Exchange Rates and the Adjustment
     Process   387
     Jacques de Larosière

16. Floating as Seen from the Central Bank   395
     Henry C. Wallich

17. Improving International Performance   405
     Beryl W. Sprinkel

PART V   PRIVATE SECTOR INNOVATION AND FREE MARKETS

18.   The International Monetary Market   417
      Leo Melamed

19.   A Proposal for Resolving the U.S. Balance
      of Payments Problem; Confidential
      Memorandum to President-elect   429
      Richard Nixon
      Milton Friedman

PART VI   MACROECONOMIC COORDINATION AND FLEXIBLE EXCHANGE RATES

20.   Coordination Could Be Washed Out   441
      Alan Greenspan

21.   Turbulence in the Foreign Exchange
      Markets and Macroeconomic Policies   445
      Jacob A. Frenkel

22.   Expectations and Exchange Rate
      Dynamics   471
      Rudiger Dornbusch

23.   Flexible Exchange Rates and Excess
      Capital Mobility   489
      Rudiger Dornbusch

      The Contributors   513

      Acknowledgments   525

FOREWORD

Leo Melamed

Freshness of thought is a mark of genius.

Milton Friedman's essay, "The Case for Flexible Exchange Rates," was written when the Bretton Woods system of fixed exchange rates was just a few years old. It is properly the first selection in this anthology.

In this essay, Professor Friedman presents a compelling case for a system of exchange rates freely determined in open markets primarily by private transactions and accompanied by abandonment of direct controls over exchange transactions. Two full decades were to pass before exchange rates would float freely, before his premise was a reality. Friedman's genius with that essay is as equally insightful and relevant today as when it was written.

This anthology was conceived against a backdrop of renewed pressure in some quarters for a return to a more managed or fixed form of exchange rates. In the U.S., the movement stemmed primarily from a desire to use exchange rates as a means of achieving a more favorable trade environment for U.S. products. In addition, there was a growing belief on the part of some finance ministers of leading industrial nations and their central bankers that they could achieve a "more correct" value for world currencies by carefully manipulating the markets.

As anecdotal evidence of the current strong divergent views on the issue of fixed or managed versus flexible or floating exchange rates, I need only cite the following two items, both of which occurred on September 14, 1987. First, the lead story in the London *Financial Times* reported that the European Community finance ministers and central bankers agreed to "strengthen their intervention measures to stabilize currencies." Second, in New York, the policy statement of the Shadow Open Market Committee urged the U.S. Federal Reserve and Treasury to "cease efforts at targeting the dollar's exchange rate."

Professor Allan Meltzer, a leading member of the Shadow Committee and professor at Carnegie-Mellon, reiterated the need for the U.S. Treasury to abandon its mistaken policy of trying to support the dollar, and rather to allow market forces to work. With the benefit of hindsight, Professor Meltzer's advice takes on even greater relevance.

The stock market crash of October 19, 1987, sent everyone searching for its cause. There were a plethora of underlying candidates, but whatever final judgment may be reached about the relative importance of each, there is one dimension of the cause that should not be ignored and that underscores the fundamental reason for the Shadow Open Market Committee's concern over a policy of supporting the dollar. Tinkering with free market forces in a significant way creates unnatural economic conditions that may then beget unnatural market consequences.

For example, the Louvre Agreement. This was really a policy of not only the U.S. Treasury, but far more importantly, of the world central banks that bought (reputedly) between $60 and $80 billion to effectuate their course of action. By accumulating this large sum of dollars, the central banks of the world were able, for a time, to maintain the price of the dollar at an artificially high price. But that house of cards was bound to collapse. When it did, it produced a sharp and sudden fall in the exchange value of the U.S. dollar that could only have disturbing consequences for equity markets around the world.

Whether the collapse of the Louvre Agreement was a major or minor factor in the stock market collapse, the coincidence of the two in time certainly provides food for thought as well as further incentive for this publication.

This publication also offers a unique opportunity to include a confidential memorandum from Milton Friedman dated October 15, 1968, and submitted to President-elect Richard M. Nixon before he assumed office. The memorandum, presented now for the first time to the public, contains a bold prescription for resolving the U.S. balance of payments problem of the Johnson era. It sets forth a succinct economic rationale for commencing an immediate free float of the dollar, allowing all individuals, American and foreign alike, to "use, hold, or exchange dollars in whatever way is advantageous to them."

In urging the new President to quickly institute the recommended policy, Friedman argues that the uniqueness of the opportunity to act at the outset of the new administration is a historical rarity that should not be wasted. If there is a delay, Friedman predicts, "there will be no significant alternative to the measures proposed, but these measures will then have to be taken out of weakness and under crisis conditions . . ."

With the benefit of hindsight, it is easy to marvel at Friedman's foresight. It took the Nixon administration nearly three years before the recommended action was taken. By then, of course, crisis conditions existed.

If there is a common view to be derived from the writings in this publication, I believe it is the repetition of the simple but powerful lesson of all of economic history: market rule. Artificial values or targeted ranges for currency in international markets of this day and age will last for only so long as the market tolerates them. Ultimately, market forces will overpower any man-made method to artificially ordain the values of the dollar or any other currency.

Thus, while the world awaits the new and "relatively stable monetary regimes" Milton Friedman's Introduction promises will follow the "present transitional period" (he does not tell us how long the current phase will last), this volume strongly supports the philosophy of allowing market forces to determine currency values. As Friedman puts it, "Flexibility in exchange rates has provided a useful, indeed indispensible, shock absorber for monetary and other disturbances, and will continue to do so for the foreseeable future."

The articles selected for this publication remind us that the belief in the relative merits of a flexible international monetary system has a long and distinguished pedigree. Collected here are the classic writings on the subject by renowned scholars such as Milton Friedman, Harry Johnson, Fritz Machlup, and Gottfried Haberler; we offer a perspective from the Federal Reserve Board with Chairman Alan Greenspan and Governor Henry Wallich; we also present a view from the International Monetary Fund with Jacques de Larosière; and, finally, we provide important fresh thinking by a number of today's leading economists including Rudiger Dornbusch, Martin Feldstein, Jacob Frenkel, Beryl W. Sprinkel and others.

In certain ways, this anthology is a critique of the Bretton Woods system of fixed exchange rates. That system was instituted in 1945 because it was the only sensible thing to do in a world completely ravaged by war. For its time, the system was an astounding success. It worked because the United States represented the only remaining industrial nation with its financial system intact, because the dollar was the only remaining currency of value, because the U.S. was willing to use its financial resources to the benefit of everyone and because America could dictate its economic resolve.

But the very resources that saved the western world could not forever be drawn upon without themselves becoming weakened. The cumulative effect of fixed exchange rates so disadvantaged the United States that, by the time they were discarded in the early 1970s, this nation's financial structure was crumbling and drastic measures were in order. Consequently, we are in a position to review the financial history of the world from the perspective of both the pre and post flexible exchange rate era. Indeed, the writings collected here examine a world punctuated by unparalleled upheavals from the late 1960s to the late 1970s.

One last housekeeping note before we proceed. Of the many different organizational formats available for this publication we chose the following order: historical overview; flexible rates and international trade; balance of payments, budget deficits and flexible rates; international financial institutions and the policy of intervention; the private sector innovation of financial futures; and macroeconomic coordination.

*　*　*

As if on cue from the Friedman exhortation to move toward a freely determined system of exchange rates, Harry G. Johnson, in his 1969 essay, proposes that Great Britain unilaterally float the pound. Thus, he argues, the British economy will be freed from the "vicious circle of 'stop-go' policies" that had sought unsuccessfully to improve the British balance of payments. At the same time, Johnson urges the International Monetary Fund to be sensitive to the British economic dilemma and to be tolerant of reforms that would permit the international monetary system as a whole to survive and function more effectively.

Government, not private sector actions, caused the most serious disturbances to international economic equilibrium over the previous forty years, writes J. Carter Murphy in "Reflections on the Exchange Rate System," published in 1985. This, according to Murphy, suggests that the exchange rate system must be designed to absorb the shock of government policies and actions as well as those in the private sector. While the floating rate system was held by Murphy to be imperfect as a tool for insulating nations from the actions of each other, he found flexible exchange rates coupled with monetary and fiscal policy balance "deserving of consideration."

The best prospects for improved economic stability rest with better management of national economic policies and with greater attention to the international consequences of these policies, writes Thomas D. Willett in his 1983 essay. Willett concludes that perhaps the greatest advantage of flexible exchange rates is the system's shock-absorbing capacity which has limited the international damage from poor national policies conflicting with national objectives.

Gottfried Haberler's work, reprinted here, reminds us forcefully that markets set the pace and governments react, albeit slowly, to market realities. "It is in the nature of the political process," writes Haberler, "that governments are slow to admit mistakes and even slower to change their policies."

Haberler's 1987 articles add to the historical perspective of exchange rate determination with a discussion of the activist policies of Treasury Secretary James Baker in the second Reagan Administration. These actions, he notes, were a composite of three elements: efforts at "talking" the dollar down, concerted intervention in the foreign exchange markets, and U.S. demands for international coordination of national economic policies.

The lesson Haberler draws from this most current experience is the same as from the past. Writes Haberler: "The politicalization of exchange rates is a dangerous game. It has caused much turbulence in the foreign exchange markets. Free markets do a better job of setting exchange rates than governments do." In practice, says Haberler, the vaunted economic policy coordination of Secretary Baker boiled down to U.S. demands that Germany and Japan stimulate their economies in order to reduce their trade surpluses and U.S. deficits.

Fritz Machlup examines the question of the effects of economic growth on trade balances and/or movements in the exchange rates among the countries concerned in "Growth Rates, Trade Balances and Exchange Rates." Machlup concludes that the notion that real growth can be controlled by any kind of government policy is an illusion, and that particularly damaging is the coaxing of nations with trade surpluses to seek higher growth rates. "Such coordination," writes Machlup . . . "may do little to enhance real growth and may even inhibit it in the long run."

The paper by Jacob Frenkel and Morris Goldstein, "A Guide to Target Zones," declines to take a position for or against the adoption of target zones as an approach to exchange rate management. Yet, the issues they detail surrounding this topic are essential to any discussion of the target zone question, and allow careful assessment of the costs of fixity.

In "Unexpected Real Consequences of Floating Exchange Rates," Rachel McCulloch writes that the flexible exchange rate system functioned for its first decade in ways markedly different from the predictions of most analysts on both sides of the question. In particular, says McCulloch, it was predicted that flexible rates would be stable if national monetary policies were stable, yet. . . . "The central message of recent experience," says McCulloch, "is that the foreign exchange market is an asset market, and that the economic laws governing exchange rates are fundamentally similar to those governing other asset prices—with stock and bond markets providing obvious domestic analogies. In fact, while exchange rates have indeed been volatile, their volatility has been less than that of stock prices (Frenkel and Mussa, 1980). We live in times of too much daily economic 'news' from other sources to avoid large fluctuations in market-determined exchange rates."

Martin Feldstein's article challenges thinking on the relationship between domestic savings and international capital movements. He observes what one would expect, that capital tends to seek the highest return, but points out how that is impeded by various risk considerations including government policies. He raises the "puzzling fact that substantial gross capital flows produce relatively small net capital flows," and questions why governments impose the various capital flow restrictions they do.

"Should the United States do something to drive the dollar down to where it belongs?" This recurring question is examined as part of Paul Krugman's paper on international aspects of U.S. monetary and fiscal policy. Of the various options for bringing down the dollar, Krugman concludes that none but tighter fiscal policies seemed appealing, and that seemed politically impossible. Divergence in fiscal and monetary policies between the United States and other advanced countries led to the strong dollar and the prospect of huge U.S. external deficits. This same divergence complicated prospects for international cooperation on monetary policies, concludes Krugman.

At a conference in Zurich in June 1986 on the reform of the international monetary system, Alan Greenspan critiqued the difficulties of international economic coordination because short-term domestic policy pressures work against the longer-term yields of international cooperation. His adaptation of these remarks is included as clairvoyant of the dilemma he now faces as Chairman of the Federal Reserve Board. Alan Greenspan was also Chairman of the Council of Economic Advisors in the mid-1970s and was then called upon to assess the early years of the free float exchange process which was being roundly buffeted by international tensions and the oil embargo. Excerpts from his *Reports to the President* offer the views of the United States' lead economic policymaker at that transitional time.

Michael Mussa's paper on "The Role of Official Intervention" (1981) finds that during the first seven years of floating rates, official intervention in foreign exchange markets did not appear to have contributed to exchange rate stability. Thus the intervening central banks appeared to have been "leaning against the wind" unsuccessfully. Mussa raises helpful distinctions between "targets" and "indicators" and offers an insightful analysis of the "asset market view" of exchange rates.

Movements in the exchange rate have their main effect on trade in the U.S. by changing relative prices and making the exchange rate an efficient instrument for external adjustment. But, in Europe, changes in the exchange rate may have their main effect on domestic prices, making the exchange rate there a poor instrument for external balance. These are basic conclusions of William H. Branson in the 1983 paper "Economic Structure and Policy for External Balance."

"Exchange Rates and the Adjustment Process" is adapted from a 1979 speech by Jacques de Larosière, then managing director of the International Monetary Fund. He develops the themes that flexible exchange rates do not insulate economies in an open world, that they do not lessen the need for basic policy adjustments, and that they do not diminish the need for cooperation and active international surveillance.

Henry C. Wallich's chapter is a discussion of floating rates from the perspective of a central banker—as a member of the Board of Governors of the Federal Reserve System. In the 1984 paper, Wallich defends intervention in the exchange markets as appropriate under certain conditions but adds that this does not necessarily mean intervention will be successful. While exchange rates in most countries are in the hands of the political authorities, exchange market intervention that seeks to counter market disorder more plausibly belongs in the hands of central bankers, writes Wallich.

No economist has been more immersed in today's policy implications of demand for "exchange rate stability" than the President's Chairman of the Council of Economic Advisors, Beryl Sprinkel. His address to the Commonwealth Club in April 1987 offers a sense of the policymaker's crucible, and outlines those steps government officials can and do take when there are wrenching variances in leading nations' macroeconomic policies. Sprinkel bravely challenges quick-fix solutions, and focuses on the difficult underlying reality that "wide swings in exchange rates must be understood, not as a fault of the system, but on the undesirable policies that produced them."

Jacob A. Frenkel's article, "Turbulence in the Foreign Exchange Markets and Macroeconomic Policies," offers empirical evidence illustrating the responsiveness of exchange rates to expectations. He boldly raises the question: "Have exchange rates fluctuated excessively?" He reviews the idea that periods dominated by news developments are characterized by volatile exchange rates. As news is unpredictable, so too are exchange rates. Frenkel also explores the purchasing power parity question and the relationship between exchange rates and interest rates.

Rudiger Dornbusch's work (1977) on expectations and exchange rate dynamics helped alter traditional thinking on the subject. It sets forth a new macroeconomic framework for the study of exchange rate movements, drawing on the role of asset markets, capital mobility and expectations.

My own contribution to this publication is on a different plane than the others and underscores the fact that, lacking the "economist" credentials or expertise of my colleagues, I am not so foolish as to compete in their domain. Indeed, my title as Editor is, by itself, an overstatement since I did little more than coordinate the overall effort.

My brief essay outlines the private sector response to the demise of the Bretton Woods system: the creation of financial futures on the International Monetary Market. I take the liberty of offering a brief glance back at how and why it happened, who we were, and some of the little known but important roles of Milton Friedman, Beryl Sprinkel, and others who were critical to the IMM's success.

Finally, the reader should know that this anthology was developed as an outgrowth of an ad-hoc coalition of leaders from academia, business, and commerce who share the idea that world economic stability and viability is best achieved through adherence to free market principles. That Coalition, the American Coalition for Flexible Exchange Rates (ACFX), was formed in 1986 when there was a growing clamor for a return to a more fixed international monetary system. The ACFX had a simple premise:

- that free markets are the best arbiter of supply and demand, providing the most efficient determinant of price;
- that the free market exchange system reflects, does not cause, fundamental economic factors at work in various nations;
- that the value of a nation's currency depends upon a complicated analysis by the free market of the differences between that nation and others in price levels and inflation rates, interest rates, national money supplies, national incomes, trade and investment flows, government and private debt, and political risk;
- that these complex factors are best assessed and balanced through the flexible free market exchange system;
- that a stable international monetary system is fostered by market-driven exchange rates.

This volume exists because I, along with members of that Coalition, believe that ideas have consequences, and that the most consequential will only prevail if presented clearly and forcefully time and time again.

With a nod to Churchill's well known quote, I believe the writings collected here suggest that the floating exchange rate system, while imperfect, is the best system man can offer to sort out the complexities which make up the relative values of money.

ACKNOWLEDGMENT

I would like to acknowledge the invaluable assistance of Charles M. Seeger, Vice President-Government Relations of the Chicago Mercantile Exchange, in coordinating the efforts of this anthology.

INTRODUCTION

Milton Friedman

An exchange rate is the price of one "money" in terms of another "money." Generally, each "money" is identified with a different country: e.g., the U.S. dollar, the Japanese yen. However, the two moneys may be for a single country. Before the Federal Reserve instituted par clearance, there were internal exchange rates such as the price of New York dollars in terms of Kansas City dollars. During the Civil War greenback period, gold dollars remained the principal circulating medium in some parts of the country, notably California, while greenback dollars were dominant elsewhere. The price of a gold dollar in terms of greenback dollars was set in a free and active market. Similarly, during pre-Federal Reserve periods of "suspension of payments" by banks, a market exchange rate emerged for currency in terms of bank deposits.

The purpose of these comments is to stress that the determination of exchange rates is a by-product of monetary systems, not something that can be considered independently of them. The reason that there was a drastic change in the determination of exchange rates in the early 1970s, and that there has been heightened concern about exchange rates ever since, is because 1971 marks a sharp break in the monetary regime adopted by the major Western countries. Ever since, we have been in a transition period. The basic issue is not "flexible" versus "fixed" exchange rates—in a relevant sense, exchange rates are always "flexible"—but the monetary regime or regimes that will finally emerge from the trial and error groping that has necessarily characterized this transition. As the shape of that regime or those regimes becomes reasonably definite, the determination of exchange rates will accommodate itself, uncertainty will decline, and markets in foreign exchange will become routinized and less exciting.

Until 1971, the physical object or piece of paper or bookkeeping entry that was called "money" and generally accepted in discharge of an obligation was invariably linked to a physical commodity. The particular commodity varied widely—from the *pecu* (i.e., cattle) that gave us words like "pecuniary" to the cowrie shells or wampum of the American Indians, the stone money of the Yap islanders, the tobacco money of the early American colonists, and the more familiar copper, silver, and gold, to mention only a few of the items that have somewhere or other, or at some time or other, served as "money." At times throughout this long period the link was broken—apparently as long as two millenia ago with paper money episodes in China; more recently, with Continental currency during the American Revolution, *assignats* during the French Revolution, the departure from gold by Britain during the Napoleonic wars, greenbacks during the U.S. Civil War, and the increasingly numerous paper money episodes of more recent times. However, these breaks typically occurred as a result of revolution, war, or other crises, were expected to be temporary, and proved to be temporary—largely because, as Irving Fisher put it in 1911, "Irredeemable paper money has almost invariably proved a curse to the country employing it."[1] As monetary economies became more complex, the link to a commodity became increasingly indirect until, in the final stages, the citizens of the United States and some other countries were forbidden even to hold the supposed monetary commodity, gold, except for numismatic or industrial purposes, and the link was maintained entirely by official transactions.

This long process came to its final end on August 15, 1971 when President Nixon closed the gold window, that is, suspended the U.S. commitment to convert foreign official holdings of dollars into gold at a fixed price. As I put it elsewhere, "the commodity Cheshire cat has completely disappeared, and only the fiat grin remains."[2] Since 1971, no major currency is linked to a commodity. What economists call outside money consists entirely of government fiat, in the form of paper currency, minor coin, and bookkeeping entries such as deposits at U.S. Federal Reserve Banks.

The triumph of irredeemable paper money aroused widespread fears that history would repeat itself, that, as in most earlier paper money episodes, inflation would destroy the value of the fiat money and lead to the restoration of a commodity link. However, that is by no means a necessary implication of earlier experience. As already noted, the earlier paper money episodes almost invariably occurred as a result of crisis, and were expected to be temporary. Currently, an irredeemable paper standard is not regarded as a temporary emergency expedient. Although the major countries still genuflect to the past by retaining an entry on central bank balance sheets for the value of gold reserves, generally at an artificial "monetary" value, there is no commitment to restoring a link to a commodity and no expectations that a link will be restored. To the best of my knowledge, there is no historical precedent for the present situation. We are sailing on an uncharted sea.[3]

The earlier commodity link provided a physical anchor to the price level over the long term. The price level in Britain in 1930 was roughly the same as in 1740; in the United States in 1932 roughly the same as in 1832. This long-term predictability of the price level did not hold for shorter periods, as the fluctuation in prices over both short business cycles and much longer swings demonstrates. Nonetheless, long-term predictability had important effects on asset preferences and interest rates. Though Irving Fisher emphasized the distinction between nominal and real interest rates nearly a century ago, in practice the distinction was of little importance, especially for long-term interest rates, which displayed remarkable stability over both long and short periods. Long-term bonds were the investment of choice for "widows and orphans."

The use of the same commodity by different countries provided a physical anchor to the exchange rate between their respective currencies, and the use of different commodities (e.g., silver and gold), while not fixing a single value to the exchange rate, provided an external measure in terms of the relative price of the different commodities which served as a similar anchor. Again, the exchange rate like the price level was not fixed over short periods. The commodity link served primarily to provide longer term stability.

During the period of the commodity link, though exchange rates were regarded as fixed, and are now described as fixed, they were not in fact fixed. From 1879 to 1914, there existed a close approximation to a unified currency among most major countries because of the use of gold and convertible claims to gold as money by the several countries. Only the names attached to the claims to gold, and the physical amounts to which those names corresponded, differed from country to country. Under that regime, fluctuations in market exchange rates were limited by the cost of shipping gold—the famous "gold points." In the 1920s, the early thirties, and during the post-World War II Bretton Woods era, a unified currency was replaced by strictly national currencies linked by official exchange rates set by the several governments. These official exchange rates were held within narrow limits for long intervals by pegging operations by monetary authorities. From time to time, the official rates became unsustainable, and then were altered, typically by substantial amounts.

Under the current fiat system, the situation has been very different.

Uncertainty about the long-term behavior of the price level has almost surely increased sharply in recent years—although short-term month-to-month and year-to-year variability has apparently declined. The rates of inflation during the 1970s and early 1980s have no peacetime precedent in either the United States or the United Kingdom. The U.S. price level in 1985 was eight times its 1939 level; the U.K. price level, 20 times its 1939 level. In addition, interest rates, especially long-term interest rates, have risen to levels unprecedented in peacetime and have fluctuated widely, paralleling rates of inflation, but fluctuating more widely over short periods. No one any longer regards long-term fixed interest bonds as the investment of choice for "widows and orphans." And no one any longer disregards Fisher's distinction between nominal and real interest rates.

Governments have continued to intervene in markets for foreign exchange and some smaller countries have succeeded in pegging their currencies to a major currency for extended periods—e.g., Taiwan, Hong Kong, and Korea to the U.S. dollar—but the major countries have been unable or unwilling to peg their exchange rates for any but the briefest of periods. Flexible exchange rates—"dirty floating"—has become the rule. The European Monetary System is an attempt to maintain a pegged exchange-rate island within a sea of floating currencies. It has had only limited success, as demonstrated by repeated crises and revaluations.

Public futures markets in individual commodities—corn, wheat, etc.— have existed for a long time—indeed a futures market in rice is said to have existed in Japan as early as 1650. However, to the best of my knowledge, no public futures markets existed prior to 1971 in foreign exchange, or in financial claims such as bonds, Treasury bills, stock market indexes and the like. Commercial banks, and in some cases central banks, provided future cover for large transactions in foreign exchange, but there was no role for the kind of futures markets that existed and continue to exist for individual commodities. The reason is clear. The basic function of futures markets is to enable economic agents to deal with uncertainty. A futures market will exist only if there is the kind of uncertainty that attracts speculators and hedgers, and they are attracted by short-term, substantial, and unpredictable variability in price. Under those circumstances, even relatively small producers or consumers of the item in question have an incentive to hedge, and speculators can earn a net return by satisfying their demands. The commodities for which futures markets existed before 1971 satisfied these requirements. Foreign currencies or nominal financial claims did not. For major foreign currencies, there were occasional large changes in the exchange rate, but not the day-to-day, month-to-month variability that characterized the price of corn or wheat or hog bellies.

As already noted, that situation changed radically with the final climactic end of the link between money and a commodity and the full-fledged emergence of pure fiat standards. The International Monetary Market was the first major financial futures market to emerge. Its early emergence owed much to the foresight and initiative of Leo Melamed and his colleagues at the Chicago Mercantile Exchange. But it also owed much to the particular form that the end of a commodity link took—the publicly announced abandonment by the U.S. of the Bretton Woods system of fixed exchange rates. That action led in the first instance to uncertainty about exchange rates. Only as its more indirect consequences for nominal price levels and interest rates unfolded over time did futures markets in other financial assets develop. The final consequence has been a literal explosion of such markets.

Throughout the period since 1971, proposals have repeatedly been made for resurrecting a Bretton Woods type system or restoring a commodity link or reaching some other international arrangement directed at "stabilizing" exchange rates. But so far, that has been just talk and I confidently predict that it will continue to be. The reason is that it attacks the problem from the wrong end. The real issue is the monetary regime that will emerge from the transition we have been going through. Once that is settled, the exchange-rate regime will fall into place—which does not mean that exchange rates will settle down into the narrow ranges of fluctuation that prevailed in the "golden" age of 1880–1914 that evokes much misplaced nostalgia. Flexibility in exchange rates has provided a useful, indeed indispensible, shock absorber for monetary and other disturbances, and will continue to do so for the foreseeable future. However, if these disturbances become less violent, exchange rates will also become less volatile.

Two factors lead me to believe that the present transitional period will lead to relatively stable monetary regimes consistent with relatively stable nominal price levels, and hence with relatively stable exchange rates, though without a link to a commodity.

The first factor is that the potency of inflation as a source of government revenue has been greatly reduced, and hence so has its political appeal. The elimination of bracket creep via the indexation of income taxes, the shortening of the debt structure forced by the market's greater sensitivity to the difference between nominal and real interest rates, and the rising ratio of national income to high-powered money have all reduced the potency of inflation as a tax.[4]

The second factor is simply the impact of experience with an undisciplined random monetary walk in the immediate aftermath of the enthronement of fiat money. The accelerating inflation in the U.S. and other countries during the 1970s proved so unpopular as to make politically acceptable the disinflation of the 1980s, despite the periods of sharp recession that accompanied the disinflation. The public's memories of such episodes is long. In Germany, Austria, and other European countries that experienced hyperinflation after World War I, the collective memory remains sufficiently strong that more than sixty years later it remains highly unpopular politically to permit inflation to develop. Similarly, the accelerating inflation in Japan in the 1960s and early 1970s made a steady monetary policy consistent with bringing down inflation popular in the later 1970s and in the early 1980s. It is no accident that these countries have kept inflation under far better check than most countries that had no such earlier traumatic experiences.

The public demands a stabler price level than we have experienced in the past several decades, and the political system is sufficiently responsive to meet that demand. Control over high-powered money is the key monetary tool available to governments in an age of fiat money. Effective limits on the level and the growth of high-powered money are the basic requisite for a stabler price level, for a long-term anchor to the nominal price level. Such limits can in principle be provided in many different ways, and there is a vigorous and growing literature on alternative arrangements. I do not know what substitute will finally emerge for a commodity link as a long-term anchor to the price level. Monetary systems are not made, they grow, as Bagehot said in another connection, through the "instinctive confidence generated by use and years. . . ." It took generations for confidence in gold to erode; it may take generations for confidence in alternative anchors to emerge.

As such alternative anchors emerge, exchange rates and interest rates will settle down and become less variable. The International Monetary Market and other financial futures markets will become less active, and speculators will be driven to seek other ways to make greatest use of their rare talents.

There are some glimmerings that this process is already under way, as the cases of Japan, Germany, and Austria already mentioned suggest. Moreover, despite all the attention devoted to the recent decline of the dollar, exchange rates have become less variable in the past several years. I believe that tendency will continue.

Transition periods are always the most interesting—partly in the sense suggested by the ancient Chinese curse. This book is striking evidence of that proposition. Uncertainty about monetary regimes has produced a flood of literature on this occasion as it did during the Napoleonic period in Britain, and the greenback and "free silver" periods in the United States. When and as that uncertainty is resolved, economists, and not only operators in financial futures markets, will turn to greener fields.

Notes

1. *The Purchasing Power of Money* (1911), new and rev. ed. (New York: Macmillan, 1926), p. 121.

2. "The Resource Cost of Irredeemable Paper Money," *Journal of Political Economy* 94, part 1 (June 1986): 643.

3. See Milton Friedman, "Monetary Policy in a Fiat World," *Bank of Japan Monetary and Economic Studies* 3 (September 1985): 11–18; and Milton Friedman and Anna J. Schwartz, "Has Government Any Role in Money?" *Journal of Monetary Economics* 17 (1986): 37–62.

4. For a fuller discussion, see Friedman, "Monetary Policy in a Fiat World," pp. 16–18; and Friedman and Schwartz, pp. 55–57.

PART I

HISTORICAL OVERVIEW AND BACKGROUND

1

THE CASE FOR FLEXIBLE EXCHANGE RATES*

Milton Friedman

The Western nations seem committed to a system of international payments based on exchange rates between their national currencies fixed by governments and maintained rigid except for occasional changes to new levels. This system is embodied in the statutes of the International Monetary Fund, which provides for changes in exchange rates of less than 10 per cent by individual governments without approval of the Fund and for larger changes only with approval; it is implicit in the European Payments Union; and it is taken for granted in almost all discussions of international economic policy.

Whatever may have been the merits of this system for another day, it is ill suited to current economic and political conditions. These conditions make a system of flexible or floating exchange rates—exchange rates freely determined in an open market primarily by private dealings and, like other market prices, varying from day to day—absolutely essential for the fulfilment of our basic economic objective: the achievement and maintenance of a free and prosperous world community engaging in unrestricted multilateral trade. There is scarcely a facet of international economic policy for which the implicit acceptance of a system of rigid exchange rates does not create serious and unnecessary difficulties. Promotion of rearmament, liberalization of trade, avoidance of allocations

*This paper had its origin in a memorandum written in the fall of 1950 when I was a consultant to the Finance and Trade Division of the Office of Special Representative for Europe, United States Economic Cooperation Administration. Needless to say, the views it expresses are entirely my own. I am grateful to Joel Berenstein and Maxwell Obst for criticism of the original memorandum and to Earl J. Hamilton and Lloyd A. Metzler for criticism of a subsequent draft. The paper owes much, also, to extensive discussion of the general problem with a number of friends, particularly Aaron Director, James Meade, Lloyd Mints, and Lionel Robbins. Unfortunately, these discussions failed to produce sufficient agreement to make a disclaimer of their responsibility unnecessary.

and other direct controls both internal and external, harmonization of internal monetary and fiscal policies—all these problems take on a different cast and become far easier to solve in a world of flexible exchange rates and its corollary, free convertibility of currencies. The sooner a system of flexible exchange rates is established, the sooner unrestricted multilateral trade will become a real possibility. And it will become one without in any way interfering with the pursuit by each nation of domestic economic stability according to its own lights.[1]

Before proceeding to defend this thesis in detail, I should perhaps emphasize two points to avoid misunderstanding. First, advocacy of flexible exchange rates is *not* equivalent to advocacy of unstable exchange rates. The ultimate objective is a world in which exchange rates, while *free* to vary, are in fact highly stable. Instability of exchange rates is a symptom of instability in the underlying economic structure. Elimination of this symptom by administrative freezing of exchange rates cures none of the underlying difficulties and only makes adjustment to them more painful. Second, by unrestricted multilateral trade, I shall mean a system in which there are no direct quantitative controls over imports or exports, in which any tariffs or export bounties are reasonably stable and nondiscriminatory and are not subject to manipulation to affect the balance of payments, and in which a substantial fraction of international trade is in private (nongovernmental) hands. Though admittedly vague and subject to considerable ambiguity, this definition will do for our purposes. I shall take for granted without detailed examination that unrestricted multilateral trade in this sense[2] is a desirable objective of economic policy.[3] However, many of the arguments for flexible exchange rates remain valid even if this premise is not accepted.

I. Alternative Methods of Adjusting to Changes Affecting International Payments

Changes affecting the international trade and the balance of payments of various countries are always occurring. Some are in the "real" conditions determining international trade, such as the weather, technical conditions of production, consumer tastes, and the like. Some are in monetary conditions, such as divergent degrees of inflation or deflation in various countries.

These changes affect some commodities more than others and so tend to produce changes in the structure of relative prices—for example, rearmament by the United States impinges particularly on selected raw materials and tends to raise their prices relatively to other prices. Such effects on the relative price structure are likely to be much the same whether exchange rates are rigid or flexible and to raise much the same problem of adjustment in either case and so will receive little attention in what follows.

But, over and above these effects on particular commodities and prices, the changes in question affect each country's balance of payments, taken as a whole. Holders of foreign currencies want to exchange them for the currency of a particular country in order to purchase commodities produced in that country, or to purchase securities or other capital assets in that country, or to pay interest on or repay debts to that country, or to make gifts to citizens of that country, or simply to hold for one of these uses or for resale. The amount of currency of a particular country that is demanded per unit of time for each of these purposes will, of course, depend in the first instance on the exchange rate—the number of units of a foreign currency that must be paid to acquire one unit of the domestic currency. Other things the same, the more expensive a given currency, that is, the higher the exchange rate, the less of that currency will in general be demanded for each of these purposes. Similarly, holders of the currency of the country in question want to exchange that currency for foreign currencies for the corresponding purposes; and, again, the amount they want to exchange depends, in the first instance, on the price which they can get. The changes continuously taking place in the conditions of international trade alter the "other things" and so the desirability of using the currencies of various countries for each of the purposes listed. The aggregate effect is at one time to increase, at another to decrease, the amount of a country's currency demanded at any given rate of exchange relative to the amount offered for sale at that rate. Of course, after the event, the amount of a particular currency purchased must equal the amount sold—this is a question simply of double-entry bookkeeping. But, in advance, the amount people want to buy need not equal the amount people want to sell. The *ex post* equality involves a reconciliation of these divergent desires, either through changes in the desires themselves or through their frustration.

There is no way of avoiding this reconciliation; inconsistent desires cannot simultaneously be satisfied. The crucial question of policy is the mechanism whereby this reconciliation is brought about. Suppose the aggregate effect of changes in the conditions affecting international payments has been to increase the amount of a country's currency people want to buy with foreign currency relatively to the amount other people want to sell for foreign currency at the pre-existing exchange rate—to create an incipient surplus in the balance of payments. How can these inconsistent desires be reconciled? (1) The country's currency may be bid up, or put up, in price. This increase in the exchange rate will tend to make the currency less desirable relative to the currency of other countries and so eliminate the excess demand at the pre-existing rate.[4] (2) Prices within the country may rise, thus making its goods less desirable relative to goods in other countries, or incomes within the country may rise, thus increasing the demand for foreign currencies. (3) Direct controls over transactions involving foreign exchange may prevent holders of foreign balances from acquiring as much domestic exchange as they would otherwise like to; for example, they may be prevented from buying domestic goods by the inability to get a required export license. (4) The excess amount of domestic currency desired may be provided out of monetary reserves, the foreign currency acquired being added to reserves of foreign currencies—the monetary authorities (or exchange equalization fund or the like) may step in with a "desire" to buy or sell the difference between the amounts demanded and supplied by others.

Each of these four methods has its obvious counterpart if the effect of the changes is to create an incipient deficit. Aside from purely frictional frustrations of desires (the inability of a buyer to find a seller because of imperfections of the market), these are fundamentally the only four ways in which an *ex ante* divergence between the amount of a country's currency demanded and the amount supplied can be converted into the *ex post* equality that necessarily prevails. Let us consider each in turn.

A. Changes In Exchanges Rates

Two different mechanisms whereby exchange-rate changes may be used to maintain equilibrium in the balance of payments must be sharply distinguished: (1) flexible exchange rates as defined above and (2) official changes in temporarily rigid rates.

1. *Flexible exchange rates.*—Under flexible exchange rates freely determined in open markets, the first impact of any tendency toward a surplus or deficit in the balance of payments is on the exchange rate. If a country has an incipient surplus of receipts over payments—an excess demand for its currency—the exchange rate will tend to rise. If it has an incipient deficit, the exchange rate will tend to fall. If the conditions responsible for the rise or the fall in the exchange rate are generally regarded as temporary, actual or potential holders of the country's currency will tend to change their holdings in such a way as to moderate the movement in the exchange rate. If a rise in the exchange rate, for example, is expected to be temporary, there is an incentive for holders of the country's currency to sell some of their holdings for foreign

currency in order to buy the currency back later on at a lower price. By doing so, they provide the additional domestic currency to meet part of the excess demand responsible for the initial rise in the exchange rate; that is, they absorb some of what would have been surplus receipts of foreign currency at the former exchange rate. Conversely, if a decline is expected to be temporary, there is an incentive to buy domestic currency for resale at a higher price. Such purchases of domestic currency provide the foreign currency to meet some of what would have been a deficit of foreign currency at the former exchange rate. In this way, such "speculative" transactions in effect provide the country with reserves to absorb temporary surpluses or to meet temporary deficits. On the other hand, if the change in the exchange rate is generally regarded as produced by fundamental factors that are likely to be permanent, the incentives are the reverse of those listed above, and speculative transactions will speed up the rise or decline in the exchange rate and thus hasten its approach to its final position.

This final position depends on the effect that changes in exchange rates have on the demand for and supply of a country's currency, not to hold as balances, but for other purposes. A rise in the exchange rate produced by a tendency toward a surplus makes foreign goods cheaper in terms of domestic currency, even though their prices are unchanged in terms of their own currency, and domestic goods more expensive in terms of foreign currency, even though their prices are unchanged in terms of domestic currency. This tends to increase imports, reduce exports, and so offset the incipient surplus. Conversely, a decline in the exchange rate produced by a tendency toward a deficit makes imports more expensive to home consumers, and exports less expensive to foreigners, and so tends to offset the incipient deficit.

Because money imparts general purchasing power and is used for such a wide variety of purposes abroad as well as at home, the demand for and supply of any one country's currency is widely spread and comes from many sources. In consequence, broad, active, and nearly perfect markets have developed in foreign exchange whenever they have been permitted—and usually even when they have not been. The exchange rate is therefore potentially an extremely sensitive price. Changes in it occur rapidly, automatically, and continuously and so tend to produce corrective movements before tensions can accumulate and a crisis develop. For example, if Germany had had a flexible exchange rate in 1950, the crisis in the fall of that year would never have followed the course it did. The exchange rate would have been affected not later than July and would have started to produce corrective adaptations at once. The whole affair would never have assumed large proportions and would have shown up as a relatively minor ripple in exchange rates. As it was, with a rigid exchange rate, the warning of impending trouble was indirect and delayed, and the government took no action until three months later, by which time the disequilibrium had grown to crisis dimensions, requiring drastic action at home, international consultation, and help from abroad.

The recurrent foreign-exchange crises of the United Kingdom in the postwar period are perhaps an even more dramatic example of the kind of crises that could not develop under a system of flexible exchange rates. In each case no significant corrective action was taken until large disequilibriums had been allowed to cumulate, and then the action had to be drastic. The rigidities and discontinuities introduced by substituting administrative action for automatic market forces have seldom been demonstrated so clearly or more impressively.

2. *Official changes in exchange rates.*—These examples suggest the sharp difference between flexible exchange rates and exchange rates held temporarily rigid but subject to change by government action to meet substantial difficulties. While these exchange-rate changes have the same kind of effect on commodity trade and the like as those produced automatically under a system of flexible exchange rates, they have very different effects on speculative transactions. Partly for this reason, partly because of their innate discontinuity, each exchange-rate change tends to become the occasion for a crisis. There is no mechanism for producing changes in exchange rates of the required magnitude or for correcting mistakes, and some other mechanism must be used to maintain equilibrium during the period between exchange-rate changes—either internal price or income changes, direct controls, or monetary reserves.

Even though an exchange-rate change would not otherwise be the occasion for a crisis, speculative movements are highly likely to convert it into one, for this system practically insures a maximum of destablizing speculation. Because the exchange rate is changed infrequently and only to meet substantial difficulties, a change tends to come well after the onset of difficulty, to be postponed as long as possible, and to be made only after substantial pressure on the exchange rate has accumulated. In consequence, there is seldom any doubt about the direction in which an exchange rate will be changed, if it is changed. In the interim between the suspicion of a possible change in the rate and the actual change, there is every incentive to sell the country's currency if devaluation is expected (to export "capital" from the country) or to buy it if an appreciation is expected (to bring in "capital"); either can be done without an exchange loss and will mean an exchange gain when and if the rate is changed. This is in sharp contrast with the situation under flexible exchange rates when the decline in the exchange rate takes place along with, and as a consequence of, the sales of a currency and so discourages or penalizes sales, and conversely for purchases. With rigid rates, if the exchange rate is not changed, the only cost to the speculators is a possible loss of interest earnings from an interest-rate differential. It is no answer to this argument to say that capital flows can be restricted by direct controls, since our ultimate objective in using this method is precisely to avoid such restrictions.

In short, the system of occasional changes in temporarily rigid exchange rates seems to me the worst of two worlds: it provides neither the stability of expectations that a genuinely rigid and stable exchange rate could provide in a world of unrestricted trade and willingness and ability to adjust the internal price structure to external conditions nor the continuous sensitivity of a flexible exchange rate.

B. Changes In Internal Prices Or Income

In principle, changes in internal prices could produce the same effects on trade as changes in the exchange rate. For example, a decline of 10 per cent in every internal price in Germany (including wages, rents, etc.) with an unchanged dollar price of the mark would clearly have identically the same effects on the relative costs of domestic and foreign goods as a decline of 10 per cent in the dollar price of the mark, with all internal prices unchanged. Similarly, such price changes could have the same effects on speculative transactions. If expected to be temporary, a decline in prices would stimulate speculative purchases of goods to avoid future higher prices, thus moderating the price movement.

If internal prices were as flexible as exchange rates, it would make little economic difference whether adjustments were brought about by changes in exchange rates or by equivalent changes in internal prices. But this condition is clearly not fulfilled. The exchange rate is potentially flexible in the absence of administrative action to freeze it. At least in the modern world, internal prices are highly inflexible. They are more flexible upward than downward, but even on the upswing all prices are not equally flexible. The inflexibility of prices, or different degrees of flexibility, means a distortion of adjustments in response to changes in external conditions. The adjustment takes the form primarily of price changes in some sectors, primarily of output changes in others.

Wage rates tend to be among the less flexible prices. In consequence, an incipient deficit that is countered by a policy of permitting or forcing prices to decline is likely to produce unemployment rather than, or in addition to, wage decreases. The consequent decline in real income reduces the domestic demand for foreign goods and thus the demand for foreign currency with which to purchase these goods. In this way, it offsets the incipient deficit. But this is clearly a highly inefficient method of adjusting to external changes. If the external changes are deep-seated and persistent, the unemployment produces steady downward pressure on prices and wages, and the adjustment will not have been completed until the deflation has run its sorry course.

Despite these difficulties, the use of changes in internal prices might not be undesirable if they were called for only rarely and only as a result of changes in the real underlying conditions of trade. Such changes in underlying conditions are likely in any event to require considerable changes in relative prices of particular goods and services and only changes of a much smaller order of magnitude in the general level of internal prices. But neither condition is likely to be satisfied in the modern world. Adjustments are required continuously, and many are called for by essentially monetary phenomena, which, if promptly offset by a movement in the exchange rate, would require no change in the actual allocation of resources.

Changes in interest rates are perhaps best classified under this heading of changes in internal prices. Interest-rate changes have in the past played a particularly important role in adjustment to external changes, partly because they have been susceptible to direct influence by the monetary authorities, and partly because, under a gold standard, the initial impact of a tendency toward a deficit or surplus was a loss or gain of gold and a consequent tightening or ease in the money market. The rise in the interest rate produced in this way by an incipient deficit increased the demand for the currency for capital purposes and so offset part or all of the deficit. This reduced the rate at which the deficit had to be met by a decline in internal prices, which was itself set in motion by the loss of gold and associated decrease in the stock of money responsible for the rise in interest rates. Conversely, an incipient surplus increased the stock of gold and eased the money market. The resulting decline in the interest rate reduced the demand for the currency for capital purposes and so offset part or all of the surplus, reducing the rate at which the surplus had to be met by the rise in internal prices set in motion by the gain of gold and associated rise in the stock of money.

These interest-induced capital movements are a desirable part of a system relying primarily on changes in internal prices, since they tend to smooth out the adjustment process. They cannot, however, be relied on alone, since they come into operation only incidentally to the adjustment of internal prices.

Primary reliance on changes in internal prices and incomes was tolerable in the nineteenth century partly because the key countries of the Western world placed much heavier emphasis on freedom from government interference at home and unrestricted multilateral trade abroad than on domestic stability; thus they were willing to allow domestic economic policy to be dominated by the requirements of fixed exchange rates and free convertibility of currencies. But, equally important, this very emphasis gave holders of balances confidence in the maintenance of the system and so made them willing to let small differences in interest rates determine the currency in which they held their balances. Furthermore, the emphasis on freedom from government interference at home gave less scope to internal monetary management and so meant that most changes affecting international trade reflected real changes in underlying conditions, or else monetary changes, such as gold discoveries, more or less common to the major nations. Modern conditions, with the widespread emphasis on full employment at home and the extensive intervention of government into economic affairs, are clearly very different and much less favorable to this method of adjustment.

C. Direct Controls

In principle, direct controls on imports, exports, and capital movements could bring about the same effects on trade and the balance of payments as changes in exchange rates or in internal prices and incomes. The final adjustment will, after all, involve a change in the composition of imports and exports, along with specifiable capital transactions. If these could be predicted in advance, and if it were technically possible to control selectively each category of imports, exports, and capital transactions, direct controls could be used to produce the required adjustment.

It is clear, however, that the changes in imports and exports and the required capital transactions cannot be predicted; the fact that each new foreign-exchange crisis in a country like Britain is officially regarded as a bolt from the blue is ample evidence for this proposition. Even if they could be predicted, direct control of imports, exports, and capital transactions by techniques other than the price system[5] necessarily means extending such control to many internal matters and interfering with the efficiency of the distribution and production of goods—some means must be found for rationing imports that are being held down in amount or disposing of increased imports and for allocating reduced exports or getting increased exports.

Aside from the many unfortunate results of such a process which are by now abundantly clear, it has a perverse effect on the foreign-payments problem itself, particularly when direct controls are used, as they have been primarily, to counter an actual or incipient deficit. The apparent deficit that has to be closed by direct controls is larger than the deficit that would emerge at the same exchange rate without the direct controls and, indeed, might be eliminated entirely or converted into a surplus if the direct controls on imports and exports and their inevitable domestic accompaniments were removed. The mere existence of the direct controls makes the currency less desirable for many purposes because of the limitations it places on what holders of the currency may do with it, and this is likely to reduce the demand for the currency more than it would be reduced by the fluctuations in exchange rates or other adaptive mechanisms substituted for the direct controls. In addition, permitted imports are generally distributed at prices lower than those that would clear the market and so are used wastefully and in the wrong places, increasing apparent import "requirements"; similarly, the composition of imports is determined by administrative decisions that tend to have the same effect. Both of these are particularly important in hindering exports, because export industries are not likely to get so large a fraction of the imports as they would bid away in a free market, even if the government supposedly favors export industries, and cannot make their influence fully felt in determining the composition of imports; and the direct controls have a tendency to make the incentive to export lower than it would otherwise be.[6]

The considerations mentioned in the preceding paragraph may help to reconcile—and, indeed, their elaboration was stimulated by my own need to reconcile—the impression of casual visitors to England, and the conclusions of some careful students of the subject, that the pound is currently (1952) undervalued in purchasing power terms with the recurrent pressures on the pound and the restrictive measures that seem to be required to maintain the pound at its present rate. They show that there is no necessary inconsistency between the following two assertions: (1) the market value of the pound would be higher than $2.80 if all exchange restrictions and associated controls were removed and the exchange rate were allowed to be determined by primarily private dealings in a free market; (2) given the retention of an official exchange rate and of the existing *system* of exchange restrictions and associated internal controls, an *easing* of restrictions would produce pressure on the exchange rate and require a rate lower than $2.80 to keep exchange reserves from being depleted. Both statements may not, in fact, be correct; but there is no such obvious contradiction between them as there appears to be at first sight.

Finally, whatever the desirability of direct controls, there are political and administrative limits to the extent to which it is possible to impose and enforce such controls. These limits are narrower in some countries than in others, but they are present in all. Given sufficient incentive to do so, ways will be found to evade or avoid the controls. A race develops between officials seeking to plug legal loopholes and to discover and punish illegal evasions of the controls and the ever numerous individuals whose inventive talents are directed toward discovering or opening up new loopholes by the opportunities for large returns or whose respect for law and fear of punishment are overcome by the same opportunities. And the race is by no means always to the officials, even when they are honest and able. In particular, it has proved extremely difficult in all countries to prevent capital movements by direct controls.

D. Use of Monetary Reserves

Given adequate reserves, tendencies toward a surplus or a deficit can be allowed to produce an actual surplus or deficit in transactions other than those of the monetary authority (or exchange equalization fund, or whatever the name may be) without a change in exchange rates, internal prices or incomes, or direct controls, the additional domestic or foreign currency demanded being supplied by the monetary authority. This device is feasible and not undesirable for movements that are small and temporary, though, if it is clear that the movements are small and temporary, it is largely unnecessary, since, with flexible exchange rates, private speculative transactions will provide the additional domestic or foreign currency demanded with only minor movements in exchange rates.

The exclusive use of reserves is much less desirable, if possible at all, for movements of large magnitude and long duration. If the problem is a deficit, the ability of the monetary authorities to meet the deficit is immediately limited by the size of their reserves of foreign currency or the equivalent plus whatever additional sums they can or are willing to borrow or acquire in other ways from holders of foreign currency. Moreover, if the internal price level (or level of employment) is to be kept stable, the proceeds from the sales of foreign-exchange reserves must not be impounded or used in other deflationary ways. This assumes, of course, that the deficit is not itself produced by internal inflationary policies but occurs despite a stable internal price level. The proceeds must be used to retire debt or to finance a deficit in the budget to whatever extent is necessary to prevent a price decline.

If the problem is a surplus, the monetary authorities must be prepared to accumulate foreign exchange indefinitely, providing all the domestic currency that is demanded. Moreover, if the internal price level is to be maintained constant, it must obtain the domestic currency it sells for foreign currency in noninflationary ways. It can print or create the currency only to the extent that is consistent with stable prices. For the rest it must get the amount required by borrowing at whatever interest rates are necessary to keep domestic prices stable or from a surplus of the appropriate amount in the government budget. Entirely aside from the technical problems of monetary management involved, the community is unlikely to be willing to exchange indefinitely part of its product for unproductive currency hoards, particularly if the source of the surplus is monetary inflation abroad, and thus the foreign currency is decreasing in real value.

Traditionally, of course, monetary reserves have not been used as the primary method of adjusting to changes in external conditions but as a shock absorber pending changes in internal prices and incomes. A deficit has been met out of monetary reserves in the first instance, but the proceeds or even a multiple of the proceeds have been, as it were, impounded; that is, the stock of money has been allowed or made to decrease as a result of the decline of monetary reserves, with a consequent rise in interest rates and downward pressure on internal prices. Similarly, the domestic currency exchanged for a surplus of foreign currency has, as it were, been created and allowed to or made to increase the stock of money by the same amount or a multiple of that amount, with a consequent decline in interest rates and upward pressure on internal prices.[7]

Since the end of the first World War, nations have become increasingly unwilling to use reserves in this way and to allow the effect to be transmitted directly and immediately to internal monetary conditions and prices. Already during the 1920's, the United States, to cite one outstanding and critical example, refused to allow its surplus, which took the form of gold imports, to raise domestic prices in the way the supposed rules of the gold standard demanded; instead, it "sterilized" gold imports. Especially after the Great Depression completed the elevation of full employment to the primary goal of economic policy, nations have been unwilling to allow deficits to exert any deflationary effect.

The use of monetary reserves as the sole reliance to meet small and temporary strains on balances of payments and of other devices to meet larger and more extended or more basic strains is an understandable objective of economic policy and comes close to summarizing the philosophy underlying the International Monetary Fund. Unfortunately, it is not a realistic, feasible, or desirable policy. It is seldom possible to know in advance or even soon after the event whether any given strain in the balance of payments is likely to be reversed rapidly or not; that is, whether it is a result of temporary or permanent factors. Reserves must be very large indeed if they are to be the sole reliance in meeting changes in external conditions until the magnitude and probable duration of the changes can be diagnosed with confidence and more fundamental correctives undertaken in light of the diagnosis, far larger than if they serve the function they did under the classical gold standard. Except perhaps for the United States, and even for the United States only so long as gold is freely acceptable as an international currency, reserves are nothing like this large. Under the circumstances there is a strong tendency to rely on reserves too long for comfort yet not long enough for confident diagnosis and reasoned action. Corrective steps are postponed in the hope that things will right themselves until the state of the reserves forces drastic and frequently ill-advised action.

E. A Comparison

One or another of the methods of adjustment just described must in fact be used to meet changes in conditions affecting external trade; there is no avoiding this necessity short of the complete elimination of external trade, and even this would be an extreme form of direct controls over imports and exports. On the basis of the analysis so far, flexible exchange rates seem clearly the technique of adjustment best suited to current conditions: the use of reserves is not by itself a feasible device; direct controls are cumbrous and inefficient and, I venture to predict, will ultimately prove ineffective in a free society; changes in internal prices and incomes are undesirable because of rigidities in internal prices, especially wages, and the emergence of full employment—or independence of internal monetary policy—as a major goal of policy.

The argument for flexible exchange rates is, strange to say, very nearly identical with the argument for daylight saving time. Isn't it absurd to change the clock in summer when exactly the same result could be achieved by having each individual change his habits? All that is required is that everyone decide to come to his office an hour earlier, have lunch an hour earlier, etc. But obviously it is much simpler to change the clock that guides all than to have each individual separately change his pattern of reaction to the clock, even though all want to do so. The situation is exactly the same in the exchange market. It is far simpler to allow one price to change, namely, the price of foreign exchange, than to rely upon changes in the multitude of prices that together constitute the internal price structure.

II. Objections to Flexible Exchange Rates

Three major criticisms have been made of the proposal to establish a system of flexible exchange rates: first, that flexible exchange rates may increase the degree of uncertainty in the economic scene; second, that flexible exchange rates will not work because they will produce offsetting changes in domestic prices; and, third, that flexible exchange rates will not produce the best attainable timing or pace of adjustment. The first objection takes many different forms, and it will promote clarity to deal with some of these separately, even though this means considerable overlapping.

A. Flexible Exchange Rates and Uncertainty

1. *Flexible exchange rates mean instability rather than stability.*—On the naïve level on which this objection is frequently made, it involves the already-mentioned mistake of confusing the sympton of difficulties with the difficulties themselves. A flexible exchange rate need not be an unstable exchange rate. If it is, it is primarily because there is underlying instability in the economic conditions governing international trade. And a rigid exchange rate may, while itself nominally stable, perpetuate and accentuate other elements of instability in the economy. The mere fact that a rigid official exchange rate does not change while a flexible rate does is no evidence that the former means greater stability in any more fundamental sense. If it does, it is for one or more of the reasons considered in the points that follow.

2. *Flexible exchange rates make it impossible for exporters and importers to be certain about the price they will have to pay or receive for foreign exchange.*—Under flexible exchange rates traders can almost always protect themselves against changes in the rate by hedging in a futures market. Such futures markets in foreign currency readily develop when exchange rates are flexible. Any uncertainty about returns will then be borne by speculators. The most that can be said for this argument, therefore, is that flexible exchange rates impose a cost of hedging on traders, namely, the price that must be paid to speculators for assuming the risk of future changes in exchange rates. But this is saying too much. The substitution of flexible for rigid exchange rates changes the form in which uncertainty in the foreign-exchange market is manifested; it may not change the extent of uncertainty at all and, indeed, may even decrease

uncertainty. For example, conditions that would tend to produce a decline in a flexible exchange rate will produce a shortage of exchange with a rigid exchange rate. This in turn will produce either internal adjustments of uncertain character or administrative allocation of exchange. Traders will then be certain about the rate but uncertain about either internal conditions or the availability of exchange. The uncertainty can be removed for some transactions by advance commitments by the authorities dispensing exchange; it clearly cannot be removed for all transactions in view of the uncertainty about the total amount of exchange available; the reduction in uncertainty for some transactions therefore involves increased uncertainty for others, since all the risk is now concentrated on them. Further, such administrative allocation of exchange is always surrounded by uncertainty about the policy that will be followed. It is by no means clear whether the uncertainty associated with a flexible rate or the uncertainty associated with a rigid rate is likely to be more disruptive to trade.

3. *Speculation in foreign-exchange markets tends to be destabilizing.*— This point is, of course, closely related to the preceding one. It is said that speculators will take a decline in the exchange rate as a signal for a further decline and will thus tend to make the movements in the exchange rate sharper than they would be in the absence of speculation. The special fear in this connection is of capital flight in response to political uncertainty or simply to movements in the exchange rate. Despite the prevailing opinion to the contrary, I am very dubious that in fact speculation in foreign exchange would be destabilizing. Evidence from some earlier experiences and from current free markets in currency in Switzerland, Tangiers, and elsewhere seems to me to suggest that, in general, speculation is stabilizing rather than the reverse, though the evidence has not yet been analyzed in sufficient detail to establish this conclusion with any confidence. People who argue that speculation is generally destabilizing seldom realize that this is largely equivalent to saying that speculators lose money, since speculation can be destabilizing in general only if speculators on the average sell when the currency is low in price and buy when it is high.[8] It does not, of course, follow that speculation is not destabilizing; professional speculators might on the average make money while a changing body of amateurs regularly lost larger sums. But, while this may happen, it is hard to see why there is any presumption that it will; the presumption is rather the opposite. To put the same point differently, if speculation were persistently destabilizing, a government body like the Exchange Equalization Fund in England in the 1930's could make a good deal of money by speculating in exchange

and in the process almost certainly eliminate the destabilizing speculation. But to suppose that speculation by governments would generally be profitable is in most cases equivalent to supposing that government officials risking funds that they do not themselves own are better judges of the likely movements in foreign-exchange markets than private individuals risking their own funds.

The widespread belief that speculation is likely to be destabilizing is doubtless a major factor accounting for the cavalier rejection of a system of flexible exchange rates in the immediate postwar period. Yet this belief does not seem to be founded on any systematic analysis of the available empirical evidence.[9] It rests rather, I believe, primarily on an oversimplified interpretation of the movements of so-called "hot" money during the 1930's. At the time, any speculative movements which threatened a depreciation of a currency (i.e., which threatened a *change* in an exchange rate) were regarded as destabilizing, and hence these movements were so considered. In retrospect, it is clear that the speculators were "right"; that forces were at work making for depreciation in the value of most European currencies relative to the dollar independently of speculative activity; that the speculative movements were anticipating this change; and, hence, that there is at least as much reason to call them "stabilizing" as to call them "destabilizing."

In addition, the interpretation of this evidence has been marred by a failure to distinguish between a system of exchange rates held temporarily rigid but subject to change from time to time by government action and a system of flexible exchange rates. Many of the capital movements regarded as demonstrating that foreign-exchange speculation is destabilizing were stimulated by the existence of rigid rates subject to change by government action and are to be attributed primarily to the absence of flexibility of rates and hence of any incentive to avoid the capital movements. This is equally true of post–World War II experience with wide swings in foreign-payments positions. For reasons noted earlier, this experience has little direct bearing on the character of the speculative movements to be expected under a regime of genuinely flexible exchange rates.

4. *Flexible exchange rates involve increased uncertainty in the internal economy.*—It is argued that in many countries there is a great fear of inflation and that people have come to regard the exchange rate as an indicator of inflation and are highly sensitive to variations in it. Exchange crises, such as would tend to occur under rigid exchange rates, will pass unnoticed, it is argued, except by people directly connected with international trade, whereas a decline in the exchange rate would attract much

attention, be taken as a signal of a future inflation, and produce anticipatory movements by the public at large. In this way a flexible exchange rate might produce additional uncertainty rather than merely change the form in which uncertainty is manifested. There is some merit to this argument, but it does not seem to me to be a substantial reason for avoiding a flexible exchange rate. Its implication is rather that it would be desirable, if possible, to make the transition to a flexible rate at a time when exchange rates of European countries relative to the dollar would be likely to move moderately and some to rise. It further would be desirable to accompany the transition by willingness to take prompt monetary action to counter any internal reactions. A fear of inflation has little or no chance of producing inflation, except in a favorable monetary environment. A demonstration that fears of inflation are groundless, and some experience with the absence of any direct and immediate connection between the day-to-day movements in the exchange rate and internal prices would very shortly reduce to negligible porportions any increase in uncertainty on purely domestic markets, as a result of flexible yet not highly unstable exchange rates. Further, public recognition that a substantial decline in the exchange rate is a symptom of or portends internal inflation is by no means an unmixed evil. It means that a flexible exchange rate would provide something of a barrier to a highly inflationary domestic policy.

Very nearly the opposite of this argument is also sometimes made against flexible exchange rates. It is said that, with a flexible exchange rate, governments will have less incentive and be in a less strong position to take firm internal action to prevent inflation. A rigid exchange rate, it is said, gives the government a symbol to fight for—it can nail its flag to the mast of a specified exchange rate and resist political pressure to take action that would be inflationary in the name of defending the exchange rate. Dramatic foreign-exchange crises establish an atmosphere in which drastic if unpopular action is possible. On the other hand, it is said, with a flexible exchange rate, there is no definite sticking point; inflationary action will simply mean a decline in the exchange rate but no dramatic crisis, and people are little affected by a change in a price, the exchange rate, in a market in which relatively few have direct dealings.

Of course, it is not impossible for both these arguments to be valid—the first in countries like Germany, which have recently experienced hyperinflations and violently fluctuating exchange rates, the second in countries like Great Britain, which have not. But, even in countries like Britain, it is far from clear that a rigid exchange rate is more conducive under present conditions to noninflationary internal economic policy than a flexible exchange rate. A rigid exchange rate thwarts any immediate manifestation of a deterioration in the foreign-payments position as a result of inflationary internal policy. With an independent monetary standard, the loss of exchange reserves does not automatically reduce the stock of money or prevent its continued increase; yet it does temporarily reduce domestic inflationary pressure by providing goods in return for the foreign-exchange reserves without any simultaneous creation of domestic income. The deterioration shows up only sometime later, in the dull tables of statistics summarizing the state of foreign-exchange reserves. Even then, the authorities in the modern world have the alternative—or think they have—of suppressing a deficit by more stringent direct controls and thus postponing still longer the necessity for taking the appropriate internal measures; and they can always find any number of special reasons for the particular deterioration other than their internal policy. While the possibilities of using direct controls and of finding plausible excuses are present equally with flexible exchange rates, at least the deterioration in the foreign-payments position shows up promptly in the more readily understandable and simpler form of a decline in the exchange rates, and there is no emergency, no suddenly discovered decline in monetary reserves to dangerous levels, to force the imposition of supposedly unavoidable direct controls.

These arguments are modern versions of an argument that no longer has much merit but was at one time a valid and potent objection to flexible exchange rates, namely, the greater scope they give for government "tampering" with the currency. When rigid exchange rates were taken seriously, and when the armory of direct controls over international trade had not yet been resurrected, the maintenance of rigid rates left little scope for independent domestic monetary policy. This was the great virtue of the gold standard and the basic, albeit hidden, source of its emotional appeal; it provided an effective defense against hyper-inflation, against government intervention of a kind that had time and again led to the debasement and depreciation of once-proud currencies. This argument may still be a source of emotional resistance to flexible exchange rates; it is clear that it does not deserve to be. Governments of "advanced" nations are no longer willing to submit themselves to the harsh discipline of the gold standard or any other standard involving rigid exchange rates. They will evade its discipline by direct controls over trade if that will suffice and will change exchange rates before they will surrender control over domestic monetary policy. Perhaps a few modern inflations will establish a climate in which such behavior does not qualify as "advanced";

in the meantime we had best recognize the necessity of allowing exchange rates to adjust to internal policies rather than the reverse.

B. Flexible Exchange Rates and Internal Prices

While I have just used the primacy of internal policy as an argument for flexible exchange rates, it has also been used as an argument against flexible exchange rates. As we have seen, flexible exchange rates promote adjustments to changes in external circumstances by producing changes in the relation between the prices of foreign and domestic goods. A decline in an exchange rate produced by a tendency toward a deficit in the balance of payments tends to make the prices of foreign goods higher in terms of domestic currency than they would otherwise have been. If domestic prices are unaffected—or affected less—this means a higher price of foreign goods relative to domestic goods, which stimulates exports and discourages imports.

The rise in prices of foreign goods will, it is argued, mean a rise in the cost of living, and this, in turn, will give rise to a demand for wage increases, setting off what is typically referred to as a "wage-price spiral"—a term that is impressive enough to conceal the emptiness of the argument that it generally adorns. In consequence, so the argument continues, prices of domestic goods rise as much as prices of foreign goods, relative prices remain unchanged, there are no market forces working toward the elimination of the deficit that initially caused the decline in the exchange rate, and so further declines in the exchange rate are inevitable until nonmarket forces are brought into play. But these might as well have been used before as after the decline in the exchange rate.

This argument clearly applies only to rather special circumstances. At most, it may be an objection to a particular country at a particular time allowing its currency to go free; it is not a general objection to a *system* of flexible exchange rates as a long-run structure. It does not apply to circumstances making for the appreciation of a currency and applies only to some circumstances making for depreciation. Suppose, for example, that the tendency toward a deficit were produced by monetary deflations in other countries. The depreciation of the currency would then prevent the fall in external prices from being transmitted to the country in question; it would prevent prices of foreign goods from being forced down in terms of domestic currency. There is no way of eliminating the effect of the lowered "real" income of other countries; flexible exchange rates prevent this effect from being magnified by monetary disturbances. Similarly, the argument has little relevance if the decline in exchange rates reflects an open inflationary movement at home; the depreciation is then an obvious result of inflation rather than a cause. The argument has perhaps most relevance in either of two cases: an inflationary situation being repressed by direct controls or a depreciation produced by a change in the "real" conditions of trade.

Even in these cases, however, the argument cannot be fully granted. The crucial fallacy is the so-called "wage-price spiral." The rise in prices of foreign goods may add to the always plentiful list of excuses for wage increases; it does not in and of itself provide the economic conditions for a wage rise—or, at any rate, for a wage rise without unemployment. A general wage rise—or a general rise in domestic prices—becomes possible only if the monetary authorities create the additional money to finance the higher level of prices.[10] But if the monetary authorities are ready to do so to validate any rise in particular prices or wages, then the situation is fundamentally unstable without a change in the exchange rate, since a wage rise for any other excuse would lead to similar consequences. The assumption is that to him who asks will be given, and there is never a shortage of willingness to ask under such circumstances.

It will be answered that this innate instability is held in check by some sort of political compromise and that this compromise would be disturbed by the change in the exchange rate. This is a special case of the general argument considered earlier that the government is more likely to resist political pressure to take inflationary action if it nails its flag to the mast of a rigid exchange rate than if it lets the exchange rate fluctuate. But note that the forces leading to a changed exchange rate are not eliminated by freezing the rate; foreign exchange will have to be acquired or economized somehow. The "real" adjustment must be made in one way or another; the question is only how. Why should this way of making the adjustment destroy the compromise while other ways do not? Or, if this is true for a time, can it be expected to continue to be true? If, as we have argued, flexible exchange rates are the least costly way of making the adjustment, will not other methods be even more likely to destroy a tenuous political compromise?

C. Flexible Exchange Rates and the Timing of Adjustment

The ultimate adjustment to a change in external circumstances will consist of a change in the allocation of productive resources and in the composition of the goods available for consumption and investment. But this ultimate change will not be achieved immediately. It takes time to shift from the production of goods for domestic consumption to the production of goods for export, or conversely; it takes time to establish new markets abroad or to persuade consumers to substitute a foreign for a domestic good to which they have been accustomed; and so on in endless variety. The time required will vary widely: some types of adaptations can take place instantaneously (e.g., curtailment by a high price of the purchase of imported cheese, though even here the price rise required to achieve a given curtailment will be higher at first than after a time when people have had a chance to adapt their habitual pattern of consumption to the new price); other types of adaptation may take a generation (e.g., the development of a new domestic industry to produce goods formerly imported).

Suppose a substantial change in (real) external circumstances to occur and, to keep matters simple, circumstances thereafter to remain essentially unchanged for a lengthy period, so that we can (conceptually) isolate the adaptation to this one change. Suppose, further, that exchange rates are flexible and that international "capital" or "speculative" transactions are impossible, so that payments on current account must balance—a condition it is admittedly difficult to define precisely in any way susceptible to observation. It is clear that the initial change in exchange rates will be greater than the ultimate change required, for, to begin with, all the adjustment will have to be borne in those directions in which prompt adjustment is possible and relatively easy. As time passes, the slower-moving adjustments will take over part of the burden, permitting exchange rates to rebound toward a final position which is between the position prior to the external change and the position shortly thereafter. This is, of course, a highly oversimplified picture: the actual path of adjustment may involve repeated overshooting and undershooting of the final position, giving rise to a series of cycles around it or to a variety of other patterns. We are here entering into an area of economics about which we know very little, so it is fortunate that a precise discussion of the path is not essential for our purposes.

Under these circumstances it clearly might be in the interests of the community to pay something to avoid some of the initial temporary adjustments: if the exchange rate depreciates, to borrow from abroad at the going interest rate to pay for an excess of imports while the slower-moving adjustments take place rather than making the full immediate adjustment by curtailing those imports that can be readily curtailed and forcing out those exports that can be readily increased; if the exchange rate appreciates, to lend abroad at the going interest rate to finance an excess of exports while the slower-moving adjustments take place rather than making the full immediate adjustment by expanding those imports that can be readily expanded and curtailing those exports that can be readily curtailed. It would not, however, be worth doing this indefinitely, even if it were possible. For, if it were carried to the point at which the exchange rate remained unchanged, no other adjustments at all would take place. Yet the change in external circumstances makes a new allocation of resources and composition of goods optimal for the country concerned. That is, there is some optimum pace and timing of adjustment through exchange-rate-induced changes in the allocation of resources which is neither at the extreme of full immediate adjustment in this way alone nor at the other extreme of complete avoidance of adjustment.

Under the flexible exchange-rate system with a reasonably broad and free market in foreign exchange and with correct foresight on the part of speculators, just such an intermediate pace and timing of adjustment is produced even if there is no explicit negotiation of foreign loans. If the exchange rate depreciates, for example, the tendency for the exchange rate to fall further initially than ultimately offers an opportunity to make a profit by buying the currency now and reselling it later at a higher price. But this is precisely equivalent to lending by speculators to the country whose currency has depreciated. The return to the speculators is equal to the rate at which the currency they hold appreciates. In a free market with correct foresight, this will tend, aside from the minor costs of buying or selling the foreign exchange, to approach the interest rate that speculators could earn in other ways. If the currency appreciates at more than this rate, speculators still have an incentive to add to their holdings; if it appreciates at less than this rate, it is costing the speculators more in foregone interest to hold the balances than they are gaining in the appreciation of the exchange rate. In this way, speculation with a flexible exchange rate produces the same effect as explicit borrowing by a country whose currency has depreciated or explicit lending by one whose currency has appreciated. In practice, of course, there will be both explicit lending or borrowing and implicit lending or borrowing through exchange speculation. Moreover, the prospect of appreciation of a currency is equivalent to a higher interest rate for loans to the country and thus serves the same function in attracting capital to that country as the rises in interest rate that took place under the gold standard when a country was losing gold. There is, however, this important difference: under flexible exchange rates the inducement to foreign lenders need involve no change in the interest rate on domestic loans; under the gold standard, it did—a particular example of the independence of domestic monetary policy under flexible exchange rates.

But is the pace and timing of adjustment achieved in this way under flexible exchange rates an approximation to the optimum? This is an exceedingly difficult question to answer, depending as it does on whether the interest rate implicitly paid in the form of the appreciation or depreciation of the currency reflects the full relevant costs of too rapid or too slow adjustment. About all one can say without much more extensive analysis, and perhaps even with such analysis, is that there seems no reason to expect the timing or pace of adjustment under the assumed conditions to be systematically biased in one direction or the other from the optimum or to expect that other techniques of adaptation—through internal price changes, direct controls, and the use of monetary reserves with rigid exchange rates—would lead to a more nearly optimum pace and timing of adjustment.

This much would probably be granted by most persons who argue that flexible exchange rates lead to an undesirable pace and timing of adjustment. But, they would maintain, the foreign-exchange market is not nearly so perfect, or the foresight of speculators so good, as has been assumed to this point. The argument already considered, that speculation in foreign exchanges is destabilizing, is an extreme form of this objection. For, in that case, the immediate change in the foreign-exchange rate must go far enough to produce an immediate adaptation sufficient not only to balance current transactions but also to provide payment in foreign currencies for the balances of domestic currency that speculators perversely insist on liquidating when the exchange rate falls, or to provide the domestic currency for the balances speculators perversely insist on accumulating when the exchange rate rises. The country lends, as it were, when it should be borrowing and borrows when it should be lending.

But one need not go this far. Speculation may be stabilizing on balance, yet the market for foreign exchange, it can be said, is so narrow, foresight so imperfect, and private speculation so dominated by socially irrelevant political considerations that there is an insufficient smoothing-out of the adjustment process. For this to be a valid argument against flexible exchange rates, even if true, there must be some alternative that promises a better pace and timing of adjustment. We have already considered several other possibilities. We have seen that direct controls with a rigid exchange rate and the official use of monetary reserves have striking defects of their own, at least under modern conditions; they are likely to produce a highly erratic pace and timing of adjustment with alternate fits of unduly slow and unduly rapid adjustments, and direct controls are besides likely to produce the wrong kind of adjustments. Private capital movements in response to interest-rate differentials were at one time a real alternative but have been rendered largely unavailable by the unwillingness of monetary authorities to permit the required changes in interest rates, by the loss of confidence in the indefinite maintenance of the fixed exchange rates, and by the fear of restrictions on the use of exchange. In any event, such capital movements are, as we have seen, available and at least as likely to take place under flexible exchange rates.

The plausibility of the view that private exchange speculation produces too little smoothing of exchange-rate fluctuations derives, I believe, primarily from an implicit tendency to regard any slowing-down of the adjustment process as an improvement; that is, implicitly to regard no adjustment at all or an indefinitely prolonged one as the ideal.[11] This is the counterpart of the tendency to believe that internal monetary policy can and should avoid all internal adjustments in the level of income.[12] And both, I suspect, are a manifestation of the urge for security that is so outstanding a feature of the modern world and that is itself a major source of insecurity by promoting measures that reduce the adaptability of our economic systems to change without eliminating the changes themselves.

III. Special Problems in the Establishment and Operation of a Flexible Exchange-Rate System

A. Role of Governments in the Exchange Market

The argument that private exchange speculation will not produce a sufficient smoothing of exchange fluctuations is sometimes used to justify, not rigid exchange rates, but extensive intervention by individual governments or international agencies in the exchange market to even out minor fluctuations in exchange rates and to counter capital flights.[13] Such intervention, it should be noted, is in no way necessary for the operation of a flexible exchange-rate system; the issue is solely whether it is desirable. Private traders could buy and sell exchange at prices determined entirely by private demands and offers. Arbitrageurs would keep cross-rates in line. Futures markets would exist—and should be encouraged—to provide facilities for hedging. Markets like these now exist wherever they are permitted, and there is ample experience to demonstrate that they would expand rapidly and efficiently as the area in which they were permitted to operate widened.

Two separate issues are involved in judging the desirability of governmental intervention:[14] first, what, if any, restrictions on governments are desirable as part of an international agreement for establishing a system of flexible exchange rates; second, what behavior is desirable for an individual nation in its own interests.

From the international point of view, the fundamental requirement is that governments not use restrictions on trade of any kind to protect exchange rates. If they wish to use their reserves to speculate in exchange markets, that is primarily their business, provided they do not use the weapons of exchange controls, trade restrictions, and the like to protect their speculations. If they make money in exchange speculations without using such weapons, they perform the useful social function of smoothing out temporary fluctuations. If they lose money, they make gifts to other speculators or traders, and the primary cost—though not quite the whole cost—is borne by them.

From the national point of view, on balance it seems to me undesirable for a country to engage in transactions on the exchange market for the purpose of affecting the rate of exchange. I see no reason to expect that government officials will be better judges than private speculators of the likely movements in underlying conditions of trade and, hence, no reason to expect that government speculation will be more successful than private speculation in promoting a desirable pace and timing of adjustment. There is every reason to expect an extensive exchange market to develop and, hence, no need for government participation to assure sufficient speculation. A positive disadvantage of government speculation is the danger that government authorities operating under strong political pressures will try to peg the exchange rate, thereby converting a flexible exchange-rate system into a system of rigid rates subject to change from time to time by official action. Even if this does not occur, the continuous possibility that it may is likely to hinder the fullest development of a private market.

At the same time one cannot be dogmatic about this issue. It may be that private speculation is at times destabilizing for reasons that would not lead government speculation to be destabilizing; for example, government officials may have access to information that cannot readily be made available, for security or similar reasons, to private speculators. In any event, it would do little harm for a government agency to speculate in the exchange market provided it held to the objective of smoothing out temporary fluctuations and not interfering with fundamental adjustments. And there should be a simple criterion of success—whether the agency makes or loses money.

There is one qualification that needs to be made to this generally negative conclusion about the desirability of government intervention: a case can be made for government speculation in response to a capital flight produced by a threat of successful invasion of one country by another, and this even if private individuals correctly assess the threat.

Suppose everybody agrees that there is, say, one chance in four of a successful invasion. Private individuals will have a strong incentive separately to get capital out of the country. They cannot, of course, in the aggregate do so except in so far as they can literally ship physical goods out of the country into storage elsewhere or can induce foreigners to purchase from them physical capital (or claims to it) in the country. In the attempt to do the latter, they would drive down the rate of exchange. Suppose now that the government has reserves of foreign exchange. It can transfer these to its citizens by buying its own currency and thereby keep up the rate of exchange. If the invasion does not occur, the foreign-exchange reserves will tend to be repatriated, and the government will make money. On the other hand, if the invasion does occur and is successful, the government will lose, in a bookkeeping sense, and the expected loss will be greater than the expected gain. However, in this case the government may figure that all is lost anyway and that, if it had not transferred its reserves to its citizens, it would be forced to transfer them to the enemy. The incentives may therefore be different to the government than to its private citizens considered separately. Even this case, however, is not thoroughly clear. If there is hope of resistance, the government will want to mobilize all the foreign exchange it can to use in promoting the military effort.

B. Role of European Payments Union and International Monetary Fund in a System of Flexible Exchange Rates

The transition to flexible exchange rates might be organized in stages involving, first, the introduction of flexible exchange rates and free convertibility within Europe with a continuance of discrimination against the dollar and, as a later stage, free convertibility with the dollar. If this were done, the European Payments Union would retain the extremely important function of policing such a separation. When the separation was removed, EPU would lose its special functions. If it were continued at all, its only remaining functions would be as a check-clearing institution and as a body able to give advice to individual countries and to facilitate international consultation.

On the other hand, it is worth emphasizing that there is nothing essential in EPU arrangements that would be an obstacle to flexible exchange rates. The debits and credits could perfectly well be calculated in terms of an exchange rate changing from day to day. The only cost would be complication of the arithmetical calculations.

These comments apply equally to the International Monetary Fund, with, however, one important difference. The statutes of the IMF are designed for a world of exchange rates determined by government action and subject to major change only after consultation and discussion (changes of 10 per cent are permitted without consultation); indeed, the decision to adopt this technique of exchange-rate determination is, I believe, the major mistake made in postwar international economic policy. The explicit adoption of a system of flexible exchange rates might therefore require a major rewriting of the statutes of the IMF.

There is some evidence, however, that the IMF is giving way on its former insistence on announced parities. Most recently, it has acceded to the Canadian decision to have a floating rate for the Canadian dollar— with, it is true, the qualification that the floating rate is to be regarded as a temporary expedient until a satisfactory parity rate can be determined. Given the will, it may well be that some means could be found of interpreting the present statutes so that they would offer no effective obstacle to a system of flexible rates. And the apparent success of the Canadian experiment may help to produce the will.

There remains the question what, if any, functions the IMF would have in a world of flexible rates. As implied earlier, some proponents of flexible rates would have the IMF act as an international exchange equalization fund, speculating in exchange markets under instruction to make as much money as possible. This seems to me highly undesirable; any doubts about the advisability of national equalization funds are multiplied many fold for an international fund subject to political pressures from many governments. Could it, for example, really be in a position to sell a depreciating currency of a major country because of a belief that unwise internal policy would lead to still further depreciation?

If it is not given this function, the ones that might remain are to serve as a short-term international lender of funds along commercial lines, though I see no particular need for such an institution in a world of fully convertible currencies; to provide advice about internal monetary and fiscal policy; and possibly to serve as some kind of clearing agency.

C. Role of Gold in a System of Flexible Exchange Rates

A system of flexible exchange rates is incompatible with the existence in more than one country of a fixed nominal price of gold and free convertibility of currency into gold and gold into currency. The logical domestic counterpart of flexible exchange rates is a strict fiduciary currency changed in quantity in accordance with rules designed to promote domestic stability.[15] Gold could be used as part of the "backing" for such a currency, provided it was not bought and sold at a fixed price; its monetary role would then be purely fictional and psychological, designed to promote "confidence."

A fixed price for gold could, however, be maintained in one country without interfering with flexible exchange rates. The United States now has such a fixed price, and it could retain it. If it did so, other countries could use gold for the settlement of international payments, since this would be equivalent to using dollars. In so far as the United States bought gold net, it would be providing dollars to other countries, getting in return gold to be added to its hoards in Fort Knox; and, conversely, if it sold gold. There seems no reason why the United States should follow this policy. It seems better that any dollar aid that it gives should be given directly and openly on the basis of explicit legislative authorization, without requiring other countries to use resources in acquiring gold, ultimately in digging it out of the ground so that it can be reburied in Fort Knox.

A much better alternative is to have a free gold market. There is no reason why people who want to hold gold should not be permitted to do so and no reason why speculation in gold should be discouraged. In this case, gold would lose its place in official monetary systems and become a commodity like all others. For a long time, however, it would be a rather special commodity, widely regarded as a highly safe means of keeping a liquid reserve—safer than most domestic currencies in terms of real value. Its availability for this purpose would serve the useful function of inhibiting inflationary currency issue, at the cost, however, of introducing an additional element of instability. Any fear of inflation would lead to widespread substitution of gold for currency, thereby speeding up the inflation but also reducing the resources capable of being acquired by inflationary currency issue and hence the pressure to resort to it.

These are highly dogmatic statements on an exceedingly complex issue. They are included here primarily to indicate the range of problems involved rather than as a comprehensive analysis of them.

D. The Sterling Area

The sterling area raises a rather special problem in connection with the establishment of flexible exchange rates, since the sterling area includes a number of different currencies linked by fixed exchange rates and convertible one into the other. Sterling could be integrated into a world of flexible exchange rates in either of two ways: (1) flexible exchange rates could be instituted within the sterling area as well as between sterling and other currencies or (2) fixed exchange rates could be retained within the sterling area.

The above analysis of a world of flexible exchange rates applies in full to the first method of handling the sterling area. However, for both financial and political reasons there is likely to be a strong and entirely understandable preference on the part of the British for the second method. As the center of the sterling area, Britain can make the most out of its banking facilities and experience, command relatively cheap credit, and exercise a considerable degree of commercial and political influence, to mention only the most obvious reasons.

In principle there is no objection to a mixed system of fixed exchange rates within the sterling area and freely flexible rates between sterling and other countries, *provided* that the fixed rates within the sterling area can be maintained without trade restrictions. There are numerous examples of such mixed systems in the past.[16] And it may well be desirable to take the attainment of such a mixed system as the immediate goal of policy. Its attainment would remove the obstacle presented by fixed exchange rates to the liberalization of trade by continental European countries and would permit observation of the operation of the two different systems side by side.

At the same time the dangers inherent in such a policy objective should be clearly recognized. These are of two kinds: (1) such a mixed system may not be viable under current political and economic conditions and (2) Britain may be unwilling to accept such a mixed system, since it may feel that freeing the exchange rate of the pound sterling would increase the difficulty of maintaining the sterling area.

The problem of maintaining fixed exchange rates within the sterling area without restrictions on trade differs only in degree from the corresponding problem for the world as a whole. In both cases the area includes a number of sovereign political units with independent final monetary and fiscal authority. In consequence, in both cases, the permanent maintenance of a system of fixed rates without trade restrictions requires the harmonization of internal monetary and fiscal policies and a willingness and ability to meet at least substantial changes in external conditions by adjustments in the internal price and wage structure.

The differences in degree are, of course, important. The smaller extent of the area involved has somewhat divergent effects. On the one hand, it reduces the problem of harmonizing potentially divergent policies; on the other, it means that the area is subjected to larger strains from outside. The composition of the area is perhaps more important than its mere extent. It includes political units that have a long tradition of close co-operation and of mutual confidence, many of the areas are dependencies whose internal policies can be fairly well controlled from the center, and the financial relations among the members of the area are of long standing and have withstood severe strain. The preservation of these relations is considered extremely important, and, in consequence, there is a very real willingness on the part of its members to go a long way in adapting internal policies to common needs. Finally, the area has relatively large currency reserves that can be used to meet temporary strains, and its members have shown considerable willingness to accumulate balances in the currencies of other members.

Many of these differences are, of course, themselves the product of the prior existence of fixed and stable exchange rates. Whatever their cause, there can, I think, be little doubt that on balance they mean that a system of fixed exchange rates has more chance of surviving without trade restrictions in the sterling area than in the world as a whole. But, granted that the prospects are better for the sterling area than for the world as a whole, it does not follow that they are very good. There have already been substantial strains within the sterling area, most notably the drain of supposedly frozen balances and the strains within the sterling area that were among the immediate reasons for devaluation in 1949. Direct quantitative restrictions on trade have been imposed by some members on imports from others, and indirect restrictions have arisen, through some aspects of state trading and of other selective policies aimed at the foreign balance.

It is hard to see how further serious strains can be avoided in the future. Members of the sterling area are clearly not going to be willing to accumulate indefinitely balances in the currencies of other members. Reserves, no matter how large, cannot eliminate the necessity of adapting to fundamental changes in external conditions. Yet the United Kingdom and most other members of the sterling area are strongly committed to a full-employment policy which greatly limits the possibility of using changes in the internal price and wage structure as a means of adjusting to changes in external conditions. Thus within the sterling area, as in the rest of the world, if exchange-rate adjustments are ruled out, substantial strains are likely to be met sooner or later by direct controls over international trade. In consequence, I am inclined to be pessimistic about the long-run viability without trade restrictions of a sterling area with fixed exchange rates.

There remains the question whether the freeing of the pound would on balance make it more or less difficult to maintain the sterling area. The answer to this question reached in Britain is certain to be a major factor in Britain's willingness to free the pound.

The freeing of the rate for the pound, together with the removal of exchange restrictions and accompanying internal direct controls, would relieve the stress on the sterling area in some ways; in others, increase it.

It would relieve the stress by insulating the sterling area as a whole from outside disturbances, and the experience of the 1930's shows how important this can be; by producing a more efficient use of imports and a better allocation of resources between the production of goods for export and for domestic use; and by making sterling a more desirable and useful currency and so increasing the willingness to hold sterling balances. On the other hand, it might increase the stress, at least initially, because of the danger that holders of the present large sterling balances would seek to convert them into dollars or other currencies and because the substitution of a flexible for a nominally fixed rate might reduce the willingness to hold balances more than the elimination of restrictions on use of balances increased the willingness to hold them. If there were any immediate, widespread attempt to shift out of sterling, the rate for the pound might fall drastically unless Britain were willing to use a large part of its reserves to prevent the pound from falling.

This is an exceedingly complex problem that deserves much better-informed and more extensive analysis. The above highly tentative remarks on it are, however, perhaps sufficient to justify the qualified conclusion that, if the immediate problem of the transition could be surmounted, the longer-run effect of a floating pound would be to reduce the stress on the sterling area and thereby increase the chance that it could be viable without trade restrictions—though, even so, the chances do not seem to me to be high.

IV. Some Examples of the Importance of a System of Flexible Exchange Rates

It cannot be too strongly emphasized that the structure and method of determining exchange rates have a vital bearing on almost every problem of international economic relations. It will illustrate this basic proposition and at the same time help to bring out some of the implications of the preceding analysis if we consider the relation of flexible exchange rates to three specific problems of great current importance: (a) the promotion of unrestricted multilateral trade; (b) the harmonization of internal monetary and fiscal policies; and (c) the rearmament drive.

A. Unrestricted International Trade

We have seen that flexible exchange rates are entirely consistent with unrestricted multilateral trade. On the other hand, the absence of flexible exchange rates is almost certain to be incompatible with unrestricted multilateral trade. With rigid exchange rates, any changes in conditions of trade can be met only by changes in reserves, internal prices and monetary conditions, or direct controls over imports, exports, and other exchange transactions. With few exceptions, reserves of European countries are small, and, in any event, the use of reserves is a feasible device only for mild and temporary movements. Primary reliance on changes in the internal price level is undesirable, and largely for this reason, there is great political reluctance to rely on such changes. Germany, Belgium, and Italy might perhaps be willing to go some way in this direction. England, France, Norway, and some other countries would almost certainly be completely unwilling to allow the level of prices and employment at home to be determined primarily by the vagaries of foreign trade.

The only other alternative to movements in exchange rates is direct control of foreign trade. Such control is therefore almost certain to be the primary technique adopted to meet substantial movements in conditions of international trade so long as exchange rates are maintained rigid. The implicit or explicit recognition of this fact is clearly one of the chief sources of difficulty in attempts to achieve a greater degree of liberalization of trade in Europe; it is reflected in the extensive escape clauses of all recent international agreements; it is dramatically demonstrated by the ultimately successful pressure on the Germans to use direct controls in the exchange crisis of the fall of 1950, despite the general belief that the crisis was temporary and would be over in a matter of months. It is part of the explanation of the pressures for direct controls produced by the rearmament drive.

Suppose that, by some fortunate turn of events, complete liberalization of trade and convertibility of currencies were achieved tomorrow and resulted in equilibrium in the balance of payments of all European countries at existing exchange rates without American aid. Suppose, in consequence, American aid and pressure were permanently removed. I have no hesitancy in predicting that, given the existing system of determination of exchange rates and the present general political and economic environment, direct controls over exports and imports would be reimposed on a large scale within two or three years at the most.

But even this understates the problem raised by fixed exchange rates. Not only is ultimate liberalization of trade almost certain to be inconsistent with rigid and fixed exchange rates in the present state of the world; equally important, the process of moving toward this objective is rendered unduly difficult. There is no way of predicting in advance the precise economic effects of meaningful reductions of trade barriers. All that is clear is that the impact of such reductions will vary from country to country and industry to industry and that many of the impacts will be highly indirect and not at all in the particular areas liberalized. The very process of liberalization will therefore add substantial and unpredictable pressures on balances of payments over and above those that would occur in any event. These pressures would make any system of rigid exchange rates appropriate to the initial position almost certainly inappropriate to the final position and to intermediate positions. And there seems no way to decide on the appropriate final exchange rates in advance; they must be reached by trial and error. Thus, even if the ultimate goal were a new system of rigid exchange rates, it seems almost essential to have flexibility in the interim period. In the absence of such flexibility, liberalization is likely to be brought to an untimely end by the very consequences of any initial successes.

The current political reluctance to use changes in internal price levels and employment to meet external changes is matched by a political reluctance to use changes in exchange rates. But I submit that the reluctance to use changes in exchange rates is on a different level and has a different basis than the reluctance to use internal changes. The reluctance to use changes in exchange rates reflects a cultural lag, the survival of a belief the bases for which have disappeared; it is a consequence of tradition and lack of understanding. The reluctance to use changes in internal price levels and employment, on the other hand, is a new development, a product of harsh experience of the recent past and, for the moment at least, in tune with current economic conditions.

B. Harmonization of Internal Monetary and Fiscal Policies

The positive side of the reluctance to use changes in internal price levels and employment to meet external changes is the promotion of internal monetary stability—the avoidance of either inflation or deflation. This is clearly a highly desirable objective for each country separately. But, under a system of rigid exchange rates and unrestricted trade, no country can attain this objective unless *every* other important country with which it is linked directly or indirectly by trade does so as well. If any one country inflates, for example, this tends to increase its imports and reduce its exports. Other countries now start to accumulate currency balances of the inflating country. They must either be willing to accumulate such balances indefinitely—which means they must be willing to continue shipping out goods without a return flow and thus in effect subsidize the inflating country—or they must follow the inflation themselves (or impose import controls). Hence the strong pressure to achieve harmonization of internal monetary policies.

But this pressure has understandably not been matched by a willingness of all countries to submit their internal policy to external control. Why should a country do so when the failure of any one country to co-operate or to behave "properly" would destroy the whole structure and permit it to transmit its difficulties to its neighbors? Really effective "co-ordination" would require essentially either that nations adopt a common commodity monetary standard like gold and agree to submit unwaveringly to its discipline or that some international body control the supply of money in each country, which in turn implies control over at least interest-rate policy and budgetary policy. The first alternative is neither currently feasible nor particularly desirable in the light of our past experience with the gold standard.[17] As to the second alternative, whether feasible or not, is it desirable that such far-reaching powers be surrendered to any authority other than an effective federal government democratically elected and responsible to the electorate?

A system of flexible exchange rates eliminates the necessity for such far-reaching co-ordination of internal monetary and fiscal policy in order for any country separately to follow a stable internal monetary policy. If, under such a system, any one country inflates, the primary effect is a depreciation in its exchange rate. This offsets the effect of internal inflation on its international trade position and weakens or eliminates the tendency for the inflation to be transmitted to its neighbors; and conversely with deflation. Inflation and deflation in any one country will then affect other countries primarily in so far as it affects the real income position of the initial country; there will be little or no effect through purely monetary channels.

In effect, flexible exchange rates are a means of combining interdependence among countries through trade with a maximum of internal monetary independence; they are a means of permitting each country to seek for monetary stability according to its own lights, without either imposiing its mistakes on its neighbors or having their mistakes imposed on it. If all countries succeeded, the result would be a system of reasonably stable exchange rates; the substance of effective harmonization would be attained without the risks of formal but ineffective harmonization.

The chance that all countries would succeed is far greater with flexible exchange rates than with a system of rigid exchange rates that is not also a strict commodity standard. For not only do the laggards tend to call the tune under rigid exchange rates by infecting the other countries with which they are linked but also the very existence of this link gives each country an incentive to engage in inflationary action that it would not otherwise have. For, at least in the initial stages, inflationary currency issue enables the issuers to acquire resources not only from within the country but also from without: the rigid rates mean, as we have seen, that other countries accumulate balances of the currency of the inflating country. Under reasonably stable but not rigid rates, this incentive is largely removed, since the rates will remain stable only so long as countries avoid inflationary action. Once they embark on it, a decline in the exchange rates for their currency will replace the accumulation of balances that would have to take place to keep the rates rigid.

C. The Current Rearmament Drive

A particular example of the preceding problem is provided by the present rearmament drive. A really serious rearmament drive is almost certain to produce inflationary pressure, differing in degree from country to country because of differences in fiscal structures, monetary systems, temper of the people, the size of the rearmament effort, etc. With rigid exchange rates, these divergent pressures introduce strains and stresses that are likely to interfere with the armament effort. Country A, let us say, has more inflationary pressure than B, and B more than C. B will tend to find its exports to A expanding at the same time that its exports to C are falling and its imports from C expanding. Over all it may be in balance, but it is not in particular industries. It will be under strong pressure to impose export controls on products that it tends to export to A and at the same time import controls on products it imports from C. Under flexible exchange rates neither might have been necessary; its currency would appreciate relative to A's currency and depreciate relative to B's, thus offsetting both distortions in its trade patterns—distortions because by assumption the changes were produced primarily by differences in the rate of monetary expansion.

This kind of phenomenon is, I believe, one of the important factors that has made for resistance to the removal of import controls and for renewed pressure for export controls, though clearly there are other factors involved as well.

Of course, the rearmament drive will require changes in the structure of trade for technical and physical reasons and not merely for monetary reasons. It is essential for the efficiency of the armament effort that such changes be permitted. Under flexible exchange rates they would tend to be the primary ones. Monetary expansion in any country produces a general increase in demand for imports and a general reduction in supply of exports and so, with flexible exchange rates, is reflected primarily in exchange rates. On the other hand, the rearmament effort involves a shift of demand from some products to others and need involve no change in aggregate money demand. In consequence, particular prices rise relative to other prices, thereby providing the incentive for the required changes in production and trade. Even if the rearmament effort is financed by means that involve an increased aggregate money demand, it will mean a much greater increase in demand for some products than others and so can still lead to the required changes in *relative* prices.

V. Conclusion

The nations of the world cannot prevent changes from occurring in the circumstances affecting international transactions. And they would not if they could. For many changes reflect natural changes in weather conditions and the like; others arise from the freedom of countless individuals to order their lives as they will, which it is our ultimate goal to preserve and widen; and yet others contain the seeds of progress and development. The prison and the graveyard alone provide even a close approximation to certainty.

The major aim of policy is not to prevent such changes from occurring but to develop an efficient system of adapting to them—of using their potentialities for good while minimizing their disruptive effects. There is widespread agreement, at least in the Western world, that relatively free and unrestricted multilateral trade is a major component of such a system, besides having political advantages of a rather different kind. Yet resounding failure has so far marked repeated attempts to eliminate or reduce the extensive and complex restrictions on international trade that proliferated during and immediately after World War II. Failure will continue to mark such attempts so long as we allow implicit acceptance of an essentially minor goal—rigid exchange rates—to prevent simultaneous attainment of two major goals: unrestricted multilateral trade and freedom of each country to pursue internal stability after its own lights.

There are, after all, only four ways in which the pressures on balances of payments produced by changes in the circumstances affecting international transactions can be met: (1) by counterbalancing changes in currency reserves; (2) by adjustments in the general level of internal prices and incomes; (3) by adjustments in exchange rates; and (4) by direct controls over transactions involving foreign exchange.

The paucity of existing currency reserves makes the first impractical for all but very minor changes unless some means can be found to increase the currency reserves of the world enormously. The failure of several noble experiments in this direction is testimony to the difficulty of this solution.

The primacy everywhere attached to internal stability makes the second method one that would not be permitted to operate; the institutional rigidities in internal price structures make it undesirable that it should be the major means of adjustment.

The third—at least in the form of a thoroughgoing system of flexible rates—has been ruled out in recent years without extensive explicit consideration, partly because of a questionable interpretation of limited historical evidence; partly, I believe, because it was condemned alike by traditionalists, whose ideal was a gold standard that either ran itself or was run by international central bankers but in either case determined internal policy, and by the dominant strain of reformers, who distrusted the price system in all its manifestations—a curious coalition of the most unreconstructed believers in the price system, in all its other roles, and its most extreme opponents.

The fourth method—direct controls over transactions involving foreign exchange—has in this way, by default rather than intention, been left the only avenue whereby pressures on balances of payments can be met. Little wonder that these controls have so stubbornly resisted elimination despite the repeated protestations that they would be eliminated. Yet this method is, in my view, by all odds the least desirable of the four.

There are no major economic difficulties to prevent the prompt establishment by countries separately or jointly of a system of exchange rates freely determined in open markets, primarily by private transactions, and the simultaneous abandonment of direct controls over exchange transactions. A move in this direction is the fundamental prerequisite for the economic integration of the free world through multilateral trade.

Notes

1. Indeed, I have elsewhere argued that flexible exchange rates are the logical international counterpart of the monetary and fiscal framework for economic stability that seems to me the most promising. See "A Monetary and Fiscal Framework for Economic Stability," *supra*, pp. 133–56.

2. And indeed in the even more extreme sense of trade free from all barriers, including tariffs and export bounties.

3. In brief, it is desirable in its own right as one of the basic freedoms we cherish; it promotes the efficient use of resources through an appropriate international division of labor and increases consumer welfare by maximizing the range of alternatives on which consumers can spend their incomes; it facilitates

international political amity by removing potent sources of conflict between governments.

4. It is conceivable that, under some conditions and for some range of exchange rates, a rise in exchange rates would increase the excess demand. Though this possibility has received considerable attention, it will be neglected in what follows as of little practical relevance. As a purely theoretical matter, there will always be some set or sets of rates that will clear the market, and, in the neighborhood of at least one of these sets of rates a rise in the rate will mean a decline in excess demand (i.e., a negative excess demand); a fall, a rise in excess demand. Exchange rates can remain in a region in which this is not true only if they are not free to move and if some nonprice mechanism is used to ration domestic or foreign currency. As a practical matter, the conditions necessary for any relevant range of rates to have the property that a rise increases excess demand seem to me highly unlikely to occur. But, if they should occur, it would merely mean that there might be two possible positions of equilibrium, one above, the other below, the existing controlled rate. If the higher is regarded as preferable, the implication for policy would be first to appreciate the controlled rate and then to set it free.

5. Note that a tariff of a uniform percentage on all imports used to pay a subsidy of a uniform percentage on all exports is equivalent to a depreciation in the exchange rate by the corresponding percentage; and, similarly, a subsidy of a uniform percentage on all imports financed by a tax of a uniform percentage on all exports is equivalent to an appreciation in the exchange rate by the corresponding percentage. Thus devices such as these should be classified under exchange-rate changes rather than direct controls.

6. Selling import licenses at a price that would clear the market would eliminate the first effect; it would not eliminate the second and third unless the permits were not for specific commodities but for foreign exchange to be used in any way desired. Even this would not eliminate the fourth unless the proceeds were used to pay a percentage subsidy to exports and other transactions leading to the acquisition of foreign exchange. This final system is, as indicated in the preceding note, identical with a change in the exchange rate. If the price of permits to use foreign exchange and the subsidy for acquiring it were determined in a free market so as to make total receipts equal total payments, the result is equivalent to or identical with a system of flexible exchange rates.

7. Under a pure gold standard, these effects follow automatically, since any international claims not settled otherwise are settled by gold, which, in case of a deficit, is bodily extracted from the monetary stock and, in case of a surplus, bodily added to it.

8. A warning is perhaps in order that this is a simplified generalization on a complex problem. A full analysis encounters difficulties in separating "speculative" from other transactions, defining precisely and satisfactorily "destabilizing speculation," and taking account of the effects of the mere existence of a system of flexible rates as contrasted with the effects of actual speculative transactions under such a system.

9. Perhaps the most ambitious attempt to summarize the evidence is that by Ragnar Nurkse, *International Currency Experience* (Geneva: League of Nations, 1944), pp. 117–22. Nurkse concludes from interwar experience that speculation can be expected in general to be destabilizing. However, the evidence he cites is by itself inadequate to justify any conclusion. Nurkse examines only one episode in anything approaching the required detail, the depreciation of the French franc from 1922 to 1926. For the rest, he simply lists episodes during which exchange rates were flexible and asserts that in each case speculation was destabilizing. These episodes may or may not support his conclusion; it is impossible to tell from his discussion of them; and the list is clearly highly selective, excluding some cases that seem prima facie to point in the opposite direction.

Even for the French episode, the evidence given by Nurkse does not justify any firm conclusion. Indeed, so far as it goes, it seems to me clearly less favorable to the conclusion Nurkse draws, that speculation was destabilizing, than to the opposite conclusion, that speculation was stabilizing.

In general, Nurkse's discussion of the effects of speculation is thoroughly unsatisfactory. At times, he seems to regard any transactions which threaten the existing value of a currency as destabilizing even if underlying forces would produce a changed value in the absence of speculation. At another point, he asserts that destabilizing transactions may occur on *both* capital and current accounts simultaneously, in a context in which these two accounts exhaust the balance of payments, so that his statement is an arithmetical impossibility (pp. 210–11). It is a sorry reflection on the scientific basis for generally held economic beliefs that Nurkse's analysis is so often cited as "the" basis or "proof" of the belief in destabilizing speculation.

10. In principle, there are other possibilities related to the "velocity of circulation" of money that I neglect to simplify the argument; they do not change its essence.

11. An interesting example is provided by an argument for 100 per cent banking reserves under a gold standard given by James E. Meade, *The Balance of Payments*, Vol. I of *The Theory of International Economic Policy* (Oxford: Oxford University Press, 1951), p. 185. Meade argues correctly that with 100 per cent reserves the internal adaptations consequent on an external change of any given size will be at a slower rate than with a lower reserve ratio. On this ground, he says, 100 per cent reserves are better than fractional reserves. But this conclusion follows only if any slowing-down in the rate of internal adaptation is an improvement, in which case 200 per cent reserves or their equivalent ("sterilization" of gold imports and exports) would be better than 100 per cent, and so on indefinitely. Given that there is some optimum rate of adjustment, all one can say is that there exists some reserve ratio that would tend to produce this rate of adjustment and so be optimal on these grounds alone; I see no way of knowing on the basis of the considerations Meade presents whether this ratio would be 5 per cent or 500 per cent.

12. See "The Effects of a Full-Employment Policy on Economic Stability: A

Formal Analysis," *supra*, pp. 117–32, for a more detailed consideration of the formal problem involved in both internal and external policy and for some examples of this tendency.

13. See Meade, *op. cit.*, pp. 218–31.

14. I owe this distinction to Robert Triffin.

15. See "A Monetary and Fiscal Framework for Economic Stability," *supra*, pp. 133–56, and "Commodity-Reserve Currency," *infra*, pp. 204–50.

16. In a sense, any flexible exchange system is such a mixed system, since there are rigid rates between the different sections of one nation—between, say, the different states of the United States. The key difference for present purposes between the different states of the United States, on the one hand, and the different members of the sterling area, on the other, is that the former are, while the latter are not, all effectively subject to a single central fiscal and monetary authority—the federal government—having ultimate fiscal and monetary powers. In addition, the former have, while the latter have not, effectively surrendered the right to impose restrictions on the movements of goods, people, or capital between one another. This is a major factor explaining why a central monetary authority is able to operate without producing serious sectional strains. Of course, these are questions of economic fact, not of political form, and of degree, not of kind. A group of politically independent nations all of which firmly adhered to, say, the gold standard would thereby in effect submit themselves to a central monetary authority, albeit an impersonal one. If, in addition, they firmly adhered to the free movement of goods, people, and capital without restrictions, and economic conditions rendered such movement easy, they would, in effect, be an economic unit for which a single currency—which is the equivalent of rigid exchange rates—would be appropriate.

17. See "Commodity-Reserve Currency," *infra*, pp. 204–50, for a more extensive discussion of the advantages and disadvantages of a commodity standard.

2

THE CASE FOR FLEXIBLE EXCHANGE RATES, 1969*

Harry G. Johnson

I. Introduction

By 'flexible exchange rates' is meant rates of foreign exchange that are determined daily in the markets for foreign exchange by the forces of demand and supply, without restrictions on the extent to which rates can move imposed by governmental policy. Flexible exchange rates are, thus, to be distinguished from the present system, (the International Monetary Fund system) of internatioanl monetary organization, under which countries commit themselves to maintain the foreign values of their currencies within a narrow margin of a fixed par value by acting as residual buyers or sellers of currency in the foreign-exchange market, subject to the possibility of effecting a change in the par value itself in case of 'fundamental disequilibrium'; this system is frequently described as the 'adjustable-peg' system. Flexible exchange rates should also be distinguished from a spectral system frequently conjured up by opponents of rate flexibility; wildly fluctuating or 'unstable' exchange rates. The freedom of rates to move in response to market forces does not imply that they will

* The title acknowledges the indebtedness of all serious writers on this subject to Milton Friedman's modern, classic essay, 'The Case for Flexible Exchange Rates', written in 1950 and published in 1953 (M. Friedman, *Essays in Positive Economics* [Chicago: University of Chicago Press, 1953], pp. 157–203; abridged in R. E. Caves and H. G. Johnson [eds], *Readings in International Economics* [Homewood, Ill.: Richard D. Irwin, for the American Economic Association, 1968], Ch. 25, pp. 413–37). This chapter was first published in Harry G. Johnson and John E. Nash, *UK and Floating Exchanges* (London: The Institute of Economic Affairs, 1969), pp. 9–37; and subsequently in *The Federal Reserve Bank of St. Louis Review*, Vol. 51, No. 6 (June 1969), pp. 12–24; and in George N. Halm [ed.], *Approaches to Greater Flexibility of Exchange Rates* (Princeton; Princeton University Press, 1970), Ch. 8, pp. 91–111.

in fact move significantly or erratically; they will do so only if the underlying forces governing demand and supply are themselves erratic, and in that case any international monetary system would be in serious difficulty. Flexible exchange rates do not necessarily imply that the national monetary authorities must refrain from any intervention in the exchange markets; whether they should intervene or not depends on whether the authorities are likely to be more, or less, intelligent and efficient speculators than the private speculators in foreign exchange, a matter on which empirical judgement is frequently inseparable from fundamental political attitudes.

The fundamental argument for flexible exchange rates is that they would allow countries autonomy with respect to their use of monetary, fiscal and other policy instruments, consistent with the maintenance of whatever degree of freedom in international transactions they chose to allow their citizens, by automatically ensuring the preservation of external equilibrium. Since, in the absence of balance-of-payments reasons for interfering in international trade and payments, and given autonomy of domestic policy, there is an overwhelmingly strong case for the maximum possible freedom of international transactions to permit exploitation of the economies of international specialization and division of labour, the argument for flexible exchange rates can be put more strongly still: flexible exchange rates are essential to the preservation of national autonomy and independence consistent with efficient organization and development of the world economy.

The case for flexible exchange rates on these grounds has been understood and propounded by economists since the work of Keynes and others on the monetary disturbances that followed the First World War. Yet that case is consistently ridiculed, if not dismissed out of hand, by 'practical' men concerned with international monetary affairs; and there is a strong revealed preference for the fixed exchange-rate system. For this, one might suggest two reasons: first, successful men of affairs are successful because they understand and can work with the intricacies of the prevalent fixed rate system, but being 'practical', they find it almost impossible to conceive how a hypothetical alternative system would, or even could, work in practice; second, the fixed exchange-rate system gives considerable prestige and, more important, political power over national governments to the central bankers entrusted with managing the system, power that they naturally credit themselves with exercising more 'responsibly' than the politicans would do, and that they naturally resist surrendering. Consequently, public interest in and discussion of flexible exchange rates generally appears only when the fixed rate system is obviously under

serious strain, and the capacity of the central bankers and other responsible officials to avoid a crisis is losing credibility.

The present period of the late 1960s has this character, from two points
of view. On the one hand, from the point of view of the international
economy, the long-sustained sterling crisis that culminated in the devaluation of November 1967, the speculative doubts about the dollar that
culminated in the gold crisis of March 1968, and the franc-mark crisis
that was left unresolved by the Bonn meeting of November 1968 and still
hangs over the system, have all emphasized a serious defect of the present
international monetary system. This is the lack of an adequate adjustment
mechanism, i.e. a mechanism for adjusting international imbalances of
payments towards equilibrium sufficiently rapidly as not to put intolerable strains on the willingness of the central banks to supplement existing
international reserves with additional credits, while not requiring countries to deflate or inflate their economies beyond politically tolerable
limits. The obviously available mechanism is greater automatic flexibility
of exchange rates (as distinct from adjustments of the 'pegs'). Consequently, there has been a rapidly growing interest in techniques for
achieving greater automatic flexibility, while retaining the form and
assumed advantages of a fixed rate system. The chief contenders in this
connection are the 'band' proposal, under which the permitted range of
exchange rate variation around parity would be widened from the present
1 per cent or less to, say, 5 per cent each way, and the so-called 'crawling-
peg' proposal, under which the parity for any day would be determined
by an average of past rates established in the market. The actual rate each
day could diverge from the parity within the present band or a widened
band, and the parity would, thus, crawl in the direction in which a fully
flexible rate would move more rapidly.

Either of these proposals, if adopted, would constitute a move towards
a flexible rate system for the world economy as a whole. On the other
hand, from the point of view of the British economy alone, there has
been growing interest in the possibility of a floating rate for the pound.
This interest has been prompted by the shock of devaluation, doubts
about whether the devaluation was sufficient or may need to be repeated,
resentment of the increasing subordination of domestic policy to international requirements since 1964, and general discontent with the policies
into which the commitment to maintain a fixed exchange rate has driven
successive governments: 'stop-go', higher average unemployment policies, incomes policy, and a host of other domestic and international
interventions.

From both the international and the purely domestic point of view, therefore, it is apposite to re-examine the case for flexible exchange rates. That is the purpose of this chapter. Because of space limitation, the argument will be conducted at a general level of principle, with minimum attention to technical details and complexities. It is convenient to begin with the case for fixed exchange rates; this case has to be constructed, since little reasoned defence of it has been produced beyond the fact that it exists and functions after a fashion, and the contention that any change would be for the worse. Consideration of the case for fixed rates leads into the contrary case for flexible rates. Certain common objections to flexible rates are then discussed. Finally, some comments are offered on the specific questions mentioned above, of providing for greater rate flexibility in the framework of the IMF system and of floating the pound by itself.

II.   The Case for Fixed Exchange Rates

A reasoned case for fixed international rates of exchange must run from analogy with the case for a common national currency, since the effect of fixing the rate at which one currency can be converted into another is, subject to qualifications to be discussed later, to establish the equivalent of a single currency for those countries of the world economy adhering to fixed exchange rates. The advantages of a single currency within a nation's frontiers are, broadly, that it simplifies the profit-maximizing computations of producers and traders, facilitates competition among producers located in different parts of the country, and promotes the integration of the economy into a connected series of markets, these markets including both the markets for products and the markets for the factors of production (capital and labour). The argument for fixed exchange rates, by analogy, is that they will similarly encourage the integration of the national markets that compose the world economy into an international network of connected markets with similarly beneficial effects on economic efficiency and growth. In other words, the case for fixed rates is part of a more general argument for national economic policies conductive to international economic integration.

The argument by analogy with the domestic economy, however, is seriously defective for several reasons. In the first place, in the domestic economy the factors of production as well as goods and services are free to move throughout the market area. In the international economy the movement of labour is certainly subject to serious barriers created by national immigration policies (and in some cases restraints on emigration as well), and the freedom of movement of capital is also restricted by barriers created by national laws. The freedom of movement of goods is also restricted by tariffs and other barriers to trade. It is true that there are artificial barriers of certain kinds to the movement of goods and factors internally to a national economy (apart from natural barriers created by distance and cultural differences) created sometimes by national policy, e.g. by regional development policies, and sometimes by the existence of state or provincial governments with protective policies of their own. But these are probably negligible by comparison with the barriers to the international mobility of goods and factors of production. The existence of these barriers means that the system of fixed exchange rates does not really establish the equivalent of a single international money, in the sense of a currency whose purchasing power and usefulness tends to equality throughout the market area. A more important point, to be discussed later, is that if the fixity of exchange rates is maintained, not by appropriate adjustments of the relative purchasing power of the various national currencies, but by variations in the national barriers to trade and payments, it is in contradiction with the basic argument for fixed rates as a means of attaining the advantages internationally that are provided domestically by a single currency.

In the second place, as is well known from the prevalence of regional development policies in the various countries, acceptance of a single currency and its implications is not necessarily beneficial to particular regions within a nation. The pressures of competition in the product and factor markets facilitated by the common currency frequently result instead in prolonged regional distress, in spite of the apparent full freedom of labour and capital to migrate to more remunerative locations. On the national scale, the solution usually applied, rightly or wrongly, is to relieve regional distress by transfers from the rest of the country, effected through the central government. On the international scale, the probability of regional (that is, national in this context) distress is substantially greater because of the barriers to mobility of both factors and goods mentioned previously; yet there is no international government, nor any effective substitute through international co-operation, to compensate and assist nations or regions of nations suffering through the effects of economic change occurring in the environment of a single currency. (It should be noted that existing arrangements for financing balance-of-payments deficits by credit from the surplus countries in no sense fulfil this function, since deficits and surpluses do not necessarily reflect, respectively, distress in the relevant sense, and its absence.)

Third, the beneficent effects of a single national currency on economic integration and growth depend on the maintenance of reasonable stability of its real value; the adjective 'reasonable' is meant to allow for mild inflationary or deflationary trends of prices over time. Stability in turn is provided under contemporary institutional arrangements through centralization of control of the money supply and monetary conditions in the hands of the central bank, which is responsible for using its powers of control for this purpose. (Formerly, it was provided by the use of precious metals, the quantity of which normally changed very slowly.) The system of fixed rates of international exchange, in contrast to a single national money, provides no centralized control of the overall quantity of international money and international monetary conditions. Under the ideal old-fashioned gold standard, in theory at least, overall international monetary control was exercised automatically by the available quantity of monetary gold and its rate of growth, neither of which could be readily influenced by national governments, operating on national money supplies through the obligation incumbent on each country to maintain a gold reserve adequate to guarantee the convertibility of its currency under all circumstances at the fixed exchange rate. That system has come to be regarded as barbarous, because it required domestic employment objectives to be subordinated to the requirements of international balance; and nations have come to insist on their right to use interventions in international trade and payments, and in the last resort to devalue their currencies, rather than proceed farther than they find politically tolerable with deflationary adjustment policies.

The result is that the automatic mechanisms of overall monetary control in the international system have been abandoned, without those mechanisms being replaced by a discretionary mechanism of international control comparable to the national central bank in the domestic economic system, to the dictates of which the national central banks, as providers of the currency of the 'regions' of the international economy, are obliged to conform. Instead, what control remains is the outcome on the one hand of the jostling among surplus and deficit countries, each of which has appreciable discretion with respect to how far it will accept or evade pressures on its domestic policies mediated through pressures on its balance of payments, and, on the other hand, of the ability of the system as a system to free itself from the remnants of the constraint formerly exercised by gold as the ultimate international reserve, by using national currencies and various kinds of international credit arrangements as substitutes for gold in international reserves.

In consequence, the present international monetary system of fixed exchange rates fails to conform to the analogy with a single national currency in two important respects. First, regions of the system are able to resist the integrative pressures of the single currency by varying the barriers to international transactions and, hence, the usefulness of the local variant of that currency, and, in the last resort, by changing the terms of conversion of the local variant into other variants; moreover, they have reason to do so in the absence of an international mechanism for compensating excessively distressed regions and a mechanism for providing centralized and responsible control of overall monetary conditions. Second, in contrast to a national monetary system, there is no responsible, centralized, institutional arrangement for monetary control of the system.

This latter point can be rephrased in terms of the commonly held belief that the fixed rate system exercises 'discipline' over the nations involved in it, and prevents them from pursuing 'irresponsible' domestic policies. This belief might have been tenable with respect to the historical gold standard, under which nations were permanently committed to maintaining their exchange rates and had not yet developed the battery of interventions in trade and payments that are now commonly employed. It is a myth, however, when nations have the option of evading discipline by using interventions or devaluation. It becomes an even more pernicious myth when one recognizes that abiding by the discipline may entail hardships for the nation that the nation will not tolerate being applied to particular regions within itself, but will attempt to relieve by interregional transfer payments; and that the discipline is not discipline to conform to rational and internationally accepted principles of good behaviour, but discipline to conform to the average of what other nations are seeking to get away with. Specifically, there might be something to be said for an international monetary system that disciplined individual nations into conducting their policies so as to achieve price stability and permit liberal international economic policies. But there is little to be said for a system that either obliges nations to accept whatever rate of world price inflation or deflation emerges from the policies of the other nations in the world economy, or obliges or permits them to employ whatever policies of intervention in international trade and payments are considered by themselves and their neighbours not to infringe the letter of the rules of international liberalism.

The defenders of the present fixed rate system, if pressed, will generally accept these points but argue the need for a solution along two complementary lines: 'harmonization' of national economic policies in accordance with the requirements of a single-world-currency system; and progressive evolution towards international control of the growth of international liquidity, combined with 'surveillance' of national economic policies. The problem with both is that they demand a surrender of national sovereignty in domestic economic policy, which countries have shown themselves extremely reluctant to accept. The reasons for this have already been mentioned; the most important are that there is no international mechanism for compensating those who suffer from adhering to the rules of the single-currency game, and that the nations differ sharply in their views on priorities among policy objectives, most notably in respect of the relative undesirability of unemployment on the one hand and price inflation on the other. The main argument for flexible exchange rates at the present time is that they would make this surrender of sovereignty unnecessary, while at the same time making unnecessary the progressive extension of interventions in international trade and payments that failure to resolve this issue necessarily entails.

The case for fixed exchange rates, while seriously defective as a defence of the present system of international monetary organization, does have one important implication for the case of flexible exchange rates. One is accustomed to thinking of national moneys in terms of the currencies of the major countries, which currencies derive their usefulness from the great diversity of goods, services, and assets available in the national economy, into which they can be directly converted. But in the contemporary world there are many small and relatively narrowly specialized countries, whose national currencies lack usefulness in this sense, but instead derive their usefulness from their rigid convertibility at a fixed price into the currency of some major country with which the small country trades extensively or on which it depends for capital for investment. For such countries, the advantages of rigid convertibility in giving the currency usefulness and facilitating international trade and investment outweigh the relatively small advantages that might be derived from exchange rate flexibility. (In a banana republic, for example, the currency will be more useful if it is stable in terms of command over foreign goods than if it is stable in terms of command over bananas; and exchange rate flexibility would give little scope for autonomous domestic policy.) These countries, which probably constitute a substantial numerical majority of existing countries, would, therefore, probably choose, if given a free choice, to keep the value of their currency pegged to that of some major country or currency bloc. In other words, the case for flexible exchange rates is a case for flexibility of rates among the currencies of countries that are large enough to have a currency whose usefulness derives primarily from its domestic purchasing power, and for which significant autonomy of domestic policy is both possible and desired.

III. The Case for Flexible Exchange Rates

The case for flexible exchange rates derives fundamentally from the laws of demand and supply, in particular, from the principle that, left to itself, the competitive market will establish the price that equates quantity demanded with quantity supplied and, hence, clear the market. If the price rises temporarily above the competitive level, an excess of quantity supplied over quantity demanded will drive it back downwards to the equilibrium level; conversely, if the price falls temporarily below the competitive level, an excess of quantity demanded over quantity supplied will force the price upwards towards the equilibrium level. Application of this principle to governmental efforts to control or to support particular prices indicates that, unless the price happens to be fixed at the equilibrium level—in which case governmental intervention is superfluous—such efforts will predictably generate economic problems. If the price is fixed above the equilibrium level, the government will be faced with the necessity of absorbing a surplus of production over consumption. To solve this problem, eventually it will either have to reduce its support price, or devise ways either of limiting production (through quotas, taxes, and the like) or of increasing consumption (through propaganda, or distribution of surpluses on concessionary terms). If the price is fixed below the equilibrium level, the government will be faced with the necessity of meeting the excess of consumption over production out of its own stocks. Since these must be limited in extent, it must eventually either raise its control price, or devise ways either to limit consumption by rationing, or reduce the costs of production (e.g., by subsidies to producers, or by investments in increasing productivity).

Exactly the same problems arise when the government chooses to fix the price of foreign exchange in terms of the national currency, and for one reason or another that price ceases to correspond to the equilibrium price. If that price is too high, that is, if the domestic currency is undervalued, a balance-of-payments surplus develops and the country is obliged to accumulate foreign exchange. If this accumulation is unwelcome, the government's alternatives are to restrict exports and encourage imports either by allowing or promoting domestic inflation, which in a sense subsidizes imports and taxes exports, or by imposing increased taxes or controls on exports and reducing taxes or controls on imports; or to appreciate its currency to the equilibrium level. If the price of foreign exchange is too low, the domestic currency being overvalued, a balance-of-payments deficit develops and the country is obliged to run down its stocks of foreign exchange and borrow from other countries. Since its ability to do this is necessarily limited, it ultimately has to choose among the following alternatives: imposing restrictions on imports or promoting exports (including imports and exports of assets, i.e. control of international capital movements); deflating the economy to reduce the demand for imports and increase the supply of exports; deflating the economy to restrain wages and prices or attempting to control wages and prices directly, in order to make exports more and imports less profitable; and devaluing the currency.

In either event, a deliberate choice is necessary among alternatives that are all unpleasant for various reasons. Hence, the choice is likely to be deferred until the disequilibrium has reached crisis proportions; and decisions taken under crisis conditions are both unlikely to be carefully thought out, and likely to have seriously disruptive economic effects.

All of this would be unnecessary if, instead of taking a view on what the value of the currency in terms of foreign exchange should be, and being, therefore, obliged to defend this view by its policies or in the last resort surrender it, the government were to allow the price of foreign exchange to be determined by the interplay of demand and supply in the foreign exchange market. A freely flexible exchange rate would tend to remain constant so long as underlying economic conditions (including governmental policies) remained constant; random deviations from the equilibrium level would be limited by the activities of private speculators, who would step in to buy foreign exchange when its price fell (the currency appreciated in terms of foreign currencies) and to sell it when its price rose (the currency depreciated in terms of foreign currencies). On the other hand, if economic changes or policy changes occurred that under a fixed exchange rate would produce a balance-of-payments surplus or deficit, and, ultimately, a need for policy changes, the flexible exchange rate would gradually either appreciate or depreciate as required to preserve equilibrium. The movement of the rate would be facilitated and smoothed by the action of private speculators, on the basis of their reading of current and prospective economic and policy developments. If the government regarded the trend of the exchange rate as undesirable, it could take counteractive measures in the form of inflationary or deflationary policies. It would never be forced to take such measures by a balance-of-payments crisis and the pressure of foreign opinion, contrary to its own policy objectives. The balance-of-payments rationale for interventions in international trade and capital movements, and for such substitutes for exchange rate change as changes in border-tax adjustments or the imposition of futile 'incomes policy', would disappear. If the government had reason to believe that private speculators were not performing efficiently their function of stabilizing the exchange market and smoothing the movement of the rate over time, or that their speculations were based on faulty information or prediction, it could establish its own agency for speculation, in the form of an exchange stabilization fund. This possibility, however, raises the questions of whether an official agency risking the public's money is likely to be a smarter speculator than private individuals risking their own money; whether, if the assumed superiority of official speculation rests on access to inside information, it would not be preferable to publish the information for the benefit of the public rather than use it to make profits for the agency at the expense of unnecessarily ill-informed private citizens; and whether such an agency would in fact confine itself to stabilizing speculation or would try to enforce an official view of what the exchange rate should be, that is, whether the agency would not retrogress into *de facto* restoration of the adjustable-peg system.

The adoption of flexible exchange rates would have the great advantage of freeing governments to use their instruments of domestic policy for the pursuit of domestic objectives, while, at the same time, removing the pressures to intervene in international trade and payments for balance-of-payments reasons. Both of these advantages are important in contemporary circumstances. On the one hand, a great rift exists between nations like the United Kingdom and the United States, which are anxious to maintain high levels of employment and are prepared to pay a price for it in terms of domestic inflation, and other nations, notably the West German Federal Republic, which are strongly averse to inflation. Under the present fixed exchange-rate system, these nations are pitched against each other in a battle over the rate of inflation that is to prevail in the world economy, since the fixed rate system diffuses that rate of inflation to all the countries involved in it. Flexible rates would allow each country to pursue the mixture of unemployment and price trend objectives it prefers, consistent with international equilibrium, equilibrium being secured by appreciation of the currencies of 'price-stability' countries relative to the currencies of 'full-employment' countries. The maximum possible freedom of trade is not only desirable for the prosperity and growth of the major developed countries, but essential for the integration of the developing countries into the world economy and the promotion of efficient economic development of those countries. While the post-Second World War period has been characterized by the progressive reduction of the conventional barriers to international trade and payments—tariffs and quotas, inconvertibility and exchange controls—the recurrent balance-of-payments and international monetary crises under the fixed rate system have fostered the erection of barriers to international economic integration in new forms—aid-tying, preferential governmental procurement policies, controls on direct and portfolio international investment—that are in many ways more subtly damaging to efficiency and growth than the conventional barriers.

The removal of the balance-of-payments motive for restrictions on international trade and payments is an important positive contribution that the adoption of flexible exchange rates could make to the achievement of the liberal objective of an integrated international economy, which must be set against any additional barriers to international commerce and finance, in the form of increased uncertainty, that might follow from the adoption of flexible exchange rates. That such additional uncertainty would be so great as to reduce seriously the flows of international trade and investment is one of the objections to flexible rates to be discussed in section IV. At this point, it is sufficient to make the following observation. First, as pointed out in section II, under a flexible rate system most countries would probably peg their currencies to one or another major currency, so that much international trade and investment would in fact be conducted under fixed rate conditions, and uncertainty would attach only to changes in the exchange rates among a few major currencies or currency blocs (most probably a U.S. dollar bloc, a European bloc, and sterling, though in the event sterling might be included in one of the other blocs). For the same reason—because few blocs would imply that their economic domains would be large and diversified—the exchange rates between the flexible currencies would be likely to change rather slowly and steadily. This would mean that traders and investors normally would be able to predict the domestic value of their foreign currency proceeds without much difficulty. But, secondly, traders would be able to hedge foreign receipts or payments through the forward exchange markets, if they wished to avoid uncertainty; if there were a demand for more extensive forward market and hedging facilities than now exist, the competitive profit motive would bring them into existence. Third, for longer-range transactions, the economics of the situation would provide a substantial amount of automatic hedging, through the fact that long-run trends towards appreciation or depreciation of a currency are likely to be dominated by divergence of the trend of prices inside the currency area from the trend of prices elsewhere. For direct foreign investments, for example, any loss of value of foreign-currency earnings in terms of domestic currency, due to depreciation of the foreign currency, is likely to be roughly balanced by an increase in the amount of such earnings consequent on the relative inflation associated with the depreciation. Similarly, if a particular country is undergoing steady inflation and its currency is depreciating steadily in consequence, interest rates there are likely to rise sufficiently to compensate domestic investors for the inflation, and, hence, sufficiently to compensate foreign portfolio investors for their losses from the depreciation. Finally, it should be noted that the same sort of political and economic developments that would impose unexpected losses on traders and investors through depreciation under a flexible exchange-rate system, would equally impose losses in the form of devaluation, or the imposition of restrictions on trade and capital movements, under the present fixed rate system.

IV. The Case Against Flexible Exchange Rates

The case against flexible exchange rates, like the case for fixed exchange rates, is rarely if ever stated in a reasoned fashion. Instead, it typically consists of a series of unfounded assertions and allegations that derive their plausibility from two fundamentally irrelevant facts. The first is that, in the modern European economic history with which most people are familiar, flexible exchange rates are associated either with the acute monetary disorders that followed the First World War, or with the collapse of the international monetary system in the 1930s; instead of being credited with their capacity to function when the fixed exchange-rate system could not, they are debited with the disorders of national economic policies that made the fixed exchange-rate system unworkable or led to its collapse. The second, and more important at this historical distance from the disastrous experiences just mentioned, is that most people are accustomed to the fixed exchange-rate system, and are prone to assume without thinking that a system of flexible rates would simply display in an exaggerated fashion the worst features of the present fixed rate system, rather than remedy them.

The historical record is too large a topic to be discussed adequately in a brief essay. Suffice it to say that the interwar European experience was clouded by the strong belief, based on pre-First World War conditions, that fixed exchange rates at historical parity values constituted a natural order of things to which governments would seek eventually to return, and that scholarly interpretation of that experience leaned excessively and unjustifiably towards endorsement of the official view that any private speculation on the exchanges based on distrust of the ability of the authorities to hold an established parity under changing circumstances was necessarily 'destabilizing' and antisocial. It should further be remarked that European interwar experience does not constitute the whole of the historical record, and that both previously (as in the case of the U.S. dollar from 1862 to 1879) and subsquently (as in the case of the Canadian dollar from 1950 to 1962) there have been cases of a major trading country's maintaining a flexible exchange rate without any of the disastrous consequences commonly forecast by the opponents of flexible rates.

The penchant for attributing to the flexible rate system the problems of the fixed rate system can be illustrated by a closer examination of some of the arguments commonly advanced against floating exchange rates, most of which allege either that flexible rates will seriously increase uncertainty in international transactions, or that they will foster inflation.

One of the common arguments under the heading of uncertainty is that flexible rates would be extremely unstable rates, jumping wildly about from day to day. This allegation ignores the crucial point that a rate that is free to move under the influence of changes in demand and supply is not forced to move erratically, but will instead move only in response to such changes in demand and supply—including changes induced by changes in governmental policies—and normally will move only slowly and fairly predictably. Abnormally rapid and erratic movements will occur only in response to sharp and unexpected changes in circumstances; such changes in a fixed exchange-rate system would produce the same or more uncertainty-creating policy changes in the form of devaluation, deflation, or the imposition of new controls on trade and payments. The fallacy of this argument lies in its assumption that exchange rate changes occur exogenously and without apparent economic reason, an assumption that reflects the mentality of the fixed rate system, in which the exchange rate is held fixed by official intervention in the face of demand and supply pressures for change, and occasionally changed arbitrarily and at one stroke by governmental decisions whose timing and magnitude is a matter of severe uncertainty.

A related argument is that uncertainty about the domestic-currency equivalent of foreign receipts or payments would seriously inhibit international transactions of all kinds. As argued in section III, trends in exchange rates should normally be fairly slow and predictable, and their causes such as to provide more or less automatic compensation to traders and investors. Moreover, traders averse to uncertainty would be able to hedge their transactions through forward exchange markets, which would, if necessary, develop in response to demand. It is commonly argued at present, by foreign-exchange dealers and others engaged in the foreign-exchange market, that hedging facilities would be completely inadequate or that the cost of forward cover would be prohibitive. Both arguments seek to deny the economic principle that a competitive system will tend to provide any goods or services demanded, at a price that yields no more than a fair profit. They derive, moreover, from the experience of recent crises under the fixed rate system. When exchange rates are rigidly fixed by official intervention, businessmen normally do not consider the cost of forward cover worth their while, but when everyone expects the currency to be devalued, everyone seeks to hedge his risks by selling it forward, the normal balancing of forward demands and supplies ceases to prevail, the forward rate drops to a heavy discount, and the cost of forward cover becomes 'prohibitive'. Under a flexible exchange-rate system, where the spot rate is also free to move, arbitrage between the spot and forward markets, as well as speculation, would ensure that the expectation of depreciation was reflected in depreciation of the spot as well as the forward rate, and hence, tend to keep the cost of forward cover within reasonable bounds.

A further argument under the heading of uncertainty is that it will encourage 'destabilizing speculation'. The historical record provides no convincing, supporting evidence for this claim, unless 'destabilizing speculation' is erroneously defined to include any speculation against an officially pegged exchange rate, regardless of how unrealistic that rate was under the prevailing circumstances. A counter-consideration is that speculators who engage in genuinely destabilizing speculation, that is, whose speculations move the exchange rate away from rather than towards its equilibrium level, will consistently lose money, because they will consistently be buying when the rate is 'high' and selling when it is 'low' by comparison with its equilibrium value; this consideration does not, however, exclude the possibility that clever professional speculators may be able to profit by leading amateur speculators into destabilizing speculation, buying near the trough and selling near the peak, the amateur's losses being borne out of their (or their shareholders') regular income. A further counter-consideration is that under flexible rates speculation will itself move the spot rate, thus generating uncertainty in the minds of the speculators about the magnitude of prospective profits, which will depend on the relation between the spot rate and the expected future rate of exchange, neither of which will be fixed and independent of the magnitude of the speculators' transactions. By contrast, the adjustable-peg system gives the speculator a 'one-way option' in circumstances giving rise to speculation on a change in the rate, the rate can move only one way if it moves at all, and if it moves, it is certain to be changed by a significant amount—and possibly by more, the stronger is the speculation on a change. The fixed exchange-rate system courts 'destabilizing specu-lation', in the economically-incorrect sense of speculation against the permanence of the official parity, by providing this one-way position of speculating on their own ability to maintain the parity. It is obviously fallacious to assume that private speculators would speculate in the same way and on the same scale under the flexible rate system, which offers them no such easy mark to speculate against.

The argument that the flexible exchange-rate system would promote inflation comes in two major versions. The first is that under the flexible rate system governments would no longer be subject to the 'discipline' against inflationary policies exerted by the fixity of the exchange rate. This argument in large part reflects circular reasoning on the part of the fixed rate exponents: discipline against inflationary policies, if necessary for international reasons, is necessary only because rates are fixed, and domestic inflation both leads to balance-of-payments problems and im-poses inflation on other countries. Neither consequence would follow under the flexible exchange-rate system. Apart from its external reper-cussions, inflation may be regarded as undesirable for domestic reasons; but the fixed rate system imposes, not the need to maintain domestic price stability, but the obligation to conform to the average world trend of prices, which may be either inflationary or deflationary rather than stable. Moreover, under the adjustable-peg system actually existing, countries can evade the discipline against excessively rapid inflation by drawing down reserves and borrowing, by imposing restrictions on international trade and payments, and in the last resort by devaluing their currencies. The record since the First World War speaks poorly for the anti-inflationary discipline of fixed exchange rates. The reason is that the signal to governments of the need for anti-inflationary discipline comes through a loss of exchange reserves, the implications of which are understood by only a few and can be disregarded or temporized with until a crisis descends; the crisis then justifies all sorts of policy expedients other than the domestic deflation that the logic of adjustment under the fixed rate system demands. Under a flexible rate system, the conse-quences of inflationary governmental policies would be much more readily apparent to the general population, in the form of a declining foreign value of the currency and an upward trend in domestic prices; proper policies to correct the situation, if it were desired to correct it, could be argued about in an atmosphere free from crisis.

The second argument, to the effect that a flexible exchange rate would be 'inflationary', asserts that any random depreciation would, by raising the cost of living, provoke wage and price increases that would make the

initially temporarily lower foreign value of the currency the new equilibrium exchange rate. This argument clearly derives from confusion of a
flexible with a fixed exchange rate. It is under a fixed exchange rate that
wages and prices are determined in the expectation of constancy of the
domestic currency cost of foreign exchange, and that abrupt devaluations
occur that are substantial enough in their effects on the prices of imports
and of exportable goods to require compensatory revision of wage bar-
gains and price-determination calculations. Under a flexible rate system,
exchange rate adjustments would occur gradually, and would be less
likely to require drastic revisions of wage- and price-setting decisions,
especially as any general trend of the exchange rate and prices would
tend to be taken into account in the accompanying calculations of unions
and employers. Apart from this, it is erroneous to assume that increases
in the cost of living inevitably produce fully compensatory wage increases:
while such increases in the cost of living will be advanced as part of the
workers' case for higher wages, whether they will in fact result in
compensatory or in less than compensatory actual wage increases will
depend on the economic climate set by the government's fiscal and
monetary policies. It is conceivable that a government pledged to maintain full employment would maintain an economic climate in which any
money wage increase workers chose to press for would be sanctioned by
sufficient inflation of monetary demand and the money supply to prevent
it from resulting in an increase in unemployment. But in that case there
would be no restraint on wage increases and, hence, on wage and price
inflation, unless the government somehow had arrived at an understanding with the unions and employers that only wage increases compensatory
of previous cost-of-living increases (or justified by increases in productivity) would be sanctioned by easier fiscal and monetary policy. That is an
improbable situation, given the difficulties that governments have encountered with establishing and implementing an 'incomes policy' under
the fixed rate system; it is under the fixed rate system; not the flexible
rate system, that governments have a strong incentive to insist on relating
increases in money incomes to increases in productivity, and hence, are
led, on grounds of equity, to make exceptions for increases in the cost of
living. It should be noted in conclusion that one version of the argument
under discussion, which reasons from the allegation of a persistent
tendency to cost-push inflation to the prediction of a persistent tendency
towards depreciation of the currency, must be fallacious: it is logically
impossible for all currencies to be persistently depreciating against each
other.

V. Contemporary Proposals for Greater Flexibility of Exchange Rates

Increased flexibility in the IMF system

The extreme difficulties encountered in recent years in achieving appropriate adjustments of the parity values of certain major currencies within the present 'adjustable-peg' system of fixed exchange rates, as exemplified particularly in the prolonged agony of sterling from 1964 to 1967 and the failure of the 'Bonn crisis' of November 1968 to induce the German and French governments to accept the revaluations of the mark and the franc agreed on as necessary by the officials and experts concerned with the international monetary system, has generated serious interest, especially in the U.S. administration, in proposals for reforming the present IMF system so as to provide for more flexibility of exchange rates. It has been realized that under the present system, a devaluation has become a symbol of political defeat by, and revaluation (appreciation) a symbol of political surrender to, other countries, both of which the government in power will resist to the last ditch; and that this political symbolism prevents adjustments of exchange rates that otherwise would or should be accepted as necessary to the proper functioning of the international monetary system. The aim, therefore, is to reduce or remove the political element in exchange rate adjustment under the present system, by changing the system so as to allow the anonymous competitive foreign exchange market to make automatic adjustments of exchange rates within a limited range.

The two major proposals to this end are the 'wider-band' proposal and the 'crawling-peg' proposal. Under the 'wider-band' proposal, the present freedom of countries to allow the market value of their currencies to fluctuate within 1 per cent (in practice usually less) of their par values would be extended to permit variation within a much wider range (usually put at 5 per cent for argument's sake). Under the 'crawling-peg' proposal, daily fluctuations about the par value would be confined within the present or somewhat wider limits, but the parity itself would be determined by a moving average of the rates actually set in the market over some fixed period of the immediate past, and so would gradually adjust itself upwards or downwards over time to the market pressures of excess supply of or excess demand for the currency (pressures for depreciation or appreciation, rise or fall in the par value, respectively).

Both these proposals, while welcomed by advocates of the flexible exchange-rate system, to the extent that they recognize the case for flexible rates and the virtues of market determination as contracted with political determination of exchange rates, are subject to the criticism that they accept the principle of market determination of exchange rates only within politically predetermined limits, and, hence, abjure use of the prime virtue of the competitive market, its capacity to absorb and deal with unexpected economic developments. The criticism is that *either* economic developments will not be such as to make the equilibrium exchange rate fall outside the permitted range of variation, in which case the restriction on the permitted range of variation will prove unnecessary, *or* economic change will require more change in the exchange rate than the remaining restriction on exchange rate variation will permit, in which case the problems of the present system will recur (though obviously less frequently). Specifically, sooner or later the exchange rate of a major country will reach the limit of permitted variation, and the speculation-generating possibility will arise that the par value of that currency will have to be changed by a finite and substantial percentage, as a result of lack of sufficient international reserves for the monetary authorities of the country concerned to defend the par value of the currency.

In this respect, there is a crucial difference between the 'wider-band' proposal and the 'crawling-peg' proposal. The wider-band system would provide only a once-and-for-all increase in the degree of freedom of exchange rates to adjust to changing circumstances. A country that followed a more inflationary policy than other nations would find its exchange rate drifting towards the ceiling on its par value, and a country that followed a less inflationary policy than its neighbours would find its exchange rate sinking towards the floor under its par value. Once one or the other fixed limit was reached, the country would, to all intents and purposes, be back on a rigidly fixed exchange rate. The crawling-peg proposal, however, would permit a country's policy, with respect to the relative rate of inflation it preferred, to diverge permanently from that of its neighbours, but only within the limits set by the permitted range of daily variation about the daily par value and the period of averaging of past actual exchange rates specified for the determination of the par value itself. For those persuaded of the case for flexible exchange rates, the crawling peg is, thus, definitely preferable. The only question is the empirical one of whether the permitted degree of exchange rate flexibility would be adequate to eliminate the likelihood in practice of a situation which an exchange rate was so far out of equilibrium as to make it impossible for the monetary authorities to finance the period of adjustment of the rate to equilibrium by use of their international reserves and international borrowing power. This is an extremely difficult empirical question, because it involves not only the likely magnitude of disequilibrating disturbances, in relation to the permitted degree of exchange rate adjustment, but also the effects of the knowledge by government of the availability of increased possibilities of exchange rate flexibility on the speed of governmental policy response to disequilibrating developments, and the effects of the knowledge by private speculators that the effects on the exchange rate of current speculation will determine the range within which the exchange rate will be in the future, on the assumption that the crawling-peg formula continues to hold.

Evaluation of how both the wider-band and the crawling-peg proposal should work in practice requires a great deal of empirical study which, until 1969, has not been carried out on any adequate scale. In the meantime, those persuaded of the case for flexible exchange rates would probably be better advised to advocate experimentation with limited rate flexibility, in the hope that the results will dispel the fears of the supporters of the fixed rate system, than to emphasize the dangers inherent in the residual fixity of exchange rates under either of the contemporary popular proposals for increasing the flexibility of rates under the existing fixed rate systems.

A floating pound?

The argument of the preceding sections strongly suggests the advisability of a change in British exchange rate policy from a fixed exchange rate to a market-determined, flexible exchange rate. The main arguments for this change are that a flexible exchange rate would free British economic policy from the apparent necessity to pursue otherwise irrational and difficult policy objectives for the sake of improving the balance of payments, and that it would release the country from the vicious circle of 'stop-go' policies of control of aggregate demand.

A flexible exchange rate is not, of course, a panacea; it simply provides an extra degree of freedom, by removing the balance-of-payments constraints on policy formation. In so doing, it does not and cannot remove the constraint on policy imposed by the limitation of total available national resources and the consequent necessity of choice among available alternatives; it simply brings this choice, rather than the external consequences of choices made, to the forefront of the policy debate.

The British economy is at present riddled with inefficiencies consequential on, and politically justified by, decisions based on the aim of improving the balance of payments. In this connection, one can cite, from many possible examples, the heavy protection of domestic agriculture, the protection of domestic fuel resources by the taxation of imported oil, the subsidization of manufacturing as against the service trades through the Selective Employment Tax, and various other subsidies to manufacturing effected through tax credits. One can also cite the politically arduous effort to implement an incomes policy, which amounts to an effort to avoid, by political pressure on individual wage- and price-setting decisions, the need for an adjustment that would be effected automatically by a flexible exchange rate. A flexible exchange rate would make an incomes policy unneccessary. It would also permit policy towards industry, agriculture, and the service trades to concentrate on the achievement of greater economic efficiency, without the biases imparted by the basically economically-irrelevant objectives of increasing exports or substituting for imports.

The adoption of flexible exchange rates would also make unnecessary, or at least less harmful, the disruptive cycle of 'stop-go' aggregate demand policies, which has characterized British economic policy for many years. British governments are under a persistently strong incentive to try to break out of the limitations of available resources and relatively slow economic growth by policies of demand expansion. This incentive is reinforced, before elections, by the temptation to expand demand in order to win votes, in the knowledge that international reserves and international borrowing power can be drawn down to finance the purchase of votes without the electorate knowing that it is being bribed with its own money, i.e. until after the election, when the successful party is obliged to clean up the mess so created by introducing deflationary policies, with political safety if it is a returned government, and with political embarrassment if it is an opposition party newly come to power. If the country were on a flexible exchange rate, the generation of the 'political cycle' would be inhibited by the fact that the effort to buy votes by pre-election inflationary policies would soon be reflected in a depreciation of the exchange rate and a rise in the cost of living. Even if this were avoided by use of the government's control of the country's international reserves and borrowing powers to stabilize the exchange rate, a newly elected government of either complexion would not be faced with the absolute necessity of introducing deflationary economic policies to restore its international reserves. It could instead allow the exchange rate to depreciate while it made up its mind what to do. Apart from the question of winning elections, governments that believed in demand expansion as a means of promoting growth could pursue this policy à outrance, without being forced to reverse it by a balance-of-payments crisis, so long as they and the public were prepared to accept the consequential depreciation of the currency; governments that believed instead in other kinds of policies would have to argue for and defend them on their merits, without being able to pass them off as imposed on the country by the need to secure equilibrium in the balance of payments.

While these and other elements of the case for a floating pound have frequently been recognized and advocated, it has been much more common to argue that a flexible exchange rate for sterling is 'impossible', either because the position of sterling as an international reserve currency precludes it, or because the International Monetary Fund would not permit it. But most of the arguments for the presumed international importance of a fixed international value of sterling have been rendered irrelevant by the deterioration of sterling's international position subsequent to the 1967 devaluation, and in particular by the Basle Facility and the sterling-area agreements concluded in the autumn of 1968, which, by giving a dollar guarantee on most of the overseas sterling area holdings of sterling, have freed the British authorities to change the foreign-exchange value of sterling without fear of recrimination from its official holders. Moreover, the relative decline in the international role of sterling, and in the relative importance of Britain in world trade, finance, and investments, characteristic of the post-Second World War period, has made it both possible and necessary to think of Britain as a relatively small component of the international monetary system, more a country whose difficulties require special treatment than a lynch-pin of the system, the fixed value of whose currency must be supported by other countries in the interests of survival of the system as a whole. Under the present circumstances, adoption of a floating exchange rate for the pound would constitute, not a definitive reversal of the essential nature of the IMF system of predominantly fixed exchange rates, but recognition of and accommodation to a situation in which the chronic weakness of the pound is a major source of tension within the established system. The International Monetary Fund is commonly depicted in Britain as an ignorantly dogmatic but politically powerful opponent of sensible changes that have the drawback of conflicting with the ideology written into its Charter. But there is no reason to believe that the Fund as the dispassionate administrator of an international monetary system established nearly a quarter of a century ago to serve the needs of the international economy, is insensitive to the tensions of the contemporary situation and blindly hostile to reforms that would permit the system as a whole to survive and function more effectively.

Appendix

THE PANAMANIAN MONETARY SYSTEM*

Panama is unique or virtually so among the independent nations of the world with respect to its monetary system. While a national currency standard (the Balboa) exists, and subsidiary coinage denominated in this unit is issued, the Balboa has been exactly equal in value to one U.S. dollar ever since the completion of the Panama Canal six decades ago, and all the paper currency in circulation consists of U.S. dollar currency notes, there being no locally-issued paper Balboas.

This currency system was voluntarily adopted by the 'Convention of the Republic of Panama', which exercised legislative power for the Republic, in 1904, in agreement with the U.S. Secretary of War. But in the Panamanian popular mind it is associated with much-resented treaty of 1903 between Panama and the United States that established the Canal Zone. Now that the treaty is under renegotiation in Washington, it is natural that the question of the benefits and costs of the currency system should be raised in Panama.

The Panamanian monetary system has one great advantage—absolutely guaranteed stability of the currency in terms of the U.S. dollar, the country's largest trading partner in both directions. This absolute stability is important both for the inward private foreign investment on which developing countries have had increasingly to depend for external development assistance, and for Panama's burgeoning tourist trade, most of which consists either of American tourists or of other foreigners used to making transactions in U.S. dollars. In addition, the system has undoubtedly been strategic to Panama's rapid emergence as a regional financial centre.

As against these benefits, the system has two disadvantages. The first, and primarily sentimental rather than economic, one is that it is offensive to Panamanian national pride (of course in widely varying degrees) to use

---

*Reprinted from *Euromoney*, Vol. 3, No. 8 (January 1972), pp. 48–52.

a foreign currency for domestic transactions. The second, and economic, one is that dollars in circulation in Panama constitute an interest-free loan to the government of the United States. The resource loss to Panama involved depends on the interest rate at which the money could otherwise be invested. This interest rate obviously depends both on the type of asset in which the money could be invested, and on the rate of inflation in the world economy in general. As regards the first point, which will be discussed in more detail below, different possible conceptions of prudent banking practice in holding reserves against currency could lead to widely different results. As regards the second, the higher the rate of inflation in the world, sooner or later the higher will be world interest rates, as asset-holders who can choose between holding fixed-interest securities and holding equities come to realize that fixed-interest securities are losing real value from the inflation and demand higher interest rates to compensate them.

Currency in circulation in Panama has been variously estimated as of the order of $25 to $50 million. Taking the higher figure for illustrative purposes, at a 6 per cent average rate of return, obtainable otherwise, this would represent a loss of real resources of $3 million a year, and $6m, at a 12 per cent average alternative rate of return, resources which could in principle be captured by the Panamanian government issuing its own currency. These figures represent roughly 1.6 per cent and 3.2 per cent of the annual Panamanian budget, though only about .025 to 0.50 per cent of gross domestic product. These sums are certainly not negligible; but they are not magically large either. The 6 per cent assumption represents a probably high estimate of what could be gained by investing the $50 million in a fairly liquid portfolio of U.S. government securities; the 12 per cent assumption is a probably high estimate of the social value of investing it either in Panamanian enterprises or in Panamanian government debt—in the latter case on the assumption that the interest rate on such debt understates the social rate of return on Panamanian government investments in infrastructure and social-betterment projects.

It is apparently widely believed that the government of Panama could easily capture these potential gains for itself by establishing a central bank, which would issue Balboas in place of dollars. This belief, however, overlooks some important relevant considerations.

The primary problem is the loss from the interest-free loan to the United States. This loss could be largely (though not entirely) removed without establishing a central bank, by establishing instead a currency board which would issue Balboas in exchange for dollars, and invest the dollars so obtained in a range of U.S. securities. The currency board would have to keep its portfolio liquid enough to meet any demands for the conversion of circulating Balboas into dollars.

In the Panamanian context, a currency board would have the appeal of representing a logical and primarily technical extension beyond the issue of subsidiary coins to the issue of Panamanian paper money, while preserving the aforementioned advantages of guaranteed absolute fixity of the exchange rate between the Balboa and the dollar. A central bank, by contrast, carries the threat of monetary mismanagement's ending up in exchange and payments restrictions and devaluation. At a more practical level, a currency board has the great advantage over a central bank that its operations can be made fairly automatic, so that it need not require a comparable expenditure on both administrative staff and prestigious directors and a governor able and obliged to attend the annual meetings of the International Monetary Fund and make fittingly portentous speeches prepared by high-priced research staff. Nor does it require an impressive building. It should be possible to run a currency board with a small staff and one to three commissioners who need to meet only two to four times a year.

Even so, the gain would probably not be anything like the $3 million a year mentioned above, for four reasons. (1) Prudent maintenance of a liquid portfolio, including actual dollars on deposit at the Federal Reserve as well as liquid U.S. government securities, might yield an average rate of return considerably below the 6 per cent gross assumed in the preceding calculation. (2) Even if the administration were on the most modest possible scale, its total costs for staff and office accommodation might be substantial in relation to the yield achieved. (3) Once Panama began to issue Balboa currency notes it would have to bear the costs of printing and reprinting the notes; what these costs would be in relation to the interest earned would depend on the average denomination and average life of a note, and since Panama is a poor country the average denomination would be low (probably one Balboa would be the most frequently used denomination) though against the notes in circulation in rural and remote districts might remain outstanding for a period of many years. (4) Once Panama issued its own Balboas it would have to cope with the probability of forgery and the costs of preventing or controlling it.

The foregoing remarks suggest five empirical questions that should be investigated before any decision is taken on the establishment of a currency board. These are: (i) how far the Balboas would in fact be accepted instead of dollars—the replacement of course could be fostered by various government actions, but these would have some administrative cost and nuisance value; (ii) what the expected average rate of return on the portfolio of U.S. dollar assets would be; (iii) what the staff and office costs of administration would be; (iv) what the cost of printing and reprinting notes would be; (v) what costs would be involved in policing against forgery.

The proposal to establish a central bank in Panama is associated with the idea, more ambitious than that of establishing a currency board, of capturing for Panama the potential gains from being able to invest the real resources represented by the Panamanian currency circulation in domestic projects of one kind or another—essentially, given the way central banks operate, of lending these resources to the government by purchasing government debt. This would involve the same questions of returns and costs as would arise with a currency board, except that on the one hand the gross returns on the portfolio might be substantially higher, and on the other hand the directorate, staff and building costs of a central bank would undoubtedly be much higher. Further questions would arise from the fact that such a central bank, like other central banks, would most probably impose requirements in terms of its notes and deposits on the commercial banks. This would capture a part of bank deposits, as well as the currency issue, for the central bank to invest, thereby increasing the resources acquired above what a currency board would command—though it should be noted that reserve requirements are essentially a special kind of tax ultimately falling on bank depositors. On the other hand, the result would likely be that the commercial banks would come to rely on the central bank to provide them with foreign currencies in case of need, rather than holding their own portfolios of foreign liquid assets; and this might involve a considerable net loss, since the central bank is likely to be a less efficient portfolio manager than the commercial banks.

The central and fundamental issue raised by the proposal for a central bank, however, is whether a central bank—and more specifically the government whose instrument it would be—could be trusted to follow investment policies that would in fact guarantee the absolute stability of the Balboa in terms of the U.S. dollar. Monetary history is full of cases where governments hungry for money that they wanted to spend on projects they considered desirable, obtained the money not by taxes but by pressing their central bank to buy more government debt than was prudent from the point of view of defending the stability of the currency. As a result in such cases, the central bank runs its international reserves and liquidity position dangerously low, and the government is driven into exchange and trade controls and eventually into currency devaluation. Both involve not only deceit and robbery of the domestic public, whose money is reduced in value by a sort of arbitrary tax imposed on it, but perhaps more important the destruction of foreign confidence in the currency and in the country and its government, which is harmful especially to foreign investment in the country's economic development. For countries short of domestic savings and dependent on foreign capital for economic development, this highly probable long-run effect is a costly price to pay for capturing the returns on the investment of the real resources represented by the domestic money supply. For Panama, there is another cogent consideration: its emerging position as a regional financial centre would probably be seriously jeopardized if it became merely another small country with its own national currency and central bank.

For these reasons, it would seem desirable for Panama at most—and still consistently with the satisfaction of national pride—to consider seriously the question of instituting a currency board, and not to involve itself in the expensive and politically dangerous business of establishing a central bank. Even the question of a currency board should be looked into very cautiously, for two reasons. First, there are the empirical questions listed above, which will determine the probable amount of net profit that might be obtained. Second, there is the possibility that even a carefully set up and limited currency board could be converted by a determined and irresponsible government into a temporary source of easy finance for its programmes.

In view of these considerations, it might be wiser for the government of Panama to retain the present monetary system of the country, but to seek compensation for the obvious inequity of interest-free lending from a poor country to a rich one in some other way. There is a fairly close parallel here with the currency-board system that used to be characteristic of the British colonies. The argument in that case was that the low-interest (not interest-free) loans implicit in the currency-board system of investing in short-term British government securities were compensated for by British development assistance and by special rights of access to the British capital market. In the case of Panama these two forms of compensation do not seem relevant. However, Panama might ask *either* for a reasonable share of the profits of the U.S. Federal Reserve System, calculated on the basis of the estimated circulation of U.S. dollars in Panama and the profits made by the Federal Reserve per dollar in circulation, *or* for a swap loan from the Federal Reserve or some similar device designed to enable Panama to cope more efficiently with the large seasonal swings in her balance of payments.

As a final remark, these notes have been concerned only with the currency circulation of Panama. Probably a much larger volume of Panama's financial transactions is conducted through deposits at banks. As already mentioned, these depositors could be taxed through the imposition of a reserve requirement in terms of central bank notes and deposits. Apart from that, and assuming that the banking system is reasonably competitive, there would be nothing to gain by persuading or forcing it to denominate its deposits and loans in Balboas instead of dollars, because presumably the Panamanian holders of dollar-denominated bank deposits receive services from the banks that represent the returns the banks get from investing those deposits minus their costs of operation. Indeed, insisting on the Balboa as the unit of bank accounting might seriously hamper Panama's development as a regional financial centre.

3

REFLECTIONS ON THE EXCHANGE RATE SYSTEM

J. Carter Murphy

It is tempting to compare the effectiveness of fixed and flexible exchange rate systems by contrasting the performance of the world economy under the original Bretton Woods rules with economic performance since 1973. Coincidence of events in time, however, does not lead to an inference that the events are casually related. In fact, strong economic performance over a part of the IMF's first twenty-five years and poorer performance since that time are both the results of fundamental forces having little to do with fixed or flexible exchange rates. Here I shall briefly discuss those forces and then comment on proposals that would return us to some form of preannounced official targeting of the rates. This provides me an opportunity to raise some useful questions concerning the functions we want the exchange rates to perform.

I. The Postwar Boom and Bretton Woods

In a book of a few years ago (1979) I detailed some causes of the breakdown of the original Bretton Woods arrangements, and in the limited space available to me here I must summarize that history. The policy choices of governments were dominated by inflationary biases from World War II to the late 1970's. During the 1950's, inflation was more endemic to Europe and the developing world than to North America, and the effects of the expansionary excesses abroad were offset by periodic devaluations of the inflated currencies against the dollar. When, in the mid-1960's, the United States became, among industrialized countries, the region with greater relative inflation, dollar devaluation against other currencies proved difficult for many reasons, and, in the end, the gold exchange system centered on the dollar failed when flight from the dollar made the fixed gold-dollar exchange rate untenable. Subsequent efforts to restore currency par values at realigned exchange rates then proved impossible because governmental pledges to support pegged rates lacked credibility. The uneven inflation process was continuing, and inflationary expectations were on the rise.

The crux of the problem was that governments, quite predictably, responded to the constituencies that elected them (and with the limitations of their national political institutions), rather than to the requirements of a particular exchange rate structure whenever internal and external goals conflicted. The ragged inflation that resulted induced massive capital transfers in anticipation of changes in the par value exchange rates. In the end the violence of these transfers wrecked the system's tie to gold and made even continued fixed exchange rates on the dollar untenable for most countries.

To look back now with undue nostalgia on the Bretton Woods arrangements is, I think, a mistake. I like Peter Gray's (1974, p. 16) characterization of the Bretton Woods period as one in which the dollar moved from being an undervalued currency in the late 1940's and early 1950's to one roughly in equilibrium from the mid-1950's to the mid-1960's and finally to a position of overvaluation. In the first of these periods there was widespread discrimination against dollar goods and investments; in the second, progress was made toward trade and investment liberalization; the third saw a strong revival of protectionism in the United States and capital controls abroad.

The disorder that has plagued economic life during the *post*-1973 period of managed floating exchange rates is largely a legacy of the same inflationary excesses that brought the original Bretton Woods rules to an end. Considering older textbook predictions to the contrary, it is ironic that the great inflation of the 1970's originated in the period of pegged exchange rates while the 1980's policies of disinflation have come in the period of floating rates. The structural maladjustments termed "stagflation" in the early 1970's were exacerbated by ill-fated efforts in Europe and North America to dictate wages and prices and then reinforced by the petroleum crises that began in 1973–74; all these were related to the chronic inflationary management of demand. While the uneven inflation (that supported real economic growth for a time but later became a source of distortion) cannot be blamed on the system of fixed exchange rates, it also cannot be attributed to floating. It was in fact due to economic ideas that concentrated too much on aggregate demand for current output and provided politicians an easy rationale for spending without taxing and for pegging nominal interest rates below equilibrium levels.

II. Disillusionment with Flexible Exchange Rates

The disorders of the international economy since 1973 have made many economists disillusioned with managed floating and have led some to call for a return to pegging, or at least "targeting," the exchange rates (for example, John Williamson, 1983; Otmar Emminger, 1982; and Atlantic Council, 1983.) Excessive volatility in the rates is said to result from speculative activity based on changing expectations (or in some cases the absence of speculative activity), from lags in price adjustments following exchange rate changes, and from small short-run supply and demand responses to price changes. Protracted misalignments in the rates, an even more serious problem, are attributed to various causes including the following: 1) international capital transfers induced by macro- and microeconomic policies of governments; 2) public and private currency substitutions, motivated by changing appraisals of risks and returns in different currency denominations; 3) lags in sectoral price adjustments; 4) flow-stock mechanics in portfolio adjustments, in which initial portfolio balancing shifts are larger relative to more permanent redistributions of savings flows; 5) asymmetries in market access to information; 6) lagged price and quantity adjustments due to long-term contracts; and 7) oligopolies. (There are reviews of this literature in Williamson, and in Robert Dunn, 1983.) Such a list of complaints begs the question: what do we want the exchange rate system to do?

I believe we want the system: (a) to facilitate an international allocation of resources and pattern of trade that is "efficient"; (b) to encourage the movement of real and financial capital from points of lower to higher value; (c) to deal with systemic risks at low social cost and to assign the burdens of risk taking equitably; and (d) to adjust to disturbances in a low-cost way and to distribute the burden of adjustment costs equitably.

The desire for efficient resource allocation and trade does not imply that the exchange rates should be at purchasing power parity (*PPP*). The *PPP* calculations are behind most allegations of misalignment in the rates even when it is acknowledged that the rates must do more than achieve a goods and services market equilibrium. Williamson goes further than most when he defines a "fundamental equilibrium exchange rate" to be one which is "expected to generate a current account surplus or deficit equal to the underlying capital flow over the cycle, given that the country is pursuing 'internal balance' as best it can and not restricting trade for balance of payments reasons" (p. 14).

Still, what else might the exchange rate accomplish? Do we not want this price to reflect changing expectations as we want other prices to do?

It is well established that speculative positions *correctly* taken in advance of uncertain events lead to actions which prepare for the event and have social value. While numerous studies have shown that forward (and, with interest parity, spot) exchange rates are imperfect predictors of future rates and are, to that degree, inefficient, have we experience that an officially targeted rate does better? Even though the "noise" of daily aberations in a flexible rate is a nuisance, I am skeptical of the view that assumes experts have greater wisdom to gauge market tendencies than market participants have. While I have no difficulty rationalizing small government interventions to interrupt exchange rate runs or to give depth to thin and hesitant markets, such interventions are very different from exchange rate targeting.

It is clear that exchange rates will "overshoot" their long-run equilibria when exchange rates are free to adjust rapidly while other adjustments in the system are slow. The relevant question is: is such overshooting uneconomic? Overshooting may accelerate other desired responses throughout the system, in the same way that Alfred Marshall (1890) saw his exaggerated short-term price adjustments inducing proper long-term adjustments of supply. Is not every market price in every real world adjustment part of what is at most a "second-best" solution, with the "first-best" solution denied by constraints on rates of adjustment of some variables? Have we much yet to say about the welfare properties of alternative adjustment paths in disequilibrium periods? In view of our ignorance on these matters, I see the evidence on overshooting as useful data on the dynamic properties of national economic systems, but not grounds for rejecting flexible exchange rates in favor of rates more fixed.

Let us turn next to the roles the exchange rate plays in directing real flows of investment. For investment flows to be efficient, it is not required that they be from regions where fixed capital is relatively abundant toward regions where fixed capital is scarce, or from "rich" countries to "poor." The allocation of saving, and also the portion of the existing capital stock that is liquid, is directed by its price and the expected variance of that price. These values are sensitive in different regions to changing time preferences, changing liquidity supply and demand, and changing perceptions of risk, as well as to changes in the efficiency with which investment contributes to the production of goods.

When there are changes in one country's excess demand for liquidity, time preference, or apparent ability to provide safety to capital returns, as compared to other countries, it is, in my view, efficient from a global perspective for capital to move toward the area of improved or safer returns. One may want to distinguish analytically between changes that originate in the private sector and those that are implemented through government policies—changes in money demand as opposed to government controlled money supply, for example, or changes in aggregate time preference resulting from individuals' savings choices as opposed those due to government managed income redistributions—and I return to this matter below. But I think one should not deny that capital movements induced by changing time preferences, liquidity adequacy, and perceptions of security are "appropriate" and that the exchange rates that accommodate the transfers are efficient rates.

The allegation that recent movements of capital to the United States have sought, among other things, a "safe haven," suggests, however, a further point. The safety sought by these investors has been perhaps in some degree safety from expropriatory governmental regulation. While confiscatory risks are real enough to individuals or firms as investors, they refer to wealth transfers, not losses, from the viewpoint of nations and the world as a whole. If international transfers based on this fear, then, are to be considered socially efficient, the rationale must be in terms of individual liberty and the importance of property rights rather than in terms of other needs.

The subject of risk in the economy, and who should bear it and how, is an especially difficult one, but it is an issue in arguments over the exchange rate regime. When the foreign exchange rate is held within a predesignated range by official intervention, risks in the system are transferred from some in society to others. Awareness that intervention will prevent a currency's depreciation, for example, relieves those who would be directly affected by such a change (users and producers of internationally traded goods and holders of money and nominal money claims). It also increases risk to others—at home and abroad—including those for whom the likelihood rises that governments will use alternative policy measures to deal with the balance of payments. While the provision of reserve assets for the world economy as a whole need not be costly (if fiduciary rather than "real" assets are used for this purpose), and even the holding of reserves by one country is costly only in the degree that the reserves are held in assets which yield less return than optimal real investments, *use* of reserves by any government is costly to those who must forego absorption when the reserve stocks are rebuilt and to those whose absorption is impaired by trade at an officially selected but inappropriate exchange rate. Exchange market intervention by governments, therefore, does not reduce risk; it reassigns it (Milton Friedman, 1953).

A flexible exchange rate spreads adjustment burdens—and the risk of uncertain burdens—*between* countries more than does a stabilized rate because with stablized rates deficit countries more commonly have to initiate policy changes. On the whole, greater international participation in such burden sharing is probably desirable on grounds of spreading the costs and their attendant risks as widely as possible. One cannot be unequivocal about even this, however, since it can plausibly be argued that adjustment burdens resulting from "bad" policies should be borne in the country responsible for the bad policies, where the policies can be changed.

Business people have deplored since 1973 the increased risks of international trade and investment they have been asked to bear. We are told of the multifaceted adjustments they have made to minimize the costs of their new risks (for example, Marina Whitman, 1984). I do not, however believe that the fact that these burdens and adjustments are being borne by traders and investors is a proper argument against flexible exchange rates. The exchange rate has been described as a "system variable par excellence" (Val Koromzay et al., 1984); it reflects changes that have occurred, are occurring, or are expected to occur in many parts of the world economy. Might it not be best for the uncertainty surrounding these events to be borne, in the first instance, by those most likely to have information about them? In particular, is it not desirable that they be borne to the maximum extent possible by those persons who have less risk aversion and are willing to take speculative positions in the market, rather than by those who are passive gainers or losers from governments' successes or failures as exchange speculators? Broad price level changes— and their risks and burdens—that accompany significant exchange rate swings are of course.passed on by traders in a flexible rate regime; the evidence nevertheless is clear that the effects of many small exchange rate moves are absorbed by the professionals in such a setting. Generally, I feel that risk taking ought to be a market activity, rather than a socialized one, except where significant externalities can be demonstrated.

III. Which System Best Bears Shocks?

How does the system bear shocks, and can anything be said about the contributions of alternative exchange rate regimes in this connection? Clearly neither fixed nor flexible exchange rates is best at minimizing adjustment costs to *all* types of disturbance. One must, therefore, weigh the seriousness of disturbances the system must absorb and consider what exchange rate design copes best with the more serious shocks. In this vein I suggest that by far the most damaging disturbances to international economic equilibrium during the past forty years have emanated from the public sector, not the private. While many of us were raised in an era in which it was accepted that the *private* sector was the source of economic instability and the *public* sector was the home of policy instruments for countervailing the private sector disturbances, I am sadly driven to doubt the old views. Perhaps a time will come when democratic governments will tax and spend and manage money in a way that is stabilizing to society. But experience since World War II suggests that we should give thought to system designs that absorb shocks from this area as well as the private sector. Furthermore, it is worth noting that to seek a system that protects one national economy from unexpected policy shifts in another is not the same thing as desiring a system that facilitates as much as possible governmental use of the macroeconomic policy instruments.

The ease with which one or another exchange rate regime handles the macroeconomic aspects of public policy disturbances depends, in the first instance, on the way the regime handles the international capital transfers involved, as the asset approach to exchange rate determination has shown us. Now the important thing about a flexible exchange rate regime is that in it net transfers of capital claims immediately become real transfers because international net sales of capital claims affect exchange rates and generate current account surpluses or deficits to mirror the claims flow. In a system where the exchange rate is wholly or partly stabilized, on the other hand, international shifts in capital claims are wholly or partly financed by reserve transfers, avoiding to that degree a disturbance to production and trade. This is, I think, a central argument for stabilized exchange rates, and it is applicable when disturbances are temporary and of sufficiently small magnitude that they can be financed by modest monetary reserve movements. Where a disturbance is large and enduring, a flexible exchange rate is almost certainly preferable because it avoids the production and consumption distortions that are due to a too long maintained nominal exchange rate, and it provides a useful degree of flexibility to real prices and wages at home and abroad.

Since, of course, no one knows whether a government policy change is going to be large or durable until after the event, one must consider the costs involved in a wrong forecast. What is clear here is that the very costly adjustments are the large ones, and they are the ones that must not be missed. Failure to recognize and accommodate them early enough was a critical weakness in the Bretton Woods arrangements. It is this line of thought that persuades me we must have a system among the industrialized countries that has a significant degree of exchange rate flexibility.

Correct expectations and speculation on those disturbances that prove reversible can give even a flexible exchange rate regime the advantages of a fixed rate system. Incorrect expectations or inadequate speculation, on the other hand, expose the weaknesses in the flexible system. Exploration of crawling rate systems (see my 1965 article) and other compromise arrangements should not be ruled out. But a high degree of exchange rate responsiveness to market pressures is, I believe, an important safeguard against delaying real economic adjustments too long.

IV. Containing Public Sector Shocks

It is clear from much of the literature on exchange rate arrangements that the authors seek global adjustments to disturbances that arise in the private sector but minimal external accommodation of disturbances from the public sector. It is not clear to me that all shifts in public sector actions have any less claim to accommodation through world market adjustments than have private sector shifts. Yet the view that one government should not impose the results of its economic policy choices on other nations is widely accepted. It is, I think, the basis for the lament seen in recent economic writings (Whitman; Dunn) that floating exchange rates have not secured isolation for national economies from external changes, and it is the justification for the grant by governments of surveillance authority to the IMF to inhibit beggar-thy-neighbor policy choices. The truth probably is that we don't want bad policies exported, but we do want good policies shared.

Is there any institutional arrangement that, without too great cost, will contain the macroeconomic effects of all government monetary and fiscal changes? Clearly a regime of floating exchange rates will not do so alone, although in a more naive age there was hope for it. Severe restrictions on international capital movements would protect the current account in a flexible exchange rate setting but would be unable to distinguish between government induced capital movements and those serving strictly private sector needs; they would also raise a harvest of other problems. The IMF surveillance of nations' economic policy mixes with a view to discouraging clear beggar-thy-neighbor choices can be helpful, but the IMF's ability to influence the policies of major countries so far remains small (William Hood, 1982).

One promising guideline for evaluating governments' macroeconomic policy choices calls for fiscal and monetary changes to be "balanced." Equal proportional changes in a nation's monetary base and in face value of public debt instruments outstanding (by maturity class) would go far toward neutralizing the impact of demand management changes on real interest rates in the nation where the changes take place and hence on induced international capital transfers. In a regime of flexible exchange rates, any nation, or all nations simultaneously pursuing such a rule, could follow expansive or restraining overall monetary and fiscal policies of their choice without disturbing the international current and capital account balances much (see my book, 1979). Yet the markets would remain free to accommodate shifts in costs and private preferences of all kinds. Under fixed exchange rates, the monetary-fiscal policy mix of each country is pulled automatically toward the balance of other countries because money stocks move internationally toward countries with the lowest ratio of money to debt growth. But this alone does not prevent policy shifts in one country from impinging upon others.

I do not hold out much hope in the near future for guidelines calling for fiscal and monetary balance because fiscal policies are the result of microeconomic political pressures as much as of macroeconomic needs, and central banks will, for reasons, some of which are good, be reluctant to yield up their independence to pursue their own policy objectives. Nevertheless, if we continue to have activist government policies and at the same time wish to limit their impact abroad, we must create new images for the public concerning what constitutes good policy. In this case, flexible exchange rates with monetary and fiscal policy balance provides one of the few packages around that is deserving of consideration.

References

Dunn, Robert M., Jr., *The Many Disappointments of Flexible Exchange Rates*, Essays in International Finance, No. 154, Princeton University, 1983.

Emminger, Otmar, *Exchange Rate Policy Reconsidered*, Occasional Papers 10, Group of Thirty, New York, 1982.

Friedman, Milton, "The Case for Flexible Exchange Rates," in his *Essays in Positive Economics*, Chicago: University of Chicago Press, 1953.

Gray, H. Peter, *An Aggregate Theory of International Payments Adjustment*, Lexington: D. C. Heath, 1974.

Hood, William, C., "Surveillance Over Exchange Rates," *Finance and Development*, March 1982, 19, 9–12.

Koromzay, Val, Llewellyn, John and Potter, Stephen, "Exchange Rate Rules and Policy Choices: Some Lessons from Interdependence in a Multilateral Perspective," *American Economic Review Proceedings*, May 1984, 74, 311–15.

Marshall, Alfred, *Principles of Economics (1890)*, 8th ed., London: Macmillan, 1946.

Murphy, J. Carter, *The International Monetary System: Beyond the First Stage of Reform*, Washington: American Enterprise Institute, 1979.

———, "Moderated Exchange Rate Variability," *National Banking Review*, December 1965, 2, 151–61.

Whitman, Marina v. N., "Assessing Greater Variability of Exchange Rates: A Private Sector Perspective," *American Economic Review Proceedings*, May 1984, 74, 298–304

Williamson, John, *The Exchange Rate System*, Washington: Institute for International Economics, 1983.

Atlantic Council, "Policy Paper on the International Monetary System: Exchange Rates and International Indebtedness," Working Group on International Monetary Affairs, Washington, 1983.

4

FUNCTIONING OF THE CURRENT INTERNATIONAL FINANCIAL SYSTEM: STRENGTHS, WEAKNESSES, AND CRITERIA FOR EVALUATION

Thomas D. Willett*

The organizers of this conference asked me to focus in this paper on three topics: (1) describing the key aspects of the functioning of our present multicurrency international monetary system; (2) providing a framework for assessing the system's performance; and (3) evaluating the system's strengths, weaknesses, and potential for change. This is a tall order, and I cannot possibly present a fully comprehensive treatment of these topics, since at a minimum this would require foreknowledge of the outcomes of the discussion of the various major issue areas highlighted in the following sessions of this conference. I shall settle for the more limited objective of presenting what I hope will be useful background analysis for the discussion of these specific issues and for the evaluation of the international monetary system as a whole.

In overview papers, there is always the major question of how to organize the discussion of numerous topics which interrelate in a complex manner. My plan of attack will be first to consider criteria and perspectives for assessing the performance of international monetary systems, and then to attempt to describe and evaluate the current international monetary system and possibilities for further reform against the background of postwar international monetary evolution. In the process, I shall attempt to focus on most of the main issues of controversy among experts and policymakers about the international monetary system and

*I am indebted to Mark Bremer, Benjamin Cohen, Jacob Dreyer, Randall Hinshaw, Alexander Swoboda, Edward Tower, and George von Furstenberg for helpful comments and to the Keck Institute for International Strategic Studies and the Lincoln Foundation for research support.

to consider many of the key reasons for differences of view. Thus, a major theme running through this paper will be an attempt to analyze in a systematic manner some of the major reasons why there has been (and, in my judgment, there will continue to be) so much controversy about international monetary issues.

Differences of view about such issues can be categorized under three main headings: (1) differences about the overall objectives of the international monetary system or the relative weights given to these objectives, (2) concern with distributional aspects of the operation of the system, and (3) differences in judgment about how various regimes would operate in terms of the first two categories. The first two of these categories are explicitly normative, while the third is positive. However, uncertainties about positive aspects of evaluation often lead to a subtle interaction of normative and positive analysis, even within this third category. There is also the possibility of direct overlaps between the categories, as there are, for example, in a normative value judgment that explicit distributional objectives, such as the transfer of real resources from industrial to developing countries, should be a major objective of international liquidity creation. Still, I believe that thinking of the sources of controversy in terms of these three categories will prove useful.

While I shall indicate my own views on numerous questions, I shall not attempt to weigh systematically the relative importance of the various major reasons for international monetary controversy. I find myself somewhere in between the judgments of Richard Cooper (1975) and Benjamin Cohen (1977) in their recent analyses of these questions.[1] Cohen argues (p. 49) that "The problem of distribution is undoubtedly the most fundamental source of controversy in world monetary affairs." Cooper's view (p. 64) is that "If [my] essay carries any principal message, it is that sources of disagreement do not generally derive from divergent interests, but rather from diverse perspectives and hence different conjectures about the consequences of one regime as compared with another. In short, disagreement arises mainly from ignorance about true effects, so that we must use reasoned conjecture rather than solid fact to guide our choices." Like Cooper, I am very much struck by the considerable extent to which there are vast differences in the positive analysis invoked to support alternative positions in the international monetary area. While ultimately such differences involve the interpretation of past or future facts, I have also been very impressed by the extent to which the conceptual frameworks adopted by different analysts and the ways they phrase their questions influence their ultimate empirical judgments.

In discussing international monetary issues today, we find two radically different perspectives often being adopted. One views our current international monetary arrangements as being fundamentally unsound and requiring basic reform. The second views the framework of our international monetary system as sound and focuses on how we may reduce current international monetary problems by policy changes or evolutionary institutional innovations within the context of our current framework. Of course, not all views fall neatly into one or the other of these categories, and one person's fundamental reform may seem quite marginal to another expert. It is also important to distinguish clearly between evaluation of the structure of the international monetary system itself and evaluation of the general performance of economic policies and the world economy under any particular system. There is general agreement that the global economic performance of the past decade has been dismal. The relevant questions from the standpoint of international monetary reform, however, are the extent to which the structure of the international monetary system has contributed to this poor economic performance and what changes in that structure can be expected to improve future economic performance. The judgments of supporters and critics of the current system obviously differ greatly on these issues.

Even those (such as myself) who believe that the basic framework of our current system is relatively sound will typically see numerous areas in which improvements are needed. Obviously, the current third world international debt problems present an enormous challenge to international financial management and cooperation. Likewise, no one would argue that recent records of inflation, unemployment, and exchange rate volatility have been satisfactory. Nor are our provisions for international economic policy coordination and safeguards against beggar-thy-neighbor policies as strong as many of us would like. Still, one may see the best practical hope for reducing such problems as lying with an evolutionary process within the framework of the current system.

Others hold the view that the current system is fundamentally unsound, indeed, that it is best termed a nonsystem.[2] Critiques from this perspective frequently argue that exchange rate volatility and uncontrolled international liquidity creation have been the major causes of world-wide stagflation, that the Jamaica international monetary reforms were fundamentally incomplete, and that we are far from the degree of internationally centralized control of the international monetary system that is needed.

One of the most important (although by no means the only substantive) reasons for such differing views stems from the extent to which one adopts a historical political economy approach, which stresses the difficulties of reaching political agreement and tends frequently to judge current institutional arrangements in terms of whether they are stronger or weaker than those they preceded, or what might be called an optimal policy approach, which tends to ignore problems of collective decision making and policy implementation and focuses on deviations between real-world arrangements and theoretical ideals.[3] As the following brief historical review indicates, it is quite possible to conclude that the current international monetary system is a substantial improvement over its predecessors, yet still falls far short of the ideal.

We may highlight the major differences among alternative international monetary systems in terms of their relationships with respect to (1) exchange rate regimes and the balance of payments adjustment process, (2) mechanisms for international liquidity creation and balance of payments financing, and (3) the structure of decision-making authority. The Bretton Woods negotiators sought (successfully, I believe) to create a system which avoided the major difficulties of its predecessors—the gold standard and the nationalist system of independent economic policy that prevailed during the interwar period.[4]

While it can be argued that, in practice, the rules of the game were seldom followed all that closely, the gold standard generally worked quite well in terms of the international criteria of fostering international exchange and facilitating relatively harmonious potential relationships among countries. Its fatal flaw was the substantial loss of domestic macroeconomic control which it implied. The interwar system went much too far to the other extreme of nationalist economic policymaking designed to gain short-term advantages, and predictable disasters duly ensued.

Bretton Woods was based on the twin economic principles that exchange rates and balance of payments policies were matters of international as well as national concern and that countries should not be required to subject their economies to major inflations or deflations in order to balance payments. It also established a formal apparatus for collective interpretation and decision making through the International Monetary Fund. These principles and the international cooperation which they helped foster have served us well and continue as the basis for our current international monetary system.

For many years, the Bretton Woods system operated quite satisfactorily. It was certainly instrumental in avoiding a repeat of the 1930s. Over time, however, a number of serious deficiencies in the system became increasingly apparent and were, in turn, exacerbated by structural changes in the world economy.

Political biases against prompt adjustment of par values, combined with increasing use of activist macroeconomic policies in the pursuit of full employment and the growth of international capital mobility made the exchange rate system increasingly crisis-prone. At the same time, the slower-than-expected rate of gold production, the political infeasibility of using the provisions for universal par value adjustments to increase the value of gold, and the expanding role of the dollar as a reserve currency combined to create the Triffin dilemma: to meet the growing needs of international liquidity, further expansion of official dollar holdings were needed, but, given the level of gold backing of the dollar, this would be likely to undermine confidence and lead to an international monetary crisis.[5] With the development of a full-fledged dollar standard ruled out on political grounds, the needed remedies for these difficulties in the Bretton Woods structure involved both the creation of a new international source of reserve holdings (the special drawing right (SDR)) and substantial improvements in the operation of the adjustment process. The failure to make major progress in the latter area combined with the substantially increased strains on the system created by overheating of the U.S. economy, induced by the financing of the Viet Nam War, led to an uncontrolled explosion of international liquidity and the breakdown of the system.

I believe that the widespread adoption of flexible exchange rates has made major contributions to ameliorating all three of the problems of the Bretton Woods system—adjustment, liquidity, and confidence. Greater exchange rate flexibility has improved the operation of the adjustment process, both by offering many countries the easier use of an effective means of adjustment and by reducing the political biases against adjustment which existed under the par value system. It has improved the international liquidity problem by offering countries greater flexibility in accumulating reserves and in shielding themselves from undesired reserve accumulations. The confidence problem has been lessened by substantially reducing the availability of one-way speculative options.

Flexible rates do not provide the complete solution to all international monetary problems, however. Even with ideal private speculation, not all countries would want to float freely because of optimum-currency-area considerations.[6] Furthermore, the evidence that private speculation has always been strongly stabilizing is far from strong, and there may be macroeconomic externality arguments for official intervention by independent floaters even where private speculation is efficient in an ex ante sense.[7] Thus, a zero intervention rule for exchange rate surveillance is not a viable option. Therefore, in addition to questions of domestic macroeconomic policy coordination, issues of international liquidity management and international surveillance of the adjustment process remain.

Views on the nature and seriousness of these issues vary tremendously. Apart from direct distributional considerations, I believe that most of the controversy over the adequacy of our current international monetary arrangements has stemmed from two major sources: differences in view about (1) the best exchange rate and macroeconomic policy strategies, and (2) about the degree of effective international control over international liquidity and adjustment matters.

Section I will discuss in more detail a number of the major economic and political objectives frequently advocated for the international monetary system. This discussion will form the basis for indicating the types of criteria used for evaluating international monetary questions. The discussions of different criteria for evaluation are illustrated with applications to particular international monetary issues.

I. Objectives for the International Monetary System and Framework for Analysis

The performance of the international monetary system must be judged in terms of how well it meets the objectives delineated for the system. From an economic perspective, these objectives parallel those of domestic monetary systems to help facilitate the process of specialization and exchange and the full utilization of resources. The need for an international monetary system arises from the existence of sovereign states whose domains do not exhaust the potential benefits from specialization and exchange.

From a positive perspective, the economic objectives of the international monetary system are usually expounded as the promotion of microeconomic efficiency in the allocation of resources (including the usefulness of money) and the macroeconomic objectives of achieving a satisfactory combination of low inflation and unemployment and high rates of economic growth.[8] Viewed from an alternative perspective, international monetary systems have also been frequently evaluated in terms of their ability to handle particular problems which may arise from the operation of the system, particularly the problems of international liquidity, confidence, and adjustment. International monetary relations also have important political components. These include concerns with distributional effects and constraints on national sovereignty and more general political objectives, such as the enhancement of national power and prestige.

The emphasis on a political economy perspective also has implications crucial for the positive analysis of the behavior of governments in the operation of the international monetary system. This, in turn, has important implications for the practical relevance of various normative proposals. For example, there is a tremendous difference in the agenda for policy coordination and international monetary reform implied by an optimal economic policy framework which ignores collective decision making and implementation problems and one implied by a public choice approach which emphasizes such difficulties.

This section begins with discussion of the traditional economic criteria for evaluating the performance of the international monetary system: promoting microeconomic and macroeconomic efficiency and minimizing international liquidity, confidence, and adjustment problems. It then moves on to the analysis of distributional issues, national sovereignty, and other political considerations.

Microeconomic Efficiency

Our standard microeconomic criteria for judging microeconomic efficiency is the extent to which marginal social costs and benefits are equalized. Our theory suggests that with well-informed decision makers, competitive markets will tend to approximate this outcome in the absence of such conditions as externalities and public goods. In the international sphere, our analysis indicates a presumption in favor of free trade and investment in the absence of persuasive arguments that specific market failures exist.[9] It furthermore shows that on economic efficiency grounds, the first-best solution to most market failures associated with arguments for international restrictions involve domestic, rather than international, policy measures. For example, the first-best policy measure for stimulating an infant industry is generally a direct subsidy rather than tariff protection. Where exchange rates are at equilibrium levels, it seems not unreasonable to use the extent of international trade and payments restrictions as a crude index of the magnitude of deviations from global microeconomic efficiency in international exchange. (It is, of course, possible for international restrictions to raise the economic welfare of one country at the expense of others.) However, where exchange rates deviate from equilibrium levels, there is a distortion in the price signals given to private economic actors which will tend to generate differences between private and social costs and benefits. In such circumstances, selective measures which tend to compensate partially for overvaluations or undervaluations of currencies may lead to increases, rather than decreases, in economic efficiency. Furthermore, even in the absence of disequilibrium exchange rates, economists' views on the economic welfare effects of free international capital flows have been much more mixed than their views on the welfare effects of free international trade flows. The principal designers of the Bretton Woods system, John Maynard Keynes and Harry Dexter White, were both skeptical of the benefits of free international capital flows under many circumstances, and such views are still shared by a number of economists.[10] For example, it has been argued that interest rate differentials often are not a good reflection of differences in the marginal productivity of capital and, hence, that taxes or controls to dampen international capital flows may carry relatively low efficiency costs.

While it is clear that stable equilibrium exchange rates are conducive to efficiency and that exchange rate fluctuations due to destabilizing speculation are harmful, there has been relatively little analysis of the effects of exchange rate volatility that reflects changes in underlying economic developments and expectations about future developments. Using the criterion of efficient information processing that is frequently adopted in modern financial theory and the rational expectations literature, it is clear that such exchange rate movements, even if highly volatile, promote economic efficiency given underlying circumstances. This approach suggests that the focus of those concerned with improving economic performance should be on reducing this volatility of underlying economic conditions. Skepticism about the implications of this efficient-market view has focused both on the extent to which exchange rate movements have been dominated by efficient speculation and on whether there are not important externalities and rigidities in the goods and labor markets which would impose efficiency costs in other sectors of the economy. So far, relatively little progress has been made toward reconciling these opposing points of view.

While it is now generally accepted that we cannot safely assume that unchanged nominal exchange rates are a good guide to equilibrium exchange rates or that large, rapid movements in rates are necessarily the result of destabilizing speculation rather than reasonable shifts in expectations about economic fundamentals, wide divergencies of opinion exist about how closely the movements of flexible exchange rates have approximated equilibrium rates. In my judgment, the considerable amount of technical research on these issues has served primarily to suggest that one should be cautious about making statements that a particular exchange rate clearly is, or is not, close to an equilibrium level.[11] As will be discussed further below, different views about the predominant causes of the exchange rate fluctuations are probably the major cause of differences in judgments about how well flexible rates have worked.

Nor have we made considerable progress to date in evaluating the welfare costs of different patterns of deviations from equilibrium exchange rates. For example, what are the comparative efficiency costs of small, but persistent and growing, one-sided deviations from equilibrium, as might occur under a sticky adjustable peg, versus frequent large deviations which are of limited duration and which tend to average out.[12] Many have argued that there have been frequent large deviations under flexible exchange rates because of imperfections in private speculation or exchange rate overshooting owing to short-term variations in monetary policy.

We likewise still have not solved the decades-old controversy about whether pegged or flexible exchange rates are likely to stimulate more trade restrictions. My own view is that without the flexibility of exchange rates which we enjoyed (or suffered) over the past decade, we would have faced a higher level of restrictions. However, flexible rates certainly did not lead to as much liberalization as many advocates had hoped, and there have been cases in which it can be argued that exchange rate fluctuations have stimulated restrictions. Perhaps the strongest conclusion we can draw at this point is that whether the shift from the adjustable peg system to more widespread floating has led ceteris paribus to a marginal increase or decrease in the efficiency of international exchange, the effects do not appear to have been extremely large, especially in comparison with the beggar-thy-neighbor independent nationalistic economic policies of the 1930s.[13] The evidence also seems consistent with the view that the choice of exchange rate regime is not one of the most important determinants of international restrictions.

Macroeconomic Goals

Traditionally, the macroeconomic aspects of the operation of the international monetary system have been considered in terms of the constraints which balance of payments adjustment requirements have placed on domestic macroeconomic policies. One of the major objectives of the Bretton Woods negotiators was to construct a system in which countries would not be forced to accept major inflations or recessions in order to convert disequilibrium nominal exchange rates into equilibrium ones. In such cases of fundamental disequilibrium, internal considerations were to have primacy over external ones, subject of course to the avoidance of beggar-thy-neighbor policies.

This desire to keep the requirements for international monetary balance from seriously impinging on domestic macroeconomic objectives typically has been shared both by Keynesians and monetarists. It is not a universally held view, however. A number of writers have been quite suspicious of the types of macroeconomic policies which may be stimulated by democratic politics and have sought to have the international monetary system impose discipline over domestic financial policies. Although most often associated with advocates of the return to some form of gold standard, such arguments are also frequently made for an international or regional return to pegged exchange rates per se. While it is not clear that flexible exchange rates will necessarily impose less discipline and stimulate greater inflationary pressures than typical forms of pegged-rate systems, the objectives of most of those who have engaged in the debate over discipline clearly fall into two diametrically opposed camps—those who seek to increase, and those who seek to constrain, the freedom of domestic macroeconomic decision makers.[14] There is a similar opposition between those who view accommodation of divergent national priorities as a major objective and those who advocate instead a forced harmonization of policies. The arguments in both of these areas involve economic and political aspects which cannot be adequately resolved here. Suffice it to say that these different schools of thought will hold quite different views about the desirability of the degree of macroeconomic permissiveness of the international monetary system.

In recent years, the traditional view of balance of payments considerations as a constraint on domestic macroeconomic policies has at least partially given way to analysis from the standpoint of open economy macroeconomics. This perspective emphasizes the short-term and medium-term effects of exchange rate and balance of payments developments on inflation-unemployment relationships and on the state of activity in the economy. The adoption of flexible exchange rates has been perhaps the major force behind this shift in perspective, although analysis along these lines was quite prevalent well before the 1970s. Ideally, from the perspective of a single country, an international monetary system which serves as an automatic stabilizer for domestic economic fluctuations, while limiting the importation of disturbances from abroad, would be preferred. From a global perspective, it would be preferable to have a system which does not itself generate disturbances and which, on average, yields a net stabilizing influence from uncontrolled disturbances while preserving countries' freedom to engage in domestic policy actions to counter the effects of disturbances, whether of domestic or foreign origin.

The different aspects of these criteria may, of course, conflict in

particular situations. Depending on the particular patterns of disturbances and the structure of the economies in question, either pegged or
flexible exchange rates may provide the best-short run macroeconomic
environment for a particular country or aggregation of countries.[15] In
two-country Keynesian models, it has been shown that depending on the
particular disturbance in question, both countries could enjoy more stable
output with pegged exchange rates or with flexible rates, or there might
be conflicts of short-run interest so that one country would be better off
with a pegged rate and the other with a flexible rate. The analysis
becomes even more complicated when inflation-unemployment relationships are taken into account. In general, exchange rate movements which
worsen inflation in the short run will stimulate output (once the initial
perverse J-curve effects on the trade balance are reversed) and vice versa,
but there has been relatively little analysis of possible effects on differences in medium-term inflation-unemployment trade-offs, and the short-
term and medium-term effects may be quite different. For example,
maintaining a pegged rate in a booming economy may have the favorable
effect of reducing inflation in the short run, but at the expense of
contributing to an artificial ratcheting-up of real wages which will worsen
future inflation-unemployment relationships.

The choice of international monetary regimes may also have important
influences on the effects of macroeconomic policy instruments. In traditional IS-LM, open-economy theoretical models, a shift from pegged to
flexible exchange rates will strengthen the effects of monetary policy on
aggregate spending, while the strength of fiscal policy will be increased
or decreased, depending whether international capital mobility is low or
high.[16] Similarly, with respect to international policy coordination, under
pegged exchange rates expansionary monetary or fiscal policy at home
generally will have an expansionary effect abroad (although the magnitude
of these effects is often a matter of some dispute), while under flexible
rates, expansionary monetary policy will have a contractionary effect
abroad. Fiscal policy will still influence foreign economies in the same
direction as at home, but the magnitude of transmission will be influenced by whether the degree of capital mobility leads to an appreciation
or depreciation of the exchange rate.

The international monetary regime can also have an important influence on the way in which spending changes break down between price
and output effects in the short run. For example, with exchange rate
flexibility, the effects of exchange rate movements on the prices of traded
goods will speed up the aggregate price responses to changes in monetary
policy, steepening the short-run inflation-unemployment trade-off. While

this has often been taken as an argument that flexible rates will be more inflationary than pegged rates, it should also be recognized that disinflationary effects are also speeded up. This acceleration may make it more feasible politically to follow anti-inflationary policies through to completion and may reduce the possible inflationary bias owing to differences between short-run and long-run inflation-unemployment trade-offs which is emphasized in the literature on political business cycles.[17]

All of these considerations are further complicated when the important distinction is made between the effects of anticipated and unanticipated policy changes. As has been emphasized by the rational expectations revolution, in the absence of institutional rigidities such as long-term contracts, monetary expansions which are fully anticipated should affect only prices and not real magnitudes. In such circumstances, exchange rates would adjust along with domestic prices, completely insulating national economies from each other's monetary policies. In other words, under the assumptions necessary for the domestic-policy-ineffectiveness theorems of the rational expectations literature to hold, international monetary interactions cease to be a matter of concern. While most economists would probably argue that the assumptions of the policy-ineffectiveness theorems are not sufficiently close to reality to make this approach a sound guide to policy, the emphasis they place on the role of expectations captures an important element of truth which cannot safely be ignored.

These considerations complicate further the tasks of identifying the types of disturbances to which economies are being subjected and the effects of alternative policy responses. For example, we cannot safely predict whether rising interest rates will lead a currency to appreciate or depreciate; it may do either, depending whether the increase in interest rates was due primarily to an increase in inflationary expectations or a tightening of monetary policy. Given the wide diversity of expectations which may be quite plausible in particular circumstances, it is often difficult to evaluate developments accurately ex post, much less contemporaneously, as would be required for discretionary policy responses. Increased recognition of such difficulties in short-run discretionary policy implementation has led to a rather widespread reduction in the scope for policy activism that is viewed as feasible, but the implications of this development for the choice of international monetary regimes are not entirely clear.

It has sometimes been argued that while optimal policy strategies for particular situations may be quite complicated, as long as the aggregate world economy is relatively stable, then there is an argument for pegged exchange rates on the risk-reducing, portfolio-diversification principle that the typical country will gain more in stability by being able to disperse abroad, at least partially, the effects of its local disturbances than it will lose by importing net disturbances from abroad. Given the high degree of aggregate instability in the world economy in recent years, there must be some question about the current applicability of this argument. Perhaps more importantly, the same types of argument which explain why flexible exchange rates have not provided as much economic insulation and policy independence as was widely anticipated also imply that domestic disturbances may be spread out over the world economy, rather than being entirely bottled up, even under flexible exchange rates. Indeed, with very high international capital mobility, the spreading out of the effects of a domestic boom or slump in aggregate demand via the Keynesian trade balance mechanism can be greater under flexible than under pegged exchange rates (see, for example, Modigliani and Askari (1973)). As has been pointed out many times, to the extent that private speculation is stabilizing and trends in equilibrium exchange rates are not prevalent, the differences between pegged and flexible exchange rates may be minimal.[18] Substantial differences in inflation trends among countries, however, make the maintenance of pegged rates difficult, while destabilizing or insufficiently stabilizing speculation makes pegged rates or substantial official intervention more desirable. In a world of both substantial differences in inflation trends and poorly behaved speculation, managed flexibility of some form (which could include some type of crawling-peg regime) would seem to be the only feasible type of policy, as long as the trends cannot be substantially altered.

Flexible exchange rates have frequently been blamed for contributing substantially to world inflation through the generation of vicious circles of inflation and depreciation. My own research suggests that while exchange rate depreciation can, at times, contribute to domestic inflation and the difficulties of macroeconomic management, the charges that flexible rates have been a major cause of world-wide inflation are greatly overstated. Often depreciation is just a reflection of domestic inflationary pressures and, at times, as noted above, flexible rates can contribute to, rather than have negative effects upon, domestic macroeconomic stability.[19]

The major source of policy disagreement in such an environment involves the issue of whether changes in the international monetary regime can be used to force changes in underlying policy trends and lower the transition costs of re-establishing financial stability because, as has been emphasized by the recent literature on expectations, the more widely believed are announcements of disinflationary policies, the lower will be the transitional unemployment costs that these policies generate. This is a particular formulation of the discipline and policy harmonization arguments considered above. Whether exchange rate pegging should lead or follow dometic macroeconomic policy harmonization has, of course, been an important topic of debate surrounding the various efforts at European monetary integration.[20] While Europe's experience must make one skeptical of the strength of exchange rate pegging strategies for inducing desired changes in domestic macroeconomic policies, it is certainly possible, at times, for such regime commitments to help promote stability. The credibility of such commitments becomes perhaps the most crucial issue here. Unfortunately, over the past two decades, few governments have been able to avoid suffering serious erosion of the credibility of their macroeconomic policy pronouncements.

While the Fund's seal of approval on international stabilization policy has also suffered some decline in credibility over this period, it has lost much less than the policy announcements of most national governments. Thus, as a practical matter, the credibility of the International Monetary Fund (and ad hoc groups of official lenders) may enable it to have a major influence in helping to promote the restoration of global financial stability.

As the previous discussion illustrates, it is difficult to draw strong conclusions about the contributions of alternative international monetary regimes to macroeconomic stability. Those who have drawn strong conclusions on the subject have typically focused on only a particular subset of relevant considerations. As a practical matter, at the present time, perhaps the strongest conclusion which we can reasonably draw is the negative one that to the extent feasible, the international monetary system should avoid the creation or magnification of instabilities and should not force major sustained inflationary or deflationary pressures on individual countries.

Minimizing International Liquidity, Confidence, and Adjustment Problems

Indeed, we are used to analyzing the international monetary system from a negative perspective, in particular from the standpoint of avoiding or minimizing the instabilities generated by the three problems of international adjustment, liquidity, and confidence (see, for example, Machlup (1962)). It has become standard to analyze alternative international monetary systems in terms of how they deal with these problems. The efforts to reform the Bretton Woods system during the 1960s were heavily influenced by this perspective.[21] The interrelationships among these problems are, of course, important. With a system of instantaneous adjustment, international liquidity problems could not arise and confidence problems would be unlikely to arise. On the other hand, the slower and more uncertain is the adjustment process, the greater is the need for international liquidity and the greater are the prospects for confidence problems resulting from concerns about the prospects for individual national currencies and the relationships among multiple reserve assets. Likewise, the nature and rate of international liquidity creation may substantially influence both the speed of balance of payments adjustment and its distribution between surplus and deficit countries.

A textbook automatic gold standard solves all three of these international monetary problems but at the expense of forcing domestic macroeconomic policies to adjust to the balance of payments and the growth of the global gold supply.[22] Bretton Woods sought to reduce the strength of the balance of payments constraint over domestic policies by providing for the adjustment of par values. It did not provide a strong system for determining adjustment responsibilities, however, with the consequence that the exchange rate system became much more sticky than was originally envisioned, and par value adjustments generally occurred only after a series of cumulating crises.

The failure of the Bretton Woods agreement's provisions for the growth of international liquidity over time has been widely discussed in terms of the Triffin dilemma. While expansion of dollar holdings initially met the needs for expanding international liquidity, the continuation of this process brought into question the sustainability of the convertibility of the dollar into gold at $35 an ounce. Termination of the dollar deficits would have produced a shortage of international liquidity, while continuation was viewed as leading inevitably to a crisis of confidence. The proposed solution was the creation of a new centrally managed international reserve asset, and international negotiations culminated in the creation of the special drawing right.

However, as some had warned, the principal deficiency of the Bretton Woods system was less its lack of adequate provisions for international liquidity than its lack of adequate provisions for balance of payments adjustments. It was rather ironic that the Bretton Woods system broke down during the first period of SDR allocation. The breakdown was primarily caused by the large U.S. balance of payments deficit, generated by the way in which the Viet Nam War was financed, and was precipitated by massive private capital outflows. While my research suggests that the resulting international liquidity explosion was not responsible for as high a proportion of the subsequent acceleration of world-wide inflation as global monetarist explanations imply, this was certainly the type of massive generation and magnification of instability which a well-functioning international monetary system should avoid. (See Willett (1980 a) and Laney and Willett (1982).)

Our post-Bretton Woods international monetary system as ratified at Jamaica has also been charged with failing to solve liquidity, confidence, and adjustment problems. While perhaps most analysts grant that the widespread adoption of flexible exchange rates has substantially improved the operation of the international adjustment process, some question this and further argue that flexible rates have generated continuing crises because of their instability and have, themselves, been a further major cause of world inflation through the generation of vicious circles of depreciation and inflation. And even a number of those who have been relatively sanguine about the adjustment effects of flexible rates have argued that the Jamaica reforms have left essentially untouched the international liquidity and confidence problems that plagued the Bretton Woods system. It is certainly true that managed floating does not present the complete solution to these three problems that either freely floating rates or an automatic gold standard would provide. Such critiques have frequently tended to overlook, however, the extent to which the adoption of widespread flexibility reduces the problems of international liquidity, confidence, and conflicts over balance of payments adjustment as they existed under Bretton Woods or as they would have existed under the Committee of Twenty blueprint for return to dollar convertibility and a "new look" par value system. Flexible exchange rates did not lead to the avoidance of a second international liquidity explosion in the late 1970s, associated primarily with foreign intervention to limit the fall of the dollar, but countries had a great deal more freedom to decide upon their mix of responses to the weakness of the dollar between official intervention and exchange rate changes, taking into account the effects of both on domestic economic objectives. Likewise, flexible exchange rates did not eliminate concern about reserve switching but, by reducing the one-way speculative option frequently generated under the Bretton Woods adjustable peg, tended to reduce the incentives for frequent switching.

In such an analysis, it is important to make clear one's standard of comparison. In my judgment, our current system has made substantial improvements over Bretton Woods in handling the problems of international adjustment, liquidity, and confidence; but these problems are certainly not completely solved.[23] Strategies for further improvements in handling these problems will be discussed in Section III.

National Sovereignty and Distributional Concerns

The previous discussions have focused primarily on various aspects of economic efficiency. The international monetary system is composed, however, not only of private economic actors but also of sovereign nation-states whose governments are often more concerned with the distributional effects of the system's operation on their particular countries than with seeking global economic efficiency and who view international monetary relations as just one aspect of their overall strategies of international diplomacy. From a purely economic perspective, the operation of the international monetary system is a mixed-motive game. All gain from the efficient operation of the international monetary system and avoidance of severe breakdowns in international monetary cooperation. But within this context, there are often substantial conflicts of interest over who adjusts their policies with respect to whom; whether the emphasis should be on balance of payments adjustment or macroeconomic stabilization; and how to distribute the costs of joint undertakings, such as the transfer of resources to the developing countries.

Governments will typically wish to retain a good deal of at least nominal freedom of action, even if this leads to persistent aggregate inefficiencies, as long as their magnitude is not overwhelming. The disasters of the 1930s led to substantive modifications in the domains of effective national sovereignty in international monetary affairs claimed by major countries, so that blatant beggar-thy-neighbor policies are today much less of a problem. However, the willingness of most countries to cede substantial decision-making power to international bodies and to engage in positive discretionary acts of international monetary cooperation is still rather limited. As a result, there is a strong presumption that international monetary cooperation will be less than optimal from the standpoint of global economic efficiency.

The uncertainties about the issues of positive economic analysis discussed above further increase the difficulties of implementing strategies to achieve global economic efficiency. The more complicated and uncertain the technical issues, the less likely it is that a set of well-defined rules will prove effective in promoting efficiency. As a consequence, greater reliance is likely to be placed on case-by-case discretionary decision making. I have argued elsewhere that while a number of objective indicators can be useful presumptive criteria in the analysis of international balance of payments and exchange rate surveillance, none is likely to work well enough to form the basis of binding rules. (See Willett (1977, Chapter 4) and (1978 b).) As a result, a good deal of discretionary case-by-case analysis is needed.

By ceding strong authority to international decision makers, countries would forgo an uncertain—and potentially quite substantial—amount of national sovereignty. Without going so far as to claim that governments engage only in worst-case analysis, my experience is that they tend to display a considerable degree of risk aversion in such situations and thus are willing to bear a considerable degree of expected efficiency loss in order to preserve options for greater national influence.

This must be accepted as a basic fact of international life in any realistic efforts to improve the international monetary system. It also implies that we should not necessarily be greatly concerned about every economic analysis which concludes that the system or patterns of policy actions are operating with less than ideal efficiency, or that some future contingency is possible that current mechanisms and procedures cannot handle well. This does not mean, however, that considerable effort should not be made to attempt to promote more effective international cooperation. Analysts should continue to emphasize the prospective gains which could be made, or losses which could be avoided, on average, through greater willingness of countries to engage in collective actions.

We may also hope that good experiences with current mechanisms will foster greater trust in international decision making. This could help induce countries to support a gradual strengthening of the scope for international authority over time.[24] This process can work both ways, however. Furthermore, to the degree that international monetary affairs become increasingly politicized, it may become more difficult to strengthen our international monetary organizations. Attempts to lock oneself into an environment which requires major increases in the degree of cooperative behavior to maintain stability frequently prove counterproductive.

Recognition of the political realities of countries concerned with national sovereignty and distributional considerations and of the difficulties of collective decision making has important implications for the design of effective international agreements and collective decision-making structures. One is that since the degree of international cooperation is likely to be quite limited, it is important to focus international negotiations on the most important issues which have a reasonable chance of resolution. Of course, reasonable people may differ on the ranking of issues at any particular point in time, but it is still important that this perspective be adopted. Concern with distributional aspects also calls for focusing on limiting the liabilities of the agreeing parties and for seeking a tolerable degree of balance in the distributional effects of proposals.

The difficulties of providing compensation for losers (whether in relative or absolute terms) is one of the most severe impediments to reaching agreement on potential welfare-improving policies. One crude, but useful method which is already widely employed in international negotiations is the linking of issues with different perceived distributional effects. Contrary to the frequent interpretation of such linkages in the international relations literature as examples of power politics, such linkages may often offer a cooperative method of securing better balance in distributional effects and consequently may play a very constructive role in international negotiations (see Tollison and Willett (1979)). Such issues need to receive a good deal more attention.

Another implication of such distributional concerns is that often countries will be willing to cooperate much more fully on a bilateral or small-group basis than on a global level. This means that while the International Monetary Fund should play a crucial role in the management of the international monetary system, making it the exclusive focus of international monetary cooperation would involve a substantial reduction in overall international cooperation. While the current overlapping pattern of cooperative discussions and actions—including bilateral discussions, regional groupings, economic summits, the Group of Ten, the Organization for Economic Cooperation and Development (OECD), the Group of 77, and the Fund—is extremely untidy and clearly in part elitist, it is nevertheless necessary.

Some Additional Political Considerations and Their Implications

Up to this point, the discussion in this section has focused primarily on the distribution of economic effects at national levels. The political aspects of international monetary relations go considerably beyond this, however, and include both domestic distributional considerations and noneconomic objectives. One of the basic insights of public choice theory is that rational governments seeking re-election may pursue objectives which deviate systematically from aggregate economic efficiency. Even if government decision makers are well informed about the aggregate economic effects of various policies, a substantial portion of the electorate may not be, and well-organized interest groups may carry far greater influence in the political process than is implied by the mere number of voters they represent. Even governments with a great deal of insulation from immediate domestic political pressures may seek to use international monetary issues to obtain diplomatic objectives and to give considerable weight to symbolic considerations and the appearance of political balance rather than simply to deal with questions of global economic efficiency and international economic distribution effects. Typically, the rationale for such emphasis will be to obtain greater domestic political support by attempting to shift the blame for economic difficulties to others and to rally nationalistic support for attacks on various types of perceived foreign imperialism.

It is porbably true, as Benjamin Cohen argues (1977, p. 231), that Americans tend to pay too little attention to such matters, as do economists in general. It is not surprising that economists typically feel quite frustrated in having to deal with such matters, for not only do they in general make international cooperation and the implementation of economically efficient policies more difficult but often these politically motivated statements and analyses are based on questionable economic reasoning or greatly exaggerated implicit estimates of the magnitude of various effects. Yet economists interested in improving the operation of the international monetary system must pay serious attention to such considerations because they often have major influences on countries' positions and the prospects for substantive international cooperation.

I suggest that economists should take a two-pronged strategy in dealing with such political considerations. We need to continue to analyze the economic content of such positions and highlight where they are based on questionable or exaggerated economics. Examples include the tendency of national political statements to imply that their national economies are being dominated by adverse international economic developments to a far greater extent than is suggested by most careful empirical research and to exaggerate the amounts of seigniorage which the United States has gained from the international reserve position of the dollar. The latter discussions frequently overlook the fact that the United States pays competitive rates of interest on most foreign official dollar holdings. While the special role of the dollar probably does reduce the interest cost of financing U.S. deficits, the magnitude of this effect is quite small in relation to the amount of attention it has received. (See, for example, Cooper (1975, pp. 67–71).)

Second, we need to recognize that such political considerations play a legitimate role in international monetary relations and need to be taken into account in proposals for particular policy strategies and institutional reforms. One may quite consistently engage in persuasive attempts to reduce over time the degree of nationalistic political activism in international monetary discussions, while at the same time recognizing that viable policy proposals must, at present at least, give considerable weight to such considerations. At one level, this analysis suggests that we must learn to live with a good deal of political posturing in international forums and should attempt to make provisions for these widely-felt needs in ways which have minimal influences on actual international cooperation and substantive economic policies. In other words, we need to learn not to be offended by a great deal of public political posturing and to try to minimize the impediments which these create for substantive cooperative action. Examples of successful applications of this approach include the semantic brilliance of the first two amendments of the Articles of Agreement of the International Monetary Fund. While both amendments were of substantive importance in creating the SDR and legalizing and strengthening our current system based on flexible exchange rates, they contained sufficient compromise on wording and details to permit all major negotiating parties to claim at least symbolic victories.[25]

Not all such aspects of political objectives can be handled so easily, however. Some may require much more fundamental compromises. While adopting a political economy perspective will not be sufficient to avoid all political conflicts through diplomatic skill, it has extremely important implications for analysis of how the international monetary system works and for formulation of realistic strategies for international monetary reform in areas of more fundamental conflict as well. A few of these implications will be briefly discussed below.

While economists quite appropriately focus on opportunity costs in their analysis of economic efficiency, political officials typically believe, with some justification, that their constituents, based on rationally limited information, will focus more on positive acts which governments take than on actions which they fail to take and will place much heavier weight on how satisfactory current developments are than how they might have been if alternative policies had been adopted. Thus, models of government decision making which emphasize satisfying behavior, with a strong bias toward preservation of the status quo, have a great deal of explanatory power. One implication of such behavior in the international monetary area is the prediction that many national governments will behave in a manner more "Keynesian" than "monetarist" with respect to international reserve developments—that is, will view reserve positions more as a constraint than as a variable in the government's utility function (see Sweeney and Willett (1977) and Willett (1980 a)).

The first application is important, since it implies that control of international reserve aggregates may have only very limited usefulness as a strategy for controlling the macroeconomic behavior of the world economy. Both the short-run and long-run effects of a given change in aggregate international reserves will depend importantly on its distribution among countries and developments in their own overall financial positions. Thus, we cannot expect to have nearly as close a relationship between international reserve aggregates and global macroeconomic developments as there is between national money supplies and national spending (see Willett (1980a)).

A second implication is the need to pay attention to who initiates adjustment actions, in addition to what the ultimate economic effects will be. This emphasis yields important implications for the breakdown of Bretton Woods and the case for flexible exchange rates. Under fixed exchange rates, there is a strong (although, of course, not perfect) correspondence between who takes adjustment actions and how the costs of adjustment are distributed. It is not surprising that deficit countries typically prefer adjustment to mutual payments imbalances to come from macroeconomic expansion in surplus countries, while surplus countries prefer restraint in the deficit countries.

With exchange rate adjustments, the distribution of economic effects is much less closely related to who initiates the adjustments. However, under the Bretton Woods system, national officials typically felt that political blame and international status were closely related to who initiated adjustment. Devaluations were widely viewed as a blow to national prestige and an admission of policy failure, and even revaluations carried political costs in terms of opposition of export interests and perceptions that revaluation meant giving in to the deficit countries (see Marris (1970)). As a consequence, a strong bias toward inaction developed with respect to exchange rate adjustments as well as macroeconomic policy adjustments. In my judgment, these fundamental political considerations tend to be underemphasized considerably by advocates of the view that under the "new look" par value system envisioned in the Committee of Twenty blueprint for international monetary reform, adjustments would be made much more promptly and effectively than under the old adjustable peg system. (This is not to deny that some learning behavior can be expected to take place. The adjustable pegs within the European Monetary System have certainly been used a good deal more flexibly than under the Bretton Woods system.) Still, apart from their strictly economic merits (and limitations), flexible exchange rates have played an extremely useful role in helping to reduce the politicization of exchange rate adjustments.

The Search for Symmetry

The search for symmetry is a fundamental political aspect of the debate over international monetary reform. Quite apart from whatever economic advantages the special role of the dollar has given the United States, the desire to scale down the role of the dollar is an understandable concern of countries that care about status and political appearances. Yet in an asymmetrical world, the search for complete symmetry runs into severe practical difficulties, even apart from questions of power relationships whereby countries occupy privileged positions they are reluctant to give up. From the beginning, some critics, such as John Williamson, were skeptical of the attempt at universality embodied in Bretton Woods. The evolution of the special role of the dollar was consistent with his predictions, as is the increased recognition, embodied in the Jamaica reforms, that size, openness, and other factors as enumerated in the theory of optimum currency areas (see, for example, Tower and Willett (1976)) imply that different exchange rate regimes will be preferable for different countries.

The Bretton Woods system had formal symmetry, since any country was free to choose either option for its exchange rate obligations, maintaining fixed price convertibility with gold or with a currency pegged to gold. But, in practice, the United States was the only country to select the former option, and the dollar clearly took on a special role over time. Likewise, the current system of permissive exchange rate flexibility provides formal symmetry, but the dollar still plays a special, if somewhat reduced, role. While a strong economic case can be made for various forms of dollar standard and the distribution of economic benefits from these systems would be considerably more balanced than critics of dollar imperialism typically imply, in political terms it is easy to understand why many would find such a system objectionable.[26] Many of the charges leveled against such a system are overstated. For instance, the seigniorage gains to the dollar are quite small; and a flexible rate dollar standard would not give U.S. policy the dominance in the determination of the monetary policies of other countries that would result from a fixed rate dollar standard under which the U.S. faced no effective balance of payments constraint (the type of system which critics frequently seem to have in mind).

Furthermore, while the adoption of a passive exchange rate and balance of payments policy by the United States Government would relieve it of the political cost of initiating adjustments, it would also subject it to greater political pressures from domestic mercantilist forces who might argue that overvaluation of the dollar was causing unemployment and undermining the U.S. industrial base. Still, the political imagery of anything looking like a dollar standard carries negative connotations. In this context, the creation of the SDR has been of considerable symbolic, if not yet substantive, advantage by creating the impression of a more symmetrically based international monetary system.

The SDR also gives us a better basis for developing a more symmetrical and centralized international monetary system. Progress in this direction has been rather limited, however, largely because of other fundamental political considerations. Some have interpreted the failure of international monetary negotiations to reach agreement on reforms along the lines of the Committee of Twenty's Outline of Reform to the parochial efforts of the United States to preserve its privileged position and its consequent insistence on greater tightness in the rules for adjustment than in the rules for convertibility.

I believe that there is an element of truth in this view, but that it was not one of the fundamental causes of the failure of the Committee of Twenty's blueprint to gain official acceptance. Essentially, we never came close enough to agreement on effective reform of a par value system for the particular concerns of the United States to have blocked the process. While there is considerable reason to doubt whether this approach would have proved workable, even with strong international control, it is clear that implementation of the Committee of Twenty's convertibility, par value approach would have required a high degree of international control over the adjustment policies and reserve management behavior of member countries. Thus, the political objective of creating an international monetary system that was more symmetrical in appearance came into direct conflict with another major political goal—preserving a considerable degree of national sovereignty over adjustment and reserve management policies.

A benign interpretation of the primary emphasis of the U.S. position (which, I believe, contains a great deal of truth) was the need for consistency (or symmetry) between the degree of tightness of centralized control of the adjustment process and the provisions for convertibility. U.S. officials indicated a willingness to go along with a system which was either consistently loose or consistently tight; but they argued—correctly, I believe—that a system with much tighter rules for convertibility than for international supervision of the adjustment process would soon break down. Faced with this dilemma and the mounting evidence that flexible rates were much more workable than many had anticipated, most countries indicated a strong revealed preference for preserving a high degree of national sovereignty. Thus, we adopted a loose system based on exchange rate flexibility for the dollar and resisted the political attractions of a more structural and symmetrical-looking tight system based on some form of convertibility of the dollar into reserve assets (including the possibility of indirect conversions through the Fund rather than direct conversion of dollar holdings by national governments) and substantial international control over national adjustment and reserve management questions.

It is possible that had a substantial proportion of countries given priority to creating a tighter, more symmetrical system, the negotiations would still have failed because of disagreements over technical considerations (such as the disagreements over the merits of the specific U.S. reserve indicator proposals) or disagreements with the United States over what constituted a balanced and consistent relationship between convertibility and adjustment provisions. As it happened, however, the negotiations never really came close to achieving this degree of finality. The failure to negotiate a highly symmetrical centralized system along the lines of the Committee of Twenty's blueprint reflected widespread unwillingness to cede the necessary degree of authority to international rules and/or discretionary decision making and not just an unwillingness of the United States to give up international monetary privileges.[27]

This outcome assures that there will be continuing complaints about dollar dominance and lack of symmetry in the current international monetary system, but the frequency of such complaints cannot be taken as strong evidence of widespread support for substantial increases in the degree of centralized authority over the operation of the international monetary system. Attitudes may, of course, change over time, but I am convinced that for some time to come the most productive approaches to improving the operation of the international monetary system will be those which focus on specific innovations within the current loose framework, rather than those which emphasize a massive restructuring and more centralized control of the system.

II. Improving International Monetary Analysis

Because of the diversity of objectives, the importance of political constraints, and the inconclusiveness of a great deal of the positive analysis discussed above, it should not be surprising that there is so much disagreement over international monetary issues. What seems less justified is the strength with which opposing views are often put forward. In my judgment, this has often been the result of seriously incomplete or defective analysis.

A distressingly high proportion of the conclusions drawn in international monetary writings and political discussions is based on erroneous analysis. While increased exposure of such misstatements and overstatements will not, by itself, yield correct answers, it is an important step toward improving the quality of international monetary debate and facilitating progress toward finding such answers. Furthermore, greater recognition of the complexity of many of these issues may make a small contribution to promoting international monetary harmony by helping to mute the vehemence of some disputes. This section offers several illustrations of fallacies put forward or overstatements made in international monetary discussions.

As was indicated in Section I, views about equilibrium exchange rates are crucial to the analysis of alternative exchange rate systems in terms of both microeconomic and macroeconomic efficiency. While there is little disagreement that major exchange rates have displayed a great deal of volatility at times since the adoption of floating, supporters of flexible rates have tended to interpret these fluctuations as primarily reflecting reasonable responses to volatile underlying economic and financial conditions, while critics have tended to view them as major independent sources of instability stimulated by frequent episodes of destabilizing or insufficiently stabilizing private speculation. Differences in belief about the relative explanatory power of these two hypotheses is perhaps the major source of disagreement among those who advocate a generalized return to pegged rates, heavy managed floating, or relatively free floating. (Of course, even in a system of relatively free floating among major currencies, smaller countries may want a considerably higher degree of exchange rate management on optimum-currency-area grounds.)

How can we narrow this range of dispute? There has been no dearth of statements that this or that currency has become clearly overvalued or undervalued. Frequently, however, such statements are based explicitly or implicitly on some simple criterion such as purchasing-power-parity calculations or relative rates of monetary growth. Recent research has clearly indicated that while such considerations are certainly relevant to exchange rate determination, they are not sound guides to either short-run or long-run equilibrium exchange rates. Modern analysis shows that expectations and real shocks also have important effects on equilibrium exchange rates. Given uncertainties about plausible ranges of expectations and structural relationships, the width of the zone of plausible estimates of equilibrium rates is typically quite wide. With such a wide gray area and the substantial differences in a priori beliefs about the correct hypothesis, it is not surprising that there is such a range of opinion. It is important to keep in mind, however, that evidence which is found to be not inconsistent with a particular hypothesis is quite different from evidence which strongly supports one hypothesis and appears to be inconsistent with another.

Despite the correctness of the view that the purpose of central banks is not to make money, tests of the profitability of official intervention and the existence of unexploited profit opportunities for speculation can give us useful information on whether official intervention and private speculation have been stabilizing or not.[28] Such testing has cast considerable doubt on the extreme hypothesis that the major foreign exchange markets have been systematically dominated by major bandwagon effects. It has also cast doubt on the alternative extreme hypothesis that exchange rates are always at their equilibrium levels and that official attempts to influence exchange rates through sterilized intervention have no effects, even in the short run. The use of filter rules and autocorrelation analysis to study systematically the time patterns of exchange rate movements since generalized floating generally does not suggest the predictable reversibility of the large swings in exchange rates that would be consistent with views that massive destabilizing bandwagon effects have been a dominant cause of exchange rate volatility. On the other hand, neither does such testing find as strong support for the efficient markets hypothesis in the major foreign exchange markets as has been found for the U.S. stock market. Coupled with judgmental assessments of the thinness of the foreign exchange markets at times and the findings of frequent losses on official interventions by central banks, this suggests the possibility that excessive leaning against the wind by central banks combined with private speculation which is unable to dominate the market (as it does in efficient markets models) may be a major cause of the inefficiencies (unexploited profit opportunities) suggested by recent testing. At this point, such a conclusion is itself quite speculative, however. At present, we are left with rather wide sway for differing interpretations of the role for official exchange market intervention.

In addition to the tendency to overgeneralize from specific pieces of empirical evidence, there is a similar tendency with respect to the results of particular theoretical exercises. Both the microeconomic and macroeconomic effects of exchange rate changes often depend crucially on the causes of the changes (see Willett (1982 a)). It is easy to construct scenarios in which a particular disturbance or pattern of disturbances, combined with particular assumptions about the structure of the economy, can make either fixed or flexible rates more inflationary or less conducive to the stability of output. Analyses which draw strong conclusions about alternative exchange rate systems on these grounds have typically relied on a quite limited number of scenarios (often only one) without attempting to investigate the full range of likely possibilities and their relative probabilities.

Another common set of fallacies involves the failure to consider how relationships may change as the system moves from pegged to flexible exchange rates. One example was the tendency to charge that the exchange rate flexibility embodied in the Jamaica reforms dealt only with adjustment problems and made no contribution to reducing the liquidity and confidence problems. While reasonable people can certainly differ over whether the Jamaica reforms made sufficient progress in these latter areas, it cannot be argued that the removal of adjustably pegged prices among reserve assets does not reduce the confidence problem. (Remember that Gresham's Law was developed to explain behavior toward moneys with pegged, not flexible, rates of exchange.) Likewise, while flexible exchange rates certainly do not offer complete monetary independence, they clearly do offer countries at least somewhat greater protection against the effects of liquidity creation in the rest of the world.

Another example is some of the early versions of the so-called locomotive proposals for internationally coordinated economic expansion by the major industrial countries. These failed to consider the extent to which flexible exchange rates might dampen international transmission and how monetary and fiscal policy combinations might have substantially different short-run effects under flexible rates than under pegged rates (see Willett (1978a)). In none of these examples just considered can we safely assume that the adoption of flexible rates completely solves the policy issue at hand, but it is important to recognize how analysis developed in a pegged-rate context may need to change under flexible rates.

A somewhat similar difficulty results from the tendency to reverse ends-means relationships over time. To the Bretton Woods negotiators, the par value exchange rate system was clearly seen as a means of achieving broader ends; but, over time, in the minds of many officials and international monetary specialists, it became such a symbol of international monetary cooperation that the system was widely viewed as almost an end in itself, with many people (fortunately incorrectly) believing that the termination of the par value system would lead to a major breakdown in international financial cooperation. Some have likewise tended to view convertibility of reserve assets as a basic international monetary objective rather than as one particular method of regulating international monetary relationships.

Promotion of the SDR sometimes seems to be viewed in a similar vein. While this seems a perfectly legitimate end in itself in political terms, it is sometimes combined with a failure to distinguish between marginal and inframarginal effects to imply that there is a prospect of more substantial economic effects than thorough analysis suggests are likely to occur. For example, expansion of the role of the SDR is sometimes advocated as a means of gaining control of international liquidity creation. The major sources of uncontrolled international liquidity creation result from exchange market intervention decisions and official borrowing from the private international financial markets. Better centralized control over these activities requires international surveillance and influence over these national activities, which would be little influenced if the proportion of SDRs in official international liquidity rose from 5 to 10, or even to 50, percent. The establishment of a strict ratio between SDRs and total reserve holdings would, of course, be quite another matter, but the previous analysis suggests that adoption of such a constraint over national reserve management is quite unlikely to be politically acceptable to most countries, at least in the near term. There are also important technical questions about whether this would be the most effective type of approach, even if such increased centralization of authority did prove feasible.

A similar tendency to exaggerate substantially the benefits of international actions has sometimes occurred with proposals to regulate the Euro-currency markets and to create a Fund substitution account to convert official foreign exchange holdings into SDRs. Advocates of international regulation of the Eurocurrency markets sometimes talk as if measures such as harmonization of reserve requirements would substantially increase the degree of international financial independence. A good case can be made that an international agreement on reserve requirements for Eurobanks would be desirable, but it would do relatively little to reduce international capital mobility, which is the major source of loss of domestic financial autonomy.

Likewise, I believe that a good case can be made for a Fund substitution account (see Willett (1980 a)), but it would likely make only a modest, rather than a major, contribution to increasing international financial stability. Despite the attention it has received, the magnitude of official reserve switching has been relatively small comparerd with private currency switching and has tended to respond to the same types of incentives. The elimination of exchange market effects of official reserve switching would likely only modestly reduce exchange rate instability, which, in my judgment, is influenced primarily by private responses to expectations about underlying economic and financial conditions.

One last difficulty I would like to mention is the frequency with which the establishment of a theoretical interdependence leads analysts to accord it major policy significance without considering empirical magnitudes and the feasibility of policy responses. For example, while it is true that extremely high elasticities of currency substitution would make flexible exchange rates between these currencies, as well as interest rates in the countries concerned, unstable, it does not follow that the detection of statistically significant (but relatively low) degrees of substitution implies such instability (see Laney, Radcliffe, and Willett (1982)). The degree of optimal discretionary international policy coordination under the assumptions of perfect information and no collective decision-making costs vastly exceeds the degree that is practically feasible.

While abstract theoretical modeling obviously can be extremely valuable, its translation into effective policy advice requires a good deal of judgment and common sense. On the one hand, there is danger that unrealistic attempts to strive for theoretical maxima may be counterproductive; pursuit of the best may sometimes be the enemy of the good. On the other hand, we must guard against becoming so overwhelmed by the practical difficulties of decision making that we become excessively complacent and view any status quo short of disaster as being optimal from a practical perspective. Avoiding these extremes is the essence of good applied policy analysis.

While the complexity of international monetary issues assures that our knowledge will always be a great deal less than is desired, there is still tremendous scope for improving the technical quality of international monetary discussions and our knowledge of key aspects of how the international monetary system is working. While a good deal of progress has been made, we still have a long way to go in better integrating policy-level discussions and technical research. There is enormous scope for mutually beneficial interactions, expecially in guiding empirical work toward our most pressing policy concerns and in increasing the capability and willingness of high-level officials to make use of such research (see Willett (1982 b)).

III. Evaluating the Current System: A Summing Up

The preceding sections have discussed a number of important elements which I believe must be taken into account in evaluating international monetary issues and have illustrated their application to a wide range of international monetary considerations. This section seeks to pull the major strands of this analysis together in a summary evaluation of the current international monetary system and the prospects for strengthening it.

A major theme of the preceding analysis is that there is such a vast range of both normative and positive reasons for differing evaluations of international monetary questions that controversy will always be with us and therefore that its presence per se cannot be taken as a strong indication that the system is not working fairly well.

It is clear that the operation of any real-world international monetary system will fall far short of the ideals perceived by any particular theorist. The system will always be in need of improvement from any one particular perspective, but the directions of change suggested by different legitimate perspectives will often conflict. The limited willingness of national governments to cede power to centralized authority reflects not only shortsighted concerns about maintaining traditional degrees of national sovereignty but also genuine concerns about what the outcomes of centralized decisions should be, even if purely national concerns were put aside. It is inevitable that any international monetary system will reflect compromises among different objectives, perceptions, and degrees of willingness to engage in cooperative action to gain long-term advantages by forgoing some short-term advantages.

In my judgment, the evidence to date is broadly consistent with my initial view (Willett (1977)) that our new international monetary system, ratified by the Jamaica agreements, represents a substantial improvement over its predecessors. It has kept much of the best of the institutional structure and spirit of international obligations and cooperation of the Bretton Woods system and provides a more flexible exchange rate mechanism.

A worrisome aspect of the current system is that there is not strong enough centralized international control over the operation of the international monetary system to offer absolute assurance that we will avoid severe beggar-thy-neighbor problems, excessive international liquidity creation, and short-term financial crises. But it is often forgotten what a relatively modest degree of effective international control was available under Bretton Woods. In the absence of a willingness to cede substantially greater power to international authority, the Jamaica agreements represent a sound response which reduces somewhat the amount of international control needed to keep the system working tolerably well. The adoption of greater exchange rate flexibility has made substantial contributions to reducing important aspects of the international liquidity, confidence, and adjustment problems. Except for very small, open economies, exchange rate changes are an effective (although certainly not a painless) instrument of balance of payments adjustment, and greater exchange rate flexibility has helped to reduce the problem of deciding how mutual adjustment responsibilities should be shared. Likewise, flexible rates have reduced (although, of course, they have not eliminated) the incentives for reserve switching compared with those existing under the adjustable peg and have given countries greater scope to protect themselves from excessive international liquidity creation. It is more difficult to judge its effects on microeconomic and macroeconomic efficiency, but I do not believe that charges that flexible rates have had a disastrous effect on international trade and investment and have been a major cause of global stagflation are supported by the available evidence. While the macroeconomic performance of most countries has been quite unsatisfactory, I believe that this has been due much more to basic domestic political and economic causes than to the operation of the international monetary system and that flexible exchange rates probably give individual countries a greater opportunity to take the lead in restoring domestic stability. While the substantial appreciation of the dollar which has accompanied the recent U.S. anti-inflation efforts has had painful effects abroad (as the efforts have had painful effects at home), it has helped to speed the decline of inflation in the United States, which, in turn, has made it more feasible to carry these efforts through to a successful conclusion.

To date, international cooperation under our current loose system has been sufficient to avoid the major disastes many of the critics of the Jamica agreements foresaw. But we certainly have no reason for complacency. Even apart from questions of the ability to head off the possibilities of financial collapse and economic warfare, management of the system today is particularly complicated. The substantial increase in underlying instabilities, both in macroeconomic conditions and international economic relations (such as those brought about by the oil shocks), has made the design of optimal economic policies much more difficult. The growth of official borrowing from private international financial markets has greatly reduced the "special privilege" of the United States of financing balance of payments deficits by increasing liabilities rather than reducing assets and has played a major beneficial role in the recycling of the oil surpluses. It has substantially weakened, however, the already weak relationship between international reserve aggregates and the behavior of the world economy. Similarly, while the move toward diversification of reserve holdings across a wide range of currencies is beneficial from the standpoint of efficient risk reduction, it also further increases the complexities of operating the system. Simple rules for the management of international reserve aggregates are unlikely to be effective.

At the same time, the substantial increase in the number of individual countries and groups of countries which have a major influence on international monetary developments has substantially increased the difficulties of formal collective decision making. While the move away from hegemony is desirable based on global political criteria, it does substantially increase the scope for "blocking coalitions" which can frustrate attempts at positive international agreements. The increased complexities of operating the current system make the formulation of clearcut rules to deal with issues of exchange rate and balance of payments adjustment and international liquidity management increasingly difficult. Apart from an understanding of the realities of national political considerations, what is primarily needed to strengthen the efficiency of the operation of the system is either a highly structured set of limitations on national behavior which would make international rules more workable or greater discretionatory central control over countries' balance of payments financing and adjustment and reserve management policies.

The prospects for such radical revision in the scope of authority given to international rules and/or discretionary decision making are not bright, at least for the near future. However, for the reasons indicated in this paper, with some increase in the financial resources available for crisis management and to deal with the developing countries' debt problem and with good luck, I believe that the current level of international control is likely to prove adequate, even if far less than optimal. Over the past decade of generalized floating, global macroeconomic performance has certainly been dismal, but I think that the contribution of deficiencies in the operation of the international monetary system per se have been small rather than large. Thus, I believe that the best prospects for improved global economic stability rest with better management of national economic policies, including paying better attention to, and coordination of, the international consequences of these policies.

Perhaps the greatest advantage of the current system is that while optimal policymaking is probably more difficult than it was under the Bretton Woods system, the current system has shown substantial shock-absorbing capabilities which have substantially limited the international damage generated by poor national policies and the inconsistencies among national objectives. Thus, I see the most productive strategy for improving the operation of the international monetary system as one involving continuing efforts to increase gradually over time the influence of the International Monetary Fund in the surveillance of countries' balance of payments adjustment and financing policies. Because of the important influence of Fund attitudes and policies on the willingness of private lenders to provide credit, the Fund already has much greater leverage than is implied by its formal authority; but such control is far from perfect, and efforts to increase this leverage further deserve high priority.[29]

Likewise, on account of its expertise and role as an honest broker, the Fund may be able to play a highly beneficial role in the discussion of exchange rate and macroeconomic policy coordination issues among the major industrial countries. While the quality of technical analysis which is used as a basis for national official discussions of such questions has risen substantially over the past decade, it is still often distressingly low. Better technical analysis will certainly not eliminate all disputes and will often suggest that it is difficult to know what the best policy is. But even an understanding of such difficulties can make a substantial positive contribution to efforts to achieve international cooperation when the alternative is, as it frequently has been, disagreements among disputants who are strongly convinced that they are clearly right and their opponents are clearly wrong. From the standpoint of improving the technical quality of official international monetary analysis, it seems particularly regrettable that the Fund does not appear to be playing a substantial role in the review of official intervention policies of the major industrial countries, an activity deemed important at the Versailles economic summit.

Given the limitations on the willingness of most countries to give up substantially increased amounts of national sovereignty, I believe that our basic strategy should be to focus on attempting to secure marginal improvements in the structure and operation of the current system and to keep our fingers crossed that conflicts of national objectives and/or international financial crises do not produce greater strains than the system can handle. In practice, the likelihood of ad hoc coordination among the major industrial countries makes their capacity to handle substantial international financial crises much greater than is implied by the formal structure of current arrangements. Still, there is strong case for substantially increasing the emergency borrowing and lending powers of the Fund, both to reduce further the likelihood of emergency cooperation among the major financial powers breaking down and to allow a greater proportion of such crisis management to take place through formal international channels.

With respect to international liquidity and reserve management issues, I see a strong case for a sustained modest rate of SDR creation, as much (or more) for political as for economic reasons. Even with managed floating, there is a secular increase in the demand for owned international reserves over time. I see no compelling reason why the issuance of SDRs should not be the main method of meeting this increased demand. I also believe, however, that there should be a substantial tilt in official international liquidity creation away from owned reserves and unconditional borrowing provisions and toward conditional loans. The requirement that the Fund's conditional loans be based on sound stabilization programs should play an important role in helping to restore greater global economic stability. Assuming that major crises are avoided, this may be the most important positive role which international monetary institutions can play in improving the operation of the world economy. It should be remembered, however, that the effectiveness of the Fund's lending and its "seal of approval" in reducing the cost of restoring greater stability rests crucially on the continued credibility of such policies.

Given the apparent widespread preferences for autonomy in national reserve management, I see little prospect of the SDR becoming the principal reserve asset in the system; nor would this have major economic effects unless we moved to a system with very strong central control. On political grounds, however, it is probably useful to maintain this stated objective. Furthermore, some of the actions which should be taken on their own merits, such as facilitation of greater private market use of the SDR and the creation of a Fund substitution facility, are likely to contribute to a gradual shift toward increasing use of the SDR.

I continue to believe that creation of a Fund substitution facility would be desirable, although I would expect the effects to be marginal rather than major. International interest in such a facility seems to wax and wane with the ups and downs of the dollar. I likewise believe that national governments and the Fund should support, rather than discourage, the growth of private SDR use. There is a good microeconomic case for the use of composite currency units, and the new five-currency SDR basket may make the unit an attractive candidate for many private transactions. International financial innovation seems likely to continue, and one is likely to see both greater use of composite units and greater diversification across currencies in the future.

Paradoxically, greater diversification marginally reduces, rather than increases, exchange rate instability over time. While it is clear that going from one to two currencies (or reserve assets) contributes to a confidence or stability problem, it is not clear that going from two to three currencies, from three to four currencies, and so on will further increase the potential instability. With more diversified portfolios, the changing prospects of individual assets might lead to less, rather than more, asset switching. Since it is extremely unlikely agreement will be reached on a single-reserve-asset system, we have to learn to live in a multi-asset system. While conceptually it would be desirable to have improved mechanisms for minimizing the exchange rate consequences of autonomous shifts in both private and official asset preferences, it is not clear how important such autonomous currency switching has been compared with shifts generated by changing expectations. Likewise, there has been little analysis of how well such shifts could be identified in the time available to governments for deciding on accommodating policy actions. These issues, along with questions about the effectiveness of alternative strategies of national official intervention and macroeconomic policy coordination, should be major topics of further international policy research and analysis.

In summary, I believe that the current system should be evaluated quite favorably in light of historical comparisons and political realities. In the absence of the most extreme combinations of severe shocks and bad luck, the current formal and informal structure of the system should remain basically sound. Thus, while I view the prospects for radical reform of the system as being extremely remote because of basic political considerations, I do not see this as a major cause for alarm. Our basic strategy, in my judgment, should be to improve the operation of the current system. Within this content, there is considerable scope for improvement. While hopes of creating a more stable international environment must rest in large part on the future course of national economic policies, there is also considerable room for strengthening our international monetary institutions and the influences they have over time. The political prospects of such improvements are difficult to evaluate, but continuing efforts along these lines should certainly be made.

Notes

1. I should add that my delineation of issues in this paper draws heavily in places on the treatments of international monetary controversy by these two authors.

2. I shall use the terms international monetary or international financial system, regime, and order interchangeably to refer to the international monetary arrangements which exist at any particular point in time or to proposals for major changes in these arrangements. While granting the point that such arrangements may at times be neither systematic nor orderly, I shall not emphasize semantic distinctions about the minimal levels of structure necessary to call a set of arrangements a system, although there has been considerable controversy over whether our current arrangements should be called a system or a nonsystem. For further discussion and references on this set of issues, see Cooper (1975) and Willett (1977).

3. For discussion of these alternative approaches to international economic policy issues, see Tollison and Willett (1976) and Willett (1981). A number of writers have recently emphasized the need to blend economic and political considerations in international monetary analysis. See, for example, Aliber (1980), Cohen (1977), Cooper (1975), and Strange (1976).

4. For more detailed discussion of the historical development of the international monetary system, see Willett (1977) and the many references cited therein.

5. See Triffin (1960). For recent analyses and references to the subsequent discussion of this issue, see Cumby (1983); Part I of "The Evolving Role of the SDR in the International Monetary System," which is Chapter 11 in this volume; and Willett (1977).

6. For discussion and references, see Tower and Willett (1976).

7. The analysis of this issue is still in its infancy. See Willett (1978 b) and the references cited therein.

8. For more detailed discussions, see, for example, Cooper (1975) and Tower and Willett (1976).

9. See, for example, Corden (1982).

10. Such a distinction between the case for free international trade and the case for free international capital flows was made by the major negotiators at Bretton Woods. See, for example, Willett (1977, and the references cited therein). For recent discussions and references on views about the freedom of international capital flows, see Cooper (1975) and Dornbusch (1982).

11. For discussion of, and references to, the extensive literature on exchange market efficiency and exchange rate modeling, see Dornbusch (1980); Dreyer, Haberler, and Willett (1982, Parts II and III); Levich (1979); Mussa (1980); and Willett (1980 a). This question will be discussed further in Section II.

12. For further discussion and extensive references to the literature on these issues, see Pigott, Sweeney, and Willett (1982) and Thursby and Willett (1982).

13. For discussion and references to the evidence on this point, see Thursby and Willett (1982) and Willett (1982 a).

14. My own view is that a rather strong case can be made for some constitutional constraints on the freedom of domestic monetary and fiscal authorities but that return to a gold standard is not an efficient approach to this problem. For further discussion and references on these issues, see Willett (1983); Willett and Mullen (1982); and United States, Commission on the Role of Gold in the Domestic and International Monetary Systems (1982).

15. For recent analysis and references to the literature on this subject, see Bryant (1980), Henderson (1982), and Tower and Willett (1976).

16. For a discussion of the original analysis of these issues by J. Marcus Fleming and Robert A. Mundell and more recent contributions, see Dornbusch (1980 b) and Willett (1976).

17. On these issues, see Dornbusch and Krugman (1976) and Willett and Mullen (1982).

18. See Tower and Willett (1976) and Enders and Lapan (1979).

19. For discussion and references on the vicious circle debate, see Willett and Wolf (1983). See also Goldstein (1980).

20. See, for example, the discussion of this issue in Halm (1970) and Katz (1979).

21. For discussion and references, see Cumby (1983), Dam (1982), Solomon (1982), and Willett (1977 and 1980 a).

22. With a full-fledged gold standard, gold is the source of international liquidity to which the world economy adjusts; and since adjustment to gold flows is automatic, there are no problems of confidence or the distribution of adjustment responsibilites. Of course, real-world gold standards have included substantial elements of discretion, and confidence and adjustment issues have not been entirely absent.

23. I have presented my reasons for this judgment in more detail in Willett (1977 and 1980 a). See also the discussion in Mundell and Polak (1977) and Dreyer, Haberler, and Willett (1982).

There are three main arguments to the effect that exchange rate flexibility has not improved the adjustment process. One, associated with the global monetarists, is that exchange rate changes cannot have real effects and, hence, cannot induce adjustment. While this may be true for very small, open economies (as emphasized in the theory of optimum currency areas), there is considerable evidence that exchange rate changes can have real effects on medium-sized and large countries (see Willett (1982)).

The second argument is that flexible exchange rates have often been pushed to disequilibrium levels. The third argument is that safeguards against beggar-thy-neighbor adjustment policies have been loosened. The evidence on speculation and equilibrium exchange rates is discussed in Section II. Concerning the third argument, my judgment is that while it would be desirable to further strengthen international surveillance of exchange rates and the adjustment process, it should also be recognized that the adoption of flexible exchange rates has not caused a net increase in beggar-thy-neighbor problems. An additional consideration is that although managed flexibility has not always prevented countries from postponing necessary adjustment, it would be difficult to argue that maintenance of the Bretton Woods regime would have reduced this problem.

24. For a useful discussion of the role of trust and risk aversion in international monetary issues, see Cooper (1975).

25. For discussion and references, see Solomon (1982) and Willett (1977).

26. For discussion and references to this literature, see Willett (1977, Chapter 3).

27. For further discussion of the details of the Committee of Twenty's negotiations, see Solomon (1982), Willett (1977), and Williamson (1977) and (1982).

28. For discussion and references on testing for unexploited profit opportunities in the foreign exchange markets, see Sweeney (1982 a) and (1982 b) and Willett (1982 a). On the profitability (or lack thereof) of official intervention, see Argy (1982) and Taylor (1982).

29. For a recent evaluation of the relationship between official and private financing of balance of payments deficits, see Cohen (1981).

Bibliography

Aliber, Robert Z., "Issues in U.S. International Monetary Policies" in *International Economic Policy Research: Papers and Proceedings of a Colloquium Held in Washington, D.C., October 3, 4, 1980,* Washington: National Science Foundation, 1980, pp. I–59–75. (Hereinafter this book will be referred to as *International Economic Policy Research*.)

Argy, Victor E., *Exchange-Rate Management in Theory and Practice,* Studies in International Finance, No. 50 (Princeton, New Jersey: International Finance Section, Princeton University, 1982).

Bryant, Ralph C., *Money and Monetary Policy in Independent Nations* (Washington: Brookings Institution, 1980).

Cohen, Benjamin J., *Organizing the World's Money: The Political Economy of International Monetary Relations* (New York: Basic Books, 1977).

————, in collaboration with Fabio Basagni, *Banks and the Balance of Payments: Private Lending in the International Adjustment Process* (Montclair, New Jersey: Allanheld, Osmun and Company, 1981).

Cooper, Richard N., "Prolegomena to the Choice of an International Monetary System," in *World Politics and International Economics,* ed. by C. Fred Bergsten and Lawrence B. Krause (Washington: Brookings Institution, 1975), pp. 63–97.

Corden, W. Max, "The Normative Theory of International Trade," University of Stockholm, Institute for International Economic Studies, Seminar Paper No. 230 (November 1982), forthcoming as Chapter 2 in R. W. Jones and P. B. Kenen, eds., *Handbook of International Economics,* Vol. 1 (Amsterdam: North-Holland Publishing Company, to be published in 1984).

Cumby, Robert E., "Special Drawing Rights and Plans for Reform of the International Monetary System: A Survey," Chapter 10 in this volume.

Dam, Kenneth W., *The Rules of the Game: Reform and Evolution of the International Monetary System* (Chicago: University of Chicago Press, 1982).

Dornbusch, Rudiger (1980 a), "Exchange Rate Economics: Where Do We Stand?" *Brookings Papers on Economic Activity: 1* (1980), pp. 143–85.

———— (1980 b), *Open Economy Macroeconomics* (New York: Basic Books, 1980).

————, Flexible Exchange Rates and Interdependence, National Bureau of Economic Research, Working Paper No. 135 (Cambridge, Massachusetts, November 1982).

————, and Paul Krugman (1976), "Flexible Exchange Rates in the Short Run," *Brookings Papers on Economic Activity: 3* (1976), pp. 537–84.

Dreyer, Jacob S., Gottfried Haberler, and Thomas D. Willett, eds., *The International Monetary System: A Time of Turbulence* (Washington: American Enterprise Institute for Public Policy Research, 1982). (Hereinafter this book is referred to as *The International Monetary System*.)

Enders, Walter, and Harvey E. Lapan, "Stability, Random Disturbance and the Exchange Rate Regime," *Southern Economic Journal,* Vol. 46 (July 1979), pp. 49–70.

Goldstein, Morris, *Have Flexible Exchange Rates Handicapped Macroeconomic Policy?* Special Papers in International Economics, No. 14 (Princeton, New Jersey: International Finance Section, Princeton University, 1980).

Halm, George N., ed., *Approaches to Greater Flexibility of Exchange Rates: The Bürgenstock Papers* (Princeton, New Jersey: Princeton University Press, 1970).

Henderson, Dale, "The Role of Intervention Policy in Open Economy Financial Policy: A Macroeconomic Perspective," in *Political Economy of International and Domestic Monetary Relations,* ed. by Raymond E. Lombra and Willard E. Witte (Ames, Iowa: Iowa State University Press, 1982), pp. 261–89.

Katz, Samuel I., ed., *U.S.-European Monetary Relations* (Washington: American Enterprise Institute for Public Policy Research, 1979).

Laney, Leroy O., and Thomas D. Willett, "The International Liquidity Explosion and Worldwide Inflation: The Evidence from Sterilization Coefficient Estimates," *Journal of International Money and Finance,* Vol. 1 (August 1982), pp. 141–52.

Laney, Leroy, Chris Radcliffe, and Thomas D. Willett, *International Currency Substitution by Americans Is Not High: A Comment on Miles,* Claremont Working Papers, No 27 (Claremont, California: Claremont Graduate School, 1982). This paper will be published in a forthcoming issue of the *Southern Economic Journal.*

Levich, Richard. "The Efficiency of Markets for Foreign Exchange," in Rudiger Dornbusch and Jacob A. Frenkel, eds., *International Economic Policy: Theory and Evidence* (Baltimore: Johns Hopkins University Press, 1979), pp. 246–67.

Lombra, Raymond E., and Willard Witte, eds., *Political Economy of International and Domestic Monetary Relations* (Ames, Iowa: Iowa State University Press, 1982). (Hereinafter this book is referred to as *Political Economy of Monetary Relations.*)

Machlup, Fritz, *Plans for Reform of the International Monetary System,* Special Papers in International Economics, No. 3 (Princeton, New Jersey: International Finance Section, Princeton University, 1962).

Marris, Stephen N., "Decision-Making on Exchange Rates," in *Approaches to Greater Flexibility of Exchange Rates: The Bürgenstock Papers,* ed. by George N. Halm (Princeton, New Jersey: Princeton University Press, 1970), pp. 77–88.

Modigliani, Franco, and Hossein Askari, "The International Transfer of Capital and the Propagation of Domestic Disturbances Under Alternative Payment Systems," Banca Nazionale del Lavoro, *Quarterly Review,* Vol. 26 (December 1973), pp. 295–310.

Mussa, Michael, "Public Policy Issues in International Finance," in *International Economic Policy Research,* pp. I–76–104.

Mundell, Robert A., and Jacques J. Polak, eds., *The International Monetary System* (New York: Columbia University Press, 1977).

Pigott, Charles, Richard J. Sweeney, and Thomas D. Willett, *The Costs of Disequilibrium Under Pegged and Flexible Exchange Rates*, Claremont Working Papers, No. 46 (Claremont, California: Claremont Graduate School, 1982).

Solomon, Robert, *The International Monetary System, 1945–1981* (New York: Harper and Row, 1982).

Strange, Susan, *International Monetary Relations* (London: Oxford University Press, 1976).

Sweeney, Richard J. (1982 a), "Intervention Strategy Implications of Purchasing Power Parity and Tests of Spot Exchange-Market Efficiency," in *The International Monetary System*, pp. 65–109.

———— (1982 b), "Speculation: Stabilizing or Destabilizing," Claremont Working Papers, No. 59 (Claremont, California: Claremont Graduate School, 1982).

————, and Thomas D. Willett, "Eurodollars, Petrodollars, and Problems of World Liquidity and Inflation," in *Stabilizing of the Domestic and International Economy*, ed. by Karl Brunner and Allan H. Meltzer, Carnegie-Rochester Conference Series on Public Policy, Vol. 5 (Amsterdam: North-Holland Publishing Company, 1977), pp. 277–310.

Taylor, Dean, "Official Intervention in the Foreign Exchange Market, or, Bet Against the Central Bank," *Journal of Political Economy*, Vol. 90 (April 1982), pp. 356–68.

Thursby, Marie, and Thomas D. Willett, *The Effects of Flexible Exchange Rates on International Trade and Investment: A Survey of Historical Views and Recent Evidence*, Claremont Working Papers, No. 62 (Claremont, California: Claremont Graduate School, 1982).

Tollison, Robert D., and Thomas D. Willett, "Institutional Mechanisms for Dealing With International Externalities; A Public Choice Perspective," in *The Law of the Sea*, ed. by Ryan C. Amacher and Richard J. Sweeney (Washington: American Enterprise Institute for Public Policy Research, 1976), pp. 77–101.

———— "An Economic Theory of Mutually Advantageous Issue Linkages in International Negotiations," *International Organization*, Vol. 33 (Autumn 1979), pp. 425–50.

Tower, Edward, and Thomas D. Willett, *The Theory of Optimum Currency Areas and Exchange-Rate Flexibility*, Special Papers in International Economics, No. 11 (Princeton, New Jersey: International Finance Section, Princeton University, May 1976).

Triffin, Robert, *Gold and the Dollar Crisis: The Future of Convertibility* (New Haven, Connecticut: Yale University Press, 1960).

United States, Commission on the Role of Gold in the Domestic and International Monetary Systems, *Report to the U.S. Congress*, Vols. I and II (Washington: Government Printing Office, 1982).

Willett, Thomas D., "The Eurocurrency Market, Exchange-Rate Systems, and National Financial Policies," in *Eurocurrencies and the International Monetary System*, ed. by Carl H. Stem, John H. Makin, and Dennis E. Logue (Washington: American Enterprise Institute for Public Policy Research, 1976), pp. 193–221.

――――, *Floating Exchange Rates and International Monetary Reform* (Washington: American Enterprise Institute for Public Policy Research, 1977).

―――― (1978 a), "It's Too Simple To Blame the Countries with a Surplus," *Euromoney* (February 1978), pp. 89–96.

―――― (1978 b), "Alternative Approaches to International Surveillance of Exchange-Rate Policies," in *Managed Exchange-Rate Flexibility: The Recent Experience* (Boston: Federal Reserve Bank of Boston, October 1978), pp. 148–72.

―――― (1980 a), *International Liquidity Issues* (Washington: American Enterprise Institute for Public Policy Research, 1980).

―――― (1980 b), "Policy Research Issues in a Floating Rate World: An Assessment of Policy-Relevant Research on the Effects of International Monetary Institutions and Behavior on Macroeconomic Performance," in *International Economic Policy Research*, pp. I–24–45.

―――― "The Causes and Effects of Exchange Rate Volatility," in *The International Monetary System*, pp. 24–64.

―――― *A New Monetary Constitution*, Claremont Working Papers, No. 71 (Claremont, California: Claremont Graduate School, 1981). This paper will be included in Alvin Rabushka and W. Craig Stubblebine, eds., *Constraining Federal Taxing and Spending* (Palo Alto, California: Hoover Institution Press, forthcoming in 1983).

――――, and John Mullen, "The Effects of Alternative International Monetary Systems on Macroeconomic Discipline and Inflationary Biases," in *Political Economy of Monetary Relations*, pp. 143–59.

Willett, Thomas D., and Matthias Wolf, *The Vicious Circle Debate: Some Conceptual Distinctions*, Claremont Working Paper, No. 81 (Claremont, California: Claremont Graduate School, 1983). This paper will be published in a forthcoming issue of *Kyklos*.

Williamson, John H., *The Failure of World Monetary Reform, 1971–74* (New York: New York University Press, 1977).

――――, "The Failure of World Monetary Reform: A Reassessment," in *The International Monetary System Under Flexible Exchange Rates: Global, Regional, and National*, ed. by Richard N. Cooper, Peter B. Kenen, Jorge Braga de Macedo, and Jacques van Ypersele (Cambridge, Massachusetts: Ballinger, 1982), pp. 297–307.

PART II

FLEXIBLE EXCHANGE RATES AND INTERNATIONAL TRADE

5

THE INTERNATIONAL MONETARY SYSTEM AND PROPOSALS FOR INTERNATIONAL POLICY COORDINATION

Gottfried Haberler

Prologue as an Epilogue

Some dramatic developments came too late to be considered in the text below. The outstanding one is the sharply increased volatility of exchange rates. On October 31, 1986, Secretary Baker and his Japanese counterpart Mr. Miyazawa declared the dollar/yen exchange rate "broadly consistent with the underlying fundamentals." Yet two months later the dollar slumped. On January 21, 1987, Baker and Miyazawa held an emergency meeting. The dollar plunged again. Two typical news headlines: "If the Dollar Cracks" (The Economist, February 7, 1987); "Dollar Battered in Hectic Day" (New York Times, February 10, 1987).

Whatever the outcome, a lengthy period of uncertainty and turmoil is not the best way to set exchange rates. U.S. policy of pressuring Germany and Japan to expand suffers from two serious weaknesses. First, the United States still needs foreign capital to finance budget deficits. Second, even a large noninflationary expansion of the German and Japanese economies would have only a minor effect on U.S. trade deficits. All this supports the principal conclusions of the present paper: Large U.S. budget deficits are the main cause of the trade deficit. Governments do a poor job setting exchange rates. Markets, too, make mistakes, but if left alone markets do much better than governments. Ergo, the system of floating exchange rates should continue.

Summary

After James Baker became secretary of the Treasury in February 1985, the Reagan administration's balance-of-payments policy took a sharp turn from a passive, laissez-faire, benign-neglect approach to an activist, interventionist one. Under Baker's predecessor market forces were allowed to set the exchange value of the dollar. Under Baker the policy was first to talk the dollar down and then to push it down by internationally concerted interventions in the foreign exchange market.

The reason for the switch is well known. From 1980 to February 1985 the dollar appreciated sharply relative to all foreign currencies. The strong dollar stimulated imports and discouraged exports, producing huge trade deficits causing unemployment in export and import competing industries, which triggered strong protectionist pressures in Congress. True, the market had turned around and in March 1985 the dollar started on a lengthy decline. But that was not immediately clear. So Secretary Baker organized the surprise meeting of the Group of Five (the United States, England, France, Germany, and Japan) at the Plaza Hotel in New York, where it was decided to bring the dollar further down by concerted interventions in the foreign exchange market.

Parallel with the initiative on the monetary front, the United States has been pushing for "international policy coordination." This theme was taken up by the Tokyo Economic Summit in May 1986. The heads of state of seven nations (the Group of Five plus Canada and Italy) instructed their seven ministers of finance to meet at least once a year to check the "mutual compatibility" of their policies. The ministers conducted "their first exercise of multilateral surveillance" in September 1986 and issued a bland statement, a collection of generalities: the ministers agreed to continue to promote noninflationary growth, to continue to remove structural rigidities, to resist protectionist pressures, and so on.

In practice, the vaunted international policy coordination has boiled down to the increasingly urgent and impatient demand by the United States that Germany and Japan stimulate their economies in order to reduce their trade surpluses and U.S. deficits, threatening them with a further decline of the dollar and with a protectionist explosion in the U.S. Congress. The United States and Japan, dubbed the Group of Two, have reached an agreement. On October 31, 1986, after a secret meeting, Mr. Baker and the Japanese Minister of Finance Kiichi Miyazawa issued a "Statement on Economic Cooperation." Apart from the usual phrases about "the importance of continuing cooperative action" and the like, the substantive content is: The Bank of Japan reduced the discount rate from 3½ percent to 3 percent, and the Japanese government promised to submit to the Diet a fiscal package of 3.6 trillion yen (about $22 billion) in additional expenditures spread over several years and a sizable reduction of marginal tax rates. Actually, these reforms had been announced *earlier. The United States promised to "remain fully committed" to reducing the budget deficit and, most important, agreed that the dollar-yen rate is "now broadly consistent with the present underlying fundamentals." In plain English, the United States will, for the time being, not ask for any further appreciation of the yen. But the agreement is not a return to fixed exchange rates. Nothing has been said about defending the exchange rate or about what should be done when the fundamentals change.*

The U.S.-Japanese agreement demonstrates the superiority of quiet diplomacy. It was easier for the United States to reach an agreement with Japan than with Germany because Prime Minister Nakasone, unlike German Chancellor Helmut Kohl, was not confronted with an early election. But the American policy of pressuring the Germans and the Japanese to get rid of their trade surpluses suffers from two serious weaknesses: First, the United States still needs foreign capital to finance its huge budget deficits and, second, several econometric studies—by the IMF, the Federal Reserve Board, and private analysts—indicate that even a substantial increase of the German and Japanese GNP growth will have only a small effect on the U.S. trade deficit. The correction of the U.S. external deficit must go hand in hand with the reduction of the budget deficit, which reflects the insufficiency of domestic savings to finance both private-sector investment and public-sector borrowing. The United States cannot go on indefinitely importing capital on a large scale. First, sooner or later investors will get nervous and there may develop a stampede out of the dollar; second, the rapidly mounting service charge on the foreign debt will make it necessary to reduce the trade deficit and turn it into a surplus. These changes will make it necessary to devote a growing portion of output to exports and import substitution, implying a squeeze on consumption and investment—in other words, a reduction in the living standard, which with rigid wages would pose a serious problem.

No modern government relishes unemployment and all want growth. Much of the high European unemployment is structural, not Keynesian. The conclusion that I draw from all this is that each country should make its own judgment. Criticism and advice of other countries should be given quietly through institutions such as the OECD, BIS, and the IMF. Public criticism, echoed by the media in cruder form, is internationally counterproductive.

The U.S. switch to an activist balance-of-payments policy reflects a fairly widespread disenchantment with floating exchange rates. Floating was forced on most reluctant policy makers by the breakdown of the Bretton Woods system in the late 1960s and 1970s. But it was never fully accepted. It was blamed for the wide swings of the dollar and the huge U.S. trade deficits.

It is easy to see that we were lucky to have entered the 1980s with floating exchange rates. If the world had been on fixed exchange rates when capital flowed into the United States on a large scale, Europe would have suffered a massive loss of international reserves and intense deflationary pressure. The fixed-rate system would have broken down, which would have caused a severe recession. Thanks to floating, this did not happen.

The strong dollar and large U.S. trade deficits were not a gigantic market failure. On the contrary, up to a point they were highly beneficial and pulled the world economy out of the recession. I say up to a point, because with the benefit of hindsight we can say that in 1984 the market did overshoot. But the market corrected itself and the dollar started to decline in March 1985, well before the U.S. policy changed.

The budget deficits, too, were a blessing up to a point; they pulled the U.S. economy out of the recession. But unlike the markets, a reversal of government policy is not yet in sight, although there is now almost universal agreement that deficit spending has gone much too far. It is in the nature of the political process that governments are slow to admit mistakes and that the legislative machinery delays corrective action.

The determination of exchange rates should therefore be left to the markets; in other words, the system of floating exchange rates should continue. Jacob Dreyer argues convincingly in this volume that economists simply do not know enough about the determination of exchange rates to identify the "correct" rate. This is strikingly demonstrated by the fact that there is no agreement among experts on whether the dollar has declined far enough to eliminate or sharply reduce the U.S. trade deficit, let alone on how much it should decline. There is even no agreement on how much the dollar has already declined overall. We know, of course, how much it has declined against individual currencies; there exist many sharply divergent indexes of the overall decline, but there is none that is generally accepted as the best of the lot, let alone the correct one.

From all this it follows that a return to some sort of fixed exchange rate is out of the question. It is hardly necessary to explain at length that a return to the gold standard is also out of the question. Who would want to entrust the international monetary system to the mercies of South Africa and the Soviet Union, the two by far most important producers of gold? A Bretton Woods type of fixed but adjustable exchange rate is very vulnerable to destabilizing speculation. If the members of the Group of

Five are unable to agree on the pattern of exchange rates of their currencies, how could it be done in a wider circle?

Early in 1987, the European Monetary System (EMS) was shaken by an acute crisis. The French franc was very weak because of widespread strikes in France. The German mark was strong. Prime Minister Jacques Chirac insisted that this was "a mark crisis, not a franc crisis" and called on the German authorities to "do what is necessary:" either upvalue the mark or reduce interest rates and stimulate the economy—in plain English, create a little inflation. After hectic negotiation, the ministers of finance papered over the cracks in the system with a token 3 percent appreciation of the mark and the Dutch guilder and a 2 percent appreciation of the Belgian franc against the other European currencies. The situation has been made more troublesome by a sharp slide of the dollar against the mark and the yen despite the Baker-Miyazawa agreement. According to press reports, that is what the U.S. administration wants in order to keep the pressure on Germany to expand. It is true that sufficient inflation in the surplus countries, Germany and Japan, would let the deficit countries, the United States and France, off the hook. But it would be like infecting the healthy instead of curing the sick. Worldwide inflation is not a sound basis for the world economy. All this provides a classic demonstration of the dangers of politicization of exchange rates. Markets do a better job than governments in setting exchange rates.

Introduction

Since the breakdown of the Bretton Woods system of stable but adjustable exchange rates early in the 1970s, the international monetary system and its reform have been under almost continuous discussion. The system of floating exchange rates instituted in 1973 has never been fully accepted. In the past two or three years the criticism of floating has sharply increased and the call for monetary reform become more and more intense. The wide swings of the dollar, rising from June 1980 to February 1985 by 19 percent against the Japanese yen and 89 percent against the German mark, and then declining rapidly from February 1985 to September 1986 by 41 percent against the yen and 39 percent against the German mark; the huge trade and current-account deficits; and the resulting protectionist pressure have been most disturbing events. All had been blamed on the system of floating exchange rates.

Before continuing the story it must be pointed out that, while the appreciation and depreciation of the dollar in terms of single currencies is clear-cut, measuring the overall appreciation or depreciation of the dollar presents very difficult index number problems. I confine myself to some general remarks. Interested readers should consult the preceding chapter by Jacob Dreyer and the literature cited there.

There exist many indexes of the value of the dollar; in fact, the number has sharply increased in the past year. These indexes are weighted averages of the changes of the value of the dollar relative to individual currencies, the weights being the volume of trade—trade-weighted indexes. The various indexes differ with respect to the currencies covered, the system of weighting, and some other characteristics. The indexes are either bilaterally weighted, using as weights each country's volume of trade with the United States, or multilaterally weighted, using as weights each country's total trade or some more sophisticated system. The indexes yield divergent measures for the overall change of the dollar's value, the divergence being much greater for the decline of the dollar since 1985 than for the preceding appreciation. The reason for this asymmetry is that from 1980 to 1985 the dollar rose with respect to all currencies. After February 1985 the dollar did not decline against all currencies. The currencies of Taiwan, South Korea, and Hong Kong, for example, did not rise against the dollar, and the currencies of inflationary countries in Latin America and elsewhere declined.

Until recently the most widely used indexes were the Federal Reserve Board index (ten countries, multilateral weights), the Morgan Guaranty Trust index (fifteen countries, bilateral weights), the International Monetary Fund index (seventeen countries, sophisticated multilateral weighting system), and the U.S. Department of the Treasury index (twenty-two countries, bilateral weights). The four indexes cover the countries of the Organization for Economic Cooperation and Development (OECD), Western Europe, Japan, and Canada (the Treasury index adds Finland, Greece, Iceland, Ireland, and Turkey). All four indexes leave out South Korea, Taiwan, Hong Kong, Singapore, and the rest of the world. Thus they give an exaggerated impression of the magnitude of the decline of the dollar since February 1985.

Several attempts have been made to broaden the coverage of the indexes. I mention three. The first was presented by Michael Cox, "A New Alternative Trade-Weighted Dollar Exchange Rate Index."[1] This index covers all 131 U.S. trading partners and uses bilateral weights, reaching the conclusion that "only about a 6 percent depreciation of the dollar has occurred" from January 1980 to May 1986. This probably understates the decline of the dollar because the index is (as the author points out) in purely *nominal* terms and does not allow for inflation. Specifically, the inclusion of the highly inflationary Latin American countries vitiates the outcome. It is true that the four indexes mentioned above, too, are formally in nominal terms. But in the OECD countries inflation rates did not diverge very much during the 1980s, so that these indexes can be regarded as a close approximation to a real—that is, to an inflation-corrected—index.

The second comprehensive, "Why Our Trade Gap Persists," was presented by Irwin L. Kellner.[2] According to this index the dollar has hardly declined since March 1985. Since the index is in nominal terms (not corrected for inflation), it probably understates the decline of the dollar. But according to the author, preliminary calculations suggest that adjustment for inflation changes the result only marginally.

The third attempt to broaden the geographic base of the index has been presented by Jeffrey A. Rosensweig, "A New Dollar Index: Capturing A More Global Perspective."[3] This index includes the Asian countries of Taiwan, South Korea, Hong Kong, and Singapore. It excludes the Latin American countries because of their high inflation rate. This index yields a depreciation of the dollar by about 20 percent.

Each of the existing indexes has its strong and weak points, and I believe that there is no good reason to single out one of them as the best of the lot or the correct one. This is unfortunate, because it means that we simply do not know by how much the dollar has declined overall since February 1985. It is true that attempts are under way in several places to construct a comprehensive inflation-corrected index. I doubt, however, that this will settle the question of how much the dollar has declined overall. The difficulties of such an inflation-corrected index are formidable because, for example, most of the highly inflationary countries have exchange controls and multiple rates. Mexico, the third largest trade partner of the United States, is a striking example.

An important implication of this conclusion is the following: policy makers and their economic advisers are confronted with the question whether the dollar has already declined sufficiently to eliminate the balance-of-payments deficit. The answer depends partly on how much the dollar actually has declined. The uncertainty about this has important implications for economic policy. More on this later.

The changed outlook on the balance of payments and exchange rates is highlighted by the sharp reversal of the Reagan administration's policy since the arrival of James Baker at the Treasury Department in February 1986. Under Baker's predecessor, the team of Donald Regan and Beryl Sprinkel in the Treasury, U.S. policy was one of laissez-faire, hands-off benign neglect of the balance of payments.[4] It opposed official interventions in the foreign exchange markets. The policy of benign neglect, also called a "passive" policy with respect to the balance of payments and exchange rates, was well stated in the Economic Report of the President for 1984:

> In the 1950s and 1960s central banks were committed to maintaining their countries' exchange rates at fixed levels. This effort became increasingly difficult over time, due particularly to divergent inflation rates among countries. By 1971 the dollar had become unsustainably overvalued in the sense that the supply of dollars greatly exceeded the private demand for dollars. Central banks made up the difference, buying unwanted dollars in exchange for foreign currencies. The effort was abandoned in 1973 and the major currencies moved on to a system of floating, i.e., market-determined, exchange rates. When exchange rates float, there is no such thing as undervaluation or evaluation, in the sense of excess market supply or demand for currencies. The value of the currency is whatever the market dictates that it should be.
>
> It is nearly impossible to imagine the world economy going through the past 10 years in the straightjacket of fixed exchange rates. Given the events of this period, notably the large changes in oil prices and the divergent macroeconomic policies among the industrialized countries, floating exchange rates have performed well.[5]

In spring 1985, under the James Baker-Richard Darman team in the Treasury, the stance of U.S. policy turned sharply from a passive-laissez-faire approach to an active-interventionist one. The reasons for the change are not hard to find; they are the understandable concern about the strong dollar, the huge trade and current-account deficits that in a few years have made the United States the world's largest debtor and, above all, the fear of a protectionist explosion. That this fear is not groundless has been demonstrated by the Democratic omnibus trade bill that was passed by the House of Representatives with a large bipartisan majority.[6]

The first big success of the new policy was the agreement of the Group of Five at the surprise meeting in the Plaza Hotel, New York City, September 22, 1985. The five members agreed that "some further orderly appreciation of the main non-dollar currencies against the dollar is desirable,"—in other words, that the dollar should be pushed down by internationally concerted interventions in the foreign exchange markets. The decision of the Group of Five was endorsed by the Economic Summit in Tokyo in May 1986.

In his State of the Union Message in February 1986 President Reagan went a step further. He said:

> The constant expansion of our economy and exports requires a sound and stable dollar at home and reliable exchange rates around the world. We

must never again permit wild currency swings to cripple our farmers and other exporters. . . . We've begun coordinating economic and monetary policy among our major trading partners. But there's more to do, and tonight I am directing Treasury Secretary Jim Baker to determine if the nations of the world should convene to discuss the role and relationship of our currencies.

This seems to say that it may be possible to organize a Bretton Woods type international conference to negotiate a return to some sort of fixed exchanges. A brief reflection leads to the conclusion that this is practically out of the question. It is, therefore, not surprising that Secretary Baker changed his mind after talking things over with his European colleagues. On December 11, 1986, he said there was no need at that time for the United States to call an international monetary conference to consider changing the present floating exchange rate system.

How Floating Was Forced on Reluctant Policy Makers

Since the memories of most policy makers are so short, it is well to recall once again, very briefly, how floating was forced on most reluctant policy makers.

During the first fifteen to seventeen years after World War II the value of the dollar was unquestioned, the dollar was convertible into gold, and the Bretton Woods system of stable but adjustable exchange rates had practically become a dollar standard: "The dollar is better than gold" was the slogan. True, in 1958 and 1959 the U.S. balance of payments developed deficits of $3.4 and $3.9 billion, which was then regarded as alarming.[7] The Eisenhower administration promptly took anti-inflationary measures, which caused a mild recession in April 1960–February 1961, the balance of payments improved, and prices remained stable until 1965.

Thereafter the picture changed when President Johnson, ignoring the advice of his economic advisers, financed the escalating cost of the war in Vietnam and of the equally expensive domestic Great Society programs with inflationary bank credit rather than with higher taxes. True, the rising inflation (less than 10 percent) was not very high compared with what came ten years later. But the international situation had changed. There had been a fairly drastic realignment of currencies: in 1949 the British pound and numerous other currencies in the sterling area were devalued, and in 1958 the French franc was sharply devalued. Even more important, the war-ravaged countries in Europe and Asia had recovered. Especially in Germany and Japan what Keynes called the "classical medicine" of sound money and sound public finance (which he said should be given a chance) had produced the German and Japanese economic "miracles." So the dollar lost its unique position; it was no longer as good as gold. The crucial fact was that the U.S. inflation rate was higher than the three strong-currency countries—Germany, Japan, and Switzerland—were ready to accept. The balance of payments weakened, and the gold reserve declined.

The policy response of successive administrations was to impose increasingly severe restrictions and controls. Duty-free allowances for returning U.S. tourists were reduced from $500 to $100, for example; American foreign aid that used to be granted "un-tied" was tied to purchases in the United States—a sort of "buy American" policy. Similarly, to reduce foreign exchange costs of military expenditures abroad, shipments from the United States were substituted for foreign supplies, although this policy involved a sharp increase in real cost. These measures were described in the literature as a de facto depreciation of the "foreign aid dollar," "the tourist dollar," etc. Unsurprisingly, these measures and "voluntary" restraints on capital exports (direct investments as well as bank lending) were ineffective. In the fourth quarter of 1967 confidence in the dollar was shaken by the devaluation of the British pound and by a large balance-of-payments deficit.

So on January 1, 1968, President Johnson dramatically announced a sweeping seven-point "program of action" which, if it had been fully enacted, would have put the United States under full-fledged exchange control. To indicate the flavor of the official thinking at that time I mention a few of the points. Mandatory tight capital export controls, based on the Trading with the Enemy Act of 1917, were put into effect by executive order. (It came as a surprise to most Americans that they had been living under a state of "national emergency" ever since President Truman had proclaimed it during the Korean War December 19, 1950.) Border taxes on all imports and similar refunds (subsidies) for exports were imposed to offset U.S. indirect taxes. A "tourist tax," graduated according to the amount spent per day, was proposed to be levied on American tourists traveling outside the Western Hemisphere. This tax was supposed to reduce the "tourist deficit" in the balance of payments by $500 million. Fortunately, this proposal was rejected by Congress.

Late in 1969 and 1970 the pressure on the dollar was alleviated a little by the 9.3 percent "upvaluation" of the German mark in September–October 1969 and by the U.S. recession of December 1969–November 1970, which brought down the rate of inflation from 5.7 percent in 1969 to 3.1 percent in 1972. Despite all that, to hold the line foreign central banks, especially the German Bundesbank, were forced to intervene massively in foreign exchange markets by buying many billions of dollars until February 1973 when floating started.

On August 15, 1971, President Nixon declared the dollar inconvertible into gold for foreign central banks, imposed a surcharge of 10 percent on all imports, and introduced wage and price controls in the United States to force a realignment of exchange rates. This was accomplished at the Smithsonian Conference in December 1971. The devaluation of the dollar was about 8 percent against most major currencies.

President Nixon called the Smithsonian Agreement "the most significant monetary agreement in the history of the world." Unfortunately, it did not last very long. In June 1972 the British pound was set afloat, taking with it many currencies in the sterling area. The pressure on the dollar rose again sharply. Investors (speculators) all over the world had learned their lesson: under fixed but adjustable exchange rates a currency under pressure can only go down, not up, and the chances are that it will be devalued sharply because the authorities want to be sure that they will not have to repeat the painful operation in the near future. This situation is ideal for the speculator: if he has guesed right, he makes a large profit; if he has guessed wrong, he loses only the cost of the transaction. Under floating, speculation obviously is a much more risky business.

To make a long story short, the pressure on the dollar continued, and foreign central banks had to buy billions of dollars to hold the line. The end came early in 1973. On January 23, 1973, the Swiss National Bank stopped buying dollars and let the franc float up. So a flood of dollars swept into Germany. In four days (February 5–9, 1973) the Bundesbank bought $5 billion to hold the line. That was the last gasp of the system of "stable but adjustable" exchange rates under Bretton Woods.

The Floating Dollar in the 1970s

Since 1973 the international monetary system, or nonsystem, as some critics call it, has been one of widespread floating; all major currencies and many others float. There are, of course, areas of stable exchange rates; according to IMF statistics some thirty-four countries peg their currencies to the dollar, others to the D-mark, the yen, and the French franc; and the European monetary system (EMS) maintains a precarious stability among the members of the European Community (EC), minus

Britain. But "two thirds to four fifths of world trade is conducted at floating rates."[8]

Central banks were slow to get used to floating rates. While the Bretton Woods system was disintegrating, a prestigious IMF committee, the Committee of Twenty, was working on monetary reform. Right to the end it stuck to the position that "the reformed system should be based on stable but adjustable par values."[9]

But in January 1974, on the occasion of the first oil shock, J. H. Witteveen, then managing director of the IMF, said in a major policy speech: "In the present situation, a large measure of floating is unavoidable and indeed desirable."[10] Otmar Emminger added, "I think this is still valid today, after the second oil shock." It is safe to say that no system other than widespread floating could have coped with the turbulent period of the 1970s and early 1980s. The oil shocks certainly were highly disturbing, but their importance has been greatly exaggerated. The fact is that the two oil shocks were preceded and accompanied by highly inflationary cyclical booms, which, in turn, were superimposed on an inflationary groundswell that had started in the middle 1960s.[11]

The dollar was weak through the 1970s because inflation was high. In June 1974 the annual rate of inflation in the United States reached 12 percent, the highest ever in peacetime. Inflation was world-wide; even Switzerland had an inflation rate of 10 percent. Although anti-inflationary measures and the severe recession of November 1973–March 1975 brought U.S. inflation down to about 5 percent in 1976, inflation reaccelerated when the Carter administration switched from fighting inflation to expansion, reaching a peak of close to 20 percent in 1980. The strong-currency countries, Germany, Japan, and Switzerland, however, continued to fight against inflation. Switzerland applied monetary shock treatment, bringing the rate of inflation down abruptly to zero, and accepting a short but severe recession (A GNP drop of 7 percent) as the cost of price stability.[12] The German reaction was essentially the same, though a little less drastic than the Swiss.

No wonder that the dollar was weak all those years. In the fall of 1978 a "dollar rescue operation" was organized, with the United States, in effect, borrowing about $30 billion in foreign currencies to hold the line. The pressure on the dollar eased, but there was no lasting improvement because there was no sustained tightening of monetary policy. In 1979 the situation deteriorated rapidly, inducing President Carter to appoint Paul Volcker chairman of the Federal Reserve System. At the annual meeting of the IMF in Belgrade Volcker was told by foreign central bankers that they would stop supporting the dollar unless the United

States took credible measures to curb inflation. Volcker stepped on the monetary brake, a real turning point. But a price had to be paid for stability: the severe twin recessions of the early 1980s (January 1980–July 1980 and July 1981–November 1982).

In the 1970s every spell of weakness of the dollar gave rise to an outburst of criticism of floating. Floating and excessive volatility of exchange rates, it was said, were responsible for the high inflation. Actually, the opposite is true. Inflation forced floating on reluctant policy makers. High inflation is incompatible with fixed exchanges for the following reason: Under fixed exchanges all participating countries must have approximately the same rate of inflation. It is, however, impossible for sovereign countries to agree on an inflation rate of, say, 6, 7, or more percent. There will always be some who will find it excessive and let their currencies appreciate. The same is true of deflation.

There are many examples. In the 1970s Germany, Japan, Switzerland, and some other countries did not accept the rate of inflation that a fixed exchange rate with the dollar would have imposed on them. In other words, floating protected them from imported inflation. Similarly, in the 1930s floating (or at that time devaluation of currencies against gold and the dollar) enabled many countries to extricate themselves from the deflation that raged in the United States.

All this disproves another argument against floating. It has been said and is still said that floating has not provided countries the freedom, which advocates of floating had promised, to pursue the macroeconomic policy they want; in other words, floating rates do not protect countries from disturbances from abroad.[13]

Floating protects a country from purely monetary disturbances from abroad; no country can be forced to inflate its economy or to deflate it, as they have been forced under fixed exchanges. But floating does not protect against *real* disturbances from abroad. Real disturbances are not merely exogenous events, such as oil shocks or protectionist measures abroad, but also real changes caused by monetary forces. Deflation, for instance, causes unemployment, which in turn leads to a decline of the deflating country's *real* demand for the exports of its trade partners.

But contrary to what critics often say, floating has an anti-inflationary disciplinary effect. Central bankers know that if they yield to inflationary pressures they risk a run on the currency, with painful real effects. Unfortunately, floating does not provide full protection against inflation, for a strong inducement to resist inflationary pressure can be overwhelmed by an even stronger propensity to inflate. Examples are not hard to find.

The Strong Dollar: 1980 to February 1985

The dollar's spectacular ascent started late in 1980. It reached its high point in February 1985 and was followed by a rapid decline. The causes of the strong dollar are still being debated. The late Otmar Emminger, former president of the German Bundesbank, called the persistent strength of the dollar "the most over-explained—and maybe least understood—economic event of our time."[14] With the benefit of hindsight it is possible, I submit, to identify the most important factors and to explain certain baffling features that make the strong dollar almost a unique event.

The rise in interest rates and growing confidence that under the chairmanship of Paul Volcker the Federal Reserve would bring inflation down certainly was an important factor explaining the upturn of the dollar late in 1980, two years before the U.S. economy turned up from the recession. But it is difficult to avoid the conclusion that the dollar's rise also had something to do with the election of Ronald Reagan, that it was a vote of confidence of the market for the incoming conservative administration. This view is perfectly compatible with the widely accepted proposition that triple-digit budget deficits caused by the tax cuts of 1981 produced the strong dollar by driving up interest rates, which led to a huge net capital inflow. The strong dollar, in turn, stimulates imports and restrains exports; in other words, it creates a trade deficit. There is still another way in which the government deficit increased the trade deficit. The budget deficits resulting from tax cuts in 1981 and 1982 undoubtedly had a stimulating effect on the U.S. economy. The vigorous cyclical recovery of the U.S. economy, which started in November 1982 in conjunction with the sluggishness of Western Europe and the weak market for U.S. exports in debt-ridden Latin America, would have worsened the trade balance even if high interest rates had not attracted foreign capital and the dollar had not gone up. But there can be no doubt that the strong dollar was by far the most important cause of the trade deficit.

The U.S. economy from 1980 to 1985 has two baffling features. First, it is paradoxical that huge budget deficits—and trade deficits—should accompany strong currency. In innumerable cases, both in this country and elsewhere, in developed and developing countries, large budget deficits have been associated with inflation, flight of capital, and a more or less rapid decline of the currency in the foreign exchange market. Why was it different in the United States? The main reason surely is that the Federal Reserve managed to contain inflation in a period of vigorous cyclical expansion. Sound monetary policy and the credibility of the Fed's policy to hold the line against inflation were and are essential to maintain the confidence of foreign (and domestic) investors in the dollar. If the policy changed or the credibility of the Fed to stick to it eroded, the picture would change rapidly.

A second baffling feature of the period is that inflation declined. Business cycle upswings are usually associated with rising rates of inflation. Why was it different in the 1980s? The strong dollar certainly was important, because it reduced prices of imported goods and put a damper on export prices. Later, the collapse of the oil price was an anti-inflationary factor. Perhaps some credit should also be given to structural reforms and deregulation of industries, such as airlines and trucking.

These developments were influenced, as noted, by the strong performance of the U.S. economy in the 1980s, which contrasted with the sluggishness of Western Europe. The U.S. economy has created many millions of new jobs while employment in Europe has been stagnant. Unemployment is now much higher in most European countries than in the United States—9 percent in Germany, 13 percent in Britain, 15 percent in the Netherlands. All this has received much attention on both sides of the Atlantic.[15]

Analysis of the stagnation and high unemployment of the European economies has produced two alternative interpretations or explanations— a macroeconomic-Keynesian one and a microeconomic-classical one. The Keynesian one attributes the high unemployment to a deficiency of aggregate demand and assumes that it is widespread. The obvious cure is increasing aggregate demand by monetary-fiscal expansion.[16] The Keynesian interpretation seems to underlie the administration's policy of asking the Europeans to stimulate growth by expansionary measures.[17]

The microeconomic-classical interpretation regards the high European unemployment as structural and spotty due to inflexibilities, rigidities, and immobilities, especially in the labor market; concretely, it is attributable to overregulation of industries, overgenerous welfare programs, high unemployment benefits, a vast "social safety net" protecting workers and firms from losses caused by changes in demand and supply. As a consequence, the strength of the labor unions in Europe is much greater than in the United States. The result is that in nationally and (despite the Common Market) internationally fragmented labor markets, wages are too high for full employment. The high cost of these policies has led to oppressively high taxes in general and to extremely high marginal tax rates in particular.

All this is compounded by the fact that the regulations and restrictions differ from country to country, which sharply limits the scope of the Common Market. The United States enjoys the immense advantage of a real free-trade area of continental size with free mobility of capital and entrepreneurship and considerable mobility of labor. Europe cannot match that despite the Common Market. The European handicap is all the more serious because transportation, communications, electric power, airlines, railroads, telephones, and telegraph are operated by government enterprises that often are inefficient, but in any case are impervious to competition. In the United States airlines compete with each other and with railroads, buses, and trucks throughtout the country.

In the two papers cited earlier, Arthur Burns and Herbert Giersch describe the contrast between the United States and Europe in great detail, and Giersch shows that in Germany the situation has sharply deteriorated over the past fifteen or twenty years. This can be expressed by saying that in Europe the level of "natural" unemployment has sharply risen in the past fifteen to twenty years and is now much higher than in the United States.

Some counterfactual theorizing will be useful. Suppose that in 1980 the international monetary system had been one of fixed exchanges. Even more capital would have flowed into the United States than under floating because there would have been no exchange risk if the fixed rates were credible (gold standard), or if the exchange rates were "fixed but adjustable" (Bretton Woods): the investors would have known that the currency of a country that loses reserves is likely to be devalued and that the currency of a country that gains reserves is likely to be upvalued. Europe would have lost reserves and would have experienced intense deflationary pressure. The United States would have gained reserves and suffered inflation if it followed the rule of the game. The outcome surely would have been a breakdown of the system of fixed exchange rates, probably after fruitless attempts to stop the capital flow by more-or-less tight controls. Such a breakdown would have been a most disturbing event; the consequence would have been a sharp slowdown of the economy or a full-blown recession.

The outcome would have been the same if in 1980 a system of target zones had been in operation. The dollar would have hit the upper limit of the zone. Market participants would have known that the dollar could only go up, and speculators would have had a field day. The authorities would have no choice but to shift the zone and perhaps to widen it, demonstrating that his approach is no better than the parvalue (Bretton Woods) system.[18]

My conclusion is that we were lucky to enter the 1980s with floating exchange rates.

The sharp rise of the dollar is now often portrayed as a gigantic market failure. Some critics have gone so far as to say that the grossly overvalued dollar has cost the U.S. economy millions of jobs and has cut the growth rate in half. This is an enormous exaggeration. Some jobs have been lost in manufacturing, but over the whole period millions of jobs have been added.

Up to a point in 1984 when the market did overshoot, the package of a strong dollar, capital inflow, and trade deficits was an indispensable prop for U.S. prosperity. But contrary to what supply siders had promised, tax cuts did not generate sufficient savings to finance both government deficits and private investments. If the dollar had not gone up, say because investors lacked confidence in the dollar, interest rates would have gone much higher, and government borrowing would have crowded out private investment, which would have aborted the expansion.

To avoid being misunderstood, let me say that I did not then and do not now object to the tax cuts or to the budget deficits in the early 1980s. On the contrary, I think they were part of a very good policy designed to get the United States out of the severe recession. I would suggest only that there can be too much of a good thing.[19]

My overall conclusion is that the strong dollar was a good thing for the United States until some time in 1984. Furthermore, there can be no doubt that the U.S. trade deficit has been highly beneficial for the rest of the world, developed as well as less developed, for the U.S. economy was the locomotive that pulled the world economy out of the recession.

The Declining Dollar—March 1985 to . . .

We have seen that the sharp appreciation of the dollar after 1980 was a rational and highly beneficial response to the serious problem posed by the huge budget deficits. But with the benefit of hindsight a case can be made for the proposition that the appreciation of the dollar went too far in 1984; in other words, the market overshot in 1984.

The dollar reached its high point in February 1985. Then it declined rapidly. What caused the decline? There were, I believe, no powerful external shocks that would explain the turnaround of the dollar in February—March 1985. The shift in administration policy came later, and there was no sharp decline in the volume of capital inflow. It is true that there were large interventions by central banks, by the Federal Reserve, and by the central banks of other Group of Ten countries.

Between January 21 and March 1, 1985, about $10 billion were sold against D-marks, yen, and some other currencies. This sum is not negligible, but it is difficult to believe that the interventions by themselves would have brought about the downturn of the dollar. This becomes clear if we apply the modern asset-theoretic approach, also called the "portfolio adjustment" approach, to the determination of exchange rates—a stock theory rather than a flow theory, which formerly was popular. The relevant stock is that of internationally traded financial assets denominated in U.S. dollars and other major currencies.

For details of the theory see the chapter in this volume by Jacob Dreyer. I confine myself to two remarks. First, in today's highly developed international capital markets—Eurodollar and Euroyen markets, which developed after most important currencies became convertible in the 1950s, with thousands of sophisticated market participants, banks, corporate treasurers, and speculators of different kinds—in this environment the asset-theoretic approach surely is the right one. Second, whatever the precise definition of the relevant types of assets, the size of the stock undoubtedly is enormous, amounting to trillions of dollars. Compared with this, $10 billion sold by central banks is insignificant, unless these sales are part of a clear and explicit shift in policy, as happened later on in 1985.

A pronounced shift in the general outlook for the U.S. economy seems to have caused the market to change. Up to February 1985 the general outlook was optimistic. Then in March a more pessimistic reassessment of the outlook took place. The economy seemed to be slowing down and interest rates began to decline.

Discounting the importance of the interventions for the explanation of the downturn of the dollar in early 1985 does not mean that interventions in the foreign exchange market never have much effect. If the authorities make it clear that the interventions are part of a basic shift in policy, the situation is different. That is precisely what happened later in 1985 when the Treasury team of James Baker and Richard Darman abandoned the passive, laissez-faire balance-of-payments or exchange rate policy of their predecessors and developed an increasingly activist, not to say aggressive, interventionist policy of talking the dollar down and later pushing it down by interventions in the foreign exchange market.

The major motive of the change in policy was the fear of a protectionist explosion. That this fear is not groundless was demonstrated by the Democratic trade bill passed in 1986 by a large bipartisan majority in the House—an unmitigated monstrosity that President Reagan accurately described as an antitrade bill.

The first result of the new balance-of-payments policy was, as we have seen, the September 1985 decision of the Group of Five to push the dollar down by internationally concerted interventions in the foreign exchange market. The decision was unexpected and caused considerable turbulence in the market. The announcement itself pushed the dollar down sharply, before any of the central banks intervened. Private demand for dollars has fluctuated greatly since then because the new activist policy has forced market participants to speculate not only about the prospects of the economy and possible changes in domestic monetary and fiscal policy, but also about the intentions of the authorities concerning interventions.

A vivid description of the interaction of these various forces and the resulting shifts in the foreign exchange market can be found in the periodic reports of the Federal Reserve Bank of New York on Treasury and Federal Reserve foreign exchange operations. Intervention sales of dollars by the Federal Reserve and foreign central banks amounted to over $10 billion during the first two or three months after the September meeting of the Group of Five. According to the latest reports there seem to have been hardly any interventions in the first quarter of 1986.

Parallel with its drive to reform the international monetary system through concerted interventions in the foreign exchange market, the administration has stepped up its push for international coordination of "economic and monetary policies." The purpose is to avoid or minimize the emergence of international imbalances such as the large U.S. trade deficits and the Japanese and German surpluses. The reduction of the discount rate by the Federal Reserve and the German and Japanese central banks in March and April 1986 has been hailed as the "first step to international coordination."

It was generally assumed that at the Tokyo Summit in May 1986 international monetary reform and concrete proposals for coordination of policy would be the main economic topics. If they were, the official Tokyo Economic Declaration does not reveal anything about it. The seven-page Declaration is long on generalities and short on specifics. The summiteers congratulate themselves on what has been achieved since the last economic summit but recognize that "they would still face a number of difficult challenges," that "noninflationary growth is the biggest" objective, and that it "must be reinforced by policies which encourage job creation. . . It is important that there should be close and continuous coordination of policy among the seven Summit countries." The Group of Seven is the Group of Five plus Canada and Italy. The heads of state "welcome" the recent decision of the Group of Five "to change the pattern of exchange rates and to lower interest rates," but "agree that additional measures should be taken to ensure that procedures for effective coordination of international economic policy are strengthened further." What these additional measures might be is not stated, but "the Heads of State agree to form a new Group of Seven Finance Ministers" and the Group of Five is "requested" to include Canada and Italy in its meetings whenever "the international monetary system or related measures are discussed."The ministers of finance of the Group of Seven are requested "to review their economic objectives and forecasts at least once a year . . . to ensure their mutual compatibility . . . taking into account indicators such as GNP growth rates, inflation rates, interest rates," and several other generally used economic variables. The heads of state "reaffirm the undertaking at the 1982 Versailles Summit to cooperate with the International Monetary Fund in strengthening multilateral surveillance . . . and invite Finance Ministers and Central Banks to focus first and foremost on underlying policy fundamentals, while reaffirming the 1983 Williamsburg commitment to intervene in exchange markets when to do so would be helpful."

The heads of state warned against the dangers of "persistent protectionism" and made the usual pious pleas for "opening the international trading and investment system." Then they went home and did the opposite. The United States, for example, imposed a stiff import duty (35 percent) on Canadian cedar shingles. This step did, however, have a beneficial side effect: it gave the Canadian government an opportunity to teach our congressional protectionists a lesson by retaliating promptly and forcefully, slapping a stiff tariff on American computer parts, Christmas trees, tea bags, periodicals, and several other items.

Given that the IMF has for a long time been engaged in multilateral surveillance, that ministers of finance and central bankers frequently meet in the IMF, OECD, BIS (Bank for International Settlements), in the Group of Five, and Ten, and on other occasions—given all that, the creation of still another overlapping group can hardly be regarded as a great achievement.

In the light of recent developments, what are the prospects for reform of the international monetary system? As noted above, President Reagan in his State of the Union message in February 1986 asked Secretary Baker "to determine if the nations of the world should convene to discuss the role and relationship of our currencies. We must never again permit wild currency swings to cripple our farmers and other exporters."

This was widely interpreted to mean that it may be possible and desirable to hold another Bretton Woods type of international conference for the purpose of returning to some sort of fixed exchange rates. Such a proposal has been made by the French government.

The Bretton Woods conference was held in 1944 during the War. It was run by the United States and Britain. Today the power structure is entirely different. There is what may be called the Group of Three (the United States, Japan, and Western Germany); the Group of Five (the Group of Three plus Britain and France); the Group of Seven (the Group of Five plus Canada and Italy); and the Group of Ten (the Group of Seven plus Holland, Belgium, Sweden, and Switzerland). In addition, there are the less-developed countries organized in the Group of Twenty-four.

It is not surprising that Secretary Baker said he does not think that at this time "the United States needs to call an international monetary conference to consider changing the present floating exchange-rate system; instead an attempt should be made to 'refine' the international economic policy-coordinating machinery that they agreed upon at the Tokyo economic summit in May." He also said that the "finance ministers still hadn't agreed on what they might want in any new monetary system,"[20] to which I would add that they are unlikely to agree in the foreseeable future—for the following reason.

It is hardly necessary to explain at great length why a restoration of the gold standard is impossible. Who would want to entrust the future of the international monetary system to the mercies of South Africa and the Soviet Union, the two largest gold producers? Stable but adjustable exchange rates à la Bretton Woods is, as we have seen, very vulnerable to destabilizing speculation. The basic difficulty of any fixed-rate system is that it requires a high degree of mutual policy adjustment or international policy coordination, which in the present-day world can be achieved only in exceptional cases. The vaunted European monetary system (EMS) is no exception. It is a Bretton Woods–type system of stable but adjustable exchange rates, very vulnerable to disruptive capital flows. Frequent realignments of exchange rates are preceded and accompanied by destabilizing speculation, which requires tight exchange control in some participating countries—in France, for example.

Early this year, the EMS was shaken by a severe crisis, which underscores the conclusion that markets do a better job than governments in setting exchange rates. The row between two members of the EMS, France and West Germany, has provided a striking example of the dangers of politicizing exchange rates and of the unworkability of a Bretton Woods–type international monetary system.

It was not surprising that the French franc came under intense pressure after Prime Minister Jacques Chirac capitulated to student demonstration, thereby effectively telling trade unions and other pressure groups that street demonstrations and violence pay. When the franc fell, Chirac attacked the German authorities. "This is a mark crisis," he said, "not a franc crisis. Let the German authorities do what is necessary."[21] What is regarded as necessary is a realignment of exchange rates and a little inflation in Germany. The realignment was achieved after hectic negotiations and a thirteen-hour emergency meeting of the ministers of finance on January 11, 1987. The value of the German mark and the Dutch guilder increased by 3 percent and that of the Belgian franc by 2 percent against the other members of the EMS. This can only be described as a token realignment, which will make hardly a dent in the underlying disequilibrium.

The other requirement, a little inflation in Germany, was called for in an editorial of the *Wall Street Journal*, "Waiting for Bonn:" "What Germany needs is strong, domestic-led growth, which it's not going to get until it stops fixating on its inflation rate—near zero—and starts feeding some marks to its economy and advancing its tax cuts."[22] The German Socialist party, the left-wing opposition to Chancellor Helmut Kohl's conservative government, ought to be grateful for the support it gets from conservative governments and newspapers abroad.

All this caused confusion and much turbulence in the foreign exchange markets. The dollar depreciated sharply against the mark and the yen despite the Baker-Miyazawa agreement. Foreign central banks bought many billion dollars to hold the line. According to rumors and press reports (which gained credibility through belated and half-hearted official denials), the administration wanted the dollar to decline in order to bring pressure on Germany and Japan to stimulate their economies. It is true that sufficient inflation in the strong currency surplus countries, especially Germany and Japan, would let the deficit countries, the United States and France, off the hook. But it would be like infecting the healthy instead of curing the sick. Worldwide inflation is not a sound basis for the world economy.

It is instructive to reflect for a moment on why we never hear about balance-of-payments problems of different regions of large countries, say the United States, despite the occurrence from time to time of serious regional disturbances. The most important reason is that monetary policy is the same throughout the United States, ruling out the significant differential inflation that often occurs between sovereign states. Also very important are perfect mobility of capital and much higher interregional mobility of labor that can be found between sovereign states anywhere in the world, even in the European Common Market. Still another factor, which has been mentioned in the literature, is the common fiscal system. If a region in the United States is experiencing a serious disturbance, it automatically gets some relief from the reduction of its tax liabilities to the federal government and possibly some contribution from the government through unemployment benefits and the like.

I conclude from all this that floating should continue, and I am convinced that it will, for the following reason: a return to fixed exchange rates would require international agreement on the rates that should be fixed. It is not inconceivable, but it is practically impossible that a meaningful agreement on the pattern of exchange rates could be reached in the Group of Seven or even in the Group of Five. By "meaningful," I mean a set of exchange rates that the participants undertake to defend.

Consider the simplest but most important case: the exchange value of the dollar relative to a few major currencies. There is no agreement among policy makers and experts on whether the dollar has declined sufficiently to eliminate or sharply reduce the current imbalances—U.S. deficits and German and Japanese surpluses. The Germans and Japanese think it has declined sufficiently. Federal Reserve chairman Volcker agrees. Other experts, inside and outside the administration, believe that it has to decline more. Moreover, we have seen that no agreement exists even on the question of how much the dollar has already declined overall.

Specific exchange rates should not be discussed in the glare of widely advertised meetings of the Groups of Five, Seven, Ten, the economic summits, or the annual meetings of the IMF and the World Bank. Exchange rates can be quietly discussed in the OECD, the IMF, the BIS, or in bilateral meetings.

A good example is the famous agreement between the United States and Japan, the Group of Two as it was dubbed in October 1986. After a secret meeting in San Francisco, Secretary of the Treasury Baker and the Japanese Minister of Finance Kiichi Miyazawa announced the terms of the agreement: The Bank of Japan reduced the discount rate from 3½ percent to 3 percent, and the Japanese government would submit to the Diet a "supplementary budget" providing 3.6 trillion yen (about $22 billion at the rate of 160 yen per dollar) additional expenditures spread over several years, and a proposal to reduce marginal tax rates for personal and corporate income to stimulate investment. These reforms are parts of the "Miyazawa Plan" that had been proposed in 1986. Mr. Baker states that "for its part the United States remains fully committed" to reducing the budget deficit and to resisting protectionist pressures. Most important, the ministers agreed that "the dollar-yen rate is now broadly consistent with the underlying fundamentals." For the time being, therefore, the United States will not press Japan to let the yen go still higher. But the dollar-yen rate has not yet been fixed; the current relative stability cannot even be regarded as a big step toward a fixed rate. The agreement is that the rate *now* is consistent with the fundamentals. There is no indication that an agreement exists on precisely what the fundamentals are. Whatever they are, they are bound to change over time. To settle on a fixed rate, there would have to be an agreement on how to determine a change in the fundamentals and a commitment to defend the rate by interventions in the foreign exchange market. But the usual sterilized interventions that leave the money supply unchanged would not do. It would require stronger medicine: nonsterilized interventions. It is a long way to a fixed rate!

I repeat therefore: Floating should and will continue. For the foreseeable future a return to fixed rates is impossible. If the United States and Japan cannot agree on a fixed rate, how can an agreement be reached in a wide circle? Free markets do a better job than governments in setting exchange rates. True, markets do make mistakes. But in competitive markets mistakes are quickly corrected. It is in the nature of the political process that governments are slow to admit a mistake and that they delay reversing themselves, which makes the correction when it finally must be made all the more painful.

International Policy Coordination

In the past two years international policy coordination has once again been all the rage, with the United States in the driver's seat. In practice the principal concrete manifestation of the new drive for policy coordination has been the increasingly urgent and impatient American demand that Germany and Japan stimulate their economies in order to reduce their trade surpluses and the U.S. trade deficits. More on that presently. First it will be well to review very briefly the historical roots of international policy coordination or cooperation—the two terms are often used interchangeably.

Barry Eichengreen recently reminded us that early in the interwar period—not to go further back—proposals were made to improve the working of the international monetary system by policy coordination.[23] One of the resolutions of the Genoa Conference (1922) says, for example: "Measures of currency reform will be facilitated if the practice of continuous cooperation among central banks . . . can be developed. Such cooperation of central banks . . . would provide opportunities of coordinating their policy, without hampering the freedom of the several banks."[24]

Later in the 1920s the Bank for International Settlements (BIS) was established in Basle, Switzerland. Its original purpose was to manage the transfer of German reparations to the victors in World War I. It survived the Great Depression of the 1930s and even the Second World War—a monument to the staying power of international bureaucracies. It developed into an international institution for consultation, cooperation, and coordination of monetary policy. Formally it is a European institution, the club of the major European central banks, but its monthly meetings are regularly attended by a governor of the Federal Reserve System and by a high official of the Bank of Japan.

After the end of World War II, European economic cooperation and coordination received a strong push from the Marshall Plan. A large international bureaucracy was set up in Paris. This, too, managed to enlarge and to perpetuate itself. After several metamorphoses it became the OECD (Organization of Economic Cooperation and Development), representing the industrial countries, including the United States, Canada, and Japan.

It would lead too far to discuss all the other international agencies that are directly or tangentially involved in policy coordination; they include the International Monetary Fund, the United Nations and its numerous offshoots, the European Economic Commission, the Economic Commission for Latin America (ECLA), the United Nations Conference on Trade and Development (UNCTAD), etc.

The drive for international coordination of policies again went into high gear with the Tokyo economic summit of May 1986. As mentioned, the heads of state instructed the ministers of finance of the Group of Seven to meet "at least once a year" to review "the mutual compatibility" of their policy objectives and forecasts, "taking into account indicators such as GNP growth rates, inflation rates, interest rates, unemployment rates, fiscal deficit ratios, current account and trade balances, monetary growth rates, reserves, and exchange rates."

The ball has been picked up by the Interim Committee to the IMF. The April 1986 Interim Committee communiqué refers to "the possible usefulness of indicators in implementing Fund surveillance" (paragraph 6). The committee asked the executive board to explore "the formulation of a set of objective indicators related to policy actions and economic performance, which might help to identify a need for discussion of countries' policies."[25]

On September 27, 1986, just before the annual meeting of the IMF and the World Bank, the ministers of finance of Group of Seven met in Washington, D.C. "to conduct the first exercise of multilateral surveillance pursuant to the Tokyo Economic Summit Declaration of the heads of State of May 6, 1986."[26] The one-page statement is a bland document, evidently a compromise which, according to press reports, was reached after spirited and somewhat acrimonious discussions:

> The Ministers reviewed recent economic objectives and forecasts collectively, using a range of economic indicators, with a particular view to examining their mutual compatibility. The Ministers noted that progress had been made in promoting steady, noninflationary growth. The Ministers also noted, however, that the present scale of some current-account imbalances cannot be sustained. The exchange rate changes since last year are making an important contribution toward redressing these imbalances. The Ministers agreed that cooperative efforts need to be intensified in order to reduce the imbalances in the context of an open, growing world economy. They noted, in this connection, that economic growth in surplus countries was improving, but that such growth will need to be sustained. Countries with major deficits must follow policies that will foster significant reductions in their external deficits; those countries committed themselves, among other things, to make further progress in reducing their budget deficits in order to free resources to the external sector. The Ministers agreed that the policies of all countries would be formulated with the following objectives in mind: To follow sound monetary policies supporting non-inflationary growth; to continue the process of removing structural rigidities in order to increase the long-term production potential of their economies; and to continue efforts to resist protectionist pressures.

The vagueness of this statement underscores what was said above—that so far the only concrete attempt at international policy coordination has been the insistent U.S. pressure on Germany and Japan to stimulate their economies.

The current drive for international policy coordination, including U.S. pressure on Germany and Japan, is a replay of what happened in the late 1970s. The surrounding circumstances were somewhat different, but then as now the United States had what were considered enormous and intolerable trade deficits—$31 billion in 1977, $34 billion in 1978—and the policy response was the same: The surplus countries, mainly Germany and Japan, were urged by the United States to stimulate their economies. This was called the "locomotive theory," which was later expanded to the "convoy theory," a proposal for coordinated fiscal-monetary expansion in a large number of countries.[27] In an extreme form this approach was put forward by H. J. Witteveen.[28] This scenario called for real growth in the United States to average 4 percent a year from 1978 to 1980, compared with 4.5 percent in 1978; 7.5 percent real growth a year in Japan from 1978 to 1980, compared with 5.7 percent in 1978; and 4.5 percent in Germany from 1978 to 1980, compared with 3.1 percent in 1978. The consequence of these changes in the relative growth rates of the three countries, and of other changes of similar magnitude for other industrial countries, would have been to reduce the U.S. trade deficit by $1.8 billion, the Japanese surplus by $5.7 billion, and the German surplus by $4.8 billion. Herbert Stein very aptly called this approach "international fine tuning." It is not surprising that it was not implemented. I will, therefore, confine myself to a discussion of the special case—U.S. pressure on Germany and Japan to stimulate their economies.

In one important respect the economic situation in the late 1970s was very different from what it is in the 1980s. It will be recalled that an inflationary boom escalated consumer price increases from about 5 percent per year in 1976 to almóst 20 percent in 1980, because the Carter administration immediately embarked on an expansionary policy. No wonder that the dollar was weak despite large interventions in the foreign exchange market. Under these circumstances if Germany and Japan had acceded to American demands for stimulation of their economies by monetary fiscal expansion, the result would have been more rapid worldwide inflation followed by a more severe worldwide recession.

In the 1980s the U.S. economy took a different course. After the stabilization crisis of 1981–1982 the economy took off on a vigorous expansion, which passed its fourth anniversary in November 1986. Unlike earlier cyclical expansions, the current one has been marked by declining rather than rising rates of inflation. But the huge trade deficits still dominate the scene, and the United States continues to press Germany and Japan to stimulate their economies. Addressing the annual meeting of the IMF and the World Bank on September 30, 1986, in Washington, President Reagan said faster growth "is the key" to the major problems of the world economy. The United States has done its part. U.S. economic recovery has pulled the world out of the recession; now "other industrial nations must also contribute their share for world recovery and adopt more growth oriented policies." Secretary Baker still insists that there are only two solutions to the global trade imbalance. Either the other industrial countries must grow faster or the dollar has to decline further to make U.S. industries competitive. Since the famous U.S.-Japanese agreement in the Baker-Miyazawa accord of October 31, 1986, U.S. criticism is now addressed mainly to Germany. The official criticism has been echoed in sharper forms in the media. Anthony M. Solomon, former president of the New York Federal Reserve Bank, wrote in early 1986,

> Now that exchange rates are on a more reasonable course and oil prices are declining, there is every likelihood the inflation rate in Germany will be negative in 1986. Clearly, that ought to offer immense opportunity for German authorities to provide stimulus to lower the current-account surplus, to lower unemployment and to contribute to a better balance in the world economy without threatening any outbreak of inflation. Instead, from German officials we get stonewalling because the economic thinking that pervades is every bit as ideological, every bit as divorced from the realities of the time, as we have seen on occasions in the United States in the past five years. That ideology is constructing a seemingly impenetrable intellectual roadblock to the execution of necessary policy changes.[29]

All this is hardly convincing. The conservative German government of Helmut Kohl would like nothing better than to approach the 1987 election with rising output and employment—all the more so since they are criticized by the left-wing opposition and the labor unions with the same largely Keynesian arguments that the conservative U.S. administration uses. They are afraid, however, of giving the impression that they have caved in to American pressures.

The American policy suffers from two weaknesses: first, reproaching Germany and Japan for their large export surpluses ignores the fact that the U.S. external deficits represent an inflow of foreign capital, which the U.S. economy still needs because domestic savings are insufficient to finance both private investments and huge budget deficits. Second, several econometric studies have concluded that the effects of even a substantial increase in the rate of growth in Germany and Japan on the U.S. external deficit would be minimal. The *IMF World Economic Outlook* concludes:

> Unfortunately, the effects on the U.S. current account of shifts in growth rates abroad appear to be relatively small. It is unlikely that a 1 percentage point increase in domestic growth in Japan and the Federal Republic of Germany (maintained over a three-year period and with allowance for induced effects on growth in other countries) would alter the U.S. trade balance by more than $5–10 billion.[30]

Note that the study makes allowance for indirect effects and that a rise of real growth by one percentage point, say from 3½ to 4½ percent, over three years is quite substantial.

This does not deny that faster noninflationary growth would be desirable or that in the short run pressure on the United States would be alleviated if the Germans and Japanese embarked on a highly inflationary expansion. What it does mean is that in order to bring down the external deficit the U.S. budget deficit must be reduced. This is an American responsibility, which cannot be shifted to other countries.

Now let us assume that the dollar has declined far enough to shrink the external deficit sharply; or assume that expansion abroad has reduced the U.S. deficit, which implies that capital inflow from abroad has stopped. Interest rates will rise and, if the budget deficit has not been sharply reduced and domestic savings have not increased, public sector borrowing will crowd out private sector investment. This underscores the decisive importance of the budget deficits. The September 1986 statement of the Group of Seven put it succinctly: "Countries with major deficits committed themselves to make further progress in reducing their budget deficits, *in order to free resources to the external sector*." Of course, how to reduce the budget deficit sufficiently fast without causing a recession is a difficult problem.

There is another aspect of the dollar problem that also underscores the importance of speedy action on the budget deficit. The U.S. economy is in its fifth year of expansion—one of the longest in the history of business cycles. Naturally, it shows signs of slowing down. The Federal Reserve has been under increasing pressure to reduce interest rates to prevent a slide into a recession. The Fed has insisted that it cannot go much further unless Germany and Japan go along, because there is danger that when the interest differential between the United States on the one hand, and Germany and Japan on the other, shrinks, capital inflow will stop or a net outflow will develop, causing a sharp decline of the dollar.

I think that the possibility of such a development cannot be excluded. But I still believe that an irrational stampede of investors at home and abroad out of dollars, as some experts have been predicting for the past three years, is unlikely, because the market understands that in such a case central banks, the Fed, and foreign central banks would intervene, organizing a dollar rescue operation as they did in 1978. It surely would be better, however, not to let it come to that, but to attack the evil at its root by reducing the budget deficit. For two reasons, the United States cannot go on forever importing capital from abroad: first, sooner or later investors at home and abroad will become nervous if they see no change in policy, and a run on the dollar may develop; second, the service charge on the foreign debt rises rapidly. The economy will have to do without new capital from abroad and will have to develop an export surplus to service the foreign debt, implying a sizable squeeze on what is called "domestic absorption"—that is, on consumption and investment. In other words, the standard of living will be reduced below what it otherwise would be. If the trade deficit and the associated inflow of foreign capital continue for, say, two or three more years, it has been estimated that the service charge on the foreign debt may near 1 percent of GNP. This surely would not be a crushing burden, but in a sluggish economy could well trigger a recession.

Some Policy Conclusions

No modern government is indifferent to unemployment—all of them want full employment and rapid growth. Germany and Japan are no exception. But it is also true that tolerance and fear of inflation vary somewhat from country to country. Germany, for example, with its history of destructive inflation, hyperinflation after World War I, and equally damaging repressed inflation after World War II, is more fearful of inflation than the United States is.

If this is granted, it follows, I believe, that all countries should be allowed to pursue their policies as well as they can, provided they observe the rules of the game as laid down by the IMF and the GATT. Currencies should be freely convertible at fixed or flexible exchange rates; there should be no manipulation of exchange rates, no import restrictions on balance-of-payments grounds, and the like. Let the Europeans struggle with their structural unemployment; if the Germans, the Dutch, or the Belgians think that they need two-digit unemployment to keep inflation at bay, it is their problem, not ours.

This does not mean, however, that countries should never criticize each other or should refrain from giving advice. Far from it. All governments make mistakes, all can learn from the failures and successes of others, and they should welcome friendly criticism and advice. But this is best done quietly in organizations such as the OECD, the IMF, and the BIS, or in bilateral negotiations. The superiority of quiet diplomacy has been strikingly demonstrated by the famous U.S.-Japanese agreement reached by Secretary Baker and Japanese Minister of Finance Miyazawa.

This approach is surely much better than criticizing each other publicly. Threatening other countries with a further decline of the dollar—"using the dollar as a weapon," as it was put in the press—may serve domestic political objectives but is internationally counterproductive, because no country likes doing things under pressure from abroad. The politicization of exchange rates is a dangerous game. It has caused much turbulence in the foreign exchange markets. Free markets do a better job of setting exchange rates than governments do.

Notes

An abbreviated version of the first part of this chapter appeared in *The AEI Economist*, "The International Monetary System," American Enterprise Institute, Washington, D.C. July 1986.

1. *Economic Review*, Federal Reserve Bank of Dallas, September 1986.

2. *Economic Report*, Manufacturers Hanover Trust, September 1986.

3. *Economic Review*, Federal Reserve Bank of Atlanta, June/July 1986.

4. The phrase "benign neglect" was first used by Gottfried Haberler and Thomas Willett, *A Strategy for U.S. Balance of Payments Policy* (Washington, D.C.: American Enterprise Institute, 1971), p. 15. Although the meaning was carefully explained, it was often misunderstood as neglecting or excusing the cause of the balance-of-payments troubles, namely high inflation. On that issue, see Gottfried Haberler, *U.S. Balance of Payments Policy and the International Monetary System*, AEI Reprint No. 9, American Enterprise Institute, Washington, D.C. 1973.

5. Economic Report of the President (Washington, D.C., 1984), p. 50. It is interesting that the Report for neither 1985 nor 1986 has any discussion of the exchange rate problem.

6. The product of protectionist pressure in the 99th Congress was the omnibus trade bill, H. R. 4800. Briefly summarizing its 450 pages is difficult, but the following examples indicate the flavor. Any country with a bilateral nonpetroleum trade surplus of more than $3 billion would have to cut trade by 10 percent each year. Additional industry-specific sanctions deal with a host of products including, among others, knitting needles, bicycle speedometers, steel, coal, agriculture, plums, and services. The current discretion of the executive branch in dealing with unfair trading cases referred by the International Trade Commission would also be removed. Overall, H.R. 4800 would strike a devastating blow to world trade and economic liberalism.

Another protectionist effort was the Textile and Apparel Trade Enforcement Act (1985), which includes copper, shoes, artificial fibers, dolls and, for good measure, fishing tackles to attract votes in Congress. It passed both houses of Congress with a large bipartisan majority, but the House of Representatives failed by a few votes to override the presidential veto. The act would have cut back textile imports from most countries to 1 percent of the growth of the U.S. market.

7. Measured on the so-called liquidity basis, which was then widely used. For details, see Gottfried Haberler and Thomas D. Willett, *U.S. Balance-of-Payments Policies and International Monetary Reform: A Critical Analysis* (Washington, D.C.: American Enterprise Institute, 1968), and Gottfried Haberler and Thomas D. Willett, *A Strategy for U.S. Balance of Payments Policy*. (Washington, D.C.: American Enterprise Institute, 1971).

8. See Morris Goldstein, "The Exchange Rate System: Lessons of the Past and Options for the Future," Occasional Paper 30, International Monetary Fund, Washington, D.C., July 1984, pp. 3–4.

9. *International Monetary Reform: Documents of the Committee of Twenty,* International Monetary Fund, Washington, D.C., 1974, p. 8.

10. Quoted by Otmar Emminger, then president of the German Bundesbank. See *The International Monetary System under Stress. What Can We Learn from the Past?*, AEI Reprint No. 112, Washington, D.C., May 1980, also appears in the conference volume *The International Monetary System: A Time of Turbulence,* in Jacob Dreyer, Gottfried Haberler, and Thomas Willett, eds. (Washington, D.C.: American Enterprise Institute, 1982).

11. See my paper, "Oil, Inflation, Recession and the International Monetary System," *Journal of Energy and Development* 1, no. 2 (Spring 1976), pp. 177–90, reprinted in *Selected Essays of Gottfried Haberler,* Anthony Y. C. Koo, ed. (Cambridge, Mass.: MIT Press, 1985).

12. In Switzerland the pains of disinflation were alleviated by the buffer of "guest workers" from abroad. But this is only a part of the explanation.

13. All these arguments against floating have been used by the socialist government of France of President Francois Mitterand, which has proposed a Bretton Woods type of conference to return to some sort of fixed exchanges. It is not clear yet whether the conservative government of Jacques Chirac has changed the French position.

14. See his widely quoted paper *The Dollar's Borrowed Strength,* Group of Thirty, Occasional Papers, No. 19, 1985, p. 3.

15. See, for example, Erich Grundlach and Klaus-Dieter Schmidt, "Das amerikanische Beschäftigungswunder: Was sich daraus lernen lässt" ("The American Employment Miracle: What Can We Learn from It?") Kiel Discussion Paper No. 109, Institut für Weltwirtschaft an der Universität Kiel, West Germany, July 1985; Stephen Marris, "Why Europe's Recovery is Lagging?" in *Europe Magazine of the European Community,* March–April 1984; Herbert Giersch, "Eurosclerosis," Kiel Institute of World Economics, Discussion Paper No. 112, University of Kiel, West Germany, October 1985; and Arthur Burns, "The Economic Sluggishness of Western Europe" in *The United States and Germany: A Vital Partnership* (New York: Council on Foreign Relations, 1986).

16. Some analysts would say that what is needed is a change in the monetary-fiscal mix. In my opinion this has been greatly overdone. At any rate it complicates matters greatly and makes the problem unsuitable for international coordination. Concretely, it is one thing to tell the Europeans to stimulate growth by monetary-fiscal expansion and an entirely different thing to tell them to change their monetary-fiscal mix. This would immediately lead to the further question of whether the fiscal stimulus should be brought about by lowering taxes or by increasing expenditures.

17. It is true that some officials (not to mention supply siders outside the government) sometimes urge Europeans to follow the U.S. example—to reduce taxes, deregulate industry, etc. This is good advice, but it does not lend itself to being laid down in international agreements.

18. As far as I know, "references rates" and "reference zones" were first

proposed by Wilfred Ethier and Arthur L. Bloomfield in their pamphlet, *Managing the Managed Float*, Essays in International Finance No. 112, Princeton, N.J.: 1975. The authors claim that the reference zone system is superior to the parvalue system. In my paper, "The International Monetary System after Jamaica and Manila," in William Fellner, ed., *Contemporary Economic Problems* (Washington, D.C.: American Enterprise Institute, 1977), pp. 262–264, I gave reasons why I cannot accept that claim. The theory of target zones has been further developed by John Williamson in several important papers. See especially John Williamson, "The Exchange Rate System," *Policy Analyses in International Economics* No. 5 (Washington, D.C.: 1983), Institute for International Economics, and "Exchange Rate Flexibility, Target Zones, and Policy Coordination," *World Development*, October 1986. The latest refinement is that the zones should have "soft buffers," that is to say, that the authorities are not obligated to intervene when the exchange rate leaves the zone. That brings the target zone approach close to free floating.

19. This problem cannot be further pursued in this paper. Nor is this the place to go into the question whether the recession was entirely the fault of monetary mismanagement by the Fed, as extreme monetarists and extreme supply siders assert—strange bedfellows like two scorpions in a bottle who kill each other, leaving the intended victim unscathed!

20. *The Wall Street Journal*, December 12, 1986.

21. The *Financial Times*, London, January 7, 1987. The recent row between France and Germany is reminiscent of what happened in 1968 and 1969. Then, as now, France was shaken by violent student demonstrations and strikes, the French franc was weak, and the German mark strong. President de Gaulle's minister of finance declared, "This is not, properly speaking, a French crisis. It is an international crisis," and President de Gaulle said devaluation "would be the worst form of absurdity." The Germans were equally adamant. "An official spokesman told a news conference that the decision not to upvalue the mark was 'final, unequivocal and for eternity.' " The impasse dragged on until after de Gaulle's resignation on April 28, 1969; his successor then devalued the franc by 11.1 percent on August 8, 1969. For further details see Robert Solomon, *The International Monetary System 1945–1981* (Harper & Row, New York, 1982).

22. The *Wall Street Journal*, January 7, 1987. The editorial argues that in the past year or two Germany has had negative inflation, which permits noninflationary expansion. This argument is, however, unconvincing for two reasons: First, although it is true that the price index has slightly declined, that was due to the collapse of the oil price and a price decline of some other commodities. This anti-inflationary factor has spent its force. Second, and even more important, a monetary expansion that merely restores price stability would have an insignificant effect on the global trade imbalance. Econometric studies have shown that even a sharp increase of real GNP growth in Germany and Japan would have only a minor effect on the U.S. trade deficit. The conclusion is that expansion in Germany would have to be highly inflationary to take the heat off the dollar.

23. See Barry Eichengreen, "International Policy Coordination in Historic Perspective: A View from the Interwar Years," in Willem H. Buiter and Richard C. Marston, eds., *International Economic Policy Coordination* (Cambridge, England: Cambridge University Press, for the National Bureau of Economic Research, 1985), pp. 139–83.

24. From Resolution 3 of the Report of the Financial Commission of the Genoa Conference, 1922.

25. The proposed use of "indicators" has been hailed as a new approach and a major advance of policy making in general and of international coordination of policies in particular. In my opinion there is nothing new in this "approach"; not even the term "indicators" is new. In 1973 a report for the Committee of Twenty on Reform of the International Monetary System and Related Issues by "The Technical Group on Indicators" (under the chairmanship of Robert Solomon) discussed the use of indicators in the adjustment process (see *International Monetary Reform*, IMF, Washington, D.C., 1974), pp. 51–76. Any discussion of the state, performance, and prospects of a particular economy cannot help using economic variables.

26. Quotations from the official statement of the meeting.

27. This episode was discussed in my chapter, "Reflections on the U.S. Trade Deficit and the Floating Dollar," in William Fellner, Project Director, *Contemporary Economic Problems, 1978* (American Enterprise Institute, Washington, D.C., 1978). See especially pp. 227–30 and the Postscript, pp. 240–43. See also Herbert Stein's trenchant analysis of the whole approach in "International Coordination of Domestic Economic Policies," *The AEI Economist*, June 1978, American Enterprise Institute, Washington, D.C.

28. H. J. Witteveen, "Scenario for Coordinated Growth and Payments Adjustment," presented at the IMF meeting in Mexico, May 24, 1978.

29. Anthony M. Solomon, "Germany Puts Savings Over Jobs," *Wall Street Journal*, March 24, 1986.

30. *IMF World Economic Outlook* (Washington, D.C.: International Monetary Fund, October 1986), p. 24. Several other econometric studies, too, have reached the conclusion that faster growth in Germany and Japan has little effect on the U.S. current account. See, for example, unpublished studies by the staff of the Federal Reserve Board. See also Filles Oudiz and Jeffrey Sachs, "Macroeconomic Policy Coordination among the Industrial Economies," *Brookings Papers on Economic Activity* 1, William C. Brainard and George L. Perry, eds., The Brookings Institution, Washington, D.C., 1984; and Jeffrey A. Frankel, "The Sources of Disagreement among the International Macro Models and Implications for Policy Coordination," Working Paper No. 1925, National Bureau of Economic Research, Cambridge, Massachusetts, May 1986.

6

THE INTERNATIONAL MONETARY SYSTEM— ONCE AGAIN

Gottfried Haberler

This article updates my chapter "The International Monetary System and Proposals for International Policy Coordination," which appears in the AEI volume, *Contemporary Economic Problems: Deficits, Taxes, and Economic Adjustments (CEP)*, and then analyzes the agreement reached by six major industrialized countries in Paris on February 22, 1987.

After James Baker became secretary of the Treasury in February 1985, the Reagan administration's balance-of-payments policy took a sharp turn from a passive, laissez-faire, benign-neglect approach to an activist, interventionist one. Under Baker's predecessor, market forces were allowed to set the exchange value of the dollar. Under Baker the policy was to talk the dollar down and to push it down by internationally concerted interventions in the foreign exchange market.

The reason for the switch is well known. From 1980 to February 1985 the dollar appreciated sharply relative to all foreign currencies. The strong dollar stimulated imports and discouraged exports, producing huge trade deficits causing unemployment in export- and import-competing industries, which triggered strong protectionist pressures in Congress. Although the market had turned around and in March 1985 the dollar started on a lengthy decline, that was not immediately clear. So Secretary Baker organized the famous meeting of the Group of Five (the United States, England, France, Germany, and Japan) at the Plaza Hotel in New York, where it was decided to bring the dollar further down by concerted interventions in the foreign exchange market.

Parallel with the initiative on the monetary front, the United States has been pushing for international policy coordination. This was the main theme of the Tokyo Economic Summit in May 1986. The heads of state of seven nations (the Group of Five plus Canada and Italy) instructed their ministers of finance to meet at least once a year to check the "mutual compatibility" of their policies.

In practice, the vaunted international policy coordination has boiled down to the increasingly urgent and impatient demand by the United States that Germany and Japan stimulate their economies in order to reduce their trade surpluses and U.S. deficits, warning them that a further decline of the dollar and a protectionist explosion in the U.S. Congress would be the consequence of inaction.

The U.S. switch to an activist balance-of-payments policy reflects a fairly widespread disenchantment with floating exchange rates. Stubborn misalignments of exchange rates, especially the overvaluation of the dollar, and excessive volatility of exchange rates, are blamed on the system of floating. Actually the strong dollar and the U.S. trade deficits were not a gigantic market failure; up to a point they were a rational reaction of the markets that pulled the world economy out of the recession. The U.S. budget deficits, too, were a blessing *up to a point*. But there has been too much of a good thing! It cannot be denied; markets sometimes make mistakes. Thus with the benefit of hindsight we can say that in 1984 the market did overshoot. But the market corrected itself; the dollar started to decline early in 1985, well before U.S. policy changed. It is in the nature of the political process, however, that governments are slow to admit mistakes and even slower to change their policies. This contrast is strikingly illustrated by the fact that the huge U.S. budget deficits, which are now widely regarded as the main stumbling block for a correction of the trade imbalance, are not expected to be reduced sharply for several years.

The basic trouble is that U.S. domestic savings are insufficient to finance both private sector investment and public budget deficits, which constitute negative savings. The gap has been filled by huge capital inflows from abroad (repatriated American capital and foreign capital), which is the mirror picture of the trade deficit, or more accurately of the associated current-account deficits. The capital inflow has already turned the United States from the world's largest net creditor country into the largest net debtor.

To clarify the connection between budget and trade deficits, consider three possible scenarios. First, assume the dollar has declined enough to reduce the trade deficit and the capital inflow shrinks. If the budget deficit is reduced at the same time, the supply of capital to the private sector is not changed and interest rates do not rise. In real terms it means that the reduction of the budget deficit releases the productive resources that are needed for the expansion of the export- and import-competing industries. This would be the ideal outcome.

Second, assume that the budget deficit is not reduced. In that case interest rates will rise and government spending will crowd out private sector investment. There are then several possibilities. For one thing, higher interest rates may induce a resumption of the capital inflows. But the higher interest rates would have a depressing effect on the economy, and at some point scenario two might well bring about scenario three: a loss of investors' confidence in the dollar, causing a sharp drop in capital imports or even a net outflow, a plunge of the dollar, and a sharp rise of interest rates. This would put the Federal Reserve Board on the spot. It could stand by and let private investment be crowded out, which probably would cause a recession, or it could keep interest rates down, which would cause inflation and probably a more severe recession later on.

This is not to suggest that the United States is in imminent danger of having to choose between recession and inflation; it certainly can continue borrowing abroad for some time. But the borrowing should not and cannot go on indefinitely. First, from the standpoint of the world economy it is anomalous, putting it mildly, for the richest country to borrow from the rest of the world on a large scale for a long period. Second, from the standpoint of national economic interest it is important that the service charge on the foreign debt is mounting rapidly. When borrowing abroad comes to an end, the trade balance will have to be turned around from a deficit to a surplus to permit the transfer of the service charge, implying a reduction of consumption or investment, in other words a slight decline in the standard of living. It has been estimated that if this happens at the end of the decade or soon thereafter, the burden on the economy will amount to over $200 billion a year. This is not a crushing sum in a $4,500 billion economy, but with rigid wages it would cause trouble.

That foreign capital is still needed weakens the case for the U.S. policy of pressuring Germany and Japan in order to eliminate their surpluses and the U.S. deficit. The other weakness of the U.S. position is that econometric studies by the International Monetary Fund (IMF), the Federal Reserve Board, and others have shown that even a sharp and sustained increase of noninflationary GNP growth, say from 2½ percent to 3¼ percent a year, in Germany and Japan would have only an insignificant effect on the U.S. trade deficit. An inflationary expansion would, of course, take the pressure off the dollar. But global inflation would hardly be a sound basis for the world economy.

In my *CEP* article I conclude that a return to a system of fixed but adjustable exchange rates à la Bretton Woods, let alone to the gold standard, is out of the question. It would require a high degree of policy coordination that is possible only in exceptional cases. The European Monetary System is hardly an exception. Some of its members, especially France, have tight exchange control; there are frequent realignments of exchange rates, and each change in rates is accompanied by massive speculation. I conclude that the system of floating rates should, and will, continue. If the Group of Five is unable to agree on a pattern of exchange rates of their currencies, how could it be accomplished in a wider circle?

The Paris Meeting

Now comes the question whether these conclusions have to be changed in light of the meeting in Paris of the Group of Five, dubbed Plaza II, which led to an agreement on February 22, 1987, of the Group of Six (the Group of Seven minus Italy, which stomped out of the meeting because it had not been invited to the Group of Five).

The lengthy official statement abounds in the usual generalities: "The Ministers and Governors were of the view that further progress had been made since the Tokyo summit," "The Ministers and Governors recognize that the large trade imbalances of some countries pose serious risks," and so on. The part of the agreement that has received the most attention comes in the last paragraph of the statement:

> The Ministers and Governors agreed that the substantial exchange rate changes since the Plaza Agreement will increasingly contribute to reducing external imbalances and have now brought their currencies within ranges broadly consistent with underlying economic fundamentals, given the policy commitments summarized in this statement. Further substantial exchange rate shifts among their currencies could damage growth and adjustment prospects in their countries. In current circumstances, therefore, they agreed to cooperate closely to foster stability of exchange rates around current levels.

What does it mean? For one thing, the statement is a concession on the part of the United States to Germany and Japan. The dollar is no longer seriously overvalued, and for the time being Germany and Japan are not threatened by a further appreciation of their currencies. What did the United States get in exchange for this concession? Both countries promise mildly stimulative measures—"tax reform aimed at reinforcing the incentives for private sector activity and investment," "policies that enhance market forces and investment," and things like that.

The United States for its part

will pursue policies with a view to reducing the fiscal 1988 deficit to 2.3 percent of GNP from its estimated level of 3.9 percent in fiscal 1987. For this purpose, the growth in government expenditures will be held to less than 1 percent in fiscal 1988 as part of the continuing program to reduce the share of government in GNP from its current level of 23 percent.

One can only hope that Congress will go along.

The judgment that the exchange rates of the currencies of the six are now "broadly consistent with the underlying fundamentals," implying that the dollar has declined enough to correct the trade deficit, is not shared by many experts. This judgment may well share the fate of the famous Baker–Miyazawa statement of October 31, 1986, that the dollar-yen rate was broadly consistent with underlying fundamentals, which was disproved by the facts two months later when the dollar plunged again. If this happens again, however, it will not be hard to blame it on a change in the fundamentals or on a failure of some of the six to fully live up to their "policy commitments."

The last two sentences of the statement—"Further substantial exchange rate shifts among their currencies could damage growth and adjustment prospects in their countries. In current circumstances, therefore, they [the ministers and governors] agreed to cooperate closely to foster stability of exchange rates around current levels."—have been widely interpreted to mean that the six had agreed on a target zone approach, which the French government has proposed. This is not correct. Richard Darman, deputy secretary of the Treasury, declared in a television interview that it would be counterproductive to specify at which levels of exchange rates interventions in the foreign exchange market would take place, because it would invite disturbing speculation. What it does mean is that there will be concerted interventions if there are substantial exchange rate shifts from the current levels.

This declaration seems to have had a calming effect on the market. But the calm is unlikely to last very long. The "fundamentals" are apt to change over time without notice, and it would be most surprising if the economies of the big three, let along of the five or seven, could progress in step without from time to time developing serious imbalances.

Exchange Rates and Economic Fundamentals

The trouble with the policy of interventions in the foreign exchange market is this: The usual sterilized interventions that leave the money supply unchanged can cope only with minor disturbances, with what used to be called disorderly market conditions. Over the past year or so there have been massive interventions to stop the decline of the dollar. The government of Japan alone has spent more than $40 billion worth of yen to buy dollars, implying a multibillion dollar loss to the Japanese taxpayers. The interventions, massive though they were, were completely swamped by capital flows.

It is true, nonsterilized interventions in the foreign exchange market of sufficient magnitude could in principle deal with even very large disturbances. But given the great international mobility of capital, the enormous size of the market with thousands of sophisticated investors and speculators, the interventions may well have to be so large that no modern government would carry out the policy. Suppose, for example, that the U.S. trade deficit does not quickly decline and the dollar weakens again, as the market expects the decline of the dollar to continue; in that case the United States would be forced to deflate, or the surplus countries to inflate, or both, to hold the line. Stabilizing exchange rates by nonsterilized interventions would mean returning to a system of fixed exchange rates.

Where does all this leave us? To put it bluntly, we, economists as well as Ministers and Governors, simply do not know enough to be able to say what the equilibrium exchange rate is.[1] Experts, outside and inside the administration, differ sharply on whether the dollar has declined enough to bring about a decrease of the trade deficit. The modern asset-theoretic approach to the problem of the determination of exchange rates has taught us to be modest in judging the correctness of exchange rates. This approach was thrust upon economists by the dramatic development over the past twenty years or so of international capital markets after the world's major currencies became convertible. The present financial environment is characterized by high international mobility of capital and the existence of offshore currency markets such as the Eurodollar and the Euroyen markets. It stands to reason that, in such an environment, changing expectations of the market with respect to the economic development, as well as to the intentions of policy makers and the probable course of government policies, play a major role in determining exchange rates. The foreign exchange market resembles the stock market. Stock prices, too, are swayed by changing expectations of future events, and forecasting the movement of stocks and stock indexes such as the Down Jones is a very risky business.

The conclusion I draw is that the international foreign exchange market is a very complicated mechanism, much too delicate to be manipulated by loosely organized groups of governments such as the Group of Seven. The politicization of exchange rates is a dangerous game. The activist U.S. policy seems to have increased the volatility of exchange rates. Telling the Germans and Japanese to grow faster or face a further decline of the dollar is counterproductive. No government likes to do things under pressure from abroad. No modern government is indifferent to unemployment, and all of them want faster growth. Germany and Japan are no exception. The Japanese are greatly worried by 2.5 percent unemployment; the Germans for historical reasons are more sensitive to inflation and therefore tolerate a little more unemployment than the United States. We have seen that even a sharp rise of noninflationary GNP growth in Germany and Japan has only a minor effect on the U.S. trade deficit. I believe that instead of criticizing each other publicly, each country should be allowed to grapple with its problems as well as it can.

Countries should not, however, completely abstain from criticism. Each country can learn from the failures and the successes of others. But criticism and advice should be given quietly through the Organization for Economic Cooperation and Development, the Bank for International Settlements, and the IMF, or bilaterally. Public criticism is counterproductive because it incites the media and politicians to echo the criticism in cruder form. Blaming others for our troubles diverts attention from domestic causes.

Floating exchange rates have served the world economy very well. Suppose the West had been on fixed exchange rates in the 1980s. When the U.S. economy took off on a vigorous expansion in 1982 and capital flowed in from abroad, Europe would have experienced a massive hemorrhage of reserves and would have been put under intense deflationary pressure. The fixed-rate system, with or without target zones, would have collapsed—a confidence-shattering event that probably would have brought on a serious recession. The only alternative would have been to maintain the facade of fixed rates with the help of tight controls. This happened in the 1930s with disastrous consequences. I agree with Jacob Frenkel that the United States could not have "carried out its highly successful disinflation policy of the early 1980s while committed to fixed exchange rates."[2] I repeat: markets, too, sometimes make mistakes. There have indeed been misalignments and volatility under floating. But, quoting Jacob Frenkel again, in many cases

the volatility and the misalignment of exchange rates may not be the source of the difficulties, but rather a manifestation of the prevailing package of macroeconomic policies. Fixing or manipulating the rates without introducing a significant change into the conduct of policies may not improve matters at all. It may amount to breaking the thermometer of a patient suffering from high fever instead of providing him with proper medication. The absence of the thermometer will only confuse matters and will reduce the information essential for policymaking. If volatile events and macropolicies are not allowed to be reflected in the foreign-exchange market, they are likely to be transferred to, and reflected in, other markets (such as labor markets) where they cannot be dealt with in as efficient a manner.[3]

To sum up, markets if left alone do a better job setting exchange rates than governments do. Ergo, the system of floating exchange rates should continue.

Notes

1. For a thorough discussion of this point, see Jacob Dreyer, "The Behavior of the Dollar: Causes and Consequences," in Phillip Cagan, ed., *Contemporary Economic Problems: Deficits, Taxes, and Economic Adjustments* (Washington, D.C.: American Enterprise Institute, 1987).

2. See Jacob Frenkel, "The International Monetary System: Should It Be Reformed?" *American Economic Review* (May 1987), p. 207.

3. Ibid.

7

GROWTH RATES, TRADE BALANCES, AND EXCHANGE RATES

Fritz Machlup

Few writers in the field of international monetary economics have had the deep insights and sharp foresights of Robert Triffin, the man whom I wish to honor by this modest contribution to the area of his special interest. Trade balances and exchange rates are two key words in the universe of his knowledge. The first element of the triad shown in the title of my chapter—growth rates—has not figured prominently in Triffin's work: He has not explored, as far as I know, the effects of disparate growth rates upon trade balances and equilibrium exchange rates. This will deprive me of the pleasure of pointing to his superior wisdom in avoiding many fallacies that have snared some of our respected colleagues. Triffin did not commit himself on the subject of this chapter, and this explains why references to his work will be absent from the pages that follow.

Statement of the Problem

The literature under review relates to the effects that divergent rates of economic growth are liable or likely to have on the trade balances of the countries concerned (if foreign exhange rates are kept unchanged) or on exchange rates (if these are determined by free market forces). The problem is of pragmatic significance, because it bears on national and international policies. It is also of intellectual interest to historians of economic thought. It is one of those instances where academic and official specialists find a particular answer to be cogent and "obvious" and fail to realize that some of their fellow specialists have pronounced the diametrically opposite, but equally "obvious," conclusion. Moreover, none of the partisans of the contradictory opinions seems to be aware of the fact that these pronouncements have long since been refuted and devastated by more judicious theorists. This lack of awareness, unfortunately, seems to be endemic in the economic profession: The contents of the journals of years past are disregarded or forgotten. Fallacies refuted and "safely" buried reemerge every few years, because the refutations are buried in old journal issues no longer consulted by the newer generation.

These charges need to be substantiated. First I list the two contradictory positions and their refutation. I then point out that lack of clarity in the use of terms and of tacit assumptions may be largely responsible for the confusion.[1]

Thesis. More rapid growth strengthens the trade balances of the faster growing countries and weakens the trade balances of the others.

Antithesis. More rapid growth weakens the trade balances of the faster growing countries and strengthens the trade balances of the others.

Synthesis. Whether more rapid growth will strengthen or weaken the trade balances of the faster growing countries depends on several conditions, of which the most decisive are the monetary policies of the countries concerned.

Obscurities. These statements all suffer from insufficient specifications of growth and monetary policies and from failure to stipulate whether foreign exchange rates are fixed, managed, or freely floating. It stands to reason, however, that all three positions tacitly assume fixed exchange rates and I would have to replace the words "trade balances" with "exchange rates" if the latter were freely determined in competitive markets for currencies supplied and demanded exclusively by exporters and importers of merchandise. As to monetary policies, I strongly suspect that the contradiction between thesis and antithesis is due chiefly to opposite but nonexplicit assumptions regarding relative expansions in the supplies of national moneys. The thesis is evidently based on the assumption that the more rapid real growth is not matched or exceeded by monetary expansion; the antithesis evidently takes it for granted that the faster real growth is associated with (induced, made possible by) even faster monetary expansion. The expression "faster" or "slower" monetary expansion suffers from an especially awkward ambiguity in that it seems to disregard induced changes in the demand for money balances. The references to growth rates suffer from several ambiguities, to be discussed later in the chapter. Some of the worst misunderstandings can be traced to tacit assumptions regarding supply-determined growth and demand-determined growth, where the opposing parties entertain opposite views regarding the possibility of controlling the rate of real growth by means of "demand management."

That this sketch of contradictory positions and of the underlying and disturbing obscurities is not exaggerated may be documented by quoting two highly respectable recent sources. Concerning the effects of "more rapid growth and technological advance abroad," Clarke (1980:29) states: "More rapid advance in many foreign countries than in the United States tended to weaken the country's merchandise trade balance." The antithesis, that more rapid growth abroad could strengthen, not weaken, the external position of the United States, finds strong expression in the annual reports of the International Monetary Fund (IMF) and in the periodic surveys of the Organization for Economic Cooperation and Development (OECD). The IMF report for 1978 states: "Since the divergence in rates of economic growth is one of the main causes of the present external imbalances, it is essential to achieve more coordination in this field" (p. 16); and further, "most industrial countries other than the United States—and especially the major surplus countries—should aim for growth rates . . . significantly higher than the actual rates . . ." (p. 17). Clearly, the writers of this statement attributed the weakness of the external balances of the United States to its higher rate of growth or to what they thought to be the unduly slow growth of its trading partners—especially the surplus countries, Germany and Japan.

The Thesis as Explanation
of Dollar Strength

Theories holding that disparities in rates of economic growth are responsible for imbalances in trade and/or for movements in the exchange rates among the currencies of the countries concerned were heatedly debated at various periods in the past. The thesis that faster growth strengthens and slower growth weakens a country's balance of trade was strongly argued and defended in the days of dollar shortage, or dollar strength, in the late 1940s and early 1950s. Some of the protagonists thought that the casual connection was so simple—perhaps self-evident—that no detailed explanation was needed. The country with the faster growth in output and/or productivity (the difference was usually not considered) "surely" must have a stronger currency. Why? Because faster growth made it a more "powerful" economy, or because it had more goods to supply to the more slowly growing countries, which "consequently" would have trouble finding the foreign exchange to pay for their increased imports. Even these poor reasons were sometimes not spelled out. It was simply taken for granted that the country with the faster growth in output and/or productivity would have a surplus in its trade balance, and this was, of course, the logical counterpart of a trade deficit for the more slowly growing countries. If the United States had the more rapid growth, it followed that the other countries had to suffer dollar shortage.

Thomas Balogh, a major protagonist of this position, wanted to show not only the cause but also the cure of the dollar shortage. He had rather peculiar remedies to propose. Monetary restraint on the part of deficit countries was regarded as cruel as well as unhelpful, and hence, commercial policy was proposed as the most effective remedy: The poor Europeans should adopt more stringent trade restrictions of a discriminatory sort. Foreign exchange controls, discriminating against U.S. imports, were thought to be the most effective remedy (Balogh 1950). Other currency doctors were hoping that the Europeans would eventually be able to overcome the sluggishness of their growth and reduce or close the productivity gap; in the meantime, their plight could be alleviated by a generous supply of investment, loans, and grants from the rich Americans.

At that early stage of the debate, the different concepts of growth had not yet been clarified. Those who attributed the dollar shortage to the superior economic strength of the United States and its "consequent" export surpluses were not sure how to specify that superior strength. Balogh spoke of "faster technical progress," more "aggressiveness in managerial leadership," "overwhelmingly dominant power," "advantages of greater size and wealth," "rapid development" rendering "most industries in poorer and smaller countries obsolete," greater "competitive power," "monopoly positions," and favorable "terms of trade," but he probably saw the main cause for the troublesome U.S. surpluses in its faster growth of productivity (Balogh 1946, 1950). John H. Williams, another protagonist of this position, was not any clearer, but at least in one statement he pronounced that "over time, if there are divergent rates of growth of productivity, the trade will be progressively less favorable to the countries less rapidly advancing in productivity (Williams 1954: 14). By "less favorable" he meant the trade balance—not the terms of trade— since it was dollar shortage he wanted to explain.

The thesis that faster growth of productivity could strengthen the trade position of the country concerned was partly rejected, partly qualified, by a highly sophisticated argument advanced by John R. Hicks. He distinguished between dollar shortages that could be avoided through appropriate monetary policies and others that had such profound structural causes that monetary policies would be of no avail. Thus, a U.S. trade surplus or a European trade deficit would not yield to treatment by compensatory monetary measures if the cause was found in an "import-biased" growth of productivity in the United States. If American productivity increased in the industries producing import substitutes, the consequent damage to European exporters could not be offset, reduced, or cured by any monetary adjustment (Hicks 1953). Hicks' diagnosis was that the American economy had been developing superior technologies in the goods previously imported from Europe and that this was responsible for European trade deficits and chronic dollar shortages.

The Thesis Rejected

The theories asserting that faster growth in general, or at least faster growth of productivity in particular sectors of the economy, would lead to surpluses in balances of trade of the fast-growing countries, were critically analyzed by several writers. Haberler (1948), Robertson (1954), Johnson (1954), Machlup (1954), Streeten (1955), and Komiya (1969) were among those who denied that disparities in rates of economic growth or of advances in economic productivity were strategic factors in determining the imbalances of trade of the countries involved or the relative strength of their currencies. They argued that faster growth in a country would be compatible with the emergence of a deficit, a surplus, or an even balance in its trade accounts, depending on the monetary policies of the countries concerned. It is the relative growth of money supply and aggregate spending in the various countries that is decisive in the determination of changes in their trade balances and/or exchange rates.

Not that other conditions besides monetary policies are entirely irrelevant. It may make a difference whether economic growth is the result of increases in the labor force, accumulation of capital, improvements in techniques of production and management, or intersectoral shifts of productive resources. And it may also make a difference whether technical advances occur chiefly in export industries or in import-competing industries or are well distributed over most sectors of the economy. However, all these differences are likely to impinge only on the rate of monetary expansion that would be too fast, too slow, or just right for the external balance to be unchanged at fixed exchange rates or for flexible exchange rates to remain stable. The mentioned conditions behind real growth or growth of productivity are by and large beyond the reach of governmental policy, whereas monetary expansion can be controlled, at least within limits, by the authorities. Of course, things are not easy for the authorities in as much as the rates of "adequate" monetary expansion are likely to be different in the short run, in the medium run, and in the long run.

If one accepts the proposition that the nonmonetary characteristics of real growth have a bearing on the influence that a given expansion of the money supply will have on the external balance and/or the exchange rate, one cannot consistently reject an analysis of the consequences that real growth and structural changes in the course of such growth are likely to have upon external balance with zero expansion of the money supply or with such expansion as matches the increase in the labor force or in real output or some such limiting ratio. Where the purveyors of the original thesis had gone wrong was in failing to specify what was happening on the side of money. It is impossible to say how the external position of a country or its currency will change as a result of faster growth of output or productivity unless one stipulates the relative rates of monetary expansion.

The Antithesis as Explanation of Dollar Weakness

The rejection of the thesis was soon forgotten. When, in the 1970s, it became necessary to explain dollar glut, or dollar weakness, academic and official theorists resorted again to the notion that disparities in growth rates were behind the large imbalances in foreign trade and conspicuous movements of foreign exchange rates. The thesis, however, was now converted into its obverse: The reincarnation of the theory that growth rate disparities caused external imbalances had its sign inverted; unbeknown to its proponents, the thesis had given place to the antithesis.

According to this antithesis, faster growth would now lead not to a surplus but to a deficit position; countries with higher growth rates would find themselves faced with deficits in their trade balances and/or with weakened and weakening currencies. Again, some of the theorists affirming a causal connection between divergent growth rates and external imbalances consider the proposition self-evident and thus do not take the time to explain it. Countries growing more slowly must "of course" get into surplus and have their currencies strengthened.

In the absence of explicit arguments in support of the antithesis, one has to construct one's own set of definitions and assumptions that could make the asserted effects plausible. The "growth" occurring at different rates in different countries is not, as in the earlier thesis, something that happens as a result of changes in technology and managerial organization or of differences in supply of physical and human capital; instead, it is an increase in the use of (idle or underemployed) resources induced by an increase in effective demand. In other words, faster growth, in this scenario, is brought about by fiscal and monetary expansion effecting an increase in aggregate spending. This, however, explains only nominal growth; in order to explain real growth of total output, the assumption must be made that wage rates and product prices increase less than aggregate spending. Wage inertia is supposed to ensure such a lag: There was a time when "money illusion" was thought to guarantee that all additional spending would lead to additional production with hitherto underemployed resources. Later it was thought that as much as 90 percent of the increase in nominal GNP would be "real" and 10 percent would take the form of price inflation. Now a group of empirical researchers think that the division of the demand pull between real growth and price lift may be something like 67:33 in the first year, with a possible catch-up of the price inflation in the long pull, and there are those who hold that, owing to rational expectations, all of the increase in nominal GNP will be absorbed by wage and price inflation without much of a lag. Some more sophisticated economists admit that all these possibilities exist, and just which outcome is most probable depends on the starting point of the demand pull.

The connection between demand-induced growth and trade deficits and/or currency depreciation is quite simple: One merely has to add the assumption that an increase in effect demand raises the demand for imports (and may also reduce the supply of exports), so that the countries with faster expansions of monetary demand will have their trade balances worsened and/or their currencies weakened, and the countries with slower expansion will have their trade balances improved and/or their currencies strengthened.

The assumptions regarding the wage and price lag behind the spending pull can, without being "implausible," vary between infinity and zero. Thus, the assumptions regarding the effectiveness of "macroeconomic growth policies" can vary between 100 percent and zero. If this is agreed, how is it possible for so many honest and intelligent economic advisers still to speak of specified growth targets "to be aimed at" by national governments? Yet they go on doing this, and they admonish governments to set their targets higher and, for example, to aim at growth rates 2 or 3 percent above those of last year or two years ago. Some of these advisers see an important difference between recovery from a growth recession (or an employment recession) and long-term real growth. Yet they allow their fellow economists and, particularly, their clients (government, legislature, international organization) to speak of growth even when only the question of short-term recovery should be addressed. (I shall return to the difference between short-term expansion of output and employment and long-term growth of productive capacity.) Most of the growth rate boosters believe that real growth can be controlled.

A Wide Choice of Growth Rates

Over the years we have learned that "growth" can refer to a great many things and that, in speaking of growth rates, it is wise to be specific about just which growth is being referred to. The rates of growth of several (theoretically meaningful but not always statistically obtainable) magnitudes would be on the list of the teacher of growth economics: (1) money stocks, (2) monetary demand, (3) real demand, (4) total product at current cost or market prices, (5) total product adjusted for price changes (real product), (6) real product per head, (7) real product per worker in the labor force, (8) real product per worker employed, (9) real product per labor hour, and (10) real product per unit of productive factors (including capital and land). These ten growth rates of aggregate magnitudes would have to be supplemented by some sectoral subaggregates if the analysis had to extend beyond macroeconomics. And, in any case, the time dimensions of the expansions or increases in magnitudes ought not to be disregarded.

Several of the listed macroeconomic magnitudes are purely theoretical and have no clear operational definitions. The greatest difficulties arise with the identification of demand and supply. Since expenditures are the same as receipts and quantities purchased are the same as quantities sold, the use of statistical proxies—expenditures standing in for demand and measured product for supply—is apt to erase the essential difference between the concepts of demand and supply. This makes it difficult to obtain evidence about the roles that changes and reactions on the demand side and on the supply side play in determining the outcome. Yet, even without these serious handicaps, the large number of options in selecting magnitudes for measuring growth rates interferes with clear thinking and unambiguous talking about growth.

If, for example, the theorists in the 1950s spoke of disparities or divergences in the growth of (average) productivity, they could have meant any of five magnitudes in the list above (6, 7, 8, 9, or 10). In addition, there is the question of the statistical proxy for real product: Should it be gross national product, gross domestic product, net national or domestic product, or some other aggregate? Think of improvements in quality and substitutions of new products for old ones—changes that cannot be measured and are therefore not reflected in "measured output." They may play important roles in comparative advantages in production and trade. The most likely candidate for selection, in the context of the arguments, as the representative rate of growth of productivity seems to be item 9 on the list, real product per labor hour. Any good economist will quickly realize, however, that growth in this magnitude may be offset, in its effect on competitiveness in foreign trade, by increases in hourly wage rates. The theorists who supported the thesis that faster growth of productivity would result in trade surpluses of the fast-growing countries evidently assumed that other things, including wage rates, would remain unchanged.

The theorists of the 1970s who supported the antithesis that faster growth would be liable to give trade deficits to the countries in question were most likely thinking of magnitudes 2, 3, 4, or 5. Their reasoning evidently was that total product was determined by demand and that the expansion of demand that induced or allowed the increase in domestic production would lead also to an increase in the demand for imports. Hence they concluded that fast-growing countries would find their trade in deficit and/or their currencies depreciating.

Bearing in mind that statistical concepts may be very inadequate counterparts of theoretical constructs, we may nevertheless take a glance at statistical comparisons among several growth rates (see Table 6-1). Nominal GNP, real GNP, real GNP per capita, real GNP per member of the labor force, and real GNP per worker employed are taken here as

TABLE 6-1

Rates of Growth of Gross National Product in the United States
(percent changes from previous year).

Year	(1)	(2)	(3)	(4)	(5)
1959	8.4	6.0	4.3	4.9	3.7
1965	8.2	5.9	4.6	4.0	3.5
1971	8.3	3.0	1.9	1.3	2.5
1974	8.2	−1.6	−2.3	−4.1	−3.6
1975	8.2	−1.0	−1.7	−2.7	0.4

(1) Nominal GNP total.
(2) Real GNP total.
(3) Real GNP per head of population.
(4) Real GNP per member of labor force.
(5) Real GNP per gainfully employed.
Source: U.S. Department of Commerce.

proxies for items 4, 5, 6, 7, and 8. I select five years in which the growth rate (read: percent rate of change from the previous year) of nominal GNP was almost the same. This rate was associated, however, with very different growth rates of the other four magnitudes.

Much as one tries to resist the temptation to read theories into statistical figures, one cannot help being impressed by the increasing differences between the rates of growth of nominal and real GNP: The gap between the two rates increased conspicuously over time. Thus, the same 8.2 percent growth of nominal GNP that was associated with a 5.9 percent increase in real GNP in 1965 went with a 1.6 percent decrease in real GNP in 1974.

Comparisons with the various relatives (rations to population, labor force, and employment) show little regularity. It is surely but a statistical coincidence that the rates of change of real GNP per worker in the labor force and per worker employed are virtually the same in 1965 and 1975 but with the signs reversed ($+4.0$, -4.1; $+3.5$, -3.6, respectively). The fact that the rates of growth (or change) are sometimes larger, sometimes smaller for product per head of population compared with product per member of the labor force is easily explained: The labor force increases sometimes more slowly, sometimes faster than population. Similarly, since labor force and employment may change at different rates, it is not surprising to see GNP per worker in the labor force change sometimes faster, sometimes more slowly than GNP per worker employed.

One conclusion from the few rates shown in the tabulation may be warranted: The same increase in total expenditures for goods and services measured in GNP need not be associated with similar changes in the other magnitudes and not even with the same direction of change. An increase in expenditures may be linked with negative growth of real output as a total or as a ratio to other magnitudes significant in the economics of growth.

Recovery Versus Long-Term Growth

I have promised to return to the difference between two kinds of increase in GNP: Short-term recovery from a recession and long-term sustainable growth. If an increase in real output is due only to an increase in the rate of employment of a given labor force, such increase is necessarily limited. Assume that only 92 percent of the labor force is employed and that 95 percent is regarded as the full-employment mark; the increase in GNP due to "recovery" of the employment rate cannot go on once the "gap" between actual and potential output is closed. Good economists have therefore agreed (though many seem to have forgotten) not to speak of growth as long as GNP increases only thanks to the reabsorption of the jobless into the labor force. The term "real growth," in this (more enlightened) glossary, refers only to increases in productive *capacity*.

One difficulty with this distinction is that it depends largely on judgments of what rate of unemployment should be regarded as full employment, and what part of an increase in GNP can reasonably be attributed to a growth in productive capacity (and its utilization). If measurements of capacity, or of its increase, were reliable—based on the size and quality of the labor force and on the size and efficiency of the capital stock—the concept of potential output would be empirically useful. Unfortunately it is not. Changes in the composition of the labor force with regard to skill, efficiency, perseverance, exertion of effort, etc., are not measurable and are in fact disregarded by the statisticians. (The number of years workers have spent at school is not an acceptable proxy for any of these attributes.) Changes in the stock of capital equipment and its efficiency are likewise not subject to quantification. Accumulation of capital measured by the money outlays for its construction is not a good substitute for establishing the real contribution capital can make to total output. In lieu of estimates of genuine increases in productive capacity, statisticians and econometricians have used historical data for employment and output to concoct an unacceptable proxy for "potential output," a proxy that neglects changes in the quality and composition of human resources and in the size, quality, and composition of real capital.

The general idea of separating increases in GNP resulting from demand-induced reemployment of workers made jobless in the preceding recession from increases resulting from supply-induced growth of capacity makes good economic sense in theory even if statistical data do not suffice to make the distinction in reality. Several differences may be significant:

1. In a recovery, the average productivity of labor may increase, especially because some of the employed labor had been insufficiently utilized during the recession and can now be used more nearly to capacity. The consequent reduction in labor cost per unit of output may counteract any tendencies of increased demand to pull up product prices.

Counterargument: In a later phase of the recovery, this tendency may be offset by the employment of workers of lower efficiency. The less efficient had been favored candidates for being layed off in the recession and are now being rehired; moreover, during the period of their inactivity many may have lost some of their previous skills.

2. In a recovery, starting from high rates of unemployment, increased hiring need not lead so soon to union demands for wage increases as would be the case if employers' demand for more labor increased beyond the full-employment mark.

Counterargument: This notion is associated with the belief in a trade-off between inflation and unemployment, as pictured in the popular Phillips curve. If it were true that wage boosts are rare and modest as long as unemployment is high, but frequent and sharp when "full employment" is approached, recovery and real growth would be truly different. With inflationary experiences and consequent inflationary expectations, however, the difference is apt to disappear: Wage rates are likely to be pushed up with any kind of demand pull, even if the economy is merely pulled out of a deep trough. If a strong upward pressure of wage rates is taken as a criterion of full employment, virtually any employment level or unemployment rate may qualify as full employment. We cannot really distinguish the various causes of wage increase: (a) restoration of the previous real-wage level after a period of price inflation, (b) defense against an erosion of real wages by anticipated price inflation in the next year or two, (c) participation in the gains from increased productivity in the economy as a whole or in a particular industry, or (d) an opportunity to obtain a more favorable wage contract from an industry expecting higher profits thanks to increased demand.

3. If demand-induced recovery is distinguished from supply-induced long-run real growth, a difference in the effects upon the balance of trade may be recorded. The expansion of demand (spending) during the recovery would almost certainly result in an increase in imports, whereas in the case of supply-induced growth not supported by an expansion of effective demand, the effects upon the trade balance would depend on a variety of conditions.

Counterargument: If, however, long-term growth is also supported by an expansion of effective demand, the effects upon the trade balance depend chiefly, though not exclusively, on the "relative expansiveness" of demand management, primarily monetary policy—relative to several variables, including demand management in the major trading countries.

Economic advisors who recommend policies designed to attain specified growth targets usually rely on the efficacy of fiscal and monetary policies to control what they (sloppily) call economic growth, namely, annual rates of increae of real GNP. Many believe that demand management can control not only recovery but also real economic growth, and that divergences of "growth rates" among countries are responsible for imbalances in the countries' trade accounts. Since they usually do not explicitly distinguish between recovery and long-run growth, and since, as I have tried to show, the distinction, though theoretically valid, is not operational (at least not within our present diagnostic powers), I next discuss the significance of divergent "growth rates" without the qualifications called for by different starting points of the upward movement of real GNP.

Convergent or Divergent Rates of Growth

There is no cogent reason for divergent rates of real GNP growth to induce imbalances in trade or instability of foreign exchange rates. It is conceivable that real GNP grows at a rate of 6 percent in Japan, 3 percent in West Germany, 2 percent in the United States, and 0 in Switzerland, without causing any substantial external imbalances or exchange rate movements. Indeed, this could well be a likely outcome in a world in which authorities abstain from monetary policies "aiming" to achieve faster growth.

Not divergence in rates of real growth but divergence in supposedly growth-inducing monetary policies leads to external imbalances and inordinate movements in exchange rates. Faster growth is said to have certain side effects, but these are in reality caused by so-called "growth policy"—that is, a policy claimed and believed to induce faster growth.

This so-called growth policy is neither a necessary nor a sufficient condition of real growth. Real growth can take place at falling prices and, in theory, is not incompatible with zero or negative growth of nominal GNP. However, one must admit that this has not happened in this century. Nowadays, when wage rates can easily go up but hardly ever go down, sustained growth calls for creation of monetary demand at least sufficient to induce the purchase of the labor that produces the additional output. This concession, however, does not imply that the demand expansion has to be larger than the growth in output. Many growth politicians[2] want monetary demand to be expanded enough to buy the intended increments of annual output at rising prices, and they aver that the creation of such additional monetary demand will actually bring forth the intended growth in real output. I submit that this idea of monetary growth policy has been largely responsible for the chronic price inflation that has become almost worldwide since the middle 1960s.

I further submit that the systematic adoption of growth targets to be achieved through demand management executed or supported by means of monetary expansion can lead to price inflations that may make demand expansion ineffective.[3] Large rates of growth of monetary demand are then translated into small rates of growth of real demand. Attempts to speed up the creation of monetary demand may actually result in zero rates or even negative rates of increase of real demand. Thus, the supposed growth policy may actually retard real growth some of the time. What a farce to give the name "growth policy" to a policy that may actually inhibit real growth. (It is like full-employment policy that reduces employment, and like stabilization policy that destabilizes the economy. Policies should never be named by what they are *intended* to achieve.)

Nurture Versus Control of Growth

Growth of real output (sustained, say, over a period of ten years) is the result of using more productive factors and/or using productive factors more productively. This means that the following developments can contribute to large outputs, that is, to outputs increasing year after year: increase in the labor force, increase in the labor effort per hour and in the number of hours worked per year, increase in capital equipment, improvement of management, use of better techniques of production, and reduction of nonproductive uses of productive factors (labor, land, and equipment). If it is product per labor hour, rather than total product, that one desires to grow faster, one is confined to the last four growth factors—more capital, better management, better techniques, and less waste. More capital can be obtained, for a time, through borrowing from abroad, but ultimately only through greater thrift and productive investment of nonconsumed income. Neither increases in saving nor improvements in the use of labor, land, and capital are effectively promoted by the "growth policies" recommended to our monetary authorities by national advisors as well as international organizations.

Developments that can promote real growth of measured output are possibly "nurtured" by certain government policies, none of which works in the short run: tax policies to encourage personal and corporate saving and productive investments; labor and wage policies to prevent capital consumption (inadequate replacement) and to avoid encroachments on profits (reducing the incentive to invest as well as internal generation of investible funds); industrial policies to avoid stifling regulations imposing expensive nonproductive activities and unproductive uses of investible funds; research policies to encourage and finance investments in research and development; and several kinds of policies to facilitate structural adjustments to changing conditions. Through none of these policies, however, can the government control the rate of real growth or achieve any growth targets considered desirable by its advisors, wise or unwise.

The notion that real growth can be controlled by any kind of government policy, including the mislabeled growth policy, is an illusion. Even worse, the well-meant urging that we "achieve more coordination in this field" is counterproductive. Particularly damaging is the advice that we coax surplus countries into "aiming" for higher growth rates and accelerating "the pace of economic expansion" in order to have their growth rates converge with those of deficit countries that have pursued more expansionary monetary policies. Such "coordination" is apt to support continuation of excessive monetary expansion and price inflation. It may do little to enhance real growth and may even inhibit it in the long run.

Notes

1. This may be the place to thank Richard Cooper and Peter Kenen, two of the editors of this volume, for their critical comments on the first draft of this chapter. Although they can be credited for many improvements in my formulations, they should not be held accountable for remaining weaknesses.

2. By "growth politician" I mean an advocate of policies that, in his opinion, will ensure the attainment of specified targets of real economic growth considerably above the rates that would result without the proposed policies.

3. For an attempt to show that demand expansion requires monetary expansion and cannot be engineered for a sufficiently long period (say, a year or two) by fiscal policy alone (that is, unsupported by an increase in the stock of money), see my essay on fiscal policy (Machlup 1979). For an attempt to show that expansion of monetary demand may be overtaken by price inflation, see my article on different kinds of inflation (Machlup 1978).

References

Balogh, Thomas. 1946. "The U.S. and the World Economy." *Bulletin of the Oxford Institute of Statistics* 8 (October):309–23.

———. 1948. "The United States and International Economic Equilibrium." In Seymour E. Harris, ed., *Foreign Economic Policy for the United States*, pp. 446–80. Cambridge, Massachusetts: Harvard University Press.

———. 1950. *The Dollar Crisis: Causes and Cure.* Oxford: Blackwell.

———. 1954. "The Dollar Crisis Revisited." *Oxford Economic Papers* (N.S.) 6 (September):243–84.

Clarke, Stephen V. O. 1980. "Perspective on the United States External Position

Since World War II." *Federal Reserve Bank of New York, Quarterly Review* 5, no. 2 (Summer):21–38.

Haberler, Gottfried. 1948. "Dollar Shortage?" In Seymour E. Harris, ed., *Foreign Economic Policy of the United States*, pp. 426–45. Cambridge, Massachusetts: Harvard University Press.

———. 1961. "Domestic Economic Policies and the United States Balance of Payments." In Seymour E. Harris, ed., *The Dollar in Crisis*, pp. 63–72. New York: Harcourt, Brace and World.

Hicks, John R. 1953. "An Inaugural Lecture." *Oxford Economic Papers* 5 (June):117–35.

Johnson, Harry G. 1954. "Increasing Productivity, Income-Price Trends and the Trade Balance." *Economic Journal* 64 (September):462–85. (Reprinted in his *International Trade and Economic Growth*. Cambridge, Massachusetts: Harvard University Press, 1961.)

Komiya, Ryutaro. 1969. "Economic Growth and the Balance of Payments: A Monetary Approach." *Journal of Political Economy* 77 (January–February):35–48.

Machlup, Fritz. 1954. "Dollar Shortage and Disparities in the Growth of Productvity." *Scottish Journal of Political Economy* 1 (October):250–67.

———. 1978. "Different Inflations Have Different Effects on Employment." *Banca Nazionale del Lavoro Quarterly Review* 31, no. 127 (December):291–303.

———. 1979. "The Effects of Fiscal Policy and the Choice of Definitions." In Harry I. Greenfield et al., eds., *Theory for Economic Efficiency: Essays in Honor of Abba P. Lerner*, pp. 92–109. Cambridge, Massachusetts: MIT Press.

International Monetary Fund. 1978. *Summary Proceedings of the Thirty-third Annual Meeting of the Board of Governors*, September 25–28, 1978. Report by the Managing Director, pp. 14–22. Washington, D.C.

Robertson, Dennis H. 1954. *Britain in the World Economy*. London: Allen and Unwin.

Streeten, Paul. 1955. "Productivity Growth and the Balance of Trade." *Bulletin of the Oxford University Institute of Statistics* 17 (February):11–17.

Williams, John H. 1952. *Economic Stability in the Modern World*. London: Athlone Press. (Republished as *Trade, Not Aid: A Program for World Stability*. Cambridge, Massachusetts: Harvard University Press, 1954.)

8

A GUIDE TO TARGET ZONES

Jacob A. Frenkel and Morris Goldstein

Introduction

This paper indentifies key issues surrounding the advisability and practicality of adopting "target zones" for the exchange rates of major currencies.[1]

At present there are wide differences of view on the subject of target zones. This reflects at least three factors: first, different assessments of the performance of the existing exchange rate system of managed floating; second, different evaluations of whether a system of target zones could remedy the perceived weaknesses of the existing system; and third, different conceptions of the preferred form of target zones.

The purpose of this paper is not to make the case either for or against the adoption of target zones. Indeed, we have tried to avoid expressing our own view on this central issue. Rather, the intention is to raise and discuss factors that should be considered in any serious examination of the topic. As such, the paper not only outlines potential strengths and weaknesses of various versions of the target zone approach but also confronts operational questions that would have to be faced if the target zone approach to exchange rate management were adopted.

The paper is organized as follows. Section I addresses four fundamental questions concerning the definition of and the rationale for target zones; first, what is generally meant by a target zone approach to exchange rate management and how can "hard" and "soft" versions of this approach be defined; second, what are the perceived deficiencies in the existing exchange rate system which motivate the call for the adoption of target zones; third, how might target zones remedy these deficiencies; and fourth, what factors are behind much of the skepticism over and opposition to target zones?

Section II deals with a series of operational questions and issues of a

183

more technical and specific nature that weigh heavily on the practicality of implementing a target zone approach. The issues discussed are the following: how would the target zones be calculated; what currencies would be included in the system of target zones; how wide should the target zones be and how frequently should they be revised; and what policy instruments would be employed to keep actual exchange rates within the target zones, and with what consequences for other policy objectives? A brief postscript appears as Section II of the paper.

Finally, three caveats relevant to the nature and scope of this study should be mentioned. First, there should be no presumption that advocates of target zones see this as the *only* proposal for improving exchange rate stability. Indeed, most advocates of target zones would also rely on stronger surveillance of a broader nature to help reach that objective. Second, since the paper does not attempt to compare the target zone proposal to other proposals for improving exchange rate stability, there should likewise be no presumption that the strengths and weaknesses outlined here are more or less significant than those associated with other proposals.[2] Third, since many of the precise operational features of a system of target zones remain largely conjectural (e.g., which currencies would be included, how target zones would be calculated, etc.), the views expressed on these operational features should be seen more as aids to discussion and debate than as definite conclusions.

I. The Meaning and Rationale for Target Zones

What Are Target Zones?

Target zones mean different things to different people. Perhaps the easiest way to think of them is as a *hybrid* exchange rate system that combines some of the attributes and characteristics of both pegged and flexible exchange rate systems.[3]

How Does a System of Target Zones Differ from Other Exchange Regimes?

Target zones differ from a pure system of *clean floating* in that the authorities are permitted (and indeed are likely) to intervene in the exchange market, and, more generally, are encouraged "to take a view" on the desirable level of the exchange rate. Target zones differ from the present system of *managed floating* in at least two principal respects:[4] (i) the authorities establish a target zone for the exchange rate for some future period; and (ii) the authorities are expected to keep more of an "eye" on the exchange rate in the conduct of monetary policy so as to keep the actual exchange rate within the target zone.[5] Compared to the *adjustable peg system,* target zones need *not* entail a formal commitment to intervene in all circumstances in the exchange market to keep actual rates within the zone. Indeed, the only concrete intervention guideline that is typically mentioned is that the authorities refrain from "destabilizing intervention," that is, buying their own currency when it is above the top of the zone and selling it below the bottom of the zone. This specific guideline was also included in the Fund's 1974 "Guidelines for the Management of Floating Exchange Rates."[6] Finally, target zones differ from a pure system of *rigidly fixed* exchange rates in that, in addition to the lack of a formal intervention obligation, the zones themselves are to be occasionally reviewed and changed if deemed necessary.

How Can "Hard" and "Soft" Versions of Target Zones Be Defined?

In general, various versions of target zones can be distinguished by reference to the following four characteristics:

(i) *width* of the target zones (outside of which the exchange rate is viewed as "out of line"),

(ii) the *frequency* of changes in the target zones,

(iii) the degree of *publicity* given to the zones; in this context, one may distinguish between public announcement of the target zones and confidential disclosure in official circles (for purposes of exchange rate surveillance, intervention, multilateral policy coordination, and consultation), that is, "loud zones" versus "quiet zones," and

(iv) the degree of *committment* to keeping exchange rates within the zone.

Obviously, these characteristics define a *spectrum* of possible approaches to target zones. At one end, a "hard" version of target zones might entail a monetary policy that is heavily geared to maintaining the exchange rate within the narrow, infrequently revised, and publicly announced zone. At the other end of the spectrum lies a "soft" version of target zones that might be characterizd by a monetary policy paying only limited attention to the level of the exchange rate, and by zones that are wide, frequently revised, and kept confidential. The hard and soft poles, in turn, may serve as useful benchmarks for the analysis and evaluation of intermediate versions of target zones.

The hard version of target zones shares some of the attributes of the existing European Monetary System (EMS). In particular, hard target zones can be considered a close relative of the EMS's fixed but adjustable rates with narrow margins and a "divergence indicator." However, unlike the EMS, hard target zones do not entail a formal commitment for exchange rate intervention; nor need there be an analogue to the credit facilities of the EMS. The soft version of target zones differs from existing Fund surveillance procedures (e.g., the requirement for reporting real exchange rate changes in excess of 10 percent to the Executive Board) in that the former introduces a more explicit and formal framework for defining the appropriate pattern of exchange rates and for establishing the links between exchange rates and macroeconomic policies.[7]

What Considerations Underlie the Call for Adoption of Target Zones?

Proponents of target zones proceed from two basic perceptions: first, that the present system of managed floating has exhibited serious deficiencies; and second, that the adoption of a system of target zones could remedy at least some of these deficiencies. Among the alleged deficiencies, the most attention has been paid to the following considerations.

Exchange Rates Have Been Highly Volatile and Unpredictable

Whether measured in real or nominal terms, bilateral or effective terms, the short-run variability of exchange rates over the period of managed floating has been high-indeed, significantly higher than during the previous Bretton Woods system. In addition, most exchange rate changes have been unpredictable (as suggested by market indicators like forward exchange rates). While high short-term volatility and unpredictability of exchange rates is usually deemed to be less serious than longer-term "misalignments," this volatility is still regarded as costly because it generates uncertainty, and hence leads to lower levels of investment and trade. Further, developing countries are alleged to be especially hurt by this volatility because they do not have well-developed financial markets (particularly forward cover arrangements).

Exchange Rates of Major Currencies Have Been Subject to Large and Persistent Misalignments

A second complaint against the present system is that exchange rates of major currencies have been subject to large and persistent "misalignments" over the past dozen years. Such misalignments are commonly measured by cumulative departures from purchasing power parity, or by the sheer magnitude of changes in real exchange rates themselves, or by departures from more comprehensive concepts of the "equilibrium" real exchange rate (e.g., the exchange rate that yields a cyclically adjusted current account balance equal to normal net private capital flows). Not surprisingly, charges of misalignment were particularly pronounced over the period 1981–85. A representative estimate of misalignment is provided by Williamson (1985). He estimated that by the end of 1984 the extent of misalignment in the real effective exchange rate was 39 percent (overvaluation) for the U.S. dollar and 19 percent (undervaluation) for the Japanese yen. Such misalignments are, in turn, deemed costly because they have an adverse impact on resource allocation, induce adjustment costs (including unemployment), distort optimal levels of capital formation, and encourage protectionism.

Under the Existing Exchange Rate System, Macroeconomic Policies in Major Industrial Countries Have Been Undisciplined and Uncoordinated

Perhaps the chief criticism by the proponents of target zones is that the existing system of floating exchange rates lacks an effective mechanism for ensuring policy discipline and coordination.[8] As supporting evidence, the critics cite, inter alia, the doubling of industrial-country average inflation rates as between 1963–72 and 1973–85, and the tripling of the ratio of industrial countries' government fiscal deficits to GNP over the same period. On lack of coordination, they point to the frequent conflicts among the major industrial countries on both the stance and mix of macroeconomic policies, as well as on the need for structural reform. Also, despite the efforts made at coordination, critics emphasize the absence of *binding* agreements during the floating-rate period on either rates of monetary expansion or exchange rate norms. Undisciplined and uncoordinated policies, in turn, are said to be costly because such behavior is incompatible with financial stability and sustainable growth, and also because such policies are the main driving force behind both short-term volatility and longer-term misalignment of exchange rates.

IMF Surveillance Under the Existing Exchange Rate System Has Been Largely Ineffective in Respect of Major Industrial Countries, Resulting in Asymmetry in the International Adjustment Mechanism

Yet a fourth alleged weakness of the existing system is that Fund surveillance has not been sufficiently effective in respect of the very industrial countries whose policies have the most significant "spillover effects" on the world economy, thereby producing, among other things, an asymmetric distribution in the burden of adjustment. As evidence for this position, the critics cite the magnitude and persistence of current account imbalances in the United States and Japan, especially over the past three years. The seeming inability of surveillance to bring about a correction of the structural U.S. budget deficit is regarded as another striking example of this lack of symmetry. Further, it is argued that an inappropriate mix of macroeconomic policies in the major industrial countries during the early 1980s resulted in high real interest rates and in sluggish economic activity. A consequence of this was that developing countries faced (during 1981–83) a sharp increase in debt service requirements, a significant decline in export earnings, a compression of their imports, and unusually slow growth. Thus, so it is argued, adverse spillover effects from poor policies in industrial countries were substantial, and the burden of adjustment fell disproportionately on the developing countries.

How Would the Introduction of Target Zones for the Major Currencies Remedy These Four Perceived Deficiencies of the Existing Exchange Rate System?

A central argument advanced by proponents of target zones (see, for example, Roosa (1984) is that their introduction would restore some of the useful characteristics of the Bretton Woods system without being subject to the flaws that led to the collapse of that system.

Restoring an Anchor for Medium-Term Exchange Rate Expectations

It is often argued that one reason why exchange rates have been so volatile under the present exchange rate system is that market participants lack an "anchor" for medium-term expectations about exchange rates. In such an environment, new information, rumors, or announcements can lead to large revisions of expectations about the future which in turn induce "large" changes in current exchange rates. Furthermore, under some circumstances, such events may set the stage for the emergence of "bandwagon" effects and speculative "bubbles" that can dominate the evolution of the exchange rate and divorce it increasingly from "fundamentals."

It is claimed that target zones will reduce exchange rate volatility and misalignment on two counts. First, the obligation (albeit an informal one) or the intention to keep the exchange rate within the zone provides market participants with useful information about the likely conduct of future macroeconomic policies, especially monetary policy. The easier it is to make an informed judgment about the future course of policies, the less one can expect the erroneous extrapolation of short-term events and the more forgiving will be the market of short-term deviations of policy. Second, the publication of target zones provides market participants with information on the authorities' collective estimate of future equilibrium exchange rates. Therefore, it is said to reduce the risk that market participants use the "wrong model" in translating (even perfectly foreseen) future policy changes into forecasts of future exchange rates.

Restoring Discipline and Coordination to the Conduct of
Macroeconomic Policies
Target zones are said to restore *discipline* to macroeconomic policymaking for two reasons. First, if exchange rates are maintained within the target zones, then macroeconomic policies, again particularly monetary policy, are disciplined by the exchange rate constraint. Second, even if the authorities opt to alter the target zone rather than their policies, they would still be obliged both to negotiate a new zone and to explain why a new zone is appropriate. These obligations themselves are said to introduce stronger peer pressure into policy formation.

Turning to the *coordination* of policies, the following points are noteworthy. The very fact that a system of target zones has to be negotiated and must display mutual consistency of cross exchange rates is said to enhance the degree of international policy coordination. Under a system of target zones, so it is argued, the exchange rate implications of alternative stances and mixes of policies would be directly confronted, thereby ending the undesirable current practice whereby exchange rates emerge as a "residual" of other policy actions of individual countries. Also, the requirement that target zones be negotiated and mutually agreed is said to reduce the risk of competitive devaluations.

And to the extent that target zones do restore discipline and coordination to the conduct of macroeconomic policy, they will reduce misalignment and volatility of exchange rates.

Increasing the Effectiveness of IMF Surveillance and Reducing the
Asymmetry in the Adjustment Process
Proponents of target zones argue that the need to negotiate, to ensure consistency, and to revise the zones could provide a natural focal point for multilateral Fund surveillance. Just as important, such surveillance procedures when applied to target zones will be aimed at the policies of the major industrial countries, that, in turn, are likely to constitute the membership of the target zone system. It is alleged therefore that target zones will remove the Achilles heel of the present surveillance procedures, namely, the inability to effect a meaningful change in policies of large industrial countries. Since the asymmetry of adjustment is said to depend critically on policy behavior in industrial countries, more effective surveillance of them would also produce more *symmetrical* adjustment.

The remedial properties of a target zone approach would obviously depend on the particular version adopted. The "harder" versions, by virture of being closer images of the Bretton Woods regime, clearly offer a stronger dose of external pressure on domestic policy. But, as is discussed in subsequent sections, the alleged benefits associated with the harder versions may also entail higher costs.

Proponents of the "softer" versions of the target zone approach argue that their adoption would enhance the surveillance process for at least three reasons. First, even if the zones were wide and were frequently revised, they would exert some disciplinary force on the most flagrant and persistent cases of inappropriate policies. Thus, while soft target zones may not do much to catch misalignments on the order of 10 percent or less, they will, so their supporters argue, catch the 20–40 percent real exchange rate misalignments that do most damage to the system. Second, even if the zones were not announced to the public, they still are likely to provoke helpful discussion and analysis of policy interdependence among officials of participating members. Also, such "quiet" zones provide another channel for peer pressure against inappropriate policies. Third, since the Fund's current practices in any case involve evaluating the appropriateness of members' exchange rates, supporters argue that even unpublished zones may prove useful in generating a more concrete framework for evaluating exchange rate implications of alternative macroeconomic policies.

Escaping the Same Fate as the Bretton Woods System

Supporters of target zones acknowledge that many of the factors associated with the collapse of Bretton Woods have not gone away (e.g., high international mobility of capital, larger financial resources for private speculators than for central banks, existence of large and suddenly changing interest rate differentials across countries, etc.). Nevertheless, they contend that a system of target zones can survive pressure from "hot money" flows. They argue that so long as policy adjustments are made when necessary or so long as the target zones are revised frequently to reflect inflation differentials and needs for real exchange rate adjustment, expectations of large and discontinuous exchange rate adjustments that provide the motive for speculative attacks will seldom arise. In their view, the viability of the EMS provides testimony that it is possible to operate an adjustable peg system in the 1980s provided that there is sufficient political commitment, active exchange market intervention policies, and a presumptive indicator for adjustment. Since a target zone system shares many of these characteristics, it too is viable.[9]

What Factors are Behind Much of the Skepticism About and Opposition to Target Zones?

Opposition to the adoption of target zones stems from a more sanguine appraisal of the performance of the existing system; doubts about the capacity of target zones to remedy alleged deficiencies; and concerns that target zones would introduce new problems. Each of these elements is discussed in turn.

Has the Existing System Failed?

Exchange rate volatility. While the short-run volatility of both nominal and real exchange rates has indeed been high during the period of managed floating, this begs the question of whether that volatility was "excessive." In this connection, opponents of target zones raise two points.

First, the period since 1973 has witnessed great turbulence in the world economy and great uncertainty about the future course of economic and political events. In this environment, *all* asset prices, not only exchange rates, have shown high volatility. In fact, exchange rate changes have been smaller than changes in prices of other assets (e.g., national stock market prices, changes in short-term interest rates, changes in commodity prices). As such, conclusions about the excessive nature of exchange rate fluctuations depend upon the specific yardstick selected.

Second, they note that there is an intrinsic difference between asset prices on the one hand and wages and goods prices on the other hand. The former are auction prices that depend heavily on expectations about the future whereas the latter are more sticky in the short run, reflecting in large part contractual arrangements made in the past. Thus, wages and prices of national output may not serve as a proper yardstick for assessing exchange rate volatility. Indeed, some would say that it is precisely because wages and prices are so slow to adjust to current and expected economic conditions that it is desirable to allow for "excessive" adjustment in exchange rates.

As regards the *unpredictable* nature of exchange rate changes under the present system, opponents of target zones note that the foreign exchange market is one in which risk can be covered relatively easily (via access to forward markets, options, markets, etc.) For this reason, it is argued that it may be preferable to concentrate the disturbances in this market rather than transfer them to other markets, such as labor markets, where dealing with them would be more difficult.

Turning to the *cost* of short-run volatility of exchange rates, opponents point to the sporadic nature of the evidence linking exchange rate volatility to the volume of international trade and investment.[10] They also argue that it is doubtful that the system of pegged rates could have survived in the turbulent environment of the past 15 years without severe limits on trade and capital movements being imposed by many countries.[11] Such restrictions on trade and capital flows, in turn, could well have been more costly for the world economy than the short-run volatility of exchange rates experienced under the present system.

Exchange rate misalignment. Almost all observers, even many staunch opponents of target zones, agree that there have been serious misalignments of major currency exchange rates during the past few years, particularly as regards the sharp real appreciation of the U.S. dollar. Opponents of target zones suggest however that in evaluating both the extent and the cost of such misalignments several factors ought to be recognized.

- Changes in *real economic conditions* requiring adjustments in the relative prices of different national outputs occur all the time (continuing intercountry differences in growth of labor productivity, permanent changes in the terms of trade, intercountry shifts in both the marginal productivity of capital and the propensity to save, etc.). Under a system of pegged rates, relative price adjustments are achieved through the slow changes of national price levels and through occasional changes of parity. Under floating rates, adjustments in the relative price of different national outputs occur rapidly and in anticipation of changes in economic conditions rather than after the need for adjustment has become apparent. In the absence of an explicit specification of relative costs, there is no general presumption that slow adjustment of relative prices is preferable to rapid adjustment, or that price adjustments should not occur in anticipation of events requiring such adjustments. Hence, what may seem to be misalignments may in part represent equilibrating changes.

- Critics of target zones argue that one should not overlook the fact that significant misalignment of major currency exchange rates also occurred during the Bretton Woods period, especially in its later years. In this connection, they caution that misalignment of real exchange rates can derive from too *little* nominal exchange rate flexibility as well as from too much. The frequency of misaligned real exchange rates in countries with "pegged" exchange arrangements, where there is often a reluctance to alter nominal rates in the face of large inflation differentials, should stand as a warning to the dangers involved.

- The size of estimated misalignments in major currency exchange rates is, according to defenders of the present system, highly uncertain. To take but one example, calculations of misalignment done by

Williamson (1985) and others are strongly affected by the assumption that "normal" net capital flows are zero for the United States. This assumption is important because the equilibrium exchange rate is defined in such calculations as the exchange rate that would produce a current account balance equal to the assumed normal net private capital flow. But a country that is a "normal" net capital exporter under one set of macroeconomic policies, tax considerations, and political events abroad may become a natural importer under others. In this connection, a judgment that normal net private capital flows for the United States were, say, a \$30 billion annual inflow (to reflect high expected profitability, relatively low domestic savings, and safe-haven considerations) rather than zero would reduce the estimated misalignment considerably;[12] yet the theoretical reasons for preferring the latter estimate to the former are, so the critics argue, debatable at best.

• Defenders of the present system argue that explanations that attribute long-term misalignment to a speculative bubble are highly questionable. They point out that the (narrow) theoretical models that are frequently used to generate a speculative bubble in the exchange rate (i.e., a fully expected continuous price change not justified by fundamentals) also imply that such a bubble could prevail for only a short period of time—certainly not for five years or so.

Discipline and coordination. Defenders of the current exchange rate system question the allegation that it exerts less discipline than regimes with greater fixity of exchange rates. As a theoretical matter, it is pointed out that changes in exchange rates are highly visible and are transmitted promptly into domestic prices. As a result, the consequences of undisciplined macroeconomic policies are readily apparent. In contrast, undisciplined policies under fixed exchange rates show up only in reserve changes, and then usually become public only after a significant delay. Therefore, it is argued, the supposed superior disciplining force of a fixed rate regime is not obvious. Furthermore, as an empirical matter, the 1979–86 policy experience in industrial countries can be viewed as evidence that anti-inflationary discipline can be restored *without* fixed exchange rates. Indeed, the deceleration in growth rates of narrow and broad money that took place in the face of high unemployment in most of the major industrial countries in 1979–82 coincided with relatively high variability of both nominal and real exchange rates.

As for coordination, defenders of the present system note that there have been some successful coordination efforts during the past decade.

In this context, they mention the U.S. dollar support package of November 1, 1978, agreements on short-term exchange rate management policies (e.g., intermittent joint countering of disorderly market conditions), the agreements of the Bonn economic summit of 1978, and the Group of Five agreement (of September 22, 1985) in New York on foreign exchange intervention and other policies.[13]

In addition, it can be argued that the optimal degree of coordination is less than complete. For example, the *perception* of independent monetary policy may be necessary in some countries for sustaining confidence that monetary policy will not be inflationary in the long run (particularly if not all potential partners in a target zone system have a track record of consistently sound monetary policy).[14]

In *sum*, the very point of departure for the proponents of target zones, namely, the overall appraisal that the existing system has failed, is itself not universally accepted. Opponents of target zones acknowledge that the present system has weaknesses but do not see these weaknesses as more serious than those demonstrated by earlier systems. In addition, opponents emphasize that the present system has demonstrated some "valuable strengths." Specifically, exchange rate changes are viewed as having made a positive contribution to securing effective external payments adjustment over the medium to long run. The present system is also credited with having maintained a mechanism of conflict resolution (namely, the foreign exchange market) that has *not* involved either suspension of currency convertibility or large-scale restrictions on trade and capital flows; indeed, supporters of the present system claim that floating rates allowed the removal of certain restrictions. Furthermore, it is argued that independent monetary policy, facilitated by the existing exchange rate system, permitted the application of successful disinflationary policies. Finally, it is argued that *no* exchange rate regime would have emerged unscathed from the combination of shocks, portfolio shifts, and structural and institutional changes that occurred during the years of managed floating.

Would the Introduction of Target Zones Improve Matters?

Would target zones provide an anchor? As noted earlier, one of the central arguments for the introduction of target zones is that such zones would provide an anchor for medium-term exchange rate expectations. But would it, and at what costs? Skeptics make the following points.

- If the absence of an anchor stems from lack of information about future government policies, then it is not clear that publication of target zones, rather than announcement of the future course of policies themselves, is the preferred way to provide that information. Obviously, if the zones are not published (i.e., quiet zones), then their adoption will not alleviate the policy uncertainty problem at all.[15]

- If the source of uncertainty is that market participants do not possess information on the model linking government policies with the consequent levels of exchange rates, then target zones (loud zones) do indeed provide the missing information. This presupposes, however, either that the government has superior information about the "true model" or that the government carries enough credibility to convince market participants that it will adjust its policies to consistently maintain exchange rates within the announced zone (i.e., it will adjust its policies to make the exchange rate forecast come true). Opponents of target zones see no evidence that governments have such superior information or knowledge about such a model. Further, they point out that experience with preannounced exchange rate targets in Latin America suggests that countries would probably find it difficult to adhere to such targets.[16]

- Even if the target zones were credible for some period of time, critics argue that the occasional need for revision of the target zones will invite the same type of one-way bet for speculators that ultimately felled the Bretton Woods system. Of course, since governments are not formally committed to defend the target zones, they may choose to allow exchange rates to depart from the zone (while subsequently announcing a revised zone). But in that case, the zones themselves would soon lose their credibility.

- Even if the zones are announced, critics contend that "soft" versions of target zones characterized by wide and frequently revised zones are not likely to provide a strong and reliable anchor because they will not sufficiently narrow expectations about the future rate. Yet such wide and frequently revised zones are said to be necessary (by critics) to account for our measure of ignorance about the equilibrium exchange rate and for changing real conditions.

- Even if the anchor is credible and durable, its introduction may be costly. The argument here is that the volatility or misalignment of exchange rates is not the likely source of difficulties but rather a *manifestation* of the prevailing package of macroeconomic policies. Without introducing a significant change into the conduct of policies, a manipulation of exchange rates to satisfy the zones may not improve matters at all. In fact, the absence of the exchange rate as a market gauge for assessing policies will then only confuse matters and reduce the information essential for policymaking.

Would target zones provide discipline? It is widely agreed that misalignment of real exchange rates arises to a large extent from undisciplined and uncoordinated macroeconomic policies. Hence, the ability of target zones to reduce misalignment rests in good measure on their ability to enhance discipline. Skeptics put forward the following points.

- Experience suggests to them that national governments are unlikely to adjust appreciably the conduct of domestic policies so as to satisfy the constraints imposed by the exchange rate regime. Rather, it is argued, it is more likely that the exchange rate regime adjusts to whatever discipline national governments choose to have. As an illustration, it is pointed out that other external pressures aimed at restoring discipline to policy in major industrial countries (e.g., individual Article IV consultations, Fund Executive Board discussions of the world economic outlook, Group of Five surveillance meetings, OECD country reports) have met with only limited success. Why then should target zones succeed where other similar measures have produced such limited results?
- Evidence from earlier periods during which exchange rates were more rigid does not suggest that greater fixity of exchange rates induced either lower average external imbalances, or more rapid adjustment of such imbalances, or greater symmetry of adjustment as between either surplus and deficit countries, or between reserve and nonreserve currency countries.[17] Why then should target zones provide the impetus to discipline when exchange regimes with greater formal commitment have not consistently done so?
- In a related vein, it is argued that by focusing attention on exchange rates rather than on the root cause of misalignment, namely, the stance and mix of macroeconomic policies, one may lessen the pressures for corrective action on the ultimate sources of the problem.
- Critics argue that if the nominal target zones reflect rigid targets for real exchange rates, they can destabilize the price level.[18] Take, for example, the case of a country that experiences an unexpected wage push that raises its price level relative to that abroad. Its real exchange rate will then have appreciated relative to its initial level. If the authorities attempt to restore the original real exchange rate by announcing a more depreciated nominal target zone, then the implied expansion in monetary policy (needed to keep the actual

exchange rate within the new target zone) will increase the price level. In short, critics warn that while a rigid real exchange rate may be helpful for preventing trade balance deteriorations due to eroding competitiveness, it can also present new dangers for controlling inflation. More broadly, monetary policy is not the appropriate policy response to *all* types of disturbances.

- Critics also point out that while target zones can supply information on intercountry divergences in policy, they don't provide guidance on the right stance of policy *within* a country. For example, if two countries each have inflation rates of 10 percent, the exchange rate may be stable but few would argue that monetary policy in *either* country was appropriate. Again, so the critics argue, target zones do not ensure discipline.

Would target zones enhance coordination and strengthen surveillance? In appraising the effects of the adoption of target zones on policy coordination and on Fund surveillance, skeptics make the following observations.

- Whatever the exchange rate regime, there are strong barriers to coordination for at least two reasons: (i) exchange rates are by their very nature "competitive" in the sense that one country's gain is frequently another country's loss; (ii) various compromises on growth, inflation, and income distribution at the *national* level often leave little room for further compromise on policies at the international level.[19] Target zones, so say their critics, cannot overcome these barriers.
- The process of negotiating target zones could produce dangerous frictions among the negotiating parties and could lead ultimately to a reduced level of coordination in this and other areas.
- One cannot rule out the possibility that the cumbersome negotiation of target zones would land the system back in the management delays of the latter days of the Bretton Woods system, with adverse effects on the desired flexibility of *real* exchange rates. With target zones, one loses the "safety valve" provided by the marketplace for foreign exchange as a mode of conflict resolution.
- To the extent that the adoption of target zones results in a significant loss in independence in the conduct of domestic monetary policy, the authorities may be tempted to adopt discriminatory trade practices and other measures of protection in order to compensate for the loss of a powerful policy instrument.
- Finally, the use of target zones as a possible focal point for Fund

surveillance raises three related potential problems. First, the use of the exchange rate as a primary indicator of disequilibria in macroeconomic policies could send misleading signals. Critics note that the more general Fund practice as applied to adjustment programs and financial programming is to employ a whole *set* of macroeconomic indicators for diagnostic purposes. Would exchange rate movements vis-à-vis the target zone constitute a "sufficient statistic" for monitoring macroeconomic policies? If one believes that the answer to that question is negative, then orienting Fund surveillance around that single indicator, in addition to possibly diverting attention from the root causes of disequilibria, may jeopardize the quality of surveillance.

The second problem raised by skeptics is that the target zone approach is agnostic about which policy instruments should be used to respond to departures of exchange rates from the zone. The usual presumption is that it will be monetary policy.[20] However, if the root cause of the disequilibrium is an inappropriate monetary-fiscal *policy mix*, then an excessive emphasis on monetary policy could produce compliance with the target zones and yet leave the fundamental problem unsolved. In short, critics argue that the calculation of the target zones would have to be based on an appropriate and broad set of indicators to avoid sending false signals about both the need for adjustment and the appropriate corrective measures.

Third, critics contend that target zones do not resolve the problem of how to allocate and enforce the burden of adjustment among member countries. When more than one member's (effective) exchange rate leaves the zone, it will be necessary to specify who does what if an effect and coordinated policy response is to take place. But target zones, so the critics argue, offer no solution to this "N-1 problem."

Could target zones escape the fate of the Bretton Woods system? Opponents of the target zone approach to exchange rate management remain unconvinced that target zones could escape the fate of Bretton Woods. They make essentially three arguments. First, technological advances in transferring funds across national boundaries, in combination with absence of parallel growth in official reserves, means that the capital mobility problem (hot money flows) is now even more formidable than in the early 1970s. Second, difficulties associated with negotiating mutually consistent target zones would, as before, produce large discontinuous changes in exchange rates, thus motivating strong speculation. In addition, if the timing of exchange rate changes were done unpredictably to prevent such speculation, this would destroy the *raison d'être* of the target zone scheme itself. Third, the viability of the EMS owes much to the unusual political commitment behind it, to capital controls imposed by some members, and to the structural characteristics of its members.[21] None of these factors would, according to the critics, necessarily transfer to an exchange rate arrangement among a larger and more heterogeneous group of countries. As such, to them, the viability of the EMS does not imply much about the viability or desirability of a target zone system.

II. Operational Questions Associated with the Possible Implementation of Target Zones

How Would the Target Zones Be Calculated?

An important implicit assumption in the target zone approach to exchange rate management is that the authorities can approximate the equilibrium (real) exchange rate to a useful degree. But by what methods or techniques? Three methods deserve explicit consideration.

The first is the *purchasing-power-parity* (PPP) approach. If the authorities can identify a base period when the country was in external balance, then the equilibrium value for the nominal exchange rate in the current period is the value of the exchange rate in the base period adjusted for the intercountry difference in inflation rates between the current and base periods. This is equivalent to restoring the value of the *real* exchange rate in the base period. Since the real exchange rate, in turn, is often viewed as a measure of the country's competitive position, the PPP approach can be regarded as an analysis of competitiveness as well.

The exchange rate used for such calculations would typically be an index of effective exchange rates using bilateral trade weights or more sophisticated combinations of trade weights and trade price elasticities (e.g., MERM weights). Inflation differentials could be measured by consumer price indices, or more likely, by indices of either unit labor costs or prices in manufacturing.

The PPP approach carries the advantage of simplicity and ease of computation. Arrayed against this, however, are several rather serious disadvantages for use in a target zone context.

First, PPP will be a suitable indicator of the equilibrium exchange rate when all disturbances between the base and current periods are *monetary* in origin. In this case, general price levels will be altered but relative prices (of imports and exports, or of tradables and nontradables, or of individual tradables like food or fuel) will not. In contrast, when disturbances are *real* and do alter relative prices, then it will be desirable to have a departure from PPP (i.e., a change in the real exchange rate). This point is relevant because there have been numerous real disturbances over the past 13 years of managed floating (e.g., large changes in oil prices, changes in savings and investment propensities), and there is little reason to believe that such real disturbances will not occur in the future. This means that if a PPP formula were used to compute the equilibrium rate in a target zone, there would probably have to be a manual "override option" to permit departures from PPP whenever there were real disturbances to the system. But this override option robs PPP of its simplicity and computational facility.

Another disadvantage of the PPP approach is that actual exchange rates of major currencies during the 1970s and early 1980s have *not* followed the paths implied by PPP—and for both the short and long run.[22] To most observers, the empirical failure of PPP in the short run is attributable to an intrinsic difference between exchange rates and prices of national outputs. The former are jumpy, forward-looking, auction prices that move in anticipation of future events, whereas the latter are sticky, backward-looking, administered prices that may largely reflect previous events. In the long run, structural changes and permanent supply shocks may cause PPP to miss the mark. In any case, the poor empirical track record of PPP suggest that exchange rate forecasts based on PPP might not be credible to market participants.

A third difficulty with PPP is that the results themselves appear to be quite sensitive to the choice among alternative price indices and base periods to the income levels and income growth rates of the countries involved in the comparison (i.e., the so-called productivity-bias in PPP)[23] and to the level of aggregation in the data (manufacturing versus the entire economy).[24] Such sensitivity, in turn, makes it difficult to speak with confidence about all but very large misalignments.

A second method of calculating equilibrium exchange rates for target zones is to employ an *estimated structural model of exchange rate determination* that relates the (nominal) exchange rate to "fundamentals." Two popular such models are the monetary model and the portfolio balance model. In the monetary model, the change in the exchange rate is usually explained by changes in the ratio of the demand for money at home to that abroad (where the demand for money is a function of, inter alia, real income, nominal interest rates). The portfolio balance model relates the (nominal) exchange rate to the stocks of assets denominated in the home and foreign currencies (where these asset stocks include money supplies as well as interest-bearing securities). Since the stocks of financial assets can be related to cumulative budget deficits, cumulative current account imbalances, open market operations, and exchange market intervention, the portfolio balance model provides a direct role for such policies in influencing exchange rates. In the monetary model, such policies affect exchange rates only to the extent that they affect the supply or demand for money.

Given estimates for such a structural model of exchange rates, the equilibrium exchange rate could be defined as the rate corresponding to the *desired* path of the explanatory fundamentals in the equation (i.e., money supplies, real income, interest rates, budget positions). This estimate of the equilibrium nominal exchange rate, combined with some assumed consistent path for prices at home and abroad, could then be translated into an estimate of the equilibrium real exchange rate.

This structural approach has three advantages: (i) it is forward-looking and thus compatible with the intrinsic nature of the price behavior of such assets as securities denominated in different currencies; (ii) it provides a direct link between macroeconomic policy variables and exchange rates; and (iii) it recognizes that in today's world of high international mobility of capital, the proximate determinants of exchange rates, at least in the short run, probably lie in asset markets rather than goods markets. At the same time, the structural exchange rate equation approach is subject to at least two serious deficiencies.

The most serious shortcoming is that *all* known structural models of exchange rate determination have been shown to have very limited forecasting ability. In fact, extensive empirical testing over the past few years has demonstrated that the out-of-sample performance of structural exchange rate models is frequently no better than that yielded by "naive" models (e.g., a random-walk model).[25] With the benefit of hindsight, it seems that an important reason for the poor performance of the various models is the nature of exchange rates as asset prices. As indicated above, exchange rates are very sensitive to expectations concerning future events and policies. Periods that are dominated by rumors, announcements, and "news" which alter expectations are likely to induce a relatively large degree of exchange rate volatility. Since by definition "news" cannot be predicted on the basis of past information, it follows that by and large the resulting fluctuations of exchange rates are unpredictable. In a way, this asset market perspective suggests that one should not expect to be able to forecast accurately exchange rate changes with the aid of simple structural models. The role of the simple structural models is to account for the *systematic* component of the evolution of exchange rates. In cases where the systematic, predictable component is relatively small, one may expect to account for only a small fraction of the variability of exchange rates. The main message of all this is that target zones based on exchange rate forecasts from such models might not carry sufficient credibility to act as an anchor.

Another problem with the structural exchange rate models is that the explanatory variables can be difficult to measure and interpret on a timely basis. For example, the portfolio balance model requires measurement of asset stocks by currency, by country of issuance, and by residence of the holder. But such data only become available much after the fact and estimates based on extrapolation of benchmark figures may introduce substantial error into the calculations. Similarly, in the monetary model one faces the problems of which monetary aggregate to use (in view of financial market innovations), how to forecast that aggregate over the relevant time horizon, and how to distinguish short-term movements in velocity from trends. For these reasons, the prospects of obtaining timely forecasts (target zones) from these models are not encouraging.

The third method for calculating equilibrium exchange rates is the *underlying balance* approach. In this approach, the (real) equilibrium exchange rate is defined as the rate that would make the "underlying" current account (i.e., the actual current account adjusted for temporary factors) equal to "normal" net capital flows during the next two or three years, given (i) anticipated macroeconomic policies in the subject countries, (ii) the delayed effects of past exchange rate changes, and (iii) a number of other expected developments. Furthermore, the equality between underlying current accounts and normal capital flows must *not* be achieved either by wholesale unemployment, or by artificial incentives to incoming or outgoing capital, or by undue restrictions on trade.[26] If after accounting for these factors, "underlying" current accounts are calculated to be quite different from "normal" capital flows, the implication is that either planned macroeconomic policies or present exchange rates need to change to prevent such undesirable balance of payments scenarios from taking place.

This underlying balance approach to exchange rate assessment was developed by the Fund staff in the early 1970s (see International Monetary Fund (1984b)); it similarly serves as the framework for calculation of "misalignments" in Williamson (1985). The inputs for the calculations come from various sources. Estimates of "anticipated macroeconomic policies," and their associated real growth and inflation paths, can be obtained from national projections or from the Fund's world economic outlook projections. Estimates of "normal" net capital flows typically come from an analysis of past trends adjusted for expected future structural developments (e.g., capital liberalization measures). Finally, estimates of the effect of exchange rate changes on current accounts can be derived, for example, from either of the Fund's two operating trade models, namely the multilateral exchange rate model or the world trade model.[27]

For application in a system of target zones, the underlying balance approach carries three advantages. First, it recognizes that judgments about the appropriateness of current exchange rates cannot be divorced from either future anticipated macroeconomic policies, or from delayed effects of past exchange rates that are not yet visible but are likely to emerge in the future, or from particular factors (e.g., dock strikes) that are temporary in nature. In this sense, it not only focuses attention on the root cause of misalignment (i.e., inappropriate policies) but also addresses the "time dimension" in the misalignment problem.

Second, the underlying balance approach appreciates that a desirable or sustainable payments position need not imply a zero current account balance. Specifically, it recognizes that a country with a relatively low domestic savings rate but with relatively attractive domestic investment opportunities can run a persistent current account deficit by drawing on foreign savings if (i) it invests those foreign savings wisely; and (ii) the return on domestic investments is not *artificially* high (because of special incentives for or restrictions on international capital flows, or because of unsustainably high government borrowing).

A third advantage of the underlying balance approach is that, at least in principle, it ensures that the computed equilibrium exchange rates are *consistent* across countries.[28] This is so because the trade models that underlie such exchange rate calculations are specifically designed to be used in a multilateral setting. Since target zones must be mutually consistent, this is not a trivial consideration.

Moving to the negative side of the ledger, the underlying balance approach is subject to a number of problems.

First and foremost, the concept of "normal" net private capital flows is a particularly ambiguous one; yet estimates of these capital flows play a key role in the estimate of the equilibrium real exchange rate. The reasons why the concept is so slippery include the following: (i) While private saving rates are reasonably stable over time and across countries, the geographic loci of *perceived* investment opportunities are not; the latter depend on a wide set of expected policies in both the origin and host countries—many of which can change precipitately. (ii) Various controls on capital flows make it difficult to determine what is "normal," especially when these controls change over time. (iii) Acquisition of foreign assets subjects the holder to risks (e.g., expropriation risk) that are fundamentally different from those associated with domestic assets, and therefore consideration of such risks may limit exposure even when average real rates of return on foreign assets are high. (iv) Large changes in government fiscal positions, and drastic shifts in private portfolio composition, can lead to large swings in observed capital flows, the duration of which is highly uncertain. The end result of all this is that estimates of "normal" net capital flows for the likely participants in a target zone system are subject to a considerable margin of error.

A second problem with the underlying balance approach is that it is not well suited to the analysis and diagnosis of the *mix* of macroeconomic policies. In general, macroeconomic policies influence the equilibrium exchange rate in this approach via their effect on anticipated real output and inflation paths over the next two to three years. Thus, the model will produce different estimates of the equilibrium exchange rate for different real output and inflation paths. But it cannot distinguish among policy mixes that yield the same output and inflation paths. This must be regarded as a shortcoming since the cause of misalignment may lie more with an inappropriate mix of policies (e.g., overly loose fiscal policy cum overly tight monetary policy) than with an inappropriate stance of policies (e.g., excessively expansionary monetary and fiscal policy).

The third difficulty with the underlying balance approach is that it is operationally complex. Data requirements are substantial, computations depend on large-scale trade models, the rationale behind some of the calculations is not transparent, and estimates of some key parameters (e.g., short-run and long-run trade elasticities) are uncertain.[29] All of this, in turn, might be burdensome for agreement on, and continuous revision of, target zones.

Fourth, the large-scale trade models that are likely to be used in this approach do not pay sufficient attention to either financial variables or to the important distinction between expected and unexpected values of key economic variables. These omissions render this approach somewhat remote from the mechanisms usually associated with the determination of *market* exchange rates. Therefore, target zones based on forecasts from the underlying balance approach may again be questioned by market participants.

To *summarize*, each of the three methods of calculating equilibrium exchange rates has strengths and weaknesses. It might, however, not be necessary to follow just one method. Instead, one could construct a "consensus" forecast on the basis of estimates from several methods. Such an exercise would also provide information on the comparative performance of each method which, in turn, could aid in the ultimate selection of the proper calculation method. Finally, in appraising the methods of calculating equilibrium exchange rates, it is important to recognize that such methods are already being applied to some degree whenever the Fund "takes a view" on the appropriateness of major currency exchange rates. In this sense, the problems raised are not new ones. The differences are that in a system of target zones (especially the "harder" versions) the method of calculating equilibrium exchange rates would be more explicit and subject to greater scrutiny, and that the results of such calculations would be shared with the market.

What Currencies Should Be Included in the System of Target Zones?

Another central issue for a system of target zones is the number and choice of currencies to be included. Several considerations seem paramount.

- For *administrative efficiency*, it is desirable that membership should be kept fairly small. This is because the complexity of negotiations, and the danger of conflicts that might bring about a collapse of the system, can be said to increase rapidly as the number of partners rises. This position is consistent with the view that centralized management of exchange rates is feasible only when the number of *decisions* to be made is reasonably small.[30] In this connection, it is useful to recall that although a large number of currencies were managed under the Bretton Woods system, countries took the initiative for par value changes, the Fund could only concur with or object to par value changes proposed by a member, and par values were changed rather infrequently.[31] Similarly, the present system of managed floating is a decentralized system that permits "market-based" decisions to act as a safety valve when more centralized decisions about adjustment responsibilities and exchange rate alignments do not prove possible. In short, since international decision-making on exchange rates is likely to be difficult, one should not unduly burden the system with too many players.
- For a target zone system to have an appreciable impact on conditions in foreign exchange markets, it is desirable that the membership include *major currency countries*. Although the vast majority of countries currently maintain some form of "pegged" exchange arrangements, the largest trading countries maintain either "limited flexibility" (e.g., the EMS) or "more flexible" exchange arrange-

ments, including "independent floating" by four of the largest industrial countries (Canada, Japan, the United Kingdom, and the United
States). [32] Reflecting this, it has been estimated that about two thirds
to four fifths of world trade is conducted at floating rates. [33] The key
to progressing toward more fixity in exchange rates therefore lies not
in inducing many countries to adopt constraints on exchange rate
flexibility—this is already a fact of life—but rather in inducing the
largest trading countries to accept such constraints. This consideration has no doubt influenced the leading proposals (e.g., Roosa
(1984)) that the key members of a target zone be either the three
largest industrial countries or the Group of Five (or perhaps Group
of Seven) countries.

- A further consideration is the *characteristics of the potential member
countries*. These characteristics, emphasized in the literature on so-
called optimal currency areas, are relevant not for choosing the right
number of countries for a target zone but rather for assessing the
likely membership.

The more important country characteristics are the following:

(i) The *openness* of the economy. This criterion suggests that relatively
open economies should prefer greater fixity of exchange rates because
exchange rate fluctuations induce larger domestic price changes in more
open economies, thereby complicating the task of domestic stablization
policies.

(ii) The *size* of the economy. Small economies are said to be more
inclined to join currency unions because, in the absence of such monetary
integration, their effective economic size would be suboptimal. This of
course begs the question of which currency to peg to.

(iii) The degree of *commodity diversification*. Highly diversified economies are deemed more likely candidates for greater fixity of exchange
rates because their diversification provides some natural insulation
against a variety of shocks; hence, there is less need for the insulation
properties of a flexible exchange rate.

(iv) The degree of *factor mobility*. Countries between which there is a
high degree of factor mobility are viewed as better candidates for currency unions because factor mobility provides a substitute for exchange
rate flexibility in promoting external adjustment. Since factor mobility is
in turn likely to diminish with geographic distance, this criterion is often
used to justify currency unions between small neighboring states.

(v) *Similarity of inflation rates*. The argument here is that countries
with similar tastes for inflation—and more important, similar histories of

inflation—will tend to prefer greater fixity of exchange rates. There is, however, a chicken-and-egg problem: do member countries of a currency union have similar inflation rates because they belong to the union, or have they joined the union because of their similar capacities to combat inflation?

Obviously, these country characteristics do not all point in the same direction. For example, the criteria of openness, size, and factor mobility suggest that the United States, the Federal Republic of Germany, and Japan would have relatively weak incentives to join a target zone, relative say, to the smaller European countries that are members of the EMS. On the other hand, the criteria of commodity diversification and similarity of inflation rates lean the other way.

A final consideration is the *relationship to existing currency blocs*. In thinking about the potential membership of a target zone system, it is important to recognize that most countries are already part of a currency bloc, be it via pegging to a single currency or currency basket, or via participation in an arrangement with limited exchange rate flexibility (e.g., the EMS). This raises three points: (i) where members of the target zone system are also members of other (regional) currency blocs, provision would have to be made for ensuring consistency of cross exchange rates and for coordinating intervention practices between the "core" target zone and "satellite" currency blocs; (ii) countries that already have non-exchange-rate linking arrangements (e.g., a customs union) may be reluctant to undertake additional linkages (i.e., target zones) for fear of restricting too tightly their room for independent action; and (iii) if the most natural and profitable opportunities for currency union are exploited first, then it is likely that a target zone system among major currency countries may have to operate with more flexibility (e.g., wider margins and more frequent revision of central rates) than satellite currency blocs.

How Wide Should the Target Zones Be and How Frequently Should They Be Revised?

The equilibrium exchange rate—also sometimes referred to as the *central rate*—represents only one of several parameters that characterize target zones. Two others are the *width* of the zones surrounding the central rates and the *frequency* by which the zones are revised. What considerations bear on the determination of these latter two parameters?

Concerning the *width* of the zones, four factors are relevant. First, the zones must be wide enough to accommodate transitory disturbances that do not alter long-run equilibrium real exchange rates. In this sense, the zone may be viewed as providing a buffer. The buffer not only guards against costly shifts in resources due to excessively frequent changes in central rates but also provides the authorities with breathing space to sort out permanent from transitory shocks. Second, the zone should be wide enough to reflect uncertainties about the equilibrium central rate itself. As noted earlier, there are various approaches to calculating the real equilibrium exchange rate and there are uncertainties about the parameter values in each model. To many observers, little is gained by acting as if equilibrium exchange rates could be assessed with great precision. Recognizing this, some proposals for target zones recommend initial zones on the order of 10 percentage points on each side of the central rate (see, for example, Williamson (1985)). The third factor to be considered is speculation. A well-known weakness of fixed exchange rates is that frequently they offer speculators "one-way bets" about the direction of changes in parities. Target zones must therefore be sufficiently wide to allow for occasional changes in central rates within the zone without provoking one-way speculation. Fourth, if central rates were specified in terms of a numeraire currency, then the width of the target zone linking nonnumeraire currencies will in general be different to that between each currency and the numeraire.

Also, there is no reason why the width of the zones should be constant over time. For example, if uncertainty about the equilibrium real exchange rate and about the nature of disturbances diminished with experience, then narrower zones could be adopted. On the other hand, if turbulence increased over time, wider zones could be adopted. Finally, as a corollary of the above arguments, there is no logical presumption that the width of the zone should be the same for all members. In this connection, it is relevant to note the experience of the EMS in which the currency of Italy, a country that has had relatively high inflation in the past, is subject to wider margins than other currencies. Similarly, it has been suggested that if the United Kingdom were to join the EMS, special provision should be made in the form of wider margins for the pound sterling to reflect the influence of oil price developments on the exchange rate.

Turning to the *frequency* of adjustment, a number of points need to be considered. To begin with, the frequency with which the central rates (and zones around them) are adjusted should reflect the frequency of changes in real economic conditions, as well as, of course, the size of inflation differentials across member countries. Examples of changes in real economic conditions would include permanent changes in the terms of trade, continuing intercountry differences in labor productivity, and intercountry shifts in savings and investment propensities. Because such changes in real economic conditions generally do not occur at close intervals, they are unlikely to induce frequent changes in the target zones. The size of inflation differentials depends primarily on how successful target zones are in inducing harmonization of members' macroeconomic and structural policies, particularly monetary policy. The second factor governing the desired frequency of adjustment is the flexibility of macroeconomic policy instruments. Specifically, since a change in real economic conditions can be reconciled *either* by a change in macroeconomic policies with an unchanged zone or by a change in the zone with unchanged policies, it follows that inflexible policies call for higher frequency of zone adjustment, and vice versa. Third, there is the credibility issue. Frequent revisions in the zones reduce credibility of the zones and thereby reduce their value as an anchor for expectations. On the other hand, frequent changes in macroeconomic policies designed to sustain the zones may also reduce credibility—but this time of the policies.[34] Therefore, the optimal frequency of adjustment from a credibility viewpoint involves balancing between these two considerations. Fourth, some have argued that if target zones are adjusted frequently for inflation differentials and the need for balance of payments adjustment, speculative attacks will be discouraged, since they are motivated by large discrete changes in exchange rates. Fifth, the frequency of adjustment must obviously be constrained by the availability of the data necessary for computations.

How Would Exchange Rates Be Kept Within the Zones and With What Consequences for Other Policy Objectives?

For a system of target zones to operate successfully, it is necessary that exchange rates be kept within the agreed zones, at least most of the time. But *how* could participating countries assure this result? Three policy instruments should be considered.

- The most obvious instrument is *domestic monetary policy*. Indeed, as indicated in Section I, a differentiating characteristic of target zones is that the authorities pay more attention to the exchange rate in the conduct of domestic monetary policy than they do under the present system of managed floating. What this means is that participating members will have to seek greater *coordination* of monetary policies, with a consequent reduction in the ability to independently control the money supply. For example, a member of the system that sees its nominal exchange rate fall to the bottom of the zone would be expected to slow its money growth rate and to increase its domestic interest rate vis-à-vis those of other members;[35] in this way, it would induce an appreciation in its nominal exchange rate, thereby keeping its exchange rate within the target zone. Assuming that the pass-through of nominal exchange rate changes into domestic prices is less that complete, the same monetary policy action would allow the member to satisfy its target for the real exchange rate as well.[36]

There is little doubt about the *ability* of major industrial countries to influence nominal and real exchange rates in the medium term using domestic monetary policy.[37] The key question concerns the *willingness* to do so given the implied reduction in their ability to then use domestic monetary policy for internal objectives. To many observers, it is simply naive to believe that the United States, Japan, and the Federal Republic of Germany would be willing to override internal objectives for exchange rate targets in the formulation of domestic monetary policy. Under this view, "soft" target zones are the strongest commitment one can reasonably envisage for the three largest potential members. Othes argue, however, that the independence of monetary policy is far from complete under the present system, even for those countries classified by the Fund as "independently floating." To take but one recent example, the U.K. authorities reacted to the large decline in the dollar/pound rate in early 1985 by encouraging large increases in domestic interest rates—and this even though there was strong domestic pressure for lower interest rates to help reduce unemployment. For this reason, supporters of target zones argue that all countries already have *implicit* target zones beyond which they are willing to sacrifice internal objectives for the exchange rate. It is argued therefore that the loss of monetary independence *at the margin* would be minimal.

• A second possible policy instrument for keeping exchange rates within target zones is *sterilized exchange market intervention (i.e., exchange market intervention that leaves the monetary base unchanged). Its main attraction is that, if effective, it would permit the authorities to influence exchange rates while simultaneously maintaining control of the domestic money supply*.

Unfortunately, the prognosis for using sterilized exchange market intervention as the primary instrument for controlling exchange rates is not favorable. The Jurgensen Report (1983), for example, supports the view that sterilized intervention by itself is unlikely to be an effective tool for influencing the level of the exchange rate over the medium or long term.[38] Similarly, recent empirical work on exchange rate determination indicates that while domestic and foreign currency assets may well be imperfect substitutes—a necessary condition for sterilized exchange market intervention to be effective—risk premiums in exchange markets are *not* well explained by relative asset supplies (the very variables affected by exchange market intervention).[39] In short, the effects of sterilized intervention on market exchange rates are likely to be small and uncertain in size. Nevertheless, sterilized intervention may have a useful role to play in dampening short-term volatility of exchange rates, in countering disorderly market conditions, in complementing and supporting other policies, and in expressing an attitude toward exchange markets.

- *Capital controls* represent a third instrument for keeping exchange rates within target zones. This is, however, generally not regarded as an attractive option for two reasons. First, even aggressive capital control programs, such as those of the early 1970s, were not able to stem private capital flows, and the subsequent development of offshore banking markets suggests even lower effectiveness today. Second, capital control programs are most effective in altering exchange rates when they cover all types of capital transactions. But in that case, there is no presumption that the resource allocation costs of impeding the international flow of capital would be less serious than departures of exchange rates from the zones themselves.

The preceding discussion suggests that the primary instrument for keeping exchange rates within target zones is likely to be monetary policy. If this is so, then a second relevant question emerges: with monetary policy geared more to external objectives, what policy instruments will be assigned to *internal balance* (i.e., price stability and high employment)?

One logical answer is *fiscal* policy.[40] Here, the key question is not so much whether fiscal policy *can* affect aggregate demand in major industrial countries. Experience suggests that it can. Rather, the issue is whether fiscal policy is a sufficiently *flexible* policy instrument to be used for stabilization policy in a world in which some countries have medium-term targets for reducing the share of government expenditure in overall economic activity, some are contemplating large structural changes in their tax system, some are committed to given levels of social programs and defense spending, some are wedded to preannounced public sector borrowing requirements, and some are facing legislatures that can take years (not months) to enact significant cuts in budget deficits.

A second policy option (favored for example by Meade (1984) is to use *labor market policy* for internal balance. In brief, the idea is to lower the money wage rate in any sector which has excess supply of labor and to raise it where there is excess demand. The problem, recognized by supporters, is that the implementation of such a policy would involve the substantial reform of labor market institutions. In short, although sound in its internal logic, it begs the central question of *how* to bring such a labor market policy into being in advanced industrial economies. The slow progress in reducing structural rigidities in European labor markets bears testimony to the difficulties involved.

In *sum*, because of the limitations of other policy instruments, monetary policy is often called on to serve both external and internal objectives. If a move to target zones were made, it would require shifting more of the emphasis toward external objectives. This might not create a major problem if all members of the target zone geared monetary policy toward price stability; or if coordinated, sterilized exchange market intervention could ease the external obligations of monetary policy; or if fiscal policy could be made flexible enough to deal effectively with internal balance. However, since none of these three outcomes is likely to be fully realized, members of a target zone system would probably still be faced with serious conflicts between external and internal balance. At the same time, the constraints on macroeconomic policies induced by a target zone system might make a contribution to the realization of these three outcomes.

III. Postscript

This paper, along with others that examined issues raised in the reports on the international monetary system presented by the Deputies of the Group of Ten and Group of Twenty-Four, was discussed by the Fund's Executive Board in early 1986. Since then, efforts to improve the functioning of the exchange rate system have centered on enhancing economic policy coordination among the largest economies and on strengthening the multilateral setting for Fund surveillance, including the formulation of a set of "objective indicators."

At its meeting on April 9–10, 1986, the Interim Committee agreed that "if better exchange rate performance were to be achieved on a durable basis, it would be of the essence that economic policies be conducted in a sound and mutually consistent way and that exchange rate considerations should play their part in those policies" (International Monetary Fund (1986), p. 115). The Committee also reconfirmed the key role that Fund Surveillance needs to play in the functioning of the international monetary system. "To improve the multilateral setting for surveillance, the Committee asked the Executive Board to consider ways in which its regular reviews of the world economic situation could be further adopted to improve the scope for discussing external imbalances, exchange rate developments, and policy interactions among members. An approach worth exploring further was the formulation of a set of objective indicators related to policy actions and economic performance, having regard to a medium-term framework. Such indicators might help to identify a need for discussion of economic policies" (ibid., p. 115).

The leaders of the seven major industrial countries, meeting on May 4–6, 1986 in Tokyo at the twelfth annual economic summit, reinforced this commitment to closer coordination of economic policies. They asked that their finance ministers meet at least once a year" to review their individual economic objectives and forecasts collectively, and that they use a set of quantitative indicators of economic policies and performance with a particular view to examining their mutual compatibility" (International Monetary Fund (1986), p. 145). They welcomed the recent examples of improved coordination among the Group of Five countries— including the Plaza Agreement of September 22, 1985—but felt that additional measures were needed "to ensure that procedures for effective coordination of international economic policy are strengthened further" (ibid., p. 157). Toward this goal, the leaders, together with the representatives of the European Community participating in the meeting, reaffirmed their intention "to cooperate with the IMF in strengthening multilateral surveillance, particularly among the countries (the Group of 5) whose currencies constitute the SDR" (ibid., p. 157). Further, in conducting such surveillance and in conjunction with the Managing Director of the IMF, they asked that account be taken of "such indicators as growth rates of gross national product (GNP), interest rates, inflation rates, unemployment rates, ratios of fiscal deficits to GNP, current account and trade balances, money growth rates, international reserve holdings, and exchange rates" (ibid., p. 157).

In July 1986, the Fund's Executive Board discussed a staff paper on "Surveillance-Indicators Relating to Policy Actions and Economic Performance."[41] This was followed in September 1986 by the Executive Board's discussion of the staff's world economic outlook exercise, the published version of which appeared in October. In the context of analyzing the medium-term prospects of industrial countries, that exercise contains a section which reviews certain potential sources of tension in the interaction of economic developments and considers their implications for the stance of policies.

When the Interim Committee next met on September 28, 1986 in

Washington, it once again focused, inter alia, on the use of indicators in surveillance. The Committee agreed that "a key focus of indicators should be on points of interaction among national economies, in particular developments affecting the sustainability of balance of payments positions, and on the policies underlying them" (International Monetary Fund (1986), p. 309). The Committee also asked the Fund's Executive Board "to develop further the application of indicators in the context both of the period consultations with individual member countries and of the world economic outlook so as to facilitate the multilateral appraisal and coordination of economic policies" (ibid.).

NOTES

1. At its meeting in Seoul, Korea on October 6–7, 1985, the Interim Committee of the Board of Governors of the Inernational Monetary Fund requested the Executive Board of the Fund ". . . to study the issues raised in these reports [the reports on the international monetary system presented by the Deputies of the Group of Ten and the Deputies of the Group of Twenty-Four] with a view to facilitating a substantial consideration by the Committee at its next meeting." This paper is one of the series of papers prepared in late 1985 in response to that request.

2. Some other proposals for improving exchange rate stability are analyzed in Crockett and Goldstein (1987).

3. In the Group of Ten report, target zones are described as follows: ". . . the authorities concerned would define wide margins around an adjustable set of exchange rates devised to be consistent with a sustainable pattern of balances of payments" (para. 31). (See International Monetary Fund, 1974b through 1985a.)

4. Another way of summarizing the difference between a system of target zones and the present system of managed floating would be as follows. Under target zones, authorities must come to a mutually agreed view on the appropriate zones for major currency exchange rates. In contrast, under the present system, authorities have not generally expressed their own view on appropriate zones for exchange rates, let alone come to a common view with other authorities.

5. Target zones are intended to reflect estimates of *real* equilibrium exchange rates because it is the real exchange rate that is most relevant for resource allocation decisions and for balance of payments adjustment; however, it is usually assumed that for operational purposes these real rate calculations would be translated into *nominal* exchange rate zones. The assumption is that the authorities can alter real rates by operating on nominal rates. Also, whereas a breach of the target zone is expected to initiate a review of the whole range of a country's macroeconomic and structural policies, most target zone proposals assume that monetary policy will carry the primary responsibility for managing the exchange rate.

6. International Monetary Fund (1974b).

7. Existing procedures do not rely on the assessment of appropriate zones but rather use as a starting point the last occasion on which exchange rate developments were brought to the attention of the Executive Board.

8. In what follows, coordination may be thought of as encompassing all international influences on domestic policymaking; see Polak (1981).

It might be regarded as the chief criticism because short-term volatility and longer-term misalignment of exchange rates are generally regarded as *manifestations* of the lack of discipline and coordination.

9. See Ungerer, Evans, and Nyberg (1983) for a review of the EMS experience during the 1979–82 period.

10. International Monetary Fund (1984a).

11. See, for example, Bryant (1983) and Obstfeld (1985).

12. This assumes that such an order of magnitude is compatible over the long run with a reasonable buildup of debt and with an acceptable maturity profile.

13. Critics of the present system might reply that the Group of Five agreement was a reaction to the absence of coordination and the large misalignments fostered by the present system.

14. See Solomon (1982) on this point.

15. Some observers also doubt whether in practice quiet zones could be quiet for long. They argue that it is not possible for the Fund and national authorities to know what target zones are without this information leaking out.

16. See Calvo (1983).

17. See International Monetary Fund (1984c), Tables 2 and 3.

18. See Adams and Gros (1986) for an analysis of the dangers for inflation of real exchange rate targets.

19. See Polak (1981).

20. Most proposals for target zones (e.g., Williamson 1985)) assume that fiscal policy is not well suited to be an instrument of exchange rate policy because it is too inflexible and because its (alleged) comparative advantage (vis-à-vis monetary policy) is in influencing domestic demand rather than the balance of payments.

21. See Ungerer (1984) for a discussion of the implications of the EMS for the likely success of a return to a system of fixed but adjustable exchange rates.

22. See Frenkel (1981a). Of course, to the extent that actual exchange rates have been subject to misalignments, one would not want the actual rates to closely follow a PPP path. However, divergencies from PPP have been so marked and so persistent as to raise doubts about the credibility of exchange rate forecasts based on PPP.

23. See Balassa (1964).

24. See International Monetary Fund (1984b).

25. Meese and Rogoff (1983) and Isard (1986).

26. This description of the real equilibrium exchange rate is a close relative of those outlined in Nurkse (1945) and International Monetary Fund (1970) and (1985b), par. 69.

27. See Artus and McGuirk (1981) and Deppler and Ripley (1978).

28. This advantage must be qualified in view of the large global discrepancy in current account positions. This discrepancy makes it harder to reach agreement on what constitutes an equilibrium pattern of current account positions.

29. See, for example, Goldstein and Khan (1985).

30. Of course, exchange rates established in a target zone would have clear implications for nonparticipants to which they would have to adjust and/or react.

31. The Bretton Woods system also had the U.S. dollar as the numeraire. With the dollar as anchor, exchange rate decisions could take place one-at-a-time. When this was no longer the case (e.g., August–December 1971), negotiations over exchange rates were much more difficult. It is not clear what currency or currency basket would serve as numeraire in a target zone.

32. It is worth recalling that the currencies of EMS members float against currencies of many nonmembers.

33. See International Monetary Fund (1984c) and (1985a), par. 9.

34. A counterargument is that changes in macroeconomic policies in response to real changes in the economy could act at times to enhance the credibility of policy if they were perceived as responsive to these changes.

35. It is not clear what form monetary intervention would take. Members could intervene in domestic financial markets (exchanging money for debt of the same currency of denomination) or in international financial markets (exchanging moneys of different currency denomination). If the latter were envisaged, questions could arise about the adequacy of intervention assets and about sterilization operations.

36. Obstfeld (1985) reports that month-month correlations between nominal and real exchange rates for the 1976–85 period were above 0.95 for the U.S. dollar, the Japanese yen, and the deutsche mark.

37. In the long run (say, three to five years), the ability to use monetary policy to affect the real exchange rate will be more modest. Also, even in the medium term, this ability will be lower for the smaller, more open, more highly indexed industrial countries than for the larger, less open, less indexed ones. See Goldstein and Khan (1985) for a survey of estimates of these "pass-through" effects.

38. "Intervention will normally be useful only when complementing and supporting other policies." Jurgensen Report (1983).

39. See, for example, Dooley and Isard (1983).

40. Fiscal policy also has a role to play in achieving a given real exchange rate on a sustainable basis.

41. See Crockett and Goldstein (1987) for a published version of that paper.

Bibliography

Adams, Charles, and Daniel Gros, "The Consequences of Real Exchange Rate Rules for Inflation: Some Illustrative Examples," *Staff Papers*, International Monetary Fund (Washington), Vol. 33 (September 1986), pp. 439–76.

Artus, Jacques R., and Andrew D. Crockett, *Floating Exchange Rates and the Need for Surveillance,* Essays in International Finance, No. 127 (Princeton, New Jersey: Princeton University, 1978).

Artus, Jacques R., and Anne Kenney McGuirk, "A Revised Version of the Multilateral Exchange Rate Model," *Staff Papers,* International Monetary Fund (Washington), Vol. 28 (June 1981), pp. 275–309.

Artus, Jacques R., and John H. Young, "Fixed and Flexible Exchange Rates: A Renewal of the Debate," *Staff Papers,* International Monetary Fund (Washington), Vol. 26 (December 1979), pp. 654–98.

Bergsten, C. Fred, and John Williamson, "Exchange Rates and Trade Policy," in *Trade Policy in the 1980s,* ed. by William R. Cline (Washington: Institute for International Economics, 1983).

Bergstrand, Jeffrey H., "Is Exchange Rate Volatility 'Excessive'?" Federal Reserve Bank of Boston, *New England Economic Review* (Boston, September/October 1983), pp. 5–14.

Bryant, Ralph C., "Comments and Discussion" on "Floating Exchange Rates After Ten Years," *Brookings Papers on Economic Activity: 1* (1983), The Brookings Institution (Washington), pp. 71–79.

Calvo, Guillermo, "Trying to Stabilize: Some Theoretical Reflections Based on the Case of Argentina," in *Financial Policies and the World Capital Market: The Problem of Latin American Countries,* ed. by P. Aspe, R. Dornbusch, and M. Obstfeld (Chicago: University of Chicago Press, 1983), pp. 199–216.

Cline, William R., *International Monetary Reform and the Developing Countries* (Washington: The Brookings Institution, 1976).

Crockett, Andrew D., and Morris Goldstein, *Strengthening the International Monetary System: Exchange Rates, Surveillence, and Objective Indicators,* Occasional Paper No. 50 (Washington: International Monetary Fund, forthcoming, 1987).

Deppler, Michael C., and Duncan M. Ripley, "The World Trade Model: Merchandise Trade," *Staff Papers,* International Monetary Fund (Washington), Vol. 25 (March 1978), pp. 147–206.

Dooley, Michael P., and Peter Isard, "The Portfolio-Balance Model of Exchange Rates and Some Structural Estimates of the Risk Premium," *Staff Papers,* International Monetary Fund (Washington), Vol. 30 (December, 1983), pp. 683–702.

Dornbusch, Rudiger, "Exchange Rate Economics: Where Do We Stand?" *Brookings Papers on Economic Activity: 1* (1980), The Brookings Institution (Washington), pp. 143–85.

Dunn, Robert M., *Exchange Rate Rigidity, Investment Distortions, and the Failure of Bretton Woods,* Essays in International Finance, No. 97 (Princeton, New Jersey: Princeton University, 1973).

Emminger, Otmar, *Exchange Rate Policy Reconsidered*, Occasional Paper No. 10 (New York: Group of Thirty, 1982).

———, *The Dollar's Borrowed Strength*, Occasional Paper No. 19 (New York: Group of Thrity, 1985).

Ethier, Wilfred, and Arthur I. Bloomfield, *Managing the Managed Float*, Essays in International Finance, No. 112 (Princeton, New Jersey: Princeton University, 1975).

Frenkel, Jacob A. "Reflections on European Monetary Integration," *Weltwirtschaftliches Archiv* (Kiel), Vol. 111 (No. 2, 1975), pp. 214–21.

——— (1981a), "The Collapse of Purchasing Power Parities During the 1970s," *European Economic Review* (Amsterdam), Vol. 16 (May 1981), pp. 145–65.

——— (1981b), "Flexible Exchange Rates, Prices, and the Role of 'News': Lessons from the 1970s," *Journal of Political Economy* (Chicago), Vol. 89 (August 1981), pp. 665–705.

———, "International Liquidity and Monetary Control," in *International Money and Credit: The Policy Roles*, ed by George M. von Furstenberg (Washington: International Monetary Fund, 1983), pp. 65–109.

———, "Comments on Exchange Rate Arrangements in the Eighties," in *The International Monetary System*, Federal Reserve Bank of Boston (Boston, May 1984), pp. 119–25.

———, "Seeking a Solution through Policy Coordination," in *Exchange Rate Targets: Desirable or Disastrous*, ed. by John H. Makin (Washington: American Enterprise Institute, 1986), pp. 10–22.

———, and Joshua Aizenman, "Aspects of the Optimal Management of Exchange Rates," *Journal of International Economics* (Amsterdam), Vol. 13 (November 1982), pp. 231–56.

Frenkel, Jacob A., and Michael L. Mussa, "The Efficiency of Foreign Exchange Markets and Measures of Turbulence," *American Economic Review* (Nashville, Tennessee), Vol. 60 (May 1970), pp. 374–81.

Genberg, Hans, "On Choosing the Right Rules for Exchange-Rate Management," *World Economy* (London), Vol. 7 (December 1984), pp. 391–406.

Goldstein, Morris, *Have Flexible Exchange Rates Handicapped Macroeconomic Policy?* Special Papers in International Economics, No. 14 (Princeton, New Jersey: Princeton University, 1980).

———, and Mohsin S. Khan, "Income and Price Effects in Foreign Trade," Chap. 20 in *Handbook of International Economics*, ed. by Ronald W. Jones and Peter B. Kenen (Amsterdam: North-Holland, 1985), pp. 1041–1105.

Group of Thirty, *The Foreign Exchange Markets Under Floating Rates, A Study in International Finance*, by the Exchange Markets Participants' Study Group (New York: Group of Thirty, 1980).

——, *The Problem of Exchange Rates: A Policy Statement* (New York: Group of Thirty, 1982).

Helleiner, Gerald K., *Towards a New Bretton Woods: Challenges for the World Financial and Trading System: Report by a Commonwealth Study Group* (London: Commonwealth Secretariat, 1983).

International Monetary Fund (1970), *The Role of Exchange Rates in the Adjustment of International Payments: A Report by the Executive Directors* (Washington: International Monetary Fund, 1970).

—————— (1974a), *International Monetary Reform: Documents of the Committee of Twenty* (Washington: International Monetary Fund, 1974).

—————— (1974b), "Guidelines for the Management of Floating Rates," in *Annual Report of the Executive Directors for the Fiscal Year Ended April 30, 1974* (Washington: International Monetary Fund, 1974), pp. 112–16.

—————— (1984a), *Exchange Rate Volatility and World Trade*, Occasional Paper No. 28 (Washington: International Monetary Fund, July 1984).

—————— (1984b), *Issues in the Assessment of the Exchange Rates of Industrial Countries*, Occasional Paper No. 29 (Washington: International Monetary Fund, July 1984).

—————— (1984c), *The Exchange Rate System: Lessons of the Past and Options for the Future*, Occasional Paper No. 30 (Washington: International Monetary Fund, July 1984).

—————— (1985a), "Report of the Deputies: The Functioning of the International Monetary System," *IMF Survey* (Washington), Supplement, Vol. 14 (July 1985), pp. 2–14.

—————— (1985b), "Deputies of Intergovernmental Group of 24 Call for Major Changes in Monetary System," *IMF Survey* (Washington), Supplement on Group of 24, Vol. 14 (September 1985), pp. 2–16.

—————— (1986), *IMF Survey* (Washington), Vol. 15.

Isard, Peter, "The Empirical Modeling of Exchange Rates: An Assessment of Altenative Approaches" (unpublished, International Monetary Fund, June 6, 1986).

Jurgensen Report, *Report of the Working Group on Exchange Market Intervention* (Washington: U.S. Treasury, March 1983).

Kenen, Peter, "Reforming the International Monetary System" (unpublished, New York Academy of Sciences, September 1985).

McGuirk, Anne Kenney, "Oil Price Changes and Real Exchange Rate Movements Among Industrial Countries," *Staff Papers*, International Monetary Fund (Washington), Vol. 30 (December 1983), pp. 843–84.

McKinnon, Ronald I., *An International Standard for Monetary Stabilization*, Policy Analyses in International Economics: 7 (Washington: Institute for International Economics, 1984).

Meade, James, "New Keynesian Bretton Woods," *Three Banks Review* (Edinburgh), Vol. 142 (June 1984), pp. 8–25.

Meese, Richard A., and Kenneth Rogoff, "Empirical Exchange Rate Models of the Seventies: Do They Fit Out of Sample?" *Journal of International Economics* (Amsterdam), Vol. 14 (February 1983), pp. 3–24.

Mikesell, Raymond F., and Henry N. Goldstein, *Rules for a Floating-Rate Regime*, Essays in International Finance, No. 109 (Princeton, New Jersey: Princeton University Press, 1975).

Mussa, Michael, *The Role of Official Intervention*, Group of Thirty Occasional Paper, No. 6 (New York: Group of Thirty, 1981).

——— "Empirical Regularities in the Behavior of Exchange Rates and Theories of the Foreign Exchange Market," in *Theory, Policy, Institutions: Papers from the Carnegie-Rochester Conferences on Public Policy*, ed. by Karl Brunner and Allan H. Meltzer (Amsterdam; New York: North-Holland, 1983), pp. 165–213.

Nurkse, Ragnar, *Conditions of International Monetary Equilibrium*, Essays in International Finance, No. 4 (Princeton, New Jersey: Princeton University Press, 1945).

Obstfeld, Maurice, "Floating Exchange Rates: Performance and Prospects," *Brookings Papers on Economic Activity: 2* (1985), The Brookings Institution (Washington), pp. 369–464.

Polak, Jacques J., *Coordination of National Economic Policies*, Group of Thirty Occasional Paper, No. 7 (New York: Group of Thirty, 1981).

Roosa, Robert V., "How to Create Exchange Rate Target Zones," *Journal of Commerce* (New York), June 3, 1983, p. 3.

———, "Exchange Rate Arrangements in the Eighties," in Federal Reserve Bank of Boston, *The International Monetary System: Forty Years After Bretton Woods* (Boston, May 1984), pp; 104–18.

Shafer, Jeffrey R., and Bonnie E. Loopesko, "Floating Exchange Rates After Ten Years," *Brookings Papers on Economic Activity: 1* (1983), The Brookings Institution (Washington), pp. 1–70.

Solomon, Anthony M., "International Coordination of Economic Policies: I. The Role of Economic Summitry; II. Coordinating Monetary Policy?" The David Horowitz Lectures at Tel Aviv University, Tel Aviv, and Hebrew University, Jerusalem, March 4 and 5, 1982 (unpubished).

Solomon, Robert, *Reforming the Exchange-Rate Regime*, International Economic Letter, RS Associates, Inc. (Washington), Vol. 3, No. 7 (July 18, 1983).

Tobin, James, *A Proposal for International Monetary Reform*, Cowles Foundation Discussion Paper No. 506, Cowles Foundation for Research in Economics (New Haven, Connecticut: Yale University Press, 1980).

Ungerer, Horst, Owen Evans, and Peter Nyberg, *The European Monetary System:*

The Experience, 1979–82, Occasional Paper No. 19 (Washington: International Monetary Fund, May 1983).

———, "The European Monetary System and the International Exchange Rate System' (unpublished, International Monetary Fund, January 19, 1984).

Willett, Thomas D., *Floating Exchange Rates and International Monetary Reform,* American Enterprise Institute Studies in Economic Policy (Washington: American Enterprise Institute for Public Policy Research, 1977).

Williamson, John, *The Exchange Rate System, Policy Analyses in International Economics:* 5 (Washington: Institute for International Economics, 2nd ed., 1985).

9

UNEXPECTED REAL CONSEQUENCES OF FLOATING EXCHANGE RATES

Rachel McCulloch

After a decade of floating exchange rates, international monetary reform is again in the air, and it is thus timely to ask how well (or badly) the current system is functioning. But compared to what? Because the current monetary arrangements came into effect following years of vigorous debate on the merits of exchange-rate flexibility, some observers appear to forget that these arrangements were not in reality "designed" or even "adopted" by the International Monetary Fund. Rather, the present regime was initiated by the collapse of the Bretton Woods system, following prolonged and heroic salvage efforts. As late as 1972, a report on international monetary reform by the Executive Directors of the IMF failed even to mention flexible exchange rates as a viable long-term option (IMF, 1972), while an earlier report explicitly concerned with the role of exchange rates in the adjustment process had devoted only one of seventy-eight pages to floating rates (IMF, 1970). The markedly after-the-fact Second Amendment of the IMF Articles of Agreement to legalize the status quo merely reflected recognition of member governments' inability to agree on an alternative—any system imposing even minimal restraints on national policies—rather than an affirmation of the benefits of floating.

The central and still unresolved issue in the fruitless debate over international financial arrangements was the desire to preserve national autonomy in the face of growing economic and political interdependence. Since the present time seems no more propitious than the early 1970s for the willing sacrifice of national sovereignty by IMF members, any argument for system reform must be solidly grounded in the accumulated experience with floating, not by reference to the dogmas of the Bretton Woods era. This Essay is an eclectic assessment of that experience, with particular reference to the ways in which events have confounded both advocates and critics of floating. Although there is some discussion of the consequences of the floating-rate regime for worldwide macroeconomic performance, the main focus is on microeconomic issues—specifically, the role of floating rates in facilitating or retarding the growth of world trade and investment.

International Money and the Goals of Bretton Woods

National money, in its time-honored funtions as medium of (indirect) exchange, unit of account, standard of deferred payment, and store of value, is supposed to facilitate the efficient allocation of resources in production and consumption. Although the precise nature and magnitude of the efficiency gains have never been spelled out fully in economic analyses, monetary history gives clear evidence of significant real re-source costs and unanticipated redistributions of wealth when money fails to perform its traditional functions. At the same time, control of a nation's money supply also constitutes a potent tool of macroeconomic manage-ment and an alternative to taxation as a means of financing government expenditure. Thus, conflicting objectives confront those who conduct monetary policy, and there are both microeconomic and macroeconomic bases on which to judge their performance.

Analogously, the international monetary system is supposed to facili-tate an efficient allocation of resources worldwide, presumably through trade guided by comparative advantage, but it also has important conse-quences for global macroeconomic conditions. This twofold function was explicitly recognized in the Articles of Agreement of the International Monetary Fund approved at Bretton Woods in 1944, which listed among the purposes of the Fund:

> To facilitate the expansion and balanced growth of international trade, and to contribute thereby to the promotion and maintenance of high levels of employment and real income and to the development of the productive resources of all members as primary objectives of economic policy (Articles of Agreement, Article I (ii)).

As inadequacies in the Bretton Woods system became apparent during the 1960s, criticisms and proposals for reform likewise fell into two distinct categories.

Macroeconomic Performance

The Bretton Woods system was held to impart a deflationary bias to the world economy on account of the asymmetrical positions of surplus and deficit countries—at least in the rules, if not in the actual behavior, of member nations. At a time when the prospects for "fine tuning" of national macroeconomic performance seemed bright, the obligations of member nations under the Bretton Woods rules appeared to limit the ability of elected governments to deliver the combination of inflation and unemployment desired by their constituents. Although theory suggested that control of two instruments—monetary policy and fiscal policy— should allow enlightened policymakers to achieve both "internal balance" and "external balance," thoughtful analysts stressed that other objectives, notably adequate long-run growth, could be jeopardized by this textbook solution.

Because the Bretton Woods rules appeared to constrain national governments, advocates of reform and especially of increased exchange-rate flexibility appealed to the need for greater macroeconomic independence. Most reform proposals, however, called for modification rather than scrapping of the Bretton Woods rules. Two popular evolutionary plans were the crawling peg and the widening of exchange-rate margins, the latter actually adopted in 1971 as part of the short-lived Smithsonian Agreement. Interestingly, Cooper had seen wider bands as a feasible means of increasing independence but noted a disadvantage "from the viewpoint of fostering international cooperation . . . of *not* affording an occasion for close international consultation" (1968, p. 263).

Subsequent events suggest that advocates of increased flexibility failed to distinguish adequately between institutional and economic constraints on the actions of national policymakers. The collapse of the Bretton Woods system clearly increased the national sovereignty of IMF members with regard to the conduct of macroeconomic policy but had at most a minor effect on the ability of member nations to achieve desired outcomes. Countries acquired the technical capacity to pursue autonomous monetary policies because they were no longer required to peg their exchange rates, but they were severely constrained in exercising this autonomy on account of the undesirable effects of large exchange-rate movements on their domestic economies. Furthermore, the system of flexible exchange rates could not suppress structural interdependence; the system proved to offer ample channels for the continued international transmission of macroeconomic disturbances.

Even so, the chief flaws in the standard macroeconomic arguments for flexibility had less to do with their predictions about independence than with the now-evident defects in the macroeconomic paradigms, both Keynesian and monetarist, on which they were based. That national economies failed to respond according to the predictions of ingenious

1960s models can be blamed on many aspects of human behavior that are usually assumed away for analytic convenience. Perhaps most important and surely most striking is the demonstrated capacity of market participants for profitable innovation—a description more optimistic than the pejorative "structural instability" sometimes conjured up to explain the failure of econometric models to predict human behavior in times of rapid economic and social changes.[1]

Controlling Inflation

A related issue in the pre-1973 debate concerned the implications of the exchange-rate regime for the propensity of national officials to engage in inflationary policies. According to one standard argument, "the need to defend a fixed rate or a par value induces monetary and fiscal authorities to take greater care to prevent inflation; if floating rates were adopted, discipline would be weakened and countries would be more likely to pursue inflationary policies" (Solomon, 1977, p. 287). Indeed, the case for flexibility as a means of increasing macroeconomic independence implies precisely that some nations will opt for higher inflation rates when freed from the "external constraint" of a fixed parity. A similar but distinct argument is that a democratic government (or even one that is not so democratic) may find defense of a par value a politically acceptable reason to resist the competing claims of various domestic groups for increased shares of a relatively fixed national income (Caves and Jones, 1973, p. 444). As Caves and Jones note, however, a government might just as well point to "disgraceful" depreciation of a flexible rate. In the post-1973 period some have done exactly that.

The standard arguments sometimes acknowledged the inflationary potential of exchange-rate changes themselves, whether rates are flexible or adjustable, but only after 1973 did attention shift to this line of causation and thus away from the "nail-the-flag-to-the-masthead" argument for fixed rates. Although the inflationary pressures attending any devaluation or depreciation had long been emphasized by experts on less-developed countries, analyses for the industrialized nations tended to ignore the possibility, perhaps because of their Keynesian underpinnings. For example, the "absorption" literature stressed the importance of aggregate excess capacity in determining the degree to which the effects of a devaluation would be quickly offset by induced inflation.

The post-1973 inflationary experience was too dramatic to be ignored. Much subsequent debate has therefore centered on whether flexibility provides an independent source of inflationary pressure via a "ratchet" mechanism that pushes up domestic prices when a currency's value declines but fails to push them down at times of currency appreciation. Despite its intuitive appeal, however, empirical evidence for the ratchet effect appears to be weak (Goldstein, 1980). One important competing explanation for the failure to anticipate fully the inflationary impact of devaluation or depreciation was the tendency to underestimate the true openness of industrial economies, or, more precisely, the strength of the linkage between international prices of traded goods and domestic prices of nontraded goods (on this linkage, see Chipman, 1981, and McKinnon, 1981).

Living with Exchange Risk

Pre-1973 microeconomic arguments for floating exchange rates stressed their role in encouraging "unrestricted multilateral trade" (Friedman, 1953, p. 137). While rigidly fixed exchange rates like those of the classical gold standard were conceded to provide many of the benefits of a single world money, the Bretton Woods system of adjustable pegs had major shortcomings. Balance-of-payments disequilibria were frequently met by direct controls on trade and capital flows rather than the domestic macroeconomic policy responses prescribed by the "gold-standard rules of the game." Advocates of exchange-rate flexibility argued that it would produce appropriate exchange-rate movements, ensure prompt balance-of-payments adjustment, and thus obviate the need for direct controls that distort global resource allocation. But although proponents of flexible rates were virtually unanimous on this point, some critics foresaw incentives for protectionism (see, e.g., Wallich's comments in Haberler et al., 1969, p. 362).

Of course, even pegged rates could and did change. Therefore, the appropriate comparison was not between floating and fixed rates but between rates changing by small amounts on a day-to-day basis and those changing by substantial percentages at longer intervals and usually only after macroeconomic policy debacles, welfare-reducing direct controls, and repeated foreign-exchange-market crises. Some critics warned, however, that the day-to-day movement of floating rates would not be small. Skeptics envisioned low price elasticities, long lags, exchange-rate over-shooting, and destabilizing speculation that would result in wide fluctuations in market-determined rates—a specter of the 1930s that (along with competitive devaluation) the IMF Articles of Agreement specifically pledged to exorcise. Large fluctuations in rates, it was said, would increase the uncertainty facing international traders and investors. Although forward markets and a variety of other, more complicated mechanisms could provide transactors with insurance against rate changes, some warned that the additional cost would push world trade back toward barter (Kindleberger, 1970, p. 224).

Subsequent events have provided ample reason for extreme modesty on the part of prognosticators in both camps. Market-determined exchange rates have exhibited instability beyond the fondest nightmares of fixed-rates fanatics, yet trade and investment flows seem relatively unaffected by these changes. Blackhurst and Tumlir (1980, pp. 13–16) have noted that the volume of world trade continued to grow more rapidly than production throughout the 1970s, consistent with their hypothesis that the major determinant of changes in the level of trade is underlying GNP growth. Examining the effects of exchange-rate uncertainty on the multilateral and bilateral trade flows of the United States, Germany, and several other industrial countries for the period 1965–75, Hooper and Kohlhagen (1978, p. 505) "found absolutely no significant effect on the volume of trade (at the 0.95 level) despite considerable effort and experimentation. . . ." They did find a significant impact on prices, suggesting that the absence of any impact on volume might reflect relatively inelastic short-run supplies of exports or, alternatively, substantial hedging by importers and exporters.

These apparently contradictory phenomena may also be reconciled by the observation that the only alternatives to risky international transactions are risky domestic transactions. Of the many large risks of all types that any commercial endeavor now entails, exchange-rate uncertainty may be relatively minor compared with the benefits of foreign trade and investment. The risk is appreciable but the profitability even more so. As foreign-exchange risk is highly diversifiable, international operations provide an important means of diluting risks associated with domestic transactions rather than an independent addition to risk.

Market-Determined Exchange Rates

The central message of recent experience is that the foreign-exchange market is an asset market and that the economic laws governing exchange rates are fundamentally similar to those governing other asset prices— with stock and bond markets providing obvious domestic analogies. In fact, while exchange rates have indeed been volatile, their volatility has been less than that of stock prices (Frenkel and Mussa, 1980). Some recent literature has attempted to judge whether the volatility of observed asset prices is "excessive," i.e., unjustified by movements in their fundamental determinants. Shiller (1981) found evidence that the volatility of stock prices is excessive in relation to underlying uncertainty about future dividends, at least if risk neutrality is assumed. Although his statistical methodology has been questioned by subsequent researchers, any similar test of exchange-rate behavior rests on still shakier ground. As Meese and Singleton (1982) have pointed out, a test of whether exchange-rate volatility is excessive must be predicated on the validity of a particular structural model, and there are several active contenders. Furthermore, as Frenkel and Mussa note, even a determination of excessive volatility has no obvious policy implications.

Related to these findings is the discovery that the celebrated "law of one price" is not strictly enforced by real-world markets and that purchasing power parity, which perhaps ought not to have held in any case, has evidently collapsed (Frenkel, 1981).[2] As a consequence, the once-prevalent notion that an exchange rate behaves like the ratio of two national price indices must be scrapped and the role of exchange-rate movements in equilibrating international transactions reevaluated.

Controls on Trade and Capital Flows

A market-determined exchange rate necessarily equates day-to-day supply and demand for a nation's currency, whether or not supplemented by official reserve transactions. Thus, the need for direct controls motivated by overall balance-of-payments considerations is indeed eliminated by floating rates. The result has been, as predicted, an important reduction in the use of capital controls for balance-of-payments purposes. But asset preferences can and do produce significant prolonged divergences between the market price of a currency and its apparent "real" worth as determined by purchasing power parity. There is therefore no reason to expect a floating-rate system to eliminate incentives for direct controls motivated by current-account considerations.

While current-account balances have exhibited surprising (though lagged) responsiveness to rate movements, the reverse effect of current-account imbalances on exchange-rate movements is evidently much weaker. Indeed, floating rates react only to the extent that current-account imbalances constitute one type of "news" affecting asset preferences. Accordingly, macroeconomic incentives for protection, to increase domestic aggregate demand as well as to achieve sector-specific goals, are largely unaffected by floating rates.

The actual post-1973 experience has been characterized by the persistence and even extension of sectoral protection in the major industrialized countries, mainly for industries that are losing their competitiveness in relation to counterparts in Japan and especially the newly industrializing countries. Although there has been no apparent trend toward the increased use of protection (or competitive devaluation) as a means of macroeconomic stimulus, an assumed net gain in aggregate employment is customarily used—as in the Bretton Woods era—to bolster the case for proposed sectoral interventions, especially when large industries such as apparel and automobiles are involved. The Cambridge Economic Policy Group has promulgated a macroeconomic case for across-the-board protection of British industry, but with no noticeable effect thus far on the policies of the Thatcher government. Japan is sometimes accused of engaging in policies to prevent appreciation of the yen, especially through restrictions on inward foreign investment. But the main evidence presented in support of this hypothesis is unbalanced bilateral trade with the United States, a condition that also accompanied an allegedly overvalued yen in previous years.

Further aspects of the relationship between protection and exchange-rate movements are considered in subsequent sections.

Implications for Foreign Direct Investment

The "overvalued" dollar of the 1960s was singled out as an important reason, even *the* important reason, for the large volume of U.S. direct investment abroad, particularly in Europe. Through acquisitions of existing national enterprises and the construction of new plant and equipment, U.S.-based multinationals achieved a major presence in the protected markets of the newly created European Economic Community—investments all the more attractive at prevailing exchange rates. This role of disequilibrium exchange rates in foreign-investment decisions was initially confirmed by events of the 1970s. As the dollar plummeted in relative value through two devaluations and subsequent market depreciation, foreign direct investment in the United States grew with unprecedented rapidity—enough to make the United States the world's leading *host* country (in absolute but not relative terms) by the end of the decade. Yet the strengthening of the dollar since 1978 has not stemmed the flow of new foreign direct investment, and exchange-rate volatility has had no noticeable impact on its volume.

Why have foreign investors been undeterred by exchange-rate turbulence? There are several plausible lines of explanation, not mutually exclusive, that invoke the *relative* advantages of multinational firms over national enterprises. Thus, the finding that foreign direct investment continued to increase after 1973 does not rule out real costs associated with increased exchange-rate uncertainty.

As already noted, one anticipated benefit of floating that has actually materialized is a marked reduction in the use of direct capital controls.

This trend facilitates new or expanded investments, while at the same time increasing their attractiveness by improving prospects for the unimpeded repatriation of profits and royalties. Moreover, direct investment decisions are based on long-term plans, for periods during which even a pegged rate might well be expected to change. Over the life of an investment, the effects of volatility on profits largely cancel out, whereas cumulative movements in exchange rates, whether pegged or floating, mainly compensate for differential rates of domestic inflation or productivity growth across countries. A floating-rate system might even stimulate investment by easing such compensating exchange-rate adjustments and thereby reducing the likelihood of new direct controls on capital or trade flows during the investment period.

Foreign direct investment is also influenced by many considerations apart from exchange risk or the lack of it. If, as past studies suggest, protection is an important motive for direct investment, the recent protectionist swing in the United States—both actual and threatened— may have elicited investments intended to protect large expenditures already incurred in the development of the lucrative U.S. market. Recent Japanese investments in the United States may fall into this category. Furthermore, the accumulation of wealth by OPEC surplus nations has increased demands for assets of all kinds, and the post-1973 "internationalization" of the supply of saving probably favors U.S. assets because of the relative size and stability of the American economy. However, official statistics are uninformative on this point, since many OPEC investments are held anonymously through third-country intermediaries.

Finally, as suggested above and exactly contrary to pre-1973 conventional wisdom, floating may provide an important independent incentive for foreign direct investment. Input-price uncertainty is a recognized motive for vertical integration; a regime of floating rates accordingly provides incentives for vertical multinational integration. Together with centralized management, vertical integration allows a substantial reduction in the variability of profits due to exchange-rate movements between input-source countries and the downstream user.[3] This explanation fits the Canadian floating-rate period, which was marked by continued expansion of U.S. direct investments in Canadian extractive industries. Likewise, the reduction of input-price uncertainty may be a second motive (in addition to increased actual and threatened protection) for recent Japanese investments in the United States. Horizontal global expansion may similarly be favored by floating rates. For production operations in which minimum efficient scale is relatively low or scale economies unimportant, global diversification of production facilities allows firms some opportunity to optimize with respect to medium-term movements in real exchange rates as well as enhanced leverage in dealings with national labor unions.[4]

The vertical and horizontal expansions motivated by exchange-rate variability help to explain the rapid growth of intra-industry and intra-firm trade during the 1970s. They have opposite implications, however, for the responsiveness of trade flows to movements in exchange rates. While vertical integration allows a firm to ignore changes in the rate, horizontal integration offers opportunities to profit from them through adjustments in trade flows.

Exchange Rates, Relative Prices, and Competitiveness

A major surprise of the 1970s was the discovery that the United States is not a closed economy. The old and erroneous characterization (see, e.g., comments by Wallich in Haberler *et al.*, 1969, pp. 360–361) rested in part on a confusion of *traded* with *tradable* goods; for a large country like the United States, openness is consistent with low ratios of exports and imports to total domestic shipments.[5] Closely linked was the failure to anticipate the importance of exchange-rate changes for domestic prices. Early and crude estimates of the inflationary impact of dollar devaluation assumed that the prices of imported goods would be the only ones affected.

Elasticities and the Law of One Price

Analysts had been misled in part by the traditional elasticities approach to exchange-rate changes. The elasticities approach entailed a basically Keynesian view of price movements. Domestic-currency prices (or supply curves) for exports and import substitutes were assumed to be independent of the exchange rate. A related assumption, crucial but always implicit, was that domestic and foreign goods are not highly substitutable, so that domestic producers of tradables face appreciably downward-sloping demand curves for their outputs even in the long run. Given these assumptions, the primary effect of a devaluation would be to alter the relative prices of domestic goods and their foreign counterparts, shifting domestic and foreign demands toward domestic goods. A devaluing nation with some excess capacity could therefore expect a durable improvement in the international price competitiveness of its export and import-competing industries and a resulting durable improvement in its trade balance. The same logic was carried over to open-economy versions of Keynesian macroeconomic models, in which the exchange rate served as a policy instrument for switching aggregate expenditure between foreign and domestic markets.

The unexpectedly large impact of exchange-rate changes on domestic prices in the United States, along with the many cases in which devaluation failed to produce a durable improvement in the trade balance, led analysts to discard the elasticities approach and its underlying assumptions. With considerable fanfare, the era of the monetary approach was ushered in. Central to the elasticities approach is the implicit assumption that the law of one price is not applicable; domestic-currency prices of domestically produced tradables can move independently of the domestic-currency prices of their foreign counterparts. Exponents of the monetary approach chose an opposite but equally extreme assumption, making the law of one price the centerpiece of their models. Domestically produced exports and import-competing goods were now taken to be perfect substitutes for their foreign counterparts; accordingly, their domestic-currency prices were necessarily identical at all times.

Under these new assumptions, a devaluation must increase the prices of domestically produced tradables to restore equality with the prices of their foreign substitutes. For a small country, the domestic prices of all tradables would rise by exactly athe amount of the devaluation. Accordingly, an exchange-rate change affects primarily the prices of tradables relative to those of nontradables, rather than the prices of domestic goods relative to those of foreign goods. While the higher prices of tradables implies an increase in their domestic supply, domestic demand is shifted *away* from all tradables toward nontradables, eventually raising the prices of the latter and restoring the initial allocation of resources in domestic production. A key implication of such models is that devaluation cannot improve the internal price competitiveness of domestic suppliers.

But again events confounded theories, and again the problem centered on the law of one price—unduly disregarded in the elasticities approach but exalted beyond empirical justification by advocates of the monetary approach. As producers of almost any tradable good will be happy to affirm, exchange-rate movements *are* important for the overall international competitiveness of domestic industries; for some nonnegligible period, exchange-rate movements can and do alter the prices of domestic goods relative to those of foreign goods.

While the law of one price (for any one "good") assumes a high degree of substitutability in consumption or production between domestic tradables and their foreign counterparts, as well as markets that are highly competitive, empirical investigation reveals that these conditions do not hold for most tradable goods, at least over the relatively short periods with which macroeconomic policy is concerned. Rather, for reasons having to do with product differentiation, trade barriers, delivery lags, distribution, and servicing, tradables are heterogeneous in their adherence to the law of one price, or, more precisely, in their adherence to its preconditions. "Substantial changes in exchange rates typically have substantial and persistent effects on the relative common currency prices of closely matched manufactures produced in different countries" (Isard, 1977, p. 948).

Recognizing that tradable goods are heterogeneous brings the analysis almost full circle to a framework in which elasticities again play a key role. Am important implication is that the price effects of devaluation are not typically uniform across industries producing tradable goods.

Sectoral Consequences of Changes in Exchange Rates

Sector-specific consequences within the aggregate of "tradables" attracted the attention of econometric modelers first (see, e.g., Hooper and Lowrey, 1979). More recently, theorists have also begun to explore the crucial role of "structural" characteristics such as supply elasticities and wage rigidities or wage indexation in open-economy macroeconomic analysis, thereby sacrificing some of the simplicity and elegance of highly aggregated models but shedding new light on sectoral effects (see Branson, 1982, and references cited there).

Where substitutability and therefore cross-price elasticities are high and markets competitive, there will be strong forces equating the domestic-currency prices of foreign-produced goods with those of domestically produced versions. A devaluation will therefore cause domestic prices to rise—by the full amount of a devaluation in the case of a small country that has no appreciable effect on international prices. Domestic supply, employment, and profits will rise; domestic consumption will fall.

For an industry in which domestic and foreign versions are highly imperfect substitutes, devaluation has much weaker short-run consequences for the domestic price. The increased domestic-currency price of the imperfect foreign substitute results in an outward shift in the domestic industry's downward-sloping demand curve. The effects on equilibrium price thus depend crucially on conditions of domestic supply. Domestic output, employment, and profits will rise; domestic and foreign consumption of the industry's output will rise on account of the favorable movement in its relative price. Moreover, with goods or services that are highly differentiated, each *producer* faces a distinctly downward-sloping demand curve, so that markets may be characterized by price discrimination. In such markets, an exchange-rate change may actually have a "perverse" effect on output and price, although not on profits.

Exchange-rate changes also affect industry supply curves through their consequences for the domestic-currency prices of tradable inputs. As noted above, the size of price changes depends critically upon the extent to which foreign and domestic versions are highly substitutable; the speed with which these price changes are reflected in higher production costs depends on the extent to which suppliers are bound by long-term commitments. One measure of the total impact of devaluation on a given industry through both output and input markets is the *net* effect on industry value added. As in the analysis of the "effective protection" that a nation's tariff schedule provides to a particular industry, i.e., the percentage by which industry value added per unit of output can exceed its free-trade level, a calculation can in principle be made of the *net* effect of "exchange-rate protection" on an industry's value added. A devaluation will raise domestic-currency value added by exactly the percentage of the devaluation only for an industry in which domestic and foreign goods are highly substitutable on both the output and input sides *and* effects on world prices of the industry's output sales and input purchases are negligible. Otherwise, either a smaller or larger increment is possible.

A last dimension of the sectoral consequences of devaluation concerns the division of increased industry value added between industry-specific and mobile factors. If the supply of mobile factors ("labor") is available at a fixed nominal reward, as in the case of a binding minimum wage, industry profits will increase by the full increment in value added. But because devaluation raises the cost of living and also tends to increase the demand for variable factors of production, there may be some upward adjustment in wages, whether determined by a competitive market, union contract negotiation, or legislation of a real minimum wage. On the other hand, devaluation—as opposed to depreciation of a floating rate—is often accompanied by an "incomes policy" intended to hold down wage adjustments, thus reducing the real wage and raising the proportion of increased industry value added accruing as profits.

Adjustments to Real Shocks

Although real shocks were hardly new in the 1970s, their interaction with a floating-rate system provided beleaguered policy analysts with considerable food for thought. As predicted, floating rates prevented the recurring exchange-market crises that no doubt would otherwise have accompanied the OPEC price shocks and ill-advised policy responses to them. And, although floating rates themselves did little to ease the adjustment of less-developed oil importers, most of which still peg their rates in any case, a largely private recycling process solved the immediate problem of inadequate balance-of-payments financing. Indeed, even critics of floating rates are usually quick to acknowledge that no alternative system could have survived the stormy 1970s. On the other hand, the actual adjustment process was quite different from that anticipated by most analysts, principally because of the unexpected ways in which OPEC surplus nations spent their vastly increased earnings.

According to the standard pre-1973 debate, flexible rates were supposed to insulate a country from external shocks, while fixed rates would allow the burden of internal shocks to be shared with trading partners. As already noted, the increased macroeconomic independence offered by flexible rates proved to be largely illusory. Moreover, the standard fixed vs. flexible arguments, based on conclusions from one-sector macroeconomic models, necessarily ignored the sector-specific impact of many shocks and thus obscured the sector-specific aspects of the resulting adjustment process. In response to this latter discovery, enterprising theorists have recently come forward with models of such hitherto uncelebrated maladies as "Dutch disease" (see, e.g., Corden, 1981, and Neary, 1982).

As in the analysis of exchange-rate changes, the crucial missing insight was that "the" tradables sector is in fact a set of heterogeneous industries. Furthermore, each has at any time a collection of industry-specific factors that can be shifted elsewhere only at considerable cost. Therefore, in a floating-rate system, the good fortune of one tradable-goods industry, whether technological progress, a mineral discovery, or a favorable price movement in the world market, can become bad news for other tradable-goods industries through two mechanisms: exchange-rate appreciation and the bidding up of rewards to factors mobile between sectors. The result is "Dutch disease" or "de-industrialization" or the problem of "lagging sectors," i.e., ones in which output falls and the rewards to industry-specific factors decline. Moreover, "the decline in the relative size of non-booming sectors is a necessary component of the economy's adjustment toward a higher level of income" (Neary, 1982, p. 20). Thus, a conflict arises between efficient resource allocation and certain other national objectives, such as developing and maintaining an industrial sector of a certain size or maintaining the incomes of sector-specific factors.

All this assumes, of course, that the exchange rate moves in the direction suggested by the effect on the current-account balance, an effect that may be weak in practice. Furthermore, a national government wishing to avoid the consequences of appreciation can intervene in the foreign-exchange market, directly or indirectly, thus protecting other tradables sectors from injury. Corden (1981) has suggested that this is a primary motive for "exchange-rate protection." In such a case, or with a pegged rate that is not revised upward, the good news means reserve accumulation and attendant inflationary pressure rather than appreciation. Thus, the problem of adjustment can at least be postponed—for better or worse. It would be for better if the good news were temporary or reversible, because a stable rate could eliminate the unpleasant and perhaps undesirable squeeze on other tradables, although probably at the cost of some inflation.

While a sensible comparison of effects under the two regimes requires some specification of the way in which private and official agents form expectations, the outcomes may be quite similar in the long run. The reason is that a macroeconomic policy cannot eradicate the "supercompetitiveness" of one tradable-goods sector over the rest. Through internal mechanisms such as competition for inputs, the less-competitive sectors will still be squeezed. For example, it is noteworthy that the balance (in current dollars) of U.S. trade in "high-technology" goods has grown almost exponentially since 1960, while the trade balance in all other manufactures is roughly its mirror image. There is no apparent discontinuity in this pattern between the 1960s and 1970s, except for a higher variability in the 1970s that probably reflects underlying macroeconomic fluctuations and large jumps in real exchange rates. But for a government determined to slow the movement of resources out of uncompetitive tradables industries, there is still an obvious solution in the form of sectoral intervention or "industrial policy."

Causes and Consequences of Protection

Freer trade was one widely anticipated advantage of flexible exchange rates that failed to materialize. The conventional wisdom predicted that exchange-rate flexibility would facilitate trade liberalization (e.g., Baldwin, 1970, pp. 20–21, and Bergsten, 1972, pp. 8–9). Yet the post-1973 period has in fact been marked by the proliferation of new and subtle trade-distorting measures. Furthermore, Bergsten and Williamson (1982) offer evidence that exchange-rate volatility has actually intensified the ever-present clamor for more and better protection from foreign competition.

According to the usual pre-1973 argument, exchange-rate flexibility would eliminate the perceived need for protection and in any case neutralize its benefits. This argument rested on errors concerning both the motives for protection and its consequences in a flexible-rate system.

A floating rate obviates the perceived need for direct controls on foreign transactions only to the extent that protection is motivated by overall balance-of-payments considerations; it does not eliminate incentives for protection as a tool of macroeconomic stabilization or to achieve sector-specific goals. The implicit assumption that balance-of-payments considerations dominated trade-policy choices before 1973 may have stemmed from a confusion of the underlying motives for protection with the public rhetoric used to justify it.[6] Since overall balance-of-payments considerations were in most instances merely a secondary motive for protection, the elimination of this motive has had only minor consequences for its use.

Sectoral Consequences of Protection

Gains achieved by protected domestic industries would be completely offset by resulting exchange-rate movements only under highly implausible circumstances. The notion that it is somehow irrational for industries to seek protection because it will be offset by currency appreciation (Friedman, 1981) is another example of the misleading conclusions that are drawn from macroeconomic models with insufficient "structure." In both industrialized and developing countries, real-world protection is a microeconomic, industry-specific phenomenon. Although broad coalitions may form to support or oppose major changes in national trade legislation, the level and type of actual protection are almost always determined on an industry-by-industry basis. Even the "across-the-board" tariff cuts achieved in the Kennedy Round of multilateral trade negotiations singled out numerous specific industries for exemptions from cuts. Too many recent macroeconomic analyses of protection are based on models in which only one good is produced domestically (e.g., Eichengreen, 1981). These models provide useful insights concerning asset-market channels through which protection can have unanticipated and complex general-equilibrium consequences. But, because they necessarily omit the important sector-specific effects that are at the very heart of trade policy, they can provide only partial, and sometimes misleading, information concerning the real-world policies that presumably motivate their construction.

As soon as its industry-specific nature is recognized, the analysis of protection becomes identical to that of the industry-specific shocks discussed in the previous section. Protection of some tradables is likely to worsen the economic prospects of other, less-favored tradables. As before, whether the protection of some industries transforms others into lagging sectors depends in part on whether the exchange rate actually appreciates. In the case of protection, however, the outcome has an additional element of ambiguity, since some protective devices, such as "voluntary" export restraints, can cause a deterioration rather than an improvement in the trade balance and hence a depreciation rather than an appreciation (to the extent that the trade balance does influence the exchange rate); see Meade's classic analysis (1951, Chap. XXI) and Richardson's (1982) treatment of "modern" commercial policy. Adequate analysis of industry-specific effects requires a model with at least two sectors producing tradable outputs.

Identification of sectoral consequences also helps to clarify the underlying rational motives for apparently irrational policies. One particularly interesting example is the prevalence of overvalued exchange rates among developing countries, along with extensive trade and credit controls. Taken together as a coherent policy package, this adds up to a hefty subsidy to a preferred sector, typically import-competing industrial production. While trade barriers protect domestic markets, an overvalued exchange rate allows required capital equipment and intermediate inputs to be purchased at bargain prices, and capital-export prohibitions facilitate access to low-cost credit. The resulting disadvantage to producers of other tradables is one important reason for the much-remarked failure of third-world agriculture to achieve the production levels suggested by its obvious comparative advantage. Like all generalizations regarding developing countries, this one clearly disregards many important national differences. However, the pattern seems to fit a large number of countries.

Volatility and Protectionism

The volatility of the dollar since 1973 has resulted in prolonged departures from purchasing power parity and large exogenous swings in the international competitiveness of U.S. producers of tradable goods. The unexpected increase in protectionism over the same period raises the question whether the current system has actually been an important *cause* of increased protectionism.

Bergsten and Williamson (1982) have recently suggested that there is a "ratchet" effect of exchange-rate fluctuations on the average level of protection.[7] While prolonged overvaluation of the dollar gives rise to new arguments for all manner of sectoral protection, as in 1981 and 1982, any new protection is likely to persist long after the overvaluation has disappeared. Moreover, they argue, even undervaluation might add to protectionist pressures by attracting resources into industries with secularly declining international competitiveness, or at least slowing their exit. When the inappropriately low currency value finally moves upward again, protection will be demanded.

While this hypothesis is intuitively appealing and seems consistent with the recent protectionist fever in the U.S. Congress, there is again a problem of distinguishing appropriately between the underlying motives for protection and its public justification. The quest for favorable government intervention (in all forms, including, but certainly not limited to, trade policies) is a fact of economic life. As long as governments are responsive to demands for sectoral intervention, efforts to obtain, retain, and increase such benefits represent a capital investment comparable to research and development, advertising, and other intangibles that have a favorable impact on profits. (The analogy is imperfect, however, because investment in obtaining favorable government intervention is usually undertaken by a trade association or labor union and therefore has a "free rider" aspect that does not occur with most advertising or R & D.) However, managers, union officials, and the public do tend to view asymmetrically profits vs. losses and overtime vs. layoffs. Therefore, both the industry "demand" for government intervention and its politically determined "supply" may be expected to increase when national unemployment is high, as in 1981–82. Furthermore, while protection is only one possible type of favorable legislative or administrative action among many (including government procurement, regulatory or tax relief, technical assistance, and subsidized credit), the political cost of intervention in this particular form is probably less when the exchange rate is widely acknowledged to be overvalued, as in 1981–82. For these political-economic reasons, it is plausible to expect industry-specific intervention to increase when national unemployment is high and to take the specific form of new trade barriers when the dollar is overvalued.

Yet the actual cases cited to support this link between protection and overvaluation (e.g., textiles, steel, sugar, shoes) are ones with chronic competitiveness problems, not fundamentally healthy industries put temporarily into the red by an overvalued dollar. For some, protection from imports is a national vice extending back into the 1950s. This suggests that exchange-rate overvaluation can provide the politically expedient occasion for new protection of declining industries, interacting with other determinants of increased protectionism, without being the fundamental cause. It must also be noted that the empirical evidence for the persistence of sectoral intervention seems to be weak. Because of strong domestic lobbies against, as well as in favor of, protection, import relief provides only a brief respite for many industries from the consequences of shifting comparative advantage.

Concluding Remarks

Much of the pre-1973 debate on international monetary reform proved to be irrelevant, for two reasons. First, international political realities precluded the "choice" or "design" of a new system. Perhaps Bretton Woods was a unique phenomenon, at least for modern times. But, more important, the post-1973 system of flexible exchange rates has functioned in ways that are markedly different from the predictions of most analysts on either side of the debate.

In many regards, the academic arguments in favor of increased flexibility never improved on Friedman's pioneering (1953) case. Yet Friedman, as well as most others, erred in their most fundamental prediction, that flexible rates would be stable if national monetary policies were stable. We live in times of too much daily economic "news" from other sources to avoid large fluctuations in market-determined exchange rates. As Mussa aptly remarked, "The smoothly adjusting exchange rate is, like the unicorn, a mythical beast" (1979, p. 9). Moreover, while these fluctuations probably do imply significant real costs to those engaged in international commerce, their effects on trade and investment flows are very different than anticipated. In particular, day-to-day movements in currency values offer an independent motive for international transactions, as a means of diversifying exchange risk.

If there is a single salient lesson to be learned by scrutinizing academic research on exchange rates in the light of post-1973 events in the international monetary system, it is the great mischief that can come from paying insufficient attention to economic structure in macroeconomic analysis. While theorists necessarily strip reality down to a bare minimum of basic relationships, the same basics are not appropriate for all questions. For the large number of policy issues arising from the interactions of individual industries within a single economy, macroeconomic models with only one aggregate tradable can provide at best a partial understanding and sometimes a seriously flawed account.

Notes

1. Meese and Rogoff (1983) found that a random walk performed as well out of sample as any estimated structural model of exchange-rate determination. In an earlier version of the same paper (Meese and Rogoff, 1981), the authors attributed the poor out-of-sample performance of these models to "structural instability." But the authors noted in the revised version that it is more accurate to describe the problem as one of omitted variables or other misspecifications of the under-

lying structural relationships. In other words, simple models cannot predict complex responses.

2. Although there is a rich literature spanning at least four decades on the reasons why purchasing power parity need not hold over short or even long time periods (see, e.g., Chipman, 1981), the notion persists that its absence somehow violates fundamental precepts of rational economic behavior.

3. Centralized management also facilitates optimization of foreign-exchange exposure, reducing the need for forward-market cover. Aliber (1983) has suggested that the lower cost of internal cover provides an advantage to multinational firms over domestic ones.

4. Expanded international operations in the 1970s may also reflect efforts to minimize the impact of exchange-rate movements on reported profits. Despite all the good reasons adduced by economic theorists to show that rational managers should be indifferent to the variability of accounting profits, managers persist in their concern about period-to-period fluctuations in reported earnings. F.A.S.B. Statement Number 8, the Financial Accounting Standards Board's first attempt to develop standardized accounting principles for a world of day-to-day movements in exchange rates, resulted in large and probably meaningless fluctuations in reported earnings (Hekman, 1981). The resulting storm of protests produced F.A.S.B. Statement Number 52, which broadens the definition of exposure and calls for an adjustment to net worth rather than to earnings.

5. Openness also increased in the 1970s, but authors of textbooks on macroeconomics nonetheless continue to relegate any consideration of openness to the final chapters.

6. Two indirect pieces of evidence for the dominance of other motives are levels of protection that vary markedly across industries and the use of quantitative restrictions with ambiguous balance-of-payments consequences. However, any positive balance-of-payments consequences can be viewed as reducing the political cost of providing protection to favored sectors.

7. Bergsten and Williamson call for policies to ensure that the value of the dollar does not stray too far from its "fundamental equilibrium rate," defined by analogy to the Bretton Woods criterion of fundamental disequilibrium for a parity change and distinguished from day-to-day market equilibrium. But while uncontroversial arguments in favor of greater stability constitute much of the paper, there is no indication of how the authors' proposed solution (which amounts to a wide-band peg and would thus appear to share many of the flaws that led to the end of the Bretton Woods system) could be successfully implemented.

References

Aliber, Robert Z., "Money, Multinationals, and Sovereigns," in Charles P. Kindleberger and David B. Audretsch, eds., *The Multinational Corporation in the 1980s*, Cambridge, Mass., MIT Press, 1983 forthcoming.

Baldwin, Robert, *Non-Tariff Distortions of International Trade*, Washington, D.C., The Brookings Institution, 1970.

Bergsten, C. Fred, *The Cost of Import Restrictions to American Consumers*, New York, American Importers Association, 1972.

Bergsten, C. Fred, and John Williamson, "Exchange Rates and Trade Policy," paper prepared for the Institute for International Economics Conference on Trade Policy in the Eighties, Washington, D.C., June 23–25, 1982.

Blackhurst, Richard, and Jan Tumlir, *Trade Relations under Flexible Exchange Rates*, Geneva, General Agreement on Tariffs and Trade, September 1980.

Branson, William H., "Economic Structure and Policy for External Balance," paper prepared for the NBER/IMF Conference on Policy Interdependence, Washington, D.C., Aug. 31, 1982.

Caves, Richard E., and Ronald W. Jones, *World Trade and payments*. Boston, Little, Brown, 1973.

Chipman, John, "Internal-External Price Relationships in the West German Economy, 1958–79," *Zeitschrift für die gesamte Staatswissenschaft*, 137 (September 1981), pp. 612–637.

Cooper, Richard N., *The Economics of Interdependence*, New York, McGraw-Hill for the Council on Foreign Relations, 1968.

Corden, W. M., "Exchange Rate Protection," in R. N. Cooper *et al.*, eds., *The International Monetary System under Flexible Exchange Rates: Global, Regional, and National*, Cambridge, Mass., Ballinger, 1981.

Eichengreen, Barry, "A Dynamic Model of Tariffs, Output and Employment under Flexible Exchange Rates," *Journal of International Economics*, II (August 1981), pp. 341–359.

Frenkel, Jacob A., "The Collapse of Purchasing Power Parities during the 1970s," *European Economic Review*, 16 (May 1981), pp. 145–165.

Frenkel, Jacob A., and Michael L. Mussa, "The Efficiency of Foreign Exchange Markets and Measures of Turbulence," *American Economic Review*, 70 (May 1980), pp. 374–381.

Friedman, Milton, "The Case for Flexible Exchange Rates," in *Essays in Positive Economics*, Chicago, University of Chicago Press, 1953.

———, "Do Imports Cost Jobs?" *Newsweek* (Feb. 9, 1981), p. 77.

Goldstein, Morris, *Have Flexible Exchange Rates Handicapped Macroeconomic Policy?* Special Papers in International Economics No. 14, Princeton, N.J., Princeton University, International Finance Section, 1980.

Haberler, Gottfried, Henry C. Wallich, Peter B. Kenen, and Fritz Machlup, "Round Table on Exchange Rate Policy," *American Economic Review*, 59 (May 1969), pp. 357–369.

Hekman, Christine R., "Foreign Exchange Risk: Relevance and Management," *Managerial and Decision Economics*, 2 (1981), pp. 256–262.

Hooper, Peter, and Steven W. Kohlhagen, "The Effect of Exchange Rate Uncertainty on the Prices and Volume of International Trade," *Journal of International Economics*, 8 (November 1978), pp. 483–511.

Hooper, Peter, and Barbara Lowrey, "Impact of the Dollar Depreciation on the U.S. Price level: An Analytical Survey of Empirical Estimates," International Finance Discussion Paper No. 128, Washington, D.C., Board of Governors of the Federal Reserve System, January 1979.

International Monetary Fund, *The Role of Exchange Rates in the Adjustment of International Payments*, Washington, D.C., 1970.

———, *Reform of the International Monetary System*, Washington, D.C., 1972.

Isard, Peter, "How Far Can We Push the 'Law of One Price'?" *American Economic Review*, 67 (December 1977), pp. 942–948.

Kindleberger. Charles P., *Power and Money*, New York, Basic Books, 1970.

McKinnon, Ronald I., "The Exchange Rate and Macroeconomic Policy: Changing Postwar Perceptions," *Journal of Economic Literature*, 19 (June 1981), pp. 531–557.

Meade, James E., *The Balance of Payments*, London, Oxford University Press, 1951.

Meese, Richard, and Kenneth Rogoff, "Empirical Exchange Rate Models of the Seventies: Are Any Fit to Survive?" International Finance Discussion Paper No. 184, Washington, D.C., Board of Governors of the Federal Reserve System, June 1981.

———, "Empirical Exchange Rate Models of the Seventies: Do They Fit out of Sample?" *Journal of International Economics*, 14 (February 1983), pp. 3–24.

Meese, Richard A., and Kenneth J. Singleton, "Rational Expectations and the Volatility of Floating Exchange Rates," unpublished paper, 1982.

Mussa, Michael, "Empirical Regularities in the Behavior of Exchange Rates and Theories of the Foreign Exchange Market," *Carnegie-Rochester Conference Series on Public Policy*, 11 (1979), pp. 9–55.

Neary, J. Peter, "Real and Monetary Aspects of the 'Dutch Disease'," paper prepared for the International Economic Association Conference on Structural Adjustment in Trade-Dependent Advanced Economies, Yxtaholm, Sweden, Aug. 2–6, 1982.

Richardson, J. David, "Four Observations on Modern International Commercial Policy under Floating Exchange Rates," *Carnegie-Rochester Conference Series on Public Policy*, 16 (Spring 1982), pp. 187–220.

Shiller, Robert J., "Do Stock Prices Move Too Much to Be Justified by Subsequent Changes in Dividends?" *American Economic Review*, 71 (June 1981), pp. 421–436.

Solomon, Robert, *The International Monetary System, 1945–1976*, New York, Harper & Row, 1977.

PART III

BALANCE OF PAYMENTS, BUDGET DEFICITS AND FLEXIBLE EXCHANGE RATES

10

DOMESTIC SAVING AND INTERNATIONAL CAPITAL MOVEMENTS IN THE LONG RUN AND THE SHORT RUN*

Martin Feldstein

1. Introduction

A nearly universal assumption in international economic analysis is that capital flows freely among countries to keep the return to capital equal in all places. The implications of this assumption of perfect capital mobility are not only extremely important but are also contrary to most economists' beliefs about the behavior of national economies. Perfect capital mobility implies, for example, that the burden of corporate income taxes falls primarily on labor, that government deficits do not crowd out private investment, that increases in saving do not raise domestic investment, and that monetary and tax policies cannot alter the real net rate of return on domestic capital. To avoid such intellectual schizophrenia, we must either modify the assumption of perfect capital mobility or abandon the view that national monetary and fiscal policies that alter domestic saving can thereby influence the process of domestic capital formation.

An alternative view of the international economy recognizes that capital mobility is less perfect. Capital tends to flow in the direction of higher returns but risk considerations, institutional barriers and government policies impede that flow. For private lenders and portfolio investors, foreign stocks and bond are a very imperfect substitute for domestic securities. The profitability of foreign direct investment reflects not only the factor proportions in the host country but also firm-specific consider-

*The research is part of the Bureau's project on Productivity and Industrial Change in the World Economy. I am grateful to Glenn Hubbard for assistance with this work and the several colleagues, especially Jeffrey Sachs, for discussions.

ations of marketing, tariff barriers, tax rules, etc. Foreign direct investment also involves political risks that are fundamentally different from investing in the home country. Further, government policies may seek to encourage or prevent capital inflows or outflows during long periods of time. These restrictions on perfect capital mobility imply that national economic policies that affect domestic saving can also influence domestic capital formation.

In an earlier paper, Charles Horioka and I presented a direct test of the perfect capital mobility assumption [Feldstein and Horioka (1980)]. We reasoned that with perfect capital mobility there should be no relation between a country's domestic saving rate and its domestic rate of investment. Instead, a sustained increase in saving in any one country should add funds to the world capital market. These funds would then be divided among countries in a way that depends on the relative size of each country's initial capital stock and the elasticity of its marginal efficiency of capital schedule, but that does not depend on which country did the additional saving.

We used data for the industrial countries that are members of the Organization for Economic Cooperation and Development (OECD) to test this implication of perfect capital mobility. We showed first that there are substantial differences in domestic saving rates among these countries and that these differences remain stable over a long period of time. We then estimated regression equations relating the ratio of domestic investment to gross domestic product as the dependent variable to the ratio of domestic saving to GNP as the independent variable. To reduce the impact of cyclical variations and random shocks, both variables were averaged over a minimum of five years.

The evidence overwhelmingly rejected the implication of perfect capital mobility. The relation between the investment ratio and the savings ratio is significantly different from zero in every period that we examined at significance levels that were always less than 0.001. Indeed, the coefficients were always greater than 0.85 and within two standard errors of 1.0. The conclusion was unavoidable that, contrary to the implication of the perfect capital mobility assumption, a sustained increase in the domestic saving ratio caused an almost equal increase in the domestic investment ratio.

The Feldstein-Horioka analysis explicitly assumed that intercountry differences in savings rates are caused by differences in demographic structure, population growth rates and social security retirement income programs. This specification, based on earlier work by Modigliani (1970) and Feldstein (1977), permitted using a simultaneous equations approach to estimating the investment equation with the savings ratio treated as endogenous. These estimates confirmed the ordinary least squares results.[1]

The findings of the Feldstein-Horioka study should not however be overinterpreted. They do not imply that there is no capital mobility nor that there is no tendency of capital to shift toward countries where it can earn a high after-tax rate of return.[2] Strictly interpreted, the Feldstein-Horioka paper only claims to be a test of the extreme hypothesis of perfect capital mobility. More generally, however, it is reasonable to interpret the Feldstein-Horioka findings as evidence that there are substantial imperfections in the international capital market and that a very large share of domestic savings tends to remain in the home country. This implies further that sustained government deficits to reduce domestic capital formation and that corporate income taxes can reduce the net return to capital.[3]

The Feldstein-Horioka study used data for the fifteen year period from 1960 through 1974. The sample period ended just as the dramatic 1973 OPEC price increase had begun to alter substantially the current account deficits of the industrial nations and therefore the international flow of capital. Government interference with international capital movements was also reduced in some countries in the 1970s; the United States, for example, ended its interest equalization tax on foreign borrowing in the United States in 1974, and reduced the pressure on U.S. multinationals to finance overseas investment by borrowing abroad.

One major purpose of the present study is to extend the sample period to the end of the 1970s. The evidence presented in section 2 confirms that the second half of the 1970s was a period of substantially greater international capital flows. Nevertheless, the earlier finding that international differences in saving rates are associated with nearly equal differences in investment rates is reconfirmed. There is no more support for the perfect capital mobility hypothesis in the regression estimates for 1974 through 1979 than there was in the previous fifteen years.

Since net foreign investment is equal to the difference between domestic savings and domestic investment, the strong association between domestic investment and domestic savings implies that there is only a weak association between net foreign investment and domestic savings. The empirical analysis presented in section 3 decomposes net foreign investment and examines the relation between each of the major components of net foreign investment and the domestic saving rate. A different type of decomposition is suggested by the essential equality of net foreign investment and the current account surplus. Section 3 also examines the relation between the components of the current account balance and the domestic saving rate. Neither of these analyses suggests any change in the basic conclusion about the long-run independence of international capital flows from domestic savings rates.

Since domestic savings and domestic investment are parts of an inter-dependent economic system, the regression of investment ratios on savings ratios raises problems of estimation and interpretation. Section 4 discusses the issues of identification and estimation with the help of a minimal theoretical model of investment, savings and international capital flows. The analysis indicates why cross-country data averaged over sub-stantial periods are likely to be a much more reliable basis for testing the hypothesis of perfect capital mobility and for estimating structural para-meters than time series data for individual countries.

Section 5 then examines an explicit model of portfolio choice that shows why sustained changes in domestic savings may have only a small effect on net foreign investment in the long run and yet may also have a more substantial effect on capital flows in the short run.

There is a brief concluding section that comments on some of the limitations of the current paper and that suggests direction for future research.

2. The effect of saving on domestic investment

The basic data for the present analysis are the ratios of investment to GDP and savings to GDP for seventeen OECD countries.[4] These ratios are calculated using the current dollar magnitudes published by the OECD (1981) and therefore adjusted by the OECD to a common set of statistical definitions.

Table 1 presents the values of the saving and investment ratios and of the differences between them. All of the figures refer to gross investment and saving. The first three columns show the mean values of these ratios for each country in the 15-year period from 1960 through 1974.[5] The comparable ratios for the post-OPEC years 1975 through 1979 are shown in the next three columns.

These figures show a striking increase in the absolute differences between the domestic savings rate and the domestic investment rate. In the fifteen years ending in 1974, the difference between the average savings ratio and the average investment ratio ranged from—0.030 (in Greece) to 0.018 (in the Netherlands) with a mean of 0.007 and a standard deviation of 0.016. in contrast, in the second half of the 1970s the range

TABLE 1
Savings and investment ratios in OECD countries.[a]

	Mean values, 1960–1974			Mean values, 1975–1979		
	S/Y	I/Y	S/Y–I/Y	S/Y	I/Y	S/Y–I/Y
Australia	0.245	0.267	−0.022	0.217	0.231	−0.014
Austria	0.287	0.284	0.003	0.250	0.267	−0.017
Belgium	0.233	0.224	0.009	0.201	0.215	−0.014
Canada	0.218	0.231	−0.013	0.209	0.235	−0.026
Denmark	0.220	0.248	−0.028	0.194	0.228	−0.034
Finland	0.288	0.306	−0.024	0.276	0.318	−0.042
France	0.251	0.250	0.001	0.229	0.232	−0.003
Germany	0.270	0.262	0.008	0.229	0.222	0.007
Greece	0.222	0.252	−0.030	0.247	0.276	−0.029
Ireland	0.197	0.225	−0.028	0.234	0.272	−0.038
Italy	0.237	0.227	0.010	0.221	0.214	0.007
Japan	0.366	0.358	0.008	0.305	0.317	−0.012
Netherlands	0.284	0.266	0.018	0.269	0.215	0.054
New Zealand	0.230	0.255	−0.025	0.205	0.275	−0.070
Sweden	0.243	0.241	0.002	0.195	0.211	−0.016
United Kingdom	0.189	0.193	−0.004	0.177	0.190	−0.013
United States	0.188	0.188	0.000	0.171	0.179	−0.008

[a]*Source:* 'National accounts of the OECD countries: 1950–1979' (OECD, Paris, 1981). S/Y is gross domestic savings divided by GDP, I/Y is gross domestic investment divided by GDP.

was from—0.042 (in Finland) to 0.054 (in the Netherlands) with a mean of—0.016 and a standard deviation of 0.025.

For virtually every industrial country, the second half of the 1970s represented a time when domestic investment exceeded domestic savings. This in turn implied that net foreign investment was negative and therefore that the current account was in deficit. The negative net foreign investment for the industrial countries as a whole in these years was largely a reflection of the higher prices being paid for imported oil and the resulting surpluses of the OPEC countries.

Despite the substantial increase in the size and variability of international capital flows, the second half of the 1970s showed the same strong tendency for countries with high domestic savings rates to have high rates of domestic investment. Table 2 presents estimates of the basic investment equation,

$$I_i/Y_i = \alpha + \beta[S_i/Y_i] + \epsilon_i, \qquad (1)$$

where I_i is domestic investment in country i, S_i is domestic savings, Y_i is GDP, and ϵ_i is a random disturbance. The equation is estimated with the sample of seventeen countries listed in table 1 and with the investment and savings ratios averaged over several different subperiods as well as for the entire 20-year period from 1960 through 1979.

The estimate for the second half of the 1970s indicates that an additional 'dollar' (pound, franc, mark, etc.) of domestic saving raised domestic investment by 0.865 dollars with a standard error of 0.185.[6] Comparison with the other subperiods indicates that the response of investment to savings was at least as high in this final period as in any of the earlier periods. This was true even though, as the lower $\bar{R}^2$ implies, there was more 'unpredictable' variation in domestic investment during this period.[7]

For the 20-year period as a whole, each extra 'dollar' of saving was associated with 0.796 additional dollars of investment. With a standard error of 0.112, this is clearly significantly different from zero at any relevant probability level. The alternative null hypothesis, i.e., that the coefficient of S/Y is 1.0, can be rejected at a probability level of 10 percent, implying that capital does tend to flow to countries with low savings rates although certainly much less than perfect capital mobility would imply.

The first five equations reported in table 2 refer to gross saving and gross investment. Since capital accumulation depends on net investment, it is interesting to consider also the relation between net investment and

TABLE 2
The relation between domestic savings ratios and domestic investment ratios.*

Equation	Sample period	Definition	Const.	S/Y	$\bar{R}^2$
1	1975–1979	gross	0.046 (0.042)	0.865 (0.185)	0.57
2	1970–1974	gross	0.048 (0.033)	0.826 (0.125)	0.73
3	1970–1979	gross	0.047 (0.036)	0.843 (0.146)	0.67
4	1960–1969	gross	0.059 (0.022)	0.779 (0.090)	0.82
5	1960–1979	gross	0.057 (0.028)	0.796 (0.112)	0.75
6	1960–1979	net	0.011 (0.016)	0.993 (0.111)	0.83
7	1970–1979	gross; derived	0.039 (0.027)	0.886 (0.112)	0.79

*The coefficients refer to eq. (1) in the text. Standard errors are shown in parentheses. The 'gross' equations relate gross investment and saving while the 'net' equation relates net investment and saving.

net saving. Since this requires subtracting an estimate of depreciation from both variables, any error in measuring depreciation will tend to bias the estimated coefficient toward one. This potential bias is consistent with the result presented in the sixth equation of table 2 that shows a coefficient of 0.99 for the regression of the net investment ratio on the net savings rate.

If there were no problems of measuring savings, investment and international transactions, the difference between gross domestic savings and gross domestic investment would be equal to the balance on current account (CA). This suggests that, instead of using the conventional national income account measure of domestic savings, the value of gross domestic savings could be defined as the sum of gross domestic investment and the current account balance: $\hat{S} = I + CA$.[8] The basic equation is reestimated for the decade of the 1970s with this derived measure of savings and presented in the final line of table 2. The coefficient of 0.886 is only slightly higher than the previous estimate of 0.843 for this decade and shows that this source of measurement error does not influence the basic result.

The estimation of eq. (1) with a cross-section of country averages implicitly assumes that each country's disturbance is purely random and uncorrelated with the savings ratio. If country investment rates do differ systematically for some reason that is not directly related to the savings ratio, eq. (1) should be replaced by an equation in which the constant term is allowed to differ among countries,

$$I_i/Y_i = \alpha_i + \beta(S_i/Y_i) + \epsilon_i. \tag{2}$$

If eq. (2) is the correct specification but eq. (1) is estimated, the coefficient of β will be biased if α_i is correlated with the savings ratio.

This potential source of bias can be eliminated by extending the analysis to two observations for each country so that the constant values of the α_i's can be eliminated. If eq. (2) is generalized by assuming that all investment ratios may shift by a constant amount δ between times t and t', the new specification may be written as [9]

$$I_{it}/Y_{it} - I_{it'}/Y_{it'} = \delta + \beta[S_{it}/Y_{it} - S_{it'}/Y_{it'}] + \epsilon_{it} - \epsilon_{it'}. \tag{3}$$

Defining the latter period as 1973 through 1979 (i.e., the years affected by the OPEC price shock) and the earlier period as the previous seven 'pre-OPEC' years implies an estimate of β of 1.024 with a standard error of 0.227, and an estimate of δ of 0.013 with a standard error of 0.005. The $\bar{R}^2$ for this equation is 0.55. Thus countries that increased their saving between the earlier period and the later period found that their investment increased on average by an equal amount between the two dates. There is certainly no support in this estimate for the view that increases in saving merely augmented the total world supply of funds and that such capital was allocated among countries in unconstrained pursuit of the highest rate of return.[10]

An alternative method of estimating eq. (2) is to use each of the annual observations in a pooled cross-section of time series. Using data for the entire 20-year period[11] implies an estimate of 0.771 for β with a standard error of 0.046, very similar to the estimate of 0.796 shown in table 2 and obtained when the annual data are averaged to produce a single value for each country.

The similarity of the estimates with individual constant terms and with averaged data suggests that including the individual constant terms has little effect on the estimate of β. This is confirmed when eq. (1) is re-estimated with individual annual observations for all countries for the 20-year period. The estimate of β is 0.797 with a standard error of 0.031, virtually identical to the estimates in table 2.

The use of individual annual observations makes it possible to estimate a more general dynamic relation between savings and investment. When a lagged value of the savings ratio is added to the basic specification, its coefficient is relatively small and negative.

$$I_{it}/Y_{it} = 0.074 + 0.832(S_{it} - Y_{it}) - 0.109(S_{i,t-1}/Y_{i,t-1}), \bar{R}^2 = 0.68. \qquad (4)$$
$$\qquad\qquad (0.033) \qquad\qquad (0.033)$$

The negative coefficient of the lagged savings variable suggests that investment does not adjust to savings gradually but overadjusts at first. The coefficients of further lagged values are smaller and not statistically significant. Finally, using the annual observations to estimate the average effect of year to year changes in saving among all countries indicates that

$$I_{it}/Y_{it} - I_{i,t-1}/Y_{i,t-1} = -0.0001 + 0.863[S_{it}/Y_{it} - S_{i,t-1}/Y_{i,t-1}],$$
$$\qquad\qquad (0.040) \qquad\qquad\qquad\qquad (5)$$
$$\bar{R}^2 = 0.60.$$

Thus even year to year increases in saving tend on average to be associated with increases in domestic investment in the saving country by approximately equal amounts.[12]

3. Domestic savings and the components of international capital flows

The basic investment equation can be rewritten in terms of net foreign investment and then used to analyze the relation between saving and the components of international capital flows. More specifically, subtracting the savings ratio from both sides of eq. (1) and multiplying by minus one yields

$$(S_i - I_i)/Y_i = -\alpha + (1 - \beta)(S_i/Y_i) - \epsilon_i. \tag{6}$$

The national income accounts divide the excess of domestic saving over domestic investment into net foreign investment *(NFI)* plus the statistical discrepancy in the savings-investment account *(SDS)*.[13] Substituting this into eq. (6) implies

$$NFI_i/Y_i = -\alpha + (1 - \beta)(S_i/Y_i) - SDS_i/Y_i + \epsilon_i. \tag{7}$$

If *SDS/Y* were uncorrelated with the savings ratio, the estimate of β obtained from eq. (7) would be exactly the same as the estimate obtained from eq. (1). In fact, there is a small positive association between the statistical discrepency ratio and the saving ratio in the sample, implying that the estimate of β implied by estimating eq. (7) with the decade averages of *NFI/Y* and *S/Y* for 1970 through 1979 yields

$$NFI_i/Y_i = 0.019 + 0.092(S_i/Y_i). \tag{8}$$
$$(0.002)\ (0.785)$$

The implied value of β is 0.908 and therefore slightly higher than the estimate presented in table 2. The coefficient of 0.092 implies that each extra 'dollar' of domestic saving causes a capital export of approximately 9 cents, but the very large standard error indicates that there is no statistically significant relation at all between net foreign investment and the domestic savings rate.[14]

Net foreign investment can itself be decomposed into the four major components of the international capital account (direct investment; portfolio investment; other long-term capital flows; and short-term capital flows) plus the total change in official reserves, the net errors and omissions, and a remaining minor category of the official settlements balance. The lack of a significant or substantial relation between domestic savings and net foreign investment as a whole could in principal reflect a balancing of positive and negative relationships among different components. For example, portfolio investment outflows might respond positively to the domestic savings rate only to be offset by changes in official reserves.

In fact, in each of the separate regressions, the coefficient of the savings ratio is always less than its standard error. There is no indication of a relation between sustained differences among countries in savings rates and any of the components of net foreign investment.

Net foreign investment is conceptually equal to the balance on current account.[15] This suggests another decomposition that might be useful in analyzing the effect of intercountry savings differences.[16] The relation between the current account balance and the savings ratio can be decomposed into the separate effects of savings on: merchandise exports; merchandise imports; other credits for goods, services and investment income; other debits for goods, services and investment income; private unrequited transfers; and public unrequited transfers. None of the six regression coefficients relating a current account component as a fraction of GDP to savings as a fraction of GDP had an absolute value as large as 0.1 and none was as large as its standard error. The lack of a significant relationship between the current account balance and savings reflects a lack of relation between each of its components and savings.

In short, the two decompositions that have been examined confirm the finding of section 2 that there is no relation between sustained differences in domestic savings rates and the external position of the country.

4. Parameter identification and estimation with cross-country and time-series data

The regression of the domestic investment ratio on the domestic savings ratio is an intuitively appealing test of the hypothesis of perfect capital mobility. Nevertheless, there are fundamental problems of identification and estimation that should be considered when it is recognized that both savings and investment are endogenous variables in an economic system. Feldstein and Horioka (1980) discussed the problem of simultaneous equations bias briefly and suggested that this was likely to be much less serious in estimates based on cross-country data averaged over long periods of time than in estimates based on annual time series for individual countries. As I noted in the introduction to the present paper, instrumental variable estimates suggested by a simultaneous equations model confirmed the ordinary least squares results.

The current section presents an explicit model and uses it to assess the regression of domestic investment on domestic saving as a test of the perfect capital mobility hypothesis and, when international capital mobility is less than perfect, as an estimate of the effect on domestic investment of endogenous shifts in domestic saving.

The simplest model that is adequate for this purpose requires a domestic investment function, a domestic savings function, a net foreign investment function, and a savings-investment equilibrium condition. I shall assume that all investment is financed by issuing bonds and that the demand for gross domestic investment (I) can be written as a function of the domestic real interest rate (r) plus a random shock (u),

$$I = \phi(r) + u, \tag{9}$$

with $\phi' < 0$. A similar specification of the domestic savings function,

$$S = \psi(r) + V, \tag{10}$$

provides that the supply of saving is a non-decreasing function of the real interest rate ($\psi' > 0$) plus a random shock.

Writing N for net foreign investment (i.e., the net outflow of capital from the home country), the net capital outflow in response to a higher interest rate can be written as

$$N = \eta(r) + e, \tag{11}$$

where $\eta'(r) \leqq 0$ implies that a higher real domestic interest rate reduces (or leaves unchanged if $\eta' = 0$) net foreign investment (or causes a greater net inflow from abroad, i.e., a negative net foreign investment), and e is a random shock. Perfect capital mobility implies that $\eta' = -\infty$. More generally, η' could differ between the short run and the long run and could vary among countries or time periods. Some reasons for such differences are discussed below.

Equilibrium in the goods market requires that domestic saving equal domestic investment plus net foreign investment.[17]

$$S = I + N. \tag{12}$$

These four equations determine values for the four endogenous variables I, S N and r as functions of the three random distributions u, v and e.

Substituting (9), (10) and (11) in (12) yields

$$\psi(r) + v = \phi(r) + u + \eta(r) + e. \tag{13}$$

Differentiating and solving for the change in the real interest rate implies:

$$dr = (du - dv + de)/(\psi - \phi' - \eta'). \tag{14}$$

Since $\psi' \geqq 0$, $\phi' < 0$ and $\eta' \leqq 0$, the denominator is unambiguously positive. Thus the interest rate rises when there is a positive shock to domestic investment demand ($du > 0$) or to the domestic demand for net foreign investment ($de > 0$).

The effect of investment and savings shocks on net foreign investment can be obtained by combining eqs. (11) and (14),

$$dN = \eta' \, dr + de = \eta'[du - dv + de]/(\psi' - \phi' - \eta') + de. \tag{15}$$

To interpret eq. (15) recall that $dN > 0$ means an increased capital outflow and that $\eta' \leqq 0$. Thus an increase in domestic savings ($dv > 0$) causes an increase in net foreign investment and, therefore, both a capital outflow and a current account surplus. With perfect capital mobility, $\eta' = -\infty$ and $dN/dv = 1$; in this case, all of the additional domestic saving goes abroad. Similarly, even with a finite value of η', an increase in domestic investment $(du > 0)$ causes a decrease in net foreign investment and therefore both a capital inflow and a current account deficit.[18]

This brief description of the international effects of shifts in domestic savings and investment has ignored the exchange rate movements that are likely to occur as part of the process of change. An autonomous increase in domestic investment demand (or decrease in savings) will raise the domestic interest rate and cause a real appreciation of the home currency. With this increase in the exchange rate there is a current account deficit that accommodates the capital inflow. The model is consistent with this exchange rate behavior even though the exchange rate is not explicitly modelled.

Combining eqs. (9) and (14) shows the relation between domestic investment and a shift in domestic savings.

$$dI = \phi'[du - dv + de]/(\psi' - \phi' - \eta') + du, \qquad (16)$$

which implies

$$dI/dv = \phi'/(\phi' + \eta' - \psi'). \qquad (17)$$

With perfect capital mobility, $\eta' = -\infty$ and $dI/dv = 0$. At the other extreme, if international capital movements do not respond to the interest rate, $\eta' = 0$ and

$$dI/dv = \phi'/(\phi' - \psi). \qquad (18)$$

Since $\phi' < 0$ and $\psi' \geqq 0$, in this case $dI/dv \leqq 1$. If ψ' is "small" relative to $-\phi'$, i.e., if the interest elasticity of savings is small relative to the interest elasticity of investment, dI/dv will close to 1.

Now that the theoretical relation between domestic saving and investment has been clarified it is possible to examine more explicitly the interpretation of the regression coefficient estimated by regressing the investment ratio on the savings ratio, i.e,. the coefficient of eq. (1) estimated to be approximately one in the cross-country regressions reported in table 2. The regression coefficient of eq. (1) is the ratio of the covariance between investment and saving divided by the variance of saving. The variance of savings can be approximated in terms of the current model in the following way. First, differentiate eq. (10) and eliminate dr with the help of eq. (14) to obtain

$$dS = \psi'[du - dv + de]/(\psi' - \phi' - \eta') + dv. \qquad (19)$$

Now evaluate each of the derivatives at the mean value of the corresponding variable, square both sides, and take expectations. Since the expected value of the squared deviation from the mean is the variance.

$$\sigma_{SS} = E(dS)^2$$

$$= [(\phi' + \eta')^2 \sigma_{vv} + (\psi')^2 (\sigma_{uu} + \sigma_{ee} + 2\sigma_{ue}) \qquad (20)$$

$$- 2\psi'(\phi' + \eta')(\sigma_{uv} + \sigma_{ev})]/(\psi' - \phi' - \eta')^2.$$

Similarly, combining eqs. (16) and (19) yields an approximation for the covariance between S and I.

$$\sigma_{SI} = E(dS \cdot dI)$$

$$= E[-(\phi' + \eta')dv + \psi'(du + de)]$$

$$\times [(\psi' - \eta')du - \phi'(dv - de)]/(\psi' - \phi' - \eta')^2 \qquad (21)$$

$$= [-(\phi' + \eta')(\psi' - \eta')\sigma_{uv} + \phi'(\phi' + \eta')(\sigma_{vv} - \sigma_{ev})$$

$$+ \psi'(\psi' - \eta')(\sigma_{uu} + \sigma_{ue}) - \psi'\phi'(\sigma_{uv} - \sigma_{ue}$$

$$+ \sigma_{ve} - \sigma_{ee})]/(\psi' - \phi' - \eta')^2.$$

The regression of I on S can be approximated by the ratio of σ_{SI} to σ_{SS} or

$$\hat{\beta} = [-(\phi' + \eta')(\psi' - \eta')\sigma_{uv} + \phi'(\phi' + \eta')(\sigma_{vv} - \sigma_{ev})$$

$$+ \psi'(\psi' - \eta')(\sigma_{uu} + \sigma_{ue}) - \psi'\phi'(\sigma_{uv} - \sigma_{ue} + \sigma_{ve} - \sigma_{ee})] \qquad (22)$$

$$/[(\phi' + \eta')^2 \sigma_{vv} + (\psi')^2 (\sigma_{uu} + \sigma_{ee} + 2\sigma_{ue})$$

$$- 2\psi'(\sigma' + \eta')(\sigma_{uv} + \sigma_{ev})].$$

With the help of eq. (22), we can now consider two questions. First, what is the implication of perfect capital mobility for the estimated coefficient $\hat{\beta}$? Second, what is the relation between the estimated coefficient $\hat{\beta}$ and the effect on domestic investment of a shift in domestic saving (dI/Dv)?

4.1 Testing the perfect capital mobility hypothesis

With perfect capital mobility, $\eta' = -\infty$ and eq. (22) implies that

$$\hat{\beta} = \sigma_{uv}/\sigma_{vv}. \qquad (23)$$

Thus perfect capital mobility is consistent with a positive parameter estimate only to the extent that the exogenous shifts in saving and investment are positively correlated. The likely magnitude of the correlation between savings and investment shifts depends on the nature of the data.

With time-series observations for an individual country, demand shocks could well make $\sigma_{uv} > 0$. A downturn in economic activity might cause savings to be relatively low (because consumption depends on permanent income) and might also cause investment to be relatively low (because of low capacity utilization). Similarly, a supply shock that lowers income and profitability might also reduce both saving and investment. In either of these cases, the regression coefficient $\hat{\beta}$ could be positive and substantial even if there is perfect capital mobility. Conversely time-series data for an individual country could also have $\sigma_{uv} < 0$; an exogenous temporary increase in the propensity to save ($dv > 0$) could reduce aggregate output and thereby induce a decline in investment ($du < 0$). Estimates of β based on time-series data for a single country are thus an unreliable basis for evaluating the hypothesis of perfect international capital mobility.[19]

In contrast, when the sample is a cross-section of countries and the observations for each country are averaged over a long period of time, there is no reason to expect any correlations between intercountry differences in the exogenous component of saving and in the exogenous component of investment. These intercountry saving differences reflect such things as the demographic structure of the population, the extent to which unfunded social security substitutes for private saving, the average level of government deficits, consumer credit and mortgage arrangements, and the long-term rise in income since current retirees were working and saving. Sustained differences in investment rates that are not just a reflection of savings differences (through the effect of saving on the cost of capital) reflect such things as business tax rules and the effects of unions on profitability. The intercountry variance in exogenous investment shifts is thus likely to be smaller than the intercountry variance in exogenous saving shifts ($\sigma_{uu} < \sigma_{vv}$), and the covariance between the two is likely to be small or zero. If there is a non-zero covariance, there appears to be no presumption about its sign.

Eq. (23) shows that the estimated values of β presented in table 2 are not consistent with perfect capital mobility if σ_{uv} is zero or negative. Moreover, even if there is a positive covariance between exogenous savings differences and exogenous investment differences, the high values of the estimated β's are not consistent with perfect capital mobility if the variance of the savings shifts (σ_{vv}) is large relative to the variance of the investment shifts (σ_{uu}). To see this, note that eq. (23) can be rewritten as

$$\hat{\beta} = \sigma_{uv}/\sigma_{vv}$$

$$= \rho_{uv}(\sigma_{uu}\sigma_{vv})^{\frac{1}{2}}/\sigma_{vv} \tag{24}$$

$$= \rho_{uv}[\sigma_{uu}/\sigma_{vv}]^{\frac{1}{2}},$$

where ρ is the correlation between u and v. Since $\rho \leqq 1$, with perfect capital mobility $\hat{\beta}$ is at most equal to the ratio of the standard deviation of the investment shifts to the standard deviation of the savings shifts. Since the observed estimates of β are approximately one, eq. (24) shows that the evidence is not consistent with both perfect capital mobility and a low ratio of σ_{uu}/σ_{vv}.

It is easily shown that with perfect capital mobility the correlation between savings and investment is the same as the correlation between u and v.[20] The observed correlations between saving and investment (i.e., the square root of the R^2 values reported in table 2) imply implausibly high correlations between the exogenous components of saving and investment.

In short, the identifying restriction in cross-country data that $\sigma_{uv} \leqq 0$ or that σ_{uu}/σ_{uv} is small, is sufficient to permit interpreting the observed regressions of investment on savings presented in table 2 as strong evidence against perfect capital mobility. Alternatively, the restriction that the correlation between exogenous saving and investment differences is not greater than 0.5 also implies rejection of the perfect capital mobility hypothesis.

Estimates of β based on a cross-country sample of *changes* in investment and saving provides a different type of evidence against the hypothesis of perfect capital mobility. In such a regression, any association between the *levels* of exogenous saving and investment effects is irrelevant. Instead, σ_{uv} in eq. (23) must be interpreted as a relation between shifts in saving and shifts in investment. If countries in which the exogenous component of saving has increased between two dates (or two periods) tend to be those countries in which the exogenous component of investment has also increased, $\sigma_{uv} > 0$ and the estimate of β can be high even if there is perfect capital mobility. The danger of this covariance being large is greatest when the data can reflect changes from one phase of a business cycle to the next. It is therefore reassuring that the estimate of $\beta = 1.04$ based on the changes in saving and investment reflected a comparison of two periods of six years (1968–1973 and 1974–1980) and that similar results were obtained by Feldstein and Horioka for a different set of years ($\beta = 0.724$ with a standard error of 0.158 based on the changes for 1960–1969 to 1970–1974).[21]

4.2. Estimating dI/dv

Under what plausible conditions does the estimate of β based on eq. (1) represent the effect on domestic investment of a shift in the exogenous factors influencing saving? Equivalently, when does the value of $\hat{\beta}$ given in eq. (22) equal the value of dI/dv shown in eq. (17)? And, more generally, even when exact identification is not achieved, does $\hat{\beta}$ tend to dI/dv as certain limiting conditions are achieved?

Consider first the case in which saving rates are not sensitive to the interest rate ($\psi' = 0$) and in which the exogenous differences in saving among countries are not correlated with exogenous differences in the domestic investment function or the net foreign investment function ($\sigma_{uv} = \sigma_{ve} = 0$). In this case, eqs. (22) and (17) imply that $\hat{\beta} = \phi'/(\phi' + \eta) = dI/dv$ and there is no simultaneous equation bias.[22]

Although these assumptions may not hold exactly, they may be a reasonable approximation for cross-country data based on averages over extended periods. In this context, the interest elasticities of domestic investment may be high relative to the interest elasticity of domestic savings. Similarly, the variance of domestic savings may be large relative to the covariance between exogenous savings differences and exogenous differences in investment and net foreign capital. The value of $\hat{\beta}$ in eq. (22) tends to dI/dv as ψ'/ϕ', σ_{uv}/σ_{uv} and σ_{ve}/σ_{uv} all tend to zero.

An alternative specification places no restriction on the interest sensitivity of domestic savings but posits that the exogenous differences among countries in saving rates are large relative to the exogenous differences in domestic and foreign investment: thus σ_{uu}/σ_{vv} and σ_{ee}/σ_{vv} are both small and, therefore, σ_{uv}/σ_{vv}, $\sigma_{ev}\sigma_{vv}$ and σ_{ue}/σ_{vv} are also small. Taking the limit as σ_{vv} grows relative to the other variances and covariances implies that $\hat{\beta}$ tends to $\phi'/(\phi' + \eta')$. Since the true value of dI/dv is $\phi'/(\phi' + \eta' - \psi)$, the estimate overstates the true value. More specifically, the ratio of the sample estimate ($\hat{\beta}$) to the true value of dI/dv is $(\phi' + \eta' - \psi')/(\phi' + \eta')$ $= 1 - \psi'/(\phi' + \eta')$. To express these as elasticities, let $\epsilon_{Sr} = \psi' r/S$ be the saving elasticity, $\epsilon_{Ir} = -\phi' r/I$ be the investment elasticity, and $\epsilon_{Nr} = -\eta' r/N$ be the elasticity of net foreign investment. Thus

$$\hat{\beta}/ds/dv) = 1 + S\epsilon_{Sr}/(I\epsilon_{Ir} + N\epsilon_{Nr}) \tag{25}$$
$$= 1 + (S/I)\epsilon_{Sr}/(\epsilon_{Ir} + (N/I)\epsilon_{Nr}).$$

Since S/I is approximately one and N/I is very close to zero, $\hat{\beta}/(dI/dv)$ is approximately one plus the ratio of ϵ_{Sr} to ϵ_{Ir}. Most empirical research indicates that this ratio is low and, therefore, that the relative bias in $\hat{\beta}$ is small.

4.3. The regression of savings on investment

In an interesting pair of papers, Sachs (1981a,b) emphasized the response of international capital flows to temporary shifts in domestic propensities to invest. Sachs showed that countries that increased their share of investment in GDP between 1968–1973 and 1974–1979 also experienced substantial increases in net capital inflows, i.e., substantial decreases in net foreign investment. As a leading example of this, Sachs pointed to the major flow of capital into Norway that accompanied the Norwegian investment boom caused by Norway's discovery of North Sea oil.

Eq. (26) is typical of the type of results reported by Sachs,[23]

$$\Delta[NFI/Y]_i = -0.227 - 0.561\Delta[I/Y]_i, \qquad (26)$$
$$(0.039)\ (0.148)$$
$$\overline{R}^2 = 0.46,$$

where $\Delta(NFI/Y)$ denotes the average NFI/Y ratio in country i in 1974–1979 minus that ratio in 1968–1973, and $\Delta(I/Y)$ denotes the corresponding change in the investment ratio. The paramenter estimate implies that one 'dollar' increase in domestic investment is associated with a net capital inflow of 0.56 dollars. Thus, treating I/Y as the independent variable appears to imply that net capital flows play a much more significant role.

It would be wrong, however, to interpret -0.56 as an estimate of dN/du. Unless the model is recursive with investment having no interest elasticity ($\phi' = 0$) and no covariance between shifts in domestic investment and shifts in either saving or foreign investment ($\sigma_{uv} = \sigma_{ue} = 0$), the regression coefficient will not be an unbiased estimate of dN/du. Since the equation is based on changes in domestic investment and changes in capital flows, such lack of covariance is unlikely. If, for example, a change in economic conditions between the two periods caused not only an exogenous increase in domestic investment but also a shift from foreign investment to domestic investment ($\sigma_{ue} > 0$), the absolute value of the estimated coefficient will overstate the induced capital inflow.

The ambiguity that results from using the change form of the regression can be avoided by examining the relation between the level of net foreign investment and the level of domestic investment. Since net foreign investment is essentially equal to the excess of domestic saving over domestic investment, an alternative specification is the regression of the domestic saving ratio on the domestic investment ratio, i.e., just reversing the left- and right-hand variables of eq. (1). The finding of a regression coefficient significantly less than one implies that intercountry differences in investment are associated with international capital flows to finance that investment.[24]

For the final five years of the data (1974–1979), the results with such a specification support Sachs' view. The regression coefficient in the regression of S/Y on I/Y is 0.66 with a standard error of 0.14. Taken at face value, this implies that each extra dollar of exogenous domestic investment induces a capital inflow of 34 cents.[25]

The most recent five years are, however, an unusual subperiod. For the entire 20-year period, the regression of S/Y on I/Y is 0.94 with a standard error of 0.13. The point estimate thus implies that each dollar of additional domestic investment is associated with a net capital inflow of only 6 cents; with a standard error of 13 cents, this is clearly not significantly different from zero. Similarly, for the decade of the 1960s the regression of S/Y on I/Y is 1.05 with a standard error of 0.12, while for the first half of the 1970s the regression coefficient is 0.088 with a standard error of 0.13.

One possible interpretation is that conditions have changed in the mid-1970s to make international capital flows more sensitive to differences in yields. To support this one might point to the end of the U.S. interest equalization tax in 1974, to the growth of the Eurodollar market and of the OPEC balances, and to the relaxation of restrictions on portfolio investment that were occurring in a variety of OECD countries [OECD (1980)]. Nevertheless, there is also the alternative possibility that the regression coefficient for this brief period provides a biased estimate of dS/du because of a temporary covariance among the 'exogenous' saving and investment factors during this unusual period. Only further time will tell.

It is clear, however, that for the previous fifteen years, the regressions of S/Y on I/Y as well as the regressions of I/Y on S/Y support the conclusion that higher levels of domestic investment do not induce foreign capital inflows but can only be financed by domestic saving.

5. Portfolio adjustment and capital flows in the long run and the short run

The analysis of section 4 indicates that the regression estimates are more relevant as a guide to the long-run response of international capital movements to changes in domestic savings and investment than to their short-run response. Coefficient estimates based on annual variations in savings and investment are subject to potentially severe simultaneous equation bias that is not present when annual observations are averaged over a decade or more, and the regression is estimated with a cross-country sample of these averages. The empirical estimates based on such data that were presented in sections 2 and 3 imply that, for the 1960s and 1970s as a whole, higher savings rates induce higher rates of domestic investment but virtually no increase in net foreign investment.

The behavior of capital flows in the short run may be quite different. Although the empirical analysis of sections 2 and 3 is not directly relevant, theoretical considerations suggest that the short run response of international capital flows to changes in domestic saving may be much greater than the long-run response. The essential reason for this is that the short-run capital flow is part of a once-for-all adjustment of the international portfolio. When the adjustment is complete, the rate of capital flow returns to a lower level governed by the rate of growth of the world capital stock and the share of international assets in the equilibrium portfolio.[26]

To make these ideas more precise, consider an investor who divides his portfolio between domestic and foreign assets. Domestic assets earn an uncertain return r, with subjective mean μ and subjective variance σ_{oo}. Foreign assets earn an uncertain return, r^*, with subjective mean μ^* and variance σ_{**}. The covariance between the returns is σ_{*o}. If the investor's preferences can be summarized by a utility function that is a quadratic function of the portfolio return, the investor will maximize

$$Eu[pr^* + (1-p)r)] = p\mu^* + (1-p)\mu \tag{27}$$
$$-\frac{1}{2}\gamma[p^2\sigma_{**} + (1-p)^2\sigma_{oo} + 2p(1-p)\sigma_{o*}],$$

where E is the expectations operator, p is the proportion of the portfolio invested abroad, and $\gamma > 0$ is a measure of risk aversion.

The first-order maximization condition implies that the optimal proportion invested abroad (p^*) is

$$p^* = [\mu^* - \mu - \gamma(\sigma_{o*} - \sigma_{oo})]/\gamma(\sigma_{oo} + \sigma_{**} - 2\sigma_{o*}), \tag{28}$$

the denominator is γ times the variance of $r - r^*$ and is therefore unambiguously positive. The numerator is easier to discuss if we replace σ_{o*} by $p\lambda\sigma_{oo}$ where ρ is the correlation between r and r^* and $\lambda^2 = \sigma_{**}/\sigma_{oo}$, the ratio of the foreign variance to the domestic variance. Thus

$$p^* = [\mu^* - \mu - \gamma(p\lambda - 1)\sigma_{oo}]/\gamma(\sigma_{oo} + \sigma_{**} - 2\sigma_{o*}). \tag{29}$$

It is clear that even if the foreign expected return exceeds the domestic return $(\mu^* > \mu)$, the investor may not wish to invest abroad, i.e., $\rho^* \leq 0$. This can happen only if (1) there is a positive correlation between domestic and foreign rates of return (reflecting, for example, the international business cycle or common long-term trends in productivity and profitability) and (2) the subjective variance on the foreign return exceeds the subjective variance on the domestic return. The subjective variance on the foreign return may be very large because investors lack information about the foreign economy, its individual firms, accounting practices, etc.[27] If $p^* < 0$, the investor may be constrained to a corner solution with no foreign investment. It is clear that since λ reflects *subjective* variances, investors in two countries may both decide not to invest in the other's securities.

Conversely, eq. (29) implies that p^* may be greater than zero even if $\mu^* < \mu$ if foreign investing provides a useful diversification, i.e., if $p\lambda < 1$. Thus investors in two countries may both decide to invest in the other's securities even if they have accurate assessments of the expected rates of return.

A sustained increase in the domestic saving rate raises capital intensity at home and thereby depresses the expected rate of return, μ. This unambiguously raises p^*, implying that some of the additional capital should be invested abroad.[28] If the initial p^* is negative, however, the increase in p^* may still leave the actual p at a constrained corner solution of $p^* = 0$. In this case, domestic investors do not seek to transfer any of the additional saving abroad. The increased domestic saving may nevertheless lead to an increase in net foreign investment if foreign investors respond to the lower expected return by reducing their oversease investment. In terms of eq. (29), from the point of view of foreign investors μ^* has fallen, causing an unambiguous reduction in p^*. Again, however, if foreign investors were originally not investing abroad, the reduction in the expected return would have no effect. Thus portfolio considerations alone could explain why a change in domestic saving in one country would have no effect on its net foreign investment.

Ignoring the possibility of corner solutions, a sustained exogenous increase in domestic saving will, by reducing the expected domestic rate of return, raise p^* and cause a capital outflow. This will be reinforced by foreign investors who respond to the lower expected return by reducing their overseas investment. The response of p^* to the change in μ is inversely proportional to $\gamma(\sigma_{oo} + \sigma_{**} - 2\sigma_{o*})$. The greater the risk aversion (γ) or the uncertainty about domestic and foreign rates of return (σ_{oo} and σ_{**}), the smaller will be the change in p^*. Thus, even for countries that do have overseas portfolio investments, the effect of a change in the expected return on domestic or foreign investment may be a relatively small change in the optimal allocation of assets between home and abroad.[29]

It is useful, however, to divide the response of international investment into two components. First, a sustained increase in the domestic saving rate alters $\mu^* - \mu$ and, therefore, changes p^* for both domestic and foreign investors. There is then a relatively brief period during which portfolios are readjusted to the new optimal mix.[30] During this readjustment there is a relatively large increase in the rate of net foreign investment. The shorter the time period during which the adjustment occurs, the greater will be the rate of net foreign investment per unit of time. Once the adjustment is complete, p^* remains unchanged. As the national capital stocks at home and abroad grow over time with the economies, the fraction p^* will flow abroad. Net foreign investment during this steady state growth will be the difference between the steady and state outflow of funds by domestic investment and the steady state inflow of funds from foreign investors. Although the evidence of sections 2 and 3 indicates that this long-run response to a sustained shift in domestic saving is quite small, the short-run response during a brief period of transition could be quite substantial.

6. Concluding comments

The evidence and analysis in this paper support the earlier findings of Feldstein and Horioka (1980) that sustained increases in domestic savings rates induce approximately equal increases in domestic investment rates. Although this limited extent of international capital mobility is consistent with the portfolio model developed in section 5, there are clearly other aspects of both international portfolio investment and international direct investment that should be taken into account in explaining the observed mobility.

Government policies establish the framework for private international investing. Governments of OECD countries have sought to restrict both capital inflows and capital outflows, including both direct and portfolio investment. Even the United States, perhaps the most liberal of the OECD countries in its attitude to capital movements, restricts the class of institutions that can invest abroad and thereby reduces the total volume and sensitivity of foreign investment. It would be useful to examine the capital restriction policies in detail, to evaluate their effectiveness and to understand the reasons why governments may choose to restrict international capital movements.[31]

More generally, although net capital flows do not appear to be sensitive to domestic saving rates, a stable pattern of net capital flows exists. It would be desirable to examine the reasons for this stable pattern and, in particular, to resolve the puzzling fact that substantial gross capital flows produces relatively small net capital flows.

Notes

1. The Feldstein-Horioka paper also reported several other tests that will not be repeated here, e.g., adding variables measuring country size and openess to the investment equation. Section 4 of the present paper returns to the problem of simultaneity.

2. Frisch (1981) and Hartman (1981) present some evidence that investment flows are sensitive to after-tax rates of return.

3. I interpret Harberger (1980) as essentially accepting this interpretation. In an earlier paper [Harberger (1978)], he argued that international capital markets were essentially perfect and therefore that rates of returns are equalized internationally just as 'water seeks its own level.' But by his 1980 paper, Harberger concludes: 'My own intuition does not want to accept the notion that increments of investment activity are in all or nearly all countries effectively 100 percent 'financed' by funds flowing in from abroad, and that increments in saving simply spill out into the world capital markets. I find the analogy to a hydraulic system with perhaps a viscous fluid, in which the pipes are partially clogged, and in which some vessels are separated by semipermeable membranes, to be more consonant with my image of the world than the alternative analogy to a hydraulic system where the water flows freely through the system and, essentially instantaneously, finds the same level everywhere' (p. 336). If that flow is slow enough, so that the tendency toward equalization must be measured in decades rather than months or even years, any relevant analysis must regard the capital movements as incomplete and rates of return as potentially unequal.

4. The other seven OECD countries had to be excluded from the sample because consistent data are not available for the entire period.

5. These ratios differ from the ratios presented in table 1 of Feldstein and Horioka (1980) only because of data revisions.

6. If the equation is estimated in level form rather than ratio form, the coefficient is very close to one but this reflects the pure scale effect. Only ratio equations are therefore presented in this paper.

7. These differences in domestic investment reflected such things as differences in the response of profitability and of capacity utilization to the 1973 OPEC shock and to the rising rates of inflation.

8. This is the procedure used by Sachs (1981a).

9. Although the α_i's are eliminated by first differencing in this way, they can be estimated in a second step once β and δ are estimated. The procedure is exactly equivalent to estimations with individual constant terms and two observations for each country.

10. The use of differences in saving and investment ratios may cause simulta-

neous equations bias that is not present in the estimates of table 2. This is discussed in section 4.

11. Some individual annual observations are missing, reducing the sample to 320 observations.

12. Sections 4 and 5 show that the similarity of the coefficients based on long-term averages and annual changes may be subject to different interpretations.

13. The net foreign investment of the United States thus represents the net investment abroad financed by savings in the United States.

14. The much larger standard error in eq. (8) than in table 2 reflects the importance of the statistical discrepancy.

15. In practice, the two numbers differ because of such things as the allocation of special drawing rights and the statistical treatment of gold, extraordinary military transactions, etc.

16. This analysis was suggested to me by Douglas Purvis.

17. In a simple theoretical model, this is equivalent to the equilibrium condition $S = I + X - M$, where X is exports and M is imports, since net foreign investment equals the current account surplus.

18. This is the case discussed by Sachs (1981a,b). I will return to his empirical results later in this section.

19. Feldstein and Horioka estimated time-series regressions for individual countries and presented the results in NBER Working Paper No. 310, but did not include these time-series estimates in the published version [Feldstein and Horioka (1980)] because we concluded that the problem of simultaneous-equations bias meant that these individual country coefficients could not be interpreted as estimates of the effect on investment of exogenous changes in saving.

20. With perfect capital mobility, the regression of saving on investment produces a coefficient equal to $\beta_{SI} = \sigma_{uv}/\sigma_{uu}$. Multiply this by $\beta_{IS} = \sigma_{uu}/\sigma_{vv}$ from eq. (23) and note that $\beta_{IS}\beta_{SI} = \sigma^2_{uv}/\sigma_{uu} = p^2_{uv}$. But the product of a regression coefficient and the coefficient for the reverse regression is equal to the squared correlation; i.e. $\beta_{IS}\beta_{SI} = p^2_{SI}$. Thus $P^2_{IS} = p^2_{uv}$.

21. Although the 1968–1973 to 1971–1980 comparison is influenced by the OPEC-induced slowdown, the comparison based on the earlier pair of periods is not biased by a supply shock.

22. The assumptions of $\psi' = 0$ and $\sigma_{ve} = \sigma_{vu} = 0$ make the model recursive with respect to S and, therefore, make ordinary least squares an unbiased estimator.

23. The dependent variable in Sachs' equation is actually the current account balance, but results for the current account and for NFI are very similar.

24. There are of course still identification problems in interpreting the regression coefficient as an estimate of dS/du [and therefore making inferences about $d(S - I)/du$] but these are similar to the ones discussed in sections 4.1 and 4.2.

25. See the previous footnote.

26. Although early models of Mundell (1968) and others did not distinguish between the adjustment phase and the steady state flow, the importance of

distinguishing a temporary capital flow as part of a once-for-all capital stock adjustment has been recognized at least since Branson (1970). See also Branson (1979), Cumby and Obstfeld (1982), Girton and Henderson (1977) and Obstfeld (1981).

27. A recent story in the Wall Street Journal reporting from Tokyo summarized the difficulty that foreign investors have in getting information on Japanese securities: 'A foreigner here once asked a Japanese securities salesman where to get investment advice, and this is what he was told: "We have a saying: the better the English, the worse the analysis".' [Marcom (1982)]. European investors may do more portfolio investment in the United States than *vice versa* because of the greater ease with which detailed information can be obtained about U.S. firms.

28. This is unambiguous only because I assume that the increase in domestic capital has no effect on the variance of the return or the risk aversion parameter.

29. Hartman (1980) presents evidence that international capital flows are large enough to affect rates of return on U.S. securities but not enough to equalize returns here and abroad.

30. Although such a reallocation should in principle occur instantly, institutional reasons may cause the adjustment to take a year or more.

31. One such reason, the ability of foreign governments to capture the tax revenue of foreign investment, is discussed in Feldstein (1982).

References

Branson, W. H., 1970, Monetary policy and the new view of international capital movements, Brookings Papers on Economic Activity, 235–270.

Branson, W. H., 1979, Exchange rate dynamics and monetary policy, in: A. Lindbeck, ed., Inflation and unemployment in open economics (North-Holland, Amsterdam).

Cumby, R. F. and M. Obstfeld, 1982, International interest-rate and price-level linkages under 'flexible exchange rates: A review of recent evidence.' Lecture given at the NBER conference on exchange rate theory and practice, Bellagio, Italy.

Feldstein, M., 1977, Social security and private savings: International evidence in an extended life-cycle model, in: M. Feldstein and R. Inman, eds. The economics of public services, An International Economic Association conference volume.

Feldstein, M., 1982, International tax rules, restrictions on capital mobility and domestic savings policies, forthcoming.

Feldstein, M. and C. Horioka, 1980, Domestic savings and international capital flows. The Economic Journal 90, 314–329.

Frisch, D., 1981, Issues in the taxation of foreign source income, NBER working paper no. 798 (NBER, Cambridge, MA).

Ginton, L. and D. W. Henderson, 1977, Central bank operations in foreign and domestic assets under fixed and flexible exchange rates, in: P. B. Clark, D. Logue and R. Sweeney, eds., The effects of exchange rate adjustments (U.S. Government Printing Office, Washington, D.C.).

Harberger, A. C., 1978, Perspectives on capital and technology in less developed countries, in: M. J. Artis and A. R. Nobay, eds., Contemporary economic analysis (London).

Harberger, A. C., 1980, Vignettes on the world capital market, American Economic Review, 331–337.

Hartman, D., 1980, International effects on the U.S. capital market, NBER working paper no. 581 (NBER, Cambridge, MA).

Hartman, D., 1981, Domestic tax policy and foreign investment: Some evidence, NBER working paper no. 784 (NBER, Cambridge, MA).

Marcom, J. Jr., 1982, Brokers intensify stock studies in Tokyo as more foreign investors look to Japan, Wall Street Journal, May 7.

Modigliani, F., 1970, The life cycle hypothesis of saving and intercountry differences in the saving ratio, in: W. A. Eltis et al., eds., Induction, growth and trade. Essays in honor of Sir Roy Harrod (Clarendon Press, Oxford).

Mundell, R. A., 1960, The monetary dynamics of international adjustment under fixed and flexible exchange rates. Quarterly Journal of Economics 74, 227–257.

Obstfeld, M., 1980. Imperfect asset substitutability and monetary policy under fixed exchange rates, NBER working paper no. 485 (NBER, Cambridge, MA).

OECD, 1980, Experience with controls on international portfolio operations in shares and bonds (OECD, Paris).

OECD, 1981, National accounts of the OECD countries: 1950–1979, Vols. 1 and 2 (OECD, Paris).

Sachs, J., 1981a, The curent account and macroeconomic and macroeconomics adjustment in the 1970s, Brookings Papers on Economic Activity, 201–282.

Sachs, J. D., 1981b, Aspects of the current account behavior of OECD ecconomies, NBER working paper no. 859 (NBER, Cambridge, MA).

11

INTERNATIONAL ASPECTS OF U.S. MONETARY AND FISCAL POLICY

Paul R. Krugman

Introduction

Since 1980 U.S. macroeconomic policy has diverged from that of other major industrial countries. While most countries responded to the inflationary impact of the 1979 oil shock by tightening their fiscal policies, the influence of supply-side doctrine has led the United States into a dramatic fiscal loosening. After 1979 all major countries moved towards tighter monetary policies; but until mid-1982 the United States was more determined in this respect than most others. Indeed, despite the fiscal stimulus the United States managed to have a deeper recession than the rest of the industrial world.

The impacts of this divergence in policies on the world economy in general and on U.S. trade in particular have been dramatic. But there is a good deal of disagreement about just what these impacts are, and about the appropriate response. The purpose of this paper is to lay out a framework for thinking about the effects of this kind of policy divergence, and to suggest some tentative conclusions about the current situation.

Readers should be forewarned that this is a "low-tech" paper. It neither sets out an econometric model nor develops a theoretical approach based on careful analysis of microfoundations. Instead, the empirical content, such as it is, consists of rough exploratory data analysis, while the theoretical analysis is in the Mundell-Fleming tradition of small-scale, *ad hoc* modeling. The justification for this crudity is of course that it has the compensating advantage of flexibility. We are now in an international macroeconomic situation which is quite different from anything previously experienced. In time the theory and econometric work necessary for a detailed and rigorous treatment of this situation will be done (although by that time the situation will have shifted again—generals are not alone in their tendency to be ready to fight the lost war). In the meantime, however, there is a place for ad-hockery and first-cut analysis.

The paper is in four parts. The first part is background: an account of the divergent trends in fiscal and monetary policy and of the macroeconomic and financial developments which have accompanied these trends. The second part lays out a framework for analysis. It suggests that a slightly modified version of the Mundell-Fleming or "IS-LM-BP" model is a useful way to think about recent developments. The third part of the paper addresses the problem of the strong dollar from a U.S. point of view: should the United States do something to drive the dollar down to where it belongs? Finally, the last part turns to the issue of macroeconomic interdependence and international coordination of policies.

I. Background: Monetary and Fiscal Policies in Industrial Countries

The inflationary impact of the oil shock of 1979 forced the governments of industrial countries to make a hard choice. There were (and are) only three logically consistent ways to approach a situation of uncomfortably high inflation. The first is to learn to live with it, by indexing most long-term economic arrangements to more stable measures of value. The second is to try to legislate inflation down through some kind of incomes policy. The third is to reduce inflation by creating excess capacity in the economy.

In 1979 and 1980 there was virtually a consensus that only the last choice was workable. A policy of monetary (and initially fiscal) restraint was instituted with bipartisan support in the United States and similar if generally less dramatic steps were taken in most other major countries. The three-year global recession which followed can be viewed in broad outline, if not in detail, as a choice in which a remarkably wide cross-section of leaders in the industrial world concurred.

From 1981 onward, however, it became clear that the U.S. policy *mix* was diverging from that in the rest of the industrial world. Fiscal policy, though initially tightened, shifted increasingly towards stimulus, while monetary policy was more strongly disinflationary in the United States than elsewhere.

A. Fiscal policy

During the 1970s the United States actually ran much closer to a balanced budget than other industrial countries. Table 1 shows a compar-

TABLE 1
Fiscal Policy: Actual Budget Balances, as % of GDP

	1974–81	1981	1982	1983*	1984*
	average				
United States	−.4	−1.0	−3.8	−4.4	−3.9
Japan	−3.6	−4.0	−4.1	−3.4	−2.5
Germany	−3.2	4.0	−3.9	−3.7	−3.1
France	−.8	−1.9	−2.6	−3.4	−3.3
United Kingdom	3.8	−2.5	−2.0	−2.5	−2.5
Italy	9.4	11.7	12.0	−11.6	12.4
Canada	−1.6	−1.2	−5.3	−6.5	−5.7
Non-U.S. average	−3.5	−4.0	−4.4	−4.4	−4.0

*OECD forecasts
Source: Organization for Economic Cooperation and Development.

ison of budget deficits as a share of GDP for the United States and for six other large industrial countries. Over the 1974–80 period the United States was clearly much less inclined towards deficit finance than the rest (although some of the deficits, such as Italy's, are exaggerated by inflation). It is arguable that the United States, with the lowest savings rate among the seven countries, needed to run a smaller deficit; but in any case the effect of divergent attitudes towards fiscal deficits after 1981 soon eliminated the difference. U.S. deficits grew sharply as a share of GDP, while they levelled off elsewhere.

The rise in the U.S. budget deficit was in part, of course, the result of the recession in this country. At the same time, however, recession was also tending to increase deficits abroad, so that the stability of foreign deficits actually reflected a substantial reduction in "full-employment" or "structural" deficits. Table 2 reports the OECD's estimates of those changes in budget balances not resulting from cyclical movements. Although the indicated U.S. fiscal loosening is considerably smaller than that in Table 1, there is a considerable fiscal tightening elsewhere. The *relative* movement in U.S. fiscal policy remains very large, some 4½ percent of GNP from 1981 to 1984.

B. Monetary policy and income

From 1980 through mid-1982 this country followed a more disinflationary monetary policy than other countries by any measure. The substantial loosening of our monetary policy since then has not fully made up the difference; it remains to be seen whether, as many expect, U.S. monetary policy will again tighten in the future.

The preceding paragraph was written as if the tightness of monetary

TABLE 2
Fiscal Policy: Discretionary Changes in Budget Balance
(net of cyclical factors)

	1981	1982	1983*	1984*
United States	1.0	−1.1	−0.6	−0.1
Japan	0.6	0.1	1.4	1.4
Germany	0.2	1.5	1.3	1.0
France	−1.1	0.2	0	1.2
United Kingdom	2.8	1.8	0	−.3
Italy	−2.4	1.2	1.9	0.4
Canada	1.6	0.4	−0.8	0.9
Non-U.S. average	.3	1.0	0.8	0.9

*OECD forecasts
Source: See Table 1.

TABLE 3
Monetary Policy: M1 Growth

	1980	1981	1982	Recent*
United States	9.0	5.2	4.8	14.5
Japan	.8	3.7	7.1	−.1
Germany	2.4	0.9	3.2	19.1
France	8.0	12.3	14.8	5.1
United Kingdom	4.5	10.2	8.2	12.8
Italy	15.9	11.1	12.8	16.2
Canada	3.9	3.0	0.8	14.2
Non-U.S. average	4.5	6.1	7.8	9.1

policy were something easily measured. In fact, there are a number of possible measurements. In Part II of this paper I will propose a measure which will doubtless annoy most people. For the moment, however, it will suffice to look at the more conventional measures. Table 3 shows growth rates of M1 in the United States and other major industrial countries. The table suggests a much more dramatic deceleration in this country than elsewhere until the summer of 1982, then a reversal. It is interesting to note the low recent money growth in France and Japan, both of which have (for different reasons) been strongly concerned about their exchange rates.

Differential monetary policies have had an effect on income growth which more than outweighs the effect of differential fiscal policies. Table 4 shows that the recession in the United States produced a greater shortfall of growth from its previous average than that elsewhere. If 1979 is taken to represent a year of more or less normal output, and the trend

TABLE 4
Real GDP Growth

	1973–79	1980	1981	1982	1983*
United States	2.6	−0.3	2.3	−1.7	3.0
Japan	3.6	4.9	4.0	3.0	3.3
Germany	2.4	1.9	0.2	−1.1	0.5
France	3.1	1.1	0.2	1.7	−0.5
United Kingdom	1.4	−2.0	−2.0	1.2	1.8
Italy	2.6	3.9	−0.2	−0.3	−0.5
Canada	3.3	0.5	3.8	−4.8	2.0
Non-U.S. average	2.9	2.3	1.4	0.8	1.4

*OECD forecasts

from 1973–1979 is taken as an estimte of trend growth, the U.S. GDP gap in 1982 was 7.5 percent, vs. 4.2 percent for other large industrial countries. (These numbers would be larger if we used end-of-year figures rather than annual averages).

C. Interest rates and exchange rates

Through mid-1982, the United States experienced a substantially greater increase in real short-term interest rates than other countries. The increase represented a combination of higher nominal interest rates and lower inflation, and can be explained as the result of more severe disinflationary monetary policy in this country than elsewhere.

Through mid-1982 there seemed to be a close association between the real interest differential and the dollar's exchange rate. The extraordinary rise in the dollar from its low point in 1980 to mid-1982 could in effect be explained by an equally extraordinary rise in U.S. real interest rates, not fully matched by other countries.

Events in the second half of 1982, however, caused some doubts to emerge about whether policy divergence in itself was enough to explain the dollar's strength. The reversal of U.S. monetary policy in the summer of 1982 brought about a considerable drop in interest rates; yet the dollar not only remained strong but actually rose further. This led some observers to conclude that such factors as political uncertainty, rather than purely economic factors, were the crucial determinants of the dollar's strength.

A more careful look at the evidence suggests, however, that the extent to which the exchange rate was defying economic forces in late 1982 has been exaggerated. Table 5 presents a comparison, developed by the OECD, of interest rate *changes* from June to December 1982. There are

TABLE 5
Changes in Interest Rates, end-June to end-December, 1982

	Short-Term	Long-Term
United States	−5.4	−3.3
Japan	−.2	−.6
Germany	−2.9	−1.9
France	−2.8	−.6
United Kingdom	−2.6	−2.3
Italy	−1.4	−.7
Canada	−4.2	−4.2
Non-U.S. average	−1.9	−1.4

two important points. First, the decline in U.S. interest rates was partly matched by a decline in interest rates elsewhere, so that the interest rate *differential* did not narrow as much as a look at U.S. rates alone would suggest.

Second, the interest differential on long-term securities narrowed much less than that on short-term assets. This presumably reflected the belief of the markets—a belief which turned out to be justified—that the decline in U.S. short-term rates was a temporary phenomenon.

It is argued in the appendix to this paper that the relevant interest differential for exchange rate determination is a differential on real, long-term rates. What Table 5 shows is that despite the perception of a major decline in U.S. interest rates in the second half of 1982, the long-term nominal differential fell by less than 2 percentage points. The question then becomes whether changes in relative inflation expectations offset this decline. None of the ways in which we attempt to measure inflation-ary expectations is very satisfactory. My personal impression is that the second half of 1982 was marked in this country by a revolution of falling expectations about inflation, as the true depth of the recession became apparent. If this is a correct perception, it may well be that the second half of 1982 actually saw a *rise* in the relevant interest differential between this country and other industrial countries.

This is hardly a conclusive discussion. The point is that it remains a viable working hypothesis that the strength of the dollar has basically reflected the divergence in macroeconomic policies between the United States and other industrial countries, rather than other exogenous factors.

D. U.S. external balances

The end result of the divergence in macroeconomic policies between the United States and other industrial countries is a surge in U.S. external deficits, both on merchandise trade and on the current account. In 1982, despite the strength of the dollar, these deficits increased only modestly. This was partly because the full effects of the exchange rate on trade take time to be felt. It was also importantly due to the greater depth of the recession in this country than elsewhere, which had the effect of masking the U.S. loss of competitiveness. As the U.S. economy recovers, most observers now expect record trade and current account deficits this year, unprecedented deficits next year.

II. A Framework for Analysis

In the last decade international macroeconomic theory has become an increasingly sophisticated field. The simple extensions of the IS-LM model developed by Mundell and Fleming have been followed by models which emphasize price dynamics, intertemporal optimization, and portfolio behavior under uncertainty. These newer models have yielded valuable insights. Yet bread-and-butter analysis of international macroeconomics continues to rely heavily on the older approach. For the purposes of understanding the current international situation the Mundell-Fleming model remains a useful starting point. The most important modification required is, I will argue, in our specification of the behavior of the monetary authorities rather than of private agents.

A. The Mundell-Fleming model

The basic Mundell-Fleming model is an IS-LM framework to which a rudimentary international sector has been appended. Trade flows depend on the exchange rate and income, capital flows on the interest differential. The exchange rate adjusts so as to insure a balanced flow of payments.

There are many expositions of the Mundell-Fleming model, and it need not be restated here.[1] The only important thing at this point is to recall the main conclusions about the effects of monetary and fiscal policy with a floating exchange rate.

Monetary policy: A monetary expansion leads to a lower interest rate, a capital outflow, and depreciation of the expanding country's currency. To accommodate the capital outflow the currency must depreciate so much that the trade balance actually improves, so that monetary expansion by one country actually has a contractionary effect on demand in the rest of the world.

Fiscal policy: A fiscal expansion raises the interest rate and leads to a capital inflow. Whether the currency appreciates or depreciates depends on how sensitive capital flows are to interest differentials. In either case, the counterpart of the capital inflow is a worsening of the trade balance which transmits part of the increase in demand to the rest of the world.

Few sensible observers would quarrel with the argument that monetary expansion at least temporarily lowers interest rates and leads to currency depreciation, though the perverse effect of monetary expansion on demand abroad may raise some doubts. More controversial, however, are the effects of fiscal policy. In the Mundell-Fleming model the effect of fiscal expansion on the exchange rate is ambiguous, while the effect on foreign income is clearly positive. In recent discussions of international issues, however, unqualified assertions have been made that U.S. fiscal deficits raise the value of the dollar. At the same time, many observers have claimed that U.S. fiscal deficits actually have a *contractionary* effect on the rest of the world.

These views do not by and large represent judgments about parameter values or differences of opinion about the appropriate macroeconomic model. What they reflect instead is a view about the proper characterization of monetary policy. The traditional Mundell-Fleming analysis of fiscal policy asks what happens when fiscal policy is changed, holding the money supply constant. This is a reasonable question, but in the present context it is not very relevant. To discuss the effects of fiscal policy it is necessary to ask how the monetary authorities will actually react—and this will probably not involve holding the money supply constant.

B. Restating monetary and fiscal policy: the IS-PV Model

Neither in this country nor in others have the monetary authorities held strictly to aggregate targets. Instead, they have modified their targets whenever that has seemed necessary to achieve desired macroeconomic results in terms of growth and inflation. A number of observers have called for an explicit acknowledgement of this position, and have called for targeting not of M1 or M2 but of MV—that is, of nominal GNP.

Central banks have resisted any such explicit targeting. Nonetheless, it may be reasonable as a first cut to hypothesize that monetary authorities are in effect attempting to peg nominal GNP. They are not, of course, fully successful in this, but the error seems to be uncorrelated with other policies. The Federal Reserve is at the time of writing tightening its policies to offset a strong fiscal stimulus. They may do too little, allowing an undesirably fast recovery; or they may do too much, causing the recovery to stall. But the point is that if fiscal policy were less stimulative, the Fed would feel less need to tighten, and the net effect on the *expected* pace of recovery would be ambiguous.

Beyond its rough realism, adopting the working assumption of nominal income targeting by the monetary authorities has two useful features. First, it simplifies the analysis of fiscal policy. Second, it helps clarify the discussion of exchange rate policy by making natural the distinction between questions of the *level* of output and questions of its *composition*.

Consider, then, the Mundell-Fleming model where the monetary authorities engage in nominal income targeting. The effect is to replace the conventional upward-sloping LM curve with a vertical monetary authority response function, which I will call PV curve.[2] Income is determined by the central bank; given this level of income, fiscal policy can only shift the composition of output by altering the interest rate. In effect we restore the classical full-employment view of fiscal policy even for situations when the economy is not at full employment.

What are the international trade implications of fiscal policy? Figure 1 illustrates the simple story which results. Two countries are shown, with IS curves drawn for a given exchange rate. We assume that at that initial exchange rate, external payments are in balance.

An expansionary fiscal policy in country A has the initial effect of pushing up the IS curve in that country. The resulting increase in interest rates would, however, lead to a balance of payments surplus at the initial exchange rate. Thus country A's currency appreciates. The appreciation acts directly to offset the interest differential, while at the same time acting to narrow that differential. Because A's goods have become less competitive, A's IS curve shifts down while B's shifts up.

Thus the effect of a fiscal expansion in one country is unambiguously to cause an exchange rate appreciation and also to raise interest rates both at home and in the rest of the world.

What about the assertion that U.S. fiscal deficits actually have a contractionary effect in the rest of the world? This should be understood as a statement about policy reaction functions. In the case illustrated in Figure 1, country A's fiscal expansion did not affect GNP in the rest of the world; but it did lead to a depreciation of country B's currency. Suppose that country B does not want to have a depreciating currency, perhaps because of the inflationary impact. Then to limit the fall in its currency country B must either (i) match A's fiscal expansion, or (ii) tighten its monetary policy. If fiscal policy is inflexible, monetary policy must do the job. The result is illustrated in Figure 2. The initial effect of A's fiscal expansion is to push up its IS curve; as A's currency appreciates, its IS curve shifts back down and *both* the IS and PV curves shift back in B. Thus given the hypothesized monetary authority reaction functions, concerned with nominal GNP in one country and the exchange rate

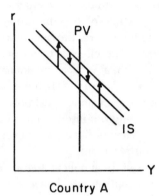

Country A

Country B

Figure 1

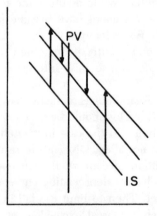

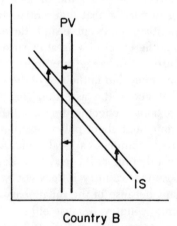

Country A

Country B

Figure 2

elsewhere, a fiscal expansion in one country actually can led to a contraction abroad.

Is this scenario reasonable? I would argue that it is for at least one major country, Japan. Japan is unwilling to see the yen depreciate for fear of provoking a protectionist response in the United States. At the same time, Japan is committed for domestic reasons to a policy of reducing budget deficits. The result is that when U.S. fiscal deficits drive up interest rates, Japan must respond by slowing money growth. In a sense which must be carefully stated but is nonetheless real, U.S. fiscal stimulus probably has a contractionary effect on activity in Japan.

C. Dynamics and expectations

To apply the simple framework just described to real-world phenomena it is necessary to make some allowance for the complications introduced by dynamics and expectations. Some of these issues, like the role played by lags in the adjustment of trade flows to the exchange rate, are not very controversial. But there has been some confusion over the appropriate treatment of expectations both of inflation and of future interest rates.

One view, associated particularly with the Council of Economic Advisers (see for example, the *Economic Report of the President* for 1983) is that the relevant interest rates for exchange rate determination are *real, long-term* rates. This view gests that anticipations of future fiscal deficits, by raising long-term rates, can tend to keep the current exchange rate high. The CEA view has, however, been challenged by many observers, who point out two aspects of actual international capital movements which seem to contradict this view. First, investors deciding in which country to place their money are deciding between two financial assets, rather than making a choice between financial and real assets, so that it seems unclear why *real* yields should matter. Second, the most volatile international investment is in short-term securities, so that it seems unclear why *long-term* yields should be emphasized.

These observations are valid, but do not necessarily contradict the CEA view. Even if investors do not care about real returns or invest in long-term instruments in a speculative market, it is still appropriate to focus on the long-term real interest differential.

A formal statement of the argument is given in the appendix. The intuitive sense behind the statement may be helped by making two points. First, high interest rates will not make for a strong currency if they are simply an offset to high inflation, suggesting that it is the real interest rate which matters—not because investors are choosing between real and financial assets, but because high inflation will be reflected other things equal in a depreciating currency, reducing the domestic financial yield measured in foreign currency. Second, an interest rate increase which is perceived as very temporary will have less effect on the exchange rate than one which is expected to persist. This suggests that what matters is a weighted average of expected future interest rates—in effect, a long-term rate. The reason is not because investors plan to buy and hold, but because the expected future course of interest rates affects the expected future course of the exchange rate—which is relevant even to short-term investors.

The emphasis on real long-term rates as determinants of the exchange rate should be interpreted, then, as shorthand for a view of the exchange market as one in which investors attempt to look forward to future fundamentals. The main objection to this view would be to question whether the markets are really that rational.

III. Policy Responses to the Strong Dollar

The first two parts of this paper have laid out some suggestive data and a simple theoretical framework on which to hang those data. The message is by and large a conventional one: actual and expected tight monetary and loose fiscal policy in the United States have led to a strong dollar and a massive U.S. trade deficit; the efforts of other countries to support their currencies in the face of the U.S. policy mix may have caused a deeper recession outside this country than would otherwise have been the case.

The next question is what to do about it. It is commonly stated that the dollar is overvalued. It is certainly unusually strong, and probably stronger than it would be given an optimal set of policies. The simple statement that the dollar is overvalued, however, seems to suggest that any policy which brings the dollar down is desirable. This is a dubious conclusion. A strong case can be made for the argument that in a *conditional* sense the strong dollar is desirable—that unless fundamental macroeconomic policies, especially fiscal policy, are changed, using other policies to reduce the value of the dollar will not be a good idea. There is also a contrary case, but it is a surprisingly shaky one.

A. Effects of the strong dollar

As a backdrop to our discussion of policy, it is useful to review the major effects of a strong dollar. These basically fall into four categories: the direct effect on U.S. competitiveness; on inflation; on aggregate demand and employment; and on interest rates and investment.

1. Competitiveness

This is not the place for a detailed discussion of econometric estimates of the impact of the exchange rate on U.S. trade. The point which is clear from most estimates is a straightforward one: essentially *all* of the actual and anticipated deterioration in U.S. external balances can be attributed to the strength of the dollar. Cyclical factors are important determinants of trade, but have so far acted to mask the effects of the strong dollar (because of the relatively deep U.S. recession) rather than to add to these effects. The expectation of growing U.S. deficits arises partly from the prospect that U.S. recovery will remove this mask, partly from lagged effects of the exchange rate. Other factors, such as the LDC debt crisis and the drop in oil prices, have been relatively small and largely offsetting. As for the alleged effects of foreign trade and industrial policies, these have had no discernible effects.

2. Inflation

Exchange rate appreciation leads to lower prices for imports and other tradable goods, thereby providing an anti-inflationary bonus. To the extent that wages are explicitly or implicitly indexed this disinflationary impact can spread to the economy as a whole. The massive appreciation of the dollar since 1980 has clearly been a significant factor in the moderation of U.S. inflation.

As Buiter and Miller (1982) have emphasized, however, this is only a transitory gain. In the long run, as the exchange rate returns to purchasing power parity, the inflation gains from exchange rate appreciation must be paid back. Indeed, a full analysis shows that they must be paid back with interest.[3]

Despite their transitory nature, however, the inflationary consequences of exchange rate changes play a crucial role in generating international macroeconomic interdependence, as discussed in Part IV of this paper.

3. Aggregate demand and employment

When we approach the question of the aggregate demand effects of the strong dollar we enter a controversial area. The *direct* impact of the strong dollar, via its effect on net exports, is of course to depress demand and employment. One's estimate of the *full* effect, however, depends on one's model of the economy and especially on one's model of the behavior of the monetary authorities.

My view should already be clear from the discussion in Part II of the paper. The Federal Reserve can, I would argue, usefully be viewed as attempting to peg GNP (if not too successfully). This implies that a decline in net exports will be met with a decline in interest rates which leads to offsetting increases in other components of demand. To a first approximation, the strong dollar thus has no effect on demand on employment.

4. Interest rates and investment

If one accepts the "PV curve" view of monetary policy, the consequences for one's view of the interest and investment impact of the strong dollar are clear. The strength of the dollar leads to lower interest rates and higher investment than would otherwise be the case. In the current context, the strength of the dollar helps limit the "crowding out" caused by the combination of loose fiscal and tight monetary policies.

One way of stating this is in terms of the adjustment shown in Figure 1. There, after fiscal expansion pushes country A's IS curve to the right, exchange rate appreciation pushes it partway back to the left. The result is a lower interest rate and, implicitly, higher investment than would have been the case had the exchange rate adjustment somehow been prevented.

Alternatively, the argument can be stated in terms of the savings-investment identity. Definitionally, U.S. investment equals private sector savings, less the government budget deficit, plus the current account deficit. In other words, the external deficit has as its counterpart a net capital inflow. This capital inflow allows a higher level of investment to be sustained for a given level of the government deficit than would otherwise be the case. In this sense, foreign capital inflow can be said to be financing part of the budget deficit—whether foreigners actually buy Treasury offerings or not.

These two ways of stating the point are equivalent, although they can be made to sound different. The important point is that the argument that the strong dollar helps sustain investment is not an outlandish concept, but a straightforward conclusion from a conventional framework.

B. Policy options

Given these effects of the strong dollar, what should be done? There are three serious options: tighter fiscal policy, looser monetary policy, and capital controls. There is also a nonserious option, exchange market intervention.

1. Fiscal policy

Given our assumptions about monetary policy, a tighter U.S. fiscal policy would lead to lower interest rates, a lower dollar, and (with some lag) an improved U.S. external position. In terms of the savings-investment identity, the reduction in government dissaving would be reflected in increases both in domestic investment and in net foreign investment.

This is a desirable outcome by almost anyone's accounting. It is not, however, something likely to happen soon. In any case, to favor a tighter fiscal policy, which would have a lower dollar as one of its consequences, is not at all the same thing as simply favoring a lower dollar.

2. Monetary policy

A loose monetary policy would clearly help drive down the dollar. The question is whether the looser policy is desirable. This depends basically on how fast you want to disinflate, and whether you like the pace the Federal Reserve has chosen. Last fall, it was relatively easy to advocate looser money; at the time of writing, with the economy growing rapidly, the case is less clear. Whatever one's views on the subject, they do not (or should not) depend primarily on the exchange rate. As is the case with fiscal policy, advocating a looser monetary policy, which would weaken the dollar, is not the same as simply advocating a lower dollar.

3. Capital controls

If one is neither able to tighten fiscal policy, nor willing to loosen monetary policy, the only practicable way to bring down the dollar is probably with capital controls—either capital import controls by the United States or capital export controls by other countries. And some influential commentators, such as Bergsten (1982) and Dornbusch (1982) have in fact advocated such controls.

There would certainly be administrative problems and microeconomic costs associated with controls, but these are not the central issue. It is probably possible to devise capital controls which would succeed in lowering the dollar. The key question is whether one wants a lower dollar, *given current monetary and fiscal policies*.

It is crucial to pose the question this way, rather than to ask in general terms whether the dollar is overvalued. If the dollar is somehow brought down without changing the underlying macroeconomic policies which brought it up, there must be a tradeoff. In particular, a weaker dollar must—as we have already seen—mean higher interest rates and lower investment.

To put it baldly, is a (say) $30 billion improvement in the trade balance worth a $30 billion reduction investment?[4] Conventional growth analysis will almost surely say that it is not. The social return on domestic investment is probably higher than on foreign investment even in normal times, because of the tax wedge. Furthermore, in the mid-1980s the crowding out of investment by budget deficits will probably mean that only relatively high return investments would have been undertaken in any case.

To make the case for capital controls one has to argue that too much of the crowding out of investment by the U.S. budget deficit is falling on net foreign investment, too little on domestic investment. If world capital markets were perfectly integrated, one would expect a fiscal deficit anywhere to crowd out investment equally around the world. Since the United States accounts for only about 40 percent of the OECD's GNP, and less of its investment, this would imply a current account deficit of at least 60 percent of the U.S. budget deficit—much more than we have observed so far or than anyone is currently forecasting. This leaves unclear by what standard the actual capital inflow may be judged as being too large.

This is not to say that no arguments can be made for trying to bring the dollar down. Several arguments are discussed below. First, however, it is necessary to treat briefly the question of exchange market intervention.

4. Exchange market intervention

Instead of using capital controls to bring the dollar down, we could attempt to use exchange market intervention. As long as such intervention is "sterilized"—that is, not allowed to affect monetary policy—it will have two problems. First, it will probably be ineffective. Second, if it is effective, it will have the same doubtfully desirable macro effects as capital controls.

The effectiveness of sterilized intervention has been the subject of a great deal of empirical work, as well as of an international summit-related study. The evidence is not as tight as one might wish, but in general there is little reason to believe that sterilized intervention can do much beyond limited smoothing of the exchange rate.

More to the point, the macroeconomic effects of intervention if it works are the same as those of capital controls: to lower the dollar while raising interest rates, and thus to trade off an improved trade balance for lower investment. It is useful in this context to think of intervention as an officially sponsored capital outflow which is being used to offset private capital inflows; the net effect is as if a restriction were simply placed on the net inflow.

If it could work, intervention might be preferable to capital controls because it is cleaner in its microeconomic effects, and because it is easier to shut off. But in macroeconomic terms, it is no different.

C. The Case for a Weaker Dollar

I have made rather strongly the case that weakening the dollar through means other than getting our monetary-fiscal house in order is not a desirable thing. Some contrary arguments, however, deserve to be briefly mentioned.

1. Adjustment costs

The strength of the dollar causes resources to move out of exporting and import-competing sectors. When the dollar declines, these resources will come back. The adjustments will have a real cost; if markets fail to perceive the temporary nature of the shift, resources will be wasted in unnecessary movement between sectors. By stabilizing the dollar these costs might be avoided.

There are two problems with this argument. First, it presumes that markets are excessively short-sighted—a shaky foundation on which to base policy. Second, it assumes that stabilizing the exchange rate would reduce total adjustment; in fact, while adjustment by tradable sectors would be less, adjustment by other interest-sensitive sectors such as construction would actually have to be larger.

2. Permanent loss of competitiveness

Many businessmen and policymakers are concerned that a sort of ratchet effect may occur in international competition: that once markets have been lost through a period of currency overvaluation, they will not be regained when the currency returns to its normal level. This cannot be true in quite the sense that it is often stated; the United States cannot permanently lose its competitiveness in everything. But there may be a valid point here: in a world where dynamic scale economies are impor- tant, as they surely are for many U.S. exports, a period of unusual strength for a country's currency may have to be followed by a period of unusual weakness as the country is obliged to reestabish market positions.

3. Political considerations

The most important argument for doing something about the dollar is not really an economic one. It is the argument that the strength of the dollar, by feeding protectionism, will lead to an irreversible breakup of the liberal trading system. A large trade deficit may be preferable to a cut in investment on purely economic grounds, but the political reper- cussions from the trade deficit will be more severe and last longer.

This is a powerful and respectable argument. It should, however, be made clearly and honestly, with full admission of the economic conse- quences. Accepting a basically undesirable policy in order to appease dangerous political forces may be good political economy; but one should be clear that is the proposal, and not go back to find reasons why the policy was good economics, too.

IV. The Scope for International Cooperation

The message of this paper so far has been that the U.S. trade deficit is part of a general crowding out of investment by tight monetary and loose fiscal policies. Without a change in these policies, there is not a compelling case—except perhaps a political one—for doing anything specifically to improve the U.S. external balance. And since monetary policy has been reasonably flexible in the last year, it is fiscal policy which is cast as the villain.

The perspective so far has, however, been a strongly U.S. centered one. One naturally wonders whether, even given the problem of U.S. fiscal policy, there is not some scope for improved results through international cooperation on monetary policies.

In this final section of the paper I will briefly sketch out a crude analysis of the possibilities for international cooperation on monetary policy. This analysis suggests that if it were not for the U.S. fiscal problem, there would be scope for coordination; but that the U.S. fiscal problem makes monetary coordination a doubtful proposition.

A. *The Interdependence of Monetary Policies: Conventional Analysis*

There is a view of international monetary interdependence which has been "in the air" in many recent discussions and has been formalized in an important recent paper by Sachs (1983). The key element in this view is the way that tight money, by inducing exchange rate appreciation, can be used to "export" inflation. In the simplest analysis, this leads countries to pursue disinflationary strategies which are individually rational but collectively too severe.

To do this analysis right requires careful distinctions between stocks and flows, and also careful treatment of dynamic issues.[5] For the purposes of this paper it is enough to do the analysis wrong but quickly.

1. *International monetary reaction functions*

Consider a world of two countries A and B, choosing levels of their nominal incomes Y_A and Y_B. We assume that the countries are attempting to work down inherited inflation, and are thus in a position where both unemployment and inflation are uncomfortably high.

From the point of view of A's monetary authority, a monetary expansion abroad is helpful because it leads to a depreciation of B's currency and thus a fall in import prices. So we can, as in Figure 3, draw a set of indifference curves in Y_A, Y_B space. If A takes B's monetary policy as given, we can draw a reaction function like AA through the bottoms of these indifference curves. In a typical model, e.g., a linear-quadratic setup, the reaction function will be upward sloping: the more expansionary B's policy, the more expansionary A's will be. We can also derive a similar schedule for B. If the countries act noncooperatively, equilibrium will be where the schedules cross.

2. The scope for cooperation

In this simple view, there are clear mutual gains even without cooperation if one country takes on a leadership role. Figure 4 illustrates the

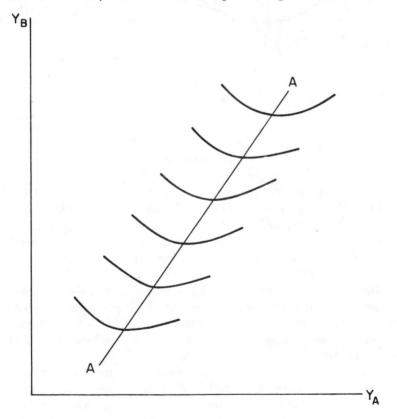

Figure 3

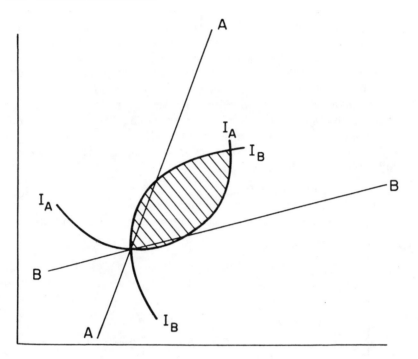

Figure 4

situation. AA and BB are the reaction functions, I_AI_A and I_BI_B the indifference curves corresponding to the noncooperative outcome. Any point in the shaded area is preferable to the noncooperative outcome for both countries. Since this area lies to the northeast of the noncooperative point, this says that in the absence of cooperation, monetary policy ends up being too tight.

The logic of this result is clear. Each country is tempted to pursue an excessively tight monetary policy because of the possibility of exporting inflation to the other,—or, more charitably, neither country is able to pursue a looser monetary policy without importing inflation via currency depreciation.

It is also worth noting that if one country recognizes the interdependence of macro policies, it can unilaterally take on a leadership role to the benefit of *both* countries. For example, it can be adopting a looser policy move to a point such as S, which is not an optimum but is still unambiguously better than the noncooperative outcome.

This analysis seems to provide a clear case for at least some coordinated monetary expansion. Unfortunately, thanks to the problem of U.S. fiscal policy, the situation is not so clear-cut.

B. The Current Dilemma

The reason why the simple analysis of international monetary interdependence is not too helpful in the current situation is that the United States has a mixed and perhaps perverse interest in foreign monetary policy. Because of expansionary U.S. fiscal policy, a monetary policy which the Federal Reserve regards as suitably anti-inflationary is associated with an unusually strong dollar. Instead of being constrained in monetary expansion by concern that the dollar will depreciate, the U.S. monetary authorities may actually be constrained in pursuing disinflationary policies by concerns about the strong dollar. For this reason, it is unclear whether this country would prefer to see looser or tighter monetary policies abroad.

Without pushing this too hard, it is worth examining the consequences if, because of an out-of-control fiscal policy, a country would actually prefer to see tight money abroad. Figure 5 illustrates the situation. Country A's indifference curves are now reversed in orientation. The zone of mutual improvement now lies *southeast* of the noncooperative solution. In other words, to strike a deal the United States would have to offer a more expansionary domestic monetary policy in return for tighter money abroad. In effect, this would be a cooperative, *unsterilized* intervention to bring down the dollar.

Note also that a sophisticated United States taking other countries' monetary reactions into account, would be inclined to follow a tighter monetary policy than otherwise, as indicated by point S. What is happening is that this country feels freer to disinflate because it knows that the induced reactions of other countries will dampen the resulting rise in the dollar. Unfortunately, U.S. sophistication about international repercussions here leads to a situation in which other countries end up worse off.

It is probably a mistake to push this analysis any further. The United States does not in fact have a clear-cut desire for tighter monetary policies abroad. Nor does it have a clear-cut desire for foreign monetary expansion. Because of its expansionary fiscal policy, this country has an ambiguous and uncertain attitude toward foreign monetary policies.

It is hard to see much realistic possibility for monetary coordination in this situation. Coordination would essentially amount to a trade, each country giving the others something they want. The United States has something other countries want—monetary expansion—but it cannot make a trade because it does not know what it wants.

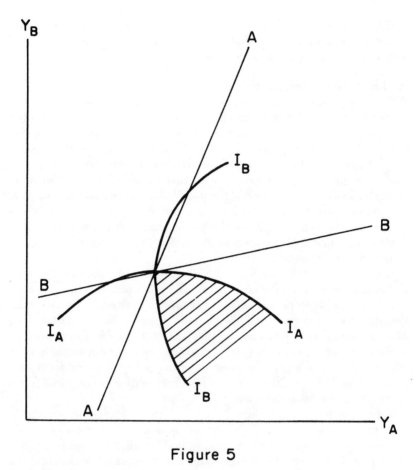

Figure 5

V. Conclusions

The divergence in monetary and fiscal policies between the United States and other advanced countries had led to an unusually strong dollar and the prospect of huge U.S. external deficits.

Of the various policy responses which might bring the dollar down, none except tighter fiscal policy seems very appealing, and that seems politically impossible. Looser money might be inflationary, while capital controls would raise interest rates and crowd out investment. The prospects for international cooperation on monetary policies, a reasonable proposal in normal circumstances, are vitiated by the effects of divergent fiscal policies.

Appendix:
Interest Rates and The Exchange Rate

The purpose of this appendix is to make algebraically the point that if investors are forward-looking, the exchange rate should depend on the differential in real, long-term interest rates.

Consider the following stripped down statement of the relationship between interest rates and the exchange rate:

(A.1) $\qquad e_t + p_t - p_t^* = \alpha + \beta[i_t - i_t^* + {}_te_{t+1} - e_t]$

where $\qquad e_t = $ log of the exchange rate

$\qquad {}_te_{t+1} = $ log of the exchange rate expected at time

$\qquad\qquad\qquad$ t to prevail at $t + 1$

$\qquad p_t, p_t^* = $ logs of domestic and foreign price levels

$\qquad i_t, i_t^* = $ domestic and foreign interest rates

As observers have urged, this equation relates the current real exchange rate to the differential in expected *nominal, short-term* returns.

Yet if investors use expectations of future fundamentals in forming their views, (A.1) can be shown to yield a relationship between the exchange rate and *real, long-term* interest rates.

Let us define

(A.2) $\qquad\qquad\qquad \widetilde{e} = e_t + p_t - p_t^*$

the real exchange rate; and

(A.3) $\qquad\qquad\qquad r_t = i_t - {}_tp_{t+1} + p_t$

the real interest rate. Then we can write (A.1) as

(A.4) $\qquad e_t = \dfrac{\alpha}{\beta + 1} + \dfrac{\beta}{\alpha + 1}[r_t - r_t^* + {}_t\widetilde{e}_{t+1}]$

so that the real exchange rate depends on real returns and the expected *future* real exchange rate. But if investors have consistent expectations about interest rates, we can rewrite once more to get

(A.5) $\qquad \widetilde{e}_t = \dfrac{\alpha}{\beta + 1} + \dfrac{\beta}{\beta + 1} \sum_{j=0}^{\infty} \left(\dfrac{\beta}{\beta + 1}\right)[{}_tr_{t+j} - {}_tr^*_{t+j}]$

The current exchange rate thus depends on a weighted average of current and future real interest differentials. If the current exchange rate is sensitive to the yield differential—i.e., β is large—the weight on future differentials will be large, and in effect the relevant rate will be a long-term rate.

Notes

1. A relatively modern exposition is given in Dornbusch and Krugman (1976).

2. For Paul Volcker.

3. A country which experiences a temporary exchange rate appreciation will have a worse current account and therefore end up with less net claims on foreigners than would otherwise have been the case. Because of this, it will eventually have lower net income from investments, and will thus ultimately have to have a *lower* real exchange rate than if it had never had the initial appreciation.

4. This is actually not quite fair. To the extent that savings respond to interest rates, part of the trade balance improvement could come at the expense of consumption.

5. The most important dynamic issue is the point, alluded to in Part III of the paper, that the inflation gains from appreciation must be given back. Sachs shows that this does not eliminate the interdependence, though it probably reduces it.

References

Bergsten, C. Fred. 1982. "What to do About the US-Japan Economic Problem," *Foreign Affairs,* vol. 60, no. 5 (Summer).

Buiter, W. H. and M. Miller, 1982. "Real Exchange Rate Overshooting and the Output Cost of Bringing Down Inflation, "*European Economic Review,* 18, #112 (May/June).

Dornbusch, R. 1983. "Flexible Exchange Rates and Interdependence," IMF *Staff Papers,* May.

———— and P. Krugman. 1976. "Flexible Exchange Rates in the Short Run," *Brookings Papers on Economic Activity,* 3.

Sachs, J. 1983. "International Policy Coordination in a Dynamic Macro- economic Model," NBER Working Paper #1166.

12

EXCERPTS FROM THE COUNCIL OF ECONOMIC ADVISERS *REPORT TO THE PRESIDENT,* 1975, 1976, 1977

Alan Greenspan

Recent Developments in International Finance

The international financial system has been fundamentally changed since August 1971, when the United States announced suspension of the convertibility into gold of dollars held by foreign monetary authorities. Following this action, major exchange rate realignments, coupled with devaluation of the dollar in terms of gold, were negotiated in December 1971 and February 1973; and negotiations were launched on a comprehensive reform of the international monetary system with establishment of the Committee of Twenty (C-20) under the auspices of the International Monetary Fund in July 1972. In March 1973, in response to great uncertainty and speculation in the foreign exchange markets following the second realignment, virtually all of the major industrial countries abandoned efforts to confine exchange rate movements within a narrow band around established par values. When the C-20 met during the IMF annual meetings in September 1973, it set July 31, 1974, as its target date for agreement on comprehensive monetary reform.

The oil price increases announced in October and December 1973, the acceleration of worldwide inflation, and *de facto* adoption of widespread floating radically altered the circumstances surrounding the C-20 negotiations. At its Rome meeting in January 1974, the C-20 shifted the focus of its negotiations. Instead of the early development of a comprehensive reform agreement, it began to work out a series of individual, less comprehensive steps that were of particular importance in the current economic situation. In mid-June the C-20 Ministers agreed on a program for immediate action and released the *Outline of Reform* and accompanying annexes that described both the status of the negotiations on longer-term reform and the direction in which the Ministers believed the system could evolve in the future.

The program of immediate action was consistent with the longer-term *Outline of Reform,* constituting in essence a proposed first step in the evolution toward a fundamentally reformed system. It included:

1. Creation of an Interim Committee of the IMF with advisory powers to guide the adjustment process and oversee the operations of the system pending the establishment, through amendment of the IMF *Articles of Agreement,* of a Ministerial Council with decision-making powers.

2. Establishment of a Development Committee, also at the ministerial level, under the joint auspices of the IMF and the International Bank for Reconstruction and Development, to deal with questions relating to the transfer of resources to developing countries.

3. Establishment of guidelines for floating exchange rates.

4. An interim change in the method of valuation of special drawing rights (SDR's) to widen the base for calculating the transactions value of SDR's so that currencies other than the dollar are included.

5. Provision for IMF members to subscribe to a declaration against taking restrictive trade or other current account measures for balance of payments purposes without IMF approval.

6. Improved measures for surveillance of the adjustment process and of developments in global liquidity.

7. A request that the Executive Directors of the IMF prepare a series of amendments to the IMF *Articles of Agreement* for consideration when IMF quotas are reviewed early in 1975.

Among other items on which draft amendments were to be prepared were: establishment of a permanent IMF Council; "legalization" of floating exchange rates; a permanent declaration against trade restrictions for balance of payments purposes; the role of gold; and various modifications of the general and SDR accounts of the IMF.

The longer-term *Outline of Reform* put forward by the C-20 called for a more effective and symmetrical system of adjustment, in which efficient operation of the adjustment mechanism would not be obstructed by controls or restrictions on current or capital account transactions for balance of payments purposes. The *Outline* envisaged that the role of the SDR would be enhanced and that the roles of gold and reserve currencies in international reserves would be reduced. At the end of 1974, the transactions value of SDR's was around $1.22 per unit of SDR.

Recognition that exchange rate flexibility must play a greater part in an efficient economic adjustment process was a key element of the reform proposals. In sharp contrast to the central role of fixed par values and narrow margins of exchange rate fluctuations around par values in the Bretton Woods system, the *Outline* called for a system in which countries could either establish adjustable par values or allow their currencies to float in response to market forces. Agreement was lacking, however, on the relative roles of floating and par values, the conditions under which the par values would be adjusted, and the provision for authorization of floating in the future system. The United States favors provisions that would permit a country to float its currency so long as it adhered to internationally agreed rules of conduct, without the need for further authorization or approval by the IMF. Some others favor a more constrained "floating option" under which floating would be limited to specified situations and subject to specific authorization by the IMF.

At its first session during the IMF annual meetings in early October 1974, the new Interim Committee of the IMF approved a work program focusing on energy-related financial problems and balance of payments adjustment in the light of the energy crisis. Pursuant to this work program, the Interim Committee, meeting in mid-January 1975, reached agreement on a broad range of key issues. The Committee agreed on:

1. A limited extension of the IMF oil facility in 1975, with borrowings of up to SDR 5 billion and with an indication that it would be appropriate to make greater use of the Fund's own resources. In conjunction with the Development Committee, the Interim Committee also endorsed a suggestion by the IMF's Managing Director that special provision be made to reduce the interest burden on oil facility borrowing by the poorest developing countries.

2. An IMF quota increase of 32.5 percent overall, "rounded up" to a new quota total of SDR 39 billion, with a doubling of the quota shares of the major oil-exporting countries as a group and no reduction of the collective share of other developing countries. No agreement was recorded on quota shares for other groups or for individual countries. It was agreed, however, that since an important purpose of increasing quotas is to strengthen the Fund's liquidity, arrangements should be made to ensure usability of all IMF currency holdings in accordance with Fund policies.

3. A request that the Executive Directors continue work on a narrowed range of amendments to the IMF *Articles of Agreement* and submit drafts to the Committee on: establishment of the Ministerial Council; legaliza-

tion of floating; improvements in the general account, including elimination of requirements to make gold payments to the IMF and establishment of arrangements to ensure the usability of IMF currency holdings; and improvements in the characteristics of the SDR.

Progress was made toward agreement on a comprehensive set of amendments on gold, including abolition of the official price and freedom for national monetary authorities to enter into gold transactions under certain specific arrangements with each other in order to ensure that the role of gold in the international monetary system would be gradually reduced. Additional agreements related to the financial support arrangement among the members of the OECD, described earlier in this chapter, and to other matters.

Managed Floating

The interim guidelines that have been recommended by the C-20 for the present situation of widespread floating represent a first effort to address in a formal way the complex issues that can arise under a floating system, as well as to develop codes of behavior that might apply under a regime of managed floating over the longer term. Under the guidelines, countries with floating rates may intervene to moderate sharp and disruptive fluctuations from day to day and from week to week in the exchange value of their currencies. Intervention should not be used, however, to moderate movements in the exchange value of any currency over longer periods like months or quarters, unless such official intervention is consistent with actual and expected world market conditions, and unless it accords also with a pattern of exchange rates considered reasonable as a medium-term norm by that country and the international community. For example, a rate of inflation substantially higher than that of a country's main trading partners or competitors would normally lead to expectations of a further depreciation of its currency. In that case, attempts to fix the exchange rate for an extended period, whether undertaken by the country itself or by its trading partners, might be viewed as violating the intent of the guidelines, since intervention for this purpose would be disequilibrating.

Even without imposing direct controls on the flow of goods and capital in international trade, official monetary agencies can modify the course of exchange rates, at least temporarily, under a system of managed floating. The techniques of management can take a variety of forms. The most common is for central banks to intervene in the international money markets by selling domestic currency for foreign currencies, thereby leaning against an appreciation of their currency. Alternately they may engage in the converse operation, possibly with exchange reserves that are supplemented through official borrowing of foreign currencies, to slow a depreciation of their currency. If, however, in the attempt to slow movements of the exchange rate in either direction by "leaning against the wind," intervention continues on the same side of the market for an extended period, the level of the exchange rate may be affected even after intervention has ceased. This would occur if persistent one-sided intervention repressed exchange rate movements substantially. Since any lasting distortion of the exchange rates achieved through one-sided intervention influences the pattern of international trade and investment after a lag, this changed pattern may reflect back on subsequent exchange rate levels.

Foreign Exchange Management Since March 1973
Although attempts to fix the exchange rates of all major countries within narrow ranges vis-a-vis the dollar were officially abandoned in March 1973, a group of European countries agreed on new sets of exchange rates, which they would maintain within 2¼ percent of the agreed parities relative to each other. The United Kingdom and Italy did not join this group, however, and the joint float was further eroded when France withdrew from the group in January 1974. By the end of 1974 only Germany, the Benelux countries, Denmark, Norway, and Sweden floated jointly against the dollar; and some other nations tied their exchange rates to those of other countries. Managed floating had thus become the rule among the industrial countries.

Since the start of generalized floating, the pattern and net amount of official intervention have not been the same as those prevailing before 1973. The direction of official intervention has changed more frequently. As exchange reserve decumulations were followed by accumulations, U.S. liabilities to foreign official institutions were only slightly higher at the end of the third quarter of 1974 than at the end of the first quarter of 1973. From that time until February 1974, the drop in U.S. liabilities to the official agencies of other industrial countries outweighed the increase in liabilities to the OPEC governments, so that total U.S. liabilities actually declined. By comparison, official claims on U.S. residents had more than quadrupled from the end of 1969 to the end of March 1973, and industrial countries accounted for almost all of this increase.

The reserves of industrial countries remained relatively stable, but only because of substantial international borrowing on the part of deficit countries. Some of this borrowing was carried out by the domestic banking system without direct governmental action; in other cases credits were raised by official entities either in the private money market or with foreign monetary authorities. Most deficit countries have used the proceeds of loans from official and private sources to counteract any large decline in their international reserves. Government-to-government loans by surplus countries to deficit countries may be treated as foreign exchange reserves by the former, whether or not they result in marketable claims on the latter. Still there was little growth in the official reserves of industrial surplus countries as exchange rates were allowed to rise to dampen inflows of funds. Specifically, of the countries whose currencies appreciated against the dollar, Canada, Germany, and Switzerland had approximately the same amount of reserves at the end of the third quarter of 1974 as at the end of the first quarter of 1973, and only a few of the countries with depreciating currencies, most notably Japan, lost reserves.

The pattern of reserve movements suggests a change in central bank behavior compared to the period prior to 1973, but a number of countries have continued to influence movements of their exchange rate through indirect forms of intervention in 1974. To slow the rise of its franc, Switzerland discouraged interest payments on nonresident deposits and maintained higher reserve requirements on nonresident than on resident deposits. In October, Switzerland lifted the interest ban but soon afterwards imposed taxes at the rate of 3 percent per quarter on nonresident deposits in excess of normal working balances, in order to discourage the inflow of funds. Other countries, however, discouraged capital outflows. For instance, France took steps to reduce franc loans to nonresidents, and Japan required the sale of private dollar holdings to the central bank for use in foreign exchange intervention. Among the deficit countries, only Italy imposed direct restrictions affecting international trade and payments when it imposed a 50 percent deposit requirement on most categories of imports in May 1974.

For short periods during 1974 disturbances originating in the private market prevented foreign exchange markets from functioning efficiently. When daily fluctuations in exchange rates become large, and severe losses by various market participants add to the uncertainty, broad participation in the exchange markets may be discouraged and the fulfillment of contracts may become less certain. Risk premiums were raised by the failure of the German Herstatt bank in June 1974 and the disclosure that large losses from private exchange trading had occurred, involving a number of other institutions not only in Germany but also in Switzerland, Britain, Italy, and the United States. Banks were less willing to take foreign exchange positions; and official efforts to discourage participation even further—for instance in Germany—made the markets thinner. Under such conditions markets are less efficient in smoothing out temporary imbalances in spot offerings or in contracts for future delivery, bid-ask spreads are likely to widen, and hence the costs of financing international trade may rise.

On the whole, however, the fact that a number of important exchange rates were no longer fixed brought several distinct advantages. With no formal commitments about exchange rates or margins, the authorities have much more flexibility in dealing with speculative exchange pressures. That is, those interested in shifting funds from one currency to another can no longer make massive purchases or sales of foreign currencies at set prices in a short period and count on the country's monetary authorities' being committed to meeting exchange demands without allowing the rate to move, as was the case in earlier years. Rather, authorities can let their rates adjust to eliminate exchange rate imbalances.

The new system has also enabled countries to manage their money supply with a greater degree of independence. Prior to the adoption of generalized floating there were periodic complaints, particularly from some European countries, that efforts to achieve domestic monetary policy objectives were being overwhelmed by movements in dollar reserves occasioned by the official intervention required to maintain the exchange rates. They system of quasi-fixed exchange rates still existed among the major trading countries at that time; and when the dollar came under pressure, foreign central banks found it difficult to offset the growth in domestic bank reserves resulting from their dollar purchases. It was therefore argued that inflation was transmitted between countries by reserve asset acquisitions on the part of the surplus countries causing their rates of monetary growth to rise while money supply growth was not allowed to fall symmetrically in the deficit countries. Yet around $30 billion, or over 40 percent of the dollars held by foreign official agencies at the end of March 1973, were acquired after the summer of 1971, when the convertibility of the dollar into gold had already been suspended. In the interim, many countries appeared disinclined to have their currencies appreciate relative to the dollar, thus revealing more concern about promoting exports than avoiding the inflationary consequences of the dollar inflows.

Since March 1973, changes in official reserve holdings have shown no consistent relation to changes in the monetary base of most countries, and official intervention has been entirely discretionary. Hence, even if international reserve flows might have raised the monetary rates of growth more than some countries desired during the period of fixed exchange rates, they cannot have had this effect since that time unless countries chose to make exchange rate objectives paramount.

Recent Exchange Rate Developments

Foreign central banks as a group ceased to observe formal intervention limits against the dollar after the international currency exchanges reopened on March 19, 1973, and the dollar declined soon afterwards. After falling through the first week of July, the value of the dollar increased in terms of most foreign currencies through August and then changed little through October.

With the cutback in oil supplies by the OPEC, the dollar soon strengthened relative to all major European currencies and the yen, since it was known that the United States was far less dependent on imported oil than Western Europe or Japan. Not only was the impact of the oil price increase on the U.S. trade balance and the domestic rate of inflation initially expected to be less, but it was widely anticipated abroad that a major share of the additional OPEC revenues would eventually be reinvested in the United States. This market assessment prompted a strong movement of short-term funds into the dollar and out of the major European currencies and the yen. Even though foreign central banks sold dollars to moderate the decline in their currencies, by mid-January the dollar prices of the German mark and the Swiss franc had fallen roughly 20 percent from their peak levels of early July 1973. Other major currencies had also declined sharply, and both the British pound and the Japanese yen were about 15 percent lower. Only the Canadian dollar remained approximately unchanged against the U.S. dollar.

The strengthening of the dollar did not continue past January 1974, because both the arrangement of substantial Eurocurrency loans to finance payments imbalances and the ending of capital controls by the United States began to depress the exchange value of the dollar. During the first half of 1974 the rate of inflation remained considerably lower in both Germany and the Netherlands than in the United States; and the trade surplus of these countries continued while the U.S. trade balance registered increasingly large deficits. The German mark, the Dutch guilder, and the Belgian and Swiss francs appreciated by about 14 percent against the dollar from mid-January to mid-May.

During the first half of 1974 the value of the dollar rose on balance in terms of the currencies of France, Italy, and Japan, because the rise of the dollar in late spring and early summer more than offset any earlier decline. The trade balances of these countries had deteriorated abruptly after the turn of the year, and inflation was much higher than in the United States. In spite of the high rates of inflation prevailing in the United Kingdom, the pound sterling rate deviated from this pattern because of unusually high short- and long-term interest rates in London and because the oil companies had expanding needs for sterling to meet tax and royalty payments to oil-exporting countries.

Around the middle of the year the United States and France were implementing some measures to reduce domestic rates of monetary growth in the hope of eventually lowering their rates of inflation, while other countries, particularly Germany, began to shift to more expansionary fiscal policies to combat rising unemployment. The French trade deficit fell and the German surplus declined, but the U.S. deficit grew little from the second to the third quarter. With interest rates reaching record levels in the United States, the dollar steadied or rose against all major currencies except the French and Swiss francs.

During the last quarter of the year, however, the dollar again declined against most currencies. The German mark recovered to its previous peak reached in May 1974, the French franc continued to rise, the Italian lira and British pound appreciated slightly, and only the Japanese yen continued to decline. Toward the end of the year the pound was jolted, but only temporarily, when Saudi Arabia announced that it would abandon its practice of taking about 25 percent of its oil payments in sterling. The effect of this statement was soon softened, however, by the Saudi announcement that it planned to continue investing in the London market. In addition, the Swiss franc rose sharply, by about 17 percent, during the fourth quarter.

Chart 11 shows that for the year as a whole the dollar depreciated against the German mark and the French franc, while it remained approximately unchanged against the British pound and appreciated against the Japanese yen. These movements were far from steady, however, during the course of the year. The Department of the Treasury's index of the change in the value of the U.S. dollar in terms of a trade-weighted basket of 22 foreign currencies indicates that the average value of the dollar declined from the end of January to May 1974: it then recovered most of its earlier losses before slipping again in the fourth quarter. At the end of 1974, the Treasury index shows the value of the dollar to have been about the same as on March 20, 1973, just after the system of managed floating had come into full operation.

Changes in International Reserves

From September 1973 through the end of March 1974, total international reserves grew very little; they subsequently increased by $22.5

Chart 11

Change in the Value of the U.S. Dollar
Relative to Selected Foreign Currencies

PERCENT CHANGE FROM MARCH 20, 1973

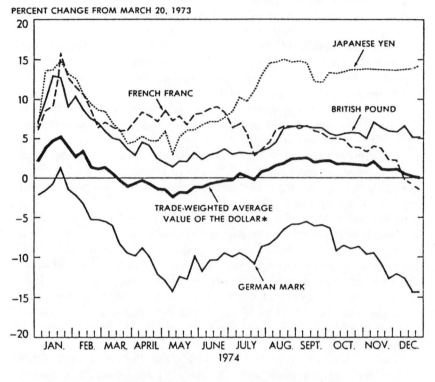

*RELATIVE TO THE 22 OECD CURRENCIES, COMPUTED BY DEPARTMENT OF THE TREASURY.
NOTE: FOR INDIVIDUAL CURRENCIES, WEDNESDAY PRICES WERE USED. FOR TRADE-WEIGHTED INDEX,
THURSDAY PRICES WERE USED UNTIL JULY 17, THEREAFTER WEDNESDAY PRICES WERE USED.
SOURCE: DEPARTMENT OF THE TREASURY.

billion from the end of March to the end of September (Table 47). All but
$3.1 billion of this increase accrued to the OPEC countries, mostly in the
form of increased foreign exchange reserves held outside the United
States. Thus, while the OPEC countries held a stable 7 percent of the
world's reserves from March through September 1973, their holdings had
increased to 10 percent by the end of March 1974 and to 18 percent by
the end of September 1974. The shift was mainly at the expense of the
industrial countries, whose share of the enlarged global reserves declined
from 65 to 56 percent although the dollar value of their reserves did not

TABLE 47

**Composition and distribution of international reserve assets, selected
months, 1973–74**

Type of reserve asset	Value of reserve assets (billions of U.S. dollars)[1]				Percent of total reserve assets			
	March 1973	September 1973	March 1974	September 1974	March 1973	September 1973	March 1974	September 1974
All Countries:[2]								
Total Reserve assets	179.2	187.6	187.8	210.3	100	100	100	100
Gold stock	43.2	43.2	43.1	42.4	24	23	23	20
SDR	10.5	10.6	10.6	10.5	6	6	6	5
Reserve position in IMF	7.5	7.5	7.5	9.0	4	4	4	4
Foreign exchange	118.0	126.3	126.5	148.3	66	67	67	71
U.S. liabilities	71.3	69.8	65.5	72.5	40	37	35	34
OPEC countries:[3]								
Total reserve assets	11.9	13.2	19.0	38.4	100	100	100	100
Gold stock	1.4	1.4	1.4	1.4	12	11	8	4
SDR	.4	.4	.4	.4	3	3	2	1
Reserve position in IMF	.3	.4	.4	1.0	3	3	2	3
Foreign exchange	9.8	11.0	16.8	35.6	82	84	88	93
Industrial countries:[4]								
Total reserve assets	120.8	121.2	113.5	117.9	100	100	100	100
Gold stock	35.9	35.9	35.9	35.3	30	30	32	30
SDR	7.9	8.0	8.0	8.0	7	7	7	7
Reserve position in IMF	5.7	5.6	5.4	6.6	5	5	5	6
Foreign exchange	71.3	71.8	64.2	67.9	59	59	57	58
Other countries:[5]								
Total reserve assets	46.6	53.1	55.3	53.9	100	100	100	100
Gold stock	5.8	5.8	5.7	5.7	13	11	10	11
SDR	2.2	2.3	2.3	2.1	5	4	4	4
Reserve position in IMF	1.5	1.6	1.7	1.4	3	3	3	3
Foreign exchange	36.9	43.4	45.6	44.8	79	82	82	83

1. End of period.
2. Total of groups of countries listed in this table. Excludes Communist countries except Yugoslavia.
3. Algeria, Ecuador, Indonesia, Iran, Iraq, Kuwait, Libya, Nigeria, Saudi Arabia, and Venezuela. Qatar and the United Arab Emirates are not included because the IMF does not publish data for these countries.
4. United States, Canada, Japan, Austria, Norway, Sweden, Switzerland, and all EEC countries except Ireland.
5. Nonindustrial countries other than OPEC countries.
Note.—Detail may not add to totals because of rounding.
Source: International Monetary Fund (IMF).

decline significantly. The share held by the nonindustrial countries
outside OPEC fell from 28 to 26 percent.

Globally, the liabilities of the United States and Britain to foreign
official institutions have risen little since March 1973, but official holdings
by the OPEC countries both in the United States and in the United
Kingdom, as well as holdings in the form of Eurodollar and other
Eurocurrency claims on private foreigners, have risen rapidly. This
increase accounted for most of the growth in international reserves in the
second and third quarters of 1974, and it changed the composition of
reserves substantially as the share of official claims on private institutions

increased relative to claims on other official institutions, including the IMF.

Another shift in the composition of international reserves could occur in 1975 if the quantity or valuation of monetary gold holdings were to change. At the end of September 1974 the industrial countries still owned 83 percent of the world's stock of monetary gold. The price of gold in the free market has been subject to large fluctuations. At the end of 1974, the London price per ounce was $186½ as compared with $112¼ at the end of 1973. Compared to alternative forms in which international reserves can be held, however, gold yields no interest, nor has it yielded liquidity services in recent years. When the two-tier gold system was adopted in March 1968, central banks agreed to refrain from buying or selling gold in the private market. Neither has it been used in official settlements since the official accounting price fell to a fraction of its free-market price. From February 1973 through June 1974, monetary gold was valued at $42.22 per ounce, while the free-market price was three to four times as high. No significant changes occurred in the distribution of gold reserves from the time that convertibility of the U.S. dollar into gold was suspended officially on August 15, 1971, until the end of 1974.

Several steps have been taken to help countries mobilize their gold holdings to assist in financing balance of payments deficits. Termination of the 1968 two-tier gold agreement in November 1973 permitted countries to sell gold on the private market, although official purchases of gold at prices above the official price of 35 SDR per ounce continued to be prohibited by the IMF. In June, 10 major industrial countries agreed in principle that gold could be used as collateral for international borrowing at a price to be determined by the borrower and the lender. Soon afterwards, Germany extended a $2-billion loan to Italy that was backed by gold valued at approximately $120 per ounce. Later in the year some countries discussed the possibility of valuing monetary gold at market prices, and France indicated that it planned to do so early in 1975. Also in January 1975, the United States sold a small amount of its monetary gold to private purchasers to satisfy demand that might have materialized after removal of the prohibition against private ownership of gold bullion, which had been in effect since 1934. Nevertheless, both the transactions value and the effective liquidity of gold in international reserves remained uncertain at the start of 1975.

From their inception the value of special drawing rights has been set at one ounce of gold equals 35 SDR's. From January 1970 through June 1974, the conversion of SDR's into dollars was made at the official U.S. price of gold. When this official price was raised from $35 to $38 per ounce as of December 1971, the transactions value of 1 SDR therefore rose from par with the dollar to $1.0857, and it rose to $1.20635 after the official price of gold had been raised to $42.22 per ounce in February 1973. In order to enhance the transferability of SDR's and to move away from exclusive reliance on the official dollar price of gold in determining the value of SDR's, the IMF decided to widen the base for calculating the transactions value of SDR's by including currencies other than the dollar after July 1, 1974. Since that date, the currencies of 16 IMF member countries whose export trade amounted to more than 1 percent of the world total in the 5-year period from 1968 through 1972 have entered into the "standard basket" valuation of the SDR. Countries whose currencies appreciate against the dollar consequently no longer find that the domestic book value of their SDR holdings with the IMF is reduced regardless of whether their currencies depreciate against third currencies that are now included in the standard basket. The relative weight of these currencies in the basket is proportional to each country's share in the world's total exports, but with some modification. Weights do compensate for the fact that the share of exports does not always accurately measure the importance of some currencies in the world economy. This applies particularly to the dollar, whose share is set at 33 percent. However, the standard basket valuation technique adopted in July 1974 represents only an interim agreement without prejudice to a new system of SDR valuation that may be negotiated in 1975.

Government Policies

Governments in most of the industrial countries responded to the deepening recession early in 1975 and the continued weakness of final demand through the summer by adopting successive measures designed to bring their economies back to more normal rates of growth. Earlier in the year, with inflation rates still high, expansionary measures, except in Germany, tended mainly to reverse earlier restrictive policies and involved, for example, the easing of credit and public expenditure ceilings. But since midyear the thrust of policy has become broadly expansionary almost everywhere except in Great Britain and Canada, where, however, policies had not been.

Faced with the great economic difficulties of 1974–75 and the threat that these might be intensified by divisive action, governments have striven to strengthen the mechanisms of international cooperation and understanding. These efforts are exemplified by the Economic Summit at Rambouillet in November 1975, a meeting of heads of government of six major industrial countries, and by the beginning in December 1975 of the Conference on International Economic Cooperation (CIEC), which involves a dialogue between industrial countries, oil producers, and non-oil LDCs. Some progress has also been made in matters involving trade and international monetary arrangements. The commitment to pursue internationally compatible policies and to avoid beggar-thy-neighbor policies may become increasingly important in months to come, since unemployment levels are likely to remain high in the early stages of the recovery and some sectors of the economy will tend to lag considerably behind a general upturn in activity. The political pressures on governments to take a narrowly nationalistic view of these problems may therefore intensify.

Trade Policies

Pressures for protectionist actions, which resulted from the worldwide recession and were latent throughout much of 1975, intensified in a number of countries toward the end of the year. Recognizing that beggar-thy-neighbor policies can only serve to make everybody ultimately poorer, the governments of the OECD countries except Portugal renewed in May 1975 the pledge they had made a year earlier to refrain from taking measures specifically aimed at improving their individual trade positions. As a result, international trading arrangements were not seriously breached during the course of 1975, and there have been few significant departures from the pledge. On the import side a number of smaller OECD countries. Portugal, Finland, Iceland, New Zealand, and Yugoslavia, have instituted import deposit or licensing schemes. (An import deposit scheme in effect in Italy was lifted in March 1975.) Among the larger countries only Australia, which had earlier cut some tariffs, imposed tariff increases or quotas on a relatively wide range of goods. Political pressure to institute protectionist measures was particularly evident in Great Britain, where the government in December imposed restrictive import measures on a limited number of products. On the export side, a number of governments, among them the French, Italian, and British, have instituted or expanded fiscal and monetary measures specifically designed to encourage exports.

Against this background, the heads of government of six major industrial countries at the Economic Summit reaffirmed their commitment to the principles of the OECD trade pledge and agreed that the time schedule of the Multilateral Trade Negotiations (MTN) now under way in Geneva should be accelerated. The MTN aim at achieving substantial tariff cuts or elimination of tariffs in some areas, a significant expansion in agricultural trade, and a reduction in nontariff barriers by the end of 1977. This constitutes an ambitious program, yet a necessary one in the current economic and political setting.

Progress in 1975 has mainly been toward laying the basis for actual negotiations in 1976 and 1977. The preparatory work for the MTN proved to be more time consuming, compared to that in preceding trade negotiations because of the larger number of participants and because for the first time a wide range of nontariff barriers are being included. Unlike preceding negotiations, the MTN have been marked by a concentrated effort within the United States to reach a broad domestic consensus on what they are to achieve.

Progress in Geneva has been made on a draft code for the regulation of product standards and the treatment of tropical products. It is expected that broad agreement will be reached in 1976 on the major elements of a tariff-negotiating plan and on the procedure for achieving a meaningful liberalization of quantitative restrictions. It is further hoped that substantial progress can be made this year on procedures for dealing with questions of subsidies, government procurement, and safeguards against injurious import penetration so that substantive negotiations can begin. The United States also continues to work toward developing improved procedures and agreed principles on assured access to supply.

The admittedly difficult area in which little movement can be discerned is agriculture. The problems in the agricultural area are well known and of long standing. First, they concern the great comparative advantage that the United States and some other primary producers have over producers in the European Community (EC). Second, there are different approaches toward maintenance of farm incomes, with the United States moving away from price stabilization and production controls and the EC firmly committed to price supports. Because of the deep-seated problems in this area, it was particularly important that the heads of government at the Economic Summit specifically emphasized their commitment to achieve a significant expansion of trade also in agriculture.

International Monetary Developments

Discussions initiated in the International Monetary Fund (IMF) in 1972 about the structure of a reformed international monetary system were quickly overtaken by events in early 1973. Growing pressures on price levels and volatile short-term capital flows led to the adoption of de facto generalized floating in March 1973. Toward the end of 1973 the quadrupling of the export price of OPEC oil brought about a fundamental change in the international payments structure. Oil-importing countries as a group began to be faced with large current account deficits vis-a-vis the oil exporters, at least for a number of years until import demand in oil-exporting countries can rise to match export revenues and until importing countries develop alternative sources of energy and succeed in economizing on energy use. Consequently financial markets and official international monetary arrangements had to adapt to rapidly changing payment patterns, including an enormous increase in capital flows connected with the financing of the so-called "oil deficits." Moreover there were wide disparities in inflation rates among countries. In these circumstances the flexibility of the exchange rate regime that had emerged after the breakdown of the parity system became increasingly important in facilitating trade and payment flows in 1974 and 1975. Of course the monetary, fiscal, and other policies that individual authorities adopt to stabilize their economies and to adapt to the higher oil import bill— whether by increasing net exports, borrowing from official or private sources, or drawing on reserve assets—constitutes "managing" their exchange rate in the wider sense of the term. It is of continuing importance that this "management" of exchange rates not lead to competitive devaluations or other self-defeating and disruptive policies, but be accomplished in an internationally cooperative manner.

The financing of the large external deficits of oil importers over the past 2 years has been accomplished considerably more smoothly than had been anticipated earlier. Financial markets turned out to be very adaptable, and the more flexible exchange rate system helped to avoid the market disruptions so often experienced during past periods of strain. Furthermore, deficits were somewhat smaller than was earlier foreseen because of a faster rise of import demand in oil-exporting countries and a reduction in the demand for oil imports resulting from resistance to high oil prices, conservation efforts, and the recession. Finally, expansion of international liquidity through increased use of IMF credit, including the creation of the Oil Facility in the IMF and increases in official lending, helped ease more serious financing strains. Traditional concepts of measurement of total international liquidity, such as those published by the Bank for International Settlements (BIS), however, have dubious applicability in today's international monetary system. Some of the currency reserve assets—for example, those accumulated by oil-exporting countries—tend to be "inactive" assets because they represent the intended accumulation of foreign investment and differ in important respects from earlier foreign currency accumulations by monetary authorities. And large-scale official borrowing in foreign financial markets has demonstrated the ability of countries to create liquidity through debt operations. The fact that not only the Eurocurrency markets but also national money markets, such as the U.S. market, are open to foreign borrowers and lenders is very important in this respect and has helped smooth the financing of external deficits.

The financial surpluses of OPEC in the first instance were largely invested in very short-term assets. But during 1975 considerable diversification of OPEC investments took place. The share of investible funds flowing into bank deposits and short-term assets was much reduced—from about one-half to perhaps one-quarter—and purchases of corporate bonds, equities, and long-term government securities rose. For the reasons discussed above, the total amount of OPEC new investible funds declined sharply in 1975.

The shrinkage in OPEC surpluses in 1975 was reflected in a large reduction in the current account deficits of the industrial countries (Tables 43 and 44). The decreased financing needs of industrial countries in 1975, however, were partly offset by an increase in import surpluses of LDCs that stemmed largely from the recession. (The financing problems of LDCs are discussed below.) Because of the smaller total external financing needs and the realization that the international financial system had been able to intermediate successfully between the large increases in the supply and demand for loanable funds, developments in international money markets in 1975 more closely reflected differential economic conditions than they had during the turbulent year of 1974. Because most other economies have lagged the United States in the cycle, interest rate relationships have shifted during the year (Charts 3 and 4). Early in 1975 short-term rates in the United States declined sharply relative to rates in

TABLE 43

Current account balances for OECD, OPEC, and other countries, 1973–76

[Billions of U.S. dollars]

Group of countries	1973	1974	1975[1]	1976[2]
OECD	2½	−36¼	−6	−17½
OPEC	3¼	56	40	43
Non-oil developing countries	−2¼	−17½	−27	−21¼
Other countries[3]	−4	−10	−14½	−13½
Discrepancy	−1¼	−7¾	−7½	−9¼

1. Estimates.
2. Projection.
3. Sino-Soviet area, South Africa, Israel, Cyprus, Malta, and Yugoslavia.

Sources: Organization for Economic Cooperation and Development, Department of the Treasury and national sources.

TABLE 44
Current account balances for OECD countries, 1974–75
[Billions of U.S. dollars; seasonally adjusted]

Country	1974		1975	
	First half	Second half	First half	Second half[1]
OECD: Total	−19.2	−17.0	−0.1	−6
United States	−1.8	−1.6	5.8	6¾
Canada	−.1	−1.5	−2.5	−2½
Japan	−4.1	−.9	.9	−1¾
France	−3.7	−2.3	.7	−1
Germany	5.2	4.4	3.5	1
Italy	−4.5	−3.3	.3	0
United Kingdom	−4.2	−4.4	−2.0	−2½
Other OECD	−6.0	−7.4	−6.8	−6

1. Estimate.
Sources: Organization for Economic Cooperation and Development and national sources.

other money-market centers. But from mid-June to September, most interest rate differentials swung the other way. Some of the resulting interest rate incentive was reversed again later in the year, but by then rate-induced capital flows to the United States were also being strengthened by the relatively better economic news here than abroad, and by the continuing high U.S. trade surplus.

Private capital transactions in the U.S. balance of payments registered sizable outflows in the first half of the year. U.S. banks increased their foreign assets by about $7½ billion, reflecting in part relatively low interest rates in the United States, and in part heavy loan demand of some foreign countries, largely LDCs. The volume of new foreign bonds issued in the United States reached record rates, reflecting to some extent extraordinary financing requirements of international agencies. But these outflows were partly offset by rising foreign purchases of U.S. corporate stocks, including sizable purchases by oil-producing countries. In the third quarter, as U.S. interest rates rose relative to rates abroad, there was some reduction in banks' acquisition of foreign assets, and the net flow of private capital was inward. The final quarter brought a resumption of net outflows through banks, as well as a sizable net outflow through transactions in securities, as placements of foreign bonds in the U.S. market, including a large issue by the International Bank for Reconstruction and Development (IBRD) more than matched a continued high volume of foreign purchases of U.S. corporate stocks. For the year as a whole net private capital outflows were probably somewhat above the net outflow of over $10 billion reported for 1974.

Interest Rates

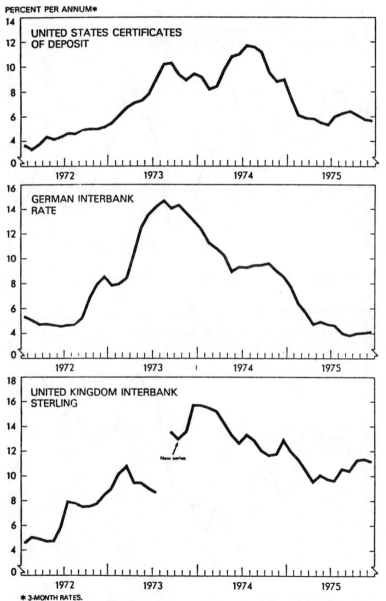

PERCENT PER ANNUM*

UNITED STATES CERTIFICATES OF DEPOSIT

14 12 10 8 6 4 0

1972   1973   1974   1975

GERMAN INTERBANK RATE

16 14 12 10 8 6 4 0

1972   1973   1974   1975

UNITED KINGDOM INTERBANK STERLING

18 16 14 12 10 8 6 4 0

New series

1972   1973   1974   1975

* 3-MONTH RATES.
SOURCE: BOARD OF GOVERNORS OF THE FEDERAL RESERVE SYSTEM.

Interest Rate Differentials

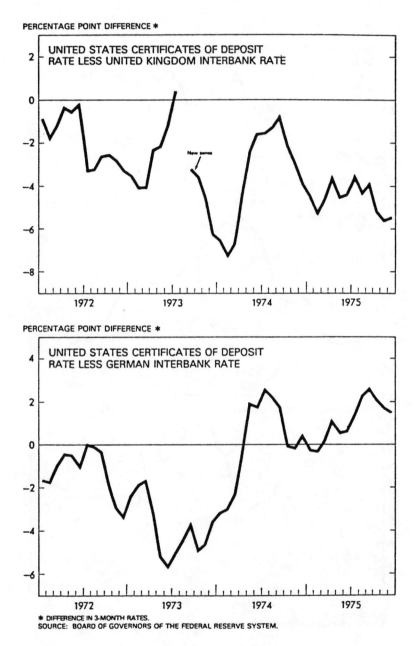

PERCENTAGE POINT DIFFERENCE *

UNITED STATES CERTIFICATES OF DEPOSIT
RATE LESS UNITED KINGDOM INTERBANK RATE

New series

PERCENTAGE POINT DIFFERENCE *

UNITED STATES CERTIFICATES OF DEPOSIT
RATE LESS GERMAN INTERBANK RATE

* DIFFERENCE IN 3-MONTH RATES.
SOURCE: BOARD OF GOVERNORS OF THE FEDERAL RESERVE SYSTEM.

Reflecting these changes in capital flows and the large surplus on trade account, noted above, the exchange value of the dollar, in terms of a trade-weighted average of major foreign currencies, first depreciated by about 4½ percent between the end of December 1974 and the end of February 1975 and then appreciated by about 12 percent from March through September 1975. During the fourth quarter of 1975 the dollar rate changed very little, drifting down by about one-half of 1 percent.

The swing in the exchange value of some individual currencies against the dollar was of course greater than is reflected in the weighted average value. In particular, movements of the European currencies against the dollar were very wide. For example, against the European currencies linked in the "snake" arrangement, the dollar depreciated by about 6 percent from the end of December, 1974 to its low early in March 1975, rose by 17½ percent to its September high, and depreciated again by 2½ percent to year-end (Chart 5).

Even though governments on the whole allowed market forces to move exchange rates rather widely, there appears to have been a considerable amount of intervention by foreign banks, particularly during the second half of the year. Gross intervention by the Federal Reserve, however, has been very limited. In order to avoid disorderly conditions and to lessen the danger of unwanted and self-defeating actions which might lead to competitive currency depreciations or other international policy conflicts, national governments recognized the need to intensify international consultation on these matters. As part of the broader international monetary negotiations, the United States and France reached an understanding at the time of the Economic Summit regarding a shared position on amendments to the Articles of Agreement of the IMF dealing with the exchange rate regime. This facilitated agreement by the Interim Committee of the IMF in January 1976 on the entire package of amendments to the IMF's Articles of Agreement which had been pending since agreement on certain parts was reached at the time of the Interim committee meeting in August 1975. The main elements of this package, in addition to amendment of the Article dealing with exchange rates, are a 33.6 percent increase in the Fund's resources to SDR 39 billion as decided in the Sixth Quota Review; the phasing out of gold with regard to Fund transactions and other gold arrangements; and the establishment of a Trust Fund for the benefit of the poorer members of the IMF.

Agreement on the outstanding IMF issues does much to help assure the adequacy of international financing arrangements in the face of the continuing large payment surpluses of the oil-exporting countries. As economic recoveries broaden, current account positions of the oil-import-

Foreign Exchange Rates

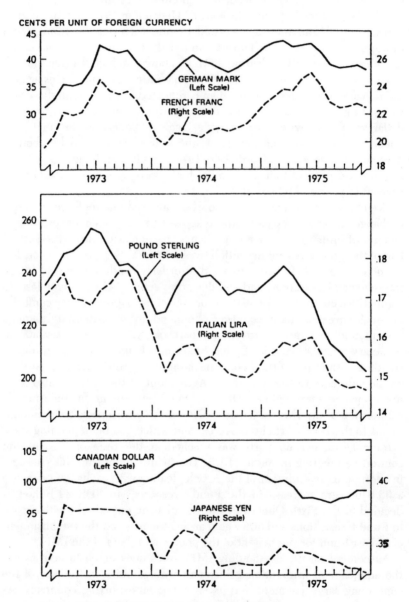

CENTS PER UNIT OF FOREIGN CURRENCY

SOURCE: BOARD OF GOVERNORS OF THE FEDERAL RESERVE SYSTEM.

ing countries as a group will move into greater deficit. This shift may put financing strains on some countries and might lead to policies that could arrest the recoveries or be mutually damaging in other ways. It is therefore important to ensure that safeguards are in place to prevent unavoidable financial difficulties from being compounded by internationally inappropriate policies. Therefore the cooperative international spirit underlying the agreements reached at the meetings in January 1976 is particularly significant.

Exchange Rate Arrangements

The agreement on amended exchange rate provisions of the IMF Articles, first worked out between the United States and France and subsequently accepted by the Interim Committee of the IMF, recognizes that the underlying economic and financial situation determines the degree of exchange rate stability that is possible. Participating members agree to endeavor to direct their economic and financial policies toward the achievement of orderly economic growth with reasonable price stability, to recognize that orderly underlying economic and financial conditions are prerequisites to stability, to avoid manipulating exchange rates or the international monetary system in order to prevent effective balance of payments adjustment or to gain an unfair competitive advantage, and to follow exchange policies compatible with these undertakings.

When formally approved by 60 percent of the member countries representing 80 percent of the votes, these general provisions will be incorporated in amended Articles of Agreement of the IMF. The agreement allows countries to choose among exchange arrangements, including: (1) The maintenance by a member of a value for its currency in terms of the Special Drawing Right or another denominator other than gold; or (2) cooperative arrangements by which members maintain the value of their currencies in relation to the value of the currency or currencies of other members; or (3) other exchange arrangements of a member's choice.

The revised Articles would authorize the Fund, upon approval by an 85 percent majority vote, to establish a system of exchange arrangements based on stable but adjustable par values when international economic conditions are appropriate. In effect such a system could not be established without the approval of the United States, which under the proposed new quotas will have approximately 20 percent of the voting strength. As far as the United States is concerned, for the foreseeable future it is thought unlikely that conditions will be appropriate for the establishment of a par value system or the setting of target rates and zones or bands within which movements in the rate of the dollar would be contained. Policies aim at achieving stable economic conditions. However, progress toward narrowing disparities among inflation rates in different countries is slow, nor can one be sure that progress once made will be lasting. Exogenous shocks to which the various economies continue to be subject also argue for a considerable degree of flexibility in the monetary system. Central bank intervention will be limited to that necessary to counter disorderly conditions or erratic fluctuations. Each country will be the judge of what constitutes an erratic fluctuation in its exchange rate.

To facilitate the achievement of internationally cooperative behavior in exchange markets, the French and the U.S. authorities have suggested an intensification of the consultative arrangements among governments and central banks of major countries. Central bank officials will exchange daily information on the foreign exchange market and their intervention activities. Finance ministry and central bank officials will at frequent intervals review exchange rate movements and intervention activities, and discuss both the underlying economic and financial conditions and the impact of policies on these conditions. Under these arrangements there may be somewhat more frequent intervention than in the past. But the main point is that decisions on intervention in exchange markets will be based on better information, and that a growing understanding may also develop which recognizes that managing the exchange rate rather than the economy may only serve to introduce disequilibria and lead to misallocation of resources.

Gold Arrangements

The agreement on gold consists of four major elements:

1. Gold no longer will be a medium of settlement in IMF transactions.

2. One-sixth of the gold holdings of the IMF will be restituted to members, that is distributed to members in proportion to their quotas.

3. One-sixth of the gold holdings of the IMF will be sold at auction over a period of 4 years to finance a Trust Fund for the benefit of the poorer members of the IMF.

4. An agreement that will be reviewed after a 2-year period has been concluded by the 10 largest industrial countries. It bars any action to peg the price of gold and provides that the total stock of gold held by the Fund and the monetary authorities of the participating countries will not be increased. Other countries may also adhere to this agreement.

The agreements on gold reflect general acceptance of the agreed upon objective to reduce the role of gold in the international monetary system. In addition, with the scheduled sale of some of the IMF's gold holdings for the purpose of financing the Trust Fund, gold may be expected to begin—gradually—to move out of the monetary system into private hands.

Some observers have argued that these new agreements may lead to a revaluation of official gold holdings at market-related prices or encourage more frequent use of gold as a medium for settlement among central banks. It is further argued that this, combined with the distribution of IMF gold to members, will have the effect of making more gold available to major countries, thus giving them greater liquidity, and perhaps adding to world inflationary pressures and reducing the likelihood that additional allocations of SDRs would be approved.

However, central banks have had the ability for some time to sell their gold holdings in the market as well as to value such holdings at market-related prices. Only one foreign central bank has actually written up its gold reserves, and there is no indication that others intend to do so. Moreover there also is no reason to expect the agreements to result in significant transactions in gold among monetary authorities. Indeed, by abolishing the official price for gold in the IMF, by strengthening the prospect of future sales of officially held gold into the market, and by establishing transitional provisions against pegging of the price, these agreements should in fact discourage widespread revaluations of official gold holdings and increase the risks associated with transactions among monetary authorities.

With the phasing of gold out of international official transactions, the danger that some authorities might seek to stabilize the price of gold is much diminished. In addition, authorities attempting to peg the price of gold, despite agreement among major countries not to do so, would find that such an effort could be exorbitantly expensive in terms of foreign currency assets needed for such operations. The cost would be higher, the smaller the number of participants.

Finally, the increases in world credit during the past several years have made it unlikely that new SDRs will be issued in the near future. Therefore, the restitution provision has been welcomed by some of the lesser developed countries which will receive 28 percent (their quota share) of the amounts to be distributed. In addition, the gold arrangements make possible the establishment of the Trust Fund, which is of crucial importance to the poorest developing countries, particularly now that the Oil Facility in the IMF is being terminated. Moreover a large number of LDCs will not make any nominal contribution to the Trust Fund, but will have that part of the profits on the gold sales by the IMF that represents their quota share in the Trust Fund distributed to them directly. Thus of the 25 million ounces of gold to be sold by the IMF, the profits on perhaps 6–7 million will go directly to LDCs, and those on 18–19 million will be used for the Trust Fund.

Exchange Rate Changes

The financing of external deficits in 1976 was accompanied by a very high rate of activity in foreign exchange markets. The trade-weighted exchange rates for certain major currencies showed considerable movement despite relatively large balance of payments financing and heavy intervention by foreign central banks in exchange markets (Chart 7). The strains experienced within the European snake arrangement were a major factor in the heavy intervention activity. Early in the year heavy pressure on the French franc led the authorities to break the link with the currencies adhering to the snake. Upward pressures on the German mark, reflecting both the large German current account surplus and the continued significantly better inflation performance of the German economy compared with its trading partners, caused considerable strain among the currencies remaining in the snake. In the fall of 1976, therefore, the central values of the currencies within the snake were realigned, with the mark appreciating by 2 percent, the Swedish krona and Norwegian krone depreciating by 1 percent, and the Danish krone depreciating by 4 percent. The largest changes in the foreign currency markets, however, involved the pound sterling, the Italian lira, and the Mexican peso, which depreciated by 16 percent, 21¾ percent and 37½ percent respectively against the U.S. dollar between the end of 1975 and the end of 1976.

International Financial Markets

The unrest in the exchange markets and the financing difficulties that surfaced during the year for a number of industrial and developing countries obscured the relative ease with which deficits of many other countries continued to be financed. Activity in the international capital market was brisk during 1976. On the demand side, expectations that borrowing costs would rise in 1977 buoyed activity; in addition, there was an exceptionally strong surge in Canadian demand for long-term funds. Concurrently the supply of funds to the bond markets was encouraged by low demand for domestic credit in the United States and Europe resulting in declines in short-term interest rates during the year. As funds became more abundant, bond yields began to fall. Medium-term credits arranged in the Euro-currency market also showed a substantial increase last year, as rising demands for finance from almost all the main categories of borrowers were met by increases in supply sufficiently large to allow borrowing costs to decline. Total borrowing in the markets for medium-term Eurocredits, Eurobonds, and foreign bonds amounted to $48 billion in the first 10 months of the year, representing an annual rate of $58 billion, an increase of more than one-third from the 1975 total.

New issues of Eurobonds during the first 10 months of the year at $12½ billion were well above the volume issued in the corresponding period of 1975, a previous peak for the Eurobond markets. Industrial countries issued 69 percent of all bonds during the first 9 months of 1976, taking a considerably lower share of loanable funds than in 1975. Japan was very active in the market, but some borrowers from countries in deficit—for example, the French, the British, and especially the Canadians—also increased their use of the Eurobond markets. Canadian issues of $2¾ billion in the first 10 months of last year were more than twice as large as in all of 1975 because of exceptional needs for long-term finance, relatively high domestic interest rates, and tax changes that facilitated foreign issues by private companies. Developing countries floated loans whose volume in the first 3 quarters of 1976 was more than twice that of the preceding year; their share of the market consequently rose to 20¼ percent, 5 percentage points of which were accounted for by oil-producing countries (Table 33).

The brisk activity in the Eurobond market was in part related to a shift in interest rate differentials that may have contributed to the willingness of investors to reduce their liquidity positions and extend the maturity of their holdings. Short-term rates exhibited a sharp cyclical decline, while long-term rates fell relatively little, partly because inflationary expectations appeared to change slowly. Thus yield differentials changed greatly. Whereas at the time of historically high short-time interest rates the differential between Eurodollar deposit rates and Eurobond yields had been as high as 3 percentage points, Eurodeposit rates in 1976 were generally below Eurobond yields.

Bank lending also rose substantially in 1976. Like the rising activity in the Eurobond market, the expansion of Eurocurrency loans and the increase in claims on foreigners by head offices reflect the high level of liquidity in the private sector in the main financial centers and the low loan demand from domestic borrowers. Although there has been considerable discussion in private and government circles regarding the struc-

TABLE 33

Borrowing in international capital markets, 1974–76

[Billions of dollars]

| Capital market | 1974 | 1975 | | | 1976 | | |
		Total	First half	Second half	First half	Third quarter[1]	October[1]
Total borrowing	40.8	42.7	19.2	23.5	30.3	11.2	6.9
Medium-term Eurocredits[2]	28.5	20.6	8.5	12.0	12.3	4.7	5.0
Industrial countries	19.0	6.4	2.8	3.6	3.6	2.5	1.5
Denmark	.4	.3	0	.3	.4	0	0
France	3.3	.5	.4	.1	.7	.1	0
Spain	1.1	1.0	.5	.6	.3	1.1	.1
United Kingdom	5.7	.6	.3	.4	1.0	.3	.6
Other	8.5	4.0	1.6	2.2	1.2	1.0	.8
Oil-exporting countries	.8	3.2	1.4	1.8	1.7	.4	1.1
Algeria	0	.5	.1	.4	.4	.1	0
Indonesia	.4	1.6	1.1	.6	.3	(3)	0
Iran	.1	.3	0	.2	.7	.2	.1
Venezuela	.1	.2	.2	0	0	0	1.0
Other	.2	.6	0	.6	.3	.1	0
Other developing countries	7.2	7.9	2.6	5.3	4.7	1.6	2.0
Argentina	.5	(1)	(2)	(3)	.1	.1	.5
Brazil	1.6	2.1	.7	1.4	1.2	.7	(2)
Mexico	1.5	2.2	.7	1.5	.7	.4	.9
Philippines	.9	.3	.1	.1	.7	.1	.1
Other	2.7	3.3	1.1	2.3	2.0	.3	.5
Nonmarket countries and organizations	1.1	2.7	1.1	1.6	1.4	.2	.3
International organizations and other	.4	.4	.3	.1	.9	(1)	.1
Eurobonds	4.5	10.2	5.6	4.6	8.4	3.1	1.0
Canada	.4	1.2	.3	.9	1.9	.6	.2
France	.3	1.3	.8	.5	.8	.3	.1
Japan	.2	1.2	.6	.6	.7	.3	.1
Other	3.6	6.5	3.9	2.6	5.0	1.9	.6
Foreign bonds	7.8	11.9	5.1	6.9	9.6	3.4	.9
Canada	2.0	3.4	1.3	2.0	3.4	1.1	.3
IBRD	3.1	2.4	.6	1.7	1.6	.5	0
Other	2.7	6.1	3.2	3.2	4.6	1.8	.6

1. Preliminary.
2. Publicized credits of over 1-year maturity; represents commitments.
3. Less than $50 million.
Source: International Bank for Reconstruction and Development (IBRD).

ture of the balance sheets of the banking system, particularly regarding the exposure vis-a-vis certain countries, bank lending to foreigners has risen briskly, at least through the third quarter of 1976 (the latest date for which overall data are available). Publicly announced Eurocurrency bank credits for 1976, at over $28½ billion, exceeded credit extensions in 1975 by 36 percent. Morgan Guaranty estimated that the size of the market, net of interbank deposits, expanded from about $250 billion at the end of 1975 to nearly $285 billion in September 1976.

In the first 10 months of last year U.S. banks increased their short-term claims on foreigners by $10½ billion, $8½ billion of which was accounted for by loans to Latin America. The continued extension of bank credits to developing countries was not confined to U.S. banks: European banks have also increased their assets vis-a-vis this group of countries. The risks associated with some of these loans are reflected in the rates that are being charged. For example, in the medium-term Eurocurrency markets the premium charged some developing countries has risen to at least ⅝ percentage point at a minimum in recent months. There seems to have been a marked shift in the way banks view the creditworthiness of certain countries. Whereas in earlier periods the fact that a government had not touched its reserve position in the IMF was taken to indicate a relatively low risk in extending loans, banks now seem to favor lending to countries operating under IMF-suggested surveillance. Because banks cannot attach macroeconomic conditions to their loans, or in any event monitor them, they apparently feel more comfortable with debtors operating under IMF conditionality.

Official Financing

Official financing flows in 1976 constituted a somewhat larger proportion of the financing of external deficits than they did in 1975. Total borrowing from the IMF in 1976 amounted to SDR 6.0 billion as compared with SDR 3.9 billion in 1975. Although this change appears relatively small, funds drawn from the IMF in 1976 reflected a higher amount of drawing on regular IMF facilities subject to stricter conditionality as the Special Oil Facility came to an end in March 1976. Access to IMF resources was eased because credit availability in the IMF had been increased temporarily by 45 percent of quotas pending the ratification of the Amendments to the Articles of Agreement, which among other things will put into effect the particular quota increases agreed upon in Jamaica at the beginning of 1976.

Access to official financial resources was also considerably increased by liberalization of the Compensatory Financing Facility in the IMF. This facility is designed to help countries overcome shortfalls in export earnings which are largely beyond their own control. During 1976 drawings approved under this facility amounted to SDR 2.3 billion compared with a total usage for the preceding 13-year period, 1963–75, of SDR 1.2 billion. The more liberal access to the Compensatory Financing Facility has clearly done much to ease external financial constraints and cyclical payments problems that non-oil primary producing countries, both developed and developing, were experiencing during the year. In fact, the non-oil LDCs as a group were able to increase their reserve positions by SDR 7½ billion during the first 10 months of 1976. However, this aggregate increase combines a number of countries that experienced increasing external financing problems with others that experienced an easing of financial constraints.

Finally, official financing resources available to developing countries are being augmented by the disposal of part of the IMF's gold holdings. One-sixth (25 million ounces) of the IMF's 150 million ounces of gold is being sold at public auction over a 4-year period for the benefit of developing countries. A portion of the profits are being transferred directly to developing countries in proportion to their quotas in the IMF. The remainder of the profits is being used to finance a Trust Fund, separate from the IMF but managed by the IMF as trustee. This Trust Fund will provide balance of payments support on concessional terms to the IMF's poorest members. An additional 25 million ounces of the IMF's gold holdings are being sold to all members in proportion to their quotas, or "restituted," at the present official price of gold in exchange for currency usable by the IMF. Restitution is being carried out in four annual installments of approximately 6¼ million ounces each.

In May of last year the IMF announced a program of 16 auctions at roughly 6-week intervals over a 2-year period covering sales of 12½ million ounces of gold, with 780,000 ounces to be offered for sale at each auction. Five auctions were conducted under this program during 1976, in which a total of 3.9 million ounces of gold was sold at an average price of $122 per ounce and at a profit for the Trust Fund of $320 million. The first loans under the Trust Fund program were being approved by the Executive Board of the IMF at the turn of the year.

In late 1976 the Executive Board of the IMF reviewed the results of the auction program and decided that it would be desirable—without disturbing any of the basic tenets of the general agreement on gold—to shift to a definite schedule involving somewhat more frequent auctions at which slight smaller amounts of gold would be sold. The first installment of restitution was to take place in the first weeks of January 1977, to be followed on January 26 by the last auction to be held at the 6-week intervals established May of last year. Beginning March 2, 1977, auctions will be conducted on the first Wednesday of each month, each involving the sale of 525,000 ounces.

The general assessment of the experience gained so far, following some initial uncertainty about the potential effects of the IMF's sales and about market interest and participation, is that the IMF's sales program has been quite successful. All of the auctions were oversubscribed, and the IMF was able to obtain prices on each occasion that were very close to prices prevailing in the market. The absence of a definite timetable for sales, however, gave rise to questions about the timing and amounts of auctions, and has raised needless questions and speculation in the market about the IMF's intentions. The IMF's announcement in late 1976 of a definite schedule of dates and amounts for auctions over the next few months should remove any remaining uncertainties about the periodicity of IMF sales or the amounts to be offered.

Adequacy of Official Financial Resources

Despite the fact that official financial resources were augmented considerably during 1976, there is some question about the adequacy of such resources for the period ahead. As noted earlier, the financing of external deficits, except in a few instances, was managed relatively smoothly during 1976. Extension of bank credit remained large, although during the year there was a growing perception of the need for banks to become increasingly selective vis-a-vis their debtors, and this was reflected in a growing desire on the part of private lenders to see commitments backed by some kind of conditionality in terms of adequate economic policies. As a result a number of authorities may have become less reluctant to draw on their credit with the IMF.

Since the large increases in OPEC's export price of oil, external debt levels in nominal terms have cumulated well beyond historical highs for many countries. The OECD has estimated that current account deficits for the OECD area since 1974, the first year of the high oil prices, have cumulated to $56 billion. The comparable figure for non-oil LDCs is $72 billion. In a number of instances debt levels are such as to make private lenders reluctant to extend further credit.

It is important that countries which have adopted satisfactory adjustment measures to deal with underlying external disequilibria and high external debt positions have access to international financial resources to carry them through the adjustment period. The need for such bridging financing is obvious because adjustments cannot take place quickly. Furthermore in the absence of such financing there is a growing risk that political pressures to institute trade restrictions cannot be resisted.

But, in addition, because of the continuing need to adjust to higher import prices for energy, further financing may need to be available. As long as OPEC surpluses persist, there can be no reversal in total debt positions. On the contrary, external debts will continue to grow. In the interest of international equilibrium and the continuation of economic growth worldwide, it is necessary that the strongest economies be willing not to resist either a widening of their current account deficits (or lessening or surpluses) or an increase in purchases of their assets by foreign investors.

For a large number of countries balance of payments financing continues to be available from private sources. But a very high proportion of such financing flows through commercial banks, which perform a large share of the intermediation between OPEC surpluses and the deficits of other countries. There are internal risks in this situation: banks may at times make financing too easy for certain countries and thus delay needed adjustment; in other instances banks may be reluctant to promote adequate financial flows to a particular country although the country in question could reasonably be expected to be able to service such flows. In terms of the world financial structure there are therefore advantages to conditional multilateral financing of some proportion of the oil-importing countries' current account deficits. The IMF is the indicated institution to provide intermediation between the strong creditor countries on the one hand (certain members of OPEC as well as certain industrial countries with strong payments positions) and the deficit countries on the other. It is important, from this point of view as well as to strengthen the IMF's liquidity position, that the enlarged quotas agreed to under the Sixth Review of Quotas should go into effect as early as possible in 1977. This will require that the second Amendment to the Articles of Agreement be ratified by many members who have not yet done so. Further, in recognition of the possible greater financing needs, the OECD countries have negotiated a Financial Support Fund, submitted to the Congress last year. In addition, the IMF has advanced the date of the normal quinquennial review of its resources by 2 years. However, needs may materialize sooner than the advanced completion date of that review would allow; and, in any case, additional means may be required to augment the IMF's resources either generally or in terms of certain currencies.

PART IV

INTERNATIONAL FINANCIAL INSTITUTIONS AND THE POLICY OF INTERVENTION UNDER FLEXIBLE EXCHANGE RATES

13

THE ROLE OF OFFICIAL INTERVENTION

Michael L. Mussa

1. Introduction

One of the striking features of our experience with floating exchange rates is that the holding and use of official foreign exchange reserves has not declined dramatically from what it was under the Bretton Woods system.[1] The enormous movements of official reserves that occurred during the breakdown of the pegged rate system have not recurred on quite the same scale as in the early 1970's. But, the world's major central banks have intervened on an active basis in foreign exchange markets, sometimes on a large scale.

In the light of this experience, it is relevant to examine what are the effects and what should be the role of official foreign exchange intervention under a regime of managed floating. This is the task to which the present paper is addressed. Specifically, the paper is concerned with official intervention by countries with liberal trade and capital market regimes that do not maintain, officially or implicity, a pegged exchange rate.

To set the stage for the discussion of official intervention, it is first useful, in section 1, to examine the general principles that govern the behavior of floating exchange rates, as embodied in the "asset market view" of exchange rate behavior. Next, it is important to distinguish between two forms of official intervention: official intervention that is allowed to affect the domestic money supply, referred to as "non-sterilized" intervention; and pure or sterilized intervention, where the effects on the domestic money supply are sterilized by offsetting operations in domestic assets by the central bank. In section 2, the role and effects of non-sterilized intervention are addressed by examining the role that exchange rates can and should play in influencing the conduct of monetary policy. In section 3, the effects of pure or sterilized intervention are examined, and the appropriate role of such intervention is discussed. Finally, section 4 is devoted to an examination of what can be learned from our experience with official intervention during the past seven years.

To provide a guide to the discussion that follows, it is useful to summarize the major points that are made later in this paper. First, from the general "asset market view" of exchange rates, it follows that exchange rates, like other asset prices, are influenced not only by current market conditions, but also to a very important extent by the expectations of market participants of future events likely to affect exchange rates, including future monetary policy, future developments in the demands to hold different national monies, and future real economic conditions affecting the relative prices of the outputs of different countries. Further, exchange rates, like other asset prices, show random fluctuations in response to "new information" that alters the expectations of market participants concerning both present and future conditions relevant for determining the appropriate relative values of different national monies.

Second, the key question with respect to non-sterilized intervention is—How should exchange rates be used as a guide for the conduct of monetary policy? To the extent that influencing the behavior of exchange rates is an important objective of government policy (and it appears to be so in many countries), it is appropriate to include exchange rate behavior as one of the "targets" of monetary policy. However, since a central bank can have only one monetary policy, exchange rates must compete with other important variables in influencing the conduct of that policy. Exchange rates may also play a useful role as "indicators" for monetary policy that is directed at other primary objectives. In particular, exchange rates may signal changes in the demands to hold different monies which it would be desirable to offset by variations in money supplies. But, because exchange rates are influenced by many factors other than shifts in money demands, no generally valid argument can be made, one way or the other, that monetary policy guided by exchange rates is superior to a monetary growth rule. In an environment of rapidly changing inflationary expectations, however, it can be argued that exchange rates should be used as at least a supplement to market interest rates as an indicator of money demand changes.

Third, pure or sterilized intervention presumably affects only the short-run behavior of exchange rates and has no significant effect, by itself, on their long-run behavior. The argument that official intervention is required to remedy the defects of private speculation, specifically excessive variation caused by "bandwagon effects," is not especially convincing, particularly in view of the possibility that official intervention may itself be responsible for the purported defects of private speculation. There is, however, a valid case for official intervention on the grounds that the authorities may have better knowledge of their own future policy intentions than private market participants. Official intervention may be called for in circumstances where the credibility of the authorities is in question and it is necessary to "buy credibility" by committing the assets of the central bank to the support of its intended future policy.

Finally, the experience of the past seven years indicates that governments have intervened quite actively in foreign exchange markets, and the presumption therefore is that the observed behavior of exchange rates reflects the direct and indirect effects of this intervention as well as the behavior of private market participants. Any defects or peculiarities in the behavior of exchange rates, therefore, cannot be automatically attributed to defects of the market mechanism. Further, the experience of the past seven years indicates that the behavior of exchange rates influences the conduct of monetary policy, but only after exchange rates have moved substantially away from what the authorities regard as their appropriate or desirable values. This pattern of monetary policy tends to induce a pattern of behavior of exchange rates that suggests the operation of "bandwagon effects," apart from any defects that may affect the expectations of private speculators. With respect to their official intervention policies, it appears that most central banks have adopted a policy of "leaning against the wind," that is, of resisting to some extent changes in exchange rates. There is no clear evidence that this policy has contributed to greater exchange rate stability in the sense that it has kept exchange rates closer to their economically appropriate values. There are, however, a number of reasonably clear cases in which official intervention could be justified on the grounds that the authorities have better knowledge about their own policy interventions than private speculators. These cases are generally associated with economic or political crises in which the credibility of the authorities is in serious question.

2. The Theory of Exchange Rate Behavior

To assess the effects and objectives of exchange rate policy, especially official intervention policy, it is essential to discuss the general analytical framework within which the behavior of exchange rates must be understood. The modern "asset market view" of exchange rates emphasizes that exchange rates are relative asset prices which, like other asset prices determined in highly organized markets, are strongly influenced not only by current events but also by the market's expectation of future events. Changes in exchange rates over brief periods, such as a day, a week, or a month, are frequently large and are largely unpredictable. This randomness of exchange rate changes is a characteristic that is shared with the prices of common stocks and other asset prices. It is a manifestation of the fact that the dominant cause of exchange rate changes is the receipt of "new information" that alters the market's view of the economically appropriate exchange rate.[2]

In connection with the present discussion of official intervention, there are five general features of the "asset market view" of exchange rates that deserve special emphasis. First, since an exchange rate is the relative price of two highly durable assets—namely two national monies—the exchange rate that the market believes appropriate in the current period is necessarily tightly linked to the exchange rates that the market expects to prevail in future periods. It follows that the economic factors relevant for determining the currently appropriate exchange rate include not only the factors that influence the immediate conditions of supply and and demand in the foreign exchange market (such as current flows of exports and imports), but also, to a much greater extent, the market's expectations of what these conditions will be in future periods.[3]

Second, since an exchange rate is the relative price of two national monies, and since central banks can ultimately control the supplies of such monies, it is clear that the monetary policies of central banks are of first order importance for the behavior of exchange rates. This does not mean that a central bank can or will always maintain precise control over its money supply, or that it could use such control to hold a close rein on the exchange rate. It does mean that a central bank's actual monetary policy and the market's perception of its likely future policy are of prime importance in determining the value of its money relative to the monies issued and controlled by other central banks.

Third, exchange rates are also strongly affected by the demands of asset holders to hold the stocks of various national monies. In an environment of "currency substitution" in which asset holders shift their money holdings between different national currencies with considerable ease and in response to relatively small differences in expected rates of return, such shifts of demand may be the dominant cause of exchange rate changes. Changes in the actual and perceived monetary policies of central banks are probably an important factor motivating shifts in the demands to hold different national currencies. Exchange rate changes resulting from such demand shifts are, therefore, ultimately attributable to the actual and expected behavior of money supplies, rather than to the more basic determinants of money demand. However, there are almost certainly many important changes in the demands to hold different national currencies that are not ultimately attributable to changes in the actual or perceived changes in money supplies; such changes in money demand will have an important impact on exchange rates.

Fourth, exchange rates play an important role in responding to changes in real economic conditions requiring adjustments in the *relative* prices of different national outputs, as well as in responding to changes in monetary conditions and associated adjustments of absolute price levels in different countries.[4] It is not the case, however, that exchange rates adjust on a moment to moment basis to maintain balance in the trade or current account. Rather, the current exchange rate reflects expectations concerning the real factors that will influence the trade balance (or the current account) in the current and in future periods. Monetary conditions aside, changes in exchange rates reflect not the level of the trade balance, but rather innovations in the trade balance which convey "new information" that alters the market's beliefs concerning the present and future behavior of the real economic factors that ultimately determine the behavior of the trade balance and the equilibrium relative price of one country's output in terms of the outputs of other countries.[5]

Fifth, the general "asset market view" of exchange rates does not necessarily imply that foreign exchange markets are perfectly efficient either in the narrow technical sense of modern finance theory or in the broader sense of economic efficiency. In the theory of finance, a market is said to be "efficient" if the current price appropriately reflects all currently available information and there are no opportunities for making extraordinary profits by further exploiting such information. Empirical tests of the hypothesis of market efficiency for various foreign exchange markets have yielded conflicting conclusions, with some studies reporting significant divergences from the conditions of market efficiency. This evidence of the possible existence of market inefficiencies, however, does not conflict with the general view that exchange rates behave much like the prices of other assets traded in organized markets where price changes are frequently large and random, and occur primarily in response to new information received by market participants. Further, the acceptance or rejection of the hypothesis of market efficiency does not establish either the optimality or non-optimality of exchange rate policies. The policies of national governments determine an important part of the environment in which foreign exchange markets operate. Technical deficiencies in the functioning of these markets that are induced by the policies of national governments are not evidence of market failures requiring further intervention. On the other hand, technical efficiency of foreign exchange markets, within the environment created by government policies, does not necessarily indicate that these policies are creating the socially optimal environment.

3. Exchange Rates and Monetary Policy

Official intervention occurs when a central bank buys and sells foreign exchange for the purpose of affecting the foreign exchange value of its own money.[6] For analytical purposes, it is important to distinguish between "sterilized" and "non-sterilized" intervention. With sterilized intervention, the domestic money stock is insulated from the foreign exchange operation by an offsetting sale or purchase of domestic assets by the central bank. With non-sterilized intervention, the foreign exchange operation is permitted to affect the stock of high-powered money and hence the domestic money supply. The two forms of intervention share whatever is the "direct" effect of official purchases and sales of foreign exchange on the foreign exchange market. They differ only in the important respect that non-sterilized intervention is associated with changes in the domestic money supply. It is convenient to focus first on this key difference and to examine, in this section, the role of non-sterilized intervention as a form of monetary policy.

From the discussion of the "asset market view" of exchange rates, it is apparent that non-sterilized intervention can profoundly affect the behavior of exchange rates, precisely because it affects the behavior of national money supplies. In examining the role of such intervention, however, it is not particularly convenient to ask how monetary policies should be used to affect exchange rates. Rather, it is more fruitful to turn the question around and to ask how exchange rates should be used as a guide for the conduct of monetary policy. Since, in the end, a country can have only one monetary policy, it is clear from this question that the critical issue is the role that exchange rates should play, relative to other economic variables, in influencing the conduct of monetary policy.

A useful distinction in discussions of monetary policy is the distinction between "targets" and "indicators." A target is a variable that the policy authorities would ultimately like to influence, such as the inflation rate or the unemployment rate. Many such targets are not under the direct and immediate control of the central bank and hence cannot be used as day-to-day guides for the conduct of monetary policy. An indicator is a variable that may be of no ultimate interest by itself, such as the level of free reserves, but is sufficiently under the control of the central bank to be useful as an immediate guide for the actual conduct of monetary policy. In principle, exchange rates could serve as both targets and indicators for monetary policy, and their role in each of these functions needs to be evaluated.

It is not the purpose of this essay to consider the extreme case of an exchange rate as a target for monetary policy—namely, the commitment of monetary policy to the maintenance of a fixed exchange rate. Many of the arguments for a fixed exchange rate are, however, relevant in considering a more limited role for exchange rates as targets for monetary policy. The risk associated with random changes in exchange rates is a problem for firms engaged in international business. The reduction of such risk, particularly in an economy where international transactions are an important part of total business, would appear to be at least as important an objective for monetary policy as the reduction of risk arising from fluctuations in nominal interest rates. Perhaps more important is the reduction in real economic disturbances associated with fluctuations in exchange rates. In particular, we know that many changes in exchange rates are associated with changes in the relative prices of the outputs of different countries, rather than with adjustments of general price levels to the requirements of purchasing power parity. Such relative price changes can certainly be an important source of disturbance for individual industries (particularly export industries and import-competing industries) and perhaps also for the general level of economic activity. If these relative price changes are not the consequence of changes in fundamental real economic conditions, then moderation of such changes is a desirable objective for monetary policy. Finally, some economists and policy makers argue that fluctuations in exchange rates contribute to general price inflation because increases in import prices associated with exchange rate depreciation are readily built into domestic wages and material costs, but reductions in import prices associated with exchange rate appreciation are not so readily reflected in lower wages and materials costs. If this argument is correct, then monetary policy directed at moderating exchange rate fluctuations would contribute to lower general price inflation.[7]

There are two principle arguments against assigning significant weight to the behavior of exchange rates as an important target for monetary policy. First, the commitment of monetary policy to achieving objectives with respect to exchange rate behavior may conflict with the use of monetary policy to achieve other, more important objectives, in particular, objectives relating to the behavior of the inflation rate and the levels of output and employment. Second, the moderation of movements in exchange rates through the use of monetary policy may interfere with adjustments of exchange rates that are desirable to meet changes in real economic conditions requiring changes in the relative prices of the outputs of different countries.

No doubt, both of these arguments represent serious objections to the use of exchange rates as targets for monetary policy. A country that wishes to pursue its own policy with respect to its national inflation rate will find it difficult to rationalize that desire with the maintenance of stable exchange rates vis-a-vis countries with widely diverging inflation rates. A central bank that is unwilling to accept occasional sharp changes in domestic interest rates and in growth rates for monetary aggregates because it believes they will induce significant fluctuations in output and employment will find that an exchange rate target is inconvenient. Further, there is no doubt that real economic conditions do change, sometimes quite rapidly, and that movements of exchange rates can be the best way to accommodate to such real changes.

There is no magic formula to resolve these difficulties with the role of exchange rates as targets for monetary policy. Ultimately, since a central bank can have only one monetary policy, it must decide on the weight that should be given to exchange rates, relative to other policy objectives, in determining that policy, and it must recognize that attempts to influence exchange rates will occasionally go awry. It is not useful to pretend that these problems do not exist, specifically to pretend that a central bank can use exclusively sterilized intervention to influence the behavior of exchange rates, without ever committing the course of monetary policy to its exchange rate targets. Either the behavior of exchange rates is sufficiently important to influence the conduct of monetary policy, even in the presence of conflicts with other policy objectives, or their behavior is sufficiently unimportant that central banks should probably give up most attempts to influence them through any form of intervention.

Even if it is decided that the behavior of exchange rates is not sufficiently important, by itself, to influence significantly the conduct of monetary policy, it remains possible that exchange rates could provide a useful guide for the conduct of monetary policy designed to serve other objectives—that is, exchange rates could be useful as indicators for monetary policy, it is convenient to first review the case for monetary growth rates and market interest rates as indicators of monetary policy, and then consider the appropriate role for exchange rates.

Economists who argue for a money supply growth rule do not do so because the monetary growth rate is intrinsically important, but rather because they believe that a stable, preannounced monetary growth rate is the monetary policy that will lead to the greatest possible stability of national output and the price level. The argument for a money supply growth rule is based on the assertion that the demand for money is a very stable function of national output and the price level. If so, then a constant growth rate of the money supply will be consistent with a stable growth rate for national output and a stable inflation rate. Moreover, if the demand for money is stable, then a monetary policy that allows wide fluctuations in the monetary growth rate will tend to create instability in the behavior of national output and the price level.[8] This instability may be further exacerbated by fluctuations in the demand for money that are themselves induced by variations in the monetary growth rate. In particular, if the demand for money is sensitive to 'inflationary expectations which, in turn, are influenced by observed rates of monetary expansion, then fluctuations in the rate of monetary expansion may induce fluctuations in money demands that contribute to the instability of national output and the price level.

The principle argument against a money supply growth rule is that such a rule does not allow the money supply to offset fluctuations in money demand. This argument has two essential parts. First, there is an empirical assertion that there are significant fluctuations in money demand that are not the result of changes in income and prices or the induced effect of variations in the money supply. If not offset by compensating changes in the money supply, such fluctuations in money demand would induce undesirable fluctuations in output and prices. Second, there are observable economic variables whose behavior may be used to diagnose such fluctuations in money demand and to guide monetary policy in offsetting them. Clearly, if there were no such variables to act as indicators for monetary policy, there would be no operational method for implementing a policy to offset money demand fluctuations, even if such a policy were desirable in principle.

Market interest rates are widely used as an indicator for monetary policies designed to offset fluctuations in money demand.[9] The basic notion underlying this use of market interest rates is that because of the liquidity preference relationship, fluctuations in money demand are positively correlated with fluctuations in market interest rates. A monetary policy that is directed toward stabilizing interest rates, therefore, contributes to the stability of output and prices. Specifically, it is argued that an increase in money demand (at given output and prices) will tend to increase interest rates. A policy of stabilizing interest rates will lead the central bank to intervene automatically to offset this rise in interest rates by increasing the supply of money, thereby offsetting the increase in money demand.

The difficulty with market interest rates as an indicator for monetary policy is that fluctuations in interest rates do not always indicate fluctuations of money demand that should be offset by money supply changes. Following Irving Fisher, the market interest rate may be thought of as the sum of the real interest rate and the expected rate of price inflation. It is desirable for monetary policy to offset fluctuations in the real interest rate that would otherwise result from fluctuations in money demand. It is not desirable, however, to offset fluctuations in the real interest rate that result from changes in productivity and thrift. Indeed, if anything, monetary policy should seek to reinforce real interest rate changes that are associated with shifts of desired saving and desired investment, in order to stabilize output and employment.[10] The practical difficulty is that even if fluctuations in the nominal interest rate are known to correspond to fluctuations in the real interest rate, there is no completely reliable way of determining whether a particular interest rate change is due to a change in money demand or to a change in productivity and thrift.[11] For this reason, a monetary policy geared to interest rate stablilization can turn out to be destabilizing with respect to the true objectives of economic policy.

This problem becomes far worse when we consider the possibility of interest rate fluctuations resulting from changes in the expected inflation rate. There is little doubt that during periods of high and variable inflation rates, such as have been experienced in most of the industrial countries during the past decade, changes in inflationary expectations are a dominant cause of changes in nominal interest rates. In such an environment, a monetary policy directed at stabilizing nominal interest rates can go very badly wrong. In the presence of such a policy, upward pressure on the interest rate due to an increase in the expected inflation rate would lead the central bank to increase the money supply. The increase in the money supply might, in turn, lead to expectations of even higher inflation, to greater upward pressure on interest rates, and to even more rapid monetary expansion. Presumably, the central bank would ultimately react to this potentially explosive situation by an upward adjustment of its interest rate target. However, the possibility that such adjustments will be long-delayed and that their appropriate magnitude will be misjudged implies that the use of interest rates as the principal indicator for monetary policy in an environment of unstable inflationary expectations can be destabilizing for output and the inflation rate.

These defects of market interest rates as indicators for the conduct of monetary policy suggest that exchange rates might be used as an alternative or supplemental indicator of fluctuations in money demand. The "asset market view" of exchange rates indicates that fluctuations in the demand to hold domestic money ought to be reflected in the value of domestic money relative to foreign monies. Hence, a policy that links positive changes in the domestic money supply to positive changes in the foreign exchange value of domestic money ought to offset, at least to some extent, fluctuations in the demand to hold domestic money. Moreover, such a policy would not be subject to the same critical difficulties as an interest rate stabilization policy in an environment of changing inflationary expectations. An increase in the expected inflation rate would presumably mean a decrease in the perceived attractiveness of holding domestic money relative to holding foreign money, implying a tendency for domestic money to depreciate in terms of foreign exchange. In this situation, a monetary policy guided by exchange rates would lead the central bank to reduce the rate of monetary expansion. This is a stabilizing policy, especially in comparison with an interest rate policy that would lead the central bank to increase the rate of monetary expansion in response to an increase in the expected inflation rate.

Unfortunately, there are some important problems with the use of exchange rates as indicators for monetary policy. First, as discussed in connection with the "asset market view" of exchange rates, exchange rate changes occur not only in response to changes in the demand to hold domestic money, but also in response to actual and expected changes in real economic conditions requiring adjustments in the relative price of a country's output in terms of the outputs of other countries. In general, it is not desirable to allow monetary policy to be strongly influenced by exchange rate adjustments required to meet changes in real economic conditions; nor is it possible, in general, to ascertain when exchange rates are changing for this reason rather than because of changes in the demand to hold domestic money. Second, changes in exchange rates also reflect changes in the demand to hold foreign monies and the actual and expected future monetary policies of foreign central banks. In principle, we would not want to vary the supply of domestic money in response to such changes, unless they also affected the demand to hold domestic money. Again, therefore, we face the difficult problem of distinguishing the reasons for a particular change in exchange rates before we can use this change to guide monetary policy. Third, as emphasized in the "asset market view" of exchange rates, there is a complicated dynamic relationship between monetary policy and the foreign exchange value of domestic money—specifically, exchange rates react not only to what the money supply is today, but also to what it is expected to be in future periods. For this reason, it is difficult to specify the rule that should govern the adjustment of the money supply in response to changes exchange rates. The nature of the rule itself affects the way in which exchange rates will behave.

From this discussion, it follows that no general case can be made for the use of exchange rates as indicators for monetary policy, as opposed to the adoption of a fairly rigid monetary growth rule. The choice depends on what one believes about the magnitude and causes of fluctuations in money demand and fluctuations in exchange rates. If the demand to hold domestic money is quite stable (as a function of income and prices), except for fluctuations induced by actual and expected changes in money supply, then a money supply rule should work very well. Moreover, even if there are significant fluctuations in money demand, a monetary growth rule may still be the best policy, unless money demand changes are the dominant cause of exchange rate changes or can be easily isolated from other causes of exchange rates changes. On the other hand, exchange rates can provide a useful indicator for monetary policy if money demand changes are either the dominant or an easily identifiable cause of exchange rate changes. In particular, if the dominant cause of exchange rate changes is shifts in demand among national currencies, associated with the phenomenon of currency substitution, then it is entirely appropriate to allow such shifts to be absorbed primarily by shifts in the relative supplies of national monies, rather than by exchange rate changes which may be the source of further economic disturbances.

Finally, while no general case can be made for the use of exchange rates as monetary indicators, in preference to monetary growth rules, a quite general case can be made for the use of exchange rates as at least a supplement to market interest rates as a indicator of money demand changes. From both theory and experience, we know that monetary policy guided by interest rates can go badly off track when interest rate changes are dominated by changes in inflationary expectations. In particular, an increase in interest rates induced by a higher expected inflation rate can lead to a destabilizing spiral of ever increasing rates of monetary expansion and ever increasing upward pressure on interest rates. To guard against such mistakes, at least some attention should be paid to exchange rates and growth rates of monetary aggregates. If the foreign exchange value of domestic money is sinking when domestic interest rates are rising, the indication is that the increase in interest rates is probably due to expectations of higher inflation, and not to an increase in the demand to hold domestic money. In this situation it is entirely inappropriate and probably seriously destabilizing for the central bank to attempt to hold down domestic interest rates through rapid expansion of the money supply. Instead, it should recognize the signal that is being provided by the behavior of exchange rates and should allow market interest rates to rise.

In summary, non-sterilized official intervention implies a linkage between events in the foreign exchange markets and the conduct of monetary policy—specifically, the behavior of the domestic money supply. The key issue with respect to such intervention concerns the role that exchange rates should play as a guide for the conduct of monetary policy. To the extent that the behavior of exchange rates is itself an important objective of economic policy, it is appropriate to include such behavior as one of the targets toward which monetary policy is directed. Since a central bank can ultimately have only one monetary policy, however, exchange rates must compete with other important economic variables as potential targets for monetary policy. In the end, weight given to exchange rates in influencing the conduct of monetary policy necessarily means less weight given to other objectives. In addition to their possible role as targets for monetary policy, exchange rates may play a useful role as indicators for policy that is directed toward other objectives. In particular, exchange rate changes may signal changes in the demand to hold domestic money which it would be desirable to offset by variations in the supply of domestic money. But, because exchange rates are influenced by many factors other than changes in the demand to hold domestic money, no generally valid argument can be made that a monetary policy guided by exchange rates is necessarily superior to a monetary growth rule. In an environment of rapidly changing inflationary expectations, however, a general case can be made for the use of exchange rates as at least a supplement to market interest rates in guiding the conduct of monetary policy.

4. Pure Official Intervention

When the central bank does not allow its operations in the foreign exchange market to affect the domestic money supply we have the case of "pure" or "sterilized" official intervention.[12] There are two key questions that should be examined with respect to pure official intervention. First, how and to what extent can such intervention affect the behavior of foreign exchange rates? Second, what principles should guide the conduct of such intervention, particularly in relation to other economic policies?

In the case of non-sterilized intervention, which affects the domestic money supply, it is clear from the general principles of the "asset market view" of exchange rates why such intervention should be of first order importance for the behavior of exchange rates. It is much less clear, from general analytical principles, that pure intervention, which has no effect on the domestic money supply, should have a significant effect on the behavior of exchange rates, particularly in the long run. In fact, an analysis of the principle channels through which pure intervention may be presumed to operate suggests that while such intervention may be able to affect the behavior of exchange rates in the short tun, it has at best very modest capacity to affect their behavior in the long run.

There are two principle channels through which pure official intervention affects exchange rates. First, official purchases and sales of foreign exchange directly affect the flow demands and flow supplies of foreign exchange that must be balanced in determining the current exchange rate. Second, pure official intervention may influence the current exchange rate by influencing the expectations of non-official market participants concerning the likely future behavior of exchange rates.[13] This effect on expectations may come both from the direct effect on intervention on the current exchange rates and from the information that such intervention provides about the likely future behavior of the central bank with respect to its future monetary and exchange rate policies.[14]

From actual experience, there is little doubt that pure official intervention can have a significant short-run impact on the behavior of exchange rates through its direct effect on market conditions and through its effect on expectations. There is good reason to doubt, however, that pure official intervention can have a significant effect on the long-run behavior of exchange rates. Experience under both fixed and floating exchange rates indicates that when the market becomes persuaded that the authorities are attempting to maintain a disequilibrium exchange rate, the magnitude of intervention required to sustain the rate rapidly grows to enormous proportions. Usually in such situations, the authorities are ultimately forced to bow to market pressures. Knowledge of this likely outcome provides the stimulus of enormous speculation against the authorities which frequently turns out to be a self-fulfilling prophesy. Further, on theoretical grounds, there is no good reason to believe that pure official intervention should have much of an effect on the basic economic conditions that determine the long-run behavior of the exchange rate. Such intervention does not materially affect the monetary conditions that determine the long-run behavior of general price levels in different countries; nor does it affect the real economic conditions that determine the long run behavior of the relative prices of the outputs of different countries.

Given that pure official intervention can significantly affect only the short-run behavior of exchange rates, the question of which principles should govern the conduct of such intervention remains.

One simple and appealing answer is that central banks should avoid intervention and should allow foreign exchange rates to be determined by market forces. The basic rationale for this principle of non-intervention is that government authorities are, in general, no better at diagnosing changes in economic conditions requiring adjustments of exchange rates than are private market participants. Indeed, there are many instances in which government exchange rates have clearly resisted change, even after the need for change became apparent. This may be because change tends to be politically unpopular, and government authorities are sensitive to the political consequences of their actions. In contrast, private market participants who risk their own capital cannot afford to resist economically necessary changes simply because they may be unpopular with some politically important groups.

A case for official intervention is frequently made on the basis that private market participants are influenced by "bandwagon effects" and other speculative manias that lead to excessive variability and generally inappropriate behavior of exchange rates. The guiding hand of government authorities, it is argued, is essential in preventing these evils of speculation from being a serious source of disturbance to the economic system. This argument is supported, at least superficially, by the observation that floating exchange rates exhibit a fairly high degree of short run variability for which there is no easily identifiable cause and which appears to serve no obvious economic purpose. In particular, month-to-month and quarter-to-quarter changes in exchange rates appear to be largely random and bear little relationship to differentials between national inflation rates, as called for by the theory of purchasing power parity.[15] It is difficult for many economists and government officials to believe that the rather large, random changes in the relative prices of the outputs of different countries implied by such behavior of exchange rates correspond to changes in real economic conditions requiring adjustments of relative prices. Further, there is some statistical evidence that the behavior of exchange rates diverges from what should be expected in an "efficient market" and, in some cases, there is evidence of "bandwagon effects" leading to positive correlation of changes in exchange rates.[16]

In my judgment, however, the available evidence on the behavior of exchange rates does not support a convincing case for official intervention to correct the inherent evils of a speculative market. From the general theory of asset prices, we know that in an efficiently functioning market asset prices will fluctuate randomly in response to new information received by market participants. The fact that we frequently are not able to identify the specific new information that caused a particular price change does not imply that prices change without reason, or that it is desirable to resist price changes through official intervention. Further, evidence of divergences from the conditions of efficiency in foreign exchange markets is, at this stage, far from conclusive. Perhaps more important, observed inefficiencies may in many cases be the result of official intervention policies already in operation. In particular, a standard policy of "leaning against the wind" by intervening against all exchange rate changes will almost inevitably create the impression of "bandwagon effects" by converting a random sequence of exchange rate changes into a sequence with positive correlation.

A more persuasive case for official intervention can be made on the grounds that central banks possess resources and knowledge not available to private market participants. Specifically, a central bank has ultimate control over the supply of domestic money and, in principle, has a certainty of knowledge about its future monetary policy that is not available to private market participants. A central bank can use its knowledge of its own future policy to guide its speculations in foreign exchange and, if the need arises, can use its control over monetary policy to guarantee the success of its speculations. Alternatively, one might say that a central bank can use its official intervention in the foreign exchange market to guide the behavior of exchange rates in a manner that is consistent with its long-run monetary policy and, if the need arises, can adjust its monetary policy to meet its exchange rate objectives.

This, in effect, is what happens under a fixed exchange rate. The fixed exchange rate is ultimately guaranteed by the commitment of monetary policy to support the official parity. In the short run, however, monetary policy is used to a limited extent to pursue other policy objectives, and the exchange rate is maintained within its support points by official intervention. In principle, this general form of policy is relevant in a more general context where a central bank adopts a less rigid exchange rate target. The essential justification for official intervention in connection with such a general policy is that the central bank possesses a certainty of knowledge about its future monetary policy and its relationship to the behavior of exchange rates that is not available to private market participants.

It is important to recognize that in this situation, private foreign exchange speculation is not an adequate substitute for official intervention. The problem is that private speculation is limited by the moral hazard associated with the government's commitment to its own expected future policy. The government would like to influence expectations of its future policy because these expectations have significant effects on variables of current policy importance, including exchange rates, nominal interest rates, and rates of price and wage inflation. The difficulty is that once the government has persuaded people to expect that it will follow a future policy that assists in achieving its current objectives, there is nothing to insure that the government will actually follow the future policy that people expect. There is the moral hazard that in the future the government will simply choose whatever policy seems best at that time, without regard to its past commitments. Since private agents recognize that there is this moral hazard, they will not completely believe government pronouncements about future policy and will restrict activities that expose them to risk should the government not behave in accord with its announced or expected future policy. In particular, private speculators in foreign exchange will be reluctant to extend themselves on the basis of expectations concerning the future conduct of monetary policy.[17]

Official intervention provides a partial solution to this problem of moral hazard in the foreign exchange market. When a central bank intervenes on the basis of its expectations concerning its own future policy, it is not subject to the same problem of moral risk that confronts a private speculator.. Moreover, when a central bank takes an official position in the foreign exchange market it is doing more than simply announcing its future policy intentions; it is providing concrete evidence of the seriousness of those intentions by staking its capital in support of them. This function of official intervention is particularly important when the credibility of government policy is in question, either as a result of erratic past policy or as a result of political uncertainties. In effect, the central bank can purchase credibility by official intervention in foreign exchange market, perhaps including the forward market. Of necessity, private foreign exchange speculation cannot perform this function.[18]

Another reason for pure official intervention is to forestall exchange rate developments that would "create facts" having an adverse impact on economic policy. For example, a government may want to forestall the depreciation of its currency if nominal wage rates react rapidly to depreciation and monetary policy is forced to accommodate to the facts created by increases in nominal wage rates. There is a danger, however, that official intervention adopted with this rationale may be used in an attempt to sustain an economic situation that is unsustainable. The level of real wage rates can perhaps be raised, in the short run, by official intervention. But, it is not possible to sustain a higher level of real wages, except by continued official borrowing that must ultimately reach an upper limit.

Whatever else official intervention is used to accomplish, it is important that it not be used in a manner that unduly discourages or distorts private speculation. At least since Adam Smith, economists have recognized the beneficial services provided by speculators. These services are especially important in foreign exchange markets. Not only do speculators smooth exchange rates in response to what they perceive to be transitory fluctuations in supply and demand, but, more importantly, they induce exchange rates to move in response to what they perceive to be changes in economic conditions warranting such movements. This latter function is one that cannot be adequately performed by official government agencies. It is virtually inherent in the structure and motivations of official agencies that they will resist large and rapid changes in exchange rates, and they will almost certainly never promote such changes. Indeed, the 1974 Guidelines for the Management of Floating Exchange Rates adopted by the IMF, presumably with the approval of member governments, call upon a country to intervene in order to ". . . moderate sharp disruptive fluctuations . . . in the exchange value of its currency . . ., but normally not to "act aggressively" to induce changes in the foreign exchange value of its currency.[19]

Clearly, however, if governments are generally precluded from acting aggressively to promote economically appropriate changes in exchange rates, this vital function is left to the private market. Official intervention should be conducted in a manner that does not unduly impair the market's capacity to perform this vital function. Specifically, central banks should avoid "punitive" actions against foreign exchange speculators such as the "bear squeeze" carried out by the French Government in 1924. More generally, government authorities should recognize that continual, large-scale official intervention that is not based on a clear informational advantage of the authorities with respect to their own future policies or on the need to establish the credibility of those policies, can be destructive to stabilizing private speculation. In the absence of such an advantage or need, official intervention is likely, at best, to replace private speculation. At worst, it can be a serious source of disruption as private speculators devote increased attention to "psyching out" the likely intervention actions of the authorities and less attention to divining the fundamental economic forces that ought to influence the behavior of exchange rates.

Finally, there is the important question of how the intervention policies of different central banks should be coordinated and how the agreed upon rules for official intervention should be policed. There is general agreement, as expressed in the 1974 IMF Guidelines and in the 1978 amendments to the Articles of Agreement dealing with IMF surveillance of exchange rate policies, that governments should intervene in order to prevent "disorderly conditions" in foreign exchange markets, should "avoid manipulating exchange rates or the international monetary system to prevent effective balance of payments adjustment or gain unfair competitive advantage," and should "take account of the interests and policies of other countries" in conducting its own intervention. Unfortunately, the key terms in this general injunction, "disorderly conditions," "unfair competitive advantage," etc., are difficult to define in an operational manner. The contribution of the present discussion toward the definition of these terms is that the "disorderly conditions" that official intervention should especially be directed toward preventing are disorderly conditions that result from uncertainties and misperceptions of the future course of government policy. It is in this area that the authorities, in principle, have a unique and substantial advantage over the private market. It remains an empirical question whether it is possible to identify episodes and circumstances in which this advantage is relevant and important.

5. Recent Experience With Official Intervention

Recent experience with the behavior of exchange rates and the conduct of official foreign exchange market intervention illustrates a number of the principles discussed earlier in this paper. One fact that certainly stands out in our experience with floating exchange rates since March 1973 is that governments do intervene very actively to influence the behavior of exchange rates. This fact is apparent from studies of the demand for the use of international reserves. Specifically, John Williamson (1976) found that during the first three years of generalized floating, the use of international reserves by major countries (that is, the up and down movements in their reserve holdings) was smaller, but not a great deal smaller, than it had been during the last few years of the pegged rate system. In his study of the demand for reserves, Jacob Frenkel (1978) found that despite the ". . . presumption that international reserves play a fundamentally different role under a regime of floating exchange rates . . ., patterns of country holdings and usages of reserves resemble to some extent the behavior prescribed for a regime of pegged exchange rates." Moreover, even without a detailed statistical analysis, it is apparent from the reports of major central banks that there has been large scale official intervention in foreign exchange markets.

The nature and pattern of official intervention has, of course, varied significantly from country to country. The Japanese have intervened fairly consistently throughout the floating rate period to resist major movements in the yen/dollar exchange rate.[20] Initially, the Bundesbank sought to avoid intervention to counteract "fundamental trends in the market," but did intervene in fairly substantial amounts "to moderate excessive fluctuations in the deutsche mark rate vis-a-vis the U.S. dollar over extended periods of time."[21] The British and Italian authorities intervened modestly by accumulating reserves during the initial period of floating when their currencies were strong. Later, in 1975 and 1976, they intervened strongly to resist the sharp declines in the lira and the pound. After the crises had past, both countries accumulated substantial reserves as their currencies and balances of payments positions strengthen in 1977 and 1978. The general intervention policy of the French government is more difficult to discern, but it is clear that there were periods in which substantial official support was provided by the franc, in particular in early 1976.[22] Switzerland adhered to a monetary growth rule from 1973 through 1977, and avoided substantial intervention in the foreign exchange market. It did, however, adopt other measures to discourage nonresident deposits in Swiss banks. By early 1979, Switzerland officially gave up its monetary growth rule and allowed the money supply to be influenced by increases in official reserves resulting from interventions carried out to prevent further appreciation of the Swiss franc relative to the deutsche mark. Prior to 1978, official intervention by the U.S. authorities was very limited in both magnitude and objective, with the focus on "disorderly conditions" associated with extreme daily movements of exchange rates. Since 1978, especially since November 1, 1978, however, the U.S. authorities have intervened far more extensively, with the objective of affecting exchange rates on a longer term basis and correcting what are perceived to be incorrect valuations of the dollar by the private market.[23]

It follows from the fact that there has been extensive official intervention in foreign exchange markets since March 1973 that the behavior of exchange rates during this period does not reflect exclusively the actions of private market participants. The behavior of exchange rates also reflects the direct effect of interventions by official agencies and the effect of actual and expected interventions by official agencies on the behavior of private market participants. For this reason, we cannot automatically conclude that any observed peculiarities in the behavior of exchange rates necessarily indicate defects in the operation of market mechanisms. Such peculiarities might equally well indicate defects in the intervention policies of official agencies. Further, since it is now known that official agencies will intervene extensively in foreign exchange markets, this fact will inevitably influence the future behavior of private market participants. In my judgment, it will never be possible to obtain a clean test of how foreign exchange markets would function in the absence of actual and expected intervention by official agencies.

Another fact that is apparent from the experience of the past seven years is that the behavior of exchange rates does influence the conduct of monetary policy. Central banks do not only intervene on a sterilized basis to affect exchange rates; they will also, in certain circumstances, adjust their monetary policies in the light of developments in the foreign exchange markets. As a general matter, however, central banks do not allow exchange rate movements to have a smooth and systematic effect on monetary policy. Rather, they tend to adjust monetary policy only to what they see as extreme and undesirable movements of exchange rates.

Probably the most dramatic instance of policy behavior of this kind is the shift in the monetary and exchage rate policy of the United States in early November of 1978. It is noteworthy that prior to 1978, the effective exchange rate of the U.S. dollar relative to the trade-weighted basket of currencies of its major trading partners had not changed dramatically since the advent of generalized floating, despite substantial movements relative to individual currencies. From the perspective of U.S. policy makers, the behavior of the exchange rate was not a problem prior to 1978. This situation changed markedly in 1978, particularly in the late summer and early fall when the dollar declined substantially against virtually all major currencies. The decline of the dollar was regarded by the policy authorities as a serious threat to the anti-inflation program in the United States and to the efforts of European countries and Japan to expand output and employment. On November 1, 1978, after earlier suggestions of minor policy changes had proved unconvincing to the market, a significant change in U.S. monetary and exchange rate policy was announced. The discount rate was raised by a full percentage point to its highest level in history (up to then) as a signal that the Federal Reserve would pursue a tighter monetary policy, and the United States arranged to significantly expand its resources for exchange market intervention and announced that it would use those resources to support a realistic value of the dollar. On the strength of these announcements and of actual intervention, the dollar recovered sharply in November 1978, though it lost ground again in late December. The general point, however, is not the success or failure of these operations, but the fact that they were undertaken partly because of developments in the foreign exchange markets, but only after exchange rates had been pushed far from what the authorities regarded as reasonable and appropriate.

A similar pattern is apparent in the policies pursued by other countries. Sterling went through a series of depreciations in 1976, with occasional periods of support by official intervention, until the crisis of late September and early October finally forced the adoption of more restrictive fiscal and monetary policies that persuaded the market that the pound was undervalued. Italy went through a similar experience during the first six months of 1976. As previously mentioned, the Swiss National Bank ultimately gave up on its fixed monetary growth rate in order to prevent further large appreciation of the Swiss franc. Up to mid-1977, the Bundesbank was reasonably well satisfied with the operation of the floating rate system, and geared its acceptable inflation rate, In late 1977 and especially in 1978, however, the Bundesbank intervened actively to prevent substantial further appreciation of the deutsche mark and allowed its interventions to push the monetary growth rate well above its preannounced target level. Again, we have the pattern that the behavior of exchange rates influences the conduct of monetary policy, but only after exchange rates have moved far from the values that the authorities regard as appropriate.

This pattern of behavior of monetary policy could well be the explanation for peculiarities in the behavior of exchange rates that are usually attributed to the defects of private speculation. Consider the following explanation of the possible defects of private speculation that is given in a recent article by Jacques Artus (1976):

> "More forcefully than anyone else, Nurkse . . . has pointed out that . . . movement(s) in the spot rate could become self-perpetuating, at least for a while, if market participants' expectations as to the future value of the exchange rate were revised in the same direction as the actual change in the rate. Ultimately, investors would realize that the movement of the rate had gone too far and a corrective movement would begin—a corrective movement that might itself push the rate too far in the opposite direction. Speculation would become destabilizing."

If expectations of private speculators were subject to the defect described in this quotation, movements of exchange rates ought to be subject to "bandwagon effects," that is, movements in one direction would tend to lead to movements in the same direction until the exchange rate is pushed so far that a correction sets in.

The alternative explanation for such "bandwagon effects" is that they are the result of the pattern of policy pursued by the authorities. Private speculators know that if the exchange rate is pushed far enough, the authorities are likely to take effective action to limit or reverse the exchange rate movement by altering monetary policy. Private speculators do not know, however, the point at which the authorities will feel compelled to take effective corrective action, or even that they will always do so. In this situation, if there is pressure on the exchange rate in one direction, private speculators will tend to push the rate in that direction until the government acts to oppose the movement. If the initial resistence is weak or temporary, speculators will push the rate further and further until the government takes effective action—that is, action that affects not only the temporary conditions in the foreign exchange market (sterilized intervention), but also affects the basic economic determinants of the exchange rate (monetary policy). This scenario is at least broadly descriptive of the events associated with major movements in several important exchange rates.

Another regularity in policies of official foreign exchange intervention is that intervention tends to be used to "lean against the wind," that is, to resist changes in exchange rates. The Japanese authorities have probably been the most consistent practioners of this policy. In his study of Japanese intervention practices, Peter Quirk (1977) found that, on average, each one percent monthly movement in the exchange rate of the yen vs. the dollar was accompanied by net intervention of about $250 million, with the Japanese authorities buying dollars when the yen rose and selling them when the yen declined. For other countries, the pattern has been less systematic, but in general the authorities have purchased foreign exchange when their currencies were rising and have sold it when their currencies were declining. [24]

It is difficult to assess whether such policies of "leaning against the wind" have contributed to the "stability" or to the "instability" of exchange rates. Promoting stability does not mean preventing change; it means keeping exchange rates close to their "economically appropriate" values. Unfortunately, we have no measure of the "economically appropriate" values of exchange rates by which to judge the stabilizing effect of official intervention. One criterion of judgment is the principle that stabilizing intervention ought to be profitable. Judged by this criterion, official intervention has not been stabilizing; most central banks have lost money as a result of their interventions in the foreign exchange market. [24] However, there is a legitimate question as to the relevance of this profitability criterion in assessing the stabilizing effect of official intervention. Official intervention may be motivated by general policy objectives that make it desirable to move exchange rates contrary to the direction dictated by market forces. It is possible, therefore, that the losses sustained by central banks in their foreign exchange operations have been compensated by more important benefits in other areas.

In the theoretical discussion of the rationale for pure official intervention, it was argued that intervention is desirable when exchange rates do not appropriately reflect a central bank's true intentions with respect to its own future monetary policy. This is a circumstance that is likely to arise when the policy authorities have lost their credibility either as a result of erratic behavior of past policy or of some political or economic crisis. The experience of the past seven years provides several instances in which intervention could be justified on these grounds. The sharp decline of the dollar from August through October of 1978, in my judgment, reflected the fear that the authorities had lost control of the rate of monetary expansion and that the inflation rate in the United States might accelerate relative to that in other industrial countries. An announcement by the authorities that they intended to pursue a tighter monetary policy would probably not, by itself, have corrected conditions in the foreign exchange markets. The Federal Reserve had significantly exceeded its monetary growth targets in the past, and there was no way for the market to be certain that this would not happen in the future. In this situation, if the authorities were serious about their intention to bring monetary expansion under control, there was reason to provide evidence of the seriousness of that intention by supporting the dollar in the foreign exchange market. A similar situation existed, in my judgment, in Italy in the late spring and summer of 1976 and in the United Kingdom in the fall of 1976. The sharp decline of the lira in April and early May and the sharp decline of the pound in September and October reflected not primarily the actual conditions prevailing at the time, but rather the fear that the situation might deteriorate further in the future. In these situations, as with the dollar in the fall of 1978, announcements by the authorities of their policy intentions would not have corrected conditions in the foreign exchange markets. It was necessary to provide evidence of those intentions through official support for the lira and the pound.

Political unrest and uncertainty have created other cases where official intervention in the foreign exchange markets was warranted. A relevant case is that of France during the student revolution and general strike of May 1968. Under the fixed exchange rate regime that prevailed at the time, the Bank of France intervened heavily to support the franc. Clearly, had these disturbances occurred under a floating rate regime, in the absence of equally heavy intervention, the franc would have sunk like a rock. No announcement by the authorities could have prevented this decline. In order to do so it was essential that the authorities absorb the risk that private market participants perceived to arise from the political unrest and uncertainty.

A similar situation existed in Portugal after the socialist revolution of 1974. As economic conditions deteriorated and as the balance of payments deficit enlarged, the escudo came under heavy pressure. Had the Bank of Portugal simply allowed the exchange rate to be determined by market forces, the escudo would probably have declined precipitiously in 1975, 1976 and 1977, with the effect of seriously undermining efforts to achieve political and economic stability. Some downward adjustment in the foreign exchange value of the escudo (which occurred with the devaluation of early 1977) was clearly necessary. But, given the political situation, the determination of this downward adjustment could not reasonably be left to private market speculators. It was essential that the authorities absorb a substantial part of the risk created by political uncertainty.

In summary, during the past seven years, official agencies have intervened extensively in foreign exchange markets, and the behavior of exchange rates has presumably been affected by the direct and indirect effects of this official intervention. For this reason, we cannot conclude that observed peculiarities in the behavior of exchange rates necessarily reflect defects in the operation of market mechanisms. From the experience of the past seven years, it is also apparent that the behavior of exchange rates influences the conduct of monetary policy, but usually only after exchange rates have moved substantially away from what the authorities regard as their appropriate or desirable values. This pattern of policy behavior may create a pattern in the behavior of exchange rates that gives the impression that private speculation is subject to "bandwagon effects." Aside from the effect of exchange rates on monetary policy, it appears that many central banks have adopted a policy of "leaning against the wind" with respect to their official foreign exchange interventions. On the basis of the profitability criterion, it does not appear that these policies have, in general, contributed to the stability of exchange rates, in the relevant sense that intervention has moved rates in the direction of their equilibrium values. The evidence on this point, however, is far from conclusive. Finally, there appear to have been a number of important cases in which official intervention could be justified on the grounds that the authorities possessed better knowledge or greater certainty about their own future intentions than private market speculators. These cases are generally associated with economic or political crises in which, for some reason, the credibility of the authorities has come into serious question.

Notes

1. For evidence on the holding and use of international reserves see, in particular, John Williamson (1976) and Jacob Frenkel (1978).

2. The "asset market view" of exchange rates and the more specific "monetary view" has been the subject of a number of recent theoretical and empirical papers; see, in particular, Bilson (1978a) and (1978b), Dornbusch (1976a) and (1976b), Frenkel (1976), Kouri (1976), Mussa (1976), (1977), (1979a), and Stockman (1978). For a discussion of the relevance of the "asset market view" for explaining the gross empirical regularities in the behavior of exchange rates, see Frenkel (1979), Frenkel and Mussa (1980), and Mussa (1979b).

3. This basic point can be represented in a very simply formal model. Suppose that the current equilibrium value of the logarithm of the spot exchange rate, $s(t)$, is determined by

$$s(t) = x(t) + b\ E(\Delta s(t);t), \qquad b > 0,$$

where $x(t)$ summarizes the effect of the current conditions of supply and demand on $s(t)$, and $E(\Delta s(t);t) = E((s(t+1) - s(t));t)$ is the expected percentage rate of change of the exchange rate between t and $t+1$. Assuming that expectations are "rational" in the sense that they are consistent with the basic equation determining $s(t)$, it follows that $s(t)$ is determined by a weighted average of expected future values of x; specifically,

$$s(t) = (1/(1+b)) \cdot \sum_{k=0}^{\infty} (b/(1+b))^k \cdot E(x(t+k);t).$$

For further discussion of the derivation and significance of this result, see Mussa (1976) and (1979a) and Frenkel and Mussa (1980).

4. For a detailed, formal treatment of the role of real and monetary factors in influencing the dynamic behavior of exchange rates, see Mussa (1979a). For an analysis of the relationship between the exchange rate and the trade balance, see Dornbusch and Fischer (1978), Kouri (1976), Mussa (1979a), and Rodriguez (1978).

5. For a survey of the literature on foreign exchange market efficiency, see Levich (1979) and Kolhagen (1978). Also, see especially Frenkel and Clements (1980), Hansen and Hodrick (1980), Krugman (1977), and Obstfeld (1978).

6. There is wide variation in the institutional arrangements for official intervention. For simplicity in the present discussion, it is assumed that intervention is carried out by the central bank.

7. This argument presupposes that the central bank allows the money supply to expand rather than enforce a contraction of output and employment in the export sector when the exchange rate appreciates. Even with this proviso,

however, I do not assign much credibility to the argument that exchange rate fluctuations generate general price inflation. This was not the case during the 1930s; nor has it been the case with Switzerland and West Germany during the 1970s. Indeed, the adoption of floating exchange rates has clearly allowed Switzerland and West Germany to enjoy lower inflation rates than they would have experienced had they remained pegged to the dollar.

8. For further analysis on this point, see Poole (1976) and Genberg and Roth (1979).

9. It can also be argued that interest rates are important as an indicator for monetary policy because interest rates affect investment which, in turn, affects aggregate demand and the levels of output and employment. There is no essential conflict between this view and the present discussion of the role of market interest rates as indicators of money demand shifts. If interest rates are important because they affect investment, it is desirable to offset fluctuations in interest rates that would be generated by fluctuations in money demand.

10. In terms of the standard ISLM model (with a given expected inflation rate), we may distinguish between interest rate changes induced by shifts of the LM curve, due to money demand changes, and interest rate changes induced by shifts of the IS curve, due to changes in desired saving and investment. To stabilize national income, we would want to offset interest rate changes resulting from LM curve shifts, and reinforce interest rate changes resulting from IS curve shifts.

11. Once the economy falls into recession, it may be possible to diagnose the probable cause of the interest rate change. However, given the lags in the effect of monetary policy, this diagnosis may come too late.

12. If a central bank buys foreign money by creating domestic money, it can sterilize the effect of this operation by selling domestic assets from its portfolio. Alternatively, the central bank can obtain the foreign currency it wishes to supply to the market by borrowing it either from foreign central banks (perhaps through swaps) or in foreign credit markets. Such operations have no effect on the domestic money supply. Similarly, official intervention carried out by an exchange stabilization fund normally has no effect on the domestic money supply. It is also assumed that the foreign money supply is unaffected by such intervention.

13. Expectations of future exchange rates affect the current exchange rate because they affect the supply and demand for foreign exchange that will be present at any given current exchange rate. For purposes of discussion in this paper, however, it is useful to maintain the usual distinction between basic factors that affect the demand and supply of foreign exchange (imports and exports) and expectations that affect the "speculative" demand and supply of foreign exchange. Elsewhere (see Mussa (1979b), I have argued that this distinction is not particularly useful and, indeed, that the concept of the foreign exchange market as a market for flows of foreign exchange is not the most enlightening way to view this market.

14. William Day (1977) develops a model in which official intervention can affect the exchange rate through its effect on the net amount of private indebtedness that is required to finance the cumulative current account deficit. Such an effect of pure official intervention is also clearly implied by portfolio balance models of exchange rate determination (such as those discussed by Branson (1979) and Dornbusch (1980) in which an alteration in the relative supplies of securities denominated in different monies brought about by sterilized official intervention affects the equilibrium structure of yields and equilibrium exchange rates.

The potential importance of this portfolio balance mechanism for allowing a permanent effect of sterilized official intervention has been emphasized to me by Peter Kenen. While I do not dispute the potential importance of this mechanism for the effect of pure intervention, I doubt its quantitative importance for the magnitudes of interventions that have been are likely to be carried out. Specifically, I do not believe that it would make a great deal of difference to the exchange rate between the U.S. dollar and the deutsche mark if there were an additional $50 billion of U.S. government obligations already outstanding that were denominated in deutsche marks. Note, however, that an announcement that the U.S. government is prepared to borrow an additional $50 billion of deutsche marks to use in intervention operations to support the dollar may have an effect on the exchange rate through mechanisms other than its portfolio effect on the supplies of securities denominated in dollars and deutsche marks.

15. For further discussion of the random character of exchange rate changes and their relationship to changes in national price levels, see Mussa (1979b) and Frenkel and Mussa (1980).

16. The argument that private speculation is subject to "bandwagon effects" is perhaps the most widely stated reason for official intervention that "leans against the wind" in order to reduce excessive variability of exchange rates. For a discussion of this argument, see Branson (1976) and Artus (1976). For a general analysis of the effects of alternative rule for governing official intervention, see Kenen (1975). Concerning the general question of whether asset prices fluctuate excessively, also see the interesting work of Shiller (1979) and LeRoy and Porter (1980).

17. The general problem discussed in this paragraph is the problem of "policy consistency" that arises whenever expectations of future policy affect current behavior.

18. The problems of moral hazard and government credibility might not arise if the government adopted and adhered to monetary growth rule. Given the history of monetary policy in most countries, however, it would probably be difficult to persuade people that such a rule would be adhered to by the government.

19. It is relevant and desirable to adopt rules for official intervention that reduce the possibility of serious conflicts among governments. In particular, it is desirable to avoid conflict over assertions that a government is engaging in "competitive depreciation" and seeking "unfair competitive advantage" by ac-

tively inducing its currency to depreciate. The IMF strictures against "aggressive intervention" make considerable sense in this context.

20. For an analysis of the official intervention policy of the Japanese government, see Peter Quirk (1977).

21. These quotations are from the description of the intervention policy of the Bundesbank in its 1974 annual report. Bundesbank policy was also influenced by its responsibilities with the European Monetary System.

22. Official intervention by the French authorities was also carried out to support the position of the franc in the European Monetary System (the "snake"), during those periods when the France was participating in the system.

23. In 1980 and 1981, the value of the U.S. dollar in terms of European currencies was strongly influenced by movements in U.S. interest rates and, presumably, by the monetary policies and other factors that induced these movements. The Federal Reserve did not alter its monetary policy in response to the large exchange rate changes that occurred in 1980 and 1981, but continued to pursue the growth rates for monetary aggregates that it believed to be consistent with its primary objective of gradually reducing the U.S. inflation rate. European governments which faced high unemployment rates did not tighten monetary policy and raise domestic interest rates in order to prevent depreciation of their currencies vis-a-vis the U.S. dollar. Moreover, it was recognized, especially by the Bundesbank, that sterilized intervention would be of little effectiveness in countervailing large changes in the value of the U.S. dollar, given the magnitude of the movements in U.S. interest rates.

24. Dornbusch (1980) also finds that the Japanese authorities followed a policy of "leaning against the wind," and that a similar policy was followed by the West German authorities.

25. The U.S. Treasury and Federal Reserve report small net losses from their current foreign exchange operations from 1973 through 1979. The Bundesbank and the Bank of Japan have, for the period as a whole, taken substantial losses on their large dollar balances. This is true even if we exclude dollars acquired before 1973. For the period as a whole, the Bank of England has also rather large losses, first from supporting the pound during its decline in 1975 and 1976, and more recently from the dollars it acquired in 1977 and 1978.

14

ECONOMIC STRUCTURE AND POLICY FOR EXTERNAL BALANCE

William H. Branson

I. Introduction and Summary

The traditional macroeconomics of the period since World War II, as well as the more recent rational expectations and neo-Keynesian approaches, analyze one-commodity economies. Output, or real gross national product (GNP), is like the *schmoo*[1] that lived in Dogpatch. It is a single good that can be consumed, invested, or exported, and it is produced by a homogeneous labor force and capital stock. The emphasis in these marcro-economic models has typically been on the interaction between the real and financial sectors and on the role of aggregate demand policy. The international version of this model, in its simplified extreme, is the monetary model of the balance of payments or, more recently, of the exchange rate.

During the 1970s emphasis shifted to the role of structure and the supply side. Most of the shocks to the industrial economies came from relative price changes, which cannot be analyzed clearly in a model with one commodity. The oil and raw materials price increases, exchange rate changes, and growth of manufacturing output in developing countries all appear as changes in relative prices in the economies of countries of the Organization for Economic Cooperation and Development (OECD). To analyze these events, structure must be specified.

Research in open economy macroeconomics has responded to the facts. Emphasis has shifted to the supply side and the role of structure in transmitting economic disturbances and effects of policy. Most recently the literature has begun to focus on questions of optimal structure. Examples are Flood and Marion (1982) and Marston (1982), who study optimal wage indexation and choice of exchange rate regimes.

361

This paper discusses some of the more significant results of the role of economic structure in determining how disturbances are transmitted. In general, the focus is one the exchange rate as an instrument for adjustment to external balance. Section II begins with an exposition of the monetary model of the balance of payments, which assumes virtually no structure. This provides a framework for the sections that follow and that introduce structural differences into the model, one at a time. In Section III the effects of trade structure on the results of changes in exchange rates are studied. The role of supply elasticities is emphasized. In Section IV the effects of wage rigidities and indexation are discussed. In Section V the effects of financial market structure on adjustment and the choice of exchange rate regime are studied.

The basic results can be summarized briefly. First, the effects of changes in exchange rates may be asymmetric between Europe and the United States. Movements in the exchange rate have their main effect on trade in the United States, by changing relative prices, which thus makes the exchange rate an efficient instrument for external adjustment in the United States. But in Europe changes in the exchange rate may have their main effect on domestic prices, making the exchange rate a poor instrument for external balance.

Second, demand policy in countries with real wage stickiness moves the price level in those countries, but influences output only in countries with nominal wage stickiness. Again, there may be a difference between Europe, with sticky real wages, and the United States wth sticky nominal wages. Third, only countries with developed and open financial markets can expect a floating exchange rate to be stable. This may be the reason why the industrial countires tend to float, while the developing countries tend to peg their exchange rates.

II. The Monetary Model

In order to set the framework for discussion of the importance of various aspects of economic structure for international adjustment and interdependence, we begin with a simple version of the monetary model of the balance of payments that was a popular tool of analysis in the 1960s and early 1970s. The monetary model assigned virtually no role to economic structure. Much of the research since the early 1970s showing the role of structural aspects can be interpreted as modifying, or making more "realistic," the assumptions of the monetary model. It thus provides a useful organizing concept and benchmark from which to begin the analysis.

The three aspects of economic structure that will be emphasized in the following sections of the paper are (a) structure of trade, (b) wage and price determination, and (c) structure of financial markets. So in setting out the monetary model, we will emphasize the assumptions made on each of these three points. We focus on the fixed exchange rate version of the model for a single country. The exposition here follows Johnson (1972). More sophisticated and complex versions can be found in International Monetary Fund (1977). Khan and Knight (1981) provide an estimated version with more detail in specification and empirical lags, estimated on pooled time-series, cross-section data for a number of developing countries.

The first strong assumption is (a) that goods are perfect substitutes. This means there is essentially one composite commodity produced by all countries in question. If the "law of one price" holds, the domestic currency price of the good P, and the foreign currency price P^* are related by

$$P = eP^* \tag{1}$$

where e is the exchange rate in units of domestic currency. In a multi-country context, e would be an effective nominal exchange rate.

If the country being discussed is a small country, in the sense that it has no influence on world prices, P^* is exogenous and independent of e in equation (1). A modification of the strong one-good assumption is to assume that each country is specialized in producing one (composite) commodity. Then equation (1) could be interpreted as translating the domestic currency price of the domestically produced export good into foreign exchange, and vice versa for imported goods. If the small-country assumption is maintained, so that many other countries are producing the same good as the home country, then all foreign exchange prices P^* are exogenous. This specialization assumption provides the starting point of the analysis of the role of structure in goods markets in Section III below. As long as the small-country assumption is maintained, the basic results of the monetary model obtain under either the one-commodity or the specialization assumption.

The second important assumption of the monetary model is (b) flexible wages and prices. Flexible real wages are not sufficient; the system must be free of all nominal price rigidity or stickiness. In general, all relative prices must be free to move to clear the relevant markets, *and* the nominal price level must be free to adjust real demand to meet full-employment output. The assumption of wage and price flexibility sets domestic output y at its full-employment level $\bar{y}$

$$y = \bar{y} \tag{2}$$

So far we have exogenized P and y by assumptions (a) and (b). It remains to pin down the interest rate by assuming (c) that domestic and foreign interest-earning assets are perfect substitutes. In the fixed rate version of the monetary model this makes the domestic interest r equal to the exogenous world rate r^*

$$r = r^* \tag{3}$$

The law of one price plus the assumption of perfect substitutes establishes the equality; the small-country assumption in asset markets makes r^* exogenous.

Money demand in the monetary model is given by

$$\frac{M^d}{P} = m(r, y), \tag{4}$$

or

$$M^d = P{\cdot}m(r, y)$$

It can be easily seen that assumption $(a) - (c)$ have exogenized all the determinants of money demand with fixed exchange rates. Substitution of $(1) - (3)$ into (4) gives us

$$M^d = eP^*{\cdot}m(r^*, \bar{y}) \tag{5}$$

The demand for money is proportional to the exchange rate, given P^*, $r^*, \bar{y}$. It is useful to note here that wealth is not included as a determinant of money demand in (4). Addition of wealth effects invalidates most of the clear propositions that come from the simple version of the monetary model, as shown, for example, in Branson and Buiter (1982).

The money supply M^s is determined by the central bank's holdings of domestic debt D and foreign exchange reserves R in this simple stylized model

$$M^s = D + R \tag{6}$$

The money multiplier is set equal to unity here; we could multiply $(D + R)$ by a constant multiplier without influencing the results.

Equating money demand and supply gives us money market equilibrium

$$D + R = eP^*{\cdot}m(r^*, \bar{y}) \tag{7}$$

With the determinants of money demand fixed, the money stock is demand determined. In most applications of the model, movements in D are set by requirements of financing the government budget deficit, $G - T$

$$\dot{D} = \alpha(G - T) \tag{8}$$

where α is the fraction of the deficit that is monetized, and a dot over a variable denotes its time rate of change—for example, $\dot{D} = dD/dt$. With money demand fixed, equation (7) implies

$$\dot{R} = -\dot{D} \tag{9}$$

We can now describe two thought experiments that show how the model works and outline the basic policy package it implies. These are "thought experiments" because they describe the reaction of the model to changes in policy beginning from a full equilibrium position. As the purpose of policy action is generally to eliminate disequilibrium, these experiments do not describe the likely results of actual policy moves. This we will do below. But these experiments do provide a way to describe how the model works. The simulations of Khan and Knight (1981) are exactly such thought experiments.

First, consider the effects of a given expansion of the domestic debt component of the money stock, generated by a temporary government deficit. Initially this increases the money supply by the increment to the domestic debt component ΔD. With the exchange rate fixed, money demand on the right-hand side of equation (7) is unchanged. The expansion of the money supply by ΔD thus creates an excess supply of real balances, which leads to a rise in domestic absorption and a current account deficit. It also puts downward pressure on the domestic interest rate and leads to a capital outflow. Both effects reduce reserves, and the reserve loss continues until $\Delta R = -\Delta D$. This restores real balances to their original value and re-establishes equilibrium. Thus, the increase in the money supply caused by the budget deficit is eliminated by an equal reserve loss.

Second, consider the effects of a devaluation. This is represented by an increase in e given in percentage terms by $\Delta e/e$. Here the difference between the one-commodity and the complete-specialization assumptions plays a role in the analysis. In either case the rise in e reduces real balances M/eP^* by the same proportion. This reduces absorption and puts upward pressure on the interest rate, resulting in a current account surplus and a capital inflow. In addition, in the complete-specialization case there is a reduction in the price of home goods relative to foreign goods, which also stimulates a current account surplus. This is a trade elasticity effect.

The balance of payments surplus adds to reserves, and this increases the money supply until the latter has risen in proportion to the initial change in e—that is, until $\Delta M/M = \Delta e/e$. At this point, the original value of real balances is restored, and the system is back in equilibrium. A devaluation generates a temporary balance of payments surplus. This adds to reserves and increases the money supply until the system is back in equilibrium. Thus, in the monetary model exchange rate policy is really policy to manipulate reserves not the current account balance.

We can now use these properties of the model to describe a policy package for a country in an initial state of disequilibrium. The monetary model, being an equilibrium model, cannot rigorously describe what happens out of equilibrium but it is frequently used to prescribe policy in such cases.

Consider a country with an existing budget deficit, which is being monetized by the central bank, causing the money supply to increase. This generates a rise in domestic spending and inflation. The excess of absorption over domestic output yields a current account deficit, and downward pressure on real interest rates may also produce a capital outflow. Thus, the existing budget deficit generates both inflation and a payments deficit. What is the policy prescription loosely implied by the monetary model?

One draconian possibility would be to unwind the entire process. If we could go back to some initial date when the economy was in equilibrium, this alternative would require reversing to a budget surplus that would diminish the money supply, would reduce prices, and would restore the initial reserve position. This would be a policy of deflation that re-established equilibrium solely through budget and monetary policy, with no change in the exchange rate.

This policy prescription may seem too strong. This is probably because the user of the monetary model to describe long-run equilibrium also has in mind a short-run model with some stickiness in wages and prices and adjustment costs in rearranging production. An actual deflation could mean a protracted spell of unemployment. The economy, or more precisely the existing government, may not reach the long-run equilibrium toward which the policy is aimed.

A less draconian alternative would be to end the budget deficit, halting the growth in the domestic debt component of the money supply, and to devalue in order to "validate" the past increase in M. If we can estimate the parameters of the money demand function m, then for given values of P^*, r^*, and $\bar{y}$ we can estimate the percentage devaluation that would reduce real balances M/eP^* enough to restore equilibrium at the existing level of M. This would end excess absorption and validate the existing M as an equilibrium value.

This is the familiar policy package of balancing the budget to stop money growth and devaluing to end the loss in reserves. It avoids the need for actual deflation by validating the past money growth through devaluation. Preference for this policy over deflation already implies that the policymaker has some structural characteristic of the economy in mind that is not part of the monetary model.

A third alternative would provide a more gradual path to equilibrium. The budget deficit could be reduced to zero gradually. This would be accompanied by a jump devaluation to validate the existing money stock, and then further gradual devaluation at a decreasing rate to keep real balances in equilibrium as the budget deficit was reduced. An announced plan of this sort would be quite similar to the decelerating crawling peg attempts made by the "Southern Cone" countries of South America. These programs have run into a number of problems involving real appreciation of the currency, with devaluation ahead of inflation, as analyzed for example by Calvo (1981). Díaz-Alejandro (1981), Dornbusch (1980), and Krugman (1980). The explanatin for the difficulty in all these cases involves specification of structure of the economy beyond the simple monetary model.

Both alternatives to simple monetary contraction imply that at least one of the three simplifying assumptions of the monetary model does not hold, and the alternative assumptions generally require some specification of the structure of the economy. We now turn to questions of the structure of trade.

III. Trade Structure and Devaluation

Under the strong assumption of perfect goods substitution, devaluation influences the current account only through real balance effects on expenditure. To study relative price effects of devaluation, we need to assume at least two separate goods (or commodity bundles), one produced by the home country and the other by the rest of the world aggregate. This adds a channel of effect for exchange rate changes, while preserving the real balance/absorption channel of the monetary model.

In this section we will analyze in a partial equilibrium framework the effect of a devaluation on the trade balance. The framework is the familiar elasticity approach. This can be used to illustrate the impact effect on the trade balance from the change in relative prices caused by the devaluation, which leads to general equilibrium adjustments. The graphs that will be used to illustrate various cases were introduced by Haberler (1949) and were used to analyze the Smithsonian realignments of 1971 by

Branson (1972). The formal mathematics are presented in Appendix A of Branson and Katseli (1982).

We will characterize different "types" of trade structure in terms of special values for elasticities of demand or supply for exports, d_x and s_x, respectively, and imports, d_m and s_m. First we will begin with the traditional *small* country case, where d_x and s_m are infinite. The small country cannot influence world prices of its exports or imports. Then we will analyze the case of a *"semismall"* country, where s_m is infinite but d_x is not. The semismall country has "market power" on the export side; it cannot expand sales without reducing price. Most European countries may be in this category. A subcase of the semismall country is the "Keynesian small country," where all supply elasticities are infinite. This is the model of the usual statement of the Marshall-Lerner condition that $|d_x + d_m| > 1$ for a "successful" devaluation.

A third example is the *"rigid"* country, where s_x and d_m go to zero. This would be true for a developing country producing a supply inelastic agricultural export, using an intermediate import with fixed coefficients. A fourth case that combines aspects of the semismall and rigid countries would be the *"pure manufacturing"* economy that imports intermediate goods not produced at home and that exports manufactures. Here d_m may approach zero. Japan may be an example of this.

In each case we wish to examine the effect of a devaluation on the trade balance and on the terms of trade. Negative results for either may be a reason for a country to reject devaluation as a way to eliminate a trade deficit, or in general to reject the use of the exchange rate as a tool for stabilizing the current account.

Small Country

We begin with the small country, where devaluation improves the trade balance and leaves the terms of trade unchanged. This case serves to introduce the basic diagrams in Figure 1, Panel A. On the vertical axes are the home currency prices of exports and imports, P_x and P_m, relative to an overall index of domestic opportunity cost. Thus, the changes in exchange rates that are discussed below are changes in real exchange rates, as shown in Branson and Katseli (1982). Quantities are on the horizontal axes. The areas under the supply-demand intersections are the domestic currency values of exports and imports.

In the small country, the infinitely elastic demand curve for exports and supply curve for imports are shifted up by the proportion of the devaluation. This raises both P_x and P_m proportionately, leaving the terms of trade unchanged. This also increases export value but has an ambiguous effect on import value, depending on the elasticity of demand. It should be clear from the diagrams that the limiting case where the increase in import payments equals the increase in export receipts would be where the supply curve for exports and demand curve for imports are both vertical. This is the rigid country case, where we take up below.

In the small country, exchange rate changes stabilize the trade balance with no effect on the terms of trade. This is a clear example of structure that is consistent with the monetary model and with a policy that uses the exchange rate for external stabilization purposes.

Semismall Country

Next, consider the case of the country that is small on the import side, so that s_m is infinite, but not on the export side. This case is consistent with traditional trade theory, in which each country concentrates on production of goods along its lines of comparative advantage and exports these few goods, but imports the whole range of consumption. Each country might then be "large" in its export markets, but "small" in its import markets. A system of such countries has been called the "world supermarket" by de Melo, Dervis, and Robinson (1977). Each producer is large in selling to the world supermarket, but small when appearing as a consumer. Indices of market power on the export and import sides were computed in Branson and Katseli (1980), and their differences were quite significant. Many medium-sized European countries and developing countries producing agricultural output or minerals and having significant shares of the world markets for these might fit into the semismall country category.

The effects of devaluation on a semismall country are shown in Figure 1, Panel B. The diagrams are the same as in Panel A except for the export demand curve. It is evident that the terms of trade P_x/P_m deteriorate with a devaluation in this case. In general, fluctuations in the exchange rate will generate fluctuations in the terms of trade in the semismall country. The effect of this on real income and welfare was analyzed in Branson and Katseli (1980).

The same ambiguity in the effect of devaluation on import payments appears in Panels A and B, but the gain in export receipts is smaller in Panel B. In the semismall country case the full Marshall-Lerner conditions come into play. Insufficiently elastic demands can result in J-curve effects and lead to dynamic instability in the exchange markets.

A special subcase of the semismall country is the "Keynesian small country," in which the supply elasticity of exports is also infinite. (Jeffery Frankel reminded me of this terminology when the topic was discussed at the Institut Européen d'Administration des Affaires (INSEAD) in Fontainebleau in July 1982). The justification for this assumption would be that the export sector of the home country is small relative to the total economy so that resources can be moved into the sector at a constant opportunity cost. In this case the Marshall-Lerner conditions simplify to the traditional $|d_x + d_m| > 1$.

In the semismall country, exchange rate fluctuations cause fluctuations in the terms of trade and may cause J-curve effects. The latter can raise problems of dynamic stability in the foreign exchange markets, as discussed in Branson (1977) and Artus (1982). Thus, even with this seemingly minor modification of the structure to conform with the basic ideas from trade theory, the use of exchange rate changes for external stabilization can be open to question.

Rigid Country

Most analysis using small or semismall country assumptions also implicitly assumes that the traded goods are final goods that substitute in consumption and that they are also substitutes in production for home goods. Consumption substitution yields demand elasticity and production substitution yields supply elasticity. Since the oil price increase in 1973, attention has turned to cases where imports are intermediate goods that may not be produced or consumed at home. The role of intermediate imports is explored extensively in Katseli (1980). In addition, there may be only a small domestic market for some exportables, such as raw materials and minerals, and the elasticity of total supply of some exports may be low.

An illustration (in the extreme) of the difficulties these structures cause might be a (probably developing) country that produces an agriculturally based raw material with an inelastic output supply in the short run. It also uses an imported intermediate input with fixed coefficients in the short run. This makes elasticities of export supply and import demand zero.

Devaluation in the rigid country is shown in Panel C of Figure 1. The terms of trade are not affected since P_x and P_m rise by the same proportion as the devaluation, but for very different reasons than in the small country (compare Panels A and C). Import payments and export receipts both rise by the same proportion. The effect on the balance of trade depends on the initial balance. An initial deficit is magnified by the devaluation, a particularly perverse result. Most devaluations occur in an initial deficit position.

The perverse trade balance results also have macroeconomic implica-

A. Devaluation in a small country

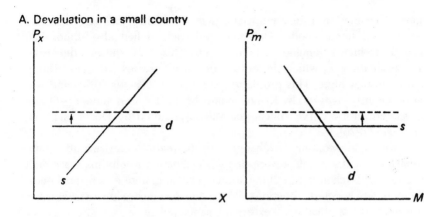

B. Devaluation in a semismall country

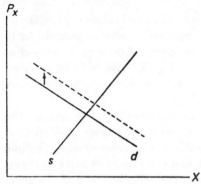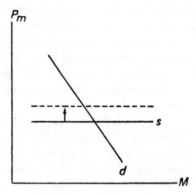

C. Devaluation in a rigid country

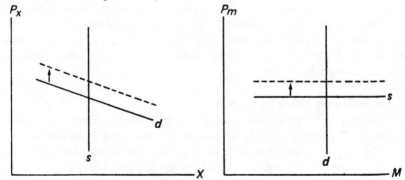

FIGURE 1. EFFECTS OF DEVALUATION

tions. Devaluation raises internal prices, reducing real balances and demand for home goods. The increased trade deficit also siphons off income, reducing demand for home goods. This can result in a deflationary devaluation, in which the devaluation itself creates a demand slump and unemployment. This problem was noted by Cooper (1971) and was more recently analyzed by Krugman and Taylor (1978). A similar problem associated with J-curve effects generally was noted by Dornbusch and Krugman (1976).

In the rigid economy, exchange rate fluctuations can magnify trade imbalances if the usual prescription of devaluation to eliminate a deficit is followed. Exchange rate fluctuations can also generate demand fluctuations in unexpected directions. This is an instance where structure is crucial for the application of external balance policy.

Pure Manufacturing Country

A final example, which is a variant on the rigid economy, is a country with imported intermediate inputs and manufacturing output. In this case export supply will have a positive slope, while import demand will be relatively inelastic. A case in point could be Japan, with 90 percent of its exports manufactured goods and 80 percent of its imports intermediate inputs.

Devaluation in this case can be analyzed with one or two modifications of Panel C in Figure 1. The effect of giving the export supply curve a positive slope is to reduce the increase in P_x; the effect of export earnings depends on the elasticity of demand. If it is inelastic, export earnings fall relative to the rigid economy case, and the effect on the trade balance is even more perverse. Thus, devaluation in this case could worsen the trade balance and cause the terms of trade to deteriorate.

Even more bizarre would be the result if intermediate inputs were tied to final output by fixed coefficients. Then the import demand curve could be positively sloped. As exports rise, intermediate imports rise. This could add to the perversity of the trade balance results while reducing the terms of trade effects.

Conclusion on Trade Structure

Traditional elasticity analyses of the effects of exchange rate changes on trade have generally implicitly assumed high supply elasticities and focused on small or semismall country cases, including the Keynesian small country. When I studied effects of the Smithsonian realignments in this framework (Branson, 1972), there was almost no literature on supply elasticities. Since the early 1970s, the problems introduced, especially by imported intermediate goods, have been recognized in the literature, and supply problems have come to the fore.

The literature on the monetary model is generally silent on elasticity conditions, which are usually presented as an alternative to the elasticity approach. The application of these conditions at the policy level, however, frequently assumes implicitly that the structure of trade meets the elasticity requirements. Their extension to the asset market approach to flexible exchange rates makes elasticity conditions important for the dynamic adjustment paths. Thus, empirical questions of trade structure have surfaced as important in the evaluation of exchange rate policy independently of the analytical approach or the degree of flexibility of the exchange rate under analysis.

IV. Wage Rigidity and Policy Interdependence

In this section the effects of sluggish adjustment, or stickiness, of wages and prices on policy interdependence are analyzed. The role of the exchange rate in the transmission of policy effects between countries will be especially focused on.

The monetary model of Section II assumes that flexible wages and prices set output equal to its full employment value. However, the idea that a nominal price or wage might be slow in adjusting to disturbances, policy or otherwise, has long been a part of the literature on output fluctuations. For example, the textbook "Keynesian" model focused on a sticky nominal wage. In the past decade there has been a resurgence of research on nominal wage stickiness as a source of real output fluctuations in the United States. Fischer (1977) and Taylor (1979) present models of multiperiod nominal wage contracts in a framework of rational expectations; the literature is surveyed by Gordon (1981).

In Europe there has been a "neo-Keynesian" development that has studied adjustment of the domestic economy to a temporary equilibrium with rigid wages and prices. While this literature is highly technical, good expositions are provided by Malinvaud (1977) and Muellbauer and Portes (1979). These approaches all share the assumption that *some* nominal price is rigid, and this rigidity results in output fluctuations.

The role of stickiness of nominal or real wages in international adjustment has been studied by Sachs (1980, 1981) and Branson and Rotemberg (1980), among others. They observed that while sticky nominal wages might be an appropriate model for the United States, a more appropriate model for many European countries would be sticky real wages. Japan might be an intermediate case. The nature of the international transmission and adjustment processes then depends crucially on which countries have which rigidities and on where the disturbances originate.

All this is bound to have implications for the use of the exchange rate as an instrument for achieving external balance, depending on the location of rigidities and degrees of indexation. These implications have been worked out in recent papers by Flood and Marion (1982) and Marston (1982). The analysis below will use Marston's graphic framework extensively.

Three aspects of recent research in this area provide excellent examples of the importance of the interaction of wage rigidity and economic structure for policy interdependence. The first is transmission with different kinds of wage rigidities. This can be seen most clearly in a one-commodity model. The second is the role of terms of trade effects in shifting aggregate supply; to study this we need at least two commodities. The third aspect is the pervasive importance of wage indexation, which can be seen by adding a nontraded good to the study. Each of these aspects will be analyzed in turn.

Transmission With Wage Rigidities

Rather than proceed with an exhaustive taxonomy, let us make the point with a single case. The problem is analyzed in detail in Branson and Rotemberg (1980). Suppose we have two countries, notionally named the United States and Europe. Nominal wages are sticky in the United States and real wages are sticky in Europe, both above their equilibrium levels. In Malinvaud's terms, unemployment in the United States is "Keynesian," and in Europe it is "classical." To make the particular point in the simplest way, let us assume both areas produce and trade the same composite commodity.

In this case, the aggregate supply curve in Europe is vertical at the level of output where the marginal product of labor equals the real wage, but in the United States it has a positive slope. These are shown in Figure 2, where P and y are, respectively, the U.S. gross domestic product (GDP) deflators and real U.S. GDP in dollars, and P^*, y^* are, respectively, the European GDP deflator and real European GDP in European currency units (ECUs). The aggregate demand curves have the usual downward slopes, and for convenience we index the \$/ECU exchange rate at unity so that $P_o = P_o^*$.

The solid lines in Figure 2 (a) and (b) show an initial equilibrium, where supply equals demand, in both diagrams, so that both current accounts are balanced. The initial price level is given by $P_o(=P_o^*)$, and outputs are given by y_o, y_o^*.

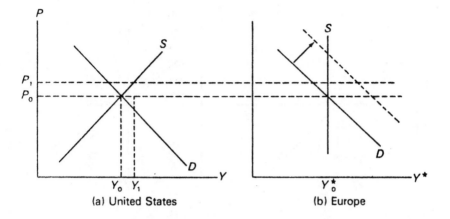

FIGURE 2. DEMAND EXPANSION IN EUROPE

Consider now a policy-induced demand expansion in Europe with the exchange rate held constant. This shifts the European demand curve to the dashed line, and raises world demand. Prices rise to $P_1(=P_1^*)$, where the United States has a current account surplus, given by its excess of supply over demand, equal to Europe's deficit. The outcome of this policy shift is a rise in prices in both areas, an increase in output and reduction in unemployment only in the United States, and a shift in the current account toward surplus in the United States and deficit in Europe.

The gain in output goes to the area with the sticky nominal wage, while the area with the sticky real wage gets inflation and a "deterioration" of the current account. It is, therefore, not surprising that the United States supported the "locomotive" approach in 1977 and Europe rejected it.

As a second policy experiment consider an appreciation of the U.S. dollar relative to the ECU. To keep the example clear we will assume this is achieved by tightening U.S. monetary policy and easing U.S. fiscal policy, which would have a neutral effect on U.S. demand in the absence of appreciation.

The results of appreciation are shown in Figure 3. Demand shifts from the United States to Europe, and prices in Europe rise relative to those in the United States. The final equilibrium shows a deficit in the United States (demand exceeds supply at P_1) equal to the surplus in Europe at P_1^*, where $P_1 = eP_1^*$ at the new exchange rate.

In the one-commodity model, an appreciation of the U.S. dollar with a demand-neutral tightening of monetary policy raises prices in Europe relative to the United States, reduces output in the United States where

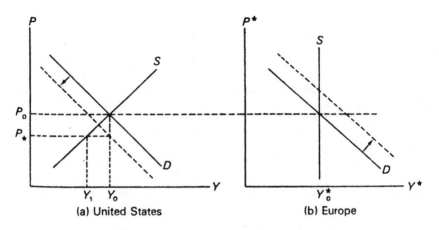

(a) United States   (b) Europe

FIGURE 3. APPRECIATION IN UNITED STATES

the nominal wage is sticky, and shifts the current account toward deficit in the United States and surplus in Europe. Except for the constancy of European output at y_o^*, this is a fairly accurate description of recent economic developments in the two areas. Movement in European output can be explained by going to a two-commodity model with terms of trade effects.

Terms of Trade Effects on Supply

Consider a more realistic case in which the United States and Europe produce different composite commodities. Then a change in the exchange rate will alter the relative price of the two commodities. Here the difference between the price that is relevant for producer decisions and the price index that defines the real wage becomes important. This point is also discussed at length in Branson and Rotemberg (1980).

In each area the producers equate the marginal product of labor to the product wage W/P^i, where P^i is the price of the output of the area. On the other hand, in our example, workers in Europe are interested in the real wage W/I, where I is a consumer price index (CPI) defined across areas' products

$$I = \alpha P^* + (1 - \alpha)\frac{P}{e} \tag{10}$$

Here α is the weight of European goods in the European CPI, and P/e is the European price of U.S. goods. We now are using P and P^* to denote the domestic currency prices of the U.S. good and the European good, respectively.

An appreciation of the U.S. dollar relative to the ECU, by reducing e, raises the European CPI defined in equation (10). With a sticky real wage W/I, the nominal wage W rises along with I. This raises the product wage W/P^* facing European employers, who react by reducing employment. The result of the dollar appreciation is a reduction in employment and output in Europe because of the terms of trade effect. This effect can be introduced into Figure 2(b), if we reinterpret P^* as the price of European output. The negative terms of trade effect shifts the vertical European supply curve to the left. This reduced European output y^* and further increases the price level P^*. Thus, the result of the U.S. appreciation in this more realistic model is stagflation in Europe—output falls, and unemployment and prices (or the rate of inflation) rise.

A structure with nominal wage stickiness in the United States and real wage stickiness in Europe is consistent both with policy differences in the 1970s and the effects of the shift in the United States toward fiscal ease and monetary tightness in 1981–82. Tentative econometric evidence has been presented by Sachs (1981), Branson and Rotemberg (1980), and Grubb, Jackman, and Layard (1982) that supports this pattern of wage stickiness. On the other hand, the quick adjustment of the real wages in the Federal Republic of Germany to the 1979–80 oil price shock, summarized in my discussion of de Menil and Westphal (Branson, 1982), suggests that real wage resistance may be dissipating in the Federal Republic of Germany. The German model of Artus (1982) assumes nominal rather than real wage stickiness in the German economy.

The basic point that comes out in the examples is that the pattern of structural differences in wage behavior across countries is important for the transmission of policy effects.

Wage Indexation and Nontraded Goods

Wage indexation can provide a channel through which exchange rate changes pass quickly into prices of nontraded goods and thus escalate the entire domestic price level. In this case, changes in nominal exchange rates have no effects on real rates or relative prices, and we are back with the monetary model that relies solely on real balance effects. This is a generally well-known point, so a simple example should suffice to establish it.

Consider a small country that produces and consumes traded and nontraded goods. The nominal wage is indexed to the CPI, and the price of nontraded goods P_N assuming constant productivity equals the wage rate plus a markup. Then we have the following structure of wage and price movements.

The change in the home currency price of traded goods is the sum of movements in the exchange rate and the world price of traded goods

$$\hat{P}_T = \hat{e} + \hat{P}* \tag{11}$$

Here $\hat{P}_T$ is the domestic currency price of traded goods, and $P*$ is the world foreign currency price. A circumflex over a variable denotes percentage rate of change—for example, $\hat{e} = \Delta e/e$.

The price of nontraded goods follows the wage rate

$$\hat{P}_N = \hat{W} \tag{12}$$

The movement in the consumer price index is given by a weighted average of home currency P_T and P_N

$$\hat{I} = \alpha\hat{P}_T + (1 - \alpha)\,\hat{P}_N \tag{13}$$

and wages are indexed to I

$$\hat{W} = \hat{I} \tag{14}$$

The combination of wage indexation in equation (14) and mark-up for prices of nontraded goods in equation (12) makes P_N follow the index I

$$\hat{P}_N = \hat{I}$$

If we substitute this into equation (13) for $\hat{P}_N$, and equation (11) into (13) for $\hat{P}_T$, we obtain

$$\hat{I} = \alpha(\hat{e} + \hat{P}*) + (1 - \alpha)\,\hat{I}$$

Solving I gives us the basic result

$$\hat{I} = \hat{e} + \hat{P}*$$

As $\hat{P}_N = \hat{I}$, $\hat{P}_N$ also equals $\hat{e} + \hat{P}*$

The combination of wage indexation and markup pricing of the non-traded good passes exchange rate changes right through into wages, prices of nontraded goods, and the entire CPI. In this example of a fully indexed economy, exchange rate changes have no effects on relative prices. Thus, any effect on equilibrium output would have to come through real balance effects, which could be achieved direct through monetary policy. In a fully indexed economy, exchange rate fluctuations serve more to destabilize prices than to stabilize the trade balance.

Conclusion on Wage Behavior

The structure of labor markets and wage behavior are important in determining the pattern of international transmission of the effects of policy shifts in any one country. In general, countries or areas with relatively sticky nominal wages will experience larger output responses and smaller price responses to demand disturbances than will areas with relatively sticky real wages. Terms of trade effects from an exchange rate change yield output effects even when real wages are sticky by shifting aggregate supply. However, in a fully indexed economy, all prices move with the exchange rate.

These results suggest a pattern of differences in adjustment to exchange rate changes between Europe and the United States. Suppose we think of the latter as having relatively sticky nominal wages and relatively less indexation than Europe. Then an exchange rate change will move relative prices and the balance on current account in the United States, and also influence output, all in the expected "stabilizing" direction. In Europe, however, the movement in the exchange rate will mainly move the overall price level, with minimal effects on the trade balance or output. So the exchange rate is reasonably viewed as an effective instrument for stabilizing the current account in the United States. In Europe, however, exchange rate fluctuations are equally reasonably viewed as essentially destabilizing the price level. The result is policy conflict based on different implicit assumptions about the underlying structure of labor markets and wage behavior.

V. Financial Markets and Exchange Rate Stability

In Section II, we presented the fixed exchange rate version of the monetary model as the initial framework for the analysis of effects of exchange rate changes in Sections III and IV. In this section we turn to the structure of financial markets and the stability of floating exchange rates.

The monetary model can be easily converted into a model of exchange rate determination. Let us retain the strong initial assumptions of the monetary model that (a) goods are perfect substitutes so $P = P^*$, (b) wages and prices are flexible so $y = \bar{y}$, and (c) assets are perfect substitutes so $r = r^*$. The last assumption, combined with floating exchange rates, implies static expectations. The usual statement of perfect asset substitutability with a floating exchange rate is $r = r^* + \bar{e}$, where $\bar{e}$ is the expected percentage change in the exchange rate. One robust empirical finding from the 1970s is that spot exchange rates roughly follow random walks. Examples of these results can be found in Branson (1982) or Frenkel (1981). As a result, the best single predictor of the future spot rate is the present spot rate. This is shown, for example, in

Bilson (1981). Thus, static expectations are a reasonable rule of thumb and we can retain the simplifying $r = r^*$ assumption.

The monetary model of Section II can be written as

$$M = eP^*m(r^*, \overline{y}) \tag{16}$$

If M is fixed as well as P^*, r^*, and $\overline{y}$, this money market equilibrium condition determines a value for the exchange rate

$$e = M/[P^* \cdot m(r^*, \overline{y})] \tag{17}$$

This is the equilibrium value of the exchange rate that clears the money market. With the assumption that assets are perfect substitutes, equation (17) is a monetary model of exchange rate determination. This serves as a useful starting point for the discussion in this section of the role of financial market structure.

The monetary model provides an interesting way to analyze the monetary policy problems of Section IV. Suppose we interpret the "home" country as Europe, so the asterisk variables are the United States. A tightening of U.S. monetary policy raises r^*. This reduces the demand for real balances in Europe, $M(r^*, \overline{y})$. To keep this excess supply of money from raising e (i.e., depreciating the ECU against the dollar), European M would have to shrink proportionately. Holding the exchange rate constant in the face of tightening monetary policy in the United States would keep the demand curve from shifting upward in Figure 3(b).

The monetary model has strong implications for the relationship between price stability and monetary stability in an open economy. These are shown in the first subsection below. Then we explore the implications of imperfect asset substitutability for monetary and exchange rate policy. Finally, we end with a brief discussion of the effect financial market structure has on the choice between floating and pegging the currency.

Monetary Versus Price Stability

Consider the problem facing the monetary authority that wishes to stabilize the domestic price level in an open economy described by the monetary model. Since $P = eP^*$, stabilizing P when P^*, the world price level, is fluctuating requires offsetting fluctuations in e. As world prices rise, e must fall, that is, the domestic currency must *appreciate*, to prevent importation of the world inflation. As P^* falls, the currency must depreciate.

How are these movements in the exchange rate to be achieved? From equation (17) we have

$$P = eP^* = M/m(r^*, \overline{y}) \tag{18}$$

Exogenous fluctuations in world interest rates (or full employment output) will move the demand for real balances $m(r^*, \bar{y})$. If fluctuations in the nominal domestic money supply meet these fluctuations in demand, the product $eP^* = P$ will be stabilized. In equation (17), the sole source of fluctuations in the excess demand for money will then be movements in P^*, and these will cause offsetting changes in e, stabilizing P.

An immediate implication of the monetary model with a floating exchange rate is that to maintain domestic price stability the domestic money supply should adjust to meet fluctuations in demand for real balances as world interest rates fluctuate. This would be consistent with a constant money supply, or with a steady growth rate of the money supply equal to $\bar{y}$, only if the international financial environment is stable.

Asset Substitutability and Monetary Policy

With $r = r^*$ (and static expectations) changes in the domestic money supply cause the exchange rate to change, as indicated in equation (17), regardless of how these changes are achieved. It makes no difference whether the central bank trades in assets denominated in domestic currency via open market operations, or assets denominated in foreign currency via foreign exchange market intervention; the two are perfect substitutes by assumption. The thing that matters is what happens to the money supply.

However, if home and foreign assets are not perfect substitutes, so that $r \neq r^*$, then it is important whether changes in the money supply are induced by open market operations or by intervention in the foreign exchange markets. Consider a given reduction in the money supply, ΔM. If this is achieved by selling domestic government debt, the interest rate will rise more, and the exchange rate will fall less, than it would if the same ΔM were achieved by selling foreign exchange reserves. This is shown formally in Branson (1977); Henderson (1982) and Obstfeld (1982) provide more up-to-date expositions, complete with rational expectations. The less substitutable the assets the more pronounced these differences will be, as is shown in Katseli and Marion (1982).

These differences could be important if the objective of the monetary restaint is to slow an existing inflation. As we saw in Section III, a reduction in e can have a direct influence on domestic prices, even with imperfect goods substitution and nontraded goods. Thus, a monetary tightening that has a maximum effect on the exchange rate will yield a direct effect on domestic prices. This could have an important influence on inflationary expectations.

The extent of imperfect asset substitution and the implied degree of freedom to conduct monetary policy are as yet unclear empirically. One line of research emphasizing calculation of optimal portfolios indicates a wide range of substitutability, and even complementarities. An example is de Macedo (1981). On the other hand, researchers looking for systematic variation of "risk premiums," or interest rate differentials as asset supplies change, lean toward the perfect substitutes result. A good example is Frankel (1982). Thus, no general empirical result on asset substitutability is yet available. Given the rapid change in structure of international financial markets in the last decade, obtaining clear empirical results may remain difficult for some time.

Financial Stability and Choice of Exchange Rate Regime

In the short run, the value of a floating exchange rate is determined by equilibrium conditions in asset markets. In the monetary model, only the money market matters; in general, the exchange rate is part of the process of general achieving equilibrium in financial markets. Thus, we should expect a floating exchange rate to exhibit the fluctuations typical of stock prices rather than goods prices, as shown by Frenkel (1981). And the short-run stability of the exchange market depends on overall stability of the financial sector, as shown in Branson (1977). The Marshall-Lerner condition must be met if there is to be dynamic stability of the feedback process from the exchange rate to the current account, but in the short run it is financial stability that matters.

This implies that free floating is feasible only for countries with financial markets that are thick enough and sufficiently well-integrated into international financial markets to convince monetary authorities that private speculation will generally be stabilizing. The argument is given in detail in Branson and Katseli (1981). In this case a floating rate can be expected to be stable, and it is possible to leave exchange rate determination to the market.

If floating is not feasible, the central bank has to "make" the market in foreign exchange. This means it has to set a price, and the problem of exchange rate policy becomes one of how to determine the equilibrium price and adjustment toward it. One of the interesting developments of the 1970s was the alignment of countries into groups of "feasible floaters" with financial stability—mainly the industrial countries—and "peggers" with exchange rates fixed against one of the major currencies or an average of several of them.

Why might floating not be feasible for any single country? Stable floating requires the existence of a number of agents in the private sector who hold the home currency as part of a portfolio diversified across currencies and who will shift out of the currency when the exchange rate rises above its expected long-run level and into the currency when the exchange rate falls below that level. Agents may hold the currency either for transactions balances or for portfolio diversification. For many countries, the trade denominated in domestic currency is so limited that there is no external transactions demand for that currency. Some small countries, such as Singapore or Switzerland, have created portfolio demand for their currencies by giving them attractive stability or covariance properties. But portfolio diversification into many currencies is minimized, either by political risk that foreign claims on home country institutions denominated in home currency may not be honored, or by capital controls that make up part of a system of financial repression that rules out capital mobility and floating.

Thus, due to underdevelopment of the local financial market structure, floating may not be a feasible option for many central banks. This had led to the advent of more or less floating currencies and blocs such as the European Monetary System, at the center of the international financial system, while countries on the periphery are pegging in many instances.

Conclusion on Financial Structure

The assumptions of free capital movement and perfect substitution are perhaps the most powerful and widely used combination in international finance. They permit the analyst to peg domestic interest rates to the world market level and to proceed with an analysis that essentially ignores the structure of financial markets. For some questions, this is the efficient way to proceed. For others—such as the choice of market for monetary policy intervention, or the decision whether to float or peg—consideration of aspects of structure in financial markets is essential. The choices that governments have made in these areas since the early 1970s attest to the governments' views that even financial market structure is important for macroeconomic policy decisions.

The short-run determination of floating exchange rates by financial market equilibrium conditions has put financial structure in the center of analyses of policy interdependence and the choice of exchange rate regimes. Sir Arthur Lewis characterized the results in his Per Jacobssen lecture at the International Monetary Fund in 1977:

> It is now the conventional wisdom that the currencies of the developed countries should float, but the currencies of the less developed countries (LDCs) should not; that is to say that each LDC should choose a more developed country (MDC) as a partner—or the SDR—and tie itself in a fixed relationship. [2]

Notes

1. Character in U.S. cartoon by Al Capp.
2. "The Less Developed Countries and Stable Exchange Rates," in *The International Monetary System in Operation* (Washington, 1977), p. 33.

References

Artus, Jacques, "Effects of U.S. Monetary Restraint on the Deutsche-Mark/Dollar Rate and the German Economy," paper presented at the National Bureau of Economic Research Conference on Exchange Rate Theory and Policy (Bellagio, 1982).

Bilson, J., "The 'Speculative Efficiency' Hypothesis," *Journal of Business*, Vol. 54 (July 1981), pp. 435–51.

Branson, William H. "The Trade Effects of the 1971 Currency Realignments," *Brookings Papers on Economic Activity*, No. 1 (1972), pp. 15–69.

———, 1977, "Asset Markets and Relative Prices in Exchange-Rate Determination," *Sozialwissenschaftliche Annalen*, Vol. 1, pp. 69–89. Reprints in International Finance No. 20 (Princeton, June 1980).

———, 1982, "Exchange Rate Policy After a Decade of Floating," paper presented at the National Bureau of Economic Research Conference on Exchange Rate Theory and Policy (Bellagio).

———, and W. H. Buiter, 1982 "Monetary and Fiscal Policy with Flexible Exchange Rates," scheduled to be published in 1982 in J. Bhandari and B. Putnam, eds., *The International Transmission of Economic Disturbances* (Massachusetts).

Branson, William H. and Lauka T. Katseli-Papaefstratiou, 1980, "Income Stability, Terms of Trade, and The Choice of Exchange-Rate Regime," *Journal of Development Economics*, Vol. 7, pp. 49–69.

———, 1981, "Exchange-Rate Policy for Developing Countries," in S. Grassman and E. Lundberg, eds., *The World Economic Order: Past and Prospects* (London), pp. 391–419.

———, 1982, "Currency Baskets and Real Effective Exchange Rates," in Carlos Díaz-Alejandro, Mark Gersovitz, Gustav Ranis, and Mark R. Rosenzweig, eds., *The Theory and Experience of Economic Development, Essays in Honor of Sir W. Arthur Lewis* (London), pp. 194–214.

Branson, William H. and J. J. Rotemberg, 1980, "International Adjustment with Wage Rigidity," *European Economic Review*, Vol. 13, pp. 309–32.

Calvo, G. A., "Trying to Stabilize: Some Theoretical Reflections based on the Case of Argentina" (unpublished manuscript, Columbia University, February 1981).

Cooper, R. N., "Currency Devaluation in Developing Countries," Princeton Essays in International Finance, No. 86 (Princeton, June 1971).

de Macedo, J. B. "Portfolio Diversification Across Currencies," in R. N. Cooper, P. B. Kenen, J. B. de Macedo, J. Van Ypersele, eds., *The International Monetary System Under Flexible Exchange Rates: Global, Regional and National* (Cambridge, 1981), pp. 69–100.

de Melo, Jaime, Kemal Dervis, and Sherman Robinson, "A Global Model of North-South Trade and Growth," Research Program in Development, Discussion Paper No. 73 (Princeton, May 1977).

de Ménil, Georges and Uwe Westphal, 1982, "The Transmission of International Disturbances: A French-German Diometric Analysis, 1972–1982," *European Economic Review*, Vol. 18 (May/June), pp. 41–73.

Díaz-Alejandro, Carlos, "Southern Cone Stabilization Plans," in W. R. K. Cline, S. Weintraub, eds., *Economic Stabilization in Developing Countries*, (Washington, 1981).

Dornbusch, Rudiger, 1980, "Monetary Stabilization, Intervention and Real Appreciation," Ch. 12 in *Open Economy Macroeconomics* (New York), pp. 215–35.

————, and P. Krugman, 1976, "Flexible Exchange Rates in the Short Run," *Brookings Papers on Economic Activity: 3*, pp. 537–75.

Fischer, S., "Long-Term Contracts, Rational Expectations, and the Optimal Money Supply," *Journal of Political Economy*, Vol. 85 (February 1977), pp. 191–205.

Flood, R. P., and N. Marion, 1982, "The Transmission of Disturbances Under Alternative Exchange-Rate Regimes with Optimal Indexing," *Quarterly Journal of Economics*, February, Vol. 96, No. 1, pp. 43–66.

Frankel, Jeffrey, "On the Mark, Pound, Franc, Yen and Canadian Dollar," paper presented at the National Bureau of Economic Research Conference on Exchange Rate Theory and Policy (Bellagio, 1982).

Frenkel, Jacob A., "Flexible Exchange Rates, Prices, and the Role of 'News': Lessons from the 1970s," *Journal of Political Economy*, Vol. 89 (August 1981), pp. 665–705.

Gordon, R. J., "Output Fluctuations and Gradual Price Adjustment," *Journal of Economic Literature*, Vol. 19 (June 1981), pp. 493–530.

Grubb, D., R. Jackman, and R. Layard, "Wage Rigidity and Unemployment in OECD Countries," Centre for Labour Economics, London School of Economics, Discussion Paper No. 135 (July 1982), presented at The International Seminar in Macroeconomics, Mannheim, June 20–22.

Haberler, G., "The Market for Foreign Exchange and the Stability of the Balance of Payments: A Theoretical Analysis," *Kyklos*, Vol. 3 (1949), pp. 193–218.

Reprinted in R. N. Cooper, ed., *International Finance* (Middlesex, 1971), pp. 107–34.

Henderson, D., "What Role for Intervention Policy," paper presented at the National Bureau of Economic Research Conference on Exchange Rate Theory and Policy (Bellagio, 1982).

International Monetary Fund, *The Monetary Approach to the Balance of Payments: A Collection of Research Papers by Members of the Staff of the International Monetary Fund* (Washington, 1977).

Johnson, H. G., *Inflation and the Monetarist Controversy*, Ch. 3 (Amsterdam, 1972), pp. 75–108.

Katseli-Papaefstratiou, Louka T., 1980, "Transmission of External Price Disturbances and the Composition of Trade," *Journal of International Economics*, Vol. 10 (August), pp. 357–75.

———, and N. P. Marion, 1982, "Adjustment to Variations in Prices of Imported Inputs: The Role of Economic Structure," *Weltwirtschaftliches Archiv*.

Khan, Mohsin S., and Malcolm D. Knight, "Stabilization Programs in Developing Countries: A Formal Framework," *Staff Papers*, Vol. 28 (March 1981), pp. 1–53.

Krugman, P., 1980, "The Capital Inflows Problem in Less Developed Countries" (unpublished manuscript, Massachusetts Institute of Technology, February).

———, and L. Taylor, 1978, "Contractionary Effects of Devaluation," *Journal of International Economics*, Vol. 8 (August), pp. 445–56.

Lewis, W. A., "The Less Developed Countries and Stable Exchange Rates," in *The International Monetary System in Operation* (Washington, 1977).

Malinvaud, E., *The Theory of Unemployment Reconsidered* (London, 1977).

Marston, R. C., "Wages, Relative Prices and the Choice Between Fixed and Flexible Exchange Rates," *Canadian Journal of Economics*, Vol. 15 (February 1982), pp. 87–103.

Muellbauer, J., and R. Portes, "Macroeconomics When Markets Do Not Clear," in W. H. Branson, *Macroeconomic Theory and Policy*, 2nd ed., (New York, 1979).

Obstfeld, M., "Can We Sterilize? Theory and Evidence," National Bureau of Economic Research Working Paper, No. 833 (January 1982).

Sachs, J. D., 1980, "Wages, Flexible Exchange Rates, and Macroeconomic Policy," *Quarterly Journal of Economics*, Vol. 94 (June), pp. 731–47.

———, 1981, "The Current Account and Macroeconomic Adjustment in the 1970s," *Brookings Papers on Economic Activity: 1*, pp. 201–68.

Taylor, J. P., "Staggered Wage Setting in a Macro Model," *American Economic Review*, Vol. 69 (May 1979), pp. 108–18.

15

EXCHANGE RATES AND THE ADJUSTMENT PROCESS

J. de Larosière

The subject I treat in this chapter is a very broad one—exchange rates and the adjustment process—and I intend to treat it broadly, offering a series of practical reflections emerging from the experience of the last half dozen years. If one is going to discuss it in terms of broad generalizations, it is useful to have an image in mind of the system being described and how it works. What is the right image of the exchange rate system we have had for the last six years? On the one hand, more than three quarters of the members of the Fund have rates that are wholly or partially pegged to another currency or to a basket of currencies. On the other hand, about three quarters of all trade, including all or a major part of the trade of every industrial country, is carried out across floating rates. While many of those rates have been heavily managed in recent years, there has been no lack of movement. Thus, we have had a system which can justly be categorized as predominantly a flexible rate system.

How then was a flexible rate system supposed to work? There clearly was no general agreement on this subject or much of the controversy over the choice of an exchange rate regime would not have taken place. Nevertheless, a widely held view on the floating system saw flexible rates as providing countries with the freedom to pursue domestic objectives without the constraint imposed by balance of payments considerations, or more broadly without the need to be directly and closely concerned with the behavior and policies of other countries. Indeed, many of the opponents of flexible rates shared this view and feared that exchange rate flexibility would diminish the external discipline on domestic management and lead to a fragmenting of the world economy.

I shall develop three themes: (1) that flexible rates do not insulate economies in an open world; (2) that they do not lessen the need for basic policy adjustments; and (3) that they do not diminish the need for cooperation and active international surveillance.

Flexible Rates Do Not Insulate Economies in an Open World

It is a matter of observation that, in today's world, a high degree of economic interdependence continues in spite of widespread floating. To some extent this is because the floating is not "clean": central bank intervention results in the transmission of monetary flows from one economy to another. This is an important and growing practice which I shall consider shortly in its own right. But even in the absence of intervention there are three fundamental reasons why flexible rates cannot fully insulate a domestic economy from external influences.

The first reason is that real activity in an economy will react to exchange rate changes only to the extent that relative costs adjust, and after the time lag that it takes for demand to respond to changes in these relative costs. It has long been recognized, of course, that exchange rate changes can only be effective if they lead to shifts in the costs of producing goods in one country as compared with others. To the extent, however, that devaluations set off movements in wages and prices that lead to offsetting increases in costs, while appreciations act in the direction of reducing costs, the effects of exchange rate changes can be limited in both time and amount. In a large number of cases changes in nominal rates have been offset by inflation differentials, and thus real exchange movements have often been small. The risk of such feedback is increased by the fact that, for many goods and services, trade volume only responds to relative cost changes over a fairly extended period. This varies from one country to another, from one time to another, and from one type of product to another. Nevertheless, for most devaluing or appreciating currencies it is generally a year or more before a noticeable change occurs in the country's real balance of trade, and a substantial additional period may be required to realize something approaching the full result of the change in the exchange rate. If during this period the relative cost improvement in devaluing countries is eroded by domestic inflation, while the relative cost deterioration in appreciating countries is dampened by reduced rates of inflation, then the full effects of the exchange rate changes will not come through and the need for adjustment will remain. Adoption of a realistic exchange rate is thus a necessary but not a sufficient condition for adjustment of a country's external accounts.

The second reason why flexible exchange rates cannot entirely insulate economies lies in the high level of external trade in relation to domestic production in many countries. Exchange rate changes cannot, especially given the lags I have mentioned, prevent the level of economic activity in one country from being affected directly by the demand for its products in its principal trading partners. In this important respect, therefore, the flexible rate system has a good deal of similarity to a pegged rate system, and those responsible for economic policy need to continue to take a close interest in economic developments in other countries.

The third aspect of interdependence which is important concerns those countries whose currencies are widely used for international trade and held by other countries in their international reserves. The domestic monetary policies of these major countries are naturally reflected in the external value of their currencies, and if these policies result in sharp fluctuations or in widespread shifts in confidence then the functioning of the world's markets and the economies of other countries are invariably and directly affected.

These, then, are three reasons for the continuing interdependence of national economies even under a regime of freely floating rates. Let me now turn to examine the type of exchange rate fluctuations we have seen in practice over the last few years, the factors that have led to the widespread adoption of "managed" floating, and the reasons why these developments in my view do not diminish the need for prompt adjustment of general economic policies compared with the position under the previous par value system.

Flexible Exchange Rates Do Not Lessen the Need for Basic Policy Adjustments

During the later years of the par value system, when balance of payments crises were receiving a good deal of attention, there were those who held that the introduction of flexible rates would banish stories about international payments and exchange rates to the back pages of the newspapers. Unfortunately, this has not turned out to be the case, and in recent years developments in exchange markets have often provided the lead stories for the media throughout the world.

Looked at retrospectively, three kinds of exchange rate changes can be identified in the recent experience: first, very short-term fluctuations of the day-to-day, month-to-month variety; second, intermediate-term fluctuations in which a change in one direction of six months to a year is subsequently reversed; and third, long-term structural changes in the pattern of rates.

It has long been held that the authorities should do what they can to smooth out very short-term fluctuations, although on occasion they may have to vary their intervention tactics to avoid being made a target by the market. There is similarly wide agreement that little can be usefully done by intervention alone to resist long-term structural rate changes.

It is, however, in the area of intermediate-term fluctuations that the test of principles becomes clearest, and here there have recently been substantial developments. Following the events of last year all countries are prepared to take a view on whether a movement in the value of their currencies is appropriate, and are prepared to use intervention and other policies to resist a potential intermediate-term change which they regard as undesirable. This is an important change in attitude, and when the commitment to the management of exchange rates reaches this level the distinction between a flexible rate system and an adjustable peg system has narrowed substantially.

The chief reasons for this adoption of "managed" floating are perhaps as follows. First, it has been accepted that exchange rates alone could not take the full strain of the severe external shocks to which economies have been subjected during the last few years. Second, governments have come to recognize that, because of the factors I described earlier, exchange rate movements cannot by themselves, or in the very short term, bring about adjustment between economies. This in itself implies that, while the management of exchange rates can make a contribution to stability, adjustment policies must go beyond intervention in exchange markets and also embrace general economic policies to tackle inflationary disorders directly. It is in the underlying economic conditions and policies that the key to exchange stability is to be found.

The recognition that changes in nominal exchange rates are an important, but not by themselves sufficient, policy tool has encouraged a search for alternatives to a system of flexible rates which would aim to coordinate intervention policies and also general policies of economic adjustment. The decision to establish the European Monetary System is an indication of a willingness to place more emphasis on the adjustment of other policies as well as exchange market intervention. It is clearly of vital importance that these other policies are in fact adjusted. Past experience with the par value system indicates that, if rates of inflation differ substantially among member countries, there is a need both to adjust exchange rates promptly and to make changes to general economic policies which prevent excessively frequent one-way movements. Similarly, exchange rate zones can make a contribution to the stability of markets, but their success depends on the timely adjustment of rates and on a readiness to adopt appropriately coordinated internal policies.

The Use of Flexible Rates Does Not Diminish the Need for Cooperation and Active International Surveillance

While the question of exchange rate arrangements is one that will continue to be followed closely in the Fund, this is an issue that the amended Articles of the Fund leave explicitly in the hands of individual members. It is clear, however, that while members are free to choose an exchange rate arrangement, the level of their exchange rates is a matter of mutual concern. Indeed, if an exchange rate is so high that it prevents "effective balance of payments adjustment" or so low that it enables the member "to gain an unfair competitive advantage over other members," the member is not fulfilling its obligations. The Fund is then required to act under its responsibility to "exercise firm surveillance over the exchange rate policies of members."

The Articles use the term surveillance to apply particularly to the exchange rate policies of members. It is clear from what has been said earlier, however, that the mere fact that a Fund member allows its exchange rate to adjust does not mean that other members can afford to be indifferent to the domestic policies it follows, or that it has no interest in the policies of other countries. Indeed, if a country cannot insulate its economy from that of others, it cannot fail to take a close interest in what happens in other countries. An increasing recognition of the fact that a high degree of interdependence remains under flexible rates has led to developments in the application of surveillance that encompass both surveillance over exchange rate policies and oversight over related economic policies which can affect the exchange rate.

The communiqué of the Interim Committee of March 1979 already reflected this wider view: "The Committee emphasized the importance of international economic cooperation, and, with this objective in mind, stressed the necessity of active surveillance by the Fund over the exchange rate and related policies of all members as a means of strengthening the adjustment process." Further encouragement for an active surveillance role for the Fund came at the recent Interim Committee Meeting in Belgrade, and the Committee's communiqué again called for an active exercise of the Fund's surveillance authority. In his address to the Annual Meetings Secretary Miller of the United States stated: "Without active surveillance, there is no system. The Fund has moved cautiously and prudently in applying its surveillance procedures. Bolder action is now required." It is widely accepted that, while regional exchange blocs have their virtues, international surveillance can make an important contribution to ensuring a degree of coherence in exchange rate and related policies throughout the system as a whole.

It is easy these days to be pessimistic about the long-run outlook. In recent years we have had a high degree of flexibility of rates combined with massive intervention in foreign exchange markets. This is a paradoxical situation, but in my view it does not arise from defects in the rules or legal arrangements of the system. Rather, we have to look to the same underlying economic policy errors that made the old par value system unsustainable. That system could tolerate modest differences in inflation rates with periodic adjustments in exchange rates but could not withstand divergence in economic policies on the scale experienced in the late 1960s and early 1970s. Now, as then, the difficulties encountered by the United States in containing its rate of inflation are central to the problems we are encountering. The United States is to be commended for the recent monetary policy changes that indicate the seriousness with which inflation is being regarded.

Conclusion

For my concluding remarks I will present a few general observations that arise from these reflections on exchange rates and the adjustment process. The first is that there has been less difference between the operation of the adjustment process under the par value system and under flexible rates than many had expected. This extends right through to the Fund's stabilization programs. Some may have thought that the nature of these stabilization programs, particularly the restraints on domestic credit expansion, would be different under flexible rates. Recent research at the Fund, however, has shown that under a flexible rate system such as the present one, in which countries exercise a degree of management over exchange rates, such a distinction does not apply.

A second observation is that, among a considerable number of swings in exchange rates, there have been over the period some significant real exchange rate changes. A substantial movement in real exchange rates occurred in the latter part of 1977 and in 1978 between the U.S. dollar and a number of other major currencies. The position stabilized in the first half of 1979 with further changes occurring recently. Balance of payments positions, in particular a much needed shift in the current account positions of the three largest industrial countries, show that these real exchange rate changes have played a role in adjustment.

A third observation is that while we are still very early in the process of applying surveillance, it can make a significant contribution to the adjustment process if used with a combination of firmness and discretion. In this connection I was very heartened in Belgrade to see that there is growing understanding in countries of the deep-seated nature of the inflationary problem confronting us. This is of particular importance in the case of the United States given the key position it occupies in the system as a whole. If the governments of the world's major trading countries persevere in the firm resolve which they have now expressed, and in a framework of active international cooperation, then the outlook must be for a smoother functioning of the exchange markets in the international adjustment process.

16

FLOATING AS SEEN FROM THE CENTRAL BANK*

Henry C. Wallich

Floating rates are discussed usually—and properly—from a general point of view. In this chapter, the approach taken will be that of a central banker. It is hoped that, in this way, some contribution can be made to a subject, the discussion of which has by now fallen into a fairly familiar pattern. At the same time, it hardly needs to be said that the occupational biases and preconceptions of central bankers are by no means monolithic.

Differences are bound to exist among views held in central banks of small countries and large countries, in reserve currency countries and nonreserve currency countries, in countries with an experience of strong currencies and of weak currencies, and in developed and developing countries. Analytical approaches will also be colored according to whether floating rates are implicitly compared with a well-working fixed rate system or with a badly working fixed rate system and by whether foreign exchange controls are regarded as a readily acceptable alternative or not. In addition, most central bankers probably would do well to admit to some bias in favor of hard money and strong currencies. Finally, central bankers are necessarily concerned about how the floating rate system affects the role of the central bank. I shall pick up the discussion at this point.

Policy Freedom

Floating exchange rates have given central banks, or the governments within which individual central banks may have a greater or lesser degree of freedom, the technical means of conducting independent monetary

---

*The views expressed are those of the author and do not necessarily reflect those of the staff or any other member of the Federal Reserve Board.

policies. Under a truly fixed rate system, money creation and extinction had to reflect the need to monesize balance of payments surpluses and deficits. Interest rate policy had to be geared in good part, although not totally, to the need to keep surpluses and deficits, including capital movements, within manageable limits. Under the floating rate system, the volume of money can be controlled without regard to the balance of payments, provided the monetary authorities are prepared to accept the consequences for the exchange rate. Interest rates, therefore, can likewise be "controlled" instead of the money supply, subject to some degree of compatibility with the expected rate of inflation. Thus, under the floating regime, many central banks found it possible and desirable to adopt money supply targets.

Substantively, the policy freedom bestowed by floating rates, as has often been noted, has been disappointingly limited. There are several reasons. First, analysts seem to have underrated the degree of policy freedom that the fixed rate system derived from the absence of a "bottling up" effect. Expansionary or contractionary policies could be pursued for a while because fixed rates permitted the country to export its inflation or unemployment and to import stability. Floating rates bottle up the effects of national policy within the domestic economy. Excess domestic demand, or a demand shortfall, tend immediately to be reflected in a movement of the exchange rate that has domestic price and income consequences.

Perhaps this development could not have been clearly foreseen prior to the onset of floating. The Bretton Woods system, after all, rested on the assumption that exchange rates should change only under conditions of fundamental disequilibrium. Minor disequilibria were to be ridden out, with reliance on reserves and IMF credit. It might have been supposed that the financial markets under floating would have taken a similar attitude and would have been ready to finance disequilibria other than fundamental ones without significant exchange rate changes. This the markets have not done, although the markets have been very ready to supply credit to monetary authorities who wanted to support their exchange rates. In the absence of managed floating aimed at effective rate stabilization, therefore, exchange rates have often if not always quickly reflected payments imbalances and changes in rates of inflation.

Second, exchange rates frequently have overshot purchasing power parity rates or almost any hypothetical longer run equilibrium rates. More will be said about this later. Markets seem to have extrapolated the effects of expansionary or contractionary policies into the distant future and moved rates sharply. "Rational expectations," which in the domestic goods market imply an implausibly high degree of price flexibility, seem to have worked only too well in the foreign exchange field.

Third, the impact of exchange rate movements on domestic prices seems to have been underestimated. Particularly for the United States, these effects revealed themselves to be surprisingly large, principally because of the impact of exchange rate fluctuations upon the prices of domestic import- and export-competing goods and because of subsequent real demand and wage-price effects. This has given rise to the phenomenon of so-called vicious and virtuous circles, in which exchange rate depreciation feeds back on domestic inflation, which in turn feeds back upon the exchange rate. It seems to be a matter of semantics whether one applies this description or epithet to cases where the real exchange rate remains constant—that is, where the nominal exchange rate moves with the domestic-foreign inflation differential. One could reserve it, alternatively, to the case of overshooting of equilibrium rates in some sense. In either case, there is an effect present that under fixed rates can be postponed so long as the fixed rate lasts.

Furthermore, the world's views of inflation have gradually been changing. The Phillips curve as a locus of long-run equilibria permitting a choice between different trade-offs of inflation and unemployment has been widely given up. The perception of the consequences of inflation has advanced, in the minds of governments that may not have thought so previously, from that of a minor nuisance to that of a major problem. Thus, policy leeway for stimulative action has become severely restricted, particularly for countries whose inflation is high already. The counterpart of this limitation of domestic policy freedom under floating has been the experience that floating does not substantially shield a country from events abroad.

Finally, the experience of vicious and virtuous circles has led to a polarization of countries that under fixed rates did not occur to the same extent. This seems, in part, to have happened because exchange rates have been determined very predominantly by the state of the current account rather than of the capital account. Thus, countries with "strong"—that is, rising—currencies have been those that had current account surpluses. Those with "weak"—that is, falling—currencies have had current account deficits. This was not preordained. One could have visualized, for instance, that countries with strong anti-inflationary policies would have had high interest rates that would have attracted capital and driven up their exchange rates. They might then have found themselves suffering current account deficits. The opposite might have happened in countries with low interest rates and declining currencies.

Given that the speed of adjustment is higher in asset markets than in goods markets, this could not have been an implausible prediction. Reality has gone the other way. Countries with strong currencies have had large surpluses, perhaps because they have intervened sufficiently to keep their currencies from rising to the point of choking off their exports and strongly stimulating imports. These problems have been aggravated by the experience noted above that floating does not substantially shield a country from most economic events abroad, any more than it bestows substantive (as opposed to technical) policy independence.

Polarization among countries, in turn, has given rise to schemes of international coordination involving locomotive countries and cabooses or convoys, with attendant international recriminations. All this is a far cry from the idyllic vision of harmless and constructive economic nationalism under floating exchange rates where each country does its own thing in a context of free trade and without damage to its neighbors.

Disenchantment with the degree of policy independence provided by floating rates has numerous implications. One of them is the recognition that a country has relatively little to lose from voluntarily surrendering some of its remaining policy independence by forming a stable currency area jointly with other countries. What it gains in so doing, of course, are some of the benefits of exchange rate stability. What may keep a country from entering such a group, such as the snake or the European Monetary System, is not so much the desire for and belief in its ability to carry out independent policies, but the possibility that it may be unable to merge and coordinate its policies, especially its rate of inflation, with those of the group.

For the United States as a reserve currency country, other implications of limited policy freedom are evident. As a reserve currency country, the United States has not normally been under the same balance of payments discipline and consequent policy constraints as most other countries. Under the fixed rate system, however, the United States was severely constrained with respect to freedom to move its exchange rate, since that was determined by the dollar peg of other countries. Floating rates have to some extent relieved the United States of this "nth currency" role. Nevertheless, the continued reserve currency role of the dollar imposes constraints upon the United States that are not necessarily inherent in a floating dollar as such. Instability in the value of the dollar makes the dollar a less desirable reserve asset and less desirable also as a trading and investment currency for private users. Under floating rates, therefore, the world role of the dollar adds one more reason to the many that make it advisable for the United States to pursue policies conducive to a strong dollar. Floating has, if anything, increased the weight of balance of payments discipline upon the United States.

The question has often been asked whether the signal and disciplinary effects emanating from falling reserves under fixed rates are more powerful than those emanating from a falling exchange rate under floating. Historically, the fear of an exchange crisis often has powerfully motivated countries to adopt measures that were politically difficult. Under a floating system, a country is spared such pressures. On the other hand, the damage foreseeable from a falling exchange rate also has been severe enough at times to trigger major policy action. The answer quite likely depends in part on the speed with which an exchange rate moves. A slow decline may have little energizing effect, whereas a sudden sharp drop may stimulate action.

Disappointing Adjustment

Current account imbalances have been protracted under the floating system, especially the surpluses of the countries with strong currencies. If this is an indictment, it should be directed to any form of exchange rate change as a means of correcting imbalances, rather than to floating as a means of bringing about such changes. Perhaps the thought that clean floating would produce rapid current account adjustments arose from the expectation that in the absence of official reserve transfers, the current account must necessarily balance. But private capital movements can, of course, sustain a current account disequilibrium indefinitely and, in the case of developing countries, which are structural capital importers, ought in fact to do so. There seems to be nothing mysterious about slow adjustment in response to exchange rate changes. Goods markets are known to clear less rapidly than assets markets. There is a J-curve effect that takes some months to overcome. Income effects are more powerful than price and exchange rate effects and in cyclical situations often dominate. The magnitude of exchange rate effects has been explored empirically, though not always conclusively. There have been the well-known schools of price elasticity optimists and pessimists, and it is not clear that floating has added a great deal to our understanding of these matters.

There are some aspects of floating, however, that do bear specifically on the speed and magnitude of adjustment. One is the need to distinguish clearly between nominal and real exchange rates, in each case focusing upon an effective (e.g., trade-weighted) rate. Large changes in nominal rates may be quite consistent with small or zero changes in real rates.

This, for instance, was the observation of the Managing Director of the International Monetary Fund, Johannes Witteveen, at the Fund's Manila meeting in October 1976, after three and one-half years of generalized floating experience. Without changes in real rates, adjustment cannot be expected to flow from floating.

If the equilibrating effects of exchange rate movements are indeed slow and small, this is an argument, if anything, in favor of a permanently fixed rate system. Adjustments would then have to be made in the old-fashioned way by controlling inflation, slowing down the growth of income, and reorienting the structure of the economy toward better balance of payments equilibrium.

Under floating rates there may be a tendency for real rates to remain stable. Policy action to drive down a floating rate could be regarded as inconsistent with the principles of Article IV of the Fund Agreement and at odds also with the common law injunction against "aggressive" inter-vention—that is, "driving" a rate in the direction in which it is already going. Under a fixed rate system, sharp sudden changes in real rates are possible, and they can set in motion strong equilibrating tendencies. This will be the case, in any event, if such rate changes are accompanied by appropriate macropolicies, which have often been lacking. A gradual movement of a floating rate, whether in nominal or real terms, may not energize a government into strong action in the same manner.

Finally, balance of payments adjustment for countries whose exchange rates move up and down may be asymmetrical. Prices and wages are sticky downward but not upward. A drop in the exchange rate is quickly translated into higher wages and prices. A subsequent rise in the ex-change rate, for whatever reasons, does not reverse the preceding infla-tion, although it presumably will slow it. The net effect is more inflation, which in turn works against balance of payments adjustment.

Overshooting and Managed Floating

Rate movements have been wide and reversals frequent. There is some danger, to be sure, of being overimpressed by observed fluctuations. Effective rates change less than bilateral rates; real rates generally change less than nominal rates. Even so, frequent reversals even of real rates have occurred and raise questions about the efficiency of the process. Wide movement and reversals have contributed to the widespread im-pression that floating rates tend to overshoot. The theoretical possibil-ity—indeed, probability—of overshooting has been demonstrated. Asset markets clear faster than goods markets. The rates required for clearing of asset markets may imply a wider move than those required for equilibrium in goods markets, because during the interval before goods prices have reached their equilibrium levels, excess supplies of or demands for money and securities are likely to arise.

Diagnosing the magnitude of rate movements is difficult. Effective weighted average rates depend on the choice of bilateral versus multilateral weighting, and real rates depend upon the choice of a price index. For some countries, these choices make substantial differences. This is the case, for instance, for the choice of bilateral versus multilateral weights in the U.S. effective rate, as well as with respect to the number of countries included in the weighting. For Japan, the choice of price index very materially affects the real valuation of the yen.

The equilibrium rate with respect to which overshooting may occur and toward which the market must ultimately be assumed to move remains vague in concept and practice. Forward premia have been poor, albeit unbiased, predictors of future spot rates. Forward rates simply have, for the most part, reflected relative interest rates. The process of current account adjustment is so long that market participants must make allowance for all kinds of exogenous events, many of them unforeseeable. Many market participants, including commercial banks, have only a limited ability to take positions reflecting their longer run hunches, in part as a result of bank regulation and changes in accounting practices. Very short-run-oriented actions, on the other hand, such as postponement and acceleration of trade payments, can quickly generate enormous capital movements. In the case of the United States, a shift in these leads and lags by one week on payments connected with total current account activity of about $350 billion annually would amount to $7 billion.

Specifying an equilibrium rate, cyclically adjusted and perhaps moving on a trend to allow for income differences and differences in income elasticities of imports and exports, to say nothing of estimating future inflation and capital movements, remains as difficult under floating as it was under fixed rates. Given this great uncertainty of rate expectations, there is a tendency on the part of the market as well as of policymakers to assume that whatever rate prevails is about right and then, after it has changed somewhat, or even appreciably, to assume that it is still right. If in the stock market, on conspicuous occasions, such as 1929 or 1974, analysts have been unable to arrive at plausible or sustainable evaluations of the present value of future cash flows discounted from here to eternity because of some short-run or cyclical event, it is not surprising that students of the exchange market should have similar difficulties. The best they can hope to do is to diagnose when a rate is seriously wrong but hardly when it is right.

Wide fluctuations and reversals have raised questions, in particular, about the merits of clean floating. Although clean floating has not yet become a dirty word, the simple faith that the market is always right has been shaken. Intervention, therefore, seems appropriate not only to counter disorder in the narrowest short-run sense, but also to correct or prevent conditions that with some degree of confidence can be diagnosed as excessive. This does not mean to say, of course, that intervention will be successful. The amounts that the market can mobilize are larger than the resources of the authorities. In 1977 and the early part of 1978, the market decisively defeated various national authorities in their efforts to prevent a rise in their currencies against the dollar. Intervention is most likely to be successful when it not only comes at a time when currency movements have become extreme, but is accompanied also by actions that convince the market of a shift in basic economic policies. The market, to be sure, may not be governed in a short-run sense by fundamentals. But over time it must be expected to be, even though its interpretation of these fundamentals may be shaky.

Management of floating with any purpose other than that of countering disorder runs the risk of very quickly coming into conflict with the interests of other countries. Small countries are less exposed to this risk than are large ones, and the United States is exposed most of all. Fears of competitive depreciation obsessed the framers of Bretton Woods. Fear of inflation and particularly of rising oil prices could lead to competitive appreciation.

Individual countries may well have current account objectives. Historically, many industrial countries have acted as if the spirit of mercantilism was not yet altogether extinct. So long as there are countries willing to import capital, especially among the developing countries, the current account objectives of industrial countries need not be irreconcilable. But such current account objectives are better implemented by policies facilitating capital outflows and allowing exchange rates to adjust to these flows than by exchange market intervention.

The Role of the Central Bank

Monetary policy was partly paralyzed under fixed rates; it has gained strength under floating. That does not mean that central banks as institutions were powerless under fixed rates or that they have become strong under floating. More nearly the opposite seems to have been the case. During the 1960s, central bankers derived influence from their ability to confront their domestic authorities with the danger of a currency crisis. Aided by the discipline of the balance of payments, they often were able to gain acceptance for their recommended policy courses. Under floating, the danger of crisis has diminished, although not disappeared. For some countries it seems to have been replaced with the near certainty of a continuing malaise. The latter is less persuasive on behalf of policies that central bankers consider sound. This shift is quite apparent in the general role played during the 1970s by finance ministers and central bankers, the ascendancy of the ministers undeniably increasing.

Exchange rates in most countries are in the hands of the political authority, running from the legislature to the chief of state to the minister of finance. The strong political nature of exchange rates decisions buttresses this relationship, even though it may not make for better decisions. Exchange market intervention to counter disorder belongs more plausibly in the hands of central bankers, with their closer contact with the financial markets. However, it should be noted that political control of the exchange rate can become a means of controlling monetary policy even in countries where the central bank has a degree of independence from the executive power. By requiring the central bank to defend an exchange rate that implies changes in money supply and interest rates, monetary policy can become subordinated to exchange rate objectives under managed floating, as, of course, it must be under a fixed rate system.

One of the defenses of central banks against such influences has been the establishment of money supply targets. These impose a certain discipline that can serve as a substitute for the discipline exerted in the past by a fixed rate. Hereafter, as international interdependence mounts, it is likely to be the broad discipline of the balance of payments, rather than that of a fixed exchange or money growth rate, that will most effectively back up central banks when they seek support for their policies.

17

IMPROVING INTERNATIONAL PERFORMANCE

Beryl W. Sprinkel

This occasion provides an opportunity to assess past accomplishments and, more important, to contemplate the challenges now facing our economy. In my opinion, the accomplishments of this Administration are considerable. We are presently enjoying the 52nd consecutive month of sustained growth—the second longest peacetime expansion in the post-war era—and inflation remains subdued. The percentage of our working-age population with jobs is now at record levels and we continue to enjoy steady employment gains.

Important challenges, however, still remain. The United States has run unprecedented trade and current account deficits in each of the last three years. At the start of 1985 we were a net creditor nation. Now we are the world's largest net debtor—and we continue to accumulate foreign debt at a rapid rate. Many of our trade-sensitive industries, especially manufacturing and agriculture, have faced severe pressures as a result of the wide and prolonged appreciation of the dollar in the 1980s. As a consequence, protectionist forces are on the rise, promoting a seductive, but undeniably false cure that threatens trade, growth, and well-being.

These problems must be and are being addressed. They did not arise overnight, and they cannot be resolved overnight. There are no quick fixes. Today, I would like to discuss the continuing efforts to resolve these problems and to improve the performance of the international economic system.

The International Monetary System

A thread that connects external imbalances of industrial countries and the development of protectionist pressures is the perceived instability of the international economic system, as reflected by wide swings in the exchange rates of major currencies.

This aspect of the international monetary system has been studied extensively. At the Williamsburg Summit in 1983, the leaders of the major industrial countries directed their Ministers of Finance to investigate the functioning of the international economic system and to identify ways in which its operation might be improved. The G-10 Deputies that prepared this report were mindful of the imperfections of the current system, but they were also aware of the challenges that wide swings in petroleum prices, differing policy priorities in various countries, and the development of the international lending crisis had presented to the system. In their final report, the G-10 Deputies concluded that:

> . . . the basic structure of the present [international monetary] system . . . has provided the essential flexibility for individual nations . . . to respond constructively to a period of major adjustment and global change . . . Flexible exchange rates among the major currencies have made a positive contribution to the adjustment process . . . in a difficult global environment . . .

We have now had about fourteen years' experience with floating exchange rates. During this time, exchange rates have shown much more short-term volatility than initially expected. Several studies, however, have shown that this short-term volatility has not resulted in a sharp contraction of world trade, as some have feared. Instead, the development or expansion of forward, futures, options, and swap markets have allowed market participants to manage exchange-rate risks.

More serious problems, however, have arisen in connection with wide swings of exchange rates over long periods, especially the spectacular rise of the dollar from the summer of 1980 until February 1985. Wide swings of exchange rates have induced substantial shifts in the allocation of resources within and between economies. In particular, traded goods industries in strong currency countries have been under heavy pressure, while such industries in weak currency countries have enjoyed a competitive edge. Weak currency countries have eventually faced painful adjustments as well. Many traded goods industries, having been encouraged to overexpand under the protection of a weak currency, have subsequently been forced to contract when currencies returned to more sustainable levels.

These problems have led some to look back nostalgically to the Bretton Woods system, but this system was also not immune to external imbalances and exchange rate swings. When economic policies and performances diverge, external imbalances emerge which are either preceeded or followed by currency realignments.

The Bretton Woods system was thrown into crisis when the United States, facing a conflict between policies thought necessary to preserve recovery from the recession of 1969–70 and those policies required to correct a growing balance-of-payments deficit, suspended official convertivility of the dollar into gold on August 15, 1971. An attempt was made to reconstruct the Bretton Woods system in the Smithsonian Agreement of December 1971. This agreement, which was immodestly hailed by President Nixon as ". . . the most significant monetary agreement in the history of the world," proved to be short-lived. Continued divergence between the relatively expansionary policy of the United States and the more anti-inflation oriented policies of other major countries led to renewed pressure on the international monetary system. In March 1973, the reconstructed Bretton Woods system collapsed, and the system of floating exchange rates among major countries was inaugurated.

It is widely held among national monetary authorities that a return to a generalized system of fixed exchange rates is not realistic at the present time. Although inflation rates in most major industrial countries have fallen appreciably, the degree of convergence of economic performance and the extent of the coordination of economic policies still appears well short of that required to sustain a return to fixed exchange rates. Determining the exact set of parities consistent with long-term balance of payments equilibrium would be a nearly impossible task. On top of that, there remains the fundamental problem that future changes in economic conditions or economic policies may significantly alter the exchange rates that are consistent with longer-run equilibrium in international payments.

Currently, defending exchange-rate parities in the presence of changing market expectations would not be feasible. The Bretton Woods system was created in an environment of limited capital mobility. Capital flows could now swamp any conceivable central bank attempts to prop up a particular set of exchange-rate parities. A danger of fixed parities, therefore, would be that governments might be tempted to reimpose capital controls in order to facilitate exchange-rate management, reversing the many gains we have made toward achieving a truly international capital market.

Fundamentally, if national economic policies are to be effectively constrained by an exchange-rate system, that must mean that conflicts are arising between the use of these policies to limit exchange rate movements and their use for other purposes. No doubt, a variety of conflicting objectives must often be balanced in formulating economic policies. But it is far from clear that drawing the appropriate balance is facilitated by a rigid commitment to defend a particular set of fixed parities.

Two recent examples serve well to illustrate the importance of this point. In the second quarter of 1980, the United States fell into a sharp but brief recession. Real output dropped, unemployment rose, interest rates fell dramatically, and the money supply declined. The foreign exchange value of the dollar also fell, reaching its lowest level ever against the G-10 countries (plus Switzerland) in late June and early July. If we were committed to defending a particular set of exchange-rate parities, action might well have been required during the second quarter of 1980 to stem this decline in the value of the dollar. This presumably would have meant a larger decline in the U.S. money supply and a sharper and more prolonged decline in economic activity. It is highly questionable, however, whether the U.S. authorities would or should have been willing to take such actions in this situation.

The opposite situation would probably have arisen in 1983 or 1984 when the dollar continued to strengthen against other major currencies. At that time, the U.S. economy was recovering very strongly from the recession of 1980–82, while inflation remained moderate. Would it have been wise to ease U.S. monetary policy substantially and risk a resurgence of inflation in order to stem the rise of the dollar? Of course, given the strength of the dollar it is reasonable to suppose that other countries, not the United States, would have been facing massive reserve losses in order to defend their exchange rate. Still, would it have been wise for European countries to tighten monetary policy to defend existing exchange-rate parities, at a time when inflation was falling and European unemployment was rising—in some cases to depression-era levels?

International Policy Coordination

These questions are difficult to answer. They suggest, however, that rigid exchange-rate systems are not the answer. Certainly, recent events demonstrate that needed reforms can be accomplished within the general structure of the present international monetary system. The wide swings in exchange rates that have bedevilled the floating exchange rate system have been a product of divergent economic policies. These swings in exchange rates can be limited by promoting the adoption of sound and compatable policies across countries. When appropriate, coordinated intervention in foreign exchange markets may also improve the performance of the international economic system. This intervention could never hope to play a dominant role in exchange markets, even temporarily, but it could signal the authorities' resolve to implement sound monetary and fiscal policies consistent with exchange rate stability.

Recent efforts at international policy coordination offer real hope of securing improved macroeconomic performance and greater exchange rate stability. Inflation has fallen substantially from earlier double-digit rates. Economic performance in the major industrial countries has generally converged. At the Tokyo Summit, leaders of the seven largest industrial democracies agreed to provide more effective procedures for the coordination of economic policies. Although the details of the system of policy coordination mandated by the Tokyo summit have not been all worked out, further progress was achieved at a meeting of Finance Ministers and Central Bank Governors from six industrial countries last month.

One of the most visible moves toward improved policy coordination took place in September 1985, when the Finance Ministers and Central Bank Governors of the five largest industrial countries (known as the G-5) agreed to pursue policies that would promote sustainable, non-inflationary growth and a ". . . further orderly appreciation of the main non-dollar currencies against the dollar." Since then, the depreciation of the dollar has substantially restored our international cost competitiveness, relative to most major foreign industrial countries. The deterioration of our trade balance appears to have abated and we are seeing growing, but still incomplete evidence that export volumes are finally strengthening. Favorable movements in trade volumes helped promote economic growth in the fourth quarter of 1986 and I am confident that further improvements in our trade performance will contribute significantly to growth in 1987.

Additional efforts will be required to reduce the U.S. trade deficit to sustainable levels, but it is clear that we are entering a new phase in this process. This new phase was signalled at the meeting of Ministers and Governors from six major industrial countries last month when they stated that, "Further substantial exchange rate shifts among their currencies could damage growth and adjustment prospects in their countries . . . therefore, they agreed to cooperate closely to foster the stability of exchange rates around current levels."

As was recognized in the Ministers' communique, meeting the combined challenge of holding down inflation, sustaining world growth, promoting exchange rate stability, and reducing external imbalances requires that we address the other fundamental causes of our trade deficit. Sole reliance on dollar depreciation to reduce our trade deficit is not desirable. It risks inflation at home and recession abroad. Instead, we must follow a coordinated strategy of strengthening internally-generated growth abroad while working resolutely to reduce the U.S. government budget deficit through spending restraint.

Stronger domestic demand growth in the major foreign industrial countries would help to give balance to the current world recovery. The U.S. expansion has been fueled by one of the strongest recoveries of domestic demand in the postwar period. In contrast, the recovery of domestic demand in Japan and Europe has been one of the weakest. In some cases, economic growth abroad during much of the recovery was maintained by increased emphasis on export-led growth. In other cases, the recovery of economic activity though much of the expansion has been weak.

Stronger domestic demand growth in the major foreign industrial countries is needed to engender the much needed expansion of U.S. export markets without having to rely on further dollar depreciation. It is also needed to maintain growing export markets for developing countries. Most importantly, stronger domestic demand growth in the major foreign industrial countries is needed to maintain satisfactory output and employment performance in these countries as the United States reduces its trade deficit, no matter how this reduction is effected. As net exports from these countries to the United States tail off, increases in foreign domestic demand will be needed to take up the slack. Many foreign industrial countries enjoyed stronger domestic demand growth in 1986, although in Japan this strengthening was not sufficient to prevent a weakening in GNP growth. Maintaining moderate rates of GNP growth abroad will require that this strengthening be sustained over the medium-term.

These efforts by foreign industrial countries to effect a growth-oriented reduction in external imbalances must be matched by corresponding efforts in the United States to reduce the Federal government budget deficit. The U.S. deficit on goods and services trade signifies that total spending on goods and services in the United States exceeds U.S. production of goods and services and that we are importing the difference. This gap between national expenditure and national income has not been associated with an unusual widening in the gap between private expenditure and income. What has been unusual is the unprecedented increase in the Federal government budget deficit during an expansion, which has been fueled by excessive expenditure growth.

Put differently, last year we borrowed on net about $140 billion from abroad to finance our current account deficit. This absorbtion of foreign saving implies that our national saving fell far short of national investment. Last year, net capital inflows from abroad corresponded to over 60 percent of net U.S. capital formation. An important reason for this dependence on foreign saving is that the general (Federal, State, and local) government deficit absorbed over 60 percent of net private saving.

Reducing the Federal government budget deficit by expenditure restraint is needed to preserve the low marginal tax rates achieved by tax reform and the promise of stronger economic growth that they bring. It will also contribute importantly to reducing our trade and current account deficits by slowing the growth of total national expenditure and narrowing the excess of national spending over national production. Substantial progress is now being made toward this goal. The Federal government deficit is expected to fall nearly $50 billion in fiscal 1987. The President has submitted a budget that would reduce the fiscal deficit to the Gramm-Rudman-Hollings target of $108 billion in fiscal 1988. Achieving this goal will be difficult, as pressures are mounting in Congress to increase expenditures. These pressures must be resisted: a vote to increase government expenditures is a vote against tax reform and against reducing our trade deficit.

Implementing a growth-oriented program for reducing our trade deficit will require efforts on two other fronts. First, pressures for protectionism must be resisted. Protectionist measures are neither appropriate nor effective for resolving trade or current account imbalances. The U.S. trade deficit is primarily a macroeconomic phenomenon. It is not primarily the product of narrow commercial policy actions taken by our trading partners. Our international trade position has deteriorated in virtually all product categories and against virtually all trading partners. This general deterioration can be reversed only by reversing the general forces that led to its creation—excessive government spending and slow foreign growth. Protectionist measures, while having superficial appeal, fail utterly in this task.

Protectionist trade restrictions, however, do introduce inefficiencies into the economy. Prices are higher, reducing our standard-of-living. Resources are shifted to sectors in which we are relatively less efficient, reducing growth. Moreover, the United States is not a small country whose actions will be ignored by others—especially in the present environment. Just as most of the deterioration of the U.S. trade balance was in manufactures, improvements in the U.S. trade balance will come about largely from a swing in manufactures trade. This development will present serious adjustment problems for U.S. trading partners, especially as the performance of manufactures output and employment in many countries, notably in Western Europe, has been weak. If we move down the protectionist path, other nations are likely to follow—as happened after the Smoot-Hawley Tariff in the 1930s. It would be singularly unfortunate to invite this kind of response, just as our trade balance is beginning to improve.

Rather than risking an outbreak of protectionism, we should strive to reduce trade restrictions and to promote a more open system of international trade. Needed adjustments in the relative attractiveness of U.S.-produced goods should be accomplished by increasing our international cost competitiveness. Dollar depreciation, of course, represents one means of improving our competiveness. The resulting increase in import prices, however, reduces our standard of living. A far better method to increase our competitiveness would be to improve our international cost competitiveness by boosting our productivity. This is the essence of the President's initiative to improve our international competitiveness—an initiative that stresses increased education and training; an initiative that stresses the elimination of burdensome regulations that impair productive efficiency; in short, an initiative that seeks to increase the amount that can be produced—and therefore earned—by Americans.

There is no reason for pessimism about the ability of U.S. firms to compete in international markets. The decline in U.S. international competitiveness experienced in the 1980s resulted primarily from the strong appreciation of the dollar. Growth of labor productivity in manufacturing during this Administration has been faster than its postwar average. Wage increases have been moderate. These developments, combined with the depreciation of the dollar and efforts to spur productivity growth even further, will promote a vigorous and competitive economy.

Conclusion

To recap, important strides are being made to reduce external imbalances. The need for stronger, internally-generated growth abroad is now recognized. Real progress is finally being made in reducing our Federal government budget deficit and further initiatives are being promoted to improve our productivity and competitiveness. These developments, combined with further progress in international policy coordination, offer real hope for reducing exchange-rate fluctuations. In the end, it must be recognized that no international monetary system can compensate for bad economic policy. The wide swings in exchange rates must be understood not as a fault of the system, but of the undesirable policies that produced them. Better, more stable, more consistent policies, directed toward the key objective of sustainable and non-inflationary growth, will also ensure the smooth performance of the international monetary system.

PART V

PRIVATE SECTOR INNOVATION AND FREE MARKETS

18

THE INTERNATIONAL MONETARY MARKET

Leo Melamed

Few things are more symbolic of flexible exchange rates than the International Monetary Market (IMM) in Chicago. Indeed, the birth of this futures exchange on May 16, 1972 is inextricably intertwined with the death of Bretton Woods, occurring as it did but a few months after President Nixon officially closed the gold window and ended the system of fixed exchange rates.

Yet, the IMM represented much more than a new economic era or the successful introduction of currency futures. In May of 1986, precisely fourteen years after its inception, Merton H. Miller, Distinguished Service Professor of Finance at the University of Chicago Graduate School of Business, bestowed upon the IMM a supreme and unparalleled honor—he nominated financial futures as "the most significant financial innovation of the last twenty years."[1]

It is not my place to admit or deny this distinction. Professor Miller and others of his distinguished credentials are eminently more qualified than I to make such determinations. Rather, I am best placed to reflect on the events surrounding the birth of our currency market, to recall some of the noteworthy moments of the IMM's formative years and to answer questions about who we were, and whether we knew what we were doing.

I dare say, if ever one needed proof of the sagacity of "Necessity is the mother of invention,"[2] one need only review the economic disorders leading to and following the creation of our new exchange. These events proved beyond anything we could say that the IMM was an invention made necessary by the dictates of the times.

The date most observers would mark as the official onset of financial upheaval would be August 15, 1971. That day, President Nixon announced his economic emergency package which included a wage and price freeze, a 10% import surcharge, and the suspension of dollar convertibility into gold and other reserve assets. Unquestionably, the closing of the gold window was a seismic shock that unleashed financial reverberations that were felt even a decade later. It is unfair, however, to characterize any one event as critical to the actual beginning.[3] No one factor is responsible for the chain of events that culminated in the financial tumult of the 1970s and early 1980s, except, of course, the 1945 Bretton Woods Agreement itself.

In my humble opinion, Bretton Woods was a short-term solution uniquely suited for post-World War II reconstruction. If applied much beyond that, as it was, then its basic and fundamental flaw—its rigidity— was destined to become its undoing. A fixed exchange rate system could not forever effectively cope with the continual change in currency values resulting from the daily flows of political and economic stresses between the member nations of Bretton Woods. The different external and internal interests of the participants—their different rates of economic growth; their different fiscal and monetary policies, beholden to different forms of governments; their different work force considerations; their different election timetables and political pressures—all would combine to destroy a system dependent upon a unified opinion regarding respective exchange values.

Milton Friedman knew this from the beginning:

> . . . , from the time Bretton Woods became effective, it was inevitable it would break down . . . It tried to achieve incompatible objectives: freedom of countries to pursue an independent internal monetary policy; fixed exchange rates; and relatively free international movement of goods and capital . . . As one of the architects of Bretton Woods, Keynes tried to resolve the incompatibility by providing for flexibility of exchange rates through what he intended to be frequent and fairly easily achieved changes in official parities. In practice, this hope was doomed because maintaining the an- nounced parity became a matter of prestige and political controversy. Countries therefore held on to a parity as long as they could, in the process letting minor problems grow into major crises and then making large changes . . .[4]

By December 1971, when the IMM was officially incorporated as an independent financial exchange, it was obvious to some of us that the imbalances created and pent up by fixed exchange rates were about to erupt. President Nixon's economic measures were only one of those effects and were immediately followed by a number of joint international actions and pious pronouncements which, for the most part, turned out to be futile. These were followed by a series of amendments and counter-measures that proved equally useless and simply added to the general confusion.

The "Smithsonian Agreements"[5] proposed currency realignments as well as dollar devaluation. These attempts at a new foreign exchange value standard were doomed from the outset since they were not much more than a reshaping of Bretton Woods in a slightly more flexible form.

The Basle Agreement for the European Economic Community (EEC) established the so-called "snake"[6] for EEC currencies. This regime was novel in that it allowed EEC currencies to jointly float against the dollar while the movement between each currency was restricted to a predetermined band. The concept has, of course, survived to this day. Nevertheless, there were an unending series of currency revaluations and devaluations, entering and leaving the snake, IMF agreements, amendments and inevitable disagreements—all proving that the world was in serious difficulty.

The centerpiece of the unfolding disarray occurred in 1973. In October of that year, the oil embargo, oil price increases and the Arab-Israeli war set in motion economic distortions that would dramatically change the world financial fabric for a long time to come. What followed was an era of financial turmoil rarely equaled in modern history; turmoil that tested the very foundations of western society: the U.S. dollar plunged precipitously; U.S. unemployment reached in excess of 10%; oil prices skyrocketed to $39 a barrel; the Dow Jones Industrial Average fell to 570; gold reached $800 an ounce; U.S. inflation climbed to an unprecedented peacetime rate of 20%; interest rates went even higher.

These events ensured that the formula for successful invention based on necessity would be applicable to the IMM. Indeed, if one could ordain the perfect backdrop for the creation of a new financial futures exchange designed to help manage the risk of currency and interest rate price movement, one could not have bettered what actually happened.

Moreover, it seems our exchange had embraced the single most effective remedy for the dramatic shocks of the next decade and a half. Here is the International Monetary Fund's assessment of floating exchange rates as published in its Occasional Paper, July, 1984:

> Given the events of the past decade, it is easy to be impressed by the resiliency of the present system . . . Indeed, in such an environment, managed floating might well have been the only system that could have functioned continuously.

Similarly, an even stronger statement was issued by the Group of Ten, as published June 21, 1985, ". . . it is questionable whether any less flexible system would have survived the strains of the past decade . . ."

Can we claim that we anticipated the exact nature of the turbulence that followed the IMM's creation? Of course not. It was simply that, as traders with an ear to the ground, we had heard the inner rumblings and knew there was trouble ahead. Did we grasp the vast potential of the idea? I believe so. This was the precise query pressed upon me by Milton Friedman when he served as guest of honor at the occasion of the IMM's tenth anniversary. Did we, he asked, actually envision the scope of our invention at the time of its launch?

The answer was easy to locate. It can be found in the Annual Reports to the members of the Chicago Mercantile Exchange (CME), the entity that spawned the IMM.

The 1972 Annual Report, the first to speak officially of its offspring, was not at all bashful in its assessment of what it had wrought:

> The opening of the International Monetary Market on May 16, 1972 was as revolutionary a step as the establishment of the first organized commodity exchange when that event occurred . . .
> . . . we believe the IMM is larger in scope than currency futures alone, and accordingly we hope to bring to our threshold many other contracts and commodities that relate directly to monetary matters and that would complement the economics of money futures.[7]

One year later, the first International Monetary Market Annual Report also focused on the era ushered in by the new exchange:

> The new era will afford us the opportunity to expand our potential into other areas within the monetary frame of reference. That was the essence of the philosophy that fostered the IMM. Our new market was specifically designed to encompass as many viable trading vehicles in the world of finance as practicable. We must be willing and ready to explore all possibilities.[8]

Thus, while our grammatical prowess may have been less than perfect, our eyesight was 20/20. We were fully aware of the revolutionary nature of financial futures and equally cognizant of their vast potential. Nor did we delude ourselves about the difficulties that lay ahead.

"It's ludicrous to think that foreign exchange can be entrusted to a bunch of pork belly crapshooters," proclaimed a prominent New York banker on the eve of the Merc's launch of the IMM.

"The New Currency Market: Strictly for Crapshooters," echoed *Business Week,* condemning us from the start and preaching that "if you fancy yourself an international money speculator but lack the resources . . . your day has come."[9] Not what you would describe as a friendly endorsement. Indeed, the world not only misread our purpose, but our potential as well.

In retrospect, the antagonism stemmed from three factors: misunderstanding the depth and power of financial forces pent up by twenty-five years of fixed exchange rates, misreading the nature and value of the idea we had spawned, and miscalculating who we were.

Of course, there were some notable exceptions. For one, Milton Friedman, who not only provided us with the intellectual courage to proceed undaunted by the sea of skepticism about us, but also lent our concept his esteemed academic credentials; without this help we could not possibly have defended ourselves from the onslaught of official and unofficial negativism awaiting us.

Wrote Professor Friedman in the position paper commissioned by the CME in the fall of 1971:

> Changes in the international financial structure will create a great expansion in the demand for foreign cover. It is highly desirable that this demand be met by as broad, as deep, as resilient a futures market in foreign currencies as possible in order to facilitate foreign trade and investment.
>
> Such a wider market is almost certain to develop in response to the demand. The major open question is where. The U.S. is a natural place and it is very much in the interests of the U.S. that it should develop here.[10]

Those words and scores of subsequent supporting actions by Friedman on behalf of the IMM were invaluable in facilitating our birth, and indispensable in supporting our fragile existence during our formative years.

To begin with, although CME counsel assured us that we did not need governmental sanction to proceed,[11] we thought it prudent to acquaint the appropriate U.S. officials with our intentions. We felt, correctly as it turned out, that there were compelling reasons to touch base with our government (and later with other governments): first, to give the IMM concept the proper level of import and prominence; second, to gain, if possible, a positive reaction that we might be able to use in promoting the idea; and third, if the opposite were true, to control any negative fallout.

The first government official to receive the Friedman paper formally was George P. Shultz, who became U.S. Secretary of Treasury shortly after the launch of our market. Mr. Shultz offered immediate and warm support. While he gave the project long odds, he recognized its inherent values and embraced Friedman's philosophical rationale. No doubt his own free market views were in sync with those of his fellow Chicagoan.

In similar fashion, we paid courtesy calls on Dr. Arthur Burns, Federal Reserve Board Chairman, and Herbert Stein, Chairman of the Council of

Economic Advisors. In each instance, Friedman's paper had paved the way for a receptive encounter.

No sooner did currency futures show signs of success, than we began to consider the next logical step in the financial revolution—a futures contract on interest rates. Toward this goal we were greatly assisted by the current Chairman of the Council of Economic Advisors, Dr. Beryl W. Sprinkel, who as Vice President and Economist of Harris Bank and Trust Co., served on the IMM's original Board of Directors.[12]

I recall vividly how, in 1975, Dr. Sprinkel accompanied us to Chairman Burns to discuss our prospective Treasury bill contract. It was a momentous occasion in our history; by extending financial futures to interest rates, we would dramatically expand our horizons. Moreover, this second meeting with Dr. Burns was no longer a mere courtesy call. By then, as previously noted, new futures contracts required CFTC approval. Chairman Burns welcomed the idea.

Of course, Treasury futures faced one more hurdle, the United States Treasury. Its consent did not occur until Milton Friedman wrote a letter explicitly recommending the new contract to William E. Simon, U.S. Secretary of the Treasury in 1975. Mr. Simon readily agreed.

Still another early and avid supporter of our proposed T-bill market was the recently appointed Federal Reserve Board Chairman, Alan Greenspan, who in 1975 was Chairman of the Council of Economic Advisors. Dr. Greenspan unequivocally embraced the concept. Indeed, I recall his immediate reaction as he offered a litany of uses such a futures market could provide the business community. His list included all the reasons why T-bill futures were an instant success.

I recall also Herbert Stein's cryptic comment upon learning of this new futures contract. Quipped the former CEA Chairman, "I oppose little between two consenting adults."

While positive reactions from government officials were important, the contributions by members of the business community who served on the early IMM boards were equally meaningful. Not only did each of these gentlemen give us advice and assistance, they provided our fledgling exchange with the initial credibility it so desperately needed. In addition to Beryl W. Sprinkel, our IMM Boards[13] included such distinguished names as Richard Lyng (currently serving as U.S. Secretary of Agriculture); A. Robert Abboud, Vice Chairman, First National Bank of Chicago; William J. McDonough, Executive Vice President, First National Bank of Chicago; Robert Z. Aliber, Associate Professor, University of Chicago; Henry Jarecki, Chairman, Mocatta Metals, Inc.; and Frederick W.

Schantz, Vice President, American National Bank and Trust Company of Chicago.

Of special significance were two officers of the CME: Everette B. Harris, President of the exchange and Mark J. Powers, its Chief Economist. Each of them, in their own way, were instrumental in the IMM's ultimate success.

E. B. Harris had a vast store of accumulated futures expertise as well as friends everywhere, thereby providing invaluable advice and opening important doors to give us the needed opportunities to preach the new gospel.

Mark Powers, on the other hand, was a superb economist with a truly fertile mind. He instinctively knew what the specifications of the new currency and T-bill contracts should be; and, while those specifications have been changed over time, they are still basically traded the way Powers wrote them.

Unfortunately, all these brave soldiers represented but a handful compared with the armies who viewed the idea of financial futures with disdain. It was to be an uphill struggle for many years to come. Fortunately, its success depended more on world events and our tenacity than on views of individuals or the odds against us. Listen, if you will, to a candid appraisal of who we were and why we were so underrated.[14]

Who were we?

We were a bunch of guys who were hungry.

We were traders to whom it did not matter—whether it was eggs or gold, bellies or the British pound, turkeys or T-bills.

We were babes in the woods, innocents, in a world we did not understand, too dumb to be scared.

We were audacious, brazen, raucous pioneers—too unworldly to know we could not win.

That the odds against us were too high;

That the banks would never trust us;

That the government would never let us;

That Chicago was the wrong place.

But we were fast learners as well. While logic would dictate that unsophisticated belly, cattle and hog traders could not long survive the treacherous waters of foreign exchange when pitted against seasoned forex specialists, the odds were shortened by the simple fact that we were using our own money. That singular difference spelled a trading discipline and a thirst for knowledge that became a winning combination for those CME members who came to the IMM's currency pits.

And come they did, for they represented the quintessential ingredient. Without traders who were willing to brave the dangers of the new untested and illiquid markets, we could never have succeeded. They came and stood there day after day, learning and shouting, giving their time and money, infusing the initial liquidity that ultimately lit the IMM torch.

And we made some very smart moves, two of them decisive. The first was that the new currency contracts were not simply added to the contracts already traded at the CME. Rather, the IMM was created as a separate entity with its own unique markets. This structure allowed us to build a "financial futures" image somewhat less encumbered by the history and impressions of age-old agricultural futures.

More importantly, it enabled us to sell memberships at a much lower price to gain traders whose activities would be limited to the contracts provided by the IMM. The new members were captive of the currency pits, unable to participate in the more active meat futures complex and forced to generate business in their own arena. It was a crucial element in our growth and became the model adopted by other exchanges when the financial futures idea spread to our competitors.

The second critical component at the outset was the so-called "Class B" arbitrage device. It was a brand new approach to transaction-clearing requiring us to be bold and imaginative. In the early days, the banks would not participate directly in our markets. This meant that FX values at the IMM were not immediately connected to the real world of the interbank market. To make this connection, we created a separate class of clearing members whose sole function was to act as arbitrageurs between a bank of their choice and the IMM. The Class B firms were given special margin accommodations while the banks who dealt with them were provided unique security guarantees. It worked. And, although Class B arbitrage was destined to become obsolete as soon as the banks realized that dealing directly with the IMM was safe and profitable, the system was essential until then.

It is important to note that while, at the outset, the major money center banks generally ignored the events in Chicago, the Chicago banks did not. Their long-standing relationship with futures markets was profitable and resulted in a futures expertise within their walls. It, therefore, was easy for them to grasp the concept of a futures market in currency. It is well that this was the case since we were in desperate need of their assistance. Happily, the four major Chicago banks: Continental Illinois National Bank & Trust Company of Chicago, First National Bank of

Chicago, Harris Bank and Trust Co. and American National Bank & Trust Co. were very supportive of our IMM idea.

Indeed, the assistance of Continental, then the largest of the Chicago banks and one with a world-wide network, was critical. Continental agreed to act as the delivery agent for the new currency contracts and helped devise a secure world system for this purpose. Without a delivery mechanism, our contracts had no chance.

In retrospect, in its formative period, the IMM made few mistakes—but one of them was a whopper. The instant success of its T-bill contract in 1976 made it clear to the world that the IMM's idea represented a monumental new sphere of business activity. As nothing before, this event served to enflame the fires of competition. The IMM and its larger rival, the Chicago Board of Trade (CBOT), searched frantically for the next new futures vehicle. It was destined to be in the interest rate sector, but which instrument? The IMM chose incorrectly to go after the middle range with a 4-year Treasury note contract; the CBOT, for the long range with a 30-year Treasury bond contract. Long-term bond futures became the most actively traded futures instrument, primarily to the credit of Dr. Richard Sandor who spawned and championed the concept for the CBOT.

However, there was a silver lining. The IMM gained an insurmountable hold on the short-term interest rate sector that led it to capture the Eurodollar contract. Today, this 90-day interest rate contract represents the bellwether for international short-term interest rates. It has become one of the most actively traded instruments anywhere, and often maintains the largest open interest for any futures contract.

Eurodollar futures were representative of still another IMM innovation, one that dramatically expanded the boundaries of the original concept. The IMM's notion to settle this futures contract in terms of cash, rather than the traditional method of physical delivery, was central to the future of futures. To the credit of the CFTC, "cash settlement" was approved and paved the way to uses never before thought possible for futures contracts. Cash settlement became the gateway to the index markets.

As befits but often escapes one who is first, the IMM ultimately captured the lion's share of financial futures business as well as the most diverse complement of financial instruments. Its success catapulted its parent, the CME, from a lowly secondary position in domestic markets, to a primary role in international finance.

The IMM served the CME in yet another dimension: it infused the institution with a revolutionary spirit, spawning a heritage of innovation and experimentation. This is a quality rarely found in major financial organizations which, as a rule, opt for the safety of "status quo." The heritage lives. The latest innovation of the Chicago Mercantile Exchange is a direct descendant of the IMM revolution.

On October 6, 1987, the CME membership overwhelmingly approved a joint undertaking with Reuters Holdings PLC, the world's largest communications organization, to create a global electronic automated transaction system. Called P-M-T (Post Market Trade), it represents the first major attempt to link all of the world's financial centers with a single futures trading system, one that will utilize state-of-the-art technology, operate virtually over the entire 24-hour trading day, and whose transactions will be cleared by a single clearing entity. The bold and revolutionary concept is a comprehensive response to the damands of globalization—a trend of world markets not lost on CME officials.

The IMM spirit has remained a permanent component of CME philosophy and the critical element of its continued success. At the same time, the IMM has made financial futures an indispensible tool of risk management and gained Professor Miller's coveted nomination. And, while it is untrue that the IMM spawned flexible exchange rates, there is no denying that our currency futures market is inexorably intertwined with its occurrence. Indeed, we could not have prospered nor would the world have fared as well if the IMM had not been a necessary by-product of the same economics that ushered in the new era of flexible exchange rates.

Notes

1. *Financial Innovation: The Last Twenty Years and the Next,* Merton H. Miller, Graduate School of Business, The University of Chicago, Selected Paper Number 63, May 1986.

2. Anonymous: Latin

3. A number of scholars have catalogued the events which signaled the end of the fixed rate system. Events cited range from the erratic monetary and fiscal policy in the United States produced by the Vietnam War, the efforts of the Bank of England in 1964 and 1967 to prop up an overvalued currency, similar Bundesbank efforts, increasing demand for U.S. gold reserves, the August 15, 1971 termination of the gold window by President Nixon, the Smithsonian Agreement, the oil shocks. See: Alfred E. Eckes, Jr., *A Search for Solvency,* "Death of Bretton Woods" (Austin: University of Texas Press, 1975), pp. 237–271; W. M. Scammell, *The International Economy Since 1945,* "The Breakup of the Dollar-Exchange System" (New York: St. Martin's Press, 1983), pp. 179–201; Robert Solomon, *The International Monetary System, 1945–1976: An Insider's View* (New York: Harper & Row Publishers, 1977).

4. *There's No Such Thing as a Free Lunch,* International Economic Policy, Milton Friedman (LaSalle, Illinois: Open Court, 1975).

5. Its name stemmed from the place, the Smithsonian Institution in Washington D.C., where, on December 17 and 18, 1971, the Group of Ten ministers met in an attempt to resolve the international financial crisis.

6. A system established by the EEC countries on April 24, 1972, for the narrowing of the margins of fluctuation between EEC currencies to 2.25% in a tunnel (plus or minus 2.25%). Original participating countries included Belgium, France, Germany, Italy, Luxembourg and the Netherlands.

7. *1972 International Monetary Market Annual Report,* Message from the Chairman, Leo Melamed.

8. *1973 International Monetary Market Annual Report,* Message from the Chairman, Leo Melamed.

9. *Business Week,* April 22, 1972.

10. *The Need for Futures Markets in Currencies,* Milton Friedman, 1971.

11. In 1972, there was no federal law or agency from which we were required to receive approval before listing a new futures contract. The federal statute creating the Commodity Futures Trading Commission (CFTC) was not adopted by Congress until 1974.

One of the great ironies of this event was that, over our vehement objections, the new agency adopted a rule requiring "proof of economic justification," before a new futures contract would be approved. It is doubtful whether in 1972 the IMM could have "proved" the economic need for a futures market in foreign exchange. This is a classic example of government meddling which results in suppression of market innovation. Surely, only the marketplace itself can "prove" economic justification of a financial product.

12. Beryl W. Sprinkel was named Chairman of the Council of Economic Advisors by President Reagan on April 18, 1985. Prior to that, he served as Under Secretary of the Treasury for Monetary Affairs from April 1981 to April 1985.

13. The first IMM Board of Directors included the following: Leo Melamed, Chairman of the Board; John T. Geldermann, First Vice Chairman; Carl E. Anderson, Second Vice Chairman, Robert J. O'Brien, Secretary; Laurence M. Rosenberg, Treasurer; A. Robert Abboud; Lloyd F. Arnold; Richard E. Boerke; William E. Goldstandt; Henry G. Jarecki; Daniel R. Jesser; Marlow King; Barry J. Lind; Donald L. Minucciani; William C. Muno; Frederick W. Schantz; Beryl W. Sprinkel; Michael Weinberg, Jr.

14. From remarks by Leo Melamed on the occasion of the Tenth Anniversary Celebration of the IMM, June 4, 1982.

19

A Proposal for Resolving the U.S. Balance of Payments Problem
Confidential memorandum to President-elect Richard Nixon

Milton Friedman

1. Introduction

The first few weeks of the new administration that takes over in January, 1969, will offer a unique opportunity to set the dollar free and thereby eliminate for years to come balance of payments restraints on U.S. economic policy. If this opportunity is not seized, it will not recur. Later events may force the administration to take the same measures that it could at first take voluntarily, but if so, the measures will then involve great political and social cost.

The required measures are simple and straightforward, but it will take courage and vision to cut the dog's tail off in one stroke rather than by inches. The temptation will be to temporize, to hope that small measures will suffice, that the problems will go away of themselves. It may therefore be worth stressing at the outset: (1) the uniqueness of the opportunity; (2) the importance of seizing the opportunity.

Three strictly comparable recent events indicate how far-reaching the consequences of bold action can be. (1) On one Sunday afternoon in 1948, Ludwig Erhard abolished price controls, setting the mark free (he did it on a Sunday afternoon because the U.S., U.K., and French occupation offices were closed and so unable to countermand his order). He thereby unleashed the German economic miracle and assured the Christian

This memorandum, dated October 15, 1968, was submitted to President Richard M. Nixon in December 1968. It was confidential at the time and has never heretofore been published. It seems appropriate for publication in this volume.   M.F.

Democratic Party unquestioned political dominance for several decades. (2) Charles de Gaulle in 1959–60 devalued the franc sharply, established a new franc, and promised a sound money policy. He thereby laid the basis for the balance of payments surpluses and accumulation of gold that enabled him for the next decade to have far greater political power in world affairs than the economic and political position of France justified. He frittered away these gains by a poor internal domestic policy—but it took a decade for this to occur. (3) Harold Wilson exemplifies a wasted opportunity. If he had floated the pound on first gaining office, putting all the blame, as he could then have done, on the allegedly "irresponsible" policies of the prior Tory regime, it is very likely that he would still be firmly in the saddle, and that the Labour Party would hold unquestioned political power. His failure to take this step forced on him one unpopular expedient after another—and did not even prevent later devaluation. He got the worst of all worlds—and so did Britain.

2. The measures required

Shortly after the inauguration of a new President in January, preferably on the second or third Friday evening or Saturday thereafter (after the financial markets are closed but in time for the announcement to be absorbed over the weekend), he should proclaim the following measures:

1. All restrictions on foreign investment by U.S. corporations are abolished effective immediately and the bureaucratic apparatus for administering them will be dismantled as rapidly as possible.

2. Similarly, all restrictions on foreign lending by U.S. commercial banks are ended, effective immediately.

3. Congress is being asked to repeal the interest-equalization tax.

4. All other restrictions on payments and trade imposed on balance of payments grounds will be removed as quickly as possible.

5. The U.S. will engage in no further gold transactions. For the time being it will keep its gold stock constant, neither buying nor selling gold either from or to central banks of other countries or in the private market. (This is already almost the *de facto* situation since the establishment of the two-tier gold system last February, so this point merely makes the policy explicit and open.)

6. The U.S. will engage in no exchange transactions in order to affect the rate of exchange between the U.S. dollar and other currencies— neither to peg the rates of exchange at fixed levels nor to manipulate them. The only exchange transactions engaged in by official U.S. agencies

will be to acquire the foreign exchange necessary for foreign governmental expenditures or to dispose of foreign exchange acquired in the course of foreign governmental activity. (This point will require an exemption by I.M.F. from present obligations. However, it is an exemption that has been granted to other countries and that can hardly be refused to the U.S.)

The announcement of these measures should be accompanied by an explanation that, on coming into office, the new President was shocked at the state in which the preceding administration had left the balance of payments. Current difficulties are the product of complete mismanagement by the prior administration of both domestic and international financial policies. If someone had tried to devise deliberately a policy to make the dollar look as weak as possible, he could hardly have done better than the Johnson Administration did. The Johnson policies were policies of weakness not strength; of restrictionism not expansion; of government controls not reliance on the initiative of free men operating in free markets.

The statement should stress that the basic economic strength of the U.S. economy is very great. If this strength can be released from the fetters in which the Johnson Administration bound it, it is very likely capable of supporting present exchange rates. However, the measures taken by the Johnson Administration have so distorted the situation that it is impossible to know what the appropriate rates of exchange are. The new administration therefore proposes to put its faith in the strength of the economy and its free enterprise system, not in a growing network of bureaucratic controls. Hence it proposes to leave Americans and foreigners free to use, hold, and exchange dollars in whatever way is advantageous to them.

The measures proposed do not devalue the dollar in any sense of that complex term. They amount rather to saying: the U.S. government is not going to impose any restrictions on the use, holding, or exchange of dollars.

3. Why the measures cannot be delayed

Why take these bold measures at once? Because if they are not taken at once, the new President, or members of his administration, will inevitably make statements and commitments about gold and exchange rates that will make it very difficult to take such measures except in conditions of great crisis. Never again will the range of options be so wide. The experience of Harold Wilson is a gruesome cautionary tale indicating the dangers in this direction. The time to fix the roof is in good weather, not when it is raining.

4. The economic consequences to be expected

The precise results to be expected from this policy depend on the reactions of foreign central banks and governments. But it is worth emphasizing that no foreign governments can prevent the U.S. from taking the steps proposed. All are within the country's own competence.

However, foreign governments can determine, at least to some extent and for a time, what effects the measures will have on exchange rates. For example, they could, if they wished, continue to peg exchange rates at their present level. They could do so by being ready to add to their dollar holdings—if the U.S. balance of payments continues in deficit—or by supplying excess dollars demanded out of their balances—if the U.S. balance of payments were to move to a surplus. In order for them to succeed in this policy for long, they would have to adapt their internal policies to ours. This is the only way they could keep either the accumulation or decumulation of dollars within limits. If they followed this policy, fine. The results would be those desired by present proponents of fixed exchange rates without the U.S. having to engage in foreign exchange controls and without any long, drawn-out international negotiations.

But this is not the only or even the most probable outcome. More likely, some countries would peg their currencies to the dollar, as suggested in the preceding paragraph, forming something of a dollar bloc. Other countries would let the exchange rates of their currencies vary relative to the U.S. Germany and Switzerland would probably let their currencies appreciate vis-à-vis the dollar—and their central bankers would breathe a sigh of relief at our having given them a way out of their present dilemma of either accumulating unduly large dollar balances or inflating. France and Britain might let their exchange rates float vis-à-vis the dollar. If so, both would probably depreciate rather than appreciate relative to the dollar, and hence even more relative to the Swiss franc and the Deutschemark.

Still other possibilities exist. The Common Market or part of it might form a "gold bloc" with their currencies pegged to gold and hence to one another. In that case, there would likely emerge two or three great currency areas: the dollar area, the pound area (or possibly the dollar-pound area), and the Common Market area.

Any of these possibilities would be fine for the U.S. The only possibility that should cause concern—and it is the horror story conjured up by central bankers who are constitutionally averse to having their powers reduced by the elimination of pegged exchange rates—is the setting off in some way of a trade war with competitive imposition of restrictions on trade. This spectre is drawn from the experience of competitive devaluations of the late 1930's. But that experience has little relevance today. That was a time of widespread unemployment when each country was trying to export unemployment. Today, the worldwide problem is over-employment.

The expressed fear is that the measures outlined would produce a tendency for the dollar to depreciate relative to other currencies, perhaps exaggerated at the outset by a speculative flight from the dollar. This would make U.S. goods cheap to foreigners and foreign goods expensive to Americans. Producers of goods abroad competitive with American goods would bring pressure on their governments to impose tariffs or other barriers to U.S. goods. U.S. producers in turn, it is argued, would pressure us to retaliate, setting off a trade war.

Such an outcome, while possible, seems highly unlikely—except momentarily in response to the initial shock. For it to spread and last is equivalent to water flowing uphill.

The problem now bothering foreign governments as a whole is that they are accumulating too many dollars. There is no conceivable way in which they can accumulate fewer dollars without holders of foreign currencies spending more on U.S. goods or services or securities or holders of U.S. dollars spending less on foreign goods or services or securities. Arithmetic is arithmetic. A deficit on current account must mean a surplus on capital account and vice versa. Of course, people often want to have their cake and eat it too but they cannot succeed.

Similarly here. If foreign governments do not want to see their imports from the U.S. rise relative to their exports, they always have the alternative of keeping the exchange rate fixed by accumulating the excess dollars. Because of the removal of *our* restrictions, the new flow of dollars might be higher than before (though for reasons explained in a moment, it is more likely to be lower), in which case they might be impelled to impose restrictions to replace our restrictions. It cannot, however, be in their own interest to impose restrictions so extensive as to reduce their imports from us below the initial level. Hence the U.S. is always in a position to prevent any cumulative trade war without any damage to itself. The U.S. can and should simply take the position that it will refuse to retaliate if any restrictions are imposed.

Needless to say, irrational behavior can occur for a time. However, if the U.S. keeps its self-control and persists in a steady nondiscriminatory removal of controls, such behavior cannot last.

Unlike the short-term reactions, the long-term effect is clear: the removal of restrictions would greatly strengthen the position of the dollar as the major currency used in international trade. New York would resume its growth as the real financial center of the world. The Johnson policies have stopped that development. By making U.S. and foreign holders of dollars fearful that they will be subject to exchange control, they have stimulated the development of a Euro-dollar market. This market will shrink drastically if we remove restrictions on the holding, use, and exchange of dollars. Dollars are now the major vehicle currency in international trade and they will continue to be—provided only that the U.S. follow reasonably sensible domestic economic policies.

The events in France last May assured also that the dollar would remain the major currency in which individuals and governments would hold their liquid reserves. Again, removal of restrictions would make the dollar still more attractive for this purpose.

For both these reasons, it may well be that the dollar is today undervalued rather than overvalued, and that it appears overvalued only because the Johnson policies have unnecessarily frightened the financial community and the world.

5. Alternative policies

There are only two major alternative policies.

1. *Temporizing.* We could do nothing new, simply continuing present policies in the hope that continued inflation abroad and moderate price stability at home will produce sufficient improvement in the balance of payments to enable present restrictions to be removed gradually. These restrictions have probably worsened rather than improved our balance of payments because of their effect on confidence in the U.S. dollar. However, removing them, without the protection offered by the other elements in the proposed measures outlined above, may initially make the deficit larger.

This policy is a gamble but not a completely hopeless one. Indeed, it is considerably more promising since the French near-revolution of May than it was before. Those events destroyed the franc as an alternative to the dollar for liquid funds. More important, they caused all holders of funds to recognize how rapidly situations can change and thus indirectly weakened greatly the appeal of the mark and the Swiss franc.

The policy also has more chance of working in a Nixon Administration than in a Humphrey Administration. A Nixon Administration is far more likely to pursue moderate and restrained domestic policies and to avoid significant inflation than is a Humphrey Administration. Equally important, for the short run, this expectation is widely held at home and abroad. As a result, the election of Nixon will encourage continued capital inflows to the U.S., while the election of Humphrey may well produce a large capital outflow and bring on a crisis.

Yet even on a very generous and optimistic assessment of the possibilities, the likelihood is small that the policy will work for long in the sense of enabling the U.S. to dispense for good with restrictions. The capital inflows produced by the events in France and by a Nixon election are in good part temporary, once-for-all spurts arising from a reshuffling of liquid balances. There will remain a permanent favorable effect from the tarnishing of the appeal of marks and francs to holders of funds, but that effect, which has to do with the allocation of *additions* to liquid balances, is necessarily much smaller, measured as an annual flow, than the effect produced by a transfer of existing balances. The balance on current account has continued to deteriorate at an alarming rate, from a surplus of $7 billion on goods alone and of over $8 billion on goods and services as recently as 1964 to a zero surplus on goods alone in the first two quarters of 1968 and a surplus at the annual rate of less than $2 billion on goods and services. Once the temporary spurt of capital inflows tapers off, the balance of payments will again become a critical problem.

The most likely result of temporizing, therefore, is that within a year or two at most, and even under the best of circumstances, the balance of payments will be a running sore requiring action and capable of erupting into a crisis at any time. When and if it does, there will be no significant alternative to the measures proposed—but these measures will then have to be taken out of weakness and under crisis conditions whereas now they can be taken from strength and can prevent crisis. That there will be no other significant alternative will become clearer if we examine the chief other possibility now receiving attention—devaluation.

2. *Devaluation*. This has two different meanings: (a) A rise in the U.S. official price of gold accompanied by a similar rise in the British, French, German, etc. official price of gold so that exchange rates are unchanged. (b) A rise in the U.S. official price of gold, with an agreement by at least some other major countries (e.g., Germany, Italy, Switzerland) that they will not raise the price of gold in terms of their currencies or will not

raise it as much, so that the exchange rate of the U.S. dollar depreciates—vis-à-vis some other important currencies.

(a) *A rise in the official world price of gold.* This accomplishes very little. Even its proponents only argue that it buys time. For what? At best it raises the amount of reserves we can use to finance deficits. It does nothing whatever to reduce those deficits—unless it encourages foreign countries to inflate faster than we do. There still remains the problem of finding some way to adjust our foreign payments and receipts to changing conditions of international trade.

Politically, a rise in the official price of gold benefits primarily Russia and South Africa and the speculators who have been hoarding gold for such a rise. Perhaps it might have made some sense when we had $20 billion of gold. But now that our gold reserves are halved, we have little to gain. And it seems nearly intolerable to say to the world: "We shall buy back from you at $70 an ounce the gold we sold you for $35 an ounce."

If we adopt the measures proposed, the price of gold in private markets will be free to rise, just as it now is under the two-tier system. Very probably it will rise over time. But such a rise in the price of gold on the free market is a very different thing from a rise in the *official* price of gold. The U.S. government need have no concern whatsoever with it. It would not be committed to buying or selling gold. The price of gold would have no greater relevance for its policy than the price of lead or copper or automobiles.

(b) *A rise in the official U.S. price of gold, or depreciation of U.S. exchange rates.* This makes more sense, since at least it contributes to reducing a balance of payments deficit by making U.S. goods cheaper and foreign goods more expensive. But it has serious disadvantages. (i) There is no way to know what the right exchange rates are. (ii) Extensive negotiation is likely to be required. (iii) If the wrong rates are chosen, we are stuck back where we now are. (iv) Most important of all, by comparison with the measures recommended earlier, it may resolve *this* balance of payments problem but it does not eliminate *the* balance of payments problem, whereas those measures, by relying on market mechanisms, do. Again Britain's recent experience is an excellent cautionary tale.

Politically, this method of negotiated devaluation puts us in an undesirable position. We are a great nation. The dollar is the leading currency of the world. We should behave like a great nation, not engage in demeaning and niggling negotiations to get other countries to agree to "let" us depreciate by X per cent vis-à-vis this currency, by Y per cent vis-à-vis that currency. If we behave like a great nation, the world will rapidly move to a dollar standard. The way to behave like a great nation is to put our domestic house in order and, for the rest, say to the world: A dollar is a dollar. Borrow it, lend it, buy it, sell it, use it for trade, or for denominating long-term contracts. We shall not try to prevent you. We shall impose no restrictions on your use of the dollar. We shall let capital flow freely.

(c) *"Paper Gold" and such ilk*. It will be said by many that there is a third alternative: an international agreement to provide a world money as a substitute for gold, of which the agreement to establish SDR's is a portent. The SDR's may have some minor usefulness, but they or further measures in this direction do not offer a satisfactory solution. The belief that they do confuses the problem of liquidity with the problem of adjustment. At most, SDR's and the like would enable us to borrow more to tide over a larger deficit for a longer period. They do nothing whatsoever to end the deficit. They do nothing to improve the adjustment mechanism so as to avoid future undue deficits and surpluses.

6. Costs of adopting the suggested policy

On the economic front, there appear to be only gains and no costs from the suggested policy.

On the domestic political front, it will be argued that the policy sacrifices the "discipline" of a fixed exchange rate standard in encouraging or enforcing sound domestic monetary and fiscal policy. This argument would have merit if the alternative to the suggested policy were a true gold standard. It has no merit for the actual alternative. We are not and should not be willing to submit to the discipline of whatever monetary policies other countries choose to adopt. In any event, in the modern world, changing exchange rates are a better signal and provide more appropriate and effective discipline than pressure on exchange reserves.

On the international political front, there may be a short-term cost. Some countries may feel that we have undermined international monetary cooperation, and have not played the game by acting unilaterally. But, for the longer pull, there will be a major gain rather than cost to our international political position. This gain will come from the elimination of the frictions that are now produced by the measures of exchange control that country after country has been forced to take from time to time when faced with balance of payments problems, and, most of all, from the elimination of the unjustified political power that has accrued to surplus nations. The Johnson Administration has given General de Gaulle and the West Germans alike a political influence out of all proportion to their true strength because of its insistence on pegging the price of gold—already given up—and on pegging exchange rates—not yet given up. Any short-run political costs will largely reflect the unhappiness of Germany and France at our taking back from them the loaded guns we were so unwise as to put in their hands.

7. Conclusion

In conclusion, it may be well to emphasize again the uniqueness of the opportunity that a new adminsitration will have. Harold Wilson had such an opportunity when he first took office. The Conservatives will have another when they replace the Labour Party. Enoch Powell, the most intelligent and courageous of the Tory leaders, has already made it clear that he would jump at the chance. The other Tory leaders, less brilliant and more stodgy, may well pass it by. John Kennedy would have had such an opportunity except that he tossed it away by committing himself before his election to holding the price of gold at $35 an ounce. Johnson did not have such an opportunity because he was committed to Kennedy's policies. If this opportunity is not seized, and, if the unlikely occurs and there is no major international financial crisis that forces similar actions, the next opportunity in this country will only come when and if the Democrats capture the presidency.

It is worth emphasizing also how large are the stakes. There is probably no other economic measure that the new administration will have the power to take that can contribute anything like so much simultaneously to greater freedom of U.S. citizens from government control, increased economic prosperity, liberalization of international trade, and the freedom of maneuver of the U.S. government in foreign affairs.

PART VI

MACROECONOMIC COORDINATION AND FLEXIBLE EXCHANGE RATES

20

COORDINATION COULD BE WASHED OUT

Alan Greenspan

Economists generally argue that the ideal international economic order would include a single currency and free trade. Such a regime would maximize economic efficiency and lead to all the textbook benefits of comparative advantage and optimum allocation of capital. The 50 separate states of the United States achieved that, at least to a large extent, and certainly the Common Market supported by the European monetary system is a noteworthy effort. But common currencies and open borders to goods and services are too often in conflict with national sovereignty.

The concept of international economic coordination is essentially a notion in which sovereignty is traded off for the economic benefits of an international division of labor. One could argue, as indeed I would, that it is to everyone's advantage to engage in the benefits of international trade and finance and that the exercise of sovereignty would best serve a nation's people over the long run by freer trade and coordinated international economic policies. The problem is that national politics seemingly require a much shorter time frame for fulfillment that it takes for international cooperation to yield benefits to individual countries and their citizens. Recently the world has witnessed only a few episodes of successful economic cooperation.

Principal Obstacle

Coordination is even more difficult in the face of very strong market forces. This is especially the case in the exchange markets, and unless exchange-rate coordination is feasible, policies focused on interest-rate levels and differentials become particularly difficult.

The European monetary system has been able to hold the cross rates among the major European currencies in a relatively narrow band. No

441

such stabilization, however, is likely to be initiated soon for any of the major exchange rates relative to the U.S. dollar. The principal obstacle is the extraordinarily large stock of U.S. dollar assets held in international currency portfolios. Of the approximately $2.5 billion in international bank claims on non-residents, more than two-thirds are denominated in dollars. Moreover, about three-fourths of international bond issues are denominated in dollars. Despite Japan's dramatic rise as an international financial power, international claims denominated in yen remain a small fraction of those in dollars.

When there are relatively small amounts of cross-border claims in foreign currencies, and, hence, little in the way of financial assets held in other than domestic currencies, the demand for foreign exchange tends to mirror intercountry demand for goods and services. Under those conditions, markets generally tend to arbitrage the currencies toward levels consistent with purchasing-power parity—that is, to equalize what currencies can purchase in the way of goods and services originating in various countries. Such conditions exist, more or less, among the European currencies, and this is a major reason for the relative success in maintaining exchange-rate stability.

When substantial cross-border holdings of financial claims exist, however, the demand for one currency relative to another is the combination of demand for transaction and investment purposes. In recent years, it has become ever more obvious that investment demand is virtually swamping transactions demand in all dealings with respect to the dollar. This results from the extraordinary buildup of dollar-denominated financial assets in world markets, the demand for which changes sufficiently rapidly to overwhelm changes stimulated by shifts in the underlying purchasing power of the U.S. dollar relative to other currencies. This is not the case with other currencies, even such "strong" currencies as the yen and the mark, and is one reason it's so difficult to reach the "right" value of the dollar vis-a-vis major U.S. trading partners.

The very size of dollar investment holdings implies that relatively small random changes in the propensity to hold dollar-denominated assets create flows that swamp transaction demand shifts. Such shifts obscure pressures on the value of the currency stemming from changes in purchasing-power parities. And the limited supply of alternative currencies means any moderate change in the propensity to hold dollars will create a disproportionate change in demand for yen or mark securities relative to the available stock of such securities. This results in a major change in these currencies' bilateral exchange rates relative to the dollar. If the aggregate supply of yen among international currencies, for example, were equal to that of the U.S. dollar, exchange-rate fluctuations between the yen and the dollar would moderate, although their volatility vis-a-vis other currencies would remain.

Hence, any realistic effort to reduce the volatility of exchange rates is likely to require equalizing the available stocks of the major currencies in international financial markets and/or lowering the aggregate levels.

Obviously, it's undesirable to reduce cross-border claims between the originators of savings and the ultimate users of those savings. However, the huge interbank market proliferated beyond any expectation in the past 20 years, in part because of the differing regulatory environments for international banking. Many of these interbank deposits are vehicles to avoid national and central-bank regulations and reserve requirements (which, of course, are equivalent to taxes on banking claims).

How much reduction in redepositing is either desirable or feasible, it isn't clear. Should a substantial reduction occur, it also is unclear that the net demand for any currency relative to the dollar would change significantly. A good part of interbank depositing is merely a passive process to facilitate intermediation between the final user of funds and the initial saver.

Anticipatory claims or liabilities in the interbank market that are not immediately supported by final demand do tend to build up, however. For example, a bank anticipating a fall in the exchange rate of the dollar could accept dollar deposits, convert them to another currency and redeposit them in another bank. The transaction would weaken the dollar's exchange rate, but of course the subsequent reconversion would strengthen the dollar.

Undercutting Efficiency

In the long run, this expectations-based inventorying of funds cannot have an effect on exchange rates, since net demand and supply of funds ultimately will prevail. Nevertheless, fluctuations in interbank depositing beyond those which passively reflect underlying demand almost surely impose some degree of volatility on the foreign-exchange market.

Redepositing can't be suppressed significantly and effectively, it would appear, without undercutting the extraordinary efficiency of international financial markets. It is possible, however, that less regulation of capital flows could reduce the need for multiple redepositing in the Caribbean or other havens from regulation and taxation.

Minus some attention on this front, exchange rates against the dollar are likely to continue to be volatile. Whether anchored with some fixed standard or not, efforts at international coordination of macroeconomic policies will be difficult.

21

Turbulence in the Foreign Exchange Markets and Macroeconomic Policies*

Jacob A. Frenkel

After the move to generalized floating in 1973, U.S. inflation accelerated, interest rates rose, the value of the dollar in the market for foreign exchange fluctuated, and the volatility of exchange rates between the U.S. dollar and major foreign currencies reached new heights. These developments pose several questions: What causes the large fluctuations of exchange rates? What causes the large divergences between the external and internal values of the dollar? Have exchange rates fluctuated excessively? Did the move to a flexible exchange rate regime contribute to the deterioration of the dollar? What would be the implications of restoring fixed parities for the dollar? What would be the implications of adopting an intervention rule in the foreign exchange market? What role could the external value of the dollar play in determining the course of the Federal Reserve's policy? How could macroeconomic policy contribute to stabilizing the internal and the external values of the dollar?

The Record

To set the stage for the analysis it is useful to start with a brief review of the empirical record. This review concentrates on the evolution of and the interrelation among exchange rates, prices, and interest rates during

*This is a revised and abridged version of a paper with the same title presented on October 29, 1981, as the Henry Thornton Lecture, The City University, Centre for Banking and International Finance, London, England. This version does not include the discussions of and references to Thornton's work; it includes an updated first table as well as extended third and fifth sections. This research is part of the National Bureau of Economic Research (NBER) Program in International Studies and Economic Fluctuations. The views expressed are those of the author and not necessarily those of the NBER.

the 1970s. Subsequent sections contain the interpretation of these facts as well as the policy implications. These sections draw on Frenkel 1982 and some of the arguments draw on Frenkel 1981a, 1981b and on Frenkel and Mussa 1981, 1980.

The first set of relevant facts concerns the turbulence of the foreign exchange market. A simple measure of such turbulence is the average absolute monthly percentage changes in the various exchange rates over some interval of time. Table 1–1 reports such measures for three major exchange rates: the U.S. dollar/pound sterling, the dollar/French franc, and the dollar/Deutsche mark for the period June 1973-November 1981.[1] In all cases the average absolute change exceeded 2 percent per month. In comparison the average absolute monthly percentage change of wholesale and consumer price indices and of the ratios of national price levels were only about half that of the exchange rate.

The second set of facts concerns the predictability of these changes in exchange rates. If the forward premium on foreign exchange is regarded as a measure of the market's prediction of the future change in the exchange rate, then a comparison between actual changes and the forward premium may reveal the extent to which the market was successful in predicting these changes. Figures 1–1 and 1–2 present plots of predicted and realized monthly percentage changes of the dollar/pound sterling and the dollar/Deutsche mark exchange rates where the predicted change is measured by the lagged forward premium. The key fact emerging from these figures is that predicted changes in exchange rates account for a very small fraction of actual changes. (Figures concerning other pairs of currencies and other periods of time reveal the same characteristic.) This phenomenon is also reflected in the comparison between the variances of actual and predicted changes: In all cases the variances of the monthly percentage changes in exchange rates exceeded the variances of the monthly forward premiums by a factor that is larger than 20.

If exchange rates moved in accord with relative national price levels as suggested by a simple version of the purchasing power parity theory, the volatility of exchange rates would be regarded as a manifestation of the forces underlying the volatility of national inflation rates, and the turbulence of exchange rates would probably not be regarded as an additional source of social cost. The third set of facts relevant for this issue concerns the relation between exchange rates and prices. As illustrated in Figures 1–1 and 1–2, short-run changes in exchange rates have not been closely linked to short-run differentials in the corresponding national inflation rates. Furthermore, this loose link seems to be cumulative. As illustrated in Figures 1–3 and 1–4 divergences from purchasing power parities,

TABLE 1–1

Mean Absolute Percentage Changes in Prices and Exchange Rates Monthly Data: June 1973-November 1981

Country	Variable					
	Wholesale Price Index	Consumer Price Index	Stock Market Index	Exchange Rates against the Dollar		CPI/CPI_U.S.
				Spot	Forward	
United States	0.90	0.75	3.11	—	—	—
United Kingdom	1.25	1.17	4.82	2.30	2.35	0.66
France	1.02	0.91	5.50	2.22	2.21	0.30
Germany	0.47	0.41	2.35	2.51	2.47	0.43

Note: All variables represent the absolute values of monthly percentage changes in the data. Wholesale price index is from IFS line 63; consumer price index is from IFS line 64; and the stock market index represents the industrial share prices, from IFS line 62.
Source: *International Financial Statistics* (IFS), International Monetary Fund.

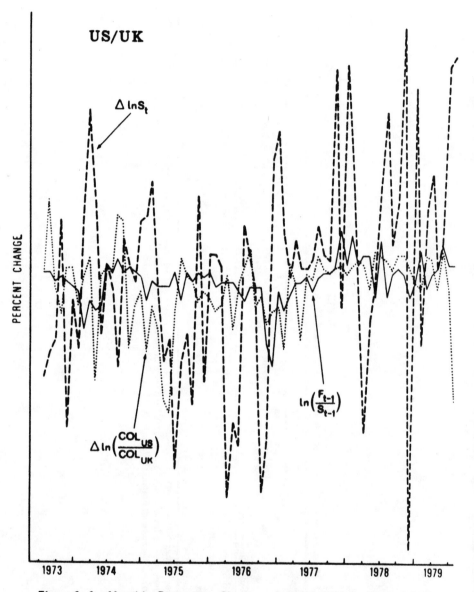

Figure 1-1. Monthly Percentage Changes of the U.S./U.K. Cost of Living Indices [$\Delta(\ln COL_{US}/COL_{UK})$], of the $/£ Exchange Rate, ($\Delta \ln S_t$), and the Monthly Forward Premium [$\ln(F_{t-1}/S_{t-1})$]: July 1973–July 1979.

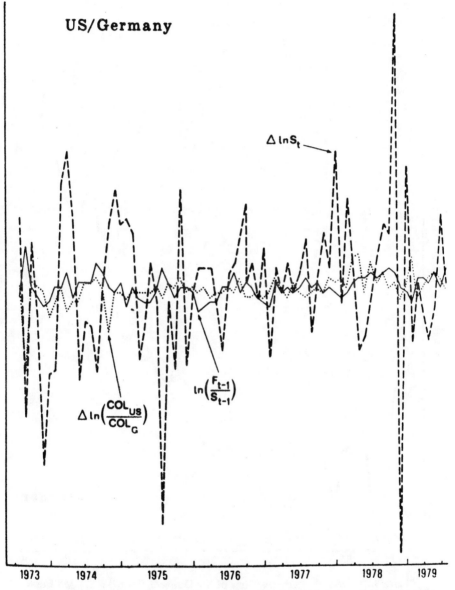

Figure 1-2. Monthly Percentage Changes of the U.S./German Cost of Living Indices [$\Delta(\ln COL_{US}/COL_G)$], of the $/DM Exchange Rate, ($\Delta \ln S_t$), and the Monthly Forward Premium [$\ln(F_{t-1}/S_{t-1})$]: July 1973–July 1979.

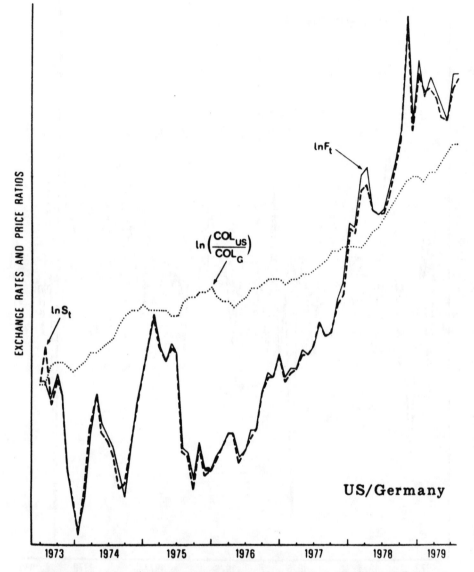

Figure 1-3. Monthly Observations of the Dollar/£ Spot ($\ln S_t$) and Forward ($\ln F_t$). Exchange Rates and the Ratio of the U.S./U.K. Cost of Living Indices [$\ln (COL_{US}/COL_{UK})$ (Scaled to Equal the Spot Exchange Rate at the Initial Month)] : June 1973–July 1979.

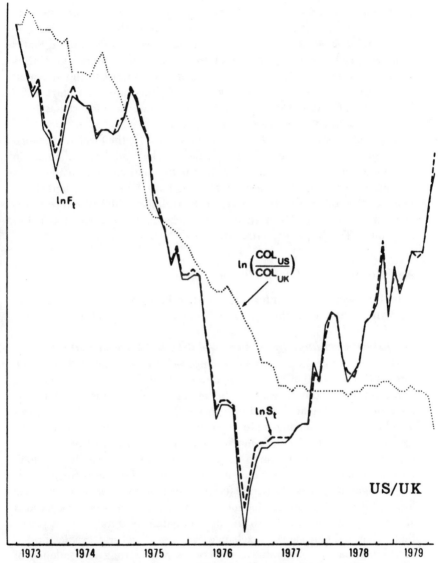

Figure 1-4. Monthly Observations of the Dollar/DM Spot ($\ell n\, S_t$) and Forward ($\ell n\, F_t$). Exchange Rates and the Ratio of the U.S./German Cost of Living Indices [$\ell n (COL_{US}/COL_G)$ (Scaled to Equal the Spot Exchange Rate at the Initial Month)] : June 1973–July 1979.

measured in terms of the relation between exchange rates and the ratio of consumer price indices, seem to persist.

The fourth and final set of facts concerns the relation between the value of the dollar and the rate of interest. The record of the 1970s (at least up to mid-1979) shows that a rise in the rate of interest in the United States (relative to the foreign rate of interest) has been associated with a depreciation of the dollar. This fact, which is in contrast to the view that a high interest rate yields a strong dollar, is illustrated in Figure 1–5.[2] Since mid-1979 the rise in the U.S. relative rate of interest has been associated with an appreciation of the dollar.

In summary the record of the 1970s shows that (1) the foreign exchange value of the dollar was highly volatile, (2) by and large changes in exchange rates were unpredictable, (3) the fluctuations in exchange rates did not conform closely to movements in national price levels, and (4) for most of the 1970s the rise in the U.S. (relative) rate of interest was associated with a decline in the foreign exchange value of the dollar, but from mid-1979 this relation reversed itself.

An Interpretation Of The Record

In this section the empirical record is interpreted in terms of the modern "asset-market theory" of exchange rate determination.

Why Have Exchange Rates Been Volatile and Unpredictable?

The central insight of the modern approach to the analysis of exchange rates is the notion that the exchange rate, being the relative price of two durable assets (monies), can best be analyzed within a framework that is appropriate for the analysis of asset prices. The volatility and the unpredictability of price changes are key characteristics of auction and organized asset markets. In such markets current prices reflect expectations concerning the future course of events, and new information, which induces changes in expectations, is immediately reflected in corresponding changes in prices, thus precluding unexploited profit opportunities from arbitrage. The strong dependence of current prices on expectations about the future is unique to the determination of durable asset prices that are traded in organized exchange; it is less of a characteristic of price determination of nondurable commodities. The strong dependence of asset prices on expectations also implies that periods that are dominated by uncertainties, new information, rumors, announcements, and "news," which induce frequent changes in expectations, are likely to be periods in which asset prices exhibit large fluctuations. It is also likely that during

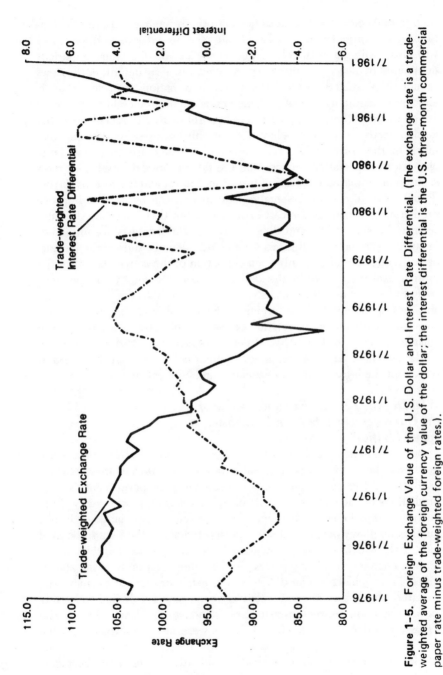

Figure 1-5. Foreign Exchange Value of the U.S. Dollar and Interest Rate Differential. (The exchange rate is a trade-weighted average of the foreign currency value of the dollar; the interest differential is the U.S. three-month commercial paper rate minus trade-weighted foreign rates.).

Source: The weights are from the *Federal Reserve Bulletin*, August 1978, p. 700.

such periods changes in expectations are the prime cause of the fluctuations in asset prices. Since exchange rates are viewed as asset prices, they will also exhibit a relatively large degree of volatility during periods dominated by news that alters expectations. Since by definition the news cannot be predicted on the basis of past information, it is clear that by and large the fluctuations of exchange rates are unpredictable.

The evidence lends support to the hypothesis that in recent years the foreign exchange market behaved as an efficient asset market and that much of the volatility of exchange rates reflected frequent and large changes in expectations concerning the future. Forward exchange rates seem to be unbiased forecasts of future spot rates, and the forecast errors do not seem to contain sysematic patterns that can be used to improve predictions. Of course, forecast errors exist, but their direction does not seem to be systematic, and thus *on average* the forecasts are unbiased. However, as indicted in Figures 1-1 and 1-2 the magnitude of the forecast errors is substantial and only a small fraction of the actual change in the foreign exchange value of the dollar is accounted for by the previous period's forward premium or discount on foreign exchange. The volatility and unpredictability of the foreign exchange value of the currency are consistent with the interpretation of the role of news. They reflect the volatile character of the 1970s, which witnessed great turbulence in the world economy, large swings in government policy, and great uncertainties about the future course of economic and political events.

Why Did the Foreign Exchange Value of the Currency Deviate from Purchasing Power Parities?

One of the striking facts concerning the relation between the price level and the foreign exchange value of currency during the 1970s (as exhibited in Figures 1-1 to 1-4) has been the poor performance of the predictions of the simple versions of the purchasing power parity (PPP) doctrine. As is known, when applied to aggregate national price levels, purchasing power parities can be expected to hold in the long run only if most of the shocks to the system are of a monetary origin and thus do not require changes in relative prices. To the extent that most of the shocks reflect "real" changes (like differential growth rates among sectors), the required changes in sectoral relative prices may result in a relatively loose connection between exchange rates and aggregate price levels. The 1970s was a decade in which real shocks were not in shortage, and the experience of the 1970s illustrates clearly the extent to which "real" shocks (oil embargo, supply shocks, commodity booms and shortages, shifts in the demand for money resulting for example from financial innovations, differential productivity growth) result in systematic deviations from purchasing power parities. These real shocks necessitated changes in real exchange rates and resulted in the persisting deviations from purchasing power parities illustrated in Figures 1-1 to 1-4. It is relevant to note however that the persistence of deviations from purchasing power parities was more pronounced for exchange rates between the U.S. dollar and the European currencies than among the European currencies themselves. This difference can be explained by noting (1) that due to transport cost, purchasing power parities are expected to hold better among the neighboring European countries than between each of these countries and the United States; (2) that changes in commercial policies and nontariff barriers to trade seem to have been more stable within Europe than between Europe and the United States; (3) that within Europe the snake agreement and later on the European Monetary System have resulted in a reduced degree of intra-European flexibility of exchange rates; and (4) that large changes seem to have occurred in the equilibrium real exchange rates between the U.S. dollar and the European currencies. It should be emphasized, however, that to some extent the overall poor performance of the purchasing power parities doctrine is specific to the 1970s. During the floating rates era of the 1920s, the doctrine seems to have been more reliable.

It is pertinent to note that in addition to the factors that account for persisting deviations from purchasing power parities, there is a presumption that, at least in the short run, as illustrated by the evidence in Figues 1-1 and 1-2, exchange rate fluctuations would not be matched by corresponding fluctuations of aggregate price levels. The arguments in the next section emphasize that in periods dominated by news that alters expectations, exchange rates are likely to be highly volatile. Aggregate price indices on the other hand are not expected to reveal such a degree of volatility since they reflect the prices of goods and services that exhibit some "stickiness" and that are less durable and therefore less sensitive to the news. It follows therefore that in periods of ample news, which induces large fluctuations in exchange rates, there will also be large, deviations from purchasing power parities. An intrinsic difference thus exists between exchange rates and national price indices. Exchange rates do not reflect only current circumstances but also reflect expectations concerning the *future*. In contrast, the prices of national outputs reflect to a large extent *present* and *past* circumstances as they are embedded in existing contracts. Consequently, when there are large and frequent changes in expectations, it is likely that the future will be expected to differ greatly from the present and the past. Under such circumstances one may find large and frequent deviations from purchasing power parities when the latter are computed using current prices.

What Accounts for the Relation between the Interest Rate and the Exchange Rate?

Prior to accounting for the empirical facts outlined previously, it is useful to recall the arguments of the conventional analysis, which predicts that high rates of interest are likely to be associated with currencies that are strong in international money markets. According to the typical explanations a higher rate of interest attracts foreign capital, which induces a surplus in the capital account of the balance of payments and thereby induces an appreciation of the domestic currency. Another variant of this approach states that the higher rate of interest lowers spending and thus induces a surplus in the current account of the balance of payments, which results in an appreciation of the currency. A third variant claims that the higher rate of interest implies (via the interest parity theory) a higher forward premium on foreign exchange and, to the extent that at a given point in time the forward exchange rate is predetermined by past history (an assumption that is clearly rejected by the evidence on the co-movements of spot and forward rates as illustrated in Figures 1-3 and 1-4), the required rise in the forward premium will be brought about by an appreciation of the domestic currency. Whatever the route, this approach predicts a positive relation between the rate of interest and the foreign exchange value of the domestic currency.

Although such a prediction might be appropriate for noninflationary environments, it is entirely inappropriate for inflationary environments like the one prevailing in the United States in recent years. Indeed, as indicated by Figure 1-5 this prediction is inconsistent with the record. During the 1970s (up to mid-1979) the secular rise in the rate of interest in the United States (relative to the foreign rate of interest) has been associated with a secular depreciation of the dollar. The same broad facts emerge from an examination of the circumstances prevailing in a cross-section of countries. Generally, countries with relatively low rates in interest (West Germany, Switzerland) have relatively strong currencies, whereas countries with relatively high rates of interest (Canada, Italy) have relatively weak currencies.

The explanation is straightforward. During an inflationary environment the primary cause for variations in rates of interest are variations in inflationary expectations. In such an environment a relatively rapid rise in prices is associated with high *nominal* rates of interest as well as with a *depreciation* of the currency in terms of foreign exchange. In an inflationary environment a rise in the nominal rate of interest may just compensate for the erosion of purchasing power without providing for a higher *real* return. Under these circumstances a rise in the U.S. rate of interest may not attract foreign capital. Capital markets are much more sophisticated than what is presumed by some of the simplistic theories. The evidence indicates that higher nominal rates of interest are associated with a forward discount on the currency in foreign exchange markets without necessarily raising *real* yields and without necessarily attracting foreign capital (except, possibly, for the very short run). The reversal of the relation between the U.S. interest and the external value of the dollar that has taken place since mid-1979 indicates that recently the prime cause for the fluctuations in U.S. interest rates has not been variations in inflationary expectations but rather variations in the *real* rate of interest occasioned by the large U.S. budget deficit.

The relation between the exchange rate, the real interest rate, and the expected rate of inflation (relative to the corresponding foreign rates) can be derived from the following basic parity conditions. Equation (1.1) describes the interest parity condition implied by covered interest arbitrage:

$$s_t = E_t s_{t+1} + i_t^* - i_t, \tag{1.1}$$

where s_t denotes the logarithm of the exchange rate in period t, E_t denotes the expectation operator (based on information available at period t) and thus, $E_t s_{t+1}$ denotes the expected (logarithm of) the exchange rate for period $t+1$ based on the information available at period t; i_t and i_t^* denote the rates of interest on domestic and foreign securities that are identical in all aspects except for the currency of denomination.

The second parity condition is the Irwin Fisher condition, which expresses the nominal rate of interest i as the sum of the real rate r and the expected inflation. Equations (1.2) and (1.3) describe this condition for the domestic and the foreign rates of interest:

$$i_t = r_t + E_t (p_{t+1} - p_t), \tag{1.2}$$

$$i_t^* = r_t^* + E_t (p_{t+1}^* - p_t^*), \tag{1.3}$$

where p_t denotes the (logarithm of) the price level in period t and where an asterisk denotes variables pertaining to the foreign country.

Using equation (1.1), the interest parity for period $t-1$ is

$$s_{t-1} = E_{t-1} s_t + i_{t-1}^* - i_{t-1}. \tag{1.4}$$

Subtracting equation (1.4) from equation (1.1) and using equations (1.2) and (1.3) yields

$$s_t = s_{t-1} + [(p_t - p_{t-1}) - (p_t^* - p_{t-1}^*)] + [(r_t^* - r_{t-1}^*$$
$$- (r_t - r_{t-1})] + (E_t s_{t+1} - E_{t-1} s_t) + (E_t p_{t+1}^* \quad (1.5)$$
$$- E_{t-1} p_t^*) - (E_t p_{t+1} - E_{t-1} p_t).$$

In deriving equation (1.5) it was assumed that the expected value of a variable for period t, based on the information available in period t, equals the actual value of that variable, e.g., $E_t p_t = p_t$.

Equation (1.5) demonstrates the relation between the exchange rate and the components of the nominal rate of interest. The framework underlying equation (1.5) is based on Isard (forthcoming). See also the discussion in Edwards (forthcoming), and in Frenkel (1983). The first bracketed term in equation (1.5) suggests that a rise in the domestic rate of inflation relative to foreign inflation is associated with a *depreciation* of the domestic currency (a rise in s_t). The second bracketed term in equation (1.5) suggests that a rise in the domestic real rate of interest relative to the foreign rate is associated with an *appreciation* of the domestic currency (a fall in s_t). The additional terms on the right-hand side of equation (1.5) describe changes in expectations concerning the exchange rate and prices. These changes in expectations are likely to be in response to new information and thus reflect the association between the exchange rate and news.

Policy Implications

The high and variable world inflation and U.S. inflation resulted in high and variable rates of interest and in volatile exchange rates. The induced turbulence of the foreign exchange value of the currency is costly, as indicated by the large and unpredictable fluctuations that did not conform closely to movements in relative national price levels. It generates capital gains and losses for holders of assets denominated in different national monies; it induces asset holders to alter behavior and expend resources in an attempt to reduce risk; it interferes with the efficiency of the price system in guiding resource allocation, and it may result in economically inappropriate patterns of production, consumption, and trade. A relevant question therefore is how government policy can be managed to stabilize the currency and reduce its costly and undesirable volatility. In this section the implications of alternative policies are analyzed.

We Should Not Restore Fixed Parities

Very few economists recommend fighting inflation by pegging the price level through direct intervention in commodity markets. Similar (though not identical) arguments could be madé against fighting the external depreciation of the dollar by pegging the exchange rate. Both dimensions of the deteriorating currency are reflections of macroeconomic policies, and both can be handled with the aid of macroeconomic policies. Prices and exchange rates are the manifestation of policies rather than tools that should be manipulated as instruments of policy.

It is clear that as a *technical* matter policy can reduce the fluctuations of the exchange rate even to the extent of a complete pegging of the rate. If the source of evil were the variability of exchange rates, then pegging the rate would have been the simple and feasible solution. The experience with the Bretton Woods system indicates that this is not the case. It may not be assumed that policies that are successful in pegging the exchange rate for a period of time are also successful in eliminating the ultimate cause underlying the fluctuations. Such policies may only transfer the effects of disturbances from the foreign exchange market to somewhere else in the economic system. For example, it is clear that a commitment to peg the rate of exchange implies reduced control over the course of monetary policy, which would have to be adjusted so as to ensure the fixity of the rate. In that case the attempt to reduce variability of exchange rates would result in an increased variability of the money supply. It follows that the relevant choice is not between costly turbulence and free tranquility but, rather, between alternative outlets to the underlying turbulence. This is one of the important constraints that the openness of the economy to international trade in goods and capital imposes on the effectiveness of monetary policy.

One could argue, however, that the obligation to peg the rate would alter fundamentally the conduct of policy by introducing discipline. Experience seems to suggest, however, that national governments are unlikely to adjust the conduct of domestic policies so as to be disciplined by the exchange rate regime. Rather, it is more reasonable to assume that the exchange rate regime is more likely to adjust to whatever discipline national governments choose to have. This is one of the more potent arguments against the restoration of the gold standard. If governments were willing to follow policies that are consistent with the maintenance of a gold standard, then the gold standard itself would not be necessary; if governments are not willing to follow such policies, however, then the introduction of the gold standard per se will not restore stability since before long the standard will have to be abandoned.

Could one make a case for transferring the effects of disturbances from the foreign exchange market? Here it is important to emphasize that there is no presumption that transferring disturbances will reduce their overall impact and lower their social cost. On the contrary, since the foreign exchange market is a market in which risk can easily be bought and sold, it may be sensible to concentrate disturbances in this market rather than transfer them to other markets, such as labor markets, where they cannot be dealt with in as efficient a manner. While it might be tempting to "solve" the problem of the fluctuating exchange rates by restoring fixed parities, this may well be a mistaken policy.

We Should Not Adopt a Rigid PPP Rule

As indicated previously, exchange rates have been far more volatile than the various aggregate price indices. This different degree of volatility resulted in large deviations from purchasing power parities (PPP) and by these standards it seems that exchange rate variations were excessive. In view of the large divergences from PPPs various proposals were made concerning rules for intervention in the foreign exchange market. Some of these proposals are variants of a PPP rule according to which the authorities are expected to intervene in the market for foreign exchange so as to assure that the path of exchange rates conforms with the path of the general price level.

There are fundamental difficulties with a PPP rule. First, as indicated in the preceding section, there are intrinsic differences between the characteristics of exchange rates and the price of national outputs. These differences, which result from the much stronger dependence of exchange rates (and other asset prices) on expectations, suggest that in assessing whether exchange rate volatility was excessive, a relevant yardstick should be variations of other asset prices, like those of securities, rather than variations in price levels. As shown in Table 1–1, the variability of exchange rates was about half that of the various stock market indices. This difference of course does not imply that exchange rates as well as stock market indices have not been too volatile; rather, it indicates that in determining whether volatility was excessive it is not enough to point to the fact that exchange rates have moved more than the price level.

Second, since in the short run the prices of national outputs do not adjust fully in response to shocks, intervention in the foreign exchange market, which ensures conformity with PPPs, would be a mistaken policy. When commodity prices are slow to adjust to current and expected economic conditions, it may be desirable to allow for "excessive" adjustment in some other prices.

Third, it is important to note that changes in real economic conditions requiring adjustment in the equilibrium relative prices of different national outputs occur continuously. Under these circumstances what may seem to be divergences from PPPs may just reflect equilibrating changes. Further, if there is short-run stickiness of prices of domestic goods in terms of national monies, then rapid exchange rate adjustments are capable of changing the relative prices of different national outputs and are a desirable response to the changing real economic conditions. An intervention rule linking changes in exchange rates rigidly to changes in domestic and foreign prices in accord with purchasing power parity ignores the occasional need for equilibrating changes in relative prices. Although it might be tempting to solve the problem of divergences from PPP by adopting a rigid PPP rule, this policy is also likely to be a mistake.

The Rate of Interest Is a Poor Monetary Indicator

The interpretation of the relation between the rate of interest and the foreign exchange value of the dollar during the 1970s rested on the distinction between nominal and real rates of interest—a distinction that is critical during inflationary periods. That discussion also provides an illustration of the potential danger of using the wrong monetary indicator. Traditionally the criterion for assessing whether monetary policy was easy or tight has been the height of the rate of interest. A high interest rate was interpreted as indicating a tight monetary policy, whereas a low interest rate was interpreted as indicating an easy monetary policy. By now it is recognized that during an inflationary period it is vital to draw a distinction between nominal and real rates of interest; as a result, during inflationary periods the rate of interest may provide a very misleading interpretation of the stance of monetary policy. The same logic also applies with respect to the analysis of the relation between exchange rates and interest rates. A rise in the interest rate will strengthen the currency if it is due to a rise in the real rate, and it will weaken the currency if it is due to a rise in inflationary expectations. In this context inflationary expectations play a central role. As a result policies that attempt to induce an appreciation of the currency can be successful only if they reduce inflationary expectations or if they raise the real rate of interest. The reduction in inflationary expectations will halt the depreciation of the currency in terms of goods and in terms of foreign exchange and will result in lower nominal rates of interest while maintaining (or even raising) real rates of interest.

Policies that Reduce Inflation Will
Strengthen the Currency

The recognition of the link between inflation, the nominal rate of interest, and the depreciation of the currency is fundamental for the analysis of policy. An excessive growth of the supply of money relative to the demand for it (for given behavior of foreign monetary aggregates) reduces the value of the money in terms of domestic goods and services (as reflected by the domestic inflation rate) as well as in terms of foreign exchange (as reflected by the decline in the external value of the currency). Since the higher inflation rate and the higher rate of depreciation of the currency are both symptoms of the same fundamental cause, there should be no conflict whatsoever between policies aimed at lowering domestic inflation and policies aimed at halting the external depreciation of the currency.

Emphasis on the fact that the external and the internal values of the currency are both endogenous variables is important in view of the recent allegation that the move to a regime of flexible exchange rates has been inflationary. Both the external and the internal values of the currency respond to the same set of shocks, and both can be influenced by a similar set of policies. The finding that typically a depreciation of the external value of the currency precedes and exceeds the depreciation of its internal value does not imply that as an economic matter the chain of causality runs from exchange rates to prices. Rather, it may just reflect the intrinsic difference between exchange rates and prices: Exchange rates adjust faster and to a larger extent to shocks than do national price levels. It seems therefore that the attribution of the rise in inflation to the move to a flexible exchange rate regime may reflect to some extent the fallacy of a belief in post hoc ergo propter hoc.

The perspective that policies that strengthen the domestic value of the currency are consistent with policies that strengthen its external value implies that the qualitative differences between policies that are introduced through the domestic desk and the external desk at the Central Bank are not as large as might have been thought. Domestic monetary policies, like open market operations, involve sales (or purchases) of domestic currency against securities. External intervention policies, like nonsterilized interventions in foreign exchange markets, ultimately involve sales (or purchases) of domestic currency against foreign exchange. Both policies result in changes in the relative supplies of the domestic currency, and both therefore are expected to alter the domestic as well as the external value of the currency. Under these circumstances the degree of coordination between the domestic and the external desks becomes an important issue. It is relevant to note that the degree of coordination between the various activities of the monetary authority is important also when the official intervention in foreign exchange markets alters only the supplies of nonmonetary assets available to the public. Such policies may influence exchange rates through portfolio effects and, possibly more important, through signaling to the public the intentions of the government concerning future policies. It is important that such signals of the external desk of the monetary authority should be consistent with the signals provided through the policies of the domestic desk.

The foregoing arguments discussed the role of monetary policy and the conduct of the monetary authority. It is important to note that this emphasis does not reflect the belief that the source of the fluctuations of the exchange rate was exclusively monetary. On the contrary, it is clear that real shocks were responsible for a significant share of the economic difficulties of the 1970s. It is believed, however, that macroeconomic policy can do little to offset changes in equilibrium levels of real income resulting from changes in relative prices of internationally traded goods (and the recent rise in the relative price of oil is a case in point). Further, while the depreciation might have been caused to some extent by real shocks, there is little doubt that the conduct of monetary policy is critical in influencing the internal and the external values of the currency.

The Role of the Exchange Rate in the Design of Monetary Policy

As was already indicated, exchange rates are influenced by the whole array of (actual and expected) government policies, especially policies affecting the demand and supply of different national monies. Exchange rates, however, are not instruments of policy that may be manipulated independently of other policy tools.

The close association between policies aimed at lowering inflation and those aimed at strengthening the currency in foreign exchange markets raises the question of what the role of the exchange rate in the design of monetary policy should be. Consideration of the external value of the currency should play a relatively minor role in the design of monetary policy. The major consideration that should guide the monetary authority should be that of achieving price stability.

This recommendation may seem to be a revival of the "benign neglect" attitude that became popular during the fixed exchange rate era, but the opposite is the case. In the past one of the major arguments for the "benign neglect" attitude in the United States was that the U.S. economy was relatively closed and the foreign trade sector was relatively unimportant. The typical statistic used to justify this position was the low share of imports in GNP. This argument was inappropriate in the past and is even less appropriate under present circumstances. The United States has always been an open economy. The relevant measure of openness to international trade in goods and services is not the share of actual trade in GNP but rather the share of tradable commodities in GNP (that is, of potential trade), which is far larger than that of actual trade. Furthermore, one of the main linkages of the United States to the world economy is operating through world capital markets with which the United States is clearly well integrated. The same principle applies to the measures of openness of most countries.

My own recommendation is based on the notion that the economy *is* open, that the external value of the currency *is* important, and that the restoration of price stability will automatically strengthen the external value of the currency. Policy that views the exchange rate as an independent target or, even worse, as an independent instrument is likely to result in unstable prices. Furthermore, if monetary policy succeeds in achieving price stability, it might be useful to allow for fluctuations of the exchange rate that provide for a partial insulation from misguided foreign monetary policies.

It is of interest that this view that policy that ensures domestic price stability also creates an environment conducive to a stable dollar was also advocated by Henry Simons over thirty years ago:

> The major need for international monetary stabilization will be simply the internal stabilization of the dollar itself. This is the central prescription from which hopeful planning should proceed. . . . If the dollar again is violently unstable in purchasing power or commodity value, and especially if it is again debased irresponsibly by tragically inopportune tariff increases or devaluations, world economic order, large international trade, and decent national behavior in commercial policies or practices will be unattainable. If we can securely and closely stabilize our own price level and prevent recurrent aberrations of inflation and deflation, we can thereby eliminate the major obstacle to reasonable stability of foreign-exchange rates. Here is perhaps the best single contribution we can make to resumption of orderly international trade—to the ending of arbitrary exchange controls (rationing of foreign exchange), bilateralism, discrimination, and direct national control of governmental monopolizing of foreign trade . . . serving well our national interest in this matter, we may also serve well the cause of world order and reconstruction, and conversely. (1948: 262)

Even when monetary policy is not guided by exchange rate targets it might attempt to offset disturbances arising from shifts in the demand for money. Such shifts in demand may be especially pronounced under a regime of flexible exchange rates. A policy that accommodates such shifts in demand by offsetting supply shifts would reduce the need for costly adjustments of exchange rates and national price levels. The difficulty with implementing this policy is in recognizing when a shift in money demand has occurred. Here the exchange rate may be useful as an indicator for monetary policy especially when frequent changes in inflationary expectations make nominal interest rates an unreliable indicator of fluctuations in money demand. Accordingly a combination of rising nominal interest rates and an appreciation of the currency, which seems to have prevailed in the United States since mid-1979, may indicate a rise in the demand for money that should be accommodated by an increase in supply; whereas the combination of rising nominal interest rates and a depreciation of the currency, which seems to have prevailed in the United States during most of the 1970s, may indicate a rise in inflationary expectations that should obviously not be fueled by an accommodative change in supply.

Monetary Policy Should Aim at Achieving Low and Stable Rates of Monetary Expansion

An important way in which government policy can make a positive contribution to restoring price stability and reducing costly and unnecessary turbulence of foreign exchange rates is by reducing high and variable rates of monetary expansion, which result, for example, from misguided attempts to stabilize nominal interest rates. This is especially important because exchange rates are affected not only by current policy actions but also by current expectations of future policy. If expectations of future policy are highly sensitive to current policy, then instability of policy can have a magnified effect on exchange rates and on the relative prices of different national outputs, thereby generating significant social costs. If the instability and unpredictability of policy, particularly monetary policy, have indeed contributed significantly to the turbulence of exchange rates since 1973, then the turbulence and its associated cost can be reduced. In order to restore order and effectiveness to economic policies, it is important that such policies be perceived as being consistent and permanent. A track record of erratic policies based on attempts to fine tune the economy will not promote such a perception.

An open economy under fixed exchange rates cannot have a monetary rule that sets an arbitrary growth of nominal balances. In such an economy the autonomy of the monetary authorities is lost to the commitment to peg the rate of exchange. This autonomy is regained under a flexible exchange rate regime but, as noted earlier, shifts in the demand for money are likely to occur. Since it might be desirable to accommodate such demand shifts, the monetary rule should be formulated with some flexibility so as to allow for occasional accommodations.

During a stabilization program it is likely that some sectors will be harmed more than others. The principles of the division of responsibilities between monetary and fiscal policies suggest that since monetary policy is an aggregate policy, it need not be guided by intersectoral considerations. These intersectoral considerations are extremely important, however. The proper instrument for dealing with sectoral difficulties is fiscal rather than monetary policy.

Recognition of these principles is critical since very frequently the period of time that the economic system needs for adjustment is likely to be longer than the period of time that the political system is willing to provide. In the past this conflict resulted in stop-and-go policies with subsequent acceleration of the rate of inflation. These costs can be avoided if the monetary authority maintains its independence from the political pressures.

Once the monetary authority adopts a stable policy, it will minimize costly side effects. Put differently, money is felt when it is out of order; when it is in order it only serves as a veil over the real equilibrium of the economy. This unique property of money is best summarized by the following quotation from John Stuart Mill:

> There cannot, in short, be intrinsically a more insignificant thing, in the economy of society, than money; except in the character of a contrivance for sparing time and labour. It is a machine for doing quickly and commodiously, what would be done, though less quickly and commodiously, without it: and like many other kinds of machinery, it only exerts a distinct and independent influence of its own when it gets out of order.

Following a predictable and stable policy will ensure that money is in order. Adopting such a course will not eliminate variations of exchange rates, nor will it ensure that exchange rates conform with the predictions of the purchasing power parity theory. It will, however, reduce some of the unnecessary and costly fluctuations that are induced by unstable and erratic policies.

Summary and Conclusions

This chapter started with an interpretation of the key facts of the empirical record. The first set of facts involving the volatility and the unpredictability of exchange rates was interpreted in terms of the modern asset market theory of exchange rate determination. Accordingly exchange rates, like the prices of other durable assets, depend on expectations about the future, and changes in expectations result in rapid and large changes in exchange rates. It was argued that periods that are dominated by news that alters expectations are likely to be characterized by volatile exchange rates. Since news is unpredictable, most of the resultant fluctuations of exchange rates are also unpredictable.

The second set of facts relating to the large deviations from purchasing power parities was interpreted by reference to the large real shocks absorbed by the system during the 1970s as well as in terms of the intrinsic differences between exchange rates and national price levels. In contrast to exchange rates, price levels are much less sensitive to changes in expectations.

The third set of facts involved the relation between exchange rates and interest rates. During most of the 1970s the secular rise in the rates of interest in the United States (relative to the foreign rates of interest) was associated with a secular depreciation of the dollar. This fact was interpreted in terms of the distinction between nominal and real rates of interest. During an inflationary environment the primary cause for variations in rates of interest is variations in inflationary expectations. During most of the 1970s, the relatively rapid rise in prices was associated with high nominal rates of interest as well as with a depreciation of the currency in terms of foreign exchange. The more recent appreciation of the dollar has been associated with a rise in the real rates of interest in the United States rather than with inflationary expectations.

The following implications were suggested in this chapter: First, restoration of fixed parities will obviously reduce exchange rate variations, but this might be achieved at excessive cost. Second, there are fundamental difficulties with the adoption of a purchasing power parity rule for exchange rate management. When commodity prices are slow to adjust to current and expected economic conditions, it might be desirable to allow for "excessive" adjustment in exchange rates. Further, changes in real economic conditions requiring adjustment in equilibrium relative prices of different national outputs occur continuously; under such circumstances, an intervention rule that links changes in exchange rates rigidly to changes in domestic and foreign prices in accord with purchasing power parity prevents the attainment of the occasional equilibrating changes in relative prices. Third, policies that will reduce inflation will also strengthen the dollar since both the high inflation and the large depreciation of the dollar are both symptoms of the same fundamental cause. This suggests that an important factor in evaluating the consistency of policies is the degree of coordination between the domestic desk and the external desk of the Federal Reserve. Fourth, the external value of the dollar may play a relatively minor role in the design of monetary policy when major consideration is given to the achievement of price stability. Fifth, the Federal Reserve could achieve low and stable rates of monetary expansion. Exchange rates are affected not only by current policy actions but also by current expectations of future policy. If expectations of future policy are highly sensitive to current policy, the instability of policy can have a magnified effect on exchange rates and on the relative prices of different national outputs, thereby generating significant social costs. In order to restore order and effectiveness to economic policies, it is important that such policies be perceived as being consistent and permanent.

Notes

1. I am indebted to Teizo Taya for preparing Table 1–1.
2. I am indebted to Dallas S. Batten for preparing this figure.

References

Edwards, Sebastian. Forthcoming. "Comments on 'An Accounting Framework and Some Issues for Modelling How Exchange Rates Respond to the News.'" In *Exchange Rates and International Macroeconomics,* ed. Jacob A. Frenkel, Chicago: University of Chicago Press.

Frenkel, Jacob A. 1983. "Comments on Exchange Rates and Interest Rates." *Annales de L'INSEE* (July–December).

———. 1982. "U.S. Inflation and the Dollar." In *Inflation: Causes and Consequences,* ed. Robert E. Hall. Chicago: University of Chicago Press.

———. 1981a. "Flexible Exchange Rates, Prices and the Role of 'News': Lessons from the 1970s." *Journal of Political Economy* 89, 4 (August): 665–705.

———. 1981b. "The Collapse of Purchasing Power Parties during the 1970s." *European Economic Review* 16, 1 (May): 145–65.

———, and Michael L. Mussa. 1981. "Monetary and Fiscal Policies in an Open Economy." *American Economic Review* 71, 2 (May): 253–58.

———. 1980. "The Efficiency of Foreign Exchange Markets and Measures of Turbulence." *American Economic Review* 70, 2 (May): 374–81.

Isard, Peter. Forthcoming. "An Accounting Framework and Some Issues for Modelling How Exchange Rates Respond to the News." In *Exchange Rates and*

International Macroeconomics, ed. Jacob A. Frenkel. Chicago: University of Chicago Press.

Mill, John S. 1871. *Principles of Political Economy.* 7th ed. London: Longmans, Green.

Simons, Henry C. 1948. *Economic Policy for a Free Society.* Chicago: University of Chicago Press.

Viner, Jacob, 1924. *Canada's Balance of International Indebtedness: 1900–1913.* Cambridge, Mass.

22

EXPECTATIONS AND EXCHANGE RATE DYNAMICS

Rudiger Dornbusch

The paper develops a theory of exchange rate movements under perfect capital mobility, a slow adjustment of goods markets relative to asset markets, and consistent expectations. The perfect foresight path is derived and it is shown that along that path a monetary expansion causes the exchange rate to depreciate. An initial overshooting of exchange rates is shown to derive from the differential adjustment speed of markets. The magnitude and persistence of the overshooting is developed in terms of the structural parameters of the model. To the extent that output responds to a monetary expansion in the short run, this acts as a dampening effect on exchange depreciation and may, in fact, lead to an increase in interest rates.

I. Introduction

The paper develops a simple macroeconomic framework for the study of exchange rate movements. The purpose is to develop a theory that is suggestive of the observed large fluctuations in exchange rates while at the same time establishing that such exchange rate movements are consistent with rational expectations formation. In developing a formal model we draw on the role of asset markets, capital mobility, and expectations that have been emphasized in recent literature.[1] We draw, too, on the fact of differential adjustment speeds in goods and asset markets. In fact, the dynamic aspects of exchange rate determination in this model arise from the assumption that exchange rates and asset markets adjust fast relative to goods markets.

I am indebted to Stanley Black, Franco Modigliani, and Edward Tower who provided the stimulus for this paper. In revising various drafts I have had the benefit of many comments. I wish, in particular, to acknowledge the helpful suggestions I have received from Wilfred Ethier, Stanley Fischer, Jacob Frenkel, and the thoughtful remarks of two anonymous referees. Financial support was provided by a grant from the Ford Foundation.

The adjustment process to a monetary expansion in this framework serves to identify several features that are suggestive of recent currency experience. In the short run, a monetary expansion is shown to induce an immediate depreciation in the exchange rate and accounts therefore for fluctuations in the exchange rate and the terms of trade. Second, during the adjustment process, rising prices may be accompanied by an appreciating exchange rate so that the trend behavior of exchange rates stands potentially in strong contrast with the cyclical behavior of exchange rates and prices. The third aspect of the adjustment process is a direct effect of the exchange rate on domestic inflation. In this context the exchange rate is identified as a critical channel for the transmission of monetary policy to aggregate demand for domestic output.

The effect of monetary policy on interest rates and exchange rates is significantly affected by the behavior of real output. If real output is fixed, a monetary expansion will, in the short run, lower interest rates and cause the exchange rate to overshoot its long-run depreciation. If output, on the contrary, responds to aggregate demand, the exchange rate and interest rate changes will be dampened. While the exchange rate will still depreciate, it may no longer overshoot, and interest rates may actually rise.

In Part II we develop a formal model in terms of explicit functional forms. That development allows us to derive an analytical solution for the time path of variables and, in Part III, for the expectations that generate the perfect foresight path. In Part IV, the model is used to investigate the effects of a monetary disturbance. While the major part of the analysis is developed for the case of fixed output, an extension to variable output is introduced in Part V.

II. The Model

We will assume a country that is small in the world capital market so that it faces a given interest rate. Capital mobility will ensure the equalization of expected net yields so that the domestic interest rate, less the expected rate of depreciation, will equal the world rate. In the goods market we will assume that the world price of imports is given. Domestic output is an imperfect substitute for imports, and aggregate demand for domestic goods, therefore, will determine their absolute and relative price.

A. Capital Mobility and Expectations

Assets denominated in terms of domestic and foreign currency are assumed to be perfect substitutes given a proper premium to offset anticipated exchange rate changes. Accordingly, if the domestic currency is expected to depreciate, interest rates on assets denominated in terms of domestic currency will exceed those abroad by the expected rate of depreciation. That relationship is expressed in (1) where r is the domestic interest rate, r^* is the given world rate of interest, and x is the expected rate of depreciation of the domestic currency, or the expected rate of increase of the domestic currency price of foreign exchange:

$$r = r^* + x. \tag{1}$$

Equation (1) is a representation of perfect capital mobility, and it is assumed that incipient capital flows will ensure that (1) holds at all times.

Consider next expectations formation. Here we distinguish between the long-run exchange rate, to which the economy will ultimately converge, and the current exchange rate. Denoting the logarithms of the current and long-run rate by e and $\bar{e}$, respectively, we assume that

$$x = 0(\bar{e} - e). \tag{2}$$

Equation (2) states that the expected rate of depreciation of the spot rate is proportional to the discrepancy between the long-run rate and the current spot rate. The coefficient of adjustment 0 is for the present taken as a parameter. The long-run exchange rate is assumed known, and an expression for it will be developed below. We note further that, while expectations formation according to (2) may appear ad hoc, it will actually be consistent with perfect foresight, as shown in Part III.

B. The Money Market

The domestic interest rate is determined by the condition of equilibrium in the domestic money market. The demand for real money balances is assumed to depend on the domestic interest rate and real income and will, in equilibrium, equal the real money supply. Assuming a conventional demand for money, the log of which is linear in the log of real income and in interest rates, we have[2]

$$-\lambda r + \phi y = m - p, \tag{3}$$

where m, p, and y denote the logs of the nominal quantity of money, the price level, and real income. For the remainder of this part we will take the nominal quantity of money and the level of real income as given.

Combining (1), (2), and (3) will give us a relationship between the spot exchange rate, the price level, and the long-run exchange rate, *given* that the money market clears and net asset yields are equalized:

$$p - m = -\phi y + \lambda r^* + \lambda 0(\bar{e} - e). \tag{4}$$

Equation (4) can be simplified by noting that with a stationary money supply long-run equilibrium will imply equality between interest rates, because current and expected exchange rates are equal. This implies that the long-run equilibrium price level, $\bar{p}$, will equal

$$\bar{p} = m + (\lambda r^* - \phi y). \tag{5}$$

Substituting (5) in (4) gives us a relationship between the exchange rate and the price level:[3]

$$e = \bar{e} - (1/\lambda\theta)(p - \bar{p}). \tag{6}$$

Equation (6) is one of the key equations of the model. For given long-run values of exchange rates and prices, it serves to determine the current spot price of foreign exchange as a function of the current level of prices. Given the level of prices, we have a domestic interest rate and an interest differential. Given the long-run exchange rate, there is a unique level of the spot rate such that the expected appreciation, or depreciation, matches the interest differential. An increase in the price level, because it raises interest rates, gives rise to an incipient capital inflow that will appreciate the spot rate to the point where the anticipated depreciation exactly offsets the increase in domestic interest rates.

C. The Goods Market

The demand for domestic output depends on the relative price of domestic goods, $e - p$, interest rates, and real income. The demand function is assumed to have the form

$$\ln D = u + \delta(e - p) + \gamma y - \sigma r, \tag{7}$$

where D denotes the demand for domestic output and where u is a shift parameter.[4] From (7) we note that a decrease in the relative price of domestic goods raises demand, as does an increase in income or a reduction in interest rates. The rate of increase in the price of domestic goods, p, is described in (8) as proportional to an excess demand measure:

$$p = \pi \ln(D/Y) = \pi[u + \delta(e - p) + (\gamma - 1)y - \sigma r]. \tag{8}$$

We note that the long-run equilibrium exchange rate implied by (8) is[5]

$$\bar{e} = \bar{p} + (1/\delta)[\sigma r^* + (1 - \gamma)y - u], \tag{9}$$

where $\bar{p}$ is defined in (5). From (9) it is apparent that the long-run exchange rate depends with the conventional homogeneity properties on monetary variables, but obviously on real variables, too.

The price equation in (8) can be simplified by using the definition of the long-run rate in (9) and the fact that interest differences equal expected depreciation, $r - r^* = \theta(\bar{e} - e)$, to become[6]

$$\dot{p} = -\pi[(\delta + \sigma\theta)/\theta\lambda + \delta](p - \bar{p}) = -v(p - \bar{p}), \qquad (10)$$

where

$$v \equiv \pi[(\delta + \sigma\theta)/\theta\lambda + \delta]. \qquad (11)$$

The price adjustment equation in (10) can be solved to yield

$$p(t) = \bar{p} + (p_0 - \bar{p}) \exp(-vt), \qquad (12)$$

which shows that the price of domestic output will converge to its long-run level at a rate determined by (11). Substitution of (12) in (6) gives the time path of the exchange rate

$$e(t) = \bar{e} - (1/\lambda 0)(p_0 - \bar{p}) \exp(-vt) \qquad (13)$$
$$= \bar{e} + (e_0 - \bar{e}) \exp(-vt).$$

From (13) the exchange rate will likewise converge to its long-run level. The rate will appreciate if prices are initially below their long-run level and, conversely, if prices initially exceed their long-run level.

D. Equilibrium Exchange Rates

The adjustment process of the economy can be described with the help of figure 1. At every point in time the money market clears and expected yields are arbitraged. This implies a relationship between prices and the spot exchange rate shown in (6) and reflected in the QQ schedule in figure 1. The positively sloped schedule $p = 0$ shows combinations of price levels and exchange rates for which the goods market and money market are in equilibrium.[7] Points above and to the left of that schedule correspond to an excess supply of goods and falling prices. Conversely, points to the right and below the schedule correspond to an excess demand. The $\dot{p} = 0$ schedule is positively sloped and flatter than a 45° line for the following reason.[8] An increase in the exchange rate creates an excess demand for domestic goods by lowering their relative price. To restore equilibrium, domestic prices will have to increase, though proportionately less, since an increase in domestic prices affects aggregate demand, both via the relative price effect and via higher interest rates.

For any given price level the exchange rate adjusts instantaneously to clear the asset market. Accordingly, we are continuously on the QQ schedule with money-market equilibrium and international arbitrage of net expected yields. Goods-market equilibrium, to the contrary, is only achieved in the long run. Conditions in the goods market, however, are

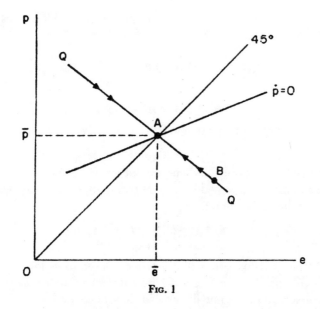

FIG. 1

critical in moving the economy to the long-run equilibrium by inducing rising or falling prices. Specifically, an initial position such as point *B*, with a price level below the long-run level and, correspondingly, an exchange rate in excess of the long-run equilibrium, implies an excess demand for goods because domestic output commands a low relative price and because the interest rate is low. Accordingly, prices will be rising, thereby inducing over time a reduction in excess demand. The path of rising prices is accompanied by an appreciation of the exchange rate. As interest rates rise, as a consequence of declining real balances, the spot rate will approach the long-run rate. Once the long-run equilibrium at point *A* is attained, interest rates are equal internationally, the goods market clear, prices are constant, and expected exchange rate changes are zero.

III. Consistent Expectations

So far we have placed no restrictions on the formation of expectations other than the assumption that the expected rate of depreciation, as shown in (2) is proportional to the discrepancy between the long-run and the current exchange rate. From (12) and (13) we note that the rate at which prices and the exchange rate converge to equilibrium is given by

v. From (11) it is apparent that the rate of convergence is a function of the expectations coefficient, θ.

Clearly, for the expectations formation process in (2) to correctly predict the actual path of exchange rates it must be true that $\theta = v$. Accordingly, the expectations coefficient, θ, that corresponds to perfect foresight, or, equivalently, that is consistent with the model is given by the solution to the equation

$$\theta = v \equiv \pi[(\delta + \sigma\theta)/\theta\lambda + \delta] \tag{14}$$

The consistent expectations coefficient, θ, obtained as the solution to (14), is a function of the structural parameters of the economy[9]

$$\bar{\theta}(\lambda, \delta, \sigma, \pi) = \pi(\sigma/\lambda + \delta)/2 + [\pi^2(\sigma/\lambda + \delta)^2/4 + \pi\delta/\lambda]^{1/2}. \tag{15}$$

Equation (15) gives the rate at which the economy will converge to long-run equilibrium along the perfect foresight path. If expectations are formed according to (2) and (15), exchange rate predictions will actually be borne out.[10] The characteristics of the perfect foresight path are that the economy will converge faster the lower the interest response of money demand and the higher the interest response of goods demand and the price elasticity of demand for domestic output. The reason is simply that with a low interest response a given change in real balances will give rise to a large change in interest rates which, in combination with a high interest response of goods demand, will give rise to a large excess demand and therefore inflationary impact. Similarly, a large price elasticity serves to translate an exchange rate change into a large excess demand and, therefore, serves to speed up the adjustment process.

IV. The Effects of a Monetary Expansion

In this part we will study the adjustment process to a monetary expansion. The analysis serves to derive substantive results but also to highlight the manner in which expectations about the future path of the economy affect the current level of the exchange rate. This link is embodied in consistent expectations and makes the impact effect of a monetary disturbance depend on the entire structure of the economy.

In figure 2 we show the economy in initial full equilibrium at point A, with a long-run price level $\bar{p}$ and a corresponding long-run exchange rate $\bar{e}$ where the level of prices is determined, according to (5), by the nominal quantity of money, real income, and the interest rate. The long-run exchange rate by (9) will depend on the level of domestic prices and characteristics of the demand for domestic goods. The asset-market equilibrium schedule QQ that combines monetary equilibrium and arbitrage of net expected yields is drawn for the initial nominal quantity of money.

An increase in the nominal quantity of money that is expected to persist will cause a goods and asset market disequilibrium at the initial exchange rate and price. To maintain asset-market equilibrium, the increased quantity of money would have to be matched by higher prices and or a depreciation in the exchange rate. The asset-market equilibrium schedule will shift out to $Q'Q'$, a shift that is (proportionately) equal to the increase in the nominal quantity of money.

It is immediately obvious that the new long-run equilibrium is at point C, where both goods and asset markets clear and exchange rate and price changes exactly reflect the increase in money.[11] This long-run homogeneity result is not surprising, since there is no source of money illusion or long-run price rigidity in the system.

Consider next the adjustment process. At the initial level of prices, the monetary expansion reduces interest rates and leads to the anticipation of a depreciation in the long run and, therefore, at the current exchange rate, to the expectation of a depreciating exchange rate. Both factors serve to reduce the attractiveness of domestic assets, lead to an incipient capital outflow, and thus cause the spot rate to depreciate. The extent of that depreciation has to be sufficient to give rise to the anticipation of appreciation at just sufficient a rate to offset the reduced domestic interest rate. The impact effect of a monetary expansion is, therefore, to induce an immediate depreciation in the spot rate and one that exceeds the long-run depreciation, since only under these circumstances will the public anticipate an appreciating exchange rate and thus be compensated for the reduced interest on domestic assets. This is shown in figure 2 by the move from point A to the short-run equilibrium at point B.

From (4), noting that $d\bar{e} = dm = d\bar{p}$, we obtain a formal expression for the impact effect of a monetary expansion on the spot exchange rate:

$$de/dm = 1 + 1/\lambda\theta. \tag{16}$$

Equation (16) confirms that in the short run the exchange rate will overshoot. The extent of the overshooting will depend on the interest response of money demand and the expectations coefficient.

A high interest response of money demand will serve to dampen the overshooting because it implies that a given expansion in the (real) quantity of money will only induce a small reduction in the interest rate. A small reduction in the interest rate in turn requires only a small expectation of appreciation to offset it and therefore, given the coefficient

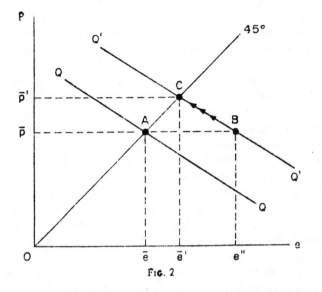

Fig. 2

of expectations and the long-run rate, only a small depreciation of the spot rate (in excess of the long-run rate) to generate that expectation. A similar interpretation applies to the coefficient of expectations in (16).

It is quite obvious from the preceding explanation that the short-term effects of a monetary expansion, in this model, are entirely dominated by asset markets and, more specifically, by capital mobility and expectations. This feature places in sharp relief the assumption that asset markets and exchange rates adjust fast relative to the goods market and the price of domestic output. It is under these circumstances that a change in the nominal quantity of money is, in fact, a change in the real quantity of money, and the spot rate adjustment serves to achieve equilibrium in the asset markets by creating the expectation of appreciation of just sufficient an extent to balance the reduced interest rate on domestic assets.

The interpretation of (16) has not so far used the restriction that expectations be rational. That restriction is introduced by substituting (15) in (16) to obtain

$$de_t dm = 1 + 1/\lambda\tilde{\theta} = 1 + \frac{1}{\pi(\sigma + \delta\lambda)/2 + [\pi^2(\sigma + \delta\lambda)^2/4 + \pi\delta\lambda]^{1/2}}.$$
$$(17)$$

Equation (17) has two implications that cannot be derived from (16). The first is that with an interet response of money demand that approaches zero the initial depreciation remains finite and, in fact, approaches de/dm

$= 1 + 1/\eta\sigma$. This result reflects the fact that, for the large interest rate changes that would result in these circumstances, the subsequent path of prices and the exchange rate is governed by the effect of interest rates on aggregate demand.

A second implication of (17) is the fact that the short-run overshooting of the exchange rate is inversely related to the speed of adjustment of the system, θ. That fact is particularly obvious for the case where the speed of adjustment of prices, η, becomes infinite and where, accordingly, the economy jumps instantaneously to the new long-run equilibrium at point C.[12] More generally, those factors that serve to speed up the adjustment process, in particular high interest rate responsiveness of money demand, or aggregate spending, or high price elasticities, will therefore serve to dampen the impact effect of a monetary expansion on the exchange rate. This effect relies entirely on expectations about the subsequent path of the economy, rather than on *current* interaction between goods and asset markets.

Consider next the adjustment process from the short-run market equilibrium at point B to long-run equilibrium at point C. We note from figure 2 that at point B there is an excess demand for goods. That excess demand arises both from the decline in domestic interest rates and from the depreciation in the exchange rate that lowers the *relative* price of domestic goods. Each factor by itself is sufficient to account for this excess demand and, in fact, they constitute independent channels through which monetary changes affect demand for domestic output.

The exchange rate channel has been identified by Fleming and Mundell as an important avenue for monetary policy to act on aggregate demand.[13] In the present context the depreciation of the spot rate that is induced by the conditions of asset-market equilibrium serves to reduce the relative price of domestic goods and thereby to raise aggregate demand and give rise to inflationary pressure as opposed to an increase in output. The importance of this channel is larger, the higher the price elasticity of demand relative to the interest response of aggregate spending.

The lower interest rates and a lower relative price of domestic goods, that are characteristics of the impact effect, will cause domestic prices to rise and therefore be reflected in falling real money balances, rising interest rates, and an appreciating exchange rate. The adjustment process of rising prices over time restores the economy to the initial real equilibrium. An important feature of that adjustment process is the fact that rising prices are accompanied by an appreciating exchange rate. In terms of figure 2, this is described by the move along $Q'Q'$ from B to C. This result is due to the fact that rising prices cause the real money supply to be falling and interest rates to be rising. The rising interest rate, in turn, gives rise to an incipient capital inflow that appreciates the exchange rate at the same rate as interest rates are rising and thus maintains expected net yields in line. The model therefore confirms the link between interest rates and exchange rates that is emphasized in popular interpretations of foreign exchange events. The observation is correct, in the present circumstances, because rising interest rates are accompanied by the expectation of an appreciating exchange rate.

In summarizing this part we note that the ultimate effect of a monetary expansion is an equiproportionate increase in prices and the exchange rate. In the short run, however, the monetary expansion does exert real effects on interest rates, the terms of trade, and aggregate demand. The details of the adjustment process will depend on the economic structure. In particular, terms of trade changes will be both larger and more persistent the lower the speed of adjustment, θ.

A key role in his analysis is played by the sluggish adjustment of prices as compared with asset markets. There is no very persuasive theoretical support for the slow adjustment of goods markets, but the facts clearly point in this direction. While the differential adjustment speed lacks theoretical backing, it implies, nevertheless, a behavior of exchange rates that is suggestive of recent experience.[14]

V. Short-Run Adjustment in Output

So far we have assumed that output is fixed at the full-employment level, $\bar{y}$. In the present part, the analysis is extended to allow for short-run adjustments in output in response to changes in aggregate demand. Therefore, we replace equation (8) by an equilibrium condition in the domestic goods market,

$$y = \ln D \equiv u + \delta(e - p) + \gamma y - \sigma r, \qquad (18)$$

where y is the log of the actual level of output that in the short run is demand determined. In addition to (18), we require a price adjustment equation which is shown in (19):

$$\dot{p} = \pi(y - \bar{y}). \qquad (19)$$

According to (19) the rate of inflation is proportional to the discrepancy between actual and full employment, or "potential" output, $\bar{y}$. This price adjustment equation is a combination of a relationship between wage and price inflation, a relation between wage inflation and unemployment as in a Phillips curve, and a relation between unemployment and the departure from potential output, $y - \bar{y}$, as described by Okun's law.

It is shown in the Appendix below that the extension that incorporates (18) and (19) in place of (8) leaves most of the analysis of adjustments to a monetary increase unchanged. In particular, the price adjustment will continue to be exponential although the speed of adjustment will depend now also on the income elasticities of demand for domestic goods and real balances, γ and ϕ.

In the present framework it continues to be true that in the short run an increase in the nominal quantity of money is an increase in the real quantity of money. Accordingly, a monetary expansion has the conventional effect of increasing in the short run the level of output and inducing inflation. Since the inflation that is induced by the expansion in real output serves to raise over time the price level, real balances will decline back to their initial level until in the long run the expansion in money is fully matched by increased prices and output has returned to the full-employment level.

The impact effect of a monetary expansion on exchange rates and interest rates may, however, differ significantly from the analysis in Part IV. The new possibility that arises from the expansion in output in the short run is that the exchange rate depreciation will fall short of the monetary expansion rather than exceed it as in (16). That possibility arises because, in the short run, the income expansion raises money demand and may do so sufficiently to actually increase interest rates. If the output expansion were sufficiently strong to raise interest rates, equalization of net yields internationally would require the expectation of a depreciation and therefore a spot rate that falls short of the long-run equilibrium rate. Since the long-run equilibrium rate increases in the same proportion as the nominal quantity of money, it follows that the spot rate would increase less than the quantity of money. The condition that gives rise to this case is

$$1 - \phi\delta/(1 - \gamma) < 0. \tag{20}$$

The term $\delta/(1 - \gamma)$ is the elasticity of equilibrium output with respect to the exchange rate. That term multiplied by the income elasticity of demand gives the increase in money demand due to a depreciation in the spot rate. Accordingly, (20) tells us whether at constant interest rates, and allowing the exchange rate to depreciate in the same proportion as the increase in money, we have an excess demand or supply of money and, accordingly, an increase or decrease in interest rates. The possibility of an excess demand and therefore an increase in interest rates is associated with a high income elasticity of money demand, high price elasticity, and a high income elasticity of demand for domestic goods.

The time path of exchange rates and the interest rate therefore depends on income and price elasticities, and the short-run overshooting of exchange rates is no longer a necessary feature of the adjustment process. In fact, if in the short run the interest rate rises and the exchange rate therefore depreciates less than proportionately to the increase in money, the adjustment process will be one of rising prices and a depreciating exchange rate. In this event, therefore, terms of trade fluctuations will be dampened as compared with the case described earlier where the exchange rate overshooting introduces large terms of trade variations in the adjustment process.

The analysis of a monetary expansion in this part confirms once more the Mundell-Fleming result that under conditions of capital mobility and flexible rates a small country can conduct, in the short run an effective monetary policy. More important, the exchange rate proves a critical channel for the transmission of monetary changes to an increase in aggregate demand and output. That channel may, in fact, prove to be the only channel since, as was shown above, the interest rate may actually rise in the transition. Unlike in the Mundell-Fleming world, extension of the analysis to the long run shows that the effects of a monetary expansion are only transitory, since the inflation that is induced by the output expansion serves to reduce real balances and thereby return interest rates, relative prices, and real income to their initial level.

The possibility of short-run output adjustment has been shown to dampen exchange rate movements and possibly reverse the interest rate effects of a monetary expansion. It is appropriate, therefore, to ask which of the assumption, fixed or variable output, is a more relevant characteristic of the adjustment process. The answer no doubt is that the fixed output adjustment is a suitable characterization of the very short run. In the very short run we would not expect output to adjust instantaneously to meet an increase in aggregate demand and, accordingly, the adjustment will be primarily confined to the asset markets and will be characterized by a decline in interest rates and overshooting of exchange rates. In the intermediate run, on the contrary, the present analysis gains relevance, since here we would expect an adjustment of both output and prices in response to increased aggregate demand. On balance, therefore, the fixed output case retains relevance, and particularly so if output adjusts sluggishly to changes in aggregate demand.

Appendix

This Appendix extends the model to include short-run supply responses. For that purpose we replace the price adjustment equation in (8) by a goods-market equilibrium condition (A1) and a price equation (A2):

$$y = \mu[u + \delta(e - p) - \sigma r]; \mu \equiv 1/(1 - \gamma) > 0, \tag{A1}$$

$$\dot{p} = \pi(y - \bar{y}), \tag{A2}$$

where $\bar{y}$ denotes the full-employment level of output and where the price adjustment equation can be thought of as arising from a Phillips-curve relation between wage inflation and unemployment combined with an Okun's-law relation between the deviation from potential output, $y - \bar{y}$, and unemployment. [15]

The specification of the money market and exchange rate expectations remains unchanged, and equation (4) that represents these relations is repeated here for convenience:

$$p - m + \phi y = \lambda r^* + \theta \lambda (\bar{e} - e). \tag{A3}$$

Noting that in long-run equilibrium we have $y = \bar{y}$ and $r = r^*$, we obtain from (A1) the long-run goods-market relationship

$$\bar{y} = \mu[u + \delta(\bar{e} = \bar{p}) - \sigma r^*], \tag{A4}$$

and subtracting (A4) from (A1) we obtain the goods-market equilibrium condition expressed in terms of deviations from long-run equilibrium,

$$y - \bar{y} = \mu(\delta + \sigma\theta)(e - \bar{e}) + \mu\delta(\bar{p} - p), \tag{A5}$$

where we have used the fact that $r^* - r = \theta(e - \bar{e})$.

Next we proceed in a similar manner for the money market and rewrite the equilibrium condition as

$$\phi(y - \bar{y}) + (p - \bar{p}) = \lambda\theta(\bar{\epsilon} - e). \tag{A6}$$

Equations (A5) and (A6) can be simultaneously solved to yield the spot exchange rate and the level of output as a function of the existing price level. These solutions are, respectively,

$$y - \bar{y} = -w(p - \bar{p}), \tag{A7}$$

where

$$w \equiv [\mu(\delta + \theta\sigma) + \mu\delta\theta\lambda]/\Delta; \Delta \equiv \phi\mu(\delta + \theta\sigma) + \theta\lambda,$$

and

$$e - \bar{e} = -[(1 - \phi\mu\delta)/\Delta](p - \bar{p}). \tag{A8}$$

Substitution of (A7) in (A2) yields the equilibrium rate of inflation as a function of the price level:

$$\dot{p} = -\pi w(p - \bar{p}).$$ (A9)

Following the procedure in Part III, rational expectations require that the expectations coefficient, θ, equal the rate at which exchange rates actually adjust, πw:

$$\theta = \pi w,$$ (A10)

which can be solved for the rational expectations coefficient of adjustment, θ.

Consider next the impact effect of a monetary expansion. Remembering that in the long run an increase in money causes an equiproportionate increase in prices and the exchange rate, we have $d\bar{e} = d\bar{p} = dm$. Therefore, from (A8) we obtain the impact effect of a monetary expansion on the exchange rate as

$$de/dm = 1 + (1 - \phi\mu\delta/\Delta > 0.$$ (A11)

Whether the exchange rate increases more or less proportionately than the nominal quantity of money depends on the condition

$$1 - \phi\mu\delta \gtrless 0,$$ (A12)

which determines, too, whether the interest rate declines or increases.

By (A7) the impact effect on real output is unambiguously positive and equal to $dy/dm = w$. The increase in the rate of inflation is given by $dp/dm = nw$.

Since from (A9) the inflation rate converges monotonically to the long-run level, we know that output declines monotonically back toward the level of full employment. The exchange rate, following the impact effect, will appreciate, or depreciate, depending on (A12).

Notes

1. For recent work on flexible exchange rates that shares some of the present emphasis, see Black (1973, 1975), Henderson (1975), Niehans (1975), Dornbush (1976a, 1976b), Frenkel (1976), Kouri (1976), and Mussa (1976). The classics remain Fleming (1962) and Mundell (1964, 1968).

2. Equation (3) is obtained by taking the logarithm of the money market equilibrium condition $M/P = Y\phi \exp(-\lambda r)$.

3. In (3) we assumed that the appropriate deflator for money balance is the price of domestic output. An alternative is provided by a deflator that is a weighted average of domestic and import prices. In such a formulation the "price

level," q, could be written as $q = ap + (1 - \alpha)e$, where a and $(1 - \alpha)$ are the expenditure shares of domestic goods and imports. With such a formulation (6) would be amended to the following equation: $e = \bar{e} - \beta(p - \bar{p})$, where $\beta \equiv \alpha/[\lambda\theta + (1 - \alpha)]$. *None of the qualitative results described below would be affected by this extension.*

4. The complete relative price argument in (7) is $(e + p^* - p)$ where p^* is the logarithm of the foreign price level. Setting the foreign price level equal to unity implies that $p^* = 0$.

5. Equation (9) is obtained by setting $p = 0$ and $r = r^*$ as is appropriate for the long run where markets clear and exchange rates are constant.

6. In (8) aggregate demand depends on the nominal interest rate. An alternative formulation allows aggregate demand to depend on the real interest rate, $r - \dot{p}$ Such a formulation requires that we substitute $p \equiv \pi/(1 - \sigma\pi) > 0$ in place of π in (11) and the equations below. The restriction that $p > 0$ is required for stability.

7. The $\dot{p} = 0$ schedule represents combined goods- and money-market equilibrium. Setting $\dot{p} = 0$ in (8) and substituting for the domestic interest rate from (3) yields the equation of the goods-market equilibrium schedule:

$$p = [\delta\lambda/(\delta\lambda + \sigma)]e + [\sigma/(\delta\lambda + \sigma)]m + [\lambda/(\delta\lambda + \sigma)][u + (1 - \gamma)y - \phi\sigma y/\lambda].$$

8. The 45° line in fig. 1 is drawn through the origin on the assumption that, by appropriate choice of units, the prices of both goods are initially equal.

9. In (16) we have taken the positive and therefore stable root of the quadratic equation implied by (14).

10. Perhaps a remark about the perfect foresight path is in order here. Why should that path command our interest rather than being a mere *curiosum?* The reason is that it is the only expectational assumption that is not arbitrary (given the model) and that does not involve persistent prediction errors. The perfect foresight path is, obviously, the deterministic equivalent of rational expectations.

11. We have not drawn in fig. 2, the $\dot{p} = 0$ schedule. It is apparent, however, from the homogeneity properties of the model that the $\dot{p} = 0$ schedule will pass through point C.

12. The slope of the QQ schedule is $dp/de = -\tilde{\theta}\lambda$, and the schedule becomes vertical as θ approaches infinity.

13. In the Mundell–Fleming model with prices and interest rates fixed, the depreciation by worsening the terms of trade creates the necessary increase in aggregate demand to support the higher level of income required by monetary equilibrium (for a further discussion see Niehans [1975] and Dornbusch [1976]).

14. An extension of this paper would draw in an explicit manner on stochastic elements to provide a rationale for the short-run stickiness of prices. At the same time, such an extension would have interesting implications for the manner in which expectations are formed. Exchange rate determination in a stochastic setting has been studied by Black (1973), Kouri (1975), and Mussa (1976). Fischer (1976) has used a stochastic framework to evaluate fixed versus flexible exchange rate systems.

15. To deal with steady-state inflation we would have to add in (A2) the long-run rate of inflation which is given by the rate of monetary growth, which in the present treatment is assumed equal to zero.

References

Black, S. *International Money Markets and Flexible Exchange Rates*. Princeton Studies in International Finance, no. 32. Princeton, N.J.: Princeton Univ. Press, 1973.

———. "Exchange Rate Policies for Less Developed Countries in a World of Floating Rates." Mimeographed. Vanderbilt Univ., 1975.

Dornbusch, R. "Exchange Rate Expectations and Monetary Policy." *J. Internat. Econ.* (1976), forthcoming. *(a)*

———. "The Theory of Flexible Exchange Rate Regimes and Macroeconomic Policy." *Scandinavian J. Econ.* 2 (May 1976): 255–75. *(b)*

Fischer, S. "Stability and Exchange Rate Systems in a Monetarist Model of the Balance of Payments." In *The Political Economy of Monetary Reform*, edited by R. Aliber. London: Macmillan, 1976.

Fleming, M. "Domestic Financial Policies under Fixed and Floating Exchange Rates." I.M.F. *Staff Papers* 9 (November 1962): 369–79.

Frenkel, J. A. "A Monetary Approach to the Exchange Rate." *Scandinavian J. Econ.* 2 (May 1976): 200–221.

Henderson, D. "Monetary, Fiscal and Exchange Rate Policy in a Two-Country, Short-Run Macroeconomic Model." Mimeographed. Board of Governors, Federal Res., 1975.

Kouri, P. *Essays on the Theory of Flexible Exchange Rates*. Ph.D. dissertation, Massachusetts Inst. Tech., 1975.

———. "The Exchange Rate and the Balance of Payments in the Short Run and in the Long Run." *Scandinavian J. Econ.* 2 (May 1976): 280–304.

Mundell, R. A. "Exchange Rate Margins and Economic Policy." In *Money in the International Order*, edited by C. Murphy. Dallas: Southern Methodist Univ. Press, 1964.

———. *International Economics*. New York: Macmillan, 1968.

Mussa, M. "The Exchange Rate, the Balance of Payments and Monetary and Fiscal Policy under a Regime of Controlled Floating." *Scandinavian J. Econ.* 2 (May 1976): 229–48.

Niehans, J. "Some Doubts about the Efficacy of Monetary Policy under Flexible Exchange Rates." *J. Internat. Econ.* 5 (August 1975): 275–81.

23

FLEXIBLE EXCHANGE RATES AND EXCESS CAPITAL MOBILITY

Rudiger Dornbusch

From 1980 to early 1985 the dollar appreciated 60 percent in real terms. Since then it has depreciated about 20 percent.[1] These exchange rate movements have made many observers wonder whether more is at work than mere changes in fundamentals, and if so, whether such large and persistent swings should be arrested by a return to the gold standard, by rigidly fixed exchange rates among the major monetary areas, or at least by target zones, either hard zones with bumpers or soft zones, implicit and discretionary. Discussion of these possibilities involves two sets of issues, views on which can be combined in a variety of ways. The issues are whether large exchange rate movements primarily reflect extravagant macroeconomic policies or poorly working markets and whether exchange rate fluctuations can be contained without the need for subordinating macroeconomic policies to the exchange rate objective.

There is only one purely market-oriented combination of views: "yes, freely flexible rates work efficiently" and "no, there should be no intervention." The agnostic position concedes that markets may not work efficiently but dismisses the possibility that managed rates would improve the performance. A third combination of views is that exchange markets do not function properly and that policymakers can and should intervene to improve performance.

	Exchange markets function efficiently	
	Yes	*No*
Manage rate movements		
Yes	Branson-Tobin	Marris-Bergsten
No	Sprinkel-Samuelson	Agnostic

The final position is that markets work reasonably but that there can nonetheless be a case for intervention. Capital flows, for example, may have to be influenced for macroeconomic reasons. Or exchange rate target zones may be useful in educating governments not to pursue policies inconsistent with more or less rigid exchange rates. The premise in both cases is that differential speeds of adjustment in goods and assets markets magnify the effects of monetary and fiscal policies beyond what would arise in a rational expectations market-equilibrium world and thus call for market intervention to avoid undesired effects on employment or inflation.

This note argues that standard theory easily explains the pattern, though perhaps not the magnitude, of exchange rate fluctuations. It argues against target zones because they would lock up monetary policy in a way that is sometimes undesirable. Ad hoc controls of international capital flows via interest equalization taxes or dual rates may be an alternative, although they are not clearly preferable to freely floating exchange rates.

Objections to Large Exchange Rate Movements

There are three basic objections to large exchange rate movements. The first is primitive, but widespread: anything that moves a lot moves too much. Asset markets, exchange markets in particular, are seen as highly speculative and not necessarily rational. Asset prices easily detach themselves for extended periods from fundamentals to go on a bubble that has important effects on resource allocation and on the macroeconomy. The argument has been applied to interest rates, and it might be applied to the stock market, but it has an extraordinary attraction when applied to exchange rates. Presumably the reason is that when wages are relatively fixed in home currency, exchange rate movements mean changes in competitiveness and hence in employment. This argument is, of course, particularly persuasive when applied to appreciation, which ultimately generates unemployment. Such unemployment may be only temporary, but there may also be permanent job loss as firms close down, move abroad, or at the very least, slow their investment. Moreover, the mere presence of exchange rate volatility might mean lower average wages because of adverse effects on profitabilty and investment.

The second objection involves inflation. Movements in exchange rates, and accompanying movements in commodity prices, represent the most important shock to an otherwise stable inflation process. Sharp appreciation is welcome from an inflation point of view because it improves the inflation-unemployment trade-off. But a bottomless decline in the home currency is rightly seen as an open-ended threat to inflation stability.

The third objection concerns the policial reaction to misaligned exchange rates. Overvalued currencies often generate threats of protectionist trade policies—threats that are not, unfortunately, counterbalanced by threats of greater trade liberalization in countries with undervalued currencies. Exchange rate misalignment therefore poses a risk to an open trading system.

These objections, even though loosely stated, make it clear that there are trade-offs. There is the question of what is "too large," and there is the issue of the costs and benefits of limiting exchange rate movements. Finally there is the practical question of whether the recommended policy instruments will work.

Why Exchange Rates Move So Much

A discussion of exchange rate management presupposes an understanding of how a well-functioning exchange market should behave a methodology for recognizing excessive volatility when it exists. In particular, one should be able to judge whether the recent volatility in the dollar can be explained by models with perfect markets and rational agents or whether it reflects a serious market failure. The same question has often been asked about bond and stock prices without ready acceptance of the market failure argument.

There are three popular explanations for the large movements in exchange rates. The first is that monetary tightening and fiscal expansion both cause an immediate large appreciation; the second focuses on safe haven effects; the third assumes that markets are irrational. According to the first two explanations, current exchange rate variations reflect a healthy floating rate regime. The theory is that exchange rate movements will be large when policy disturbances are extreme, although the exact quantitative correspondence between rate movements and disturbances remains to be established. According to the third, the dollar's volatility reflects the harsh reality of a market that makes mistakes.

Tight Money and Fiscal Expansion

The easiest explanation for large exchange rate variability comes from a Mundell-Fleming model of the effects of monetary and fiscal policy under flexible exchange rates with perfect capital mobility.

The model assumes that asset prices and exchange rates adjust instantly, while goods prices adjust sluggishly. Monetary and fiscal disturbances thus have large effects on real exchange rates. A highly simplified model of the goods and assets markets makes this point:

(1) $$m - p = \lambda 1,$$

(2) $$i = i^* + \dot{e},$$

(3) $$\dot{p} = \theta[\phi(e - p) + g],$$

(4) $$\dot{g} = -\zeta(g - \bar{g}),$$

where m, p, and e are home nominal money, the price of domestic output, and the exchange rate. The home and foreign interest rates are i and i^*, $\dot{e}$ is the expected rate of depreciation of the home currency; g is the real level of government spending. The model assumes a given output and a given foreign interest rate and ignores foreign repercussion effects of domestic disturbances. Complications are possible in all directions, but they do not substantially alter the conclusions. Equation 1 describes monetary equilibrium, and equation 2 imposes international arbitrage of interest rates, which implies that the home interest rate must equal the foreign rate plus the expected rate of depreciation. The third equation states that prices move in proportion to the excess demand for domestic output, where demand depends on the real exchange rate and on the level of government spending. Finally equation 4 specifies that government spending adjusts gradually to its steady state level.[2]

The central feature of this extended Mundell-Fleming model is the fact tht goods prices adjust only gradually, certainly not in a forward-looking manner. The sluggishness of price adjustment means that exchange rates overshoot: the nominal and real exchange rates immediately appreciate in response to a monetary contraction, and proportionally more than the change in money. Over time, as goods prices decline, the real exchange rate depreciates until, in the long run, the initial real equilibrium is regained.

An unanticipated and transitory fiscal expansion, an increase in g above $\bar{g}$ in equation 4, leads to an immediate real appreciation, as shown in figure 1. At point A', which is the short-run equilibrium, there is an excess demand for goods, and hence prices are rising. Since the interest rate is initially unchanged (the price level being given at a point in time), the nominal exchange rate at A' is unchanging. Hence at A' there must be real appreciation, since prices are rising with an unchanging nominal exchange rate.

Over time as the level of government spending falls and prices rise, the nominal interest rate increases, and hence the nominal exchange rate will

Figure 1. Effects of a Transitory Fiscal Expansion

Domestic prices

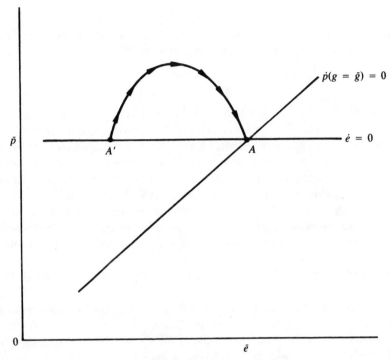

Nominal exchange rate

depreciate. At the same time there is a loss of aggregate demand because of overvaluation that is no longer offset by high government spending. Therefore the real exchange rate starts depreciating. The process continues until real spending reaches its initial level and with it interest rates, both nominal and real, as well as the real exchange rate.

Perfect substitutability of foreign and domestic capital, adjusted for expected depreciation, is expressed in equation 2 above. Adjusting nominal interest rates for the respective countries permit writing the real interest parity condition as follows:

(2a) $$r = r^* + \dot{q}.$$

The solution to equations 1 through 4 yields a relation between the expected rate of change of the real exchange rate and the deviations of government spending and the real exchange rate from their long-run equilibrium levels:[3]

$$(5) \qquad \dot{q} = \alpha(\bar{q} - q) - \beta(g - \bar{g}),$$

and hence, substituting in equation 2a, obtains a relation between real exchange rates, real interest rates, and fiscal variables:

$$(6) \qquad q = \bar{q} + \frac{1}{\alpha}(r^* - r) - \frac{\beta}{\alpha}(g - \bar{g}).$$

Equation 6 explains why there is no simple linkage between the real interest rate and the real exchange rate. Fiscal variables and other determinants of aggregate demand also affect real exchange rates. The solution to the model shows that a transitory increase in real government spending leads to an immediate real appreciation, followed for some time by a continuing real appreciation before real depreciation starts. The adjustment path for the real exchange rate is shown in figure 2. The model thus produces a coherent explanation for the exchange rate pattern experienced in the United States over the past few years. Superimposing the relative tightening of U.S. monetary policy, as measured by short-term real interest differentials, compared with policy in the rest of the world reinforces that point.

The empirical support for this interpretation comes from recent changes in the structural budget deficits of the leading industrialized countries. The 1980–85 appreciation of the dollar reflects a vast shift in the international monetary-fiscal mix, with fiscal policy in the United States shifting to a massive deficit, while fiscal consolidation abroad was unprecedented. Table 1 shows the extent of deficits and the cumulative shift in structural deficits.

The model predicts that the anticipation of a return to smaller budget deficits in the United States and a looser stance abroad would lead to dollar decline. Where the Kemp-Roth tax cuts of 1981 brought about appreciation, the anticipation of a balanced budget brought about by the Gramm-Rudman bill of 1985 must lead to depreciation.[4]

The Safe Haven Argument

A second explanation for the dollar's strength focuses on international portfolio shifts. Increased political uncertainty in Europe, a strengthening of the relative economic position of the United States under the Reagan administration, and economic disintegration in Latin America are the motivating forces in this international asset shift toward the United States.

Figure 2. Real Exchange Rate Adjustment to a Transitory Fiscal Expansion

Real exchange rate

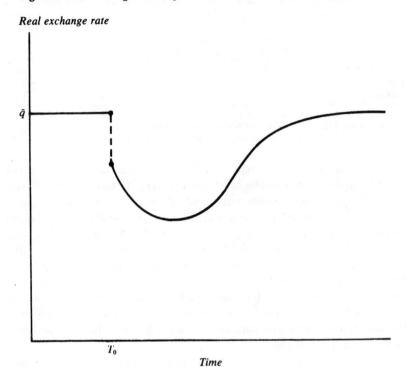

Time

The vehicles are many: a shift bank lending from the less developed countries (LDCs) to the U.S. capital market, direct investment in the United States, and flight into U.S. currency and deposits from the IMF-occupied territories.[5]

As a single explanation for the recent movements in exchange rates the safe haven argument is plainly inadequate. It works for the appreciation but has trouble explaining the sharp decline of the dollar unless it postulates an inevitable overshooting.

Irrationality

The irrationality argument in its newest form is that markets seem not to recognize the incompatibility of a strong dollar and relatively small

TABLE 1
Government Budget Deficits, United States, Japan, and Germany, 1974–85
Percent of GNP

	1974–79 average	*1980–84 average*	*1985*	*Change in structural deficit, 1980–85*[a]
United States	1.1	2.7	3.7	4.3
Japan	3.4	3.6	1.4	−3.2
Germany	3.0	3.1	1.5	−4.2

Sources: Organization for Economic Cooperation and Development, *Economic Outlook*, various issues, and *OECD Economic Studies*, no. 3 (Autumn 1984).
a. Cumulative change in inflation-adjusted structural budget deficit.

long-term interest differentials, which, from equation 2a, imply a low rate of real depreciation. The implication is that, starting from a high real value, the dollar will decline only gradually to a more competitive level and that, accordingly, the large current account imbalance will persist and accumulate with interest to give the United States, ultimately a huge debt-to-GNP ratio. Such a debt accumulation would make the United States a worse debtor than, say, Mexico. The argument goes on to say that since such an eventuality is impossible, exchange rate adjustments must come sooner and faster than is reflected in long-term real interest differentials. The irrationality of the market lies in the failure to detect the unsustainability of the path of gradual decline and the inevitability of an exchange rate collapse.[6]

The argument that small long-term interest differentials must imply a collapse has already been demonstrated over the past year. But that may not be a vindication of the approach. The calculations are highly sensitive to assumed levels of real interest rates and growth rates in the United States and abroad. They are also sensitive to the assumption that there is no risk premium. Indeed, as Dooley and Isard have noted, the portfolio shift into dollars from less developed countries may well represent a reduction of the risk premium on U.S. assets.[7] Once the existence of a risk premium is recognized, the setting of equation 2—one of perfectly substitutable capital and risk-neutral asset holders—no longer applies. The Dooley-Isard argument permits recasting the real interest equation, now including risk premium, R, on nondollar assets:

(2b) $$\dot{q} = r - r^* + R.$$

An increase in the risk premium on nondollar assets means that at given real interest differentials the U.S. currency can depreciate more rapidly. There is accordingly no longer the strong presumption that the market is on an irrational course that must end in collapse. The path may be one of rapid anticipated real depreciation, which asset holders are prepared to accept because U.S. assets yield compensating returns, psychic or otherwise.

Managed Exchange Rates: Coordination and Target Zones

The difficulties encountered last March by the United States, Germany, and Japan in obtaining a worldwide cut in interest rates dramatize the difficulty of securing international macroeconomic coordination, even in a situation where all players can come out ahead. Agreements involving sacrifices on growth or on inflation would be far more troublesome, and the near-impossibility of coordination spells trouble for any international agreement to limit the fluctuations of exchange rates. The fixed exchange rate system of the 1960s broke down because West Germany, or perhaps the United States, as one looks at it, was unwilling to agree on a consistent set of policies.

The European Monetary System might be taken as an indication that coordination works, but it is in fact nothing more than a German Monetary Area. The minor acts sacrifice their policy autonomy, presumably to improve inflation performance (perhaps at the cost of long-run fiscal problems), and attempt to adjust to the policy tone set by Germany. Occasional crises, realignments, and capital controls are the chief means by which policy incompatibility is handled.

Nevertheless, proposals to limit exchange rate fluctuations among the major currencies abound. Many seem to rest on the assumption that the job can be done without complementary domestic and international policy coordination. One especially favored proposal is a system of exchange rate target zones.

Excess Variability

One argument for a target zone system relies on the alleged excess volatility of exchange markets. Asset markets, the argument goes, put prices on assets that need not correspond to fundamentals, but that have an important impact on the economy. For the United States, an overvalued dollar leads to undesirable external indebtedness and domestic deindustrialization. If intervention can be effective, then policymakers should step in and push the exchange rate in the direction of the equilibrium value that governments can identify and point out to speculators. By deliberately creating disorder in the exchange market, they scare speculators off the wrong price and in the direction warranted by fundamentals. The action in September 1985 by the Group of Five to lower the value of the dollar relative to other major currencies would be seen as implementation and vindication of this view.

The difficulty is knowing what a disequilibrium price is, and whether and when intervention should take place in markets where mispricing is suspected. The point is best made by figure 3, which shows real stock prices for the United States in the past decade. What were the fundamentals that caused asset prices to be at a record low in 1982 and then to

Figure 3. Real Value of Stock Prices, United States, 1974–85[a]

Index, 1980 = 100

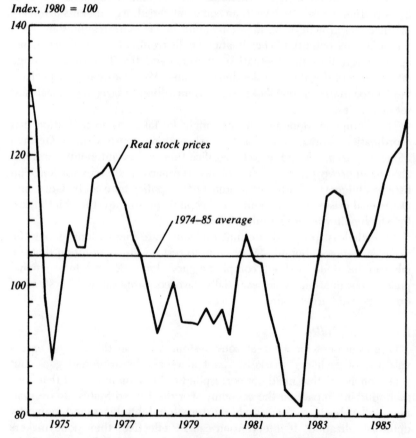

Sources: Quarterly data from Standard and Poor's Corporation and U.S. Department of Commerce, Bureau of Economic Analysis, *The National Income and Product Accounts of the United States, 1929–82 Statistical Tables* (Government Printing Office, forthcoming), and *Survey of Current Business,* vol. 66 (March 1986).

a. Standard and Poor's composite index of 500 stocks, deflated by the implicit GNP price deflator.

increase more than 50 percent in three years? Is the 1982 level too low, or the present level too high? From 1972 to 1985, stock market variability was twice as great as exchange rate variability.[8] Since the stock market is at least as significant as the exchange rate for the performance of the U.S. economy, should we have target zones to avoid erratic and irrational fluctuations in the stock market?[9] Exactly the same argument applies to long-term bond prices, which also show seemingly erratic fluctuations and have a major impact on the economy.

Many economists would be coy in responding to proposals to set target zones for interest rates or for the stock market. They would ask immediately how these target zones are to be made to stick and would certainly be concerned if the answer were monetary policy. Fixing target zones for interest rates without regard for fundamentals, they would protest, would generate inflation. The same, they would add, applies to fixing the real value of the stock market. But what is different about target zones for exchange rates? The only difference I can see is that target zones for interest rates or the stock market are discredited (perhaps excessively), while exchange rate fixing is a fad that has a way of coming back.

Even if it were quite obvious that an exchange rate was misaligned, there would still be a policy issue to be resolved. Moving the exchange rate would have macroeconomic effects on aggregate demand and on prices. Bursting an exchange rate bubble, in the U.S. case, would benefit manufacturing, which is certainly suffering from an overly strong dollar, but it would also bring about a swing of the U.S. external balance and hence create pressure on import prices. Correction of the exchange market therefore involves a macroeconomic adjustment that can easily push up inflation. In the absence of conclusive action to reduce the U.S. deficit, it is not obvious that a better-aligned exchange rate is a good trade-in for a significant increase in inflation. At a minimum, one must ask what macroeconomic policies, here and abroad, should accompany a realignment of rates. Lower world interest rates and U.S. fiscal contraction are, of course, the answer. Thus it may be impossible to avoid the coordination issue even when one thinks of bubble bursting.

Insufficient Instruments

If large changes in exchange rates primarily reflect fundamentals, the problem will be different. When fundamentals change, as in the case of a fiscal expansion, the equilibrium exchange rate also changes, and governments must explicitly or implicitly shift target zones. A serious political issue arises because now the government of a country undergoing fiscal expansion will quite overtly have to practice crowding out of the traded goods sector. The objective functioning of markets can no longer be claimed as an argument for a passive nonintervention stance. Pressures to use the target zones to counter movements in equilibrium rates will have to be resisted. The same pressures that call in the United States today for intervention or protection, rather than fiscal adjustment, will be vocal in calling for a determined effort to resist movements in market-determined exchange rates. It is difficult to see that making exchange rates more of a political issue will help make them move more often in the right direction.

The outcome would be much the same if target zones were hard rather than soft, a system that would be the practical equivalent of fixed nominal rates independent of fundamentals. Suppose a country sets out to stabilize inflation by reducing money growth. In the absence of wage-price controls, interest rates will have to rise to bring about the recession that slows inflation. The increase in interest rates in turn attracts capital and leads to currency appreciation. Pursuing a policy of rigid target zones would make it difficult to reduce inflation. To avoid the appreciation, monetary policy could not turn restrictive in the first place.

The argument is reinforced if at the very time of inflation stabilization the economy is driven by expansionary fiscal policy. In such a case, to hold the exchange rate, monetary policy would in effect have to monetize the deficits. The exchange rate would remain unchanged; there would be no crowding out except on a world scale; and there would be a maximum of inflation. This is, of course, what would have happened in the United States in 1980–85 if monetary policy had defended the 1980 value of the dollar in the face of the Kemp-Roth tax cuts. The Volcker disinflation would simply not have occurred.

The upshot of all this is that as long as legislatures or administrations reserve the privilege of enacting extravagant fiscal policies, market prices, from exchange rates to interest rates, will adjust; fixing some will quite possibly make others move even more. The lesson is that large international divergences in monetary or fiscal policy will be reflected in exchange rates. To avoid these fluctuations, bad policies must be avoided. Accommodating a poor fiscal policy by exchange-rate-oriented monetary policy simply adds yet another folly.

Institution-Building

Some analysts who favor target zones understand that an effective system of target zones requires international coordination of monetary and fiscal policies.[10] They also recognize that as yet there is no effective method of coordination. But they argue that setting target zones for exchange rates would be a first step in educating governments to pursue good policies. They seem to envision a scenario in which, when the Kemp-Roth tax cuts led to exchange rate problems, the U.S. Congress, recognizing the target zone commitment, would simply have rescinded the tax cuts. Europe, in the same way, would have abstained from fiscal consolidation.

It is difficult to believe that such conditions for international monetary and fiscal coordination are at hand. No government in a large country easily sacrifices its fiscal autonomy to an exchange rate target. The United States will not, nor will Germany, Japan, or even the United Kingdom. Promoters of target zones should be quite frank to admit that without fiscal coordination their scheme will more often than not involve abuse of monetary policy. It therefore may well introduce even more instability. The lack of fiscal convergence so far makes this almost a certainty.

It is entirely correct to try to build institutions that ultimately help promote reasonable policies. But in this respect the world economy is at a very early stage, in which the negotiation of an ad hoc consensus, for example the present one on interest rates, is the best we can hope for.

Directing and Containing Capital Flows

Whether the safe haven argument or the Mundell-Fleming model applies, when excessive incipient capital inflows move currency values, the traded goods sector, and possibly the entire macroeconomy, suffers. There are several ways out. The first is to impose a rigid exchange rate system, a prescription that assumes that fixed exchange rates can accommodate any disturbances. This is the "discipline" argument for fixed rates.

A second solution is to avoid international interest differentials by using monetary policy: whenever a fiscal expansion drives up exchange rates, a monetary expansion would keep interest rates in line internationally and thus take the pressure off exchange rates. The third possibility is to break the tight international interest rate linkages, rather than sacrifice fiscal autonomy or subordinate monetary policy to exchange rate targets.

There are in principle three ways to tamper with international interest rate linkages. The first is direct control of capital flows. A country with an incipient currency appreciation would limit capital inflows by restricting borrowing from abroad for some or all classes of assets and by precluding the repatriation of assets held abroad. Whether the strategy would work is another question. The record on capital controls is hard to interpret. The common argument is that they are circumvented the moment they are imposed, but of course the same argument was used for the income tax when it was first suggested as an important source of revenue. Some evasion is inevitable; the question is whether the controls substantially work. Even though capital controls are practiced by most countries in one form or another, they are difficult to apply for a large country with many firms that have extensive international transactions.[11]

Given these difficulties, attention centers on two market-oriented measures, the "Tobin tax" and a real interest equalization tax as proposed, for example, by Liviatan.[12] A more radical form would be a dual exchange rate regime, in which trade is conducted at a fixed rate while all capital account transactions occur in a separate market at a flexible rate. The purpose would be to reduce the dominance of capital flows over real activity and the inflation process.

The Tobin tax would reduce the incentive for short-term capital flows by imposing a small uniform tax on all foreign exchange transactions. Such a tax would tend to penalize short-term capital flows, or "hot money," and reduce their impact on exchange rates. An interest equalization tax would also narrow the net return to nonresidents and reduce incipient inflows. Of course, it would not eliminate these inflows unless it also applied to repatriation. Administrative complications could be considerable, but so are the disruptions that follow from the laissez-faire system or from second-best policies under target zones.

Ultimately, a more severe control of international capital flows may be unavoidable. Most international capital flows today involve tax sheltering or tax evasion rather than socially productive resource transfers. Shifting capital internationally in search of tax havens has become a nasty evasion of ordinary tax discipline, as is obvious in light of the massive capital flight from debtor countries—easily $100 billion—in the past ten years. This footloose capital is parked tax free in shelters, helping promote an overvalued dollar and serious fiscal and social problems in the countries of origin.

Rather than attracting capital from debtor countries by offering a tax haven, thus undermining already precarious efforts at stabilization, the United States should charge rent on the place in the sun. The same argument applies to politically motivated capital flows. And in the process of constructing a system of reasonable taxation of footloose capital, the United States would create an administrative framework that would make it possible to implement ad hoc temporary interest equalization taxes that are complements of major macroeconomic shifts in monetary or fiscal policy.

Once such policies are accepted as feasible, two issues remain. First, the international coordination necessary to help implement the scheme would raise many of the problems of achieving agreement that arise in connection with target zoning. Second, limiting the degree of exchange rate movement would affect the distribution of crowding out. For example, in the context of a fiscal expansion, exchange appreciation crowds out net exports. But if an interest equalization tax were used to limit the appreciation, home output and employment would be greater and the world interest rate higher. Crowding out would tend to take place abroad as a result of increased world interest rates, and the impact of exchange appreciation on inflation would be limited. It is not certain that such an eventuality is to be preferred to an overvaluation that crowds out net exports and contains inflation, with adjustment costs postponed until the policy comes to an end.

The main difference between target zones, reinforced by monetary accommodation, and interest equalization taxes, a Tobin tax, or dual rates is that in the latter cases monetary policy remains free for domestic stabilization. Such flexibility is to be preferred to a habitual subordination of monetary policy to exchange rate targets. Occasional ad hoc interest equalization taxes and occasional ad hoc monetary coordination seem to be a better system among the unconverged industrial countries than a promise of target zoning without an idea of how to make it stick.

Concluding Remarks

Even though ad hoc policies toward capital flows can, in principle and perhaps in practice, achieve a more favorable adjustment to disturbances, what is finally at issue is not the exchange rate system but the policy shocks. At this stage the priority must be to reduce world real interest rates, taking advantage of the leeway provided by the oil price decline to solve fiscal problems, LDC debt problems, and the problems of financial institutions.

It is worth noting that the most fervent advocates of target zones invariably have in mind sharply increased budget deficits in Japan and a much stronger yen. It is true that under a system of target zones Japan will have trade problems, which larger budget deficits and currency appreciation might be a way of preventing. We may think the average Japanese household saves too much, but it is difficult to believe that better resource allocation or full employment requires such a shift in Japan's policies. A much better case could be made for Germany, at least on the basis of the high levels of unemployment prevailing there. There is no indication, however, that either Germany or Japan sees deficit spending as a priority. Nor does sound public finance or anything else suggest that they should go on a Kemp-Roth fling. If we do not like Japanese net foreign lending and feel that we suffer because of it, we should tax it, if necessary at exorbitant rates. If that is administratively difficult we should ask our Japanese friends to do so for us and to spend the proceeds. In that way we reduce the incentives to Japanese savers or at least direct the lending to Europe or capital-starved LDCs. Insisting on their building sewers is at best a roundabout way of solving the problem.

But the main puzzle remains this: what makes it so difficult to recognize that lower interest rates, not bigger foreign deficits or an appreciating yen, are economically and politically attractive, free, and feasible? Lower interest rates solve the world's problems better than getting an extra dollar of budget deficits abroad or raising the yen another penny, whether by target zones or otherwise.

COMMENTS
AND DISCUSSION

Stanley Fischer: Each of the four papers in this symposium is extremely convincing on many points. But they differ on the central issue, whether we should return to fixed exchange rates—or their judicious equivalent, target zones for exchange rates. My comments will be directed to uncovering and evaluating the judgments that lead the authors to their different conclusions. I conclude in agreement with the Branson-Dornbusch team, though not for identical reasons, that target zones are not a good idea.

Table 1 summarizes the positions of the papers on the two key questions isolated by Rudiger Dornbusch. The agnostic entries represent positions taken in the papers for this symposium, not necessarily the views of the authors expressed on other occasions.

Here are the five points in the papers on which we should agree and on which I believe all four authors agree.

- Nominal and real exchange rates have fluctuated a great deal in the past thirteen years, far more than the proponents of flexible rates would have predicted.
- Real exchange rate appreciations bring protectionist pressures that are potentially destructive of one of the major achievements of the

TABLE 1
Anatomy of Exchange Rate Policy Positions

		Exchange markets function efficiently		
		Yes	Agnostic	No
Manage	Yes	. . .	Cooper	Williamson
rates				
directly	No	Branson	Dornbusch	. . .

post–World War II era—the restoration of world trade to the levels of the 1920s.

- From William Branson we see that manufacturing output is, other things being equal, negatively correlated with the real exchange rate, "other things" being trend, the real price of energy, and the employment ratio. This is evidence that a less valuable dollar in the past five years would have produced a different composition of U.S. output— and the point extends to agriculture and the likelihood that the farm problem would have been less severe.

- From Branson and Dornbusch, formally, and from Richard Cooper, less formally, we see that the Mundell-Fleming-Dornbusch model accounts for the real appreciation of the dollar in the past five years as the inevitable result of the world policy mix of tight fiscal policy abroad, loose fiscal policy in the United States, and tight monetary policy in the Organization for Economic Cooperation and Development.

- Exchange market intervention by itself, in the form of jawboning (Cooper) or sterilized intervention, would not be powerful enough to reduce exchange rate fluctuations substantially. At the least, monetary policy would have to be exchange-rate oriented; at best, in John Williamson's world, fiscal policies would be better coordinated than they are now.

Remarkably, the authors' policy views are nonetheless different, as outlined below.

Branson: The exchange rate has been reacting appropriately to policy. There is no prospect of fiscal policy coordination, without which monetary policy can do little. What can be achieved is best done through quiet diplomacy among the central banks. A new Bretton Woods would fail not only for lack of political will to coordinate policies, but also for lack of the analytical ability to calculate appropriate exchange rates.

Cooper: This paper is less a discussion of target zones than the others and more a discussion of the U.S. policy mix. Cooper argues that the mix has been a disaster for many firms and workers in goods-producing sectors, including agriculture. The U.S. debt, internal and external, is a major problem for the longer term. The United States should steadily tighten its fiscal policy, compensating with monetary expansion, to drive down the dollar. Jawboning helps, and the exchange rate initiatives of September 1985 were appropriate and useful.

Dornbusch: There is substantial agreement with Branson's views, but an even stronger emphasis on the impossibility of fiscal policy coordination. Dornbusch believes that the best that can be hoped for at present is ad hoc intervention, in the form of monetary policy intervention or taxes on capital flows or both. He does not express a preference between the Tobin tax on all international capital flows and the type of tax on capital inflows used by the Israelis in 1979–81 to try to prevent an attempted disinflation from producing too large an appreciation. Dornbusch argues that international capital flows are motivated in large measure by tax evasion rather than any socially useful purpose.

Williamson: Williamson wants the dollar to move another 10 percent. The world needs exchange rate target zones, agreed to by a formal group consisting of the major industrial countries and the International Monetary Fund. They will figure out zones that produce basic balance in the current account in the medium term. The zones would be 10 percent above and below the targets, and soft at the edges, which must mean 12 percent and harder at the edges. The targets would be achieved through monetary policy. Williamson's paper substantially advances the discussion by including an interesting collection of supporting judgments that reveal why he differs from the other panelists on the feasibility of the target zone approach. His most important judgment is that fiscal policy is not necessarily independent of exchange rate regimes.

How can such sensible people differ? Table 2 summarizes the judgments that divide them, using a scheme similar to that used in table 1. None of the four boxes can be ruled out a priori. If target zones could restrain inappropriate government policy—and in the mid-eighties thoughts turn to fiscal policy—there would be no contradiction between believing that exchange markets are efficient and believing that target zones are desirable. A person with those views would occupy the top left

TABLE 2
Explaining Exchange Rate Policy Positions

		Exchange markets function efficiently	
		Yes	No
Manage rates directly	Yes	Target zones will constrain government policy.	Target zones can reduce excess volatility and will constrain government policy.
	No	Markets work fine, but target zones will not constrain government policy.	Capital flows are unstoppable, and target zones will not constrain government policy.

box. John Williamson appears in the top right box, believing both that governments will be constrained by target zones and that the exchange markets are inefficient. In the bottom left-hand corner we find the essence of the Branson view, which is that the exchange markets are efficient and that governments will not be constrained by exchange rate targets. I would place myself in the bottom right-hand box, doubting that the exchange markets are efficient, but believing that governments will not be constrained by target zones and that the zones could not in any event withstand the capital flows that now move about the international financial system.

The key judgments that are being made here are on the questions of whether governments will be constrained by exchange rate rules and whether capital flows can be withstood. And underlying those questions is the basic issue that William Branson emphasizes, whether we would be better off if exchange rates were more stable. The answer is yes only if there is indeed excess volatility of exchange rates and governments have sufficient knowledge to choose the right rates, and if more stable fiscal policies are appropriate and we can constrain governments to follow such policies through exchange rate rules.

In deciding where to stand on these issues, it is useful to draw on the lessons of the breakdown of Bretton Woods and of the existence and operation of the European Monetary System.

Given that the Bretton Woods system lasted well over twenty years, the target zone system cannot be dismissed out of hand. The question is what the breakdown of the Bretton Woods system tells us about target zones. One lesson is that fiscal and monetary policies can diverge internationally even under tightly fixed exchange rates. It could be argued that was possible only because the United States was not constrained under Bretton Woods—but there is no reason to think the United States would agree to be constrained this time around either.

The Bretton Woods system became progressively less stable as the strength and volume of private capital flows increased. The second important lesson is that it is very difficult to manage a fixed exchange rate system when there are free private capital flows.

The European Monetary System was slighted in the four papers we had in this session. That institution operates substantially the way John Williamson wants the international economy to operate. It has target zones. Rudiger Dornbusch remarks that the EMS is merely the German monetary union, but that should not obscure the significant fact that countries are voluntarily in that union. The governments of France and Italy find it politically useful to operate under the constraint of German monetary policy. Thus the EMS provides some evidence in favor of the view that exchange rate targets would constrain government policies.

But there is another lesson from the EMS. Capital controls have been needed to keep the French and Italian exchange rates in line. Both Italy and France operate exchange controls, which, although not watertight, are tightened when a change in the exchange rate looks imminent. That again suggests that capital flows will be a key to the operation of a target zone system.

What should we conclude from all this? First, there is a question of how agreement will be reached on a desirable basic current account balance for each country. Richard Cooper and John Williamson talk as if the United States should have a balanced current account. That is not a good idea if Latin America is trying to pay off its debt. Agreement on the underlying balances will not be an easy matter.

Second, the big bands around the targets are a sales device. Williamson's targets are miragelike. The zone is ten percent wide, but when you get close to the edge, you can readjust the target, and, besides, it is soft at the edges. If the target zones mean anything, there will come a time when domestic policy has to be readjusted and exchange rates have to be defended, for monetary policy will not be able to withstand capital flows unless there is an appropriate policy adjustment. It is at that point that countries have to decide whether they want to subordinate their monetary or fiscal policies to the defense of the exchange rate.

Will they do it? For the United States the answer is no. When push comes to shove, the U.S. Congress is not going to change fiscal policy, or anything that matters to its constituents, in order to maintain the exchange rate. Ask yourself whether the target zones could have withstood the Reagan revolution, which is implicitly what is being argued. Or do you believe the United States would have negotiated with its trading partners for permission to move the exchange rate so it could undertake the massive Reagan tax cuts without violating the targets? The United States will not operate that way. Target zones are not a likely prospect in the United States, Germany, or Japan.

Instead we are moving at present toward a three-currency-block world. Europe is happy to operate in the EMS, which Britain may soon join. Then the three-block system will operate in the modified Branson-Dornbusch mode: there will be occasions when it is perfectly obvious that exchange rates are out of line and when they can be nudged back into line with monetary policy or with direct intervention. But mostly the blocks will operate independently, running their own monetary and fiscal policy, meeting every now and then to try to persuade the others to change policy, and occasionally surprising everyone by agreeing on the directions in which exchange rates should move and succeeding in moving them.

General Discussion

Rudiger Dornbusch reiterated his view that the most compelling reason for targeting exchange rates has to be the belief, which he does not share, that the existence of target zones would force national governments to adopt more responsible fiscal and monetary policies. Otherwise, either the target zones would have to be adjusted frequently to accommodate bad policy or the target zone system would break down entirely. Robert Gordon noted that exchange rate targeting would not have affected U.S. fiscal policy during the early 1980s because that policy was pursued on the grounds that it would produce falling deficits and interest rates. The large budget deficits actually experienced were not predicted by those responsible for the policy.

William Branson commented that the so-called misalignment of the dollar in recent years was in fact an equilibrium reaction to the change in U.S. fiscal policy under Reagan. The exchange rate movement brought about the large U.S. trade deficit that made room for the increase in the U.S. structural budget deficit. William Nordhaus challenged the view that the appreciation of the dollar could be attributed solely to U.S. fiscal policy. The dollar began to appreciate after the third quarter of 1980. But the first credible forecast of large budget deficits did not appear until the Congressional Budget Office's February 1982 report. He concluded that the explanation for the pre-1982 rise in the dollar must be traced to the October 1979 shift in monetary regime and its effect on interest rates. John Williamson acknowledged that much, though not all, of the exchange rate movement was a rational response to U.S. macroeconomic policies. But, he argued, that does not mean that those policies would have been invariant to the exchange rate regime.

Walter Salant observed that target zones have been critized both for being too flexible compared with fixed rates and for being too rigid compared with flexible rates. But he noted that this implies that they have the corresponding advantages of being less rigid than fixed rates and less volatile than flexible rates. The difficult political choice between stabilizing domestic policy and keeping the exchange rate on target would come up less frequently under a zone system than under fixed rates, especially if the zones were adjustable. And the risks of bubbles and excessive volatility would be less under a zone system than under a flexible system. In short, target zones would share the advantages as well as the disadvantages of both fixed and flexible rates. Dornbusch suggested that one reason why target zones have not attracted more political support is that they are not extreme enough. He predicted that any move away from floating rates would be back to fixed rates, not to an intermediate system. Dornbusch conceded that a target zone system would have the advantage of providing a forum for open discussion among countries about appropriate exchange rates. In a floating rate system, such discussion is unlikely to occur on any ongoing basis because the market determines exchange rates; in a fixed rate system, such discussion is avoided for fear it might provoke speculation. William Poole reflected that soft target zones would work just as money growth targets have: they would be ignored when it was convenient.

Some participants believed that exchange rate fluctuations could be excessive under floating rates and discussed taxing capital movements as a way to reduce erratic fluctuations. James Tobin commented that the basic rationale for taxing exchange transactions was to discourage short-term capital movements without impeding long-term investments. With such a transactions tax, short-term interest rates would not be so closely arbitraged across countries, so that governments would have more policy autonomy. In Tobin's view, a tax on exchange transactions would be useful not only with floating rates but also under a target zone or fixed rate regime, in that it would reduce the need to make exceptions or to change rates. However, Williamson argued that reducing short-term capital flows could cause dynamic instability of the exchange rate under either a floating rate or target zone system because it would hinder the capital flows needed to finance trade. He also noted that a transactions tax would not prevent currency misalignments coming from long-term capital movements, such as Japanese investment of long-term funds in the United States. Stanley Fischer believed that a tax on exchange transactions would be desirable for the reasons Tobin gave, but he argued that it would not work because foreign exchange transactions would merely be driven offshore. Nordhaus suggested that someone should look at whether day-to-day exchange rate volatility has changed as transactions costs have changed; his suspicion was that it has not. Poole drew an analogy to the real estate market, where transactions costs are very high. There is little day-to-day volatility in land prices, but high transactions costs have not prevented price movements that some observers believe to be speculative bubbles.

Dornbusch expressed concern over the consequences of implementing a target zone system in the current economic environment. He feared that those who favor target zones implicitly seek a large further depreciation of the dollar. Rather than adopting such a "beggar-thy-neighbor" policy that would export unemployment abroad, he would prefer to see the United States and other countries take coordinated steps to lower interest rates. Richard Cooper agreed with the need to lower worldwide interest rates but argued that the target zone proposals were a systemic reform and should not be evaluated as a current policy issue. Any target zone system would take at least three years to implement; by then, the economic environment could look quite different. Dornbusch replied that target zones could not be divorced from a current policy context. When they were first discussed seriously three years ago, they would have implied a policy of monetizing the huge impending U.S. budget deficits. Not having target zones permitted a different adjustment to the deficit.

Several participants discussed the longer run effects of large fluctuations in exchange rates. Branson noted that, in response to the dollar's real appreciation during the early 1980s, both foreign and U.S. firms developed sources of supply outside the United States in industries in which the United States had previously been competitive internationally. With these foreign sources established, some of the U.S. employment in those industries lost to foreign competition in recent years will not be recouped even if the dollar falls back to 1980 levels. Williamson observed that the existence of such irreversible effects from exchange rate fluctuations strengthens the case for target zones. Nordhaus, by contrast, observed that exchange rate fluctuations that lead to shakeouts in certain industries are not necessarily bad. By weeding out the weakest firms, such fluctuations might contribute to the economy's long-run performance, just as Schumpeter reasoned that business cycles did.

Robert Lawrence suggested that Branson's estimates of the effect of exchange rates on employment might be too large because they assume a constant employment-exchange rate elasticity. In fact, as a currency increases in value, exports of products with a high demand elasticity drop off first, and the volume of exports in the products that remain may be relatively insensitive to the exchange rate. This seems to explain why the volume of U.S. exports held up during the last stages of the dollar's appreciation. Charles Schultze noted that Branson's estimate of 1.7 million U.S. jobs lost because of the dollar appreciation did not allow for the volume of defense production, which also has important effects on manufacturing employment. Over the past fifteen years, defense spending has moved inversely with the dollar exchange rate, so that including it in the model might increase the estimated effect of the exchange rate on manufacturing employment.

THE CONTRIBUTORS

William H. Branson

William H. Branson is Professor of Economics and International Affairs at Princeton University. He received a Ph.D. degree from the Massachusetts Institute of Technology (1967), M.A. from the University of California at Berkeley (1964), and a B.S. degree from the U.S. Naval Academy at Annapolis. Dr. Branson is a member of the Advisory Board of the Institute for International Studies of Stockholm University; research associate for the Centre for Economic Policy Research, London; consultant to the World Bank on macro-stabilization programs; Director of Research in International Studies and Research Associate, National Bureau of Economic Research; a member of the Council on Foreign Relations, and senior adviser to the Brookings Panel on Economic Activity. He has been a consultant to the Federal Reserve Board, U.S. Treasury Department, Council of Economic Advisers, Organization for Economic Cooperation and Development Department of Economics and Statistics and Science Directorate, the Ministry of International Trade and Industry in Tokyo, and the Bank of Finland.

Jacques de Larosière

Jacques de Larosière is Governor of the Bank of France and a director for Renault, the National Bank of Paris, Air France and Aerospatiale. He served as managing director and chairman of the board of directors of the International Monetary Fund from 1978 to 1986. Mr. de Larosière holds degrees in arts and law from the University of Paris and a diploma from the Institute of Political Studies of Paris. Following four years at the French National School of Administration, he held a succession of positions in the French Civil Service. He was inspector of finances for the Department of External Finances Ministry; served at the French embassies in London and Algeria while with the External Finance Office; and became assistant director of the Treasury, deputy director of the Treasury, and then director of the French Treasury in 1971. Mr. de Larosière was the principal private secretary to M. Giscard d'Estaing, then Minister of Finance, in 1974. He was Undersecretary of the Treasury 1974–78. He has been chairman of the deputies of the Group of Ten and chairman of the economic development review committee of the Organization for Economic Cooperation and Development.

Rudiger Dornbusch

Rudiger Dornbusch is the Ford International Professor of Economics at the Massachusetts Institute of Technology, Cambridge, Massachusetts. He holds a Ph.D. in economics from the University of Chicago and a political science degree from the University of Geneva. Dr. Dornbusch also has held faculty positions at the University of Rochester, University of Chicago and Fundaco Getulio Vargas, Rio de Janerio. He is a research associate of the National Bureau of Economic Research; a member of the Brookings Panel on Economic Activity, the SSRC Committee on Growth and Stability, the advisory committee for the Institute for International Economics; senior fellow of the Center for European Policy Studies, and a member of the advisory council for Shearson Lehman Brothers. Dr. Dornbusch has been a fellow of the Econometric Society, recipient of the John Guggenheim Fellowship, fellow of the American Academy of Arts and Sciences, and a participant in the Gaston Eyskens Lectures, Catholic University of Leuven; Graham Lecture, Princeton University, and the Lionel Robbins Lectures, London School of Economics. He has authored and edited numerous books and articles in professional journals and editorial page articles in U.S. and foreign newspapers.

Martin Feldstein

Martin Feldstein is the George F. Baker Professor of Economics at Harvard University and President of the National Bureau of Economic Research. From 1982 through 1984, he was Chairman of the Council of Economic Advisers and President Reagan's chief economic adviser. After graduating from Harvard College in 1961, Dr. Feldstein studied at Oxford University where he became a member of the faculty and a Fellow of Nuffield College. He received a Doctor of Philosophy degree from Oxford in 1967. Dr. Feldstein joined the Harvard Economics Department as an assistant professor and became professor of economics in 1969. His research and teaching have focused on the problems of the national economy and the economics of the public sector. He is the author of more than 200 scientific articles on a wide range of economic subjects. Dr. Feldstein has received the John Bates Clark Medal of the American Economic Association. He is a Fellow of the Econometric Society and the National Association of Business Economists, the Trilateral Commission, Council on Foreign Relations and the American Academy of Arts and Sciences. He has recieved honorary doctorates from the University of Rochester and Marquette University. With his wife Kathleen, also an economist, Dr. Feldstein writes a monthly column for *The Washington Post* and *Los Angeles Times* syndicate.

Jacob A. Frenkel

Jacob A. Frenkel is the Economic Counsellor and Director of Research of the International Monetary Fund. He joined the faculty of the University of Chicago in 1973 and since 1982 has been the David Rockefeller Professor of International Economics. He has held academic posts at the Hebrew University and Tel Aviv University, Israel. Dr. Frenkel was born in Israel in 1943 and received a B.A. in economics and political science in 1965 from the Hebrew University, where he completed studies for an M.A. in economics in 1967. He received an M.A. degree in economics in 1969 and a Ph.D. in economics in 1970 from the University of Chicago. He is a Fellow of the Econometric Society and a research associate of the National Bureau of Economic Research. He was elected a Research Fellow at the Lehrman Institute, New York, and a Fellow at the Mortimer and Raymond Sackler Institute of Advanced Studies, Tel Aviv. His research has focused on issues in international economics, inflation and financial markets. He is the author or editor of several books and numerous scientific articles in professional journals and books. A member of numerous prestigious advisory commissions and boards, Dr. Frenkel is a frequent participant in international conferences of academic economists and policymakers and has lectured widely throughout the United States and abroad.

Milton Friedman

Milton Friedman, Nobel Laureate in economics, 1976, is the senior research fellow at the Hoover Institution, Stanford University. He is also professor emeritus at the University of Chicago. He received an A.B. degree from Rutgers University in 1932, A.M. Degree from the University of Chicago in 1933, and Ph.D. degree from Columbia University in

1946. At the University of Chicago, he was associate professor of economics, 1946–48; professor of economics 1948–62, and the Paul Snowden Russell distinguished service professor of economics 1962–82. Dr. Friedman is a member of the President's Economic Policy Advisory Board. He has been a member of the research staff of the National Bureau of Economic Research, visiting professor of economics at the University of Wisconsin, principal economist for the tax research division of the U.S. Treasury Department and an associate professor of economics and statistics at the University of Minnesota. He has been a Fulbright lecturer at Cambridge University, the Wesley Clair Mitchell research professor of economics at Columbia University, a fellow of the Center for Advanced Study in Behavioral Science, member of the President's Commission for the All Volunteer Army and the President's Commission on White House Fellows. He has been a visiting scholar to the Federal Reserve Bank of San Francisco. Dr. Friedman holds honorary degrees from more than 15 colleges and universities in the United States and abroad.

Morris Goldstein

Morris Goldstein is Deputy Director of the Research Department for the International Monetary Fund. He holds an A.B. degree in economics from Rutgers College and a Ph.D. in economics from New York University. He was an instructor at New York University and a research fellow in economics at the Brookings Institution. He has served in various positions within the IMF, including assistant to the Managing Director, senior economist and assistant division chief of the Research Department, and economist for the Special Studies Division. While on leave from the IMF at intermittent periods of his carrer, Dr. Goldstein has served as senior technical adviser to the Office of the Assistant Secretary for Economics Policy of the U.S. Treasury Department, and as economist for the Office of Evaluation of the U.S. Department of Labor. Dr. Goldstein has authored numerous articles published in professional journals and other publications. He is a member of the editorial board for IMF Staff Papers.

Alan Greenspan

Alan Greenspan was sworn in August 11, 1987 as Chairman of the Board of Governors of the Federal Reserve System for a four-year term. In this capacity, Dr. Greenspan also serves as Chairman of the Federal Open Market Committee, the System's principal monetary policymaking body. Dr. Greenspan received a B.S. in economics (summa cum laude) in 1948, an M.A. in economics in 1950, and a Ph.D. in economics in 1977, all from New York University. Dr. Greenspan was Chairman and President, Townsend-Greenspan & Co., Inc., 1977–1987, and 1954–1974, an economic consulting firm. From 1974 to 1977 Dr. Greenspan served as Chairman of the President's Council of Economic Advisers under President Ford, and Chairman of the National Commission on Social Security Reform from 1981 to 1983. He also served as a member of President Reagan's Economic Policy Advisory Board, a member of *Time* magazine's Board of Economists, senior adviser to the Brookings Panel on Economic Activity, and consultant to the Congressional Budget Office. His previous Presidential appointments include the President's Foreign Intelligence Advisory Board, the Commission on Financial Structure and Regulation, the Commission on an All-Volunteer Armed Force, and the Task Force on Economic Growth. He is past Chairman of the Conference of Business Economists, past President and Fellow of the National Association of Business Economists, and past Director of the National Economists Club.

Gottfried Haberler

Gottfried Haberler is a Resident Scholar at the American Enterprise Institute for Public Policy Research and Professor of Economics Emeritus at Harvard University. Born near Vienna, Austria, on July 20, 1900, Haberler earned a Doctor of Political Science, Economics, degree from the University of Vienna, in 1923 and a Doctor of Law from the University of Vienna, in 1925. Dr. Haberler came to the United States in 1936. Dr. Haberler has been a Professor of Economics and Statistics at the University of Vienna; visiting lecturer, Professor of Economics and the Galen L. Stone Professor of International Trade at Harvard. Dr. Haberler is a member of the American Economic Association and Royal Economic Society. He was President of the International Economic Association, 1950–51; President of the National Bureau of Economic Research, 1955; and President of the American Economic Association, 1963. He was a consultant to the U.S. Department of the Treasury, 1965–78. Dr. Haberler has received honorary degrees from the University of St. Gallen, Switzerland; University of the Saarland, Federal Republic of Germany; University of Innsbruck, Austria; and the Economic Univeristy, Vienna, Austria.

Harry G. Johnson

The late Harry G. Johnson, during the last several years of his academic career, was professor of economics at the University of Chicago and the

University of Geneva. He held degrees from the University of Toronto, Cambridge University and Harvard University. He was a fellow of King's College, Cambridge; professor of economic theory at Manchester University; professor of economics, the London School of Economics; a professor at the University of Toronto; and a visiting professor at Northwestern University. Johnson was president of the Canadian Political Science Association; chairman of the Association of University Teachers of Economics; a fellow of the Econometric Society, and president of the Eastern Economic Association. He received honorary degrees from St. Francis Xavier University; the University of Windsor, Ontario; Queen's University, Ontario; Carleton University; the University of Western Ontario, and Sheffield. Throughout his career Johnson authored numerous articles in economic journals on monetary theory, international trade, banking and other topics.

Paul R. Krugman

Paul R. Krugman is professor of economics at Massachusetts Institute of Technology. He holds a B.A. degree from Yale University (1974) and a Ph.D. from MIT (1977). Krugman was an assistant and associate professor at MIT from 1980 until 1984. He currently is a member of the board of advisers for the Overseas Development Council, the board of advisers for the Institute for International Economics, a rapporteur for the Panel on Advanced Technology Competition and the Industrialized Allies for the National Academy of Sciences, and a research associate for the National Bureau of Economic Research. Previously he was an assistant professor at Yale University, consultant to the U.S. State Department, international policy economist for the Council of Economic Advisers, a technical consultant to the Bank of Portugal, and a member of the research advisory board for the Committee for Economic Development. Dr. Krugman has been a consultant to the World Bank United Nations Conference on Trade and Development and to the IMF European Commission. He is a referee for numerous economic journals and has written two books and numerous professional articles and reports.

Fritz Machlup

The late Fritz Machlup was a professor of economics at New York University. Machlup was born in Austria where he graduated from the University of Vienna in 1923. For the next decade he was a businessman and held a variety of industrial positions with companies in Vienna and

Budapest. He came to the United States in 1933 and was naturalized as a U.S. citizen in 1940. He was a Rockefeller Foundation research fellow; visiting lecturer at Harvard University; the Frank H. Goodyear professor of economics at the University of Buffalo; the Abram G. Hutzler professor of political economy at Johns Hopkins, and the Walker professor of economics and international finance and director of the international finance section at Princeton University. Machlup was chief of the research and statistics division of the Office of Alien Property Custodian in Washington, 1943–46. He was president of the International Economic Association; president of the American Association of University Professors; president of the American Philosophical Society, and president of the National Academy of Education. He was a member of the Royal Economic Society and a fellow of the American Academy of Arts and Sciences and the American Association for the Advancement of Science. Machlup authored numerous books and articles on the international monetary system. He also received several honorary degrees.

Rachel McCulloch

Rachel McCulloch is Professor of International Finance at Brandeis University, having joined that faculty in September of 1987. Previously she was Professor of Economics at the University of Wisconsin and a Research Associate of the National Bureau of Economic Research, Cambridge, Massachusetts. Dr. McCulloch received an A.B. degree in mathematics from the University of Pennsylvania in 1962 and M.A. (1971) and Ph.D. (1973) degrees from the University of Chicago. Prior to joining the Wisconsin faculty in 1979, she taught for two years at the Graduate School of Business of the University of Chicago and for six years at Harvard University. Dr. McCulloch has been a visiting scholar at the Board of Governors of the Federal Reserve System, UCLA, and the Hoover Institution. A consultant and adviser to numerous government agencies and foundations, Dr. McCulloch is a member of the Technology Assessment Advisory Council of the Congressional Office of Technology Assessment, of the Advisory Committee of the Institute for International Economics, and of the Committee on International Relations Studies with the People's Republic of China. She is the author of more than forty articles and monographs on international trade, investment and technology transfer.

Leo Melamed

Leo Melamed is Chairman of the Executive Committee and Special Counsel to the Board of Governors of the Chicago Mercantile Exchange

(CME). He was first elected Chairman of the CME Board of Governors in 1969 and was responsible for the creation of the International Monetary Market (IMM) division of the CME in December 1971. The IMM, a futures market designed to deal exclusively in financial instruments, initiated the evolutionary process which spawned financial futures in currencies, interest rates and eventually index products. Melamed is widely credited with being the architect of financial futures and their international acceptance as risk management tools. Mr. Melamed's role as chief policy maker of the CME helped propel the institution to the forefront of financial markets worldwide. In 1984, he spearheaded the concept of "mutual offset" which led to the CME link with the Singapore International Monetary Exchange (SIMEX). Later, in 1987, he led the CME in expanding this concept to a global "after hours" electronic trading system (P-M-T) with Reuters Holdings PLC. As an industry leader, Mr. Melamed spurred the creation of the congressionally-sanctioned self-regulatory body, the National Futures Association (NFA) and has acted as its Chairman since its inception in 1982. Melamed is Chairman and Chief Executive Officer of Dellsher Investment Co., Inc., a futures commission merchant and clearing member of the CME and Chicago Board of Trade. He is a graduate of the University of Illinois, 1952, and received his Juris Doctor from John Marshall Law School in 1955. Melamed has written and lectured extensively on futures markets. He has also completed a science fiction novel, *The Tenth Planet*, which was published in September 1987.

J. Carter Murphy

J. Carter Murphy is Professor of Economics at Southern Methodist University. He also has been director of graduate studies in economics and chairman of the Department of Economics at SMU where he joined the faculty in 1961. Previously he was at Washington University in St. Louis for eleven years, serving as instructor, assistant professor, associate professor, chairman of the principles of economics program and director of graduate studies in economics. He was a visiting professor at the Bologna Center, School of Advanced International Studies of the Johns Hopkins University, Bologna, Italy, 1961–62; a technical assistance expert for the United Nations at the Institute of National Planning in Egypt, 1964, and a Rockefeller Foundation field staff representative and visiting professor at Thammasat University in Bangkok, Thailand, 1966–67. Dr. Murphy was a senior staff economist for the Council of Economic Advisers, 1971–72. He is an adjunct scholar for the American Enterprise

Institute. He received his Ph.D. in economics from the University of Chicago in 1955. Previously he had earned an A.M. degree in economics from the University of Chicago and an A.B. degree in music and B.S. degree in economics from North Texas State College. Dr. Murphy has authored numerous books and professional articles and has received numerous academic and professional appointments and awards.

Michael L. Mussa

Michael L. Mussa is a member of the Council of Economic Advisers, appointed by President Reagan on August 18, 1986. Prior to the appointment, Dr. Mussa was the William H. Abbott Professor of International Business at the Graduate School of Business, University of Chicago. Professor Mussa received his M.A. and Ph.D. degrees in economics from the University of Chicago and undergraduate degree from UCLA. He was on the faculty of the University of Rochester, and was a visiting faculty member at the City University of New York, London School of Economics and the Graduate Institute of International Studies in Geneva, Switzerland. In 1976, Professor Mussa joined the faculty of the Graduate School of Business of the University of Chicago as associate professor; in 1980 he was promoted to full professor and then to the Abbott Professorship. Professor Mussa's main areas of research are international trade and finance, macroeconomics and monetary economics, and municipal finance. He has served as an editor of the *Journal of Business*, a member of the Business Forecast Panel for the Graduate School of Business, and as a consultant to the World Bank.

Beryl W. Sprinkel

Beryl W. Sprinkel is Chairman of the Council of Economic Advisers, appointed by President Reagan on April 18, 1985. Prior to this appointment, Dr. Sprinkel served as Under Secretary of the Treasury for Monetary Affairs. Upon leaving the Treasury Department, he was awarded the Alexander Hamilton Award, the Department's highest honor. Previously, Dr. Sprinkel was Executive Vice President and Economist at the Harris Trust and Savings Bank in Chicago, Illinois. He was director of "Harris Economics;" a member of *Time*'s Board of Economists; chairman of the Economic Advisory Committee of the American Bankers Association; and a member of the Board of Directors of the U.S. Chamber of Commerce. Before joining Harris Bank, he taught economics and finance at the University of Chicago and at the University of Missouri School of Business and Public Administration. He has written numerous articles and is the author of two books, and co-author of a third, on the effects of monetary policy on financial markets and the economy. Dr. Sprinkel received his B.S. Degree in Public Administration from the University of Missouri in 1947; his M.B.A. degree from the University of Chicago in 1948; and his Ph.D. in economics and finance from the University of Chicago in 1952. He holds honorary degrees from four universities.

Henry C. Wallich

Henry C. Wallich served as a member of the Board of Governors of the Federal Reserve System from March 1974 to December 1986. Prior to his appointment, he was Professor of Economics at Yale University from 1951–74. While on leave from Yale, he was appointed and served as a member of the President's Council of Economic Advisers, 1959–61. He was an assistant to the Secretary of the Treasury, 1958–59, and a consultant to the Treasury Secretary, 1969–74. Dr. Wallich has been a part time editorial writer for *The Washington Post,* a columnist for *Newsweek* magazine and recipient of the John Simon Guggenheim Memorial Foundation Fellowship. He studied at Oxford University and received an M.A. from Harvard University in 1941 and a Ph.D. from Harvard in 1944. Dr. Wallich began his career in the export business in 1933, moving later to foreign security analysis with Chemical Bank and Trust Co. and a brokerage house before serving ten years with the Federal Reserve Bank of New York. He was a chief of the Foreign Research Division of the Federal Reserve Bank of New York, 1946–51. He is a member of the American Economic Association, the American Finance Association and the Council on Foreign Relations.

Thomas D. Willett

Thomas D. Willett is Director of the Claremont Center for Economic Policy Studies and Horton Professor of Economics at the Claremont Graduate School and Claremont McKenna College. He received a B.A. Degree from the College of William and Mary and Ph.D. from the University of Virginia. A former Deputy Assistant Secretary of the Treasury for International Research and Planning, he has taught at Cornell and Harvard Universities and served on the staff of the Council of Economic Advisers. He has written widely in the areas of international and monetary economics, political economy, and public policy and has served on the editorial boards of numerous economics and policy journals.

Dr. Willett is an adjunct scholar for the American Enterprise Institute for Public Policy Research. He has been an adjunct lecturer at the School of Advanced International Studies at Johns Hopkins University and an Earhart Foundation Faculty Associate. He has served as a consultant to the Cambridge Research Institute and the Sterling Institute. He was a member of the American Society of International Law Panel on International Monetary Problems (1969–71), the Council on Foreign Relations Working Group on Macroeconomic Policies and International Monetary Relations (1976), and the Burgenstock Group studying greater flexibility of exchange rates (1969–71).

ACKNOWLEDGMENTS

The editor and the publisher are grateful to the following:

The University of Chicago Press, for Milton Friedman, "The Case for Flexible Exchange Rates," reprinted from *Essays in Positive Economics* by permission of the University of Chicago Press. Copyright © 1953 by The University of Chicago.

George Allen & Unwin Ltd., for Harry G. Johnson, "The Case for Flexible Exchange Rates, 1969," reprinted from his *Further Essays in Monetary Economics*, by permission of Unwin Hyman, Ltd. Copyright © 1973 by George Allen & Unwin, Ltd.

American Economic Association, for J. Carter Murphy, "Reflections on the Exchange Rate System," reprinted from the *American Economic Review* vol. 75, pp. 68–73, May 1985. Copyright © 1985 by American Economic Association.

International Monetary Fund, for Thomas D. Willett, "Functioning of the Current International Financial System: Strengths, Weakness and Criteria for Evaluation," reprinted from George M. von Furstenberg, *International Money and Credit: The Policy Roles*, pp. 5–44, by permission of the International Monetary Fund. Copyright © 1983 by the International Monetary Fund.

American Enterprise Institute, for Gottfried Haberler, "The International Monetary System and Proposals for International Policy Coordination," reprinted from Phillip Cagan, editor, *Contemporary Economic Problems: Deficits, Taxes, and Economic Adjustments,* by permission of the American Enterprise Institute for Public Policy Research. Copyright © 1987 by the American Enterprise Institute for Policy Research.

American Enterprise Institute for Gottfried Haberler, "The International Monetary System—Once Again," reprinted from *The AEI Economist*, April 1987 by permission of the American Enterprise Institute for Public Policy Research. Copyright © 1987 by the American Enterprise Institute for Public Policy Research.

Ballinger Publishing Company, for Fritz Machlup, "Growth Rates, Trade Balances and Exchange Rates," reprinted from Cooper, *et al. International Monetary System Under Flexible Exchange Rates*, by permission of Ballinger Publishing Company. Copyright © 1982 by Ballinger Publishing Company.

International Monetary Fund, for Jacob A. Frenkel and Morris Goldstein, "A Guide to Target Zones," reprinted from IMF Staff Papers, vol. 33, no. 4, pp. 633–669, December 1986, by permission of the International Monetary Fund. Copyright © 1986 by the International Monetary Fund.

International Finance Section, Princeton University, for Rachel McCulloch, *Unexpected Real Consequences of Floating Exchange Rates*, reprinted from *Essays in International Finance* No. 153, August 1983. Copyright © 1983. Reprinted by permission of the International Finance Section of Princeton University.

Elsevier Science Publishers, for Martin Feldstein, "Domestic Saving and International Capital Movements in the Long Run and the Short Run," reprinted from *European Economic Review 21*, March/April 1983, pages 129–151. Copyright © 1983 by Elsevier Science Publishers.

Federal Reserve Bank of Boston, for Paul R. Krugman, "International Aspects of U.S. Monetary and Fiscal Policy," reprinted from The Federal Research Bank of Boston Conference Series, no. 27, pp. 112–132, October 1983.

Alan Greenspan for "Excerpts from the Council of Economic Advisors *Report to the President*, 1975, 1976, 1977.

Group of Thirty, for Michael Mussa, "The Role of Official Intervention," reprinted with permission from Occasional Paper no. 6, pp. 1–27, 1981. Copyright © 1981 by the Group of Thirty.

Ballinger Publishing Company, for William H. Branson, "Economic Structure and Policy for External Balance," reprinted with permission from Bigman and Taya's *Floating Exchange Rates and the State of World Trade and Payments*. Copyright © 1984 by Ballinger Publishing Company. Originally issued as an IMF Staff Paper, vol. 30, March 1983.

Ballinger Publishing Company, for Jacques de Larosière, "Exchange Rates and the Adjustment Process," reprinted with permission from Bigman and Taya's *Floating Exchange Rates and the State of World Trade and Payments*. Copyright © 1984 by Ballinger Publishing Company. Originally issued in IMF *Survey*, vol. 8 no. 20, pp. 333–339, October 1979.

Ballinger Publishing Company, for Henry C. Wallich, "Floating as Seen from the Central Bank," reprinted by permission from Bigman and Taya's *Floating Exchange Rates and the State of World Trade and Payments*. Copyright © 1984 by Ballinger Publishing Company.

Beryl W. Sprinkel, "Improving Economic Performance," reprinted by permission of the author from a speech before the Commonwealth Club of San Francisco, April 2, 1987.

Leo Melamed, "The International Monetary Market," prepared for this volume.

Milton Friedman, for "A Proposal for Resolving the U.S. Balance of Payments Problem (Confidential Memorandum to President-elect Richard Nixon)," published by permission of the author.

Dow Jones & Company, Inc., for Alan Greenspan, "Coordination Could be Washed Out," reprinted with permission from *The Wall Street Journal*, July 10, 1986. Copyright © 1986 by Dow Jones & Company, Inc.

Ballinger Publishing Company, for Jacob A. Frenkel, "Turbulence in the Foreign Exchange Markets and Macroeconomic Policies," reprinted with permission from Bigman and Taya's *Exchange Rate and Trade Instability: Causes, Consequences, and Remedies*. Copyright © 1983 by Ballinger Publishing Company.

The University of Chicago Press, for Rudiger Dornbusch, "Expectations and Exchange Rate Dynamics," reprinted by permission from the